D1612254

CLYMER

YAMAHA

OUTBOARD SHOP MANUAL

2-250 HP TWO-STROKE • 1996-1998 (Includes Jet Drives)

The World's Finest Publisher of Mechanical How-To Manuals

INTERTEC PUBLISHING

P.O. Box 12901, Overland Park, Kansas 66282-2901

Copyright ©1999 Intertec Publishing

FIRST EDITION
First Printing December, 1999

Printed in U.S.A.

CLYMER and colophon are registered trademarks of Intertec Publishing.

ISBN: 0-89287-727-8

Library of Congress: 99-69175

Tools shown in Chapter Two courtesy of Thorsen Tool, Dallas, Texas. Test equipment shown in Chapter Two courtesy of Dixson, Inc., Grand Junction, Colorado.

COVER: Photo courtesy of Yamaha Motor Corporation, U.S.A., Cypress, CA.

REFERENCE

The following books and guides are published by Intertec Publishing.

Contents

Quick Reference Data

ENGINE DISPLACEMENT

Model	Displacement
2 hp	43 cc (2.62 cid)
3 hp	70 cc (4.3 cid)
4 hp	83 cc (5.07 cid)
5 hp	103 cc (6.3 cid)
6, 8 hp	165 cc (10.1 cid)
9.9, 15 hp	246 cc (15.0 cid)
20, 25 hp (two-cylinder)	395 cc (24.1 cid)
C25	430 cc (26.24 cid)
25 (three-cylinder) hp	496 cc (30.27 cid)
28 jet	698 cc (42.6 cid)
C30	496 cc (30.27 cid)
30 hp (three-cylinder)	496 cc (30.27 cid)
35 jet	698 cc (42.6 cid)
C40 (two-cylinder)	592 cc (36.1 cid)
40 hp (three-cylinder)	698 cc (42.6 cid)
E48	760 cc (46.4 cid)
50 hp	698 cc (42.6 cid)
E60	849 cc (51.8 cid)
60 hp	849 cc (51.8 cid)
65 jet	1140 cc (69.6 cid)
70 hp	849 cc (51.8 cid)
75 hp	1140 cc (69.6 cid)
C80	1140 cc (69.6 cid)
80 jet	1730 cc (105.5 cid)
C85	1140 cc (69.6 cid)
90 hp	1140 cc (69.6 cid)
105 jet	2596 cc (158.4 cid)
115 hp	1730 cc (105.5 cid)
130 hp	1730 cc (105.5 cid)
150 hp	2596 cc (158.4 cid)
175 hp	2596 cc (158.4 cid)
200 hp (90°)	2596 cc (158.4 cid)
200 hp (76°)	3130 cc (191.0 cid)
225 hp (90°)	2596 cc (158.4 cid)
225 hp (76°)	3130 cc (191.0 cid)
250 hp	3130 cc (191.0 cid)

BATTERY REQUIREMENTS

Model	Cold cranking	Amp hour	Reserve
6-50 hp	210 CCA	40	59 minutes
60-200 hp	380 CCA	70	124 minutes
225 (90°)	380 CCA	100	124 minutes
200-250 hp (76°)	512 CCA	100 amp hour	182 minutes

STANDARD TIGHTENING TORQUE*

Fastener size	Standard torque
8 mm nut, M5 bolt	5.0 N•m (44.0 in.-lb.)
10 mm nut, M6 bolt	8.0 N•m (70.0 in.-lb.)
12 mm nut, M8 bolt	18.0 N•m (13.0 ft.-lb.)

(continued)

STANDARD TIGHTENING TORQUE* (continued)

Fastener size	Standard torque
14 mm nut, M10 bolt	36.0 N•m (25.0 ft.-lb.)
17 mm nut, M12 bolt	43.0 N•m (31.0 ft.-lb.)

*Check the manual for specific torque specifications. If a specific torque is not listed use these specifications

SPARK PLUG SPECIFICATIONS

Model	Spark plug type	Alternate plug	Spark plug gap
2MH	NGK B5HS	–	0.6-0.7 mm (0.024-0.028 in.)
3MHV	NGK B6HS-10	–	0.9-1.0 mm (0.035-0.039 in.)
4MH, 5MH	NGK B7HS	NGK BR7HS	0.6-0.7 mm (0.024-0.028 in.)
6, 8	NGKB7HS-10	NGK BR7HS-10	0.9-1.0 mm (0.035-0.039 in.)
9.9, 15, 20, 25 hp	NGKB7HS-10	–	0.9-1.0 mm (0.035-0.039 in.)
28 jet-50 hp	NGKB8HS-10	–	0.9-1.0 mm (0.035-0.039 in.)
30	NGK B7HS-10	–	1.0 mm (0.039 in.)
C30	NGK B8HS-10	–	1.0 mm (0.039 in.)
C40	NGK B7HS-10	–	1.0 mm (0.039 in.)
E48	NGK B7HS	NGK B8HS	0.6-0.7 mm (0.024-0.028 in.)
E75	NGK BR8HS-10	NGK B8HS-10	0.9-1.0 mm (0.035-0.039 in.)
E60, 60-90 hp	NGK B8HS	NGK BR8HS-10	0.9-1.0 mm (0.035-0.039 in.)
80 jet, 115 hp (except C115)	NGK BR8HS-10	–	0.9-1.0 mm (0.035-0.039 in.)
C115	NGK B8HS-10	–	0.9-1.0 mm (0.035-0.039 in.)
130hp	NGK BR9HS-10	–	0.9-1.0 mm (0.035-0.039 in.)
150-225 (90°)	NGK B8HS-10	–	0.9-1.0 mm (0.035-0.039 in.)
200-250 (76°)	NGK BR9HS-10	–	0.9-1.0 mm (0.035-0.039 in.)

PISTON POSITION (TIMING POINTER ADJUSTMENT)

Model	Full retard	Full advance
2 hp	*	*
3 hp	*	*
4, 5 hp	*	*
6, 8 hp	0.04-0.12 mm (0.0015-0.0047 in.) BTDC	4.53-5.05 mm (0.179-0.199 in.) BTDC
9.9, 15 hp	0.08-0.16 mm (0.003-0.007 in.) ATDC	3.95-4.50 mm (0.155-0.177 in.) BTDC
20, 25 hp (two-cylinder)	*	3.34 mm (0.13 in.)
E48	0.06-0.18 mm (0.003-0.007 in.) BTDC	2.56-3.10 mm (0.100-0.122 in.) BTDC
60 hp	*	3.23 mm (0.127 in.) BTDC
E60	0.03 (0.001in.) ATDC	2.42 mm (0.095 in.) BTDC
70 hp	*	2.68 mm (0.106 in.) BTDC
E75	0.03 (0.001 in.) ATDC	3.41 mm (0.134 in.) BTDC
75-80 (except E75, 80 jet)	*	2.83 mm (0.111 in.) BTDC
65 jet and 90 hp	*	3.41 mm (0.134 in.) BTDC
C75	*	*
C85	*	*
80 jet, 115	*	3.91 mm (0.150 in.) BTDC
130hp	*	3.05 mm (0.120 in.) BTDC
105 jet, C150,	*	2.28 mm (0.009 in.) BTDC
D150, P150	–	–
150TR, S175TR	*	3.05 mm (0.120 in.) BTDC
P175TR, P200TR	*	3.33 mm (0.130 in.) BTDC
L200TR	*	2.53 mm (0.100 in.) BTDC
200TR, 225	*	2.78 mm (0.110 in.) BTDC
200-250 (76°)	*	*

*Timing is adjusted by means other than piston position.

PICKUP TIMING SPECIFICATIONS

Model	Timing
3-5 hp	6° BTDC
6, 8 hp	4° BTDC
9.9, 15 hp	5° ATDC
20, 25 hp (two-cylinder)	3° ATDC
C25 (two-cylinder)	2° ATDC
25 hp (three-cylinder)	2° ATDC
C30 (two-cylinder)	–
30 hp (three-cylinder)	5° ATDC
28 jet, 35 jet, 40, 50 hp	7° ATDC
E48	3-5° BTDC
E60	2° ATDC
E75	2° BTDC
60 and 70 hp (except E60)	6-8° ATDC
65 jet and 75-90 hp (except 80 jet)	7-9° ATDC
80 jet, 115 and 130 hp	5° ATDC
150-200 hp (90°)	7° ATDC
225 hp (90°)	6° ATDC

MAXIMUM TIMING

Model	Maximum timing	Maximum timing speed
2 hp	16-20° BTDC	5000
3 hp	Visible in right window	5000
4, 5 hp	Visible in right window	5500
6 hp	34-36° BTDC	4700
8 hp	34-36° BTDC	5500
9.9, 15 hp	30° BTDC	5500
20 hp	25° BTDC	5000
25 hp (two-cylinder)	25° BTDC	5000
25 hp (three-cylinder)	23-27° BTDC	5000
C30 (two-cylinder)	23-27° BTDC	5000
30 hp (three-cylinder)	25° BTDC	5000
C40 (two-cylinder)	22° BTDC	5000
40, 50 hp (three-cylinder)	25° BTDC	5500
E48	19-21° BTDC	5000
E60	19-21° BTDC	5000
E75	22° BTDC	5000
60	22° BTDC	5000
70-80 hp (except E75)	19-21° BTDC	5000
65 jet and 90 hp	21-23° BTDC	5000
80 jet, 115	25° BTDC	5000
130 hp	22° BTDC	5000
105 jet, C150, D150, P150	19° BTDC	5000
150TR and S175TR	22° BTDC	5000
P175TR and P200TR	23° BTDC	5000
L200TR	20° BTDC	5000
200TR and 225 (90°)	21° BTDC	5000

PILOT SCREW ADJUSTMENT

Model	Turns out
3 hp	1-1 1/2
4 hp	1 1/2-2
5 hp	1 1/4-1 3/4
6 hp	7/8-1 3/8
	(continued)

PILOT SCREW ADJUSTMENT (continued)

Model	Turns out
8 hp	7/8-1 3/8
9.9, 15 hp	1 1/4-1 3/4
20 hp	1 3/4-3 1/4
25 hp (two-cylinder)	1 1/4-2 3/4
25 hp (three-cylinder)	1 3/4-2 1/4
C30 (two-cylinder)	1 1/4-1 3/4
30 hp (three-cylinder)	
Top carburetor	5/8-7/8
Middle carburetor	1 1/2-2
Bottom carburetor	7/8-1 1/8
C40 (two-cylinder)	1 1/2-2
40 hp (three-cylinder)	1 1/4-1 3/4
50 hp (three-cylinder) manual start	1 3/8-1 7/8
50 hp (three-cylinder) electric start	1 1/8-1 5/8
E48	1 1/8-1 5/8
E60	1 1/4-1 3/4
E75	1-1 1/2
60 hp (except E60)	1 1/4-1 3/4
70 hp	1-1 1/2
80 hp	1 1/8-1 5/8
65 jet and 90 hp	1-1 1/2
C75	1-1 1/2
C85	1-1 1/4
80 jet, 115 hp	3/8-7/8
130 hp	5/8-1 1/8
C150	3/4-1 1/4
S150TR, L150	1-1 1/2
P150, D150	
Starboard side screws	1 5/16-1 3/4
Port side screws	13/16-1 5/16
S175TR	13/16-1 5/16
P175TR	
Starboard side screws	1 3/8-1 7/8
Port side screws	7/8-1/3/8
200TR	7/8-1/3/8
S200TR	
Starboard side screws	7/8-1 3/8
Port side screws	3/8-7/8
L200TR	
Starboard side screws	7/8-1 3/8
Port side screws	3/8-7/8
P200TR	
Starboard side screws	1-1 1/2
Port side screws	1/2-1
225 hp (90°)	1-1 1/4
225, 250 hp (76°)	1/2-3/4

ENGINE IDLE SPEED

Model	Idle rpm (neutral)	Idle speed (in gear)
2 hp	–	1100-1200
3 hp	1150-1250	1050
4, 5 hp	1100-1200	1000
6, 8 hp	850-950	700-800
9.9, 15 hp	700-800	650-750
20, 25 hp (two-cylinder)	700-800	600
C25	950	850
25 hp (three-cylinder)	750	600

(continued)

ENGINE IDLE SPEED (continued)

Model	Idle rpm (neutral)	Idle speed (in gear)
C30 (two-cylinder)	1150	950
30 (three-cylinder)	750	650
C40 (two-cylinder)	1150	950
40, 50 hp (three-cylinder)	750-850	600-700
E48	1200-1300	1000-1100
E60	950-1050	800-900
E75	750-850	600-700
60-90 (except E60, 80 jet)	750-850	600-700
80 jet, 115, 130	700-800	600-700
105 jet, 150, 175 hp	675-725	550-600
200TR, S200TR, L200TR	675-725	550-600
P200TR	675-725	575-625
225 hp (90°)	725-775	575-625
225, 250 hp (76°) (except EFI models)	675-725	600-650
200-250 (76° EFI)	700-760	600-660

TEST PROPELLERS

Model	Propeller part No.
4, 5 hp	90890-01630
6, 8 hp	90890-01625
9.9, 15 hp	YB-1619
20, 25 and 30 hp (three-cylinder)	YB-1621
C30	YB-1629
40-90 hp (except C75, C85)	YB-1611
C75, C85	YB-1620
115-130 hp	YB-1624
150-175 hp	YB-1626

CLYMER®

YAMAHA

OUTBOARD SHOP MANUAL

2-250 HP TWO-STROKE • 1996-1998 (Includes Jet Drives)

Chapter One

General Information

This detailed, comprehensive manual contains complete information on maintenance, tune-up, repair and overhaul. Hundreds of photos and drawings guide you through every step-by-step procedure.

Troubleshooting, tune-up, maintenance and repair are not difficult if you know what tools and equipment to use and what to do. Anyone not afraid to get their hands dirty, of average intelligence and with some mechanical ability, can perform most of the procedures in this book. See Chapter Two for more information on tools and techniques.

A shop manual is a reference. You want to be able to find information fast. Clymer books are designed with you in mind. All chapters are thumb tabbed and important items are indexed at the end of the book. All procedures, tables, photos, etc., in this manual assume that the reader may be working on the machine or using this manual for the first time.

Keep this book handy in your tool box. It will help you to better understand how your machine runs, lower repair and maintenance costs and generally increase your enjoyment of your marine equipment.

MANUAL ORGANIZATION

This chapter provides general information useful to marine owners and mechanics.

Chapter Two discusses the tools and techniques for preventive maintenance, troubleshooting and repair.

Chapter Three describes typical equipment problems and provides logical troubleshooting procedures.

Following chapters describe specific systems, providing disassembly, repair, assembly and adjustment procedures in simple step-by-step form. Specifications concerning a specific system are included at the end of the appropriate chapter.

NOTES, CAUTIONS AND WARNINGS

The terms NOTE, CAUTION and WARNING have specific meanings in this manual. A NOTE provides additional information to make a step or procedure easier or clearer. Disregarding a NOTE could cause inconvenience, but would not cause damage or personal injury.

A CAUTION emphasizes areas where equipment damage could result. Disregarding a CAUTION could cause permanent mechanical damage; however, personal injury is unlikely.

A WARNING emphasizes areas where personal injury or even death could result from negligence. Mechanical damage may also occur. WARNINGS *are to be taken seriously.* In some cases, serious injury or death has resulted from disregarding similar warnings.

TORQUE SPECIFICATIONS

Torque specifications throughout this manual are given in foot-pounds (ft.-lb.) and either Newton meters (N.m) or meter-kilograms (mkg). Newton meters are being adopted in place of meter-kilograms in accordance with the International Modernized Metric System. Existing torque wrenches calibrated in meter-kilograms can be used by performing a simple conversion: move the decimal point one place to the right. For example, 4.7 mkg = 47 N.m. This conversion is accurate enough for mechanics' use even though the exact mathematical conversion is 3.5 mkg = 34.3 N.m.

ENGINE OPERATION

All marine engines, whether 2- or 4-stroke, gasoline or diesel, operate on the Otto cycle of intake, compression, power and exhaust phases.

4-stroke Cycle

A 4-stroke engine requires two crankshaft revolutions (4 strokes of the piston) to complete the Otto cycle. **Figure 1** shows gasoline 4-stroke engine operation. **Figure 2** shows diesel 4-stroke engine operation.

2-stroke Cycle

A 2-stroke engine requires only 1 crankshaft revolution (2 strokes of the piston) to complete the Otto cycle. **Figure 3** shows gasoline 2-stroke engine operation. Although diesel 2-strokes exist, they are not commonly used in light marine applications.

FASTENERS

The material and design of the various fasteners used on marine equipment are not arrived at by chance or accident. Fastener design determines the type of tool required to work with the fastener. Fastener material is carefully selected to decrease the possibility of physical failure or corrosion. See *Galvanic Corrosion* in this chapter for more information on marine materials.

Threads

Nuts, bolts and screws are manufactured in a wide range of thread patterns. To join a nut and bolt, the diameter of the bolt and the diameter of the hole in the nut must be the same. It is just as important that the threads on both be properly matched.

The best way to determine if the threads on two fasteners are matched is to turn the nut on the bolt (or the bolt into the threaded hole in a piece of equipment) with fingers only. Be sure both pieces are clean. If much force is required, check the thread condition on each fastener. If the thread condition is good but the fasteners jam, the threads are not compatible.

Four important specifications describe every thread:

a. Diameter.
b. Threads per inch.
c. Thread pattern.
d. Thread direction.

Figure 4 shows the first two specifications. Thread pattern is more subtle. Italian and British

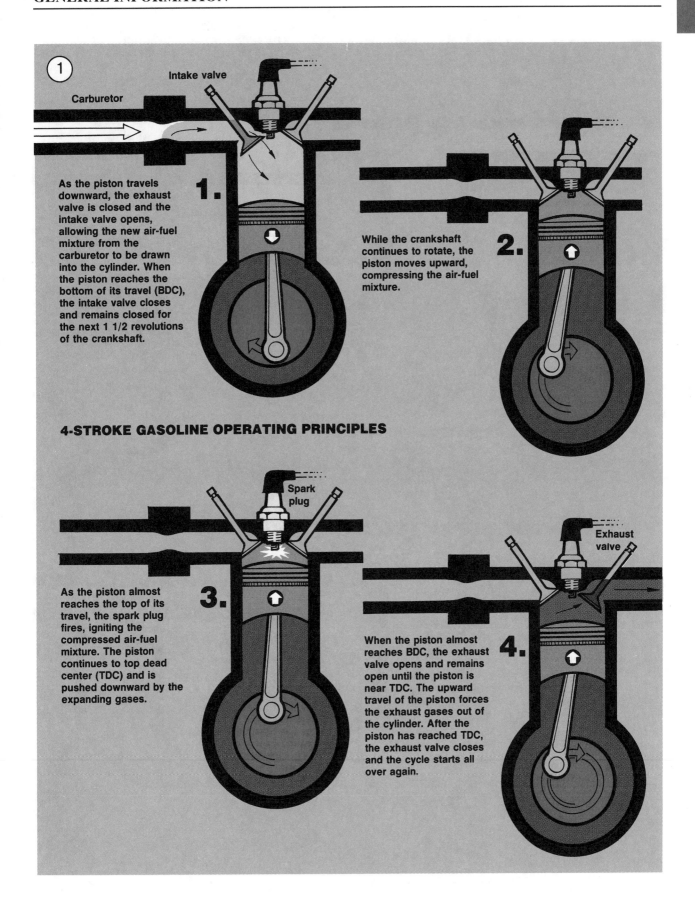

1

Carburetor

Intake valve

1.

As the piston travels downward, the exhaust valve is closed and the intake valve opens, allowing the new air-fuel mixture from the carburetor to be drawn into the cylinder. When the piston reaches the bottom of its travel (BDC), the intake valve closes and remains closed for the next 1 1/2 revolutions of the crankshaft.

2.

While the crankshaft continues to rotate, the piston moves upward, compressing the air-fuel mixture.

4-STROKE GASOLINE OPERATING PRINCIPLES

Spark plug

3.

As the piston almost reaches the top of its travel, the spark plug fires, igniting the compressed air-fuel mixture. The piston continues to top dead center (TDC) and is pushed downward by the expanding gases.

Exhaust valve

4.

When the piston almost reaches BDC, the exhaust valve opens and remains open until the piston is near TDC. The upward travel of the piston forces the exhaust gases out of the cylinder. After the piston has reached TDC, the exhaust valve closes and the cycle starts all over again.

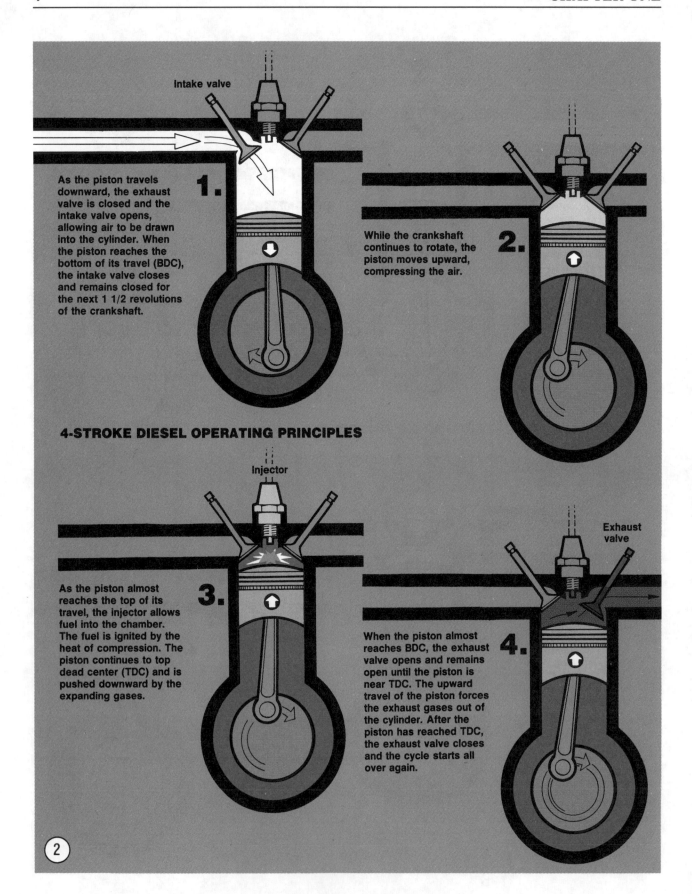

Intake valve

1. As the piston travels downward, the exhaust valve is closed and the intake valve opens, allowing air to be drawn into the cylinder. When the piston reaches the bottom of its travel (BDC), the intake valve closes and remains closed for the next 1 1/2 revolutions of the crankshaft.

2. While the crankshaft continues to rotate, the piston moves upward, compressing the air.

4-STROKE DIESEL OPERATING PRINCIPLES

Injector

3. As the piston almost reaches the top of its travel, the injector allows fuel into the chamber. The fuel is ignited by the heat of compression. The piston continues to top dead center (TDC) and is pushed downward by the expanding gases.

Exhaust valve

4. When the piston almost reaches BDC, the exhaust valve opens and remains open until the piston is near TDC. The upward travel of the piston forces the exhaust gases out of the cylinder. After the piston has reached TDC, the exhaust valve closes and the cycle starts all over again.

2

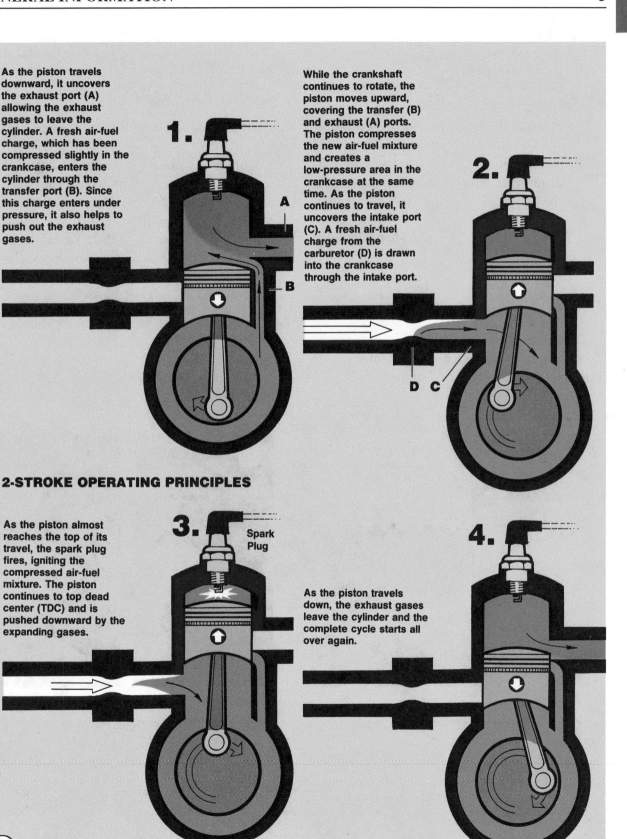

As the piston travels downward, it uncovers the exhaust port (A) allowing the exhaust gases to leave the cylinder. A fresh air-fuel charge, which has been compressed slightly in the crankcase, enters the cylinder through the transfer port (B). Since this charge enters under pressure, it also helps to push out the exhaust gases.

1.

A

B

While the crankshaft continues to rotate, the piston moves upward, covering the transfer (B) and exhaust (A) ports. The piston compresses the new air-fuel mixture and creates a low-pressure area in the crankcase at the same time. As the piston continues to travel, it uncovers the intake port (C). A fresh air-fuel charge from the carburetor (D) is drawn into the crankcase through the intake port.

2.

D C

2-STROKE OPERATING PRINCIPLES

As the piston almost reaches the top of its travel, the spark plug fires, igniting the compressed air-fuel mixture. The piston continues to top dead center (TDC) and is pushed downward by the expanding gases.

3. Spark Plug

As the piston travels down, the exhaust gases leave the cylinder and the complete cycle starts all over again.

4.

standards exist, but the most commonly used by marine equipment manufacturers are American standard and metric standard. The threads are cut differently as shown in **Figure 5**.

Most threads are cut so that the fastener must be turned clockwise to tighten it. These are called right-hand threads. Some fasteners have left-hand threads; they must be turned counterclockwise to be tightened. Left-hand threads are used in locations where normal rotation of the equipment would tend to loosen a right-hand threaded fastener.

Machine Screws

There are many different types of machine screws. **Figure 6** shows a number of screw heads requiring different types of turning tools (see Chapter Two for detailed information). Heads

are also designed to protrude above the metal (round) or to be slightly recessed in the metal (flat) (**Figure 7**).

Bolts

Commonly called bolts, the technical name for these fasteners is cap screw. They are normally described by diameter, threads per inch and length. For example, 1/4-20 × 1 indicates a bolt 1/4 in. in diameter with 20 threads per inch, 1 in. long. The measurement across two flats on the head of the bolt indicates the proper wrench size to be used.

Nuts

Nuts are manufactured in a variety of types and sizes. Most are hexagonal (6-sided) and fit

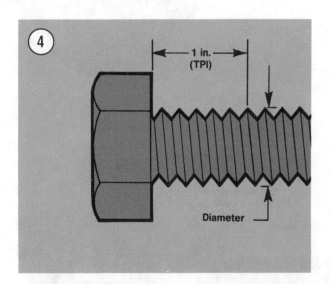

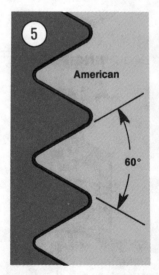

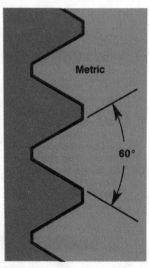

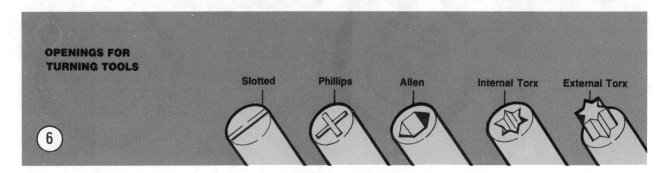

on bolts, screws and studs with the same diameter and threads per inch.

Figure 8 shows several types of nuts. The common nut is usually used with a lockwasher. Self-locking nuts have a nylon insert that prevents the nut from loosening; no lockwasher is required. Wing nuts are designed for fast removal by hand. Wing nuts are used for convenience in non-critical locations.

To indicate the size of a nut, manufacturers specify the diameter of the opening and the threads per inch. This is similar to bolt specification, but without the length dimension. The measurement across two flats on the nut indicates the proper wrench size to be used.

Washers

There are two basic types of washers: flat washers and lockwashers. Flat washers are simple discs with a hole to fit a screw or bolt. Lockwashers are designed to prevent a fastener from working loose due to vibration, expansion and contraction. **Figure 9** shows several types of lockwashers. Note that flat washers are often used between a lockwasher and a fastener to provide a smooth bearing surface. This allows the fastener to be turned easily with a tool.

Cotter Pins

Cotter pins (**Figure 10**) are used to secure special kinds of fasteners. The threaded stud

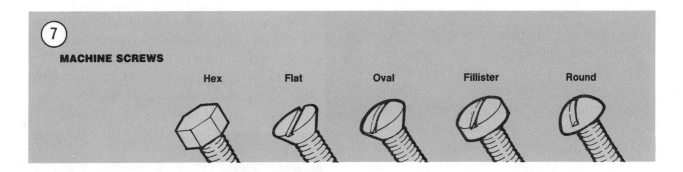

⑦ **MACHINE SCREWS**

Hex   Flat   Oval   Fillister   Round

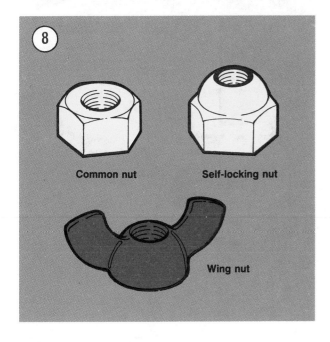

⑧

Common nut   Self-locking nut

Wing nut

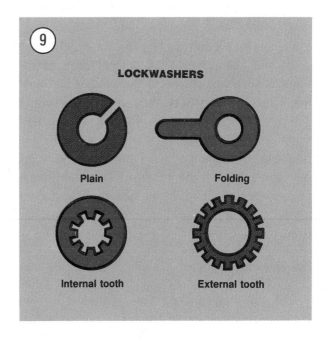

⑨ **LOCKWASHERS**

Plain   Folding

Internal tooth   External tooth

must have a hole in it; the nut or nut lock piece has projections that the cotter pin fits between. This type of nut is called a "Castellated nut." Cotter pins should not be reused after removal.

Snap Rings

Snap rings can be of an internal or external design. They are used to retain items on shafts (external type) or within tubes (internal type). Snap rings can be reused if they are not distorted during removal. In some applications, snap rings of varying thickness can be selected to control the end play of parts assemblies.

LUBRICANTS

Periodic lubrication ensures long service life for any type of equipment. It is especially important to marine equipment because it is exposed to salt or brackish water and other harsh environments. The *type* of lubricant used is just as important as the lubrication service itself; although, in an emergency, the wrong type of lubricant is better than none at all. The following paragraphs describe the types of lubricants most often used on marine equipment. Be sure to follow the equipment manufacturer's recommendations for lubricant types.

Generally, all liquid lubricants are called "oil." They may be mineral-based (including petroleum bases), natural-based (vegetable and animal bases), synthetic-based or emulsions (mixtures). "Grease" is an oil which is thickened with a metallic "soap." The resulting material is then usually enhanced with anticorrosion, antioxidant and extreme pressure (EP) additives. Grease is often classified by the type of thickener added; lithium and calcium soap are commonly used.

4-stroke Engine Oil

Oil for 4-stroke engines is graded by the American Petroleum Institute (API) and the So-

ciety of Automotive Engineers (SAE) in several categories. Oil containers display these ratings on the top or label (**Figure 11**).

API oil grade is indicated by letters, oils for gasoline engines are identified by an "S" and oils for diesel engines are identified by a "C." Most modern gasoline engines require SF or SG graded oil. Automotive and marine diesel engines use CC or CD graded oil.

Viscosity is an indication of the oil's thickness, or resistance to flow. The SAE uses numbers to indicate viscosity; thin oils have low numbers and thick oils have high numbers. A "W" after the number indicates that the viscosity testing was done at low temperature to simulate cold weather operation. Engine oils fall into the 5W-20W and 20-50 range.

Multi-grade oils (for example, 10W-40) are less viscous (thinner) at low temperatures and more viscous (thicker) at high temperatures. This allows the oil to perform efficiently across a wide range of engine operating temperatures.

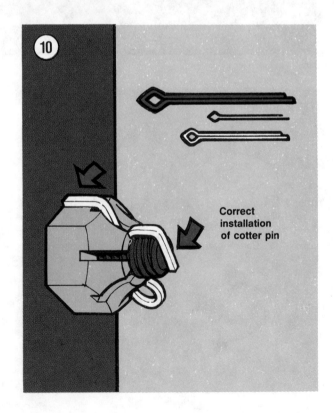

Correct installation of cotter pin

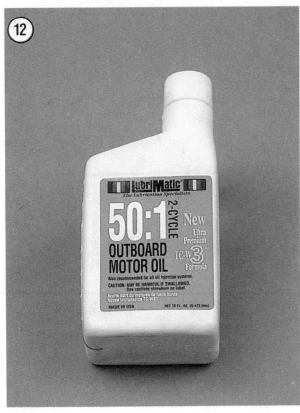

2-stroke Engine Oil

Lubrication for a 2-stroke engine is provided by oil mixed with the incoming fuel-air mixture. Some of the oil mist settles out in the crankcase, lubricating the crankshaft and lower end of the connecting rods. The rest of the oil enters the combustion chamber to lubricate the piston, rings and cylinder wall. This oil is then burned along with the fuel-air mixture during the combustion process.

Engine oil must have several special qualities to work well in a 2-stroke engine. It must mix easily and stay in suspension in gasoline. When burned, it can't leave behind excessive deposits. It must also be able to withstand the high temperatures associated with 2-stroke engines.

The National Marine Manufacturer's Association (NMMA) has set standards for oil used in 2-stroke, water-cooled engines. This is the NMMA TC-W (two-cycle, water-cooled) grade (**Figure 12**). The oil's performance in the following areas is evaluated:

a. Lubrication (prevention of wear and scuffing).
b. Spark plug fouling.
c. Preignition.
d. Piston ring sticking.
e. Piston varnish.
f. General engine condition (including deposits).
g. Exhaust port blockage.
h. Rust prevention.
i. Mixing ability with gasoline.

In addition to oil grade, manufacturers specify the ratio of gasoline to oil required during break-in and normal engine operation.

Gear Oil

Gear lubricants are assigned SAE viscosity numbers under the same system as 4-stroke engine oil. Gear lubricant falls into the SAE 72-250 range (**Figure 13**). Some gear lubricants are multi-grade; for example, SAE 85W-90.

Three types of marine gear lubricant are generally available: SAE 90 hypoid gear lubricant is designed for older manual-shift units; Type C gear lubricant contains additives designed for electric shift mechanisms; High viscosity gear lubricant is a heavier oil designed to withstand the shock loading of high-performance engines or units subjected to severe duty use. Always use a gear lubricant of the type specified by the unit's manufacturer.

Grease

Greases are graded by the National Lubricating Grease Institute (NLGI). Greases are graded by number according to the consistency of the grease; these ratings range from No. 000 to No. 6, with No. 6 being the most solid. A typical multipurpose grease is NLGI No. 2 (**Figure 14**). For specific applications, equipment manufacturers may require grease with an additive such as molybdenum disulfide (MOS^2).

GASKET SEALANT

Gasket sealant is used instead of pre-formed gaskets on some applications, or as a gasket dressing on others. Two types of gasket sealant are commonly used: room temperature vulcanizing (RTV) and anaerobic. Because these two materials have different sealing properties, they cannot be used interchangeably.

RTV Sealant

This is a silicone gel supplied in tubes (**Figure 15**). Moisture in the air causes RTV to cure. Always place the cap on the tube as soon as possible when using RTV. RTV has a shelf life of one year and will not cure properly when the shelf life has expired. Check the expiration date

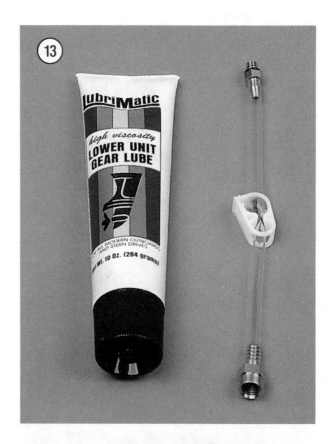

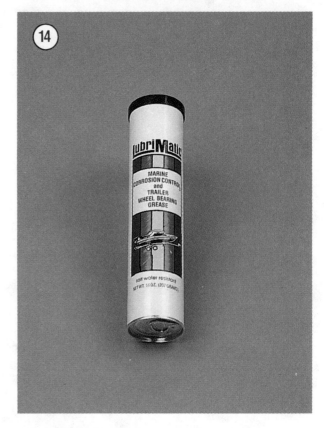

on RTV tubes before using and keep partially used tubes tightly sealed. RTV sealant can generally fill gaps up to 1/4 in. (6.3 mm) and works well on slightly flexible surfaces.

Applying RTV Sealant

Clean all gasket residue from mating surfaces. Surfaces should be clean and free of oil and dirt. Remove all RTV gasket material from blind attaching holes because it can create a "hydraulic" effect and affect bolt torque.

Apply RTV sealant in a continuous bead 2-3 mm (0.08-0.12 in.) thick. Circle all mounting holes unless otherwise specified. Torque mating parts within 10 minutes after application.

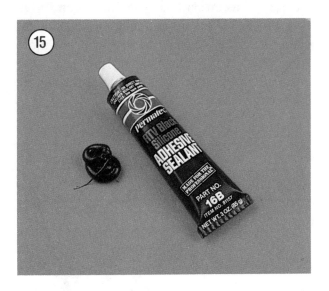

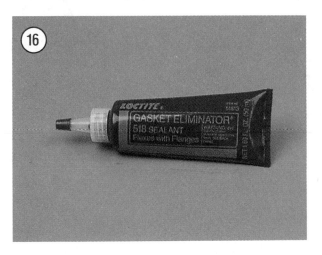

Anaerobic Sealant

This is a gel supplied in tubes (**Figure 16**). It cures only in the absence of air, as when squeezed tightly between two machined mating surfaces. For this reason, it will not spoil if the cap is left off the tube. It should not be used if one mating surface is flexible. Anaerobic sealant is able to fill gaps up to 0.030 in. (0.8 mm) and generally works best on rigid, machined flanges or surfaces.

Applying Anaerobic Sealant

Clean all gasket residue from mating surfaces. Surfaces must be clean and free of oil and dirt. Remove all gasket material from blind attaching holes, as it can cause a "hydraulic" effect and affect bolt torque.

Apply anaerobic sealant in a 1 mm or less (0.04 in.) bead to one sealing surface. Circle all mounting holes. Torque mating parts within 15 minutes after application.

GALVANIC CORROSION

A chemical reaction occurs whenever two different types of metal are joined by an electrical conductor and immersed in an electrolyte. Electrons transfer from one metal to the other through the electrolyte and return through the conductor.

The hardware on a boat is made of many different types of metal. The boat hull acts as a conductor between the metals. Even if the hull is wooden or fiberglass, the slightest film of water (electrolyte) within the hull provides conductivity. This combination creates a good environment for electron flow (**Figure 17**). Unfortunately, this electron flow results in galvanic corrosion of the metal involved, causing one of the metals to be corroded or eaten away by the process. The amount of electron flow (and, therefore, the amount of corrosion) depends on several factors:

a. The types of metal involved.

b. The efficiency of the conductor.

c. The strength of the electrolyte.

Metals

The chemical composition of the metals used in marine equipment has a significant effect on the amount and speed of galvanic corrosion. Certain metals are more resistant to corrosion than others. These electrically negative metals are commonly called "noble;" they act as the cathode in any reaction. Metals that are more subject to corrosion are electrically positive; they act as the anode in a reaction. The more noble metals include titanium, 18-8 stainless steel and nickel. Less noble metals include zinc, aluminum and magnesium. Galvanic corrosion

becomes more severe as the difference in electrical potential between the two metals increases.

In some cases, galvanic corrosion can occur within a single piece of metal. Common brass is a mixture of zinc and copper, and, when immersed in an electrolyte, the zinc portion of the mixture will corrode away as reaction occurs between the zinc and the copper particles.

Conductors

The hull of the boat often acts as the conductor between different types of metal. Marine equipment, such as an outboard motor or stern drive unit, can also act as the conductor. Large masses of metal, firmly connected together, are more efficient conductors than water. Rubber mountings and vinyl-based paint can act as insulators between pieces of metal.

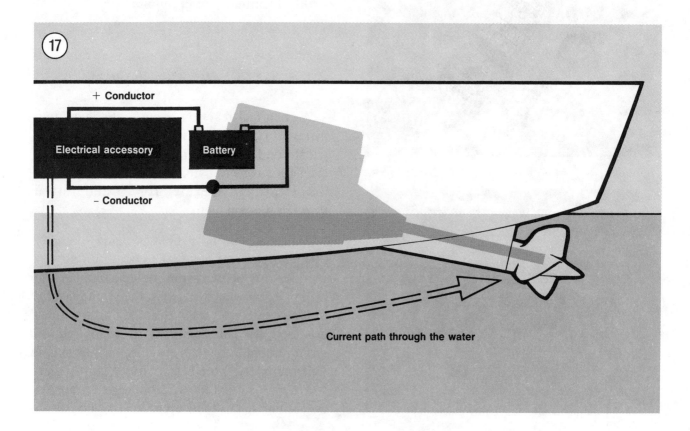

Electrolyte

The water in which a boat operates acts as the electrolyte for the galvanic corrosion process. The better a conductor the electrolyte is, the more severe and rapid the corrosion.

Cold, clean freshwater is the poorest electrolyte. As water temperature increases, its conductivity increases. Pollutants will increase conductivity; brackish or saltwater is also an efficient electrolyte. This is one of the reasons that most manufacturers recommend a freshwater flush for marine equipment after operation in saltwater, polluted or brackish water.

PROTECTION FROM GALVANIC CORROSION

Because of the environment in which marine equipment must operate, it is practically impossible to totally prevent galvanic corrosion. There are several ways by which the process can be slowed. After taking these precautions, the next step is to "fool" the process into occurring only where *you* want it to occur. This is the role of sacrificial anodes and impressed current systems.

Slowing Corrosion

Some simple precautions can help reduce the amount of corrosion taking place outside the hull. These are *not* a substitute for the corrosion protection methods discussed under *Sacrificial Anodes* and *Impressed Current Systems* in this chapter, but they can help these protection methods do their job.

Use fasteners of a metal more noble than the part they are fastening. If corrosion occurs, the larger equipment will suffer but the fastener will be protected. Because fasteners are usually very small in comparison to the equipment being fastened, the equipment can survive the loss of material. If the fastener were to corrode instead of the equipment, major problems could arise.

Keep all painted surfaces in good condition. If paint is scraped off and bare metal exposed, corrosion will rapidly increase. Use a vinyl- or plastic-based paint, which acts as an electrical insulator.

Be careful when using metal-based antifouling paints. These should not be applied to metal parts of the boat, outboard motor or stern drive unit or they will actually react with the equipment, causing corrosion between the equipment and the layer of paint. Organic-based paints are available for use on metal surfaces.

Where a corrosion protection device is used, remember that it must be immersed in the electrolyte along with the rest of the boat to have any effect. If you raise the power unit out of the water when the boat is docked, any anodes on the power unit will be removed from the corrosion cycle and will not protect the rest of the equipment that is still immersed. Also, such corrosion protection devices must not be painted because this would insulate them from the corrosion process.

Any change in the boat's equipment, such as the installation of a new stainless steel propeller, will change the electrical potential and could cause increased corrosion. Keep in mind that when you add new equipment or change materials, you should review your corrosion protection system to be sure it is up to the job.

Sacrificial Anodes

Anodes are usually made of zinc, a far from noble metal. Sacrificial anodes are specially designed to do nothing but corrode. Properly fastening such pieces to the boat will cause them to act as the anode in *any* galvanic reaction that occurs; any other metal present will act as the cathode and will not be damaged.

Anodes must be used properly to be effective. Simply fastening pieces of zinc to your boat in random locations won't do the job.

You must determine how much anode surface area is required to adequately protect the equipment's surface area. A good starting point is provided by Military Specification MIL-A-818001, which states that one square inch of new anode will protect either:

a. 800 square inches of freshly painted steel.
b. 250 square inches of bare steel or bare aluminum alloy.
c. 100 square inches of copper or copper alloy.

This rule is for a boat at rest. When underway, more anode area is required to protect the same equipment surface area.

The anode must be fastened so that it has good electrical contact with the metal to be protected. If possible, the anode can be attached directly to the other metal. If that is not possible, the entire network of metal parts in the boat should be electrically bonded together so that all pieces are protected.

Good quality anodes have inserts of some other metal around the fastener holes. Otherwise, the anode could erode away around the fastener. The anode can then become loose or even fall off, removing all protection.

Another Military Specification (MIL-A-18001) defines the type of alloy preferred that will corrode at a uniform rate without forming a crust that could reduce its efficiency after a time.

Impressed Current Systems

An impressed current system can be installed on any boat that has a battery. The system consists of an anode, a control box and a sensor. The anode in this system is coated with a very noble metal, such as platinum, so that it is almost corrosion-free and will last indefinitely. The sensor, under the boat's waterline, monitors the potential for corrosion. When it senses that

corrosion could be occurring, it transmits this information to the control box.

The control box connects the boat's battery to the anode. When the sensor signals the need, the control box applies positive battery voltage to the anode. Current from the battery flows from the anode to all other metal parts of the boat, no matter how noble or non-noble these parts may be. This battery current takes the place of any galvanic current flow.

Only a very small amount of battery current is needed to counteract galvanic corrosion. Manufacturers estimate that it would take two or three months of constant use to drain a typical marine battery, assuming the battery is never recharged.

An impressed current system is more expensive to install than simple anodes but, considering its low maintenance requirements and the excellent protection it provides, the long-term cost may actually be lower.

PROPELLERS

The propeller is the final link between the boat's drive system and the water. A perfectly

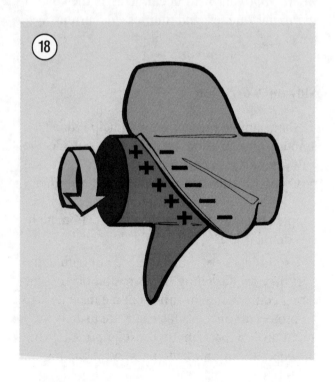

maintained engine and hull are useless if the propeller is the wrong type or has been allowed to deteriorate. Although propeller selection for a specific situation is beyond the scope of this book, the following information on propeller construction and design will allow you to discuss the subject intelligently with your marine dealer.

How a Propeller Works

As the curved blades of a propeller rotate through the water, a high-pressure area is created on one side of the blade and a low-pressure area exists on the other side of the blade (**Figure 18**). The propeller moves toward the low-pressure area, carrying the boat with it.

Propeller Parts

Although a propeller may be a one-piece unit, it is made up of several different parts (**Figure 19**). Variations in the design of these parts make different propellers suitable for different jobs.

The blade tip is the point on the blade farthest from the center of the propeller hub. The blade

tip separates the leading edge from the trailing edge.

The leading edge is the edge of the blade nearest to the boat. During normal rotation, this is the area of the blade that first cuts through the water.

The trailing edge is the edge of the blade farthest from the boat.

The blade face is the surface of the blade that faces away from the boat. During normal rotation, high pressure exists on this side of the blade.

The blade back is the surface of the blade that faces toward the boat. During normal rotation, low pressure exists on this side of the blade.

The cup is a small curve or lip on the trailing edge of the blade.

The hub is the central portion of the propeller. It connects the blades to the propeller shaft (part of the boat's drive system). On some drive systems, engine exhaust is routed through the hub; in this case, the hub is made up of an outer and an inner portion, connected by ribs.

The diffuser ring is used on through-hub exhaust models to prevent exhaust gases from entering the blade area.

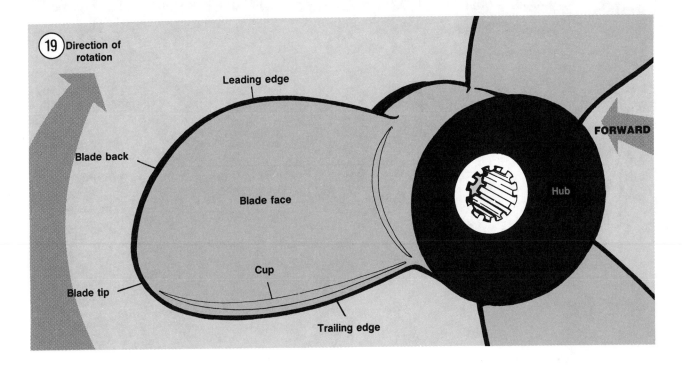

19 Direction of rotation

Leading edge

FORWARD

Blade back

Blade face

Hub

Cup

Blade tip

Trailing edge

Propeller Design

Changes in length, angle, thickness and material of propeller parts make different propellers suitable for different situations.

Diameter

Propeller diameter is the distance from the center of the hub to the blade tip, multiplied by

2. That is, it is the diameter of the circle formed by the blade tips during propeller rotation (**Figure 20**).

Pitch and rake

Propeller pitch and rake describe the placement of the blade in relation to the hub (**Figure 21**).

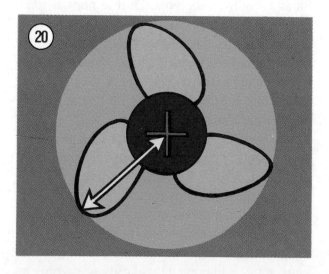

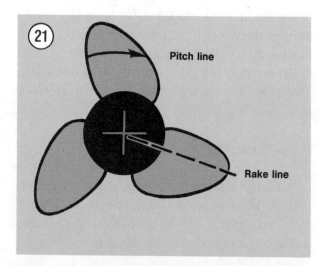

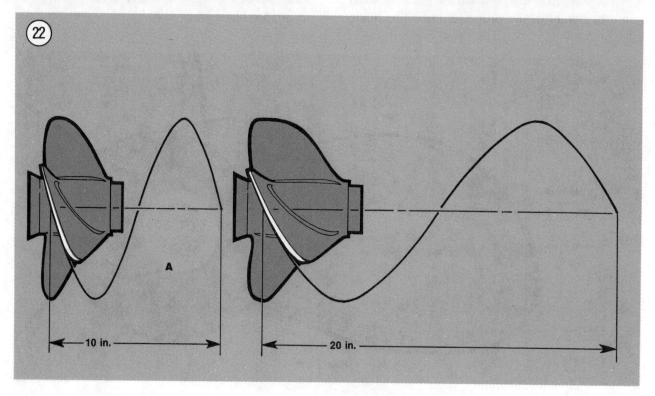

Pitch is expressed by the theoretical distance that the propeller would travel in one revolution. In A, **Figure 22**, the propeller would travel 10 inches in one revolution. In B, **Figure 22**, the propeller would travel 20 inches in one revolution. This distance is only theoretical; during actual operation, the propeller achieves about 80% of its rated travel.

Propeller blades can be constructed with constant pitch (**Figure 23**) or progressive pitch (**Figure 24**). Progressive pitch starts low at the leading edge and increases toward to trailing edge. The propeller pitch specification is the average of the pitch across the entire blade.

Blade rake is specified in degrees and is measured along a line from the center of the hub to the blade tip. A blade that is perpendicular to the hub (A, **Figure 25**) has 0° of rake. A blade that is angled from perpendicular (B, **Figure 25**) has a rake expressed by its difference from perpen-

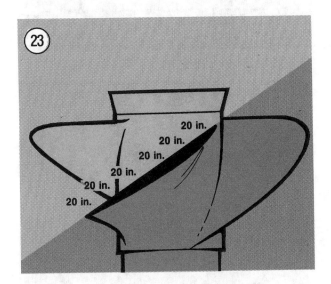

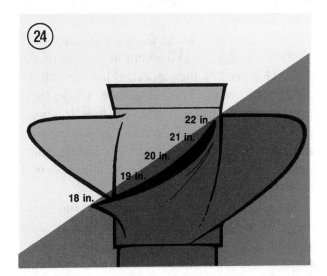

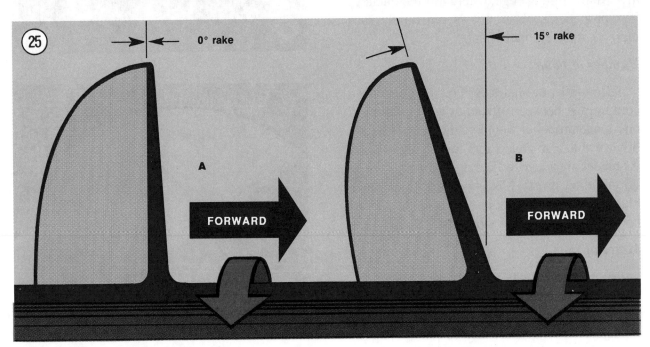

dicular. Most propellers have rakes ranging from 0-20°.

Blade thickness

Blade thickness is not uniform at all points along the blade. For efficiency, blades should be as thin as possible at all points while retaining enough strength to move the boat. Blades tend to be thicker where they meet the hub and thinner at the blade tip (**Figure 26**). This is to support the heavier loads at the hub section of the blade. This thickness is dependent on the strength of the material used.

When cut along a line from the leading edge to the trailing edge in the central portion of the blade (**Figure 27**), the propeller blade resembles an airplane wing. The blade face, where high pressure exists during normal rotation, is almost flat. The blade back, where low pressure exists during normal rotation, is curved, with the thinnest portions at the edges and the thickest portion at the center.

Propellers that run only partially submerged, as in racing applications, may have a wedge-shaped cross-section (**Figure 28**). The leading edge is very thin; the blade thickness increases toward the trailing edge, where it is the thickest. If a propeller such as this is run totally submerged, it is very inefficient.

Number of blades

The number of blades used on a propeller is a compromise between efficiency and vibration. A one-blade propeller would be the most efficient, but it would also create high levels of vibration. As blades are added, efficiency decreases, but so do vibration levels. Most propellers have three blades, representing the most practical trade-off between efficiency and vibration.

Material

Propeller materials are chosen for strength, corrosion resistance and economy. Stainless steel, aluminum and bronze are the most commonly used materials. Bronze is quite strong but

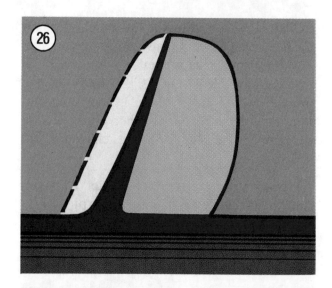

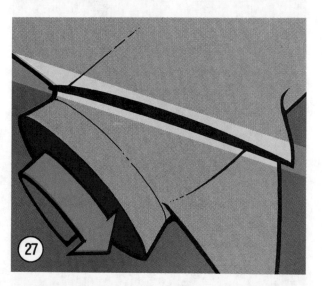

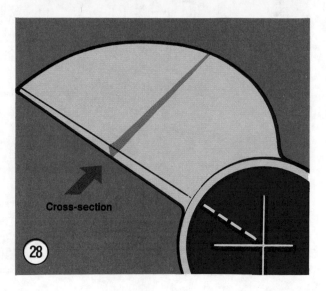

Cross-section

rather expensive. Stainless steel is more common than bronze because of its combination of strength and lower cost. Aluminum alloys are the least expensive but usually lack the strength of steel. Plastic propellers may be used in some low horsepower applications.

Direction of rotation

Propellers are made for both right-hand and left-hand rotation although right-hand is the most commonly used. When seen from behind the boat in forward motion, a right-hand propeller turns clockwise and a left-hand propeller turns counterclockwise. Off the boat, you can tell the difference by observing the angle of the blades (**Figure 29**). A right-hand propeller's blades slant from the upper left to the lower right; a left-hand propeller's blades are the opposite.

Cavitation and Ventilation

Cavitation and ventilation are *not* interchangeable terms; they refer to two distinct problems encountered during propeller operation.

To understand cavitation, you must first understand the relationship between pressure and the boiling point of water. At sea level, water will boil at 212° F. As pressure increases, such as within an engine's closed cooling system, the boiling point of water increases—it will boil at some temperature higher than 212° F. The opposite is also true. As pressure decreases, water will boil at a temperature lower than 212° F. If pressure drops low enough, water will boil at typical ambient temperatures of 50-60° F.

We have said that, during normal propeller operation, low-pressure exists on the blade back. Normally, the pressure does not drop low enough for boiling to occur. However, poor blade design

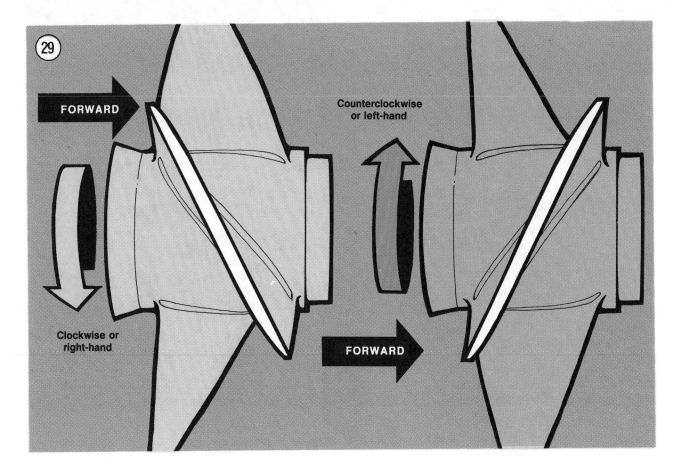

or selection, or blade damage can cause an unusual pressure drop on a small area of the blade (**Figure 30**). Boiling can occur in this small area. As the water boils, air bubbles form. As the boiling water passes to a higher pressure area of the blade, the boiling stops and the bubbles collapse. The collapsing bubbles release enough energy to erode the surface of the blade.

This entire process of pressure drop, boiling and bubble collapse is called "cavitation." The damage caused by the collapsing bubbles is called a "cavitation burn." It is important to remember that cavitation is caused by a decrease in pressure, *not* an increase in temperature.

Ventilation is not as complex a process as cavitation. Ventilation refers to air entering the blade area, either from above the surface of the water or from a through-hub exhaust system. As the blades meet the air, the propeller momentarily over-revs, losing most of its thrust. An added complication is that as the propeller over-revs, pressure on the blade back decreases and massive cavitation can occur.

Most pieces of marine equipment have a plate above the propeller area designed to keep surface air from entering the blade area (**Figure 31**). This plate is correctly called an "antiventilation plate," although you will often *see* it called an "anticavitation plate." Through hub exhaust systems also have specially designed hubs to keep exhaust gases from entering the blade area.

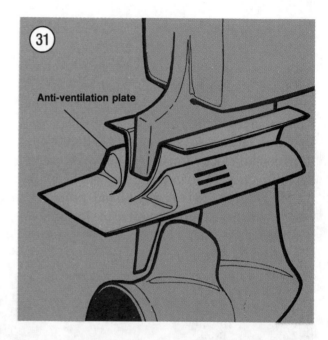

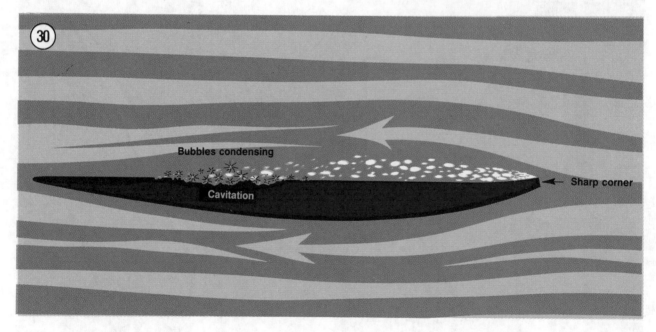

Chapter Two

Tools and Techniques

This chapter describes the common tools required for marine equipment repairs and troubleshooting. Techniques that will make your work easier and more effective are also described. Some of the procedures in this book require special skills or expertise; in some cases, you are better off entrusting the job to a dealer or qualified specialist.

SAFETY FIRST

Professional mechanics can work for years and never suffer a serious injury. If you follow a few rules of common sense and safety, you too can enjoy many safe hours servicing your marine equipment. If you ignore these rules, you can hurt yourself or damage the equipment.

1. Never use gasoline as a cleaning solvent.
2. Never smoke or use a torch near flammable liquids, such as cleaning solvent. If you are working in your home garage, remember that your home gas appliances have pilot lights.
3. Never smoke or use a torch in an area where batteries are being charged. Highly explosive hydrogen gas is formed during the charging process.

4. Use the proper size wrenches to avoid damage to fasteners and injury to yourself.
5. When loosening a tight or stuck fastener, think of what would happen if the wrench should slip. Protect yourself accordingly.
6. Keep your work area clean, uncluttered and well lighted.
7. Wear safety goggles during all operations involving drilling, grinding or the use of a cold chisel.
8. Never use worn tools.
9. Keep a Coast Guard approved fire extinguisher handy. Be sure it is rated for gasoline (Class B) and electrical (Class C) fires.

BASIC HAND TOOLS

A number of tools are required to maintain marine equipment. You may already have some of these tools for home or car repairs. There are also tools made especially for marine equipment repairs; these you will have to purchase. In any case, a wide variety of quality tools will make repairs easier and more effective.

Keep your tools clean and in a tool box. Keep them organized with the sockets and related drives together, the open end and box wrenches together, etc. After using a tool, wipe off dirt and grease with a clean cloth and place the tool in its correct place.

The following tools are required to perform virtually any repair job. Each tool is described and the recommended size given for starting a tool collection. Additional tools and some duplications may be added as you become more familiar with the equipment. You may need all standard U.S. size tools, all metric size tools or a mixture of both.

Screwdrivers

The screwdriver is a very basic tool, but if used improperly, it will do more damage than good. The slot on a screw has a definite dimension and shape. A screwdriver must be selected to conform with that shape. Use a small screwdriver for small screws and a large one for large screws or the screw head will be damaged.

Two types of screwdriver are commonly required: a common (flat-blade) screwdriver (**Figure 1**) and Phillips screwdrivers (**Figure 2**).

Screwdrivers are available in sets, which often include an assortment of common and Phillips blades. If you buy them individually, buy at least the following:

    a. Common screwdriver—5/16 × 6 in. blade.
    b. Common screwdriver—3/8 × 12 in. blade
    c. Phillips screwdriver—size 2 tip, 6 in. blade.

Use screwdrivers only for driving screws. Never use a screwdriver for prying or chiseling. Do not try to remove a Phillips or Allen head screw with a common screwdriver; you can damage the head so that the proper tool will be unable to remove it.

Keep screwdrivers in the proper condition and they will last longer and perform better. Always keep the tip of a common screwdriver in good condition. **Figure 3** shows how to grind the tip to the proper shape if it becomes damaged. Note the parallel sides of the tip.

Pliers

Pliers come in a wide range of types and sizes. Pliers are useful for cutting, bending and crimping. They should never be used to cut hardened objects or to turn bolts or nuts. **Figure 4** shows several types of pliers.

Each type of pliers has a specialized function. General purpose pliers are used mainly for holding things and for bending. Locking pliers are used as pliers or to hold objects very tightly, like a vise. Needlenose pliers are used to hold or bend small objects. Adjustable or slip-joint pliers can

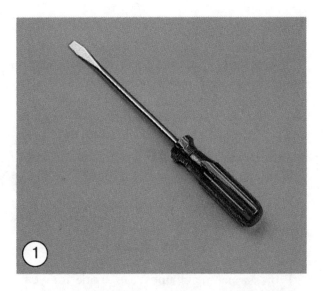

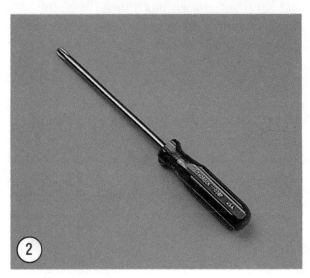

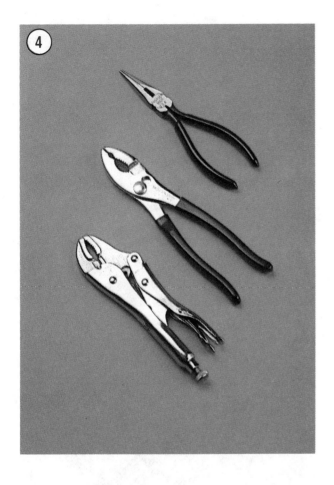

be adjusted to hold various sizes of objects; the jaws remain parallel to grip around objects such as pipe or tubing. There are many more types of pliers. The ones described here are the most commonly used.

Box and Open-end Wrenches

Box and open-end wrenches are available in sets or separately in a variety of sizes. See **Figure 5** and **Figure 6**. The number stamped near the end refers to the distance between two parallel flats on the hex head bolt or nut.

Box wrenches are usually superior to open-end wrenches. An open-end wrench grips the nut on only two flats. Unless it fits well, it may slip and round off the points on the nut. The box wrench grips all 6 flats. Both 6-point and 12-point openings on box wrenches are available. The 6-point gives superior holding power; the 12-point allows a shorter swing.

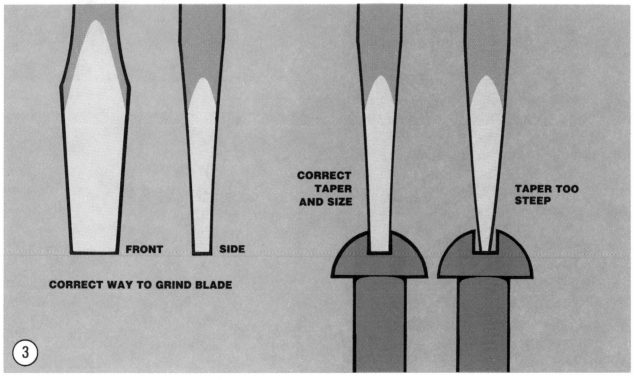

FRONT   SIDE

CORRECT WAY TO GRIND BLADE

CORRECT TAPER AND SIZE

TAPER TOO STEEP

Combination wrenches, which are open on one side and boxed on the other, are also available. Both ends are the same size.

Adjustable Wrenches

An adjustable wrench can be adjusted to fit nearly any nut or bolt head. See **Figure 7**. However, it can loosen and slip, causing damage to the nut and maybe to your knuckles. Use an adjustable wrench only when other wrenches are not available.

Adjustable wrenches come in sizes ranging from 4-18 in. overall. A 6 or 8 in. wrench is recommended as an all-purpose wrench.

Socket Wrenches

This type is undoubtedly the fastest, safest and most convenient to use. See **Figure 8**. Sockets, which attach to a suitable handle, are available with 6-point or 12-point openings and use 1/4, 3/8 and 3/4 inch drives. The drive size indicates

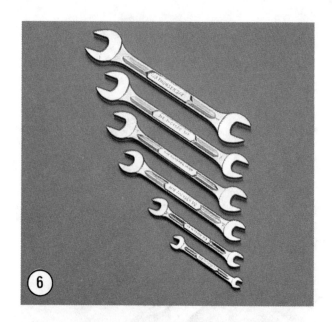

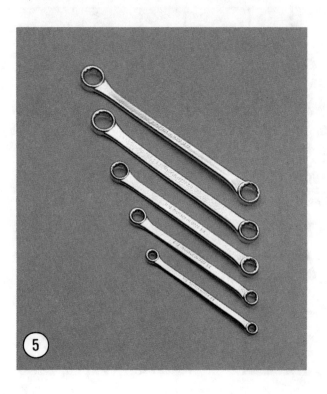

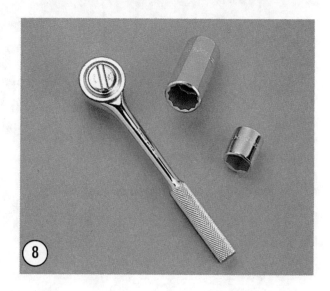

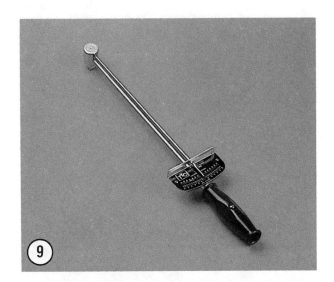

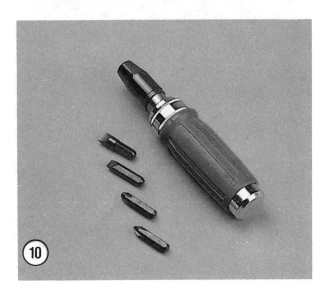

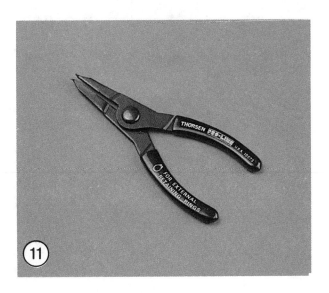

the size of the square hole that mates with the ratchet or flex handle.

2

Torque Wrench

A torque wrench (**Figure 9**) is used with a socket to measure how tight a nut or bolt is installed. They come in a wide price range and with either 3/8 or 1/2 in. square drive. The drive size indicates the size of the square drive that mates with the socket. Purchase one that measures up to 150 ft.-lb. (203 N•m).

Impact Driver

This tool (**Figure 10**) makes removal of tight fasteners easy and eliminates damage to bolts and screw slots. Impact drivers and interchangeable bits are available at most large hardware and auto parts stores.

Circlip Pliers

Circlip pliers (sometimes referred to as snapring pliers) are necessary to remove circlips. See **Figure 11**. Circlip pliers usually come with several different size tips; many designs can be switched from internal type to external type.

Hammers

The correct hammer is necessary for repairs. Use only a hammer with a face (or head) of rubber or plastic or the soft-faced type that is filled with buckshot (**Figure 12**). These are sometimes necessary in engine tear-downs. *Never* use a metal-faced hammer as severe damage will result in most cases. You can always produce the same amount of force with a soft-faced hammer.

Feeler Gauge

This tool has either flat or wire measuring gauges (**Figure 13**). Wire gauges are used to measure spark plug gap; flat gauges are used for all other measurements. A non-magnetic (brass) gauge may be specified when working around magnetized parts.

Other Special Tools

Some procedures require special tools; these are identified in the appropriate chapter. Unless otherwise specified, the part number used in this book to identify a special tool is the marine equipment manufacturer's part number.

Special tools can usually be purchased through your marine equipment dealer. Some can be made locally by a machinist, often at a much lower price. You may find certain special tools at tool rental dealers. Don't use makeshift tools if you can't locate the correct special tool; you will probably cause more damage than good.

TEST EQUIPMENT

Multimeter

This instrument (**Figure 14**) is invaluable for electrical system troubleshooting and service. It combines a voltmeter, an ohmmeter and an ammeter into one unit, so it is often called a VOM.

Two types of multimeter are available, analog and digital. Analog meters have a moving needle with marked bands indicating the volt, ohm and amperage scales. The digital meter (DVOM) is ideally suited for troubleshooting because it is easy to read, more accurate than analog, contains internal overload protection, is auto-ranging (analog meters must be recalibrated each time the scale is changed) and has automatic polarity compensation.

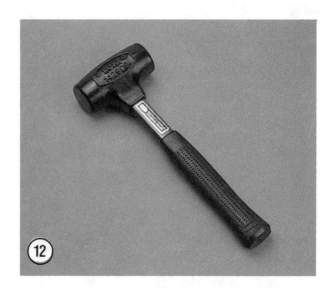

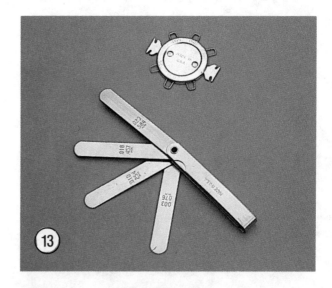

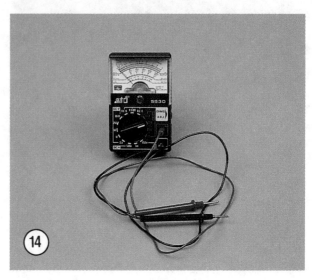

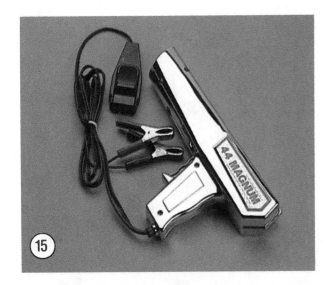

Strobe Timing Light

This instrument is necessary for dynamic tuning (setting ignition timing while the engine is running). By flashing a light at the precise instant the spark plug fires, the position of the timing mark can be seen. The flashing light makes a moving mark appear to stand still opposite a stationary mark.

Suitable lights range from inexpensive neon bulb types to powerful xenon strobe lights. See **Figure 15**. A light with an inductive pickup is best because it eliminates any possible damage to ignition wiring.

Tachometer/Dwell Meter

A portable tachometer is necessary for tuning. See **Figure 16**. Ignition timing and carburetor adjustments must be performed at the specified idle speed. The best instrument for this purpose is one with a low range of 0-1000 or 0-2000 rpm and a high range of 0-6000 rpm. Extended range (0-6000 or 0-8000 rpm) instruments lack accuracy at lower speeds. The instrument should be capable of detecting changes of 25 rpm on the low range.

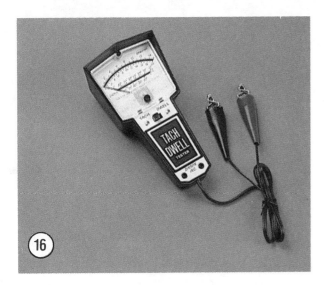

A dwell meter is often combined with a tachometer. Dwell meters are used with breaker point ignition systems to measure the amount of time the points remain closed during engine operation.

Compression Gauge

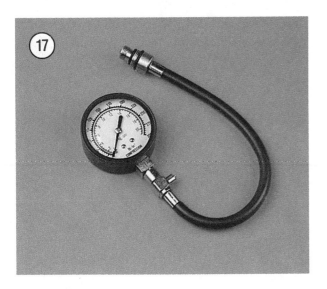

This tool (**Figure 17**) measures the amount of pressure present in the engine's combustion chamber during the compression stroke. This indicates general engine condition. Compression readings can be interpreted along with vacuum gauge readings to pinpoint specific engine mechanical problems.

The easiest type to use has screw-in adapters that fit into the spark plug holes. Press-in rubber-tipped types are also available.

Vacuum Gauge

The vacuum gauge (**Figure 18**) measures the intake manifold vacuum created by the engine's intake stroke. Manifold and valve problems (on 4-stroke engines) can be identified by interpreting the readings. When combined with compression gauge readings, other engine problems can be diagnosed.

Some vacuum gauges can also be used as fuel pressure gauges to trace fuel system problems.

Hydrometer

Battery electrolyte specific gravity is measured with a hydrometer (**Figure 19**). The specific gravity of the electrolyte indicates the battery's state of charge. The best type has automatic temperature compensation; otherwise, you must calculate the compensation yourself.

Precision Measuring Tools

Various tools are needed to make precision measurements. A dial indicator (**Figure 20**), for example, is used to determine run-out of rotating parts and end play of parts assemblies. A dial indicator can also be used to precisely measure piston position in relation to top dead center; some engines require this measurement for ignition timing adjustment.

Vernier calipers (**Figure 21**) and micrometers (**Figure 22**) are other precision measuring tools used to determine the size of parts (such as piston diameter).

Precision measuring equipment must be stored, handled and used carefully or it will not remain accurate.

SERVICE HINTS

Most of the service procedures covered in this manual are straightforward and can be performed by anyone reasonably handy with tools.

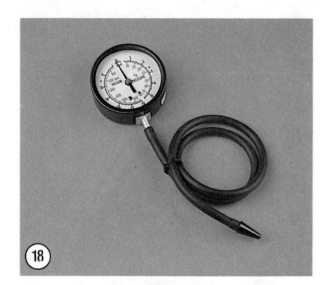

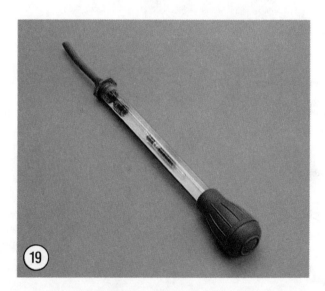

It is suggested, however, that you consider your own skills and toolbox carefully before attempting any operation involving major disassembly of the engine or gearcase.

Some operations, for example, require the use of a press. It would be wiser to have these performed by a shop equipped for such work, rather than trying to do the job yourself with makeshift equipment. Other procedures require precise measurements. Unless you have the skills and

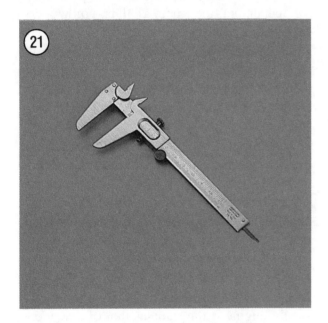

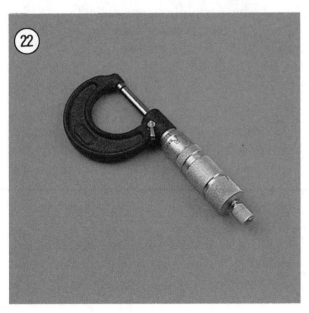

equipment required, it would be better to have a qualified repair shop make the measurements for you.

Preparation for Disassembly

Repairs go much faster and easier if the equipment is clean before you begin work. There are special cleaners, such as Gunk or Bel-Ray Degreaser, for washing the engine and related parts. Just spray or brush on the cleaning solution, let it stand, then rinse away with a garden hose. Clean all oily or greasy parts with cleaning solvent as you remove them.

> *WARNING*
> *Never use gasoline as a cleaning agent. It presents an extreme fire hazard. Be sure to work in a well-ventilated area when using cleaning solvent. Keep a Coast Guard approved fire extinguisher, rated for gasoline fires, handy in any case.*

Much of the labor charged for repairs made by dealers is for the removal and disassembly of other parts to reach the defective unit. It is frequently possible to perform the preliminary operations yourself and then take the defective unit in to the dealer for repair.

If you decide to tackle the job yourself, read the entire section in this manual that pertains to it, making sure you have identified the proper one. Study the illustrations and text until you have a good idea of what is involved in completing the job satisfactorily. If special tools or replacement parts are required, make arrangements to get them before you start. It is frustrating and time-consuming to get partly into a job and then be unable to complete it.

Disassembly Precautions

During disassembly of parts, keep a few general precautions in mind. Force is rarely needed to get things apart. If parts are a tight fit, such as a bearing in a case, there is usually a tool designed to separate them. Never use a screwdriver to pry apart parts with machined surfaces (such as cylinder heads and crankcases). You will mar the surfaces and end up with leaks.

Make diagrams (or take an instant picture) wherever similar-appearing parts are found. For example, head and crankcase bolts are often not the same length. You may think you can remember where everything came from, but mistakes are costly. There is also the possibility you may be sidetracked and not return to work for days or even weeks. In the interval, carefully laid out parts may have been disturbed.

Cover all openings after removing parts to keep small parts, dirt or other contamination from entering.

Tag all similar internal parts for location and direction. All internal components should be reinstalled in the same location and direction from which removed. Record the number and thickness of any shims as they are removed. Small parts, such as bolts, can be identified by placing them in plastic sandwich bags. Seal and label them with masking tape.

Wiring should be tagged with masking tape and marked as each wire is removed. Again, do not rely on memory alone.

Protect finished surfaces from physical damage or corrosion. Keep gasoline off painted surfaces.

Assembly Precautions

No parts, except those assembled with a press fit, require unusual force during assembly. If a part is hard to remove or install, find out why before proceeding.

When assembling two parts, start all fasteners, then tighten evenly in an alternating or crossing pattern if no specific tightening sequence is given.

When assembling parts, be sure all shims and washers are installed exactly as they came out.

Whenever a rotating part butts against a stationary part, look for a shim or washer. Use new gaskets if there is any doubt about the condition of the old ones. Unless otherwise specified, a thin coat of oil on gaskets may help them seal effectively.

Heavy grease can be used to hold small parts in place if they tend to fall out during assembly. However, keep grease and oil away from electrical components.

High spots may be sanded off a piston with sandpaper, but fine emery cloth and oil will do a much more professional job.

Carbon can be removed from the cylinder head, the piston crown and the exhaust port with a dull screwdriver. *Do not* scratch either surface. Wipe off the surface with a clean cloth when finished.

The carburetor is best cleaned by disassembling it and soaking the parts in a commercial carburetor cleaner. Never soak gaskets and rubber parts in these cleaners. Never use wire to clean out jets and air passages; they are easily damaged. Use compressed air to blow out the carburetor *after* the float has been removed.

Take your time and do the job right. Do not forget that the break-in procedure on a newly rebuilt engine is the same as that of a new one. Use the break-in oil recommendations and follow other instructions given in your owner's manual.

SPECIAL TIPS

Because of the extreme demands placed on marine equipment, several points should be kept in mind when performing service and repair. The following items are general suggestions that may improve the overall life of the machine and help avoid costly failures.

1. Unless otherwise specified, use a locking compound, such as Loctite Threadlocker, on all bolts and nuts, even if they are secured with lockwashers. Be sure to use the specified grade

of thread locking compound. A screw or bolt lost from an engine cover or bearing retainer could easily cause serious and expensive damage before its loss is noticed.

When applying thread locking compound, use a small amount. If too much is used, it can work its way down the threads and stick parts together that were not meant to be stuck together.

Keep a tube of thread locking compound in your tool box; when used properly, it is cheap insurance.

2. Use a hammer-driven impact tool to remove and install screws and bolts. These tools help prevent the rounding off of bolt heads and screw slots and ensure a tight installation.

3. When straightening the fold-over type lockwasher, use a wide-blade chisel, such as an old and dull wood chisel. Such a tool provides a better purchase on the folded tab, making straightening easier.

4. When installing the fold-over type lockwasher, always use a new washer if possible. If a new washer is not available, always fold over a part of the washer that has not been previously folded. Reusing the same fold may cause the washer to break, resulting in the loss of its locking ability and a loose piece of metal adrift in the engine.

When folding the washer, start the fold with a screwdriver and finish it with a pair of pliers. If a punch is used to make the fold, the fold may be too sharp, thereby increasing the chances of the washer breaking under stress.

These washers are relatively inexpensive and it is suggested that you keep several of each size in your tool box for repairs.

5. When replacing missing or broken fasteners (bolts, nuts and screws), always use authorized replacement parts. They are specially hardened for each application. The wrong 50-cent bolt could easily cause serious and expensive damage.

6. When installing gaskets, always use authorized replacement gaskets *without* sealer, unless designated. Many gaskets are designed to swell when they come in contact with oil. Gasket sealer will prevent the gaskets from swelling as intended and can result in oil leaks. Authorized replacement gaskets are cut from material of the precise thickness needed. Installation of a too thick or too thin gasket in a critical area could cause equipment damage.

MECHANIC'S TECHNIQUES

Removing Frozen Fasteners

When a fastener rusts and cannot be removed, several methods may be used to loosen it. First, apply penetrating oil, such as Liquid Wrench or WD-40 (available at any hardware or auto supply store). Apply it liberally and allow it penetrate for 10-15 minutes. Tap the fastener several times with a small hammer; do not hit it hard enough to cause damage. Reapply the penetrating oil if necessary.

For frozen screws, apply penetrating oil as described, then insert a screwdriver in the slot and tap the top of the screwdriver with a hammer. This loosens the rust so the screw can be removed in the normal way. If the screw head is too chewed up to use a screwdriver, grip the head with locking pliers and twist the screw out.

Avoid applying heat unless specifically instructed because it may melt, warp or remove the temper from parts.

Remedying Stripped Threads

Occasionally, threads are stripped through carelessness or impact damage. Often the threads can be cleaned up by running a tap (for internal threads on nuts) or die (for external threads on bolts) through threads. See **Figure 23**.

Removing Broken Screws or Bolts

When the head breaks off a screw or bolt, several methods are available for removing the remaining portion.

If a large portion of the remainder projects out, try gripping it with vise-grip pliers. If the projecting portion is too small, file it to fit a wrench or cut a slot in it to fit a screwdriver. See **Figure 24**.

If the head breaks off flush, use a screw extractor. To do this, centerpunch the remaining portion of the screw or bolt. Drill a small hole in the screw and tap the extractor into the hole. Back the screw out with a wrench on the extractor. See **Figure 25**.

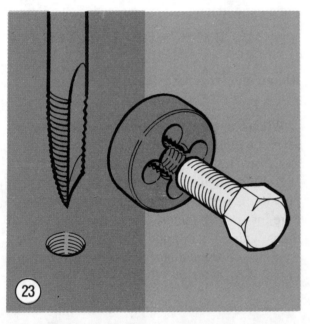

(23)

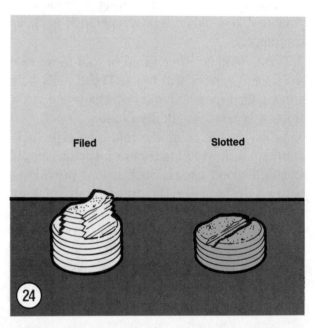

Filed   Slotted

(24)

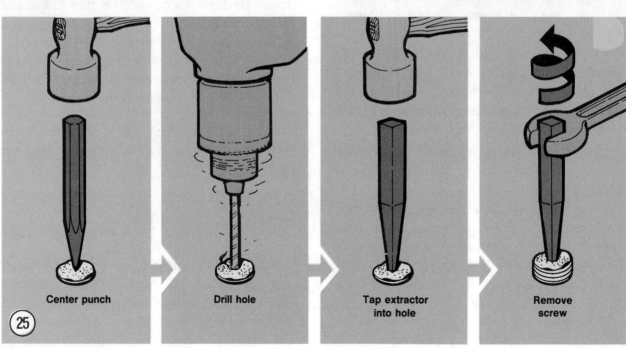

(25) Center punch   Drill hole   Tap extractor into hole   Remove screw

Chapter Three

Troubleshooting

The most successful way to troubleshoot an outboard is to take an orderly and logical approach. Taking a haphazard approach may eventually find the problem, but it can be costly in terms of wasted time and unnecessary parts replacement. Follow the step by step instructions provided in this chapter, and troubleshooting can be performed in an efficient and timely manner.

The first step in any troubleshooting procedure is to define the symptoms as closely as possible and then localize the problem. Subsequent steps involve testing and analyzing those areas that could cause the symptoms.

Never assume anything. Do not overlook the obvious. If the engine will not start, is the safety lanyard attached? Is the fuel system primed? Is the engine cranking slowly because the battery is discharged?

If the engine suddenly quits, check the easiest, most accessible problem first. Is there gasoline in the tank? Is the fuel vent check valve allowing air to enter the tank as it should?

If nothing obvious turns up in a quick check, look a little further. Learning to recognize and describe symptoms will make repairs easier for you or a mechanic at the shop. Gather as many symptoms as possible to aid in diagnosis. Note whether the engine lost power gradually or all at once, what color smoke came from the exhaust and so on.

Remember that the more complicated a machine is, the easier it is to troubleshoot because symptoms point to specific problems.

After the symptoms are defined, areas that could cause problems should be tested and analyzed. Guessing at the cause of a problem may provide the solution, but it can easily lead to frustration, wasted time and a series of expensive, unnecessary parts replacements.

You do not need expensive equipment or complicated test gear to determine whether repairs can be attempted at home. A few simple checks could save a large repair bill and lost time while your water vehicle sits in a dealer's service department. On the other hand, be realistic. Do not attempt repairs beyond your abilities. Service departments tend to charge heavily for putting together a disassembled engine that may have been abused. Some will not even take on such a job-so use common sense and do not get in over your head.

This chapter provides sections covering *test equipment, starting difficulties, troubleshooting preparation, operating requirements and systems or component testing.*

Tables 1-3 list common problems related to the starting, ignition and fuel and ignition systems. The probable cause(s) and corrective action are also listed. **Tables 1-3** may refer to the *Component Testing* section(s) of this chapter for component testing. **Tables 4-17** list specifications on various engine operating systems. **Tables 1-24** are located at the end of this chapter.

> *NOTE*
> *This manual provides procedures and specifications for standard products. This manual may not provide needed information if the product has been modified or has aftermarket equipment installed. The use of aftermarket equipment or modification of the engine can affect engine performance and tuning requirements. For information on aftermarket equipment, consult a dealership that handles such equipment or is familiar with engine modification. If necessary, contact the manufacturer of the aftermarket equipment for information. If you install any aftermarket equipment, keep all instructions with your owner's manual for future reference.*

TEST EQUIPMENT

The common tools to troubleshoot a Yamaha outboard include: multimeter, pressure/vacuum gauges, fuel pressure gauge, compression gauge and gearcase pressure tester. Descriptions of these tools and other equipment can be found in Chapter Two. Specific information on the use of this equipment is provided in this chapter and throughout this manual.

Multimeter

Modern outboards use advanced electronic engine control systems that enhance performance, reliability and fuel economy. The common multimeter is a very important diagnostic tool for electrical system troubleshooting and service. It combines a voltmeter, an ohmmeter and an ammeter into one unit. Troubleshooting procedures in this chapter will require that tests be performed using either an analog or digital multimeter. Refer to this section anytime a question arises on using a multimeter.

A digital multimeter will have the test readings displayed on a screen located on the front of the meter. An analog multimeter will have a needle that swings across the face of the meter. With analog multimeters the meter reading is determined by reading the point the needle moves to on the face of the meter. In most cases either type of meter can be used. The troubleshooting procedures will indicate when a particular type of meter is required. Make sure that the meter is equipped with fresh batteries to avoid inaccurate readings and false diagnosis. Refer to the instruction booklet that came with the meter for features,

specifications and specific instructions. Procedures for using a typical meter are provided in the following instructions.

Determining meter function

Most multimeters measure voltage, resistance and amperage. An LCD screen or the selector dial will indicate what function you have selected. For voltage the meter will display volts or V. For resistance the meter will display *ohms or resistance*. For amperage the meter will display *amps*. To select the proper function of the meter, refer to the tables that provide the desired test results. Volts, ohms or amps will be listed near the specifications. If the test results indicate continuity or no continuity, select the *ohms or resistance* settings on the meter.

> *NOTE*
> *To avoid costly errors always record the meter readings during testing. Make note of the color wires used, where the leads were connected and actual readings. Clean all*

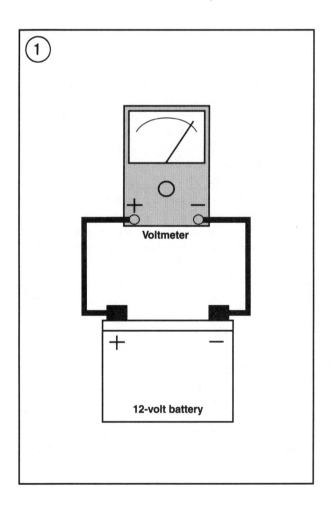

Voltmeter

12-volt battery

terminal connections before connecting test leads to them. It is a good idea to perform the test twice to verify that a fault exists before replacing any component. This important step can save time and unnecessary expense.

Determining test range

Before performing the test using the multimeter, determine the scale or range required for the test. Refer to the information provided in the tables for the test specification. Available ranges on the meter vary by model and manufacturer. Check the instruction sheet that came with the meter for specific instructions.

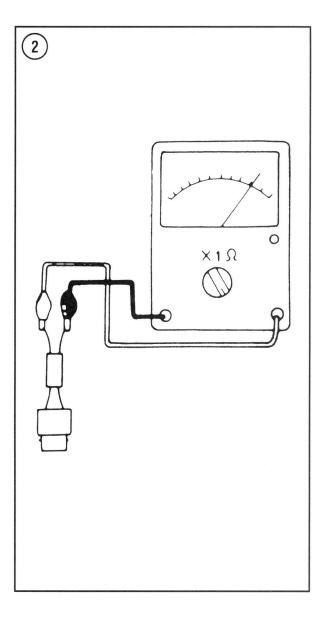

NOTE
Some digital multimeters are auto-scaling, and selection of the range is not necessary. Be aware that not all meters provide accurate readings in the millivolt, milliohm and milliamp ranges. Check the instructions provided with the meter.

Measuring voltage

To measure *voltage*, the negative lead is usually connected to the engine ground, negative battery terminal or other specified location (**Figure 1**). The positive lead is usually connected to the positive battery terminal or other specified lead/location. This connection arrangement is commonly referred to as a parallel connection. Voltage values are typically used when troubleshooting the ignition system, charging system, starting system, instruments and controls. Voltage is best described as the *potential pressure of the current* flowing in a circuit.

Measuring peak voltage

Some multimeters are provided with a *peak voltage or DVA* function. This feature allows the meter to measure voltage pulses that peak during a very short duration. Most common meters are unable to accurately measure these short duration pulses. The use of the peak voltage adapter, Yamaha part No. YU-39991/90890-03169, will provide this capability for most meters. This function is commonly used to test voltages produced by the ignition system.

WARNING
Use extreme caution when using any meter around high voltage. To help avoid potential electric shock, the probe portion of the test leads must not contact any portion of the body. Never perform the test near any source of fuel or vapor as arcing may ignite the fuel or vapor, causing a fire or explosion.

Measuring ohms

Ohms are best described as the measurement units for the resistance to current flow in a circuit. To measure *ohms or resistance*, the multimeter test leads are usually connected between two specified leads or between a specified lead and another location (**Figure 2**). This connection arrangement is commonly referred to as a series connection. Ohms tests are generally performed on ignition system components, motor windings, wire harnesses, switches and instruments.

Select the required scale and *zero* any analog meter before testing. To *zero* the meter, connect the two test leads together and rotate the adjusting knob (A, **Figure 3**) until a *0* reading (B, **Figure 3**) on the meter is attained. When an ohm value with a *K* is listed in the specifications, the resistance is 1000 times the displayed numerical value. For example (C, **Figure 3**), R × 1K (1000) would be selected if the specifications were in 1000 ohms increments. Connect the test leads to the specified locations and read the resistance on the meter. An open circuit, very high resistance or infinity, is indicated if no needle movement is noted or the digital display flashes. Essentially very little or no current would flow in this circuit. A closed circuit or short circuit, very low resistance or full continuity, is indicated if the needle swings all the way to the right or reaches the *0*. Current could easily flow in this circuit.

NOTE
When using a digital multimeter to measure very low resistance values, select the proper scale then connect the test leads together. A reading other than 0 indicates internal resis-

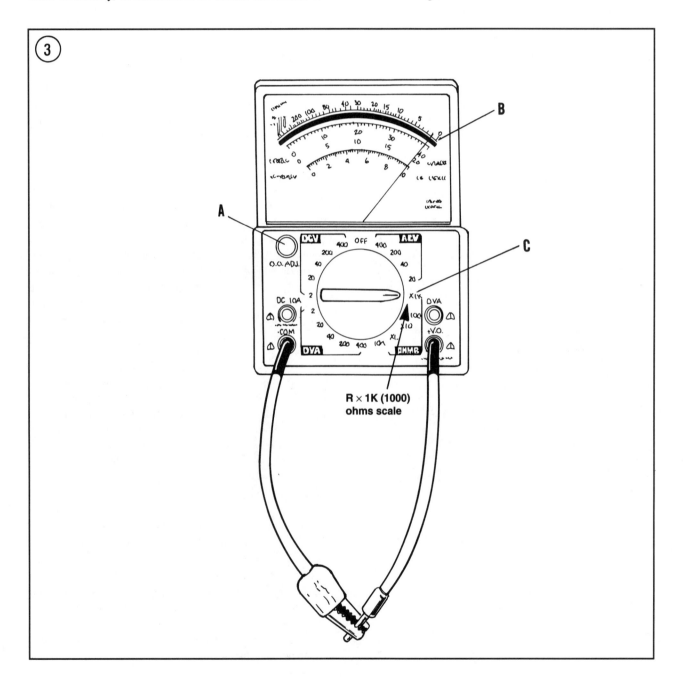

**R × 1K (1000)
ohms scale**

tance in the meter or test leads. This value must be subtracted from the reading when testing components to determine the actual resistance in a circuit.

CAUTION
Never measure ohms or resistance on any circuit or component that is connected to the battery or other source of current. The meter can suffer permanent damage.

Measuring amperage

Amperage is best described as the volume of current flowing in a circuit.

To measure *amps*, the meter test leads are usually connected between two specified leads or other locations on the engine (**Figure 4**). This connection arrangement is commonly referred to as a series connection. Pay strict attention to connecting leads to avoid inaccurate readings or possible damage to engine components. Amperage readings are typically used when troubleshooting the battery charging system or the starting system.

NOTE
Most multimeters cannot read above 10 amps. If the specification lists a value greater than 10 amps, you will need to obtain a meter that is capable of reading the required range(s).

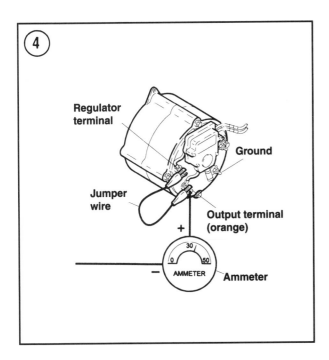

WARNING
Use extreme caution when the test requires that meter leads be connected to a battery terminal. Batteries may contain explosive hydrogen gas in and around them that can explode, resulting in death or injury. Never smoke around a battery or allow any flame or spark to occur near batteries. If testing requires that a lead be connected to a battery terminal, make certain that the final connection is made to a component other than the battery terminal. Follow all instructions carefully.

Checking diodes

Multimeters are often used to check diodes within various engine components. The ohms function is selected on most meters when checking diodes. Some meters have a diode test option. Diodes function like electrical check valves. The resistance is measured between two leads or terminals. The meter test leads are then reversed and the resistance is checked again. High resistance when connected one way and low resistance when the leads are reversed generally indicates a good diode. There is little need to be concerned about test lead polarity, as variations exist from one meter to the next. Use a meter with a diode test function if a question arises regarding the polarity of a diode.

Vacuum Pump, Pressure Pump and Gauges

Vacuum/pressure pumps and gauges, Yamaha part No. YB-35956, are used to check fuel pumps and other components of the fuel delivery system. The fuel-injected engine requires a special gauge, Yamaha part No. YB-06766/90890-06766, to test the fuel system.

Compression gauge

The compression gauge is used to measure the pressure that builds in the combustion chamber at a specified cranking speed. Specific instructions for compression testing are provided in this chapter.

Gearcase pressure tester

Gearcase pressure testers are used to find the source of water or lubricant leakage. The procedures for proper use of this type of tester are provided in this chapter.

TROUBLESHOOTING PREPARATION

Before troubleshooting the engine, verify the model name, model number, horsepower and serial number of the engine. It is absolutely essential that the model be correctly identified before performing any service to the engine. In many cases, the tables will list specifications by horsepower and/or model name. Identification tags for most models are located on the port side clamp bracket. Refer to **Figure 5** to review the various forms of information on this tag. Reference Table 14 to identify the horsepower, model name, model code, starting serial number and engine description. In addition, the information provided on the tag is required when purchasing replacement parts for your Yamaha outboard.

NOTE
*V6 models use either a 90° or 76° cylinder block. Specifications and procedures vary between these models. Refer to **Table 14** and the serial/model tag to properly identify the engine and its cylinder configuration.*

Preliminary inspection

Most engine malfunctions can be corrected by checking and correcting a few simple items. Check the following and if problems still exist refer to **Tables 1-3** for starting, ignition and fuel system troubleshooting. **Tables 1-3** indicate the necessary component testing or adjustment. Addi-

tional troubleshooting tips are provided in this chapter for the specific system or component.

1. Inspect the engine for loose, disconnected, dirty or corroded wires.
2. Provide the engine with fresh fuel and the proper mix of Yamaha TC-W3 Outboard Oil.
3. Check the battery and cables for proper and clean connections.
4. Fully charge the battery if needed.
5. Use proper equipment and test for spark at each cylinder.
6. Check spark plug condition and gap settings.
7. Position the lanyard switch in the run position.
8. Verify that the boat hull is clean and in good condition.

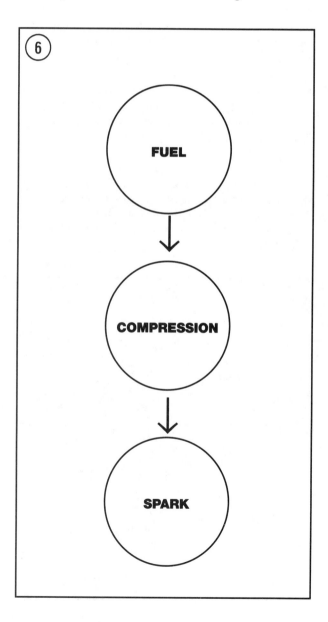

1. Model name
2. Approval model code
3. Transom height
4. Serial number

NOTE
Yamaha outboards with an L in the model name indicate a counter-rotation model. On L models, a left-hand propeller is used. Refer to the standard-rotation model (no L in the model name), of the same horsepower for procedures and specification unless designated procedures and specifications for the L models are provided.

OPERATING REQUIREMENTS

An internal combustion engine requires three basic things to run properly: a fresh supply of fuel and air in the

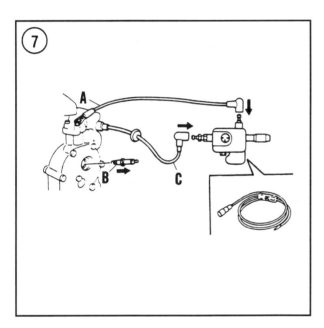

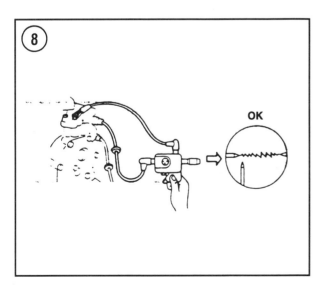

proper proportion, adequate compression in the combustion chamber and a source of ignition at the proper time (**Figure 6**). If any of these are missing, the engine will not run. If any of these are lacking, the engine will not run properly.

STARTING DIFFICULTY

Starting Procedures

If starting the engine becomes difficult, the problem may be with the engine or may be related to an improper starting procedure. The owner's manual is the best source for finding the proper starting procedure. Refer to **Table 1** to troubleshoot problems with the electric start systems. Manual or rewind starter repairs are provided in Chapter Eleven.

Determining a Fuel or Ignition Fault

It can be quite difficult to determine if a starting problem is related to fuel, ignition or other causes. If the engine will not start, it is easiest to first verify that the ignition system is operating. Check the fuel system if the ignition system is operating properly. Use a spark gap tester to indicate output from the ignition system at cranking speeds. Spark gap testers are available from a variety of sources including Yamaha part No. YM 34487/90890-06754.

Spark test

1. Connect the alligator clip test lead (A, **Figure 7**) to a suitable engine ground.
2. Remove the spark plug(s) (B, **Figure 7**).
3. Attach the spark plug leads to the spark gap tester (C, **Figure 7**).
4. Crank the engine while observing the spark tester (**Figure 8**). A strong blue spark that jumps a 9 mm (0.35 in.) gap indicates adequate spark.
5. Repeat Steps 1-4 for all cylinders. Install spark plug(s) and connect the leads when the test is complete. Refer to **Table 2** for ignition system testing if spark is lacking or weak on any cylinders. Refer to **Table 3** for fuel system troubleshooting if the ignition system is working properly, but the engine still will not start.

WARNING
High voltage is present in the ignition system. Never touch wires or connections to any part of the body. Never perform this test in wet conditions. Electric shock can be fatal or cause serious bodily injury. Never perform electrical testing when fuel or fuel vapor is

present as arcing may cause a fire or explosion.

Checking the Fuel System

Fuel-related problems are common to outboard engines. Fuels available today have a relatively short shelf life. Gasoline tends to lose some of its desirable qualities and become sour if stored for long periods. A gummy deposit may form in the carburetor and fuel passages as the fuel evaporates. These deposits may also clog fuel filters and fuel lines. Fuel stored in the tank may become contaminated with water from condensation or other sources. The water will cause the engine to run poorly or not at all.

Check the condition of the fuel if the engine has been stored for some time and refuses to start. Carefully drain the float bowl into a suitable container. Chapter Six provides drawings that indicate specific locations of the float bowl drain plugs (**Figure 9**). Unusual odor, debris, cloudy appearance or presence of water is a sure sign of a problem. If any of these conditions is noted, dispose of the old fuel in an environmentally friendly manner. Contact a local marine dealership or automotive repair facility for information on proper disposal of fuel. Clean and inspect the entire fuel system when contaminants are found in the float bowl. Problems are inevitable if the entire system is not inspected. Replace all filters in the fuel system to ensure a reliable repair. When no fuel can be drained from the float bowl, the carburetor(s) should be inspected along with the fuel lines and fuel pump. Typically, the fuel inlet needle is stuck closed or plugged with debris. Carburetor repair procedures are provided in Chapter Six. A faulty enrichment valve, choke valve or electrothermal valve may cause hard starting and performance problems. Inspect and test these components if hard starting or performance problems persist.

FUEL SYSTEM COMPONENT TESTING

Fuel Pump and Fuel Tank

The fuel tank or fuel pump is usually the culprit if the engine surges at higher speed. Boats equipped with built-in fuel tanks are equipped with some sort of anti-siphon device to prevent fuel from siphoning out of the tank if a leak occurs in the fuel line. These devices are necessary from a safety standpoint but can cause problems when they malfunction. Temporarily run the engine using a portable fuel tank with a fresh fuel/oil mixture. Inspect the fuel tank pickup, anti-siphon device and fuel tank vent if the engine

performs properly on the temporary fuel tank. Always replace corroded or plugged anti-siphon devices.

To check for a problem with the fuel pump, try gently squeezing the primer bulb when the symptom occurs. Perform a complete inspection of the fuel pump and fuel lines if the symptom improves while squeezing the primer bulb. Complete fuel system repair procedures are provided in Chapter Six. Always check for and correct fuel leaks after working with any fuel system components.

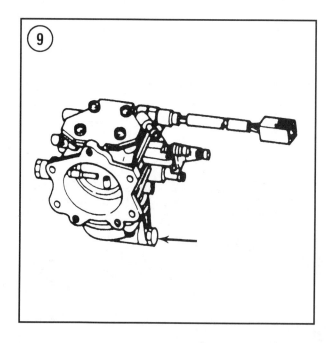

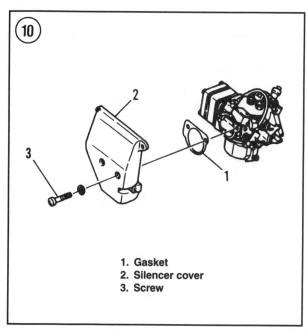

1. Gasket
2. Silencer cover
3. Screw

CAUTION
Never run an outboard without providing cooling water. Use either a test tank or flush/test device. Remove the propeller before running the engine. Install a test propeller to run the engine in a test tank.

Carburetor Malfunction

A rough running engine that smokes excessively, usually indicates a rich fuel/air mixture. The typical causes are a flooding carburetor, faulty puddle drain system, stuck choke, enrichment valve malfunction or faulty electrothermal valve. The most common cause is a flooding carburetor or improper float level adjustment. A weak spark can also cause rough running and excessive smoking.

Other conditions can cause a lean condition that leads to performance problems or bogging on acceleration. This section describes the causes and solutions for these conditions.

Flooding carburetor

To check for a flooding carburetor, perform Steps 1-4. Model variations exist in the carburetor silencer/cover and attachments. However, the testing procedures are consistent within the models. Refer to Chapter Six for specific instructions if the model being tested does not resemble the components indicated.

1. Remove the attaching screw, silencer/cover and gasket (**Figure 10**) from the front of the engine. Discard and replace damaged gaskets as required.

2. Gently squeeze the primer bulb as you look into the front of the carburetor. Engines with an integral fuel tank are not equipped with a primer bulb. Open the fuel valve and look into the opening in the front of the carburetor.

3. If fuel is observed flowing into opening of the carburetor, remove the carburetor and repair it as described in Chapter Six.

4. Install the gasket, silencer cover and screw(s) (**Figure 10**). Tighten screw(s) securely.

Plugged carburetor passages

Blocked jets, passages, orifices or vents can cause either a rich or lean condition. Operating the engine under a lean fuel condition can lead to serious power head damage. Symptoms of inadequate or excess fuel include bogging or sagging on acceleration, rough idle, poor performance at high speed or surging. If the engine experiences a bog or sag on acceleration, push in on the key switch or turn the choke switch ON to enrich the fuel mixture while accelerating the engine. The engine is operating under a lean fuel condition if the symptoms improve with the enriched fuel mixture. The engine is likely operating under a rich fuel condition if the symptoms get worse. In either case, the carburetors should be cleaned and inspected as described in Chapter Six.

Altitude adjustments

In some instances, changes to carburetor jets or carburetor adjustments are required to correct engine malfunctions. If the engine is operated at higher elevation, carburetor jet changes may be required. Operation in some environments, hot or cold climates, may require carburetor adjustments or jet changes. Contact a Yamaha dealership in the area where the engine will be operated for recommendations.

Damaged Reed Valve(s)

A chipped or broken reed valve (**Figure 11**) can cause poor idle quality and decreased performance.

The test can be performed at idle speeds only with the engine running in the water or on a flush /test device. Variations exist in the carburetor cover and attachments, but the testing procedures are consistent. Refer to Chapter Six for specific instruction if the components on the model tested do not resemble the components indicated in **Figure 10**.

1. Remove the screw(s), silencer cover, and gasket(s) (**Figure 10**). Discard and replace damaged gaskets as required.

2. Run the engine at idle speed. Fuel spitting out the front of the carburetor indicates a problem with the reed valve.

If a problem is noted, remove and inspect the reed valve assembly as described in Chapter Six.

3. Install gasket(s), silencer cover, and screw(s) (**Figure 10**). Tighten screw(s) securely.

> *WARNING*
> *Use extreme caution when working with the fuel system. Avoid damage to property, potential bodily injury or death. Never smoke around fuel or fuel vapor. Make sure that no flame or source of ignition is present in the work area. Flame or sparks can ignite the fuel or vapor resulting in fire or explosion.*

Compression Testing and Cylinder Condition

Older engines or engines with high operating hours often experience hard starting, poor idle quality or poor performance. A compression test should be performed if the fuel system and ignition system have been ruled out as causing hard starting. Avoid relying solely on the compression test to indicate the condition of the engine. Sometimes a compression test will indicate satisfactory readings when there is still something wrong. Closer inspection of the piston, rings and cylinder walls may reveal scoring or scuffing not detected by compression testing. The leak-down test is a more reliable indicator of the pistons, rings and cylinder wall condition. This equipment is far more costly and more difficult to use than a typical compression gauge. Allow a reputable marine dealer to perform this test for you if needed.

1. Remove and inspect the spark plugs from all cylinders. Clean or replace plugs as necessary.

2. Connect all spark plug leads to a suitable engine ground using jumper leads (**Figure 12**).

3. Install compression gauge into the No. 1 cylinder spark plug hole (**Figure 13**).

> *NOTE*
> *The top cylinder is the No. 1 cylinder on inline engines. On V4 or V6 engines, the top cylinder on the starboard bank is the No. 1 cylinder.*

4. Manually hold the throttle plate(s) in the wide-open position. Operate the electric starter motor or rewind starter to insure the flywheel has rotated at least six rotations.

5. Record the compression readings.

6. Repeat Steps 3-5 for the other cylinders.

7. Install original or new spark plugs and torque to the specification provided in Chapter Four.

8. Compare the compression readings noting the highest and lowest readings. Ideally the lowest reading should be within 10% of the highest reading. One or more cylinders with significantly low readings indicate a problem that deserves attention before attempting to troubleshoot or tune the engine. Power head repair procedures are provided in Chapter Eight. An engine with inadequate compression cannot be tuned properly or expected to perform correctly.

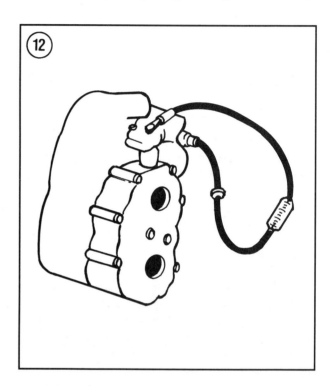

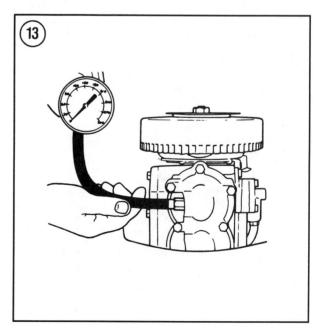

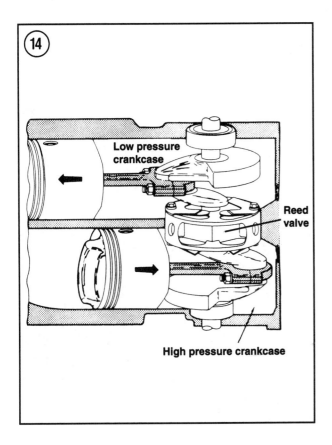

(14)

Low pressure
crankcase

Reed
valve

High pressure crankcase

Crankcase Sealing

A two-stroke engine must operate with alternating pressure and vacuum in the crankcase (**Figure 14**). As the piston moves up on the compression stroke, the volume in the crankcase increases and creates a vacuum. Atmospheric pressure forces fuel and air to flow through the carburetor, reed valve and into the crankcase (**Figure 15**) to fill the vacuum. As the piston moves down on the power stroke the volume in the crankcase decreases forming pressure (**Figure 16**). Pressure formed in the crankcase will close the reed valve (A, **Figure 16**), trapping the fuel/air mixture in the crankcase. During downward piston movement, the transfer port in the cylinder wall (B, **Figure 16**) will become exposed to the pressurized fuel/air mixture in the crankcase. The fuel/air mixture will flow into the combustion chamber providing a fresh fuel/air charge for the next cycle. Crankcase pressure and vacuum are also used to power the fuel pump on most Yamaha outboards.

Weak crankcase pressure can contribute to poor fuel pump operation during low-speed operation. Faulty pistons, rings and cylinder walls can affect crankcase pressures by allowing combustion chamber gasses to leak into the crankcase, diluting the fuel/air mixture. Likewise, faulty crankcase seals, gaskets, reed valves and cylinder

3

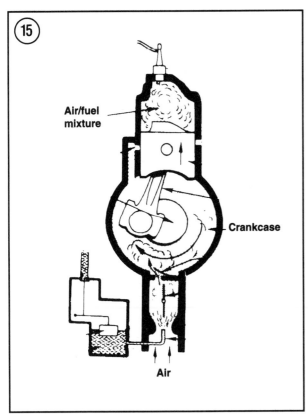

(15)

Air/fuel
mixture

Crankcase

Air

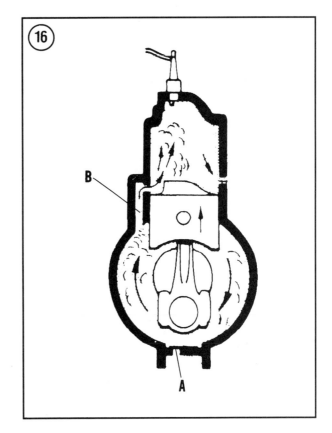

(16)

B

A

block castings can adversely affect crankcase pressures. Low crankcase pressure prevents the engine from receiving adequate fuel and air into the cylinder. The engine will produce less power thereby causing a bog on acceleration or poor idle characteristics.

If a crankcase or crankcase gasket leakage is suspected, spray a soap and water solution on the mating surfaces and castings while cranking the engine. The formation of bubbles indicates the point of the leak. On multiple cylinder engines, internal leakage can occur. The symptoms are consistent with external leakage and only disassembly and inspection will reveal the components that are causing the leakage. Typically inadequate crankcase sealing will affect engine performance at lower operating speeds. Refer to the procedures described in Chapter Eight for power head repair.

Enrichment Systems

Yamaha outboards are equipped with fuel enrichment systems to improve starting and cold engine operation. The systems include a manually operated choke valve, electrically operated choke valve (referred to as an enrichment valve) or electrothermal valve. Manual start and tiller handle models are equipped with a manually operated choke valve.

Most electric start remote control models are equipped with a solenoid actuated choke valve referred to as the *enrichment valve* (**Figure 17**). The choke valve restricts air flow into the front of the carburetor causing additional fuel to enter the engine.

Electric start oil injected 40-90 hp models are equipped with an *electrothermal valve* (**Figure 18**). The lighting coil portion of the charging system powers this carburetor-mounted valve. It allows fuel to flow from the carburetor directly into the engine during cold start/running conditions. An internal valve functions as a pump to move the fuel. The valve will cease fuel enrichment when the engine warms to operating temperature.

These devices should be tested when hard starting is noted and other systems are not at fault. Electronic fuel injected models have features that work automatically to improve starting and cold engine operation. Testing procedures for these systems are included in this chapter. Carbureted 225-250 hp (76° V) models are equipped with an enrichment system that is controlled by a microcomputer. An electric pump and valves control the fuel flowing into the engine during cold start and cold engine operation. Repair procedures for enrichment systems are provided in Chapter Six.

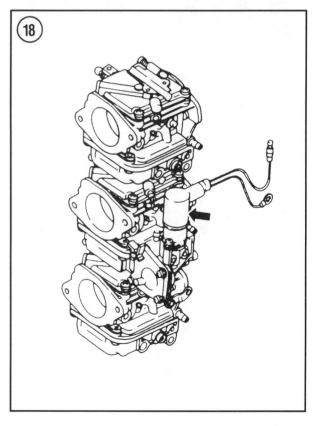

Enrichment valve/solenoid resistance test

Turn the key switch to the *ON* position and push *IN* or trip the choke switch as you observe the operation of the choke valve (**Figure 19**). The valve should move with a smooth, brisk motion. Check the resistance of the winding in the valve/solenoid following Steps 1-4. Check the wire harness and key switch if the valve falls within specifications. Replace the valve/solenoid if wire harness, valve/solenoid resistance and key switch test properly.

1. Disconnect the blue and black leads from the harness at the fuel enrichment valve (A, **Figure 20**).

2. Connect the black negative (–) lead of the meter to the black lead (B, **Figure 20**) on the fuel enrichment valve.

3. Connect the red positive (+) lead of the meter to the blue lead (C, **Figure 20**) on the fuel enrichment valve.

4. Measure the resistance as indicated. Resistance values are provided in **Table 16**. Replace the valve if its resistance is not as specified.

Electrothermal valve resistance test

Use a multimeter to measure the resistance of the winding in the electrothermal valve (**Figure 21**). Resistance

specifications are listed in **Table 16**. Refer to Chapter Six for instructions on electrothermal valve replacement. In addition the valve operation should be checked by performing the *Electrothermal valve height test* in this chapter.

1. Disconnect the blue and black leads from the electrothermal valve (**Figure 21**).

2. Connect the black meter lead (–) to the black lead on the electrothermal valve (**Figure 21**).

3. Connect the red meter lead (+) to the blue lead on the electrothermal valve (**Figure 21**).

4. Measure the resistance as indicated. Replace the valve if its resistance is out of the specified range.

Electrothermal valve operational test

The engine must be cold, at ambient temperature, when performing this test.

1. Remove the electrothermal valve from the carburetor. Refer to Chapter Six.

2. Record the measurement on the electrothermal valve at the points indicated at A, **Figure 22**.

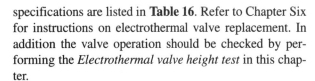

3

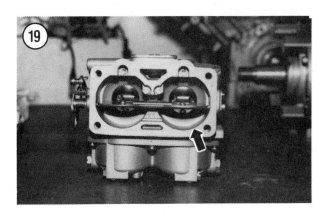

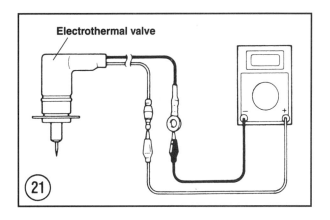

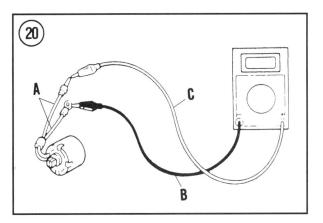

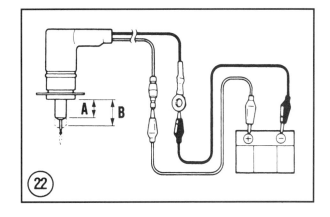

3. Using a jumper lead, connect the blue lead of the electrothermal valve to a battery positive (+) terminal (**Figure 22**).

4. Using a jumper lead connect the black lead of the electrothermal valve to a battery negative (–) terminal (**Figure 22**).

5. Maintain the connections for 5-7 minutes.

6. While still connected to the battery, record the measurement on the electrothermal valve at the points indicated at B, **Figure 22**.

7. Compare the measurement from Step 2 with measurement from Step 6. Replace the electrothermal valve if no difference in measurement is indicated.

NOTE
This enrichment system will not operate properly unless the throttle is closed while starting a cold engine.

IGNITION SYSTEM COMPONENT TESTING

The ignition system used on a Yamaha outboard is composed of reliable solid state components. Commonly used components include the flywheel, charge coil, pulser coil, CDI unit, ignition coil and spark plugs. Except for the spark plugs very little maintenance or adjustments are required. All components, except the CDI module, can be accurately tested using resistance or peak voltage testing. The best means to check a CDI unit is to use a process of elimination. If all other components of the ignition system test good, the source of the ignition system malfunction is likely the CDI unit.

Stop Circuit Test

Pushing a stop button on the tiller handle models or a key switch on the remote control models activates the stop circuit. In either case, the engine stops running because the current required to operate the ignition system is diverted to the engine ground. Some models are equipped with a safety lanyard switch in addition to the button or key switch. A failure in the stop circuit can result in the engine having no spark or not being able to stop. A multimeter is required to test the circuit.

1. Locate and *disconnect* the white wire leading into the CDI unit or microcomputer. Use the wire charts located near the end of manual to help locate the CDI unit or microcomputer.

2. Select the R × 1 or 1 ohm scale on the volt/ohm meter. Connect one meter test lead to the white wire that was disconnected from the CDI unit or microcomputer connec-

tor. Connect the other meter test lead to a good engine ground.

3. The meter should show continuity, or very low resistance, for the following conditions: key switch in the OFF position, lanyard switch in the OFF position or stop button depressed.

4. The meter should show infinity, or very high resistance, for the following conditions: key switch in the ON position, lanyard switch in the RUN position and stop button in normal run position.

5. Replace the stop button and harness (tiller models only) if incorrect readings are noted in Step 3 or Step 4.

6. Test the key switch and lanyard switch (remote control models) if failure is noted on either Step 3 or Step 4. Refer to Chapter Seven for key switch and lanyard switch testing.

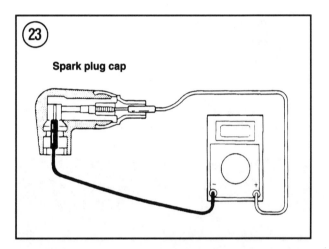

(23) Spark plug cap

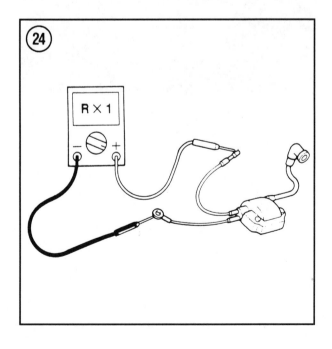

(24) R × 1

7. Repair or replace the harness (remote control models) connecting the controls to the engine if the key switch and lanyard switch test properly.

8. Perform Steps 3 and 4 to verify proper operation before operating the engine. Reconnect all leads and operate the engine to verify proper switch operation. Suspect the CDI unit if all other components test properly, but the engine has no ignition or cannot be stopped.

Spark Plug Cap

A problem with the spark plug cap can cause an ignition misfire. A current provided by the ignition system can short to ground instead of creating an arc at the plug. Often the misfire will occur only during very humid conditions. At times the cap can fail internally and cause an ignition misfire. Replace the spark plug cap if external arcing is noted at the spark plug connection. Corrosion at the connections can cause high resistance resulting in an ignition misfire. Visually inspect all spark plug caps. Replace any caps that have visual corrosion, cracks or breaks in the insulating material.

Perform a spark plug cap resistance test on the V150-V250 models with oil injection as follows:

1. Remove the spark plug cap from the spark plug

2. Turn cap counterclockwise to remove it from the spark plug wire.

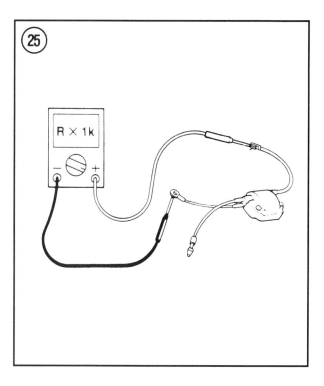

3. Select the *ohms or resistance* function of the meter. Refer to **Table 9** to determine the proper scale to use.

4. Connect the negative (–) meter test lead to the spark plug cap as shown in **Figure 23**.

5. Connect the positive (+) meter test lead to spark plug cap as shown in **Figure 23**.

6. Replace any spark plug cap if not within 4000-6000 ohms resistance.

7. Install spark plug cap onto spark plug wire by turning in a clockwise direction until properly attached. Install spark plug cap onto the spark plug.

Ignition Coil

A problem with the ignition coil can cause or contribute to an intermittent or constant ignition misfire. Perform a visual inspection on all ignition coils. Replace any coil that has corroded terminals or cracks on its body. A coil resistance test can be performed for the 2-90 hp models. Coil resistance specifications are not provided for 80 hp jet and 115-250 hp models. For these models refer to *CDI unit peak voltage test* in this chapter for procedures to follow when troubleshooting the ignition coil. Procedures for coil removal and installation are provided in Chapter Seven.

Primary resistance

1. Disconnect the primary leads and secondary lead at the ignition coil.

2. Select the ohms or resistance function of the meter.

3. Connect the negative lead of the multimeter to the black lead (**Figure 24**) of the ignition coil.

4. Connect the positive lead of the multimeter to the black/white or orange lead (**Figure 24**) of the ignition coil.

5. Compare actual reading with primary resistance specifications provided in **Table 4**.

6. Repeat the test for all ignition coils on the engine. Replace any coil that is not within the indicated specification(s).

7. Install the coil onto the power head and connect leads to proper locations.

Secondary resistance

1. Disconnect the primary leads and secondary lead at the ignition coil.

2. Select the ohms or resistance function of the multimeter.

3. Connect the negative lead of the meter to the black lead (**Figure 25**) of the ignition coil.

4. Connect the positive lead of the meter to the secondary lead (**Figure 25**) of the ignition coil.

5. Compare actual reading with secondary resistance specifications provided in **Table 4**.

6. Repeat the test for all ignition coils on the engine. Replace any coil that is not within the indicated specification(s).

7. Install coil onto the power head and connect the leads to proper location.

Pulser Coil

The pulser coil is located under the flywheel. An electrical pulse is created as magnets attached to the flywheel pass near the coil. This electrical pulse is ultimately used to signal or initiate a spark at the plug. If a pulser coil is found to be faulty, removal of the flywheel (**Figure 26**) is necessary to gain access to the coil. Flywheel removal is *not* necessary to gain access to the *pulser coil leads*. A faulty pulser coil can cause an intermittent or constant ignition misfire. Follow the testing procedures carefully to avoid misdiagnosis and unnecessary flywheel removal. Pulser coil resistance test is provided for the 3-90 hp models. Pulser coil output voltage test is provided for the 20-250 hp models. Perform both tests on the 20-90 hp models, excluding Models E48, E60 and E75, to ensure accurate test results.

Pulser coil resistance

1. Disconnect the pulser coil leads from the harness. Refer to wire charts at the end of the manual or the information provided in **Table 5** to select the proper leads.

2. Select the ohms or resistance function of the meter.

3. Connect the positive (+) and negative (–) leads of the meter (**Figure 26**) to the correct color leads as indicated in **Table 5**. Multiple pulser coils are present on some models and two or more different connections and/or readings may be required. **Table 5** will indicate the wire lead at the pulser coil harness to use for the test.

NOTE
Pulser coil resistance test results are not affected by polarity of the test leads.

4. Compare actual reading with the specification provided in **Table 5**. Replace the pulser coil if resistance is not within specification. Procedures for removal and installation of the pulser coil are provided in Chapter Seven.

5. Attach leads to the proper location(s) when testing is complete.

Pulser coil peak voltage output

When performing this test, all leads are connected into the main engine harness. The use of a test harness or the probing of wire connections (**Figure 27**) allows voltage testing while running the engine. This test can indicate a

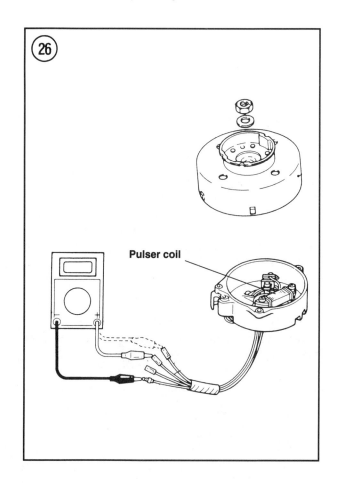

Pulser coil

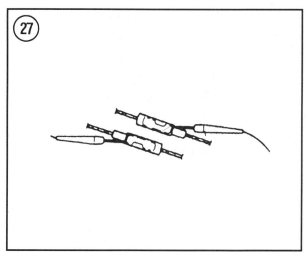

fault with the pulser coil or CDI unit during actual running conditions.

If testing 20-30 hp models, connect leads as shown in (**Figure 28**).

If testing 40-50 hp models, excluding model E48, use 3-pin test harness part No. YB-06443, 90890-06757.

If testing 60-90 hp models, except model E60 and E75, use test harness part No. YB-38831, 90890-06767.

If testing 150-200 hp models with oil injection, use test harness part No. YB-38831/90890-06771.

If testing 150-200 hp premix models, use test harness part No. YB-38832/90890-06772.

If testing 200-250 (76° V), use test harness part No. YB-39991/90890-03169.

1. Select the Peak Voltage or DVA function of the meter. Use peak volt adapter if the meter used does not have peak voltage reading capability.

2. If required, attach test harness into the engine harness at the pulser coil connector. Connect the digital volt meter with peak volt capability or adapter to the test harness (**Figure 29**) at the specified wire colors. Refer to the wire charts located at the back of the manual and the information provided in **Table 7** to identify the combinations of specified test lead connections and wire colors.

3. Run the engine on a suitable test/flush device or in a test tank. Record the voltage at the indicated rpm.

4. Compare actual reading with the specification(s) listed in **Table 7**. Replace the CDI unit if the voltage reading is above the specification. Replace the pulser coil if the reading is below the specification(s). CDI unit and/or pulser coil replacement procedures are provided in Chapter Seven.

5. Remove the test harness and attach all leads to the proper locations.

NOTE
If peak voltage reading is excessively low, reverse the polarity of the test leads and perform the test again before determining the test results.

WARNING
Stay clear of the propeller shaft while running an engine on a flush/test device. To help avoid possible bodily injury or death, remove the propeller before running the engine or while performing test. Disconnect all spark plug leads and the battery connections before removing or installing a propeller.

CAUTION
Never run an outboard without first providing cooling water. Use either a test tank or

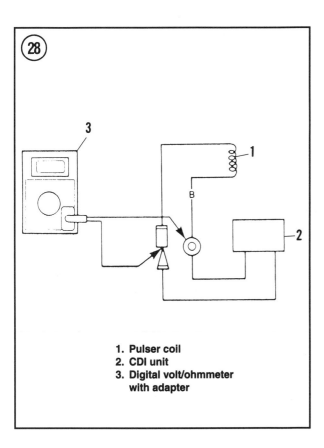

1. Pulser coil
2. CDI unit
3. Digital volt/ohmmeter
   with adapter

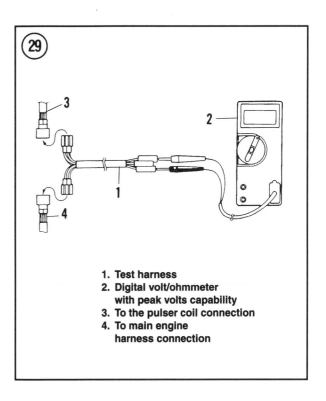

1. Test harness
2. Digital volt/ohmmeter
   with peak volts capability
3. To the pulser coil connection
4. To main engine
   harness connection

flush/test device. Remove the propeller before running the engine. Install a test propeller to run the engine in a test tank.

Ignition Charge Coil

The ignition system is powered by the ignition charge coil. An electrical current is generated as magnets attached to the flywheel rotate past the coil. This current is directed to the CDI unit where it is used to initiate a spark at the plug. A faulty ignition charge coil can cause an intermittent spark misfire or a no spark condition. On certain models the engine may operate properly at one speed and misfire at another speed due to a faulty ignition charge coil. Perform tests carefully as the flywheel must be removed to remove the charge coil. Flywheel removal is not required during testing as the coil leads are accessible.

Resistance specifications are provided for the 2-90 hp models in **Table 4**. Peak voltage readings are provided for the 20-250 hp models, except models E48 and E60, in **Table 7**. Refer to the wire charts located near the end of the manual and the information provided in **Table 4** or **Table 7** to identify the proper wire connections. Perform both tests on the 20-90 hp models, except Models E48, E60 and E75, to ensure accurate test results.

Ignition Charge Coil Resistance

1. Disconnect all ignition charge coil leads at the engine harness connection.

2. Select the resistance or ohms function and proper scale for the multimeter.

3. Connect the meter test leads to the ignition charge coil leads (**Figure 30**) as specified in **Table 4**.

4. Compare resistance reading with specification listed in **Table 4**. Replace the ignition charge coil if not within the indicated specification. Refer to Chapter Seven for the ignition charge coil removal and installation procedure.

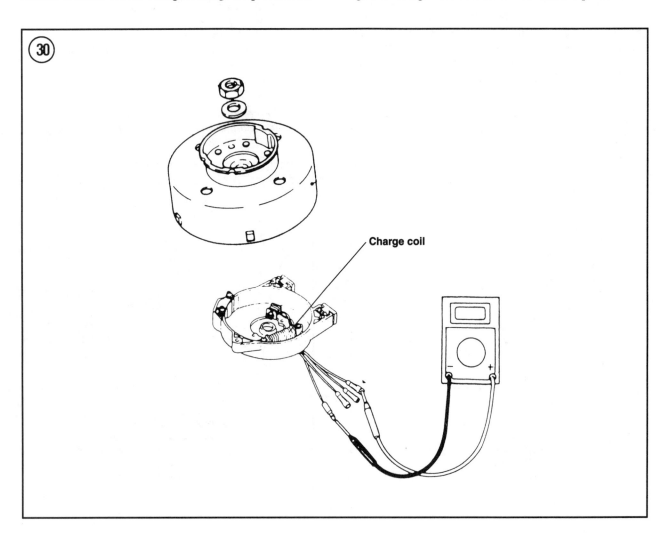

Charge coil

5. Connect all leads to the proper locations.

Ignition Charge Coil Peak Voltage Output

When performing this test, all leads must be connected into the main engine harness. The use of a test harness or the probing of wire connections (**Figure 27**) allows voltage

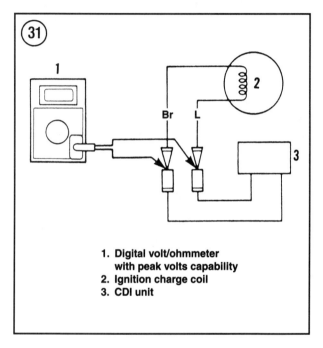

1. Digital volt/ohmmeter
   with peak volts capability
2. Ignition charge coil
3. CDI unit

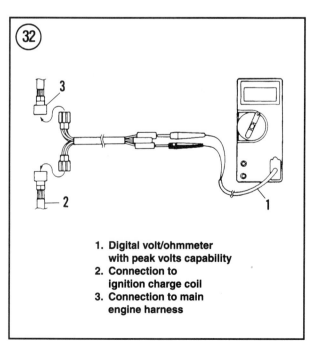

1. Digital volt/ohmmeter
   with peak volts capability
2. Connection to
   ignition charge coil
3. Connection to main
   engine harness

testing while running the engine. This test can indicate a fault with the ignition charge coil during actual running conditions.

If testing 20-50 hp models, except Model E48, connect test leads as shown (**Figure 31**).

If testing 60-70 hp models, except model 65 jet and E60, use test harness part No. YB-38831/90890-06767.

If testing a 65 jet or 75-90 hp models, except Model E75, use test harness part No. YB-06443, 90890-06757.

If testing an 85 jet or 115-130 hp models, use test harness part No. YB-38831/90890-06771.

If testing a 105 jet or 150-225 (90° V) models, except Model C150, use test harness part No. YB-38831/90890-06772.

If testing model C150, use test harness part No. YB-38832/90890-06771.

If testing a 200-250 hp (76° V) model, use test harness part No. YB- 38831/90890-06771.

WARNING
Stay clear of the propeller shaft while running an engine on a flush/test device. To avoid bodily injury or certain death, remove the propeller before running the engine or performing any test. Disconnect all spark plug leads and disconnect the battery connections before removing or installing a propeller.

CAUTION
Never run an outboard without first providing cooling water. Use either a test tank or flush/test device. Remove the propeller before running the engine. Install a test propeller to run the engine in a test tank.

1. Select the *peak voltage or DVA* function of the meter. Use a peak volt adapter if the meter used does not have peak voltage reading capability. Select the proper scale using specifications provided in **Table 7**.

2. If required, attach the test harness to engine harness at the ignition charge coil connection. Connect a digital volt meter with peak volt capability or adapter to the test harness (**Figure 32**) at the specified wire colors. Refer to the wire charts located near the back of the manual and the information provided in **Table 7** to identify the combinations of specified test lead connections and wire colors.

3. Run the engine on a suitable test/flush device at the specified rpm. Record the voltage reading.

4. Compare actual reading with specification listed in **Table 7**. Replace the ignition charge coil if reading is below specification. If reading is higher than specifications, test *pulser coil peak voltage output*. Refer to Chapter

3

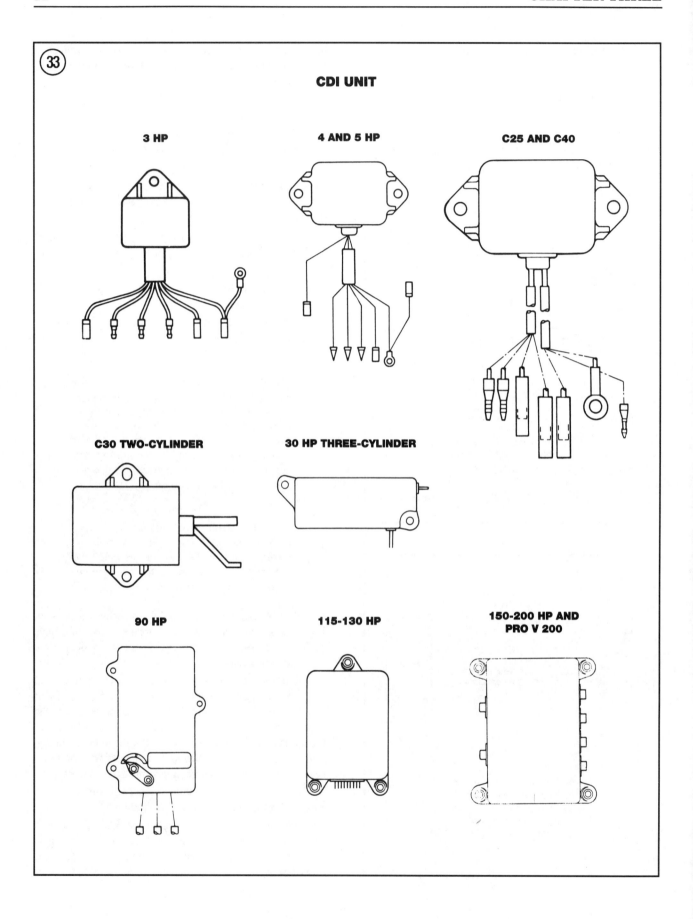

33

CDI UNIT

3 HP

4 AND 5 HP

C25 AND C40

C30 TWO-CYLINDER

30 HP THREE-CYLINDER

90 HP

115-130 HP

150-200 HP AND
PRO V 200

Seven for the ignition charge coil removal and installation procedures.

5. Attach all leads to the correct location.

NOTE
If peak voltage reading is excessively low, reverse the polarity of the test leads and perform the test again before determining the test results.

CDI Unit

The primary function of the CDI unit (**Figure 33**) is to initiate spark to the correct cylinder at the correct time. As the flywheel rotates past the charge coil, current is gener-

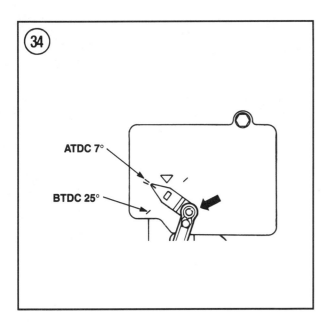

ated and stored in a capacitor within the CDI unit. As the flywheel magnets rotate past the charge coil, a current is generated and stored in a capacitor within the CDI unit. Electrical pulses generated by the pulser coil trigger the release of the stored current, which is directed to the ignition coil. The ignition coil amplifies the current to the voltage needed to jump a gap at the spark plug.

The ignition timing is advanced at higher engine speeds to improve engine performance and efficiency. On some models this is accomplished by rotating the pulser coil in relationship to the triggering magnets in the flywheel. The 40-50 hp models utilize a lever mounted on the CDI unit (**Figure 34**). The timing is advanced as the lever rotates with throttle movement. On some models the timing is advanced without mechanical devices by electronic circuits in the CDI unit. Automatic spark advance is provided with increased engine speed.

The CDI unit on some models performs other important functions in addition to ignition control. Oil injection system control and power reduction operation are performed by the CDI unit. Other models use an advanced CDI unit (**Figure 35**) commonly referred to as YMIS (Yamaha Microcomputer Ignition System). This system offers greater efficiency by using input from various engine-mounted sensors to precisely control the timing and fuel delivery for EFI models. Testing procedures for YMIS components are provided in this chapter. Timing and linkage adjustment procedures for all models are provided in Chapter Five.

The peak voltage output test provides a means of testing the CDI unit on the 20-250 hp models, except Model E48, E60 and E75. Test procedure for other models involves first testing the other components of the ignition system such as the charge coil, pulser coil, ignition coil, stop circuit and on some models the crank position sensor. Replace the CDI unit if these components test correctly and ignition problems are present. Testing the CDI unit for Models E48, E60 and E75 involves the use of expensive test equipment. It is more cost effective to have a Yamaha dealership perform this test for you.

CDI unit peak voltage

When performing this test, all leads must remain connected to the main engine harness. The use of a test harness or the probing of wires allows voltage testing while running the engine. This test can indicate a fault within a CDI unit during actual running conditions.

For 20-250 hp models, except Models E48, E60 and E75, the test leads are connected into the existing engine wire harness.

1. Select the peak voltage or DVA function of the multimeter. Use a peak volt adapter if the meter used does not have peak voltage reading capability. Select the proper scale using the specification provided in **Table 7**.

2. Connect the negative (–) meter lead to the bolt that retains the CDI unit (**Figure 36**) or to a good engine ground.

3. Probe the black/white lead at the connector (**Figure 36**) with the positive meter lead. Do not disconnect leads from the main engine harness.

4. Run the engine at the speed specified in **Table 7**. Record the output for all cylinders. Check voltage reading six times for accuracy.

5. Compare actual voltage output with specification listed in **Table 7**. If the actual reading is above the specification, replace the ignition coil and test again. If the reading is below the specification, test the charge coil and pulser coil. Replace the CDI unit if both components test correctly.

6. Attach all leads to the correct location. Check for proper operation. Check ignition timing following the procedure in Chapter Five.

> *WARNING*
> *Stay clear of the propeller shaft while running an engine on a flush/test device. To avoid possible bodily injury or death, remove the propeller before running the engine or while performing test. Disconnect all spark plug leads and the battery connections before removing the propeller.*

> *CAUTION*
> *Never run an outboard without first providing cooling water. Use either a test tank or flush/test device. Remove the propeller before running the engine. Install a test propeller to run the engine in a test tank.*

YMIS COMPONENT TESTING

YMIS is used on 1996 and later 150-250 hp models, excluding model C150. YMIS is also used on 1996 60-90 hp models (excluding models C75, C85), 1997 60-90 hp and 1998 40-90 hp models.

YMIS components used on the 40-90 hp models include the microcomputer and crankshaft position sensor.

YMIS components used on 150-225 hp 90° V models include the microcomputer, crankshaft position sensor and thermosensor.

YMIS components used on 200-250 hp (76° V) models include the microcomputer, crankshaft position sensor, thermosensor sensor, throttle position sensor, knock sensor and oxygen density sensor.

The YMIS microcomputer used on 150-250 hp models, excluding Model C150, has self-diagnosis capability. In the event of system malfunction, trouble codes are stored within the microcomputer. To read stored trouble codes use diagnostic flash harness part No. YB-06765/90890-06765. This harness attaches into the main engine harness. Codes are read by observing a flashing light located on the harness while the engine is running. Check the engine wire harness, fuse, key switch and control station to engine wire harness for dirty or faulty connections prior to replacing a suspect YMIS, microcomputer or CDI unit. Refer to **Table 22** for code description, cause and corrective action.

Reading Codes

The microcomputer will alternately turn the light ON and OFF to display stored codes. A light ON for 0.3 seconds (A, **Figure 37**), followed by a Light OFF for 5 seconds (B, **Figure 37**) and so on indicates a Code 1. A

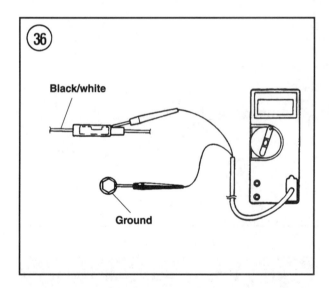

Black/white

Ground

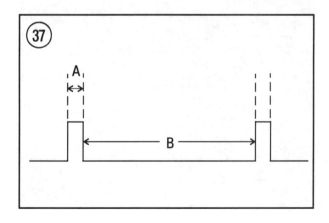

light ON for 0.3 seconds (A, **Figure 38**) followed by a light OFF for 0.3 seconds (B, **Figure 38**), then turning back on before a 1.3 second pause (C, **Figure 38**) indicates Code 2. A series of flashing lights after the pause indicates the second digit in the code (D, **Figure 38**). Additional codes may be displayed after a pause (light off) starting with the lowest number then, the next highest number and so on. Switch the engine off to clear stored codes.

Perform the diagnostic function by following Steps 1-3.

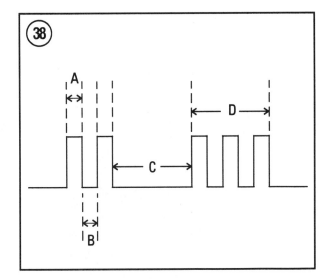

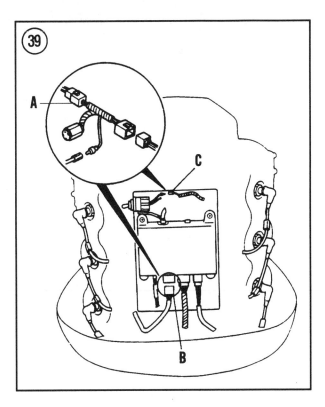

1. Connect the diagnostic test harness (A, **Figure 39**) at the indicated location (B, **Figure 39**). Disconnect the lead from the emergency switch. Connect the male connector from the diagnostic harness to the female connector that was connected to the emergency switch (C, **Figure 39**).

2. Run the engine while observing the light. Refer to **Table 15** to determine the presence and cause of the fault.

3. Stop the engine and make necessary adjustments or corrections. Refer to the section for the components or system with an indicated fault. Connect all harness leads to the proper locations.

NOTE
Higher than normal idle speed will be present when a fault exists with the crank position sensor, thermosensor sensor, knock sensor, oxygen density sensor or throttle position sensor. No code is present in the event of oxygen density sensor failure.

Crankshaft Position Sensor

The crankshaft position sensor (**Figure 40**) is located next to the flywheel to allow it to sense flywheel crankshaft position. Electrical pulses are created as raised bosses on the flywheel pass near the sensor. These pulses are used by the YMIS system to provide accurate ignition timing and rpm reference. This sensor is used on 60-90 hp models with YMIS (microcomputer) controlled ignition systems and all 150-250 hp models except Model C150. Testing involves the use of either an analog or digital multimeter and test leads. Refer to the wire charts located near the end of the manual to help locate the proper leads and components of the engine.

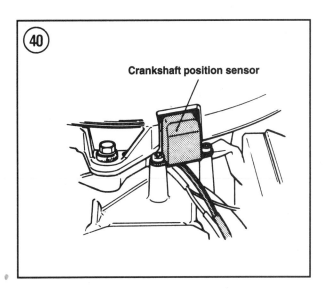

Crankshaft position sensor

1. Refer to **Table 7** to determine the required peak voltage reading.

2. Select the proper scale for the meter. Attach the required peak volt adapter if the meter does not have peak voltage reading capability.

3. Without disconnecting the leads from the harness, probe the crankshaft position sensor connectors as shown (**Figure 41**).

4. Run or crank the engine at the specified speed and record voltage output.

5. Compare actual voltage reading with specification listed in **Table 7**.

6. Replace the crankshaft position sensor if it does not meet or exceed the voltage specification.

7. Attach all leads to proper location. Check for proper operation. Check the ignition timing following the procedure in Chapter Five.

CAUTION
Never run an outboard without first providing cooling water. Use either a test tank or flush/test device. Remove the propeller before running the engine. Install a test propeller to run the engine in a test tank.

WARNING
Stay clear of the propeller shaft while running an engine on a flush/test device. To avoid possible bodily injury or death, remove the propeller before running the engine or performing test. Disconnect all spark plug leads and the battery connections before removing or installing the propeller.

Shift Cutoff Switch Test

The shift cutoff switch is used on 200-250 hp (76° V) models to help ensure smooth shift operation. The switch is activated by the shift linkage when shifting into neutral.

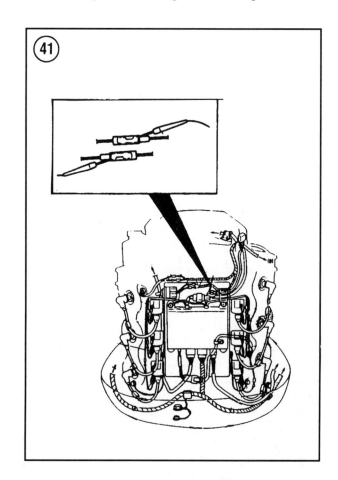

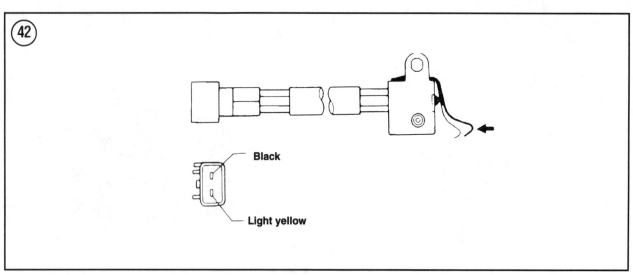

Black

Light yellow

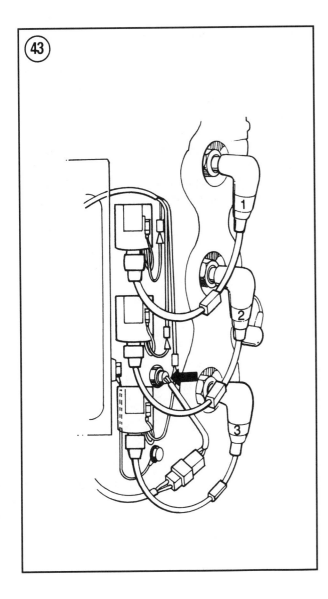

The shift cutoff switch is used on 200-250 hp 76° V models to help ensure smooth shift operation. The shift linkage activates the switch when shifting into neutral. The microcomputer interrupts the ignition on certain cylinders when the switch is depressed.

Use a multimeter set on the R × 1 scale to perform the test. Refer to the wire charts located at the end of the manual to help locate the proper lead and components of the engine.

1. Locate the shift cutoff switch and disconnect the leads from the main engine harness.

2. Connect meter test leads to the blue/yellow and black leads at the switch connector.

3. Replace the shift cutoff switch if needle movement is noted or resistance is read on the meter.

4. Push the switch lever as shown (**Figure 42**). Replace the switch if continuity is not indicated as the switch is depressed.

5. Attach all leads to the proper location.

Thermosensor Test

> *NOTE*
> *Do not confuse the thermosensor with the thermoswitch. The thermosensor is located on the starboard rear side of the power head near the lower ignition coil.*

The thermosensor (**Figure 43**) is used by the microcomputer to determine the engine temperature. This allows the microcomputer to adjust the ignition and fuel system, on EFI models only, for optimum performance under varying conditions. A digital or analog multimeter can be used to read the resistance at the indicated temperatures. Refer to the wire charts located near the end of the manual to help locate the proper leads and components on the engine.

1. Disconnect the leads and remove the thermosensor from the power head.

2. Select the proper scale on the meter and connect the negative (–) meter test lead to one of the black/yellow thermosensor leads and the positive (+) meter test lead to the other black/yellow thermosensor.

3. Suspend the thermosensor in a container of water that can be heated (**Figure 44**).

4. Pour in some tap water and check the temperature with a thermometer.

5. Add cold water if necessary or heat the container to the temperatures listed in **Table 11**.

6. Measure the resistance at the listed temperatures. Replace the thermosensor if the resistance is not within the specification for each temperature listed.

7. Install the thermosensor into proper location and reconnect the sensor leads.

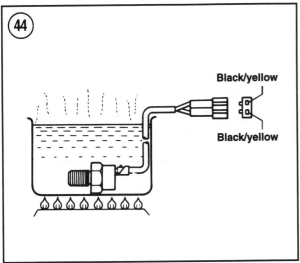

Black/yellow

Black/yellow

Throttle Position Sensor Test

The throttle position sensor is located on the upper port side of the power head (**Figure 45**). It provides a varying input to the microcomputer to indicate the amount of throttle opening. This input is used to determine and set the timing advance.

Testing and adjusting requires a digital multimeter (C, **Figure 46**) and test harness part No. YB-06443/90890-06757. Refer to the wire charts located at the end of the manual to help locate the proper lead and components of the engine.

1. Disconnect the throttle position sensor harness from the main engine harness (A, **Figure 46**). Install a test harness into disconnected leads as indicated (B, **Figure 46**).

2. Connect the meter test leads to the orange and red test harness connections. Turn the ignition key to the ON position.

3. Read the voltage on the meter. Compare the voltage readings to the *input voltage* specification listed in **Table 12**. Test the YMIS microcomputer if reading is not within the specification.

4. Connect the meter test leads to the pink and orange test harness connections. Turn the ignition key to the ON position.

5. Read the voltage on the meter. Compare the voltage readings to the *output voltage* specification listed in **Table 12**. Adjust the throttle position sensor if not within the listed specification.

6. Slowly open the throttle valve while observing the voltage reading on the meter. Replace the throttle position sensor if no change or rapid changes are noted as the valve is opened.

7. Remove test harness and attach all leads to proper locations. Adjust the throttle position sensor following the procedures in Chapter Five.

NOTE
Throttle position sensor failure on a 225 or 250 hp model will generally result in erratic timing fluctuation.

Knock Sensor Test

The knock sensor is used on 225-250 hp 76° models only. The sensor is located on the starboard cylinder head (**Figure 47**). It provides a voltage output to the microcomputer, allowing the detection of damaging spark knock or detonation. The microcomputer can alter fuel delivery and/or ignition timing to help prevent damage when knocking is detected. To test the sensor, use a digital multimeter.

1. Select the *AC millivolts scale* on the meter.

2. Disconnect the lead from the knock sensor. Connect a meter test lead to the knock sensor terminal only.

3. Connect the other meter test lead to the body of the knock sensor.

4. Lightly tap on the knock sensor body with a small screwdriver handle.

5. Replace the knock sensor if several millivolts (2-10 mV minimum) are not displayed on the meter when tapping the sensor.

6. Repeat Steps 1-5 after replacement of the sensor to verify proper operation. Attach all leads to the proper location.

45

Throttle position sensor

46

Oxygen Density Sensor

The oxygen density sensor is used on 225 and 250 hp EFI models. Input from this sensor is used by the microcomputer to fine tune the air/fuel mixture provided to the engine. Improved fuel economy and lower emissions are possible benefits provided by monitoring and reacting to oxygen density. This sensor is located on the upper starboard side of the power head near the cylinder head mounting location. Perform a *heater resistance test* followed by an *output voltage test*. Test harness part No. YB-06767/90890-06767 and a digital multimeter are required to test this sensor.

Oxygen density sensor heater resistance test

This test is performed without the engine running. It is not necessary to remove the oxygen density sensor from the power head to perform this test.

1. Locate and disconnect the oxygen density sensor connector (A, **Figure 48**).

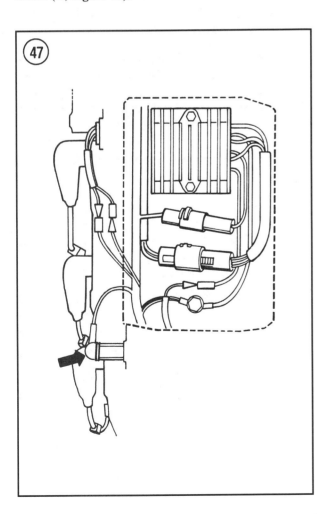

2. Select the proper ohms or resistance scale for the meter used. Connect the test harness to the sensor connector and main engine harness connector as indicated (B, **Figure 48**).

3. Connect a meter test lead to the white harness test lead. Connect the meter's other test lead to the remaining white harness test lead. Read and record the measured resistance.

4. Refer to the specification listed in **Table 14**. Replace the oxygen density sensor if resistance is not within the listed specification. Refer to Chapter Six for replacement procedure.

5. Attach all leads to the proper location.

Output voltage lower limit test

This test is performed while running the engine to verify that the oxygen density sensor provides proper output voltage. A faulty sensor or other component of the fuel system can alter the readings as well. Refer to Chapter Six for additional information.

1. Locate and disconnect the oxygen density sensor connector (A, **Figure 48**).

2. Select the proper DC voltage scale for the meter used. Connect the test harness to the sensor connector and main engine harness connector as indicated (B, **Figure 48**).

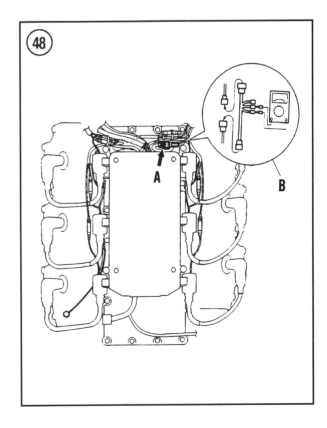

3. Connect the negative (–) meter test lead to the black or black/white test harness lead. Connect the positive (+) meter test lead to the gray harness test lead.

4. Start the engine and allow it to reach normal operating temperature. Position the throttle in the idle position. Read and record the measured voltage.

5. Refer to **Table 14** for output voltage lower limit specification. Replace the sensor if it is not within the specification. Refer to Chapter Six for replacement procedure.

6. Attach all leads to the proper location.

> *WARNING*
> *Stay clear of the propeller shaft while running an engine on a flush/test device. To avoid possible bodily injury or death, remove the propeller before running the engine. Disconnect all spark plug leads and the battery connections before removing or installing the propeller.*

> *CAUTION*
> *Never run an outboard without first providing cooling water. Use either a test tank or flush/test device. Remove the propeller before running the engine. Install a test propeller to run the engine in a test tank.*

> *NOTE*
> *If peak voltage readings are excessively low, reverse the polarity of the test leads and perform the test again before determining the test results.*

ELECTRONIC FUEL INJECTION COMPONENT TESTING

Compared to traditional carbureted outboards, advanced electronic fuel injection provides quicker starting, automatic altitude compensation, improved fuel economy and smoother overall operation. Troubleshooting the system is relatively simple if one system at a time is checked. Systems that may need attention include the low-pressure fuel system, high-pressure fuel system, sensors, the ignition system and the electronic control system which has either the Microcomputer or CDI unit. Remember to check the base engine also. Much time and expense can be wasted replacing EFI components only to find that a cylinder has low compression or a reed valve is damaged.

Troubleshooting the EFI system is separated into two sections that include the fuel supply system and the electronic control system. Always check the fuel supply system first. Perform the test on the electronic control system if all components of the fuel supply system test correctly.

Fuel System

This section covers troubleshooting the high pressure side of the fuel system. The components include the vapor separator tank, fuel rail, fuel injector, and fuel pressure regulator.

The low-pressure side of the system includes the pulse type fuel pump, fuel lines and fuel filter assembly. These components are similar to the components used on carbureted engines. Refer to *Fuel Tank and Fuel Pump* in the *Component Testing* section of this chapter for test procedures on these components.

> *WARNING*
> *Use extreme caution when working with the fuel system. Fuel can spray out under high pressure. Always use required safety gear. Never smoke or perform any test around an open flame or other source of ignition. Fuel vapors can ignite or explode resulting in damaged property, severe bodily injury or death.*

High-pressure fuel test

The most basic test to perform on a fuel-injected engine is the high-pressure fuel test. This test can verify that fuel is supplied to the fuel injectors at the required pressure. While this test can verify that the fuel pump and regulator are operating under controlled conditions, it cannot deter-

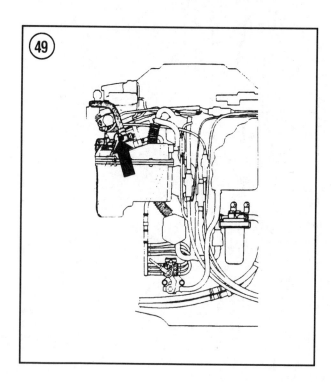

mine if fuel pressure is adequate at all engine operating ranges. Leaking fuel lines, restricted passages and blocked filters can inhibit fuel flow and reduce fuel pressure at the low pressure and high-pressure systems. When one of these conditions exists, the fuel pressure is typically correct at lower speed and will drop sharply as the throttle is increased. Engine performance will falter as the pressure drops. If this symptom is present, check all fuel filters, antisiphon valve, fuel tank pickup and low-pressure pump.

A suitable fuel pressure gauge capable of measuring pressure reaching 245 kPa (35.5 psi) or Yamaha part No YB-06766/90890-06766 is required. The engine can be ran at all speeds with the gauge attached to verify fuel pressure.

1. Locate the fuel pressure test port on the vapor separator tank. Remove the cap and install the fuel pressure gauge onto the test port (**Figure 49**).

2. Turn the key switch to the ON position and immediately check for and correct any fuel leaks. The fuel pressure should indicate 245 kPa (35.5 psi). Switch the key to the OFF position. The pressure should hold for at least one minute. Check for leaking injector, faulty fuel pressure regulator or fuel pump check valve if fuel pressure does not hold.

3. Cycle the key switch off and on to repeat the test.

4. Test and inspect the low-pressure system, vapor separator tank, fuel injectors, all filters and the fuel pressure regulator if fuel pressure is not adequate or does not hold as indicated.

5. Check for blocked or restricted hoses if fuel pressure is above the specification. Replace or inspect the fuel pressure regulator and regulator filter if the hoses check properly.

6. After testing is complete, route the bleeder tube portion (**Figure 50**) of the gauge into a suitable container. Open

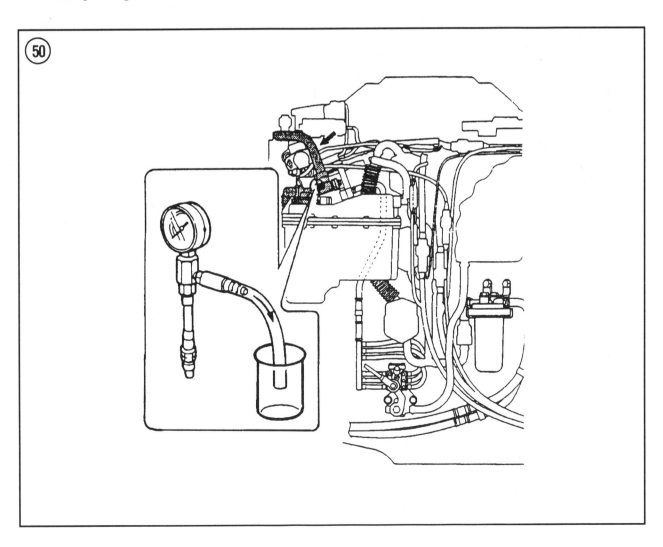

the valve on the pressure gauge to bleed off the fuel pressure. Remove the fuel connection fitting from the fuel pressure test point and install the cap. Check for and correct fuel leaks before returning the engine to service.

Vapor Separator Tank

The vapor separator tank provides a means to supply liquid fuel to the enclosed high-pressure electric fuel pump. Oil to lubricate the internal components is supplied to the vapor separator tank at a top mounted fitting. The fuel pressure regulator is mounted on top of the unit also. These tests verify that the high pressure pump is operating and the float, fuel valve, and fuel pressure regulator are operating correctly. Refer to the repair procedures in Chapter Six if faults are found in the vapor separator tank.

Flooding vapor separator tank

1. Remove the hose from the fitting on top of the tank (A, **Figure 51**).

2. Slowly squeeze the primer bulb while observing the fitting for fuel leakage.

3. Completely disassemble, inspect and reassemble the vapor separator tank following the procedures described in Chapter Six if fuel leakage is noted.

4. Connect all hose fitting to the proper location.

Checking for fuel in the vapor separator tank

This test is performed during a no-start condition to verify that fuel is entering the vapor separator tank. A fault in the low pressure system can contribute to a lack of fuel in the vapor separator tank.

1. Place a container capable of holding 1 L (1 qt.) of fuel under the vapor separator tank drain plug (B, **Figure 51**).

2. Carefully remove the plug. Discard the O-ring seal. Allow all the fuel to drain out of the vapor separator tank. Gently squeeze the primer bulb while observing the drain port.

3. Completely disassemble the vapor separator tank following the instructions provided in Chapter Six if fuel is not flowing out of the plug port when the primer bulb is squeezed.

4. Install the drain plug with new O-ring seal. Tighten plug securely. Squeeze primer bulb until firm. Inspect for and correct fuel leaks before putting engine back into service.

Testing high-pressure pump operation

This test is commonly performed when a no-start condition exists. Adequate fuel pressure must be supplied to the fuel injectors. The engine will not perform properly or in many cases will not start with inadequate fuel pressure. The high pressure electric fuel pump (**Figure 52**) moves

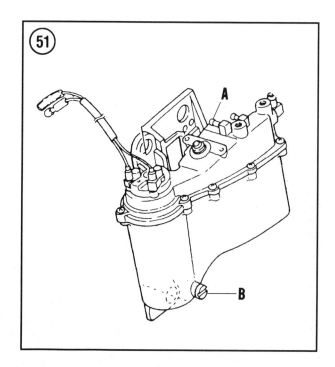

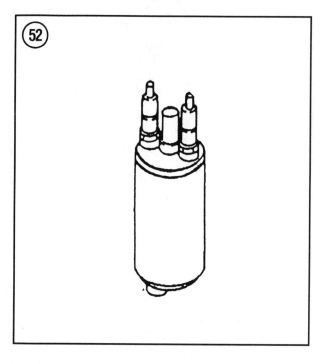

fuel from the vapor separator tank (13, **Figure 53**) to the fuel rail (14, **Figure 53**). The fuel pressure regulator (5, **Figure 53**) controls fuel pressure by restricting the fuel returning to the vapor separator tank. The microcomputer controls the fuel pump. The fuel pump will operate for a few seconds when the ignition key switch is turned on but the engine is not running, and it will continue to operate when ignition pulses are present. Verify that a spark is present at all ignition coils before performing this test.

1. Turn the ignition key to the ON position. Immediately check to see if the pump is operating. If the pump runs, refer to *high-pressure fuel test*.

3

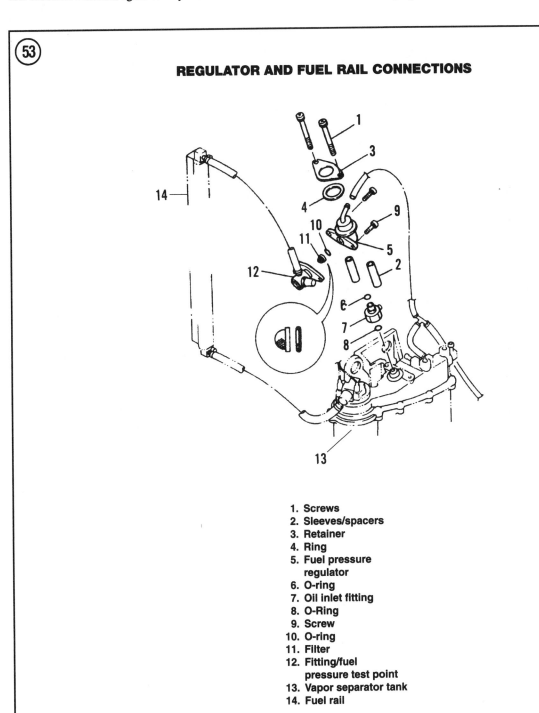

REGULATOR AND FUEL RAIL CONNECTIONS

1. Screws
2. Sleeves/spacers
3. Retainer
4. Ring
5. Fuel pressure regulator
6. O-ring
7. Oil inlet fitting
8. O-Ring
9. Screw
10. O-ring
11. Filter
12. Fitting/fuel pressure test point
13. Vapor separator tank
14. Fuel rail

FUEL RAIL AND FUEL INJECTORS

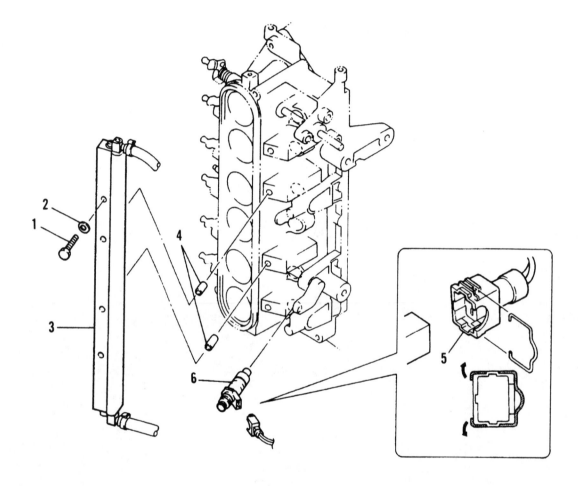

1. Bolt
2. Washer
3. Fuel rail
4. Alignment dowels
5. Fuel injector
   electrical connector
6. Fuel injector

2. If the pump does not run, check the system relay, resistor, and wire harness. Replace the fuel pump if these units check correctly. Refer to removal and installation procedures provided in Chapter Six.

Fuel rail and throttle body leak test

The fuel rail (**Figure 54**) provides a means to mount the fuel injectors as well as supplying the pressurized fuel for them. The throttle body consists of six individual throttle valves connected to the throttle linkage. The opening or closing of these valves controls air flow into the engine. Inspection of the fuel rail and throttle body is necessary when the high-pressure fuel system is unable to hold pressure.

1. Remove the silencer/cover from the front of the engine.

2. Turn the key switch to the ON position.

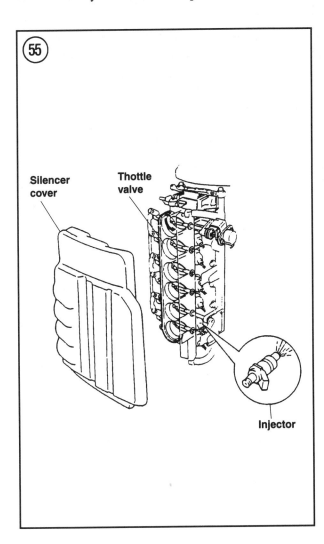

55

Silencer cover

Thottle valve

Injector

3. Fuel leaking into the throttle body valves (C, **Figure 55**) indicates the need to inspect and repair the unit as described in Chapter Six.

4. Return the key to the OFF position.

5. Replace the silencer/cover.

Injector testing

Fuel injectors are electronically operated fuel valves. Testing is commonly done to check for a leaking or failed fuel injector. Poor performance, plug fouling or lean conditions may be present when an injector is faulty.

1. Refer to the wiring charts at the end of the manual to locate the brown lead of the starter relay. Disconnect this lead and insulate the terminal with electrical tape.

2. Verify that fuel pressure in the rail is correct.

3. Remove the silencer/cover (**Figure 55**) from the front of the engine.

4. Fully open the throttle valves. While observing the fuel injectors (**Figure 55**) through the throttle body openings (**Figure 55**), have someone turn the key switch to the START position.

5. All fuel injectors should spray fuel. Check the system relay and wire harness if none of the fuel injectors are spraying fuel. Replace any fuel injector that does not spray fuel if the other injectors are functioning. Refer to Chapter Six for procedures on injector and fuel rail disassembly, inspection and assembly.

6. Install the silencer/cover (**Figure 55**). Remove the electrical tape and connect the brown lead to the proper location on the starter relay.

System relay test

When the key switch is positioned in the run position, the system relay provides current to the high pressure electric pump, fuel injectors and the microcomputer. The microcomputer supplies the current to activate the relay. To test this component, two separate test sequences are provided. The first test verifies that the relay is receiving current from the microcomputer when the key is switched on and all connecting leads are good. The second test checks the actual operation of the relay.

1. Using wire charts in the back of the manual, locate the system relay. Disconnect all leads from the relay.

2. Select the *voltage* function of a multimeter. Select a scale that can read 10-15 V. Connect the negative (–) lead of a multimeter to a good engine ground. Connect the

positive (+) lead of the meter to the red lead of the harness connector lead for the relay (**Figure 56**).

3. The meter should indicate battery voltage. Check all connections along this lead up to the battery for loose or dirty connections if voltage is not indicated. Repair as necessary.

4. Connect the negative (–) lead of the meter to the black harness connector lead for the relay (**Figure 56**). The positive (+) lead of the meter is to remain connected to the red lead of the harness connector.

5. Battery voltage should be indicated on the meter. Clean or repair wires and connectors along this lead up to the engine ground if a fault is noted.

6. Connect the positive (+) lead of the meter to the yellow harness connector lead for the relay. The black harness connector lead is to remain connected to the negative (–) meter lead.

7. Switch the key switch to the ON position. The meter should indicate battery voltage. If no or low voltage is indicated, clean or repair all connection along this lead up to the microcomputer connection. If a fault remains with the engine, test the microcomputer.

8. Connect the yellow and black harness connector leads to the system relay. Do not connect the red/yellow or red harness connector leads to the system relay.

9. Select the *ohms or resistance* and function of a multimeter position the scale so that 1-10 ohms can be read.

10. Connect the positive (+) lead of the meter to the red lead connection point on the system relay (**Figure 56**). Connect the negative (–) lead of the meter to the red/yellow connection point on the system relay (**Figure 56**).

11. With the key switch in the OFF position, the meter should indicate an open circuit, no continuity or very high resistance. Replace the system relay if meter readings indicate any continuity. Refer to Chapter Seven for replacement procedures.

12. With the key switch in the ON position, the meter should indicate a closed circuit, full continuity or very low resistance. Replace the system relay if meter readings indicate high resistance or no continuity. Refer to Chapter Seven for replacement procedures.

13. Turn the key switch to the OFF position and connect all leads to the correct location.

Resistor test

The resistor (**Figure 57**) is connected in series to the lead that connects the high pressure electric fuel pump to the microcomputer. The resistor helps reduce RFI or electrical noise in the system. A digital multimeter is required to check the resistance of this component.

1. Locate the resistor and harness connection for the resistor using the wire charts at the back of the manual. Disconnect the wire harness connector from the resistor.

2. Select the *ohms or resistance* function of the meter. Determine the correct specification in **Table 15** then select the proper scale.

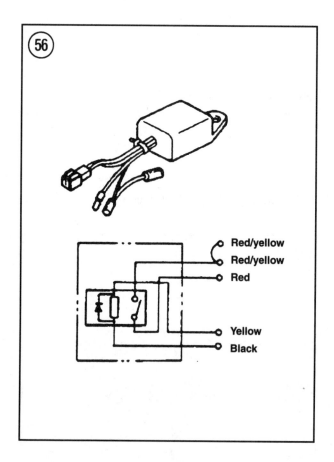

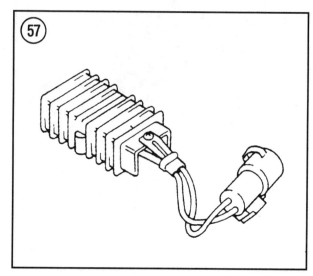

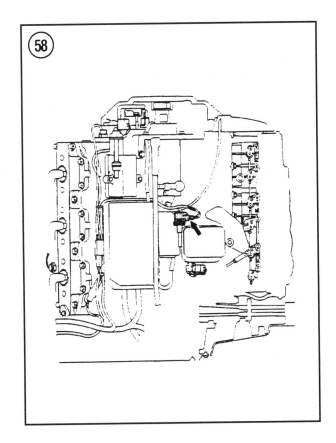

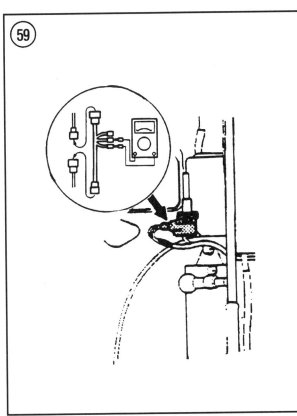

3. Connect the negative (–) lead of the meter to the brown lead to the resistor connector. Connect the positive (+) lead of the meter to the blue lead to the resistor connector. Read and record the measured resistance.

4. Replace the resistor if the resistance is above or below the listed specification. Refer to Chapter Seven for removal and installation procedures.

5. Connect all leads to the correct location.

> *NOTE*
> *When using a digital multimeter, connect the test leads together and read the displayed resistance. This indicates the amount of internal resistance in the meter and leads. Subtract the displayed measurement from any test results to determine actual resistance of a circuit.*

Pressure Sensor Testing

The pressure sensor provides the input necessary for the microcomputer to determine intake manifold air pressure. Manifold air pressure is affected by operating altitude and engine load. The microcomputer alters fuel delivery to the engine to compensate for changes in manifold air pressure. Excessive exhaust smoke, spark plug fouling, poor performance or lean running conditions can occur from a faulty pressure sensor. A test harness part No. YB-06769/90890-06769, vacuum pump/tester and digital multimeter are required to test this sensor.

Input voltage

1. Locate the pressure sensor on the mid-starboard side of the power head (**Figure 58**).

2. Disconnect the harness connector lead at the pressure sensor. Connect the test harness as indicated (**Figure 59**).

3. Select the *voltage* function of the meter. Refer to **Table 8** for test specification. Select the proper scale for the meter used.

4. Connect the positive (+) meter test lead to the orange test harness lead. Connect the negative (–) meter test lead to the black test harness lead. Turn the key switch to the ON position. Measure and record the input voltage.

5. Check the harness that connects the pressure sensor to the microcomputer for dirty or faulty connections. Check the microcomputer if harness and connections are correct.

Output voltage

1. The test harness should remain connected between the pressure sensor and main harness during these test steps.

2. Remove the pressure sensor from the power head.

3. Connect the negative (–) meter test lead to the black test harness lead. Connect the positive (+) meter test lead to the pink test harness lead as indicated (**Figure 59**).

4. Connect the hose of a vacuum tester to the fitting located on the bottom of the pressure sensor (**Figure 60**).

5. Turn the key switch to the ON position. Using the vacuum pump, apply a vacuum that equals the pressure readings listed in **Table 8**. Measure and record the voltage readings at the indicated pressures.

6. Compare the readings with the specification listed in **Table 8**. Replace the pressure sensor if it is out of the listed range. Removal and installation procedures are provided in Chapter Seven.

7. Turn the key switch OFF and connect all leads to the correct location.

Air Temperature Sensor Testing

The air temperature sensor provides input to the microcomputer to indicate the temperature of incoming air. Air temperature has a direct influence on air density and therefore changes fuel delivery requirements. Cooler air requires more fuel. Warmer air requires less fuel. Poor performance, excessive smoke, plug fouling and a lean operating condition can result from a fault with the air temperature sensor. A digital multimeter, test harness part No. YB-06768/90890-06768, and air thermometer are required to test this sensor.

Input voltage

1. Locate the air temperature sensor and disconnect the harness connection (**Figure 61**).

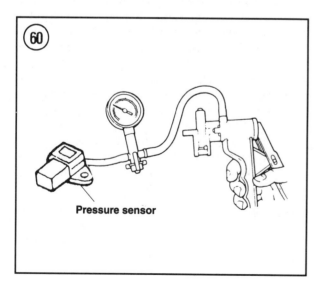

Pressure sensor

2. Connect test harness lead to engine harness connection (A, **Figure 61**). *Do not* connect test harness connection (B, **Figure 61**) to the air temperature connector.

3. Select the voltage function of the digital multimeter. Connect the positive (+) meter test lead to one of the black/yellow lead connection into the test harness. Connect the negative (–) meter test lead into the other black/yellow lead connection into the test harness.

4. Turn the key switch to the ON position. Read and record the measured voltage.

5. The voltage must be 4.75-5.25 volts. If not, check the wire harness that connects the air temperature sensor to the microcomputer for open, dirty or faulty connections.

6. Check the microcomputer if the wire harness is correct.

Output voltage

1. Remove the air temperature sensor from the power head. Connect the test harness lead to the air temperature sensor (B, **Figure 61**).

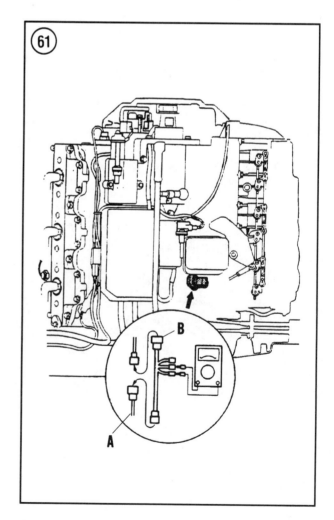

2. Determine the ambient temperature using a common air thermometer. Refer to the specifications listed in **Table 9** under *Air Temperature Sensor* to determine the correct output voltage reading for the measured ambient air temperature.

3. The air temperature can be heated or cooled to the temperatures listed in **Table 9** to test the sensor at various ranges.

4. Replace the air temperature sensor if the voltage readings are not within the indicated temperature/voltage combinations listed in **Table 9**. Removal and installation procedures are provided in Chapter Seven.

5. Install the air temperature sensor to the power head. Tighten the retaining screws securely. Turn the key switch to the OFF position. Connect all leads to the correct location.

WARNING SYSTEM

Warning systems are used on the 20-250 hp models to warn the operator of a problem with the engine. Continued operation with the warning system activated can lead to

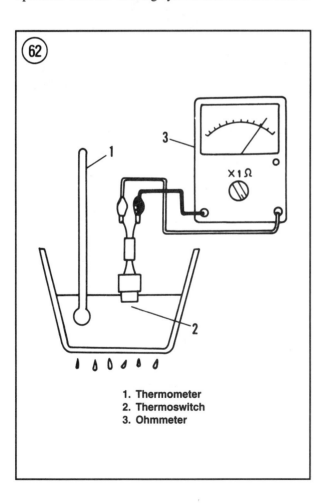

1. Thermometer
2. Thermoswitch
3. Ohmmeter

serious and expensive engine damage. The systems vary by model and horsepower. Overheat warning systems are present on the 20-250 hp models. Low oil level warning systems are present on all oil-injected models. Use the information provided on the serial number tag and refer to **Table 21** to determine if a particular model is equipped with oil injection.

The major components of the warning system include:
1. Thermoswitch.
2. Oil level sensor.
3. CDI unit.
4. Microcomputer.
5. Emergency switch.
6. Warning lamp.
7. Warning buzzer.

Thermoswitch testing

The thermoswitch is installed on all 20-250 hp engines. The thermoswitch is designed to switch to ON at a predetermined temperature and switch to OFF at a slightly lower temperature. This switch initiates the sounding of the warning horn if overheating is occurring in the power head. One thermoswitch lead is connected to the engine ground. The other lead is connected to the warning horn. This lead may also be connected to the CDI unit or Microcomputer. To test the thermoswitch, a container of water that can be heated, a multimeter and a liquid thermometer are required.

1. Locate the thermoswitch and connections. Refer to the wiring charts near the back of the manual for assistance.

2. Disconnect the thermoswitch lead and remove the thermoswitch. Fill the container with tap water and suspend the thermoswitch in the water.

3. Select the ohms or resistance function of the multimeter. Set the meter to the 1 ohm scale.

NOTE
Suspend the thermoswitch so only the tip of the switch is below the surface of the water. Inaccurate readings may occur if the switch is totally immersed in the water.

4. Connect the negative (–) meter test lead to one of the thermoswitch leads. Connect the positive (+) meter test lead to the other thermoswitch leads.

5. Suspend the thermoswitch in the water so the tip is below the surface. Place a liquid thermometer in the container with the thermoswitch (**Figure 62**).

6. The meter should indicate no continuity. Begin heating the container. Gently stir the water while observing the meter and thermometer.

7. When the meter indicates continuity, immediately record the temperature.

8. Discontinue the test if the water begins to boil before the meter reading changes. Replace the thermoswitch.

9. Allow the water in the container to cool and record the temperature when the meter reading indicates an open circuit, high resistance or no continuity.

10. Compare the switching temperature with the values listed in **Table 11**. Replace the thermoswitch if switching does not occur within the specified ranges.

11. Install the thermoswitch and connect all leads to the correct location.

Oil Level Sensor Testing

All oil-injected models use an under-the-cover oil tank to supply oil to the gear-driven oil pump. An oil level sensor is used to monitor the oil level in the tank. As the oil level changes, the float/magnet assembly passes near a magnetically activated switch. The switch is used to activate a low oil level warning system on all oil-injected models. The warning system consists of an indicator light and/or warning buzzer. On the V4 and V6 models, the switch signals the monitor unit or microcomputer to operate a pump that moves oil from a remote oil tank to the under-the-cover tank. Some models utilize special circuitry that indicates actual oil level on a gauge located at the control station. The oil level sensor consists of a single switch on 20-30 hp models, one or two switches on 40-50 hp models, two switches on 60-90 hp models and three switches on 115-250 hp models. Refer to Chapter Thirteen

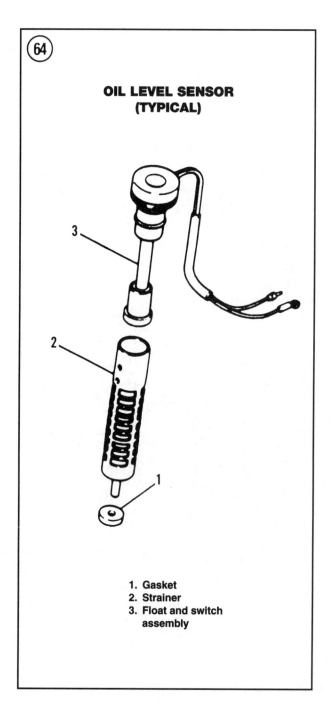

64

OIL LEVEL SENSOR (TYPICAL)

1. Gasket
2. Strainer
3. Float and switch assembly

for replacement and repair procedures on oil injection components.

A multimeter and ruler or other measuring device are required to test the oil level sensor. The test procedure is divided into four sections. Perform Steps 1 and 2 for all oil-injected models. Find the required model and perform the additional steps indicated for that model.

1. Locate the under-the-cover oil tank (**Figure 63**) and oil level sensor. Drain the oil from the tank into a suitable container by disconnecting the hose (**Figure 63**) at the top of the tank. Route the disconnected hose to the container. Place the container below the level of the tank.

2. Disconnect the harness connector plug from the oil level sensor. Gently pry the oil level sensor (**Figure 64**) from the oil tank. Retrieve and inspect the gasket (**Figure 64**) at the bottom of the strainer. Discard the gasket if damaged. Carefully remove the strainer (**Figure 64**) from the float and switch assembly. Inspect the sealing ring for a torn or damaged seal and the neck of the tank for nicks or other imperfections. Replace any damaged components.

NOTE
Significant variations exist in oil tank appearance and hose routing. Essentially all tanks contain the same type of components to include the tank itself, oil level sensor and drain hose. If instructed to remove the drain hose, it can be identified by its clear material and the connection to both the top and bottom of the oil tank. Variations exist in the means of securing the sensor to the tank. Refer to Chapter Thirteen for specific instructions on sensor removal, disassembly or installation.

CAUTION
To avoid damaging the oil tank or oil level sensor, do not use excessive force when removing the oil lever sensor from the oil tank. Handle the float and switch assembly with care to avoid accidental damage.

20-30 hp models

1. Select the ohms or resistance function on the meter used. Select the 100 ohm scale for the meter. Connect the negative (–) meter test lead to the black lead of the oil level sensor. Connect the positive (+) meter test lead to the pink lead of the oil level sensor.

2. Position the float (B, **Figure 65**) to the limit of upward travel or closest to the leads as possible. The meter should indicate no continuity. Replace the oil level sensor if a closed circuit, low resistance or continuity is indicated.

3. Slowly move the float downward or away from the leads while observing the meter. Measure the dimension indicated (A, **Figure 65**) at the point that the meter indicates continuity.

4. Replace the oil level sensor if the float travel (C, **Figure 65**) is not within 56.3-59.3 mm (2.22-2.33 in).

5. Replace the gasket (1, **Figure 64**) if needed. Follow the procedures in Chapter Thirteen to install the oil level sensor in the oil tank. Fill the oil tank with fresh oil and bleed the air from the system following the procedures listed in Chapter Thirteen.

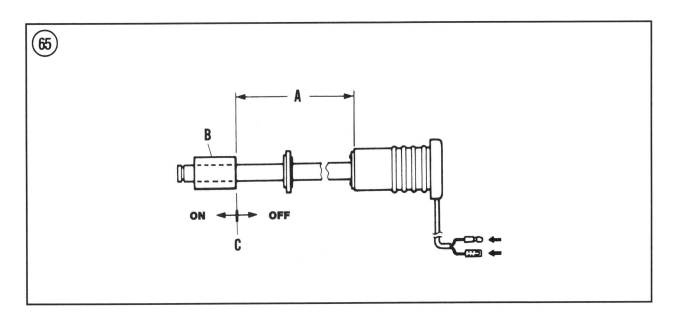

40-50 hp models

1. Select the ohms or resistance function of the meter. Select the 100 ohms scale on the meter.

2. Position the float/magnet to the upward limit or closest to the leads. Connect the negative (–) meter test lead to the black sensor lead (C, **Figure 66**) for manual start models. For electric start models connect the negative (–) meter test lead to the black sensor lead (D, **Figure 67**).

3. Connect the positive meter test lead to the pink sensor lead (A, **Figure 66**) for manual-start models or (E, **Figure 67**) for electric-start models.

4. A correct meter reading will indicate an open circuit for both manual and electric start models.

5. For electric start models only, connect the positive (+) meter test lead to the harness connector pin (C, **Figure 67**). A correct meter reading will indicate a closed circuit, or low resistance. For electric start models only, connect the positive (+) meter test lead to the harness connector pin (F, **Figure 67**). A correct meter reading will indicate an open circuit (high resistance).

6. Connect the positive (+) meter test lead to the pink sensor lead (A, **Figure 66**) for manual start models and harness connector pin (C, **Figure 67**) for electric start models. Slowly move the float downward while observing the meter. When the meter reading changes, measure and record the dimension (A, **Figure 66**) for manual start models or (A, **Figure 67**) for electric start models. The correct dimension for both models is 56.8-59.8 mm (2.24-2.35 in).

7. For electric start models only connect the positive (+) meter test lead to the harness connector pin (F, **Figure 67**). Continue to move the float/magnet downward while observing the meter. Measure and record the dimension (B, **Figure 67**) at the point the meter changed from an open reading, or high resistance, to a closed reading, or low resistance. The correct measurement is 32.8-35.8 mm (1.29-1.41 in).

60-90 hp models

1. Select the ohms or resistance function of the meter. Select the 100 ohms scale on the meter. Position the float/magnet to the upper limit of its travel or closest to the leads. Connect the negative (–) meter test lead to the sensor harness connector (E, **Figure 68**) and the positive (+) meter test lead to the other sensor harness connector (D, **Figure 68**). Correct meter readings will indicate an open circuit or high resistance.

2. Connect the negative test lead to the black sensor lead (C, **Figure 68**). Connect the positive meter test lead to the harness connector (D, **Figure 68**). Slowly move the float/magnet downward while observing the meter. A cor-

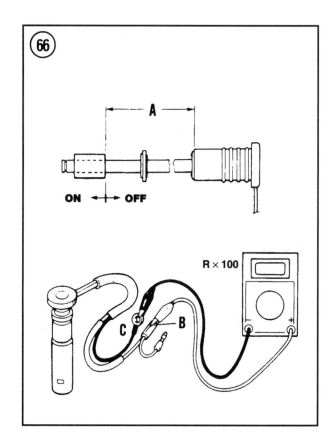

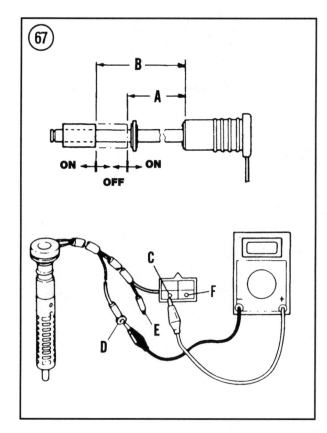

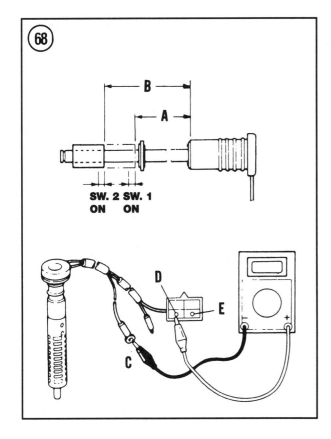

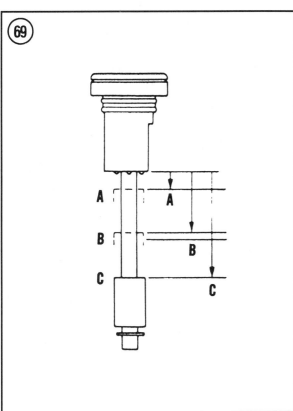

rect meter reading will indicate a closed circuit, or low resistance, at the point indicated (A, **Figure 68**). The correct measurement of position A is 79.5-82.5 mm (3.13-3.25 in) for 60-70 hp models or 5.8-8.8 mm (0.023-0.035 in) for 75-90 hp models.

3. Position the float/magnet at the correct point as indicated (B, **Figure 68**). The correct measurement of position B is 114.5-117.3 mm (4.58-4.69 in.) for 60-70 hp models and 42.3-45.3 mm (1.67-1.78 in) for 75-90 hp models.

4. Connect the negative (–) meter test lead to the sensor harness connector (E, **Figure 68**) and the positive (+) meter test lead to the black sensor lead (C, **Figure 68**). A correct meter reading will indicate 640 ohms.

5. Position the float at the upper limit of travel or closest to the leads. Connect the negative (–) meter test lead to the black sensor lead. While observing the meter, touch the positive (+) meter test lead to the sensor harness connector (E, **Figure 68**). A correct test will indicate a quick deflection of the pointer on the meter and an immediate return to an open or high resistance reading.

6. Replace the oil level sensor if an incorrect reading is noted. Refer to Chapter Thirteen for specific instruction on assembly and installation of the sensor. Fill the tank with fresh oil and bleed air from the system as required.

115-250 hp models

Although the oil level sensor is different on the 115-130 hp, 150-200 hp (90°) and 200-250 hp (76°) models, the test is similar.

1. Select the ohms or resistance function of the meter. Select the 100 ohm scale on the meter.

2. Position the float/magnet at the upper limit of travel or closest to the leads. Connect the negative (–) meter test lead to the black sensor harness lead at the connector. Connect the positive (+) meter test lead to the blue/black sensor harness lead at the connector. Correct meter reading will indicate a closed circuit or low resistance.

3. While observing the meter, slowly move the float/magnet downward or away from the leads. Measure the dimension (A, **Figure 69**) at the point where the meter reading changed to an open circuit or high resistance reading. The correct dimension is 3.3-6.3 mm (0.13-0.25 in) for 115-130 hp models, 3-6 mm (0.12-0.24 in) for 150-200 hp (90° V) models and 4-11 mm (0.16-0.43 in) for 200-250 hp (74° V) models.

4. Without disturbing the float/magnet position, connect the negative (–) meter test lead to the black sensor harness lead at the connector. Connect the positive (+) meter test lead to the blue/green sensor harness lead at the connector. Correct meter reading will indicate an open circuit or high resistance.

5. While observing the meter, slowly move the float/magnet downward until the meter indicates a closed circuit. Measure the dimension (B, **Figure 69**) at the point the meter reading changed. Correct dimension is 33.3-36.3 mm (1.31-1.43 in) for 115-130 hp models, 33-36 mm (0.12-0.24 in) for 150-200 hp 90° V models or 34-41 mm (1.4-1.6 in) for 200-250 hp 74° V models.

6. Without disturbing the float/magnet position, Connect the negative (–) meter test lead to the black sensor harness lead at the connector. Connect the positive (+) meter test lead to the blue/red sensor harness lead at the connector. Correct meter reading will indicate an open circuit.

7. Slowly move the float/magnet downward until the meter indicates a closed circuit, or low resistance reading. Measure the dimension (C, **Figure 69**) at the point the meter reading changed. Correct dimension is 53.3-56.3 mm (2.10-2.22 in) for 115-130 hp models, 53-56 mm (2.09-2.20 in) for 150-200 hp (90° V) models or 77.5-84.5 mm (3.1-3.3 in) for the 200-250 hp (74° V) models.

8. Replace the oil level sensor if an incorrect reading is noted.

Remote Oil Tank Pump

When the oil level in the under-the-cover tank drops to a given point, the CDI unit, or oil pump control unit on 115-130 hp models, activates the remote oil tank pump. This pump transfers oil from the remote tank (B, **Figure 70**) to the under-the-cover tank. The pump is turned off when the oil level in the under-the-cover tank reaches a given point. A warning system is activated in the event that oil is not available for the remote oil pump or the pump is unable to fill the under-the-cover tank. The buzzer will sound and a light will flash on models with dash-mounted gauges. An emergency switch is provided to activate the remote tank oil pump and fill the under-the-cover tank manually in the event of a system malfunction. Check the oil level sensor if the pump operates properly when the emergency switch is used.

If the pump fails to operate, check the leads that connect the oil level sensor to the CDI unit for loose or corroded connections and open or shorted leads. Test the oil level sensor as described in this section. If all other components are satisfactory and the oil pump will not operate, the likely failed component is the CDI unit, or oil control unit on 115-130 hp models.

Warning lamp

A warning lamp is used on 20-50 hp manual-start models to indicate that the engine is overheating or the oil level is low. A 1.5 volt common penlight AAA battery is required to test the lamp.

1. Remove the warning lamp from the lower engine cover/pan.

2. Using two jumper wires, connect the positive contact of the battery to the male terminal (A, **Figure 71**) of the warning lamp. Connect the negative contact of the battery to the female terminal (B, **Figure 71**). The lamp should glow.

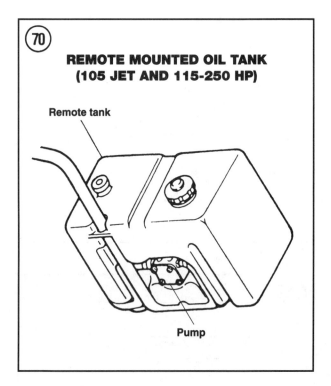

70

REMOTE MOUNTED OIL TANK (105 JET AND 115-250 HP)

Remote tank

Pump

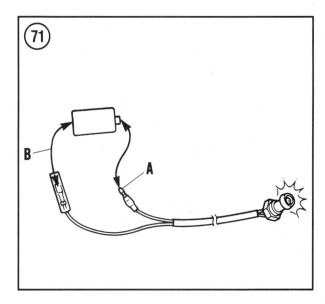

71

B

A

3. Reverse the lead connections. The lamp should not glow.

4. Replace the lamp if incorrect test results are noted.

CAUTION
Use only an ordinary 1.5 volt pen light battery to test warning lights. The use of a higher voltage battery or even an alkaline-type battery may damage the lamp.

Oil level warning lamp

Electric-start 40-50 hp models use a panel containing three LED (light emitting diode) warning lamps. The green

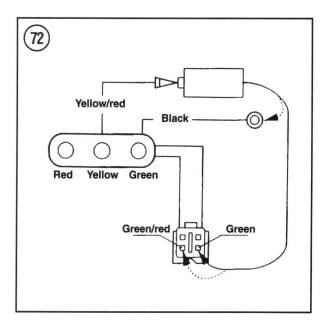

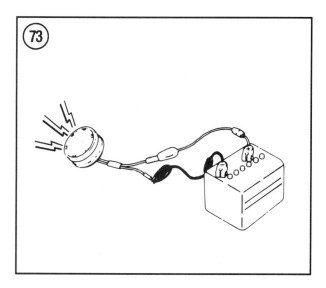

lamp indicates the tank oil level is good. The yellow lamp indicates that oil needs to be added to the tank. The red lamp indicates that the tank oil level is empty and the engine should not be operated. A common penlight battery and two short jumper wires are used to test the lamps.

1. Disconnect the harness connection and leads, then remove the LED warning panel.

2. Connect the yellow/red terminal connection to the positive (+) penlight battery contact. The yellow/red to positive (+) connection is to remain connected during Step 3 and Step 4. Using a jumper wire connect the negative (–) battery contact to the green wire harness connection (**Figure 72**). Correct test results will indicate the green LED is lit.

3. Connect the black wire connection to the negative (–) penlight battery contact. Correct test results will indicate the yellow LED is lit.

4. Using a jumper wire, connect the negative (–) penlight battery contact to the green/red wire harness connection (**Figure 72**). Correct test results will indicate the red LED had lit.

5. Replace the LED warning panel if an incorrect test result is noted.

Warning Buzzer

A warning buzzer is used on electric-start 20-250 hp models to indicate an overheat and/or low oil level condition. Connect the leads of the buzzer to battery terminal connections using jumper leads as indicated (**Figure 73**). Replace the buzzer if it fails to emit a loud warning.

WARNING
When performing tests using a battery, never make the final connection of a circuit at the battery terminal. Arcing may occur and ignite any explosive gasses that occur near the battery.

Oil Injection Component Testing

The primary oil injection components include the drive and driven gears, oil pump, check valves, hoses and fittings. Failure of any of these components can result in severe power head damage. These components should be tested when an oil related failure has occurred.

Drive/driven gear failure

Failure of the drive or driven gears will result in insufficient oil delivery to the engine. Performing an oil pump output test will indicate a failure of either gear. The pump can also be removed for inspection of the gears. Broken or missing teeth, discoloration or the presence of debris are sure signs of gear failure. Follow the instructions provided in Chapter Thirteen to remove and install the pump.

Oil pump output

A measuring container, tachometer, and a watch or clock are required to test the oil pump output.

> *NOTE*
> *The measuring container used must have 0.1 cc graduations to ensure accurate test results.*

> *CAUTION*
> *The engine must be supplied with a 50:1 fuel /oil mixture while performing the oil pump output test.*

> *CAUTION*
> *Never run an outboard without first providing cooling water. Use either a test tank or flush/test device. Remove the propeller before running the engine. Install a test propeller to run the engine in a test tank.*

> *WARNING*
> *Stay clear of the propeller shaft while running an engine on a flush/test device. To avoid possible bodily injury or death, remove the propeller before running the engine or performing tests. Disconnect all spark plug leads and the battery connections before removing or installing a propeller.*

1. Run the engine for 10 minutes on a 50:1 fuel/oil mixture then shut the engine off. Attach an accurate shop tachometer.

2. Disconnect the oil pump control linkage from the oil pump (**Figure 74**). Rotate the pump lever to the wide-open position (**Figure 75**).

3. Disconnect one of the oil pump output lines from the intake manifold connection (**Figure 76**). Route this line to the graduated container. Make sure that oil discharged from the line will not contact the side of the container (**Figure 77**).

4. Start the engine and adjust the throttle to 1500 rpm. Note and record the level of oil in the graduated container. Run the engine for exactly three additional minutes and reconnect the oil line to the fitting on the intake manifold. Shut the engine off.

5. Record the oil level in the graduated container. Subtract the early measurement from the last measurement. Compare this amount with the specification listed in **Table 24**.

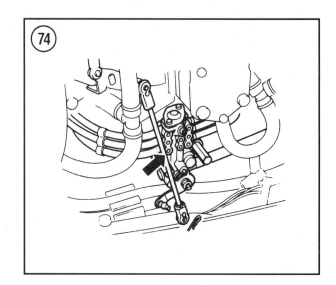

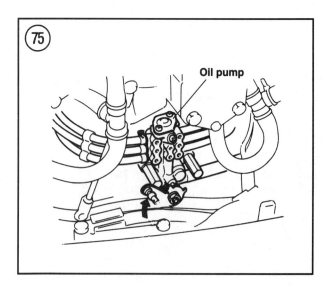

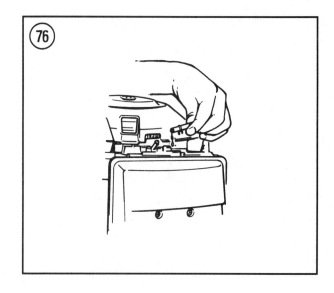

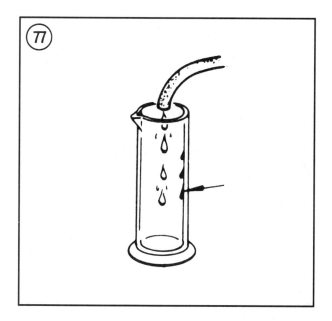

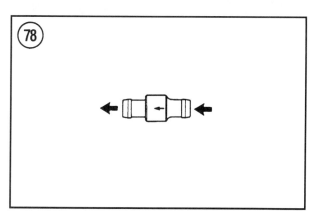

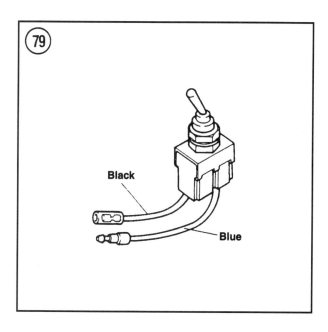

Repeat Steps 3-5 for each oil pump to intake manifold output line. If any measurement is not within the specification, check the oil pump drive/driven gears, oil line check valves and all hoses for kinks, leakage or internal restrictions. Replace the oil pump if no other faults are found.

Oil line check valves testing

An oil line check valve is used to make sure that oil will flow through the oil line in only one direction.

Failure of the check valve can result in insufficient oil flow to the engine and lead to severe power head damage. Use either a pressure tester, vacuum tester or low pressure compressed air to pass air through the check valve hose connections. Air should easily flow in the direction of the arrow on the check valve and will not flow in the direction opposite the arrow (**Figure 78**).

Emergency switch

The emergency switch (**Figure 79**) is used on 115-250 hp oil injected models to operate the on-board oil pump manually in the event of a pump control system failure. The switch is typically located on the rear of the power head and near the microcomputer. Test using a mulitmeter.

1. Disconnect the blue and black leads from the switch. Select the ohms or resistance function of the meter. Select the 1 ohm scale on the meter.

2. Connect the negative (–) meter test lead to the black switch lead (**Figure 79**) and the positive (+) meter test lead to the blue switch lead (**Figure 79**). A correct test result will indicate an open (or high resistance) circuit when the switch is in the normal (spring loaded) position.

3. Without removing the test leads, toggle the switch to the *ON* position. Correct test result will indicate a closed (low resistance) circuit.

4. Replace the switch if an incorrect test result is noted.

Overspeed Control

The overspeed control system is incorporated into the CDI unit or microcomputer on the models listed in **Table 21**. A malfunction in this system can cause an ignition misfire within the normal operating range. To check the overspeed control system, connect an accurate shop tachometer and operate the engine to verify the maximum attainable speed is within the specification listed in **Table 23**. Check all components of the ignition system. If an ignition misfire is occurring at lower than the maximum recommended rpm and all other components test correctly, the fault is likely with the CDI unit or microcomputer.

STARTING SYSTEM

The starting system on Yamaha outboards consists of a manual, or recoil type, starter only on the 2-5 hp models. Manual or electric starters are used on the 6-50 hp, 28 hp jet, E60 and E75 models. An electric starting system is used on the 60-250 hp models, excluding Model E75, and 35-105 hp jet models.

The common components of the electric starting system include the battery, start button or key switch, starter solenoid, starter motor, neutral switch, and wires.

The electric starter motor (**Figure 80**) is similar in design to what is commonly used on automotive application. Its mounting position on the power head allows the starter drive (A, **Figure 81**) to engage a flywheel mounted ring gear when the starter is operated. The neutral switch will prevent the starter motor from operating when the engine is in gear. When the starter is disengaged, the flywheel will kick the starter drive down to the starter motor with assistance of the return spring (B, **Figure 81**) mounted on the starter drive.

The electric motor portion of the starter is capable of producing a tremendous amount of torque, but only for a short period of time. To provide the torque necessary to crank the engine requires a fair amount of electrical current. Battery requirements for Yamaha outboards are listed in the Quick Reference Data at the beginning of the manual. Weak or undercharged batteries are the leading cause of starting system problems. Battery maintenance and testing procedures are provided in Chapter Four.

The operation of the start circuit begins at the ignition switch or start button. The switch or button (**Figure 82**) is connected to the positive terminal of the battery through a series of harness and lead connections. When the switch or button is operated, current is directed first to the neutral switch (**Figure 82**) and then to the starter solenoid (**Figure 82**). One terminal of the solenoid is connected to the battery positive (+) terminal with a large diameter cable (**Figure 82**). The other terminal of the solenoid is connected to a terminal on the starter motor (**Figure 82**) with a large diameter cable. When current is applied to the solenoid from the neutral switch it makes an internal connection that allows the current to flow from the battery directly to the starter motor. The solenoid arrangement allows the starter motor to be switched on or off using the shortest wires possible. The starter motor is attached to and grounded to the power head (**Figure 82**). The power head is connected to the negative (–) terminal of the battery

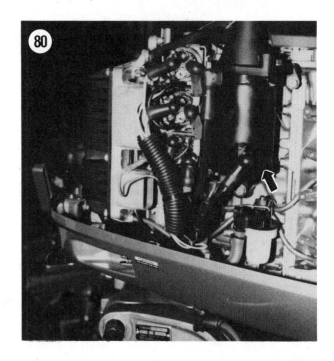

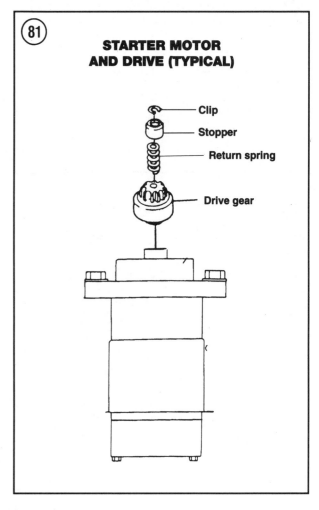

STARTER MOTOR AND DRIVE (TYPICAL)

- Clip
- Stopper
- Return spring
- Drive gear

(**Figure 82**) with a large diameter cable thereby completing the circuit. Starter motor removal, disassembly, inspection, assembly and installation procedures are provided in Chapter Seven. Refer to **Table 1** for starting system troubleshooting. Starting system component testing is provided in the following sections.

> *CAUTION*
> *Never operate the starter motor for over 10 seconds without allowing at least 2 minutes for the starter motor to cool down. Attempting to start the engine with an insufficient or*

undercharged battery can result in starter motor overheating and subsequent failure.

Starter Cranking Voltage

This test will measure the voltage delivered to the starter motor during cranking. The battery condition must be checked and corrected prior to performing this test. Refer to Chapter Seven for battery maintenance. A seized power head or gearcase must be ruled out before replacing any components.

3

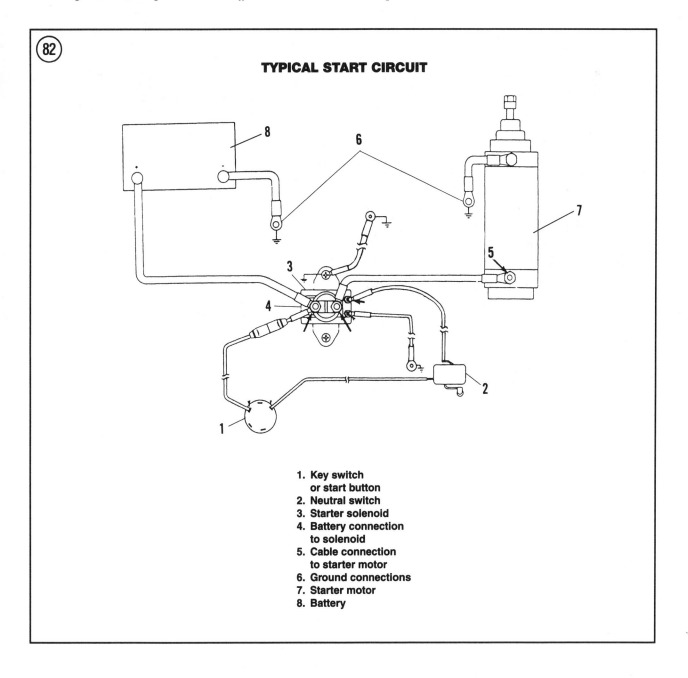

TYPICAL START CIRCUIT

1. Key switch
   or start button
2. Neutral switch
3. Starter solenoid
4. Battery connection
   to solenoid
5. Cable connection
   to starter motor
6. Ground connections
7. Starter motor
8. Battery

1. Select the voltage function of a voltmeter. Connect the positive (+) meter test lead to the large terminal at the starter motor (**Figure 83**). Connect the negative (–) meter test lead to a suitable engine ground.

2. Disconnect all spark plug leads and connect them to the engine ground. Crank the engine while observing the voltmeter.

3. Repair or replace the starter motor if the voltage indicated is 9.5 volts or greater, but the engine will not crank.

4. Test the starter solenoid and check all start system wires for faulty or dirty connections if the voltage measured is less than 9.5 volts. Test the battery again if all connections are in good condition.

Ignition Switch Testing

The ignition switch is mounted in either the dash or the remote control box (A, **Figure 84**) on all remote control models. Check the switch if the starter will not crank the engine and the neutral switch, starter solenoid, connections, fuses and battery test correctly. If equipped with a dash-mounted switch, remove the switch and perform Steps 4-7. If ignition switch is located in the control box,

partial disassembly of the control box is necessary to test the switch. Perform Steps 1-7 for a control box-mounted ignition switch.

1. Remove the control box from its mounting bracket. Remove the access cover (B, **Figure 84**) from the lower side of the control.

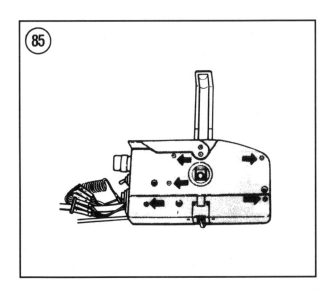

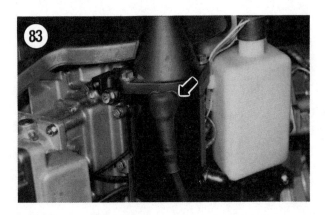

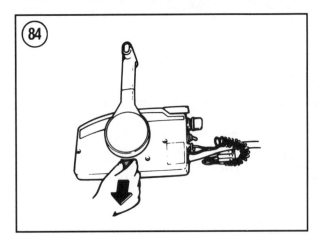

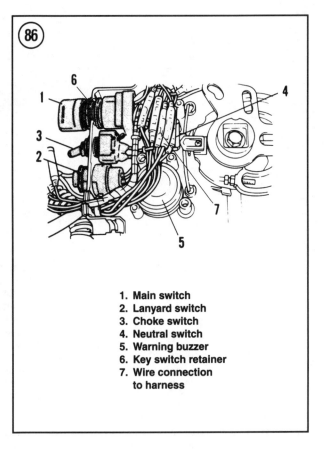

1. Main switch
2. Lanyard switch
3. Choke switch
4. Neutral switch
5. Warning buzzer
6. Key switch retainer
7. Wire connection
   to harness

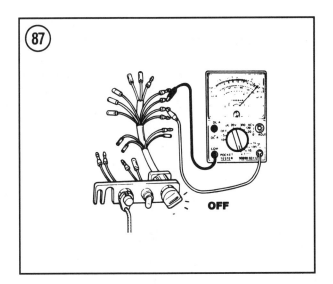

OFF

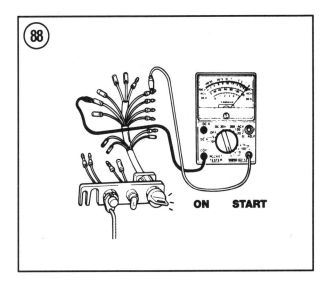

ON   START

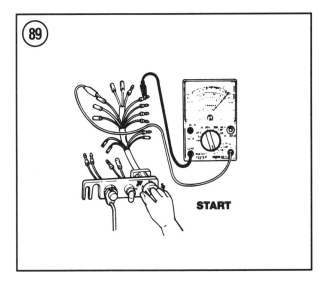

START

2. Remove the back cover screws (**Figure 85**). Remove the key from the switch. Loosen and remove the threaded retainer (6, **Figure 86**) for the ignition switch.

3. Disconnect the leads that connect the ignition switch to the harness and remove the key switch from the control box.

4. Select the ohms or resistance function of the meter. Select the 1 ohm scale. Connect the negative (–) meter test lead to the black switch lead and the positive (+) meter test lead to the white switch lead (**Figure 87**). With the switch in the OFF position, correct readings will indicate a closed circuit. With the switch in the ON position, correct reading will indicate an open circuit.

5. Connect the negative (–) meter test lead to the yellow switch lead and the positive (+) meter test lead to the red switch lead (**Figure 88**). Correct reading indicate a closed circuit with the key switch in the ON and START position. With the switch in the OFF position, correct reading will indicate an open circuit.

6. Connect the negative (–) meter test lead to the brown switch lead and the positive (+) meter test lead to the red switch lead (**Figure 89**). Correct readings will indicate a closed circuit with the switch in the START position. With the switch in the OFF or ON position, correct readings will indicate an open circuit.

7. Replace the ignition switch if an incorrect reading is noted. Connect all switch leads to the proper location and install the switch. Assemble the remote control as required.

Start Button Testing

On tiller controlled electric start models, the starter button (**Figure 90**) is mounted at the front of the lower motor pan/cover. One lead of the button is connected to the battery positive (+) terminal. The other lead is connected to the neutral switch. When the button is depressed, current

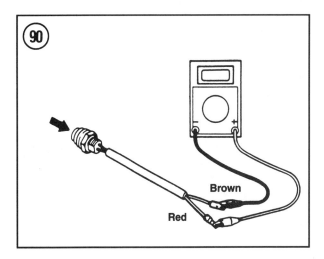

Brown

Red

is able to flow through the neutral switch and on to the starter solenoid, thus activating the starter. An analog or digital multimeter is required to test this component.

1. Disconnect the leads connecting the start button to the engine harness. Remove the threaded retainer, located inside the motor pan, and remove the button.

2. Connect the positive (+) meter test lead to the red button lead. Connect the negative (−) meter test lead to the brown button lead. A correct reading will indicate an open circuit with the button at rest.

3. Depress the button while observing the meter (**Figure 90**). Correct reading will indicate a closed circuit. Replace the button if an incorrect reading is noted. Install the button and connect all leads to the proper location.

Starter Solenoid Testing

The starter solenoid allows a large amount of current to pass from the battery to the starter motor. When the start switch or button is operated, current flows through the neutral switch and on to the solenoid. This current passes through a coil of wire in the solenoid, creating a strong magnetic force. The magnetic force moves a plunger that closes contact points in the solenoid allowing current to flow directly from the battery to the starter motor. An analog or digital multimeter and jumper leads are required to test the solenoid.

1. Remove the solenoid using the instructions provided in Chapter Seven. Connect the negative (−) meter test to one of the large terminal connections on the solenoid (**Figure 91**). Connect the positive (+) meter test lead to the other large terminal connection. A correct reading will indicate an open circuit (high resistance).

2. Using alligator clip jumper leads, connect the black lead of the solenoid to the negative (−) terminal of a fully charged battery (**Figure 91**). Connect an alligator clip jumper lead to the positive (+) terminal of a fully charged battery. While observing the meter, connect the jumper lead to the brown lead of the solenoid (**Figure 91**). Correct reading will now indicate a closed circuit.

3. Replace the solenoid if an incorrect reading is noted. Install using the instructions provided in Chapter Seven.

Neutral Switch Testing

The neutral switch is provided to prevent the starter from operating when the engine is in forward or reverse gear. A cable operated start lock mechanism is provided on 4 hp and up models with manual start. Repair procedures for these mechanisms are provided in Chapter Eleven. Electric start models with tiller control are provided with a neutral switch mounted on the engine. Verify proper neutral switch

adjustment on tiller models before testing or replacing the switch. On electric start models with remote control, the switch is located inside the control. Partial disassembly of the control is required before testing the switch. A common multimeter and measuring ruler are required to perform this test.

Remote-controlled models

1. Remove the control from its mount. Remove the cover from the lower side of the control (**Figure 84**). Remove the

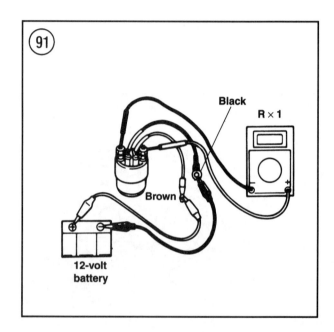

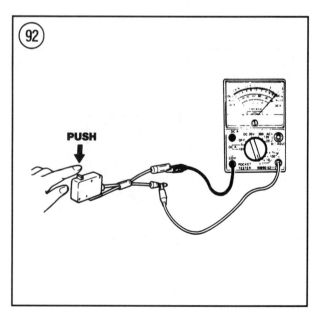

screws that retain the back cover (**Figure 85**). Disconnect the leads and remove the neutral switch (**Figure 92**).

2. Select the ohms or resistance function on the meter. Select the 1 ohm scale. Connect the positive (+) meter test lead to a brown lead on the switch. Connect the negative (–) meter test lead to the other brown lead on the switch.

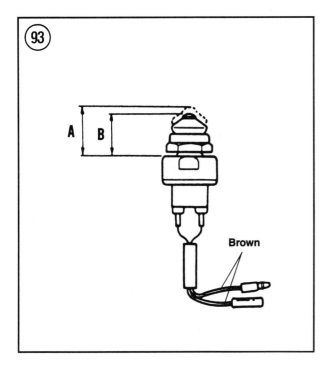

3. Correct readings will indicate an closed circuit when the switch is depressed (**Figure 92**).
4. Release the switch while observing the meter. Correct reading will indicate an open circuit with the switch released.
5. Replace the switch if an incorrect reading is noted.

Tiller-controlled models

1. Locate the neutral switch on the power head. Disconnect the neutral switch leads and remove the switch from the power head. Refer to Chapter Seven for removal procedures.
2. Select the ohms or resistance function on the meter. Select the 1 ohm scale. Connect the positive (+) meter test lead to a brown lead of the switch. Connect the negative (–) meter test lead to the other brown lead of the switch (**Figure 93**).
3. Correct meter reading will indicate an open circuit (high resistance) while the switch is released. Using a ruler, measure the dimension indicated at A, **Figure 93**. The correct measurement is 18.5-19.5 mm (0.73-0.77 in.).
4. While observing the meter, depress the switch to the dimension indicated at B, **Figure 93**. A correct meter reading will indicate a closed circuit at the measurement indicated.
5. Replace the switch if an incorrect reading is indicated. Refer to Chapter Seven for installation procedures.

Manual Start Systems

The manual start components include the recoil pulley, spring, drive pawls, drive pawl spring, rope and handle. The most common failure involves a frayed or broken rope. Before condemning a seemingly locked-up manual or recoil starter, verify that the gearcase and power head are not seized and the start lockout mechanism is functioning properly, otherwise refer to Chapter Eleven for complete repair procedures.

CHARGING SYSTEM

The components of the charging system include the flywheel, battery charging coil (**Figure 94**), rectifier (**Figure 95**) or rectifier/regulator (**Figure 96**), wires and of course the battery. The function of the charging system is to maintain the battery charge level after starting the engine and when using onboard accessories. Accessories (depth sounders, stereos, etc.) can draw considerable current from the battery. The charging system may not be able to keep up with the demand for current, leading to a battery discharge while running. The use of accessories is increasing

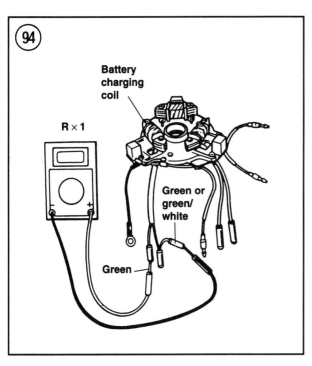

in boats thereby putting additional demand on the charging system. Check all components of the charging system if the battery fails to remain charged. Determine the total amperage of the accessories on the vessel and compare the total with the charging system output. Refer to the *Quick Reference Data* section at the front of the manual for these specifications. Keep in mind that the charging system will deliver considerably less than the maximum output when the engine is operated at lower speeds. Consider adding additional batteries or installing a greater capacity battery as a possible solution. More frequent charging of the batteries may be required. Information on battery maintenance is provided in Chapter Seven.

Engines with a manual starter generally do not use a charging system. Some models have the option of a lighting coil.

The lighting coil is positioned under the flywheel and produces alternating current as the flywheel magnets rotate past it. The current produced by the lighting coil is suitable only for operating lights. Adding a *rectifier* into a similar circuit on the E48, E60 and E75 models converts the current produced by the lighting coil to a *direct current*. This arrangement allows the charging of the cranking battery. Models with electric start, excluding Models E48, E60 and E75, use a rectifier/regulator unit. The rectifier portion of this component converts the alternating current produced by the charging coil to a direct current. The regulator portion of this component senses the voltage at the battery and prevents overcharging of the battery.

Troubleshooting the charging system requires the use of a multimeter. Use an analog multimeter when checking for open or closed circuits. To begin the troubleshooting process, verify that the charging system is not operating. Test the charging system components after verifying a charging system fault.

Charging System Output

1. Select the voltage function of the meter. Select the proper scale to measure 10-15 volts. Connect the positive (+) meter test lead to the battery positive (+) terminal. Connect the negative (–) meter test lead to a suitable engine ground. Observe and record the measured battery voltage.

2. With all test leads connected, start the engine. Observe and record measured battery voltage. A voltage equal to or less than the first measurement indicates that the charging system is not functioning. Further testing is required.

3. A voltage reading exceeding 14 volts indicates a likely overcharge condition that warrants further testing.

WARNING
Stay clear of the propeller shaft while running an engine on a flush/test device. The propeller must be removed before running the engine during testing to avoid serious bodily injury or death. Disconnect all spark plug leads and battery connections before removing or installing a propeller.

CAUTION
Never run an outboard without first providing cooling water. Use either a test tank or flush/test device. Remove the propeller before running the engine. Install a test propeller to run the engine in a test tank.

NOTE
In most, but not all, cases the tachometer will not operate when a fault occurs in the charging system. Check all components as a precaution if the charging system is suspect, but the tachometer is operating.

If a discharge or overcharge is indicated, test all components of the charging system. Many times, both the charge coil *and* the rectifier/regulator are faulty. A fault with the flywheel magnets may cause decreased charging output; however, the same magnets are used to power the ignition

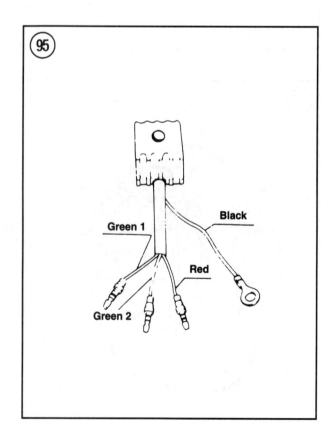

system. Problems with magnets will likely cause ignition problems as well.

Check the resistance or voltage output of the lighting coil. Then check the resistance of the rectifier or rectifier/regulator. Replace the component(s) that fail a resistance test.

Lighting/Battery Charge Coil Testing

Resistance specifications are provided for models E48, E60 and 60-90 hp models, except 80 jet. When performing

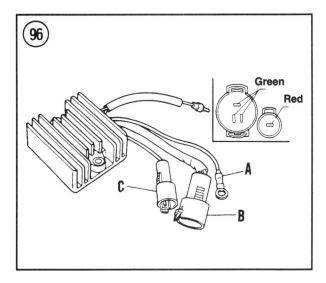

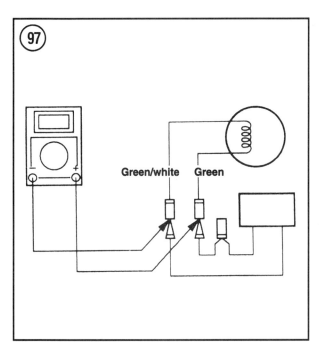

the lighting coil resistance test, remember that ambient temperature will affect the measured resistance. The resistance values specified in **Table 17**.

Voltage output test specifications are provided for 9.9-50 hp, E75 and 115-250 hp models. Operate the engine at the speed specified in **Table 17** when testing voltage output.

All charging system test specifications are provided in **Table 17**.

3

Lighting/battery charge resistance

1. Using the wiring chart at the back of the manual, locate the leads that connect the main wire harness to the lighting coil. Disconnect the leads.

2. Select the ohms or resistance function of the meter. Select the 1 ohm scale. Connect the negative (–) meter test lead to a green lighting coil lead (**Figure 94**). Connect the positive (+) meter test lead to the other green or green/white lighting coil lead.

3. Compare the meter reading with the specification listed in **Table 17**. Replace the coil if resistance is not within specified range. Follow the instructions provided in Chapter Seven for lighting coil removal and installation.

Lighting/battery charge coil voltage output test (9.9-90 hp and 115-200 hp 90° premix models)

> *NOTE*
> *The wire harness leads are to remain connected to the lighting coil when performing a voltage output test. Insert the meter test leads between the insulated connectors to make contact with the individual terminals.*

1. Select the peak voltage or DVA function of the meter. Select the proper scale or the specified voltage.

2. Locate the leads that connect the main wire harness to the lighting/coil charge using the wiring charts at the back of the manual. Connect the negative (–) meter test lead to the green/white (green lead for 9.9-30 hp models) lighting coil lead connector (**Figure 97**). Refer to **Figure 98** for 150-200 hp models. Connect the positive (+) meter test lead to the green lighting coil lead connector. Refer to **Figure 98** for 150-200 hp models.

3. Start the engine using a suitable test/flush adapter or test tank. Record the lighting coil output at the engine speed specified in **Table 17**.

4. Test and/or replace the rectifier/regulator if the lighting coil voltage is above the specification listed in **Table 17**. Replace the lighting coil if the lighting coil voltage is below the specification listed in **Table 17**.

5. Remove the test leads and check all leads for proper connections. Follow the instructions provided in Chapter Seven for lighting coil and rectifier/regulator removal and installation procedures.

Lighting/battery charge coil voltage output test (115-250 hp oil-injected models)

1. Select the peak voltage or DVA function of the meter. Select the proper scale for the specified voltage.

2. Locate the leads that connect the main wire harness to the charge coil using the wiring charts at the back of the manual. Connect the negative (–) meter test lead to a good engine ground.

3. Run the engine at each speed specified in **Table 17**. Connect the positive (+) meter test lead to each green lead that connects the lighting coil to the rectifier/regulator. Connect the positive (+) meter lead to the red regulator terminal on 200-250 (76° V) hp models. Record the peak voltage at each specified speed.

4. Replace the charge coil if the voltage is below the specification listed in **Table 17**.

5. Test or replace the rectifier/regulator if the voltage is above the specifications listed in **Table 17**.

6. Remove the test leads and check all harness leads for proper connections. Follow the instructions provided in Chapter Seven for lighting charge coil and rectifier/regulator removal and installation procedures.

Rectifier/Regulator Testing

Perform the *rectifier resistance test* on Models E48, E60 and E75, as they are not provided with a rectifier/regulator.

Perform the *rectifier/regulator resistance test* on electric start 9.9, 60-90 hp, excluding models E60 and E75, 115-130 hp and 150-200 hp (90° V) models.

Rectifier resistance test

1. Locate and disconnect the leads for the rectifier using the wire charts at the back of the manual.

2. Select the ohms or resistance function of an analog multimeter. Select the 1 ohm scale.

3. Connect the positive (+) meter test lead to a green rectifier lead and the negative (–) meter test lead to the black rectifier lead (**Figure 95**). Note meter reading, then connect the positive (+) lead to the other green rectifier lead. A correct reading will indicate a closed circuit.

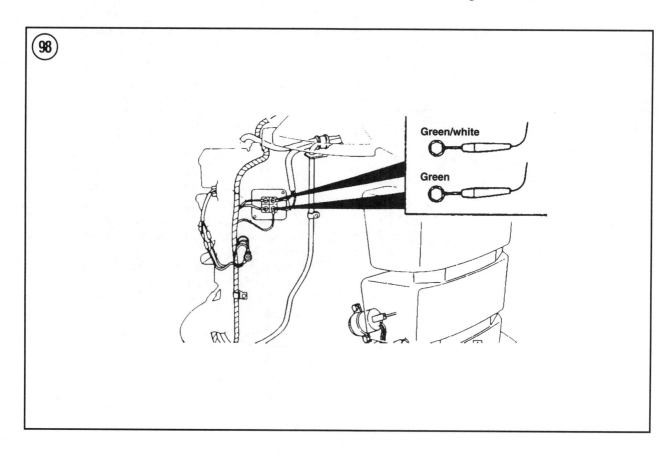

98

Green/white

Green

4. Connect the positive (+) meter test lead to the red rectifier lead and the negative (–) meter test lead to the black rectifier lead (**Figure 95**). A correct reading will indicate a closed circuit.

5. Connect the positive (+) meter test lead to the red rectifier lead and the negative (–) meter test lead to one of the green rectifier leads (**Figure 95**). Note meter reading, then switch the negative (–) meter test lead to the other green rectifier lead. A correct reading will indicate a closed circuit.

6. Connect the positive (+) meter test lead to one of the green rectifier leads and the negative (–) meter test lead to the other green rectifier lead (**Figure 95**). A correct reading will indicate an open circuit.

7. Connect the negative (–) meter test lead to the red rectifier lead and note meter readings. Switch the positive (+) meter test lead to the other green rectifier lead and note readings. A correct reading will indicate an open circuit.

8. Connect the positive (+) meter test lead to the black rectifier lead. Connect the negative (–) meter test lead to one of the green rectifier leads (**Figure 95**) and note meter reading. Switch the negative (–) meter test lead to the other green rectifier lead and note readings. Correct reading will indicate an open circuit.

9. Replace the *rectifier* if an incorrect reading is noted. Follow instructions in Chapter Seven for removal and installation procedures.

Rectifier/Regulator Resistance Test

This test procedure is divided into two sections. The first section provides test instructions for the rectifier/regulator units indicated in **Figure 96**. The second section provides test instructions for the rectifier/regulator units indicated in (**Figure 99**).

Perform Steps 1-9 for rectifier/regulator units shown in **Figure 96**.

1. Locate and disconnect the leads for the rectifier/regulator (**Figure 96**) using the wire charts at the back of the manual.

2. Select the ohms or resistance function of an analog meter. Select the 1 ohm scale.

3. Connect the positive (+) meter test lead to each green lead at the connector (B, **Figure 96**). Connect the negative (–) meter test lead to the black lead (A, **Figure 96**). A correct reading is an open circuit.

4. Connect the positive (+) meter test lead to the red lead (C, **Figure 96**) and the negative (–) meter test lead to the black lead (A, **Figure 96**). A correct meter reading is an open circuit.

5. Connect the positive (+) meter test lead to the red lead (C, **Figure 96**) and the negative (–) meter test lead to each green lead at the connector (B, **Figure 96**). A correct reading is an open circuit.

6. Connect the positive (+) meter test lead to the red lead (C, **Figure 96** and the negative (–) meter test lead to each green lead at the connector (B, **Figure 96**). A correct reading is a closed circuit.

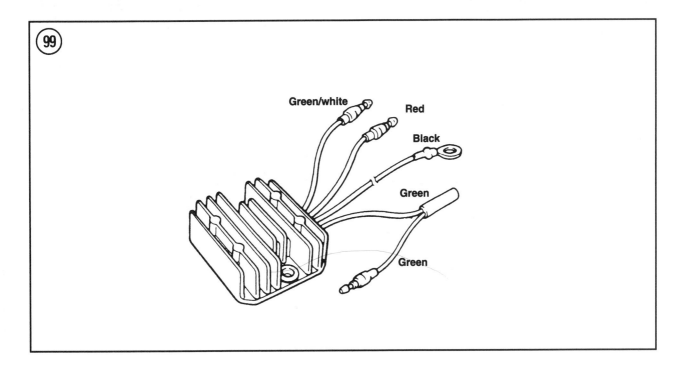

(99)

Green/white   Red

Black

Green

Green

7. Connect the positive (+) meter test lead to the black lead (A, **Figure 96**) and the negative (–) meter test lead to the red lead (C, **Figure 96**). The correct reading is a closed circuit.

8. Connect the negative (–) meter test lead to the red lead (C, **Figure 96**) and the positive (+) meter test lead to each green lead at the connection (B, **Figure 96**). The correct reading is a closed circuit, or low resistance.

9. Replace the rectifier/regulator if an incorrect reading is noted. Follow the instructions in Chapter Seven for removal and installation procedures.

Perform Steps 1-10 for the rectifer/regulator units indicated in **Figure 99**.

1. Locate and disconnect the rectifier/regulator leads (**Figure 99**) using the wire charts in the back of the manual.

2. Select the ohms or resistance function of an *analog* multimeter. Select the 1 ohm scale.

3. Connect the positive (+) meter test lead to the red lead and the negative (–) meter test lead to the green lead (**Figure 99**). Note the meter reading, then switch the negative (–) meter test lead to the green/white lead. Note the meter reading, then connect the negative (–) meter test lead to the black lead (**Figure 99**). The correct meter readings are a closed circuit.

4. Connect the positive (+) meter test lead to the black lead and the negative (–) meter test lead to the green lead (**Figure 99**). Note meter reading, then connect the negative (–) meter test lead to the red lead (**Figure 99**). The correct readings are an open circuit.

5. Connect the positive (+) meter test lead to the black lead and the negative (–) meter test lead to green/white lead (**Figure 99**). The correct reading is a closed circuit, or low resistance.

6. Connect the negative (–) meter test lead to the black lead and the positive (+) meter test lead to the green lead (**Figure 99**). Note meter reading, then switch the positive (+) meter test lead to the green/white lead (**Figure 99**). The correct readings are a closed circuit.

7. Connect the negative (–) meter test lead to the red lead and the positive (+) meter test lead to the green lead (**Figure 99**) Note meter reading, then switch the positive (+) meter test lead to the green/white lead (**Figure 99**). The correct readings are an open circuit.

8. Connect the positive (+) meter test lead to the green lead and the negative (–) meter test lead to the green/white lead (**Figure 99**). The correct reading is a closed circuit.

9. Connect the positive (+) meter test lead to the green/white lead and the negative (–) meter test lead to the green lead (**Figure 99**). The correct reading is an open circuit.

10. Replace the rectifier/regulator unit if an incorrect reading is noted. Follow the instructions in Chapter Seven for removal and installation procedures.

FUSES AND WIRE HARNESS

Fuse Testing

Fuses are used on all electric start models to protect the wire harnesses in the event of a short cicuit or overload. Never replace a fuse without performing a thorough check of the electrical system. Keep in mind that fuses are de-

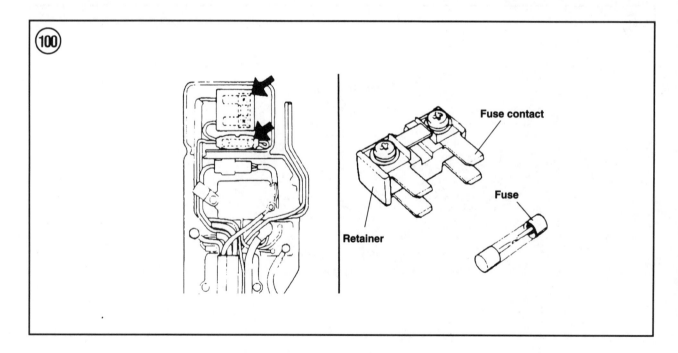

signed to open the circuit if an overload occurs. Never bypass a fuse or install a fuse with greater capacity than specified, or you may risk your safety and the safety of others. The most common symptom of a blown fuse is the engine will not crank and the instruments will not work. In some instances, the first symptom is that the trim system is not working. Use a multimeter to test fuses. Note that different types of fuse retainers are used in the various models.

1. Locate and remove the fuse (**Figure 100**) from the retainer using the wire charts at the back of the manual.

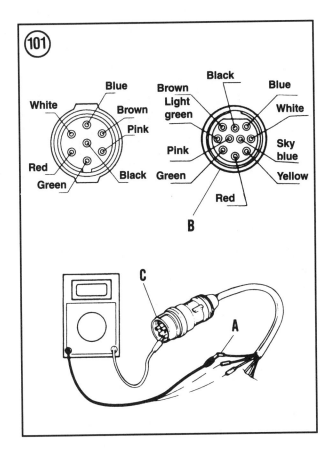

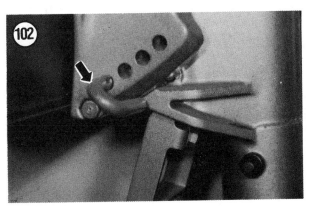

Select the ohm or resistance function of the meter. Select the 1 ohm scale.

2. Connect the positive (+) meter test lead to one of the fuse contacts (**Figure 100**) from the fuse. Connect the negative (−) meter test lead to the other contact.

3. The correct reading is a closed circuit, or very low resistance. Check all components connected to the wire harness the fuse serves. Correct any wire harness or component fault before installing a new fuse and returning the engine to service.

Wire Harness Testing

Due to the harsh operating environment, problems with the wire harness are common. A problem may occur continuously or only intermittently. When an electrical problem exists and all components test correctly, the wire harness becomes suspect. Check both the engine and instrument harnesses on remote control models. Gently twist and pull on the harness wire connectors when checking the leads for continuity. Often this is the way an intermittent fault is located.

Use an ohmmeter or self-powered test light to test the harness.

1. Disconnect the engine harness from the instrument harness if used. Disconnect wire harness leads from the engine components or instruments.

2. Select the ohms or resistance function of the meter. Select the 1 ohm scale.

3. Connect one of the meter or test light leads to a wire harness lead (A, **Figure 101**). Connect the other test lead to the connector pin (B, **Figure 101**) that corresponds to the harness lead being checked. Refer to the wire charts at the back of the manual to determine the proper connector pin for the wire color.

4. The correct reading is a closed circuit, very low resistance or test lamp lit.

5. Check and repair the connector if an open circuit, high resistance or test lamp not lit, is indicated. Replace the wire harness if the connector is not faulty.

TRIM SYSTEM TROUBLESHOOTING

Tilt Pin and Lockdown Hook

Trim and tilt systems used on Yamaha outboards vary by model and horsepower. A tilt pin and hold down hook (**Figure 102**) are used on 2-25 hp models. It allows the engine to run slightly tilted in or out to change the running attitude of the boat or to enhance shallow water operation. The hold down hook is operated when in reverse gear to prevent the prop thrust from moving the engine up or out.

The operator may notice that the unit will not hold down when in reverse or cannot tilt up when in forward or neutral when a malfunction occurs. Check the adjustment and inspect the system for broken or excessively worn components. Repair procedures and adjustments for these components are provided in Chapter Twelve.

Hydro Tilt

This hydraulic assist system is used on some 30-60 hp models (**Figure 103**). This unit is mounted between the engine clamp brackets. It provides hydraulic assistance when tilting the engine for trailering or beaching the boat. The tilt function is activated when the operator moves the lever (**Figure 104**). This system will hold the engine trim position during normal operation by trapping the fluid in the hydraulic cylinder (**Figure 104**) with internal valves. Shock absorbing valves provide controlled fluid movement that allows the cylinder to extend at a controlled rate during impact with underwater objects. This system can help minimize impact damage. The typical symptoms of a fault include:

1. Will not hold trim angle.
2. Comes up in reverse or when slowing down.
3. Leaking fluid.

This unit is not serviceable. When troubleshooting, first check the lever position. Replace the assembly if the lever is in the normal position and a fault still exists.

Power Tilt

The electrically operated power tilt system is common on the 40-50 hp models. The assembly is mounted between the engine clamp brackets (**Figure 105**). This system provides movement of the engine in the up or down direction when preparing to trailer or beach the boat. This system is not designed to trim the engine while underway. A tilt pin is used to set the desired trim position when in forward gear (**Figure 106**). Up or down movement will only occur when none or very little prop thrust is present.

The major components of this system include the electric motor (A. **Figure 105**), relays, hydraulic pump (B, **Figure 105**) and tilt cylinder (C, **Figure 105**). The bi-directional electric motor drives a hydraulic pump. Changing the electric motor direction controls fluid movement and thus the hydraulic pump direction. The hydraulic pump moves fluid to and from a single hydraulic cylinder. As the fluid move into the up side of the cylinder the engine will tilt up. Fluid returns to the pump from the down side of the cylinder when tilting up. The pump direction is changed and fluid is moved to the down side of the cylinder to tilt

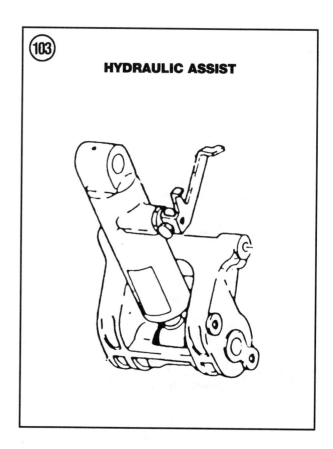

103

HYDRAULIC ASSIST

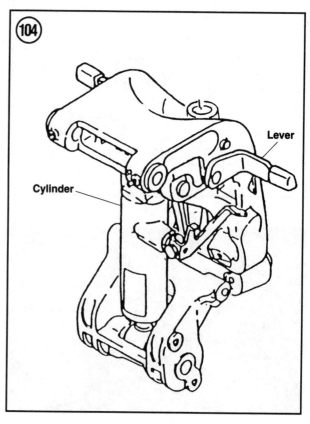

104

Lever

Cylinder

the engine down. Fluid returns to the pump from the up side of the cylinder when tilting down. Valves in the pump hold the fluid in both sides of the cylinder when the electric motor stops to prevent down or up movement during normal operation.

A relief valve is provided to allow the engine to be moved up or down manually without running the pump. Access the valve (**Figure 107**) through an opening on the

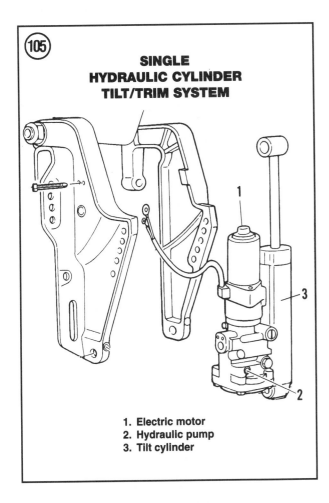

SINGLE HYDRAULIC CYLINDER TILT/TRIM SYSTEM

1. Electric motor
2. Hydraulic pump
3. Tilt cylinder

starboard clamp bracket. Always check this valve before performing other tests. Normal position is fully rotated in the clockwise direction. Turn the valve counterclockwise with a screwdriver to activate the valve.

Before performing the test, check the fluid level following the procedures provided in Chapter Four. The electric portion of this system is relatively easy to service and repair. Refer to *Electrical Testing* for electrical troubleshooting procedures. Instructions are provided in Chapter Twelve for repair of electric components along with the removal and installation procedures for major components of the trim system.

A professional should perform repair of the major components. Remove the trim system as instructed in Chapter Twelve and contact a Yamaha dealership for information. Much expense can be spared when the assembly has been removed from the engine, not to mention the inconvenience of transporting and storing the boat at the dealership. Make sure the electric motor is operating before beginning any hydraulic test.

Common symptoms indicating a possible hydraulic malfunction include :

1. The engine will not move up.
2. The engine will not move down.
3. The engine leaks down when tilted up.
4. The engine trails out when slowing down.
5. Hydraulic fluid is leaking from the system.

Single Cylinder Trim

The single cylinder trim system is common on the 40-50 hp models. It functions much like the tilt system and many

of the parts are similar in appearance. The trim system provides the capability to move the engine up/out against prop thrust, allowing the operator to change the running attitude of the boat while underway. The major components include the electric motor, relays, hydraulic pump and hydraulic cylinder. A bi-directional electric motor (**Figure 108**) drives the hydraulic pump (**Figure 109**). Reversing the motor direction controls the direction of fluid movement to and from the pump and cylinder (**Figure 110**). Fluid moves from the pump to the up side of the cylinder to trim the unit up. Fluid returns to the pump from the down side of the cylinder. Fluid is directed to the down side of the cylinder to trim the unit down. Fluid returns to the pump from the up side of the cylinder.

A relief valve (**Figure 107**) is provided to allow the engine to be moved up or down manually without running the electric motor. Always check this valve before performing other test.

Before performing any test, check the fluid level. Follow the procedure provided in Chapter Four to check the fluid level. The electrical portion of this system is relatively easy to service and repair. Refer to *Electrical Testing* for electrical troubleshooting procedures. Instructions are provided in Chapter Twelve for trim electrical repair along with removal and installation procedures for major components of the trim system.

Have major hydraulic component repair performed by a professional. Remove the trim system as instructed in Chapter Twelve and contact a Yamaha dealership for information. Much expense can be spared when the assembly has been removed from the engine, not to mention the inconvenience of transporting and storing the boat at the dealership. Make sure the electric motor is operating before beginning any hydraulic test.

Common symptoms indicating a possible hydraulic malfunction include:

1. The engine will not move up.

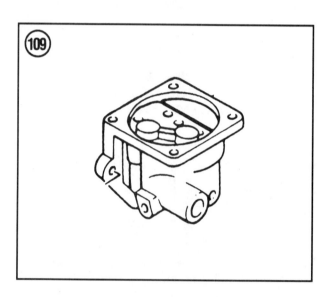

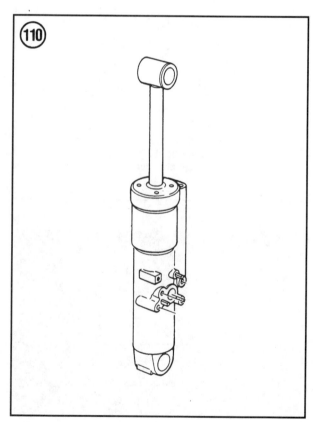

2. The engine will not move down.

3. The engine leaks down while tilted up or when underway.

4. The engine trails out when slowing down or when in reverse.

5. Hydraulic fluid is leaking from the system.

Three Ram Trim

A power trim system utilizing three hydraulic cylinders is available for 60-250 hp models. The entire hydraulic system, including the hydraulic pump, is mounted between the engine clamp brackets (**Figure 111**). Benefits derived from mounting the pump outside rather than inside the boat as on earlier systems include fewer hydraulic hoses and connections, less oil leaks and faster response due to fewer restrictions in the system. Disadvantages of the system are a greater exposure to the corrosive environment and greater difficulty in pinpointing which component is faulty when performing hydraulic tests.

The major components of this system (**Figure 112**) include the bi-directional electric motor and pump, fluid reservoir, trim rams and tilt cylinder. Engine-mounted relays control the electric motor/pump rotational direction and therefor control fluid directional movement within the system. When trimming up from a down position, fluid is moved into the up side or up cavity of both trim rams and the tilt cylinder. The end of the trim rams (**Figure 113**) contact against striker plated on the engine swivel bracket. Fluid pressure will cause all three cylinders to extend thereby moving the engine out/up. Lubricate the end of the trim rams (**Figure 113**) to prevent noisy operation when trimming up. At this point, the trim rams are fully extended and the tilt cylinder remains the only means to move the engine up/out. Less power is present from the system as only one cylinder drives the system. This has an effect of limiting the trim range while under way at high speed. The

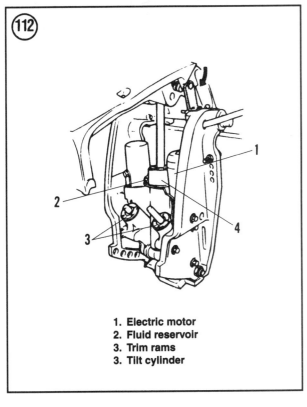

1. Electric motor
2. Fluid reservoir
3. Trim rams
3. Tilt cylinder

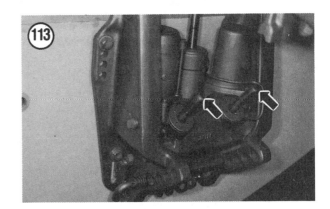

engine will, however, have a greater tilt speed as all the fluid travels to a single cylinder instead of three.

When trimming down, the motor changes direction causing fluid to flow to the down side or cavity of the cylinders. As the only cylinder connected to the engine at both ends, the tilt cylinder provides all down movement.

A manual relief valve is provided to allow manual engine movement without operating the pump. An opening on the port or starboard clamp bracket (A, **Figure 114**) provides the manual relief valve access. The fluid fill/check point (B, **Figure 114**) is located on the fluid reservoir and is only accessible when the engine is tilted up. Always check the manual relief valve and fluid level before testing or replacing components. The normal position of the manual relief valve is fully seated clockwise rotation. To activate the manual relief valve use a screwdriver and rotate the valve (**Figure 115**) counterclockwise LH three complete turns. Refer to Chapter Four for instructions for checking trim fluid level.

The electrical portion of this system is relatively easy to service and repair. Refer to *Electrical Testing* for electrical troubleshooting procedures.

Have major hydraulic component repair performed by a professional. Remove the entire system following the procedures provided in Chapter Twelve. Contact a Yamaha dealership for repair information. Considerable expense can be saved when the system has been removed from the engine not to mention the inconvenience of transporting and storing the boat at the dealership. Make sure the electric motor is operating before beginning any hydraulic test.

Common symptoms indicating a possible hydraulic malfunction include:

1. The engine will not move up.
2. The engine will not move down.
3. The engine leaks down from a full tilt position.
4. The engine leaks down when underway.
5. The engine trails out when slowing down.
6. Hydraulic fluid is leaking from the system.

> *WARNING*
> *The hydraulic system fluid may be under high pressure. Use extreme caution when removing valves or fitting. Always use safety goggles when working with the hydraulic system. Avoid exposing any portion of the body to areas where a leak is suspected.*

Hydraulic System Testing

Testing of the hydraulic system requires a pressure gauge capable of measuring pressures between 6000 kPa

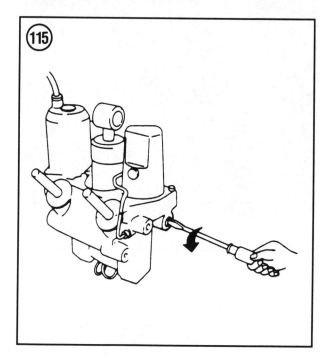

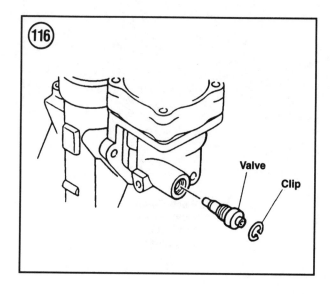

(850 psi) and 12,000 kPa (1700 psi), or Yamaha tool part No. YB-90890-06776. Testing the power trim system with three hydraulic cylinders requires special adapters, Yamaha part No. 90890-06773 and part No. 90890-06774, in addition to a pressure gauge. Pressure testing procedures are not provided for the hydraulic tilt or the single-cylinder trim system.

Perform the hydraulic system pressure test after verifying that the electrical part of the system is operating properly. Be sure the manual relief valve is in the normal operating position, the fluid level is correct and the battery is fully charged. Perform Steps 1-11 to measure the maximum *up* and *down* pressure.

Perform Steps 1-10.

1. Activate the manual relief valve and tilt the engine to the full up position. Support the engine in this position using suitable blocks or overhead cable. Check the fluid level following the procedures in Chapter Four.

2. Remove the clip (**Figure 116**) from the manual relief valve (**Figure 116**). Remove the manual relief valve

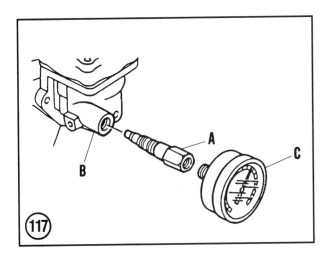

(117)

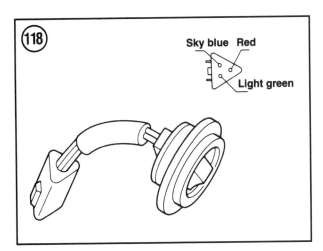

(118)

Sky blue   Red

Light green

through the access hole. Quickly install the down pressure adapter, part No. 90890-06774, (A, **Figure 117**) into the manual relief valve fitting (B, **Figure 117**).

3. Thread the hydraulic pressure gauge to the adapter and tighten securely.

4. Using caution, remove the blocks or cable supporting the engine. Run the trim system in the down direction, while observing the gauge, until all hydraulic cylinders are fully retracted. Record the maximum down pressure. Wait two minutes and read the pressure again.

5. Compare the test readings with the specification listed in **Table 12**. Correct reading will be within the specified range and will not drop significantly over a two-minute period.

6. Position the engine in the full up position and provide support for the engine.

7. Provide support for the engine. *Slowly* remove the gauge and adapter to relieve pressure within the system. *Quickly* install the up pressure adapter, part No. 9080-06773, and gauge (A and C, **Figure 117**) to minimize fluid loss. Check and correct fluid level.

8. Run the trim in the up direction while observing the gauge, until all hydraulic cylinders are fully extended. Record the maximum up pressure. Wait two minutes and read the pressure again.

9. Compare the test reading with the specification listed in **Table 19**. Correct reading will be within the specified range and will not drop significantly over a two minute period.

10. Remove the pressure gauge and adapter. Install the manual relief valve and clip (**Figure 116**). Check and correct the fluid level as indicated in Chapter Four.

11. Remove and repair the trim system if the pressure reading is not within the specified range or a significant pressure drop is noted.

Electrical Testing

The major electrical components of the trim system are the electric motor, relays, trim position sender and switches. The bi-directional electric motor is provided with a blue lead and a green lead. When up trim or tilt direction is selected, the blue lead is connected via wires and relays to the positive (+) battery terminal and the green lead is connected to ground by the same means. The motor will rotate in the direction that moves fluid toward the up side of the hydraulic cylinders. When the down direction is selected, the relays simply reverse the motor direction.

Selection of trim direction is accomplished with a remote control, dash-mounted or tiller arm-mounted trim switch (**Figure 118**). Battery voltage is supplied to the red lead of the switch assembly. When the switch is toggled to the up position, the red lead is connected to the blue lead that is also connected to the up relay. When the switch is toggled to the down selection, the red lead is connected to the green lead that is also connected to the down relay.

When voltage is applied to either one of the relays, it directs voltage to the electric motor. The other relay supplies the connection to ground for the electric motor. Both relays must make the proper connection for the electric motor to operate. Two relay arrangements are used in Yamaha outboards. The most common type is dual relays attached to a mount on the side of the power head (**Figure 119**). The other type has both relays combined in one assembly (**Figure 120**). This type has a plug-in connector or separate leads with individual connectors. The test procedures are very similar for both types.

A trim-sending unit is used with a dash-mounted gauge to give the operator a visual indication of the current trim position. A fuse is provided in the circuit that connects the positive (+) battery terminal to the trim switch. Refer to the wire charts in the back of this manual to help locate the fuse in the circuit. Test this fuse when the electric motor will not operate in the up or down direction. Refer to *Fuse Testing* in the previous section.

Use a voltmeter to check for battery voltage at the terminal before performing component testing.

1. Use the wire charts at the back of this manual to locate the relay arrangement for the model tested. Select the voltage function for the meter. Select the proper scale to read 10-20 volts.

2. Connect the negative (−) meter test lead to the black lead at the relay terminal. Connect the positive (+) meter test lead to the red lead at the relay terminal. The correct reading is battery voltage.

3. Check the battery connections and all leads and connections if an incorrect reading is noted.

When battery voltage tests are found to be correct, test the relays, trim switch, and harness. Refer to *Fuse and Harness Testing* in the previous section. The electric motor is suspect if the motor will not operate up or down and all other components test correctly. Refer to Chapter Twelve for electric motor repair.

Continuity Test (Dual Relays)

1. Locate the relay assembly using the wire charts at the back of the manual as a reference. Disconnect the positive (+) and negative (−) battery connections from the battery. Disconnect the sky blue, light green, red and black leads from the relay assembly.

2. Select the ohms or resistance function on the meter. Select the 1 ohm scale. Connect the positive (+) meter test lead to the sky blue terminal (A, **Figure 119**) and the

negative (−) meter test lead to the black terminal at the relay (B, **Figure 119**). Record the meter reading. Connect the positive (+) meter test lead to the light green terminal at the relay (C, **Figure 119**). Record the meter reading.

3. Connect the positive (+) meter test lead to the sky blue terminal (A, **Figure 119** and the negative (−) meter test lead to the light green terminal at the relay (C, **Figure 119**). Record the meter reading.

4. Connect the positive (+) meter test lead to the sky blue terminal (E, **Figure 119**) and the negative (−) meter test lead to the light green terminal (C, **Figure 119**). Record meter reading.

5. The correct meter readings in Steps 2-4 are a closed circuit, or low resistance.

6. Connect the positive (+) meter test lead to the sky blue terminal (D, **Figure 119**) and the negative (−) meter test lead to the light green terminal (E, **Figure 119**) and note meter reading. The correct reading is an open circuit, or high resistance.

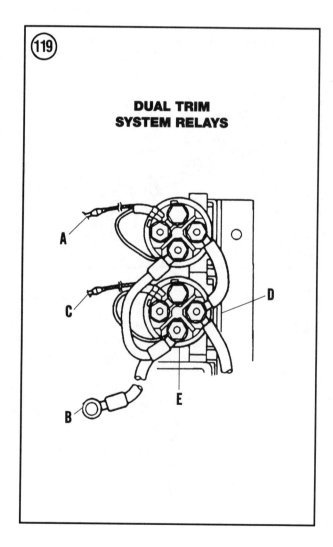

**DUAL TRIM
SYSTEM RELAYS**

7. Replace the relay or relay units if an incorrect reading is noted. Follow instructions provided in Chapter Twelve for removal and installation. Install all leads to the proper location.

Continuity Test (Combination Relay Assembly)

1. Disconnect the positive (+) and negative (−) battery terminals from the battery. Disconnect the relay harness

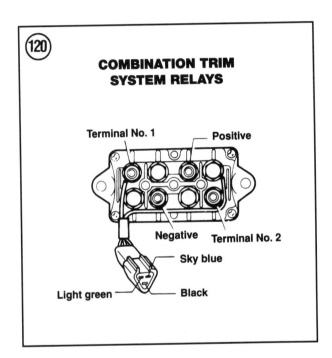

COMBINATION TRIM SYSTEM RELAYS

Terminal No. 1 — Positive

Negative — Terminal No. 2

Sky blue

Light green — Black

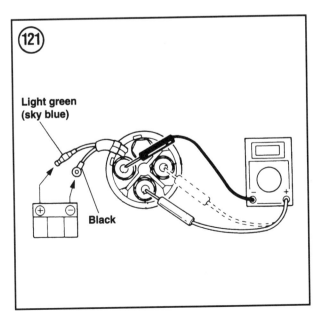

Light green (sky blue)

Black

connector or individual plug-in connectors. Select the ohms or resistance function of the meter. Select the 1 ohm scale.

2. Connect the positive (+) meter test lead to the sky blue terminal connection and the negative (−) meter test lead to the black terminal connection. Record the meter readings. Connect the positive (+) meter test lead to the light green terminal connection. Record the meter readings.

3. Connect the positive (+) meter test lead to terminal one and the negative (−) meter test lead to the Negative terminal (**Figure 120**). Record the meter readings. Connect the positive (+) meter test lead to terminal two (**Figure 120**). Record the meter reading.

4. Connect the positive (+) meter test lead to terminal one and the negative (−) meter test lead to the positive terminal (**Figure 120**). Record the meter readings. Connect the positive (+) meter test lead to terminal two and the negative (−) meter test lead to the positive terminal (**Figure 120**). Record the meter reading.

5. The correct readings are a closed circuit (low resistance) for Steps 2 and 3. The correct readings are an open circuit, or high resistance for Step 4. Replace the relays or relay unit if an incorrect reading is noted. Follow the instruction provided in Chapter Twelve for removal and installation instructions. Install all lead to the proper location.

Operational Test (Dual Relays)

1. Disconnect the positive (+) and negative (−) battery connections from the battery. Select the ohms or resistance function of the meter. Using jumper leads, connect the positive (+) battery terminal to the sky blue terminal and the negative (−) battery terminal to the black lead (**Figure 121**). Connect the positive (+) meter test lead to terminal two and the negative (−) meter test lead to terminal one (**Figure 121**). Record the meter reading.

2. With all other leads from Step 1 still attached, connect the positive (+) battery terminal to the light green terminal (**Figure 121**). Record the meter reading.

3. Connect positive (+) meter test lead to terminal 3 and the negative (−) meter test lead to terminal one (**Figure 121**) Record the meter reading.

4. Connect the (+) meter test lead to terminal two and the negative (−) meter test lead to terminal one (**Figure 121**). Record the meter reading.

5. The correct readings are a closed circuit (low resistance) for Steps 1-3 and an open circuit, or high resistance for Step 4. Replace the relays if an incorrect reading is indicated. Follow the instructions provided in Chapter Twelve for removal and installation.

Operational Test
(Combination Relay Assembly)

1. Disconnect the positive and negative battery terminals from the battery. Using jumper leads, connect the negative battery terminal to the light green terminal and the positive battery terminal to the black terminal (**Figure 122**). Select the ohms or resistance function of the meter. Select the 1 ohm scale. Connect the positive meter test lead to the positive relay terminal and the negative meter test lead to the negative relay terminal (**Figure 122**). The correct reading is an open circuit, or high resistance.

2. Using jumper leads connect the positive battery terminal to the sky blue terminal and the negative battery terminal to the black lead (**Figure 122**). Connect the positive meter test lead to the negative relay terminal and the negative meter test lead to terminal one (**Figure 122**). Record the meter readings. The correct reading is a closed circuit, or low resistance.

3. Replace the relay unit if an incorrect reading is noted. Follow the instructions provided in Chapter Twelve for removal and installation. Install all leads to the correct location.

Trim Switch Testing

The trim or tilt system is controlled by a three-position switch mounted on the remote control, dash panel or tiller handle. For operator convenience some models have an additional switch mounted in the lower engine cowl. Testing procedures are similar for all switch locations. This rocker-type switch is spring loaded into the center or OFF position. The switch can be used to activate either the UP or DOWN relay by toggling the switch to the desired position. Battery voltage is applied to the switch by a fused lead. Check the fuse or wire harness if voltage is not present on the lead. Refer to the *Fuse or Wire harness Testing* in this section. Use a multimeter to test the circuits of the switch when the unit fails to operate in one or both directions. Follow Steps 1-7 for models with the trim switch (**Figure 118**) mounted in the remote control. Follow Steps 3-7 for models with the trim switch mounted in the tiller arm. Follow Steps 4-7 for models with a dash mounted switch.

1. Disconnect the positive (+) and negative (–) battery terminals. Remove the remote control from its mounting location. Remove the wire cover (**Figure 123**), then remove the screws for the back cover (**Figure 124**).

2. Remove the back cover and disconnect the tilt/trim switch connector (**Figure 118**).

3. For tiller models or models with an engine cover-mounted switch, unplug the switch connector (**Figure 125**).

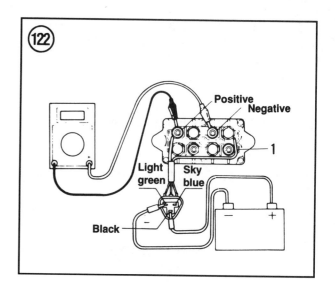

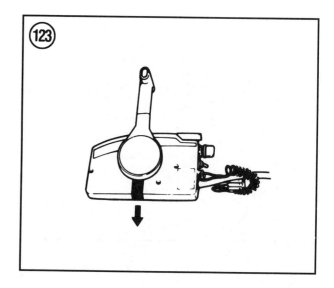

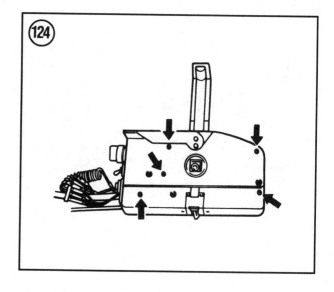

4. Select the ohms or resistance function of the meter. Select the 1 ohms scale. With the switch disconnected from any harnesses, connect the positive (+) meter test lead to the red lead connection pin at the plug. Connect the negative (−) meter test lead the sky blue lead connection pin at the plug (**Figure 118**). The correct reading is an open circuit with the switch in the middle position or toggled to the DOWN position. The correct reading is a closed circuit (low resistance) when the switch is toggled to the UP position.

5. Connect the positive (+) meter test lead to the red lead connection pin at the switch plug. Connect the negative (−) meter test lead to the light green lead connection pin at the switch plug (**Figure 118**). The correct reading is an open

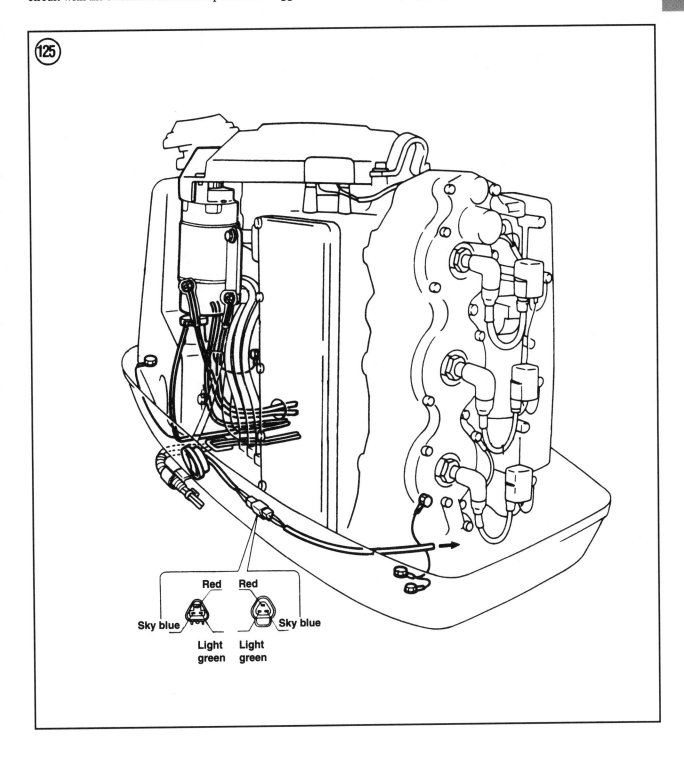

circuit with the switch in the middle position or toggled to the UP position. The correct reading is a closed circuit (low resistance) when the switch is toggled to the DOWN position.

6. Connect the negative (–) meter test lead to the sky blue lead connection at the switch plug and the positive (+) meter test lead to the light green lead connection at the switch plug (**Figure 118**). The correct reading is an open circuit at *all* switch positions.

7. Replace the trim/tilt switch if an incorrect reading is noted. Connect all leads to the proper location and install all components removed for switch access.

> *NOTE*
> *When testing a trim position sender, be aware that the resistance must be tested at 20° C (68° F). Testing the unit at temperatures other than specified can significantly affect the test results.*

Trim Position Sender Testing

A digital or analog engine trim position gauge is available for the 40-250 hp models. A trim position sender (**Figure 126**) mounted on the engine clamp bracket operates the gauge. If the gauge is not reading correctly, adjust the trim sender unit as instructed in Chapter Twelve. If the adjustment does not correct the problem, perform Steps 1-5 to test the sender unit.

1. Raise the engine to the full up position. Support the engine using an overhead cable and/or blocks to ensure that it will not drop down. Locate the trim position sender on the port clamp bracket. Disconnect the wire connector plug or individual lead connectors.

2. Loosen and remove the screw(s) that retain the sender. Carefully remove the sender from the clamp bracket. Select the ohms or resistance function of a digital multimeter. Select the proper scale for the specification provided in **Table 20**. Connect the negative (–) meter test lead to the

black sender lead connection and the positive (+) meter test lead to the pink sender lead connection (**Figure 127**).

3. Slowly move the trim sender lever while observing the meter (**Figure 128**). Record the highest and lowest resistance readings. Connect the positive (+) meter test lead to the orange sender lead connection (**Figure 128**). Slowly move the trim sender lever while observing the meter. Record the highest and lowest resistance readings.

4. Compare the measured resistance readings with the specifications listed in **Table 20**. Replace the trim sender if an incorrect reading is noted. Replace the sender if abrupt changes are noted as the lever is slowly moved. The readings must change smoothly as the lever is moved.

5. Install the trim sender and connect all leads to the proper location. Refer to the instructions provided in Chapter Twelve to install and adjust the trim sender.

POWER HEAD

This section covers troubleshooting and testing to determine if a problem is present in the power head. Areas to be

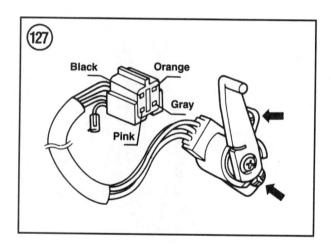

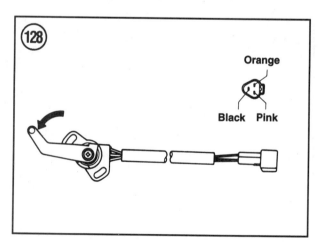

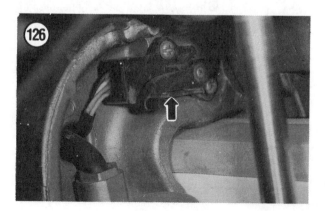

be covered include engine noises, lubrication failure, detonation, preignition, engine seizure, water entering the cylinder and puddle fuel drain system. For power head removal, repair and installation refer to Chapter Eight.

Engine Noises

Understandably, some noise will occur in the power head during normal operation. A ticking noise or a heavy knocking noise that intensifies when under load (accelerating) is a reason for concern. The ticking noise is common when a failure has occurred in one or more cylinders. Many times pieces of the piston, piston ring, or a foreign body is embedded in the piston and is striking the cylinder head. Inspect the spark plug for damage or aluminum deposits and perform a compression test as described in this chapter. Complete power head disassembly and repair is required if a problem is noted with the compression or if metal deposits are found on the spark plug. Running the

engine with an unusual noise may result in increased damage that renders a power head repair impossible.

A whirring noise that is most pronounced as the throttle is decreased is usually related to a problem with crankshaft and rod bearings. The bearing surface on the connecting rod and crankshaft may have a washboard-like surface (**Figure 129**) that causes this noise. Improper storage preparation can lead to corrosion etched surfaces at the contact point of the needle bearing to the crankshaft surface. These surfaces may later develop the washboard surface. Only major repair of the power head will correct this condition.

Sometimes the cylinder that is creating the noise can be identified by using a mechanic's stethoscope. Compare the noise emanating from one area of the power head with the noise from the same area but different cylinder. The noise will be more pronounced if the stethoscope is positioned in the cylinder head area when a problem exists in the cylinder itself. The noise will be more pronounced in the crankcase area when a problem exists in the crankshaft and connecting rod components. Special insulated pliers are available that allow spark plug lead removal while running the engine. The noise may lessen when the spark plug lead is removed on the suspect cylinder. This procedure is difficult to do and may result in damage to the electrical system. The stethoscope method is far more safe and effective for the amateur technician.

Lubrication Failure

When lubrication is insufficient, the engine faces certain damage to the internal components if not total power head failure. If the power head is not provided with oil due to oil injection failure or the operator failed to *properly* mix the correct oil in the fuel on (premix models), the engine will likely operate fine for a few minutes and then begin to slow down without moving the throttle. The engine may stop and will not crank over with the starter. On occasion the engine will start after cooling down but will likely slow down and stop again. When the engine is restarted, it will likely run rough and will not idle. Performance will be lacking as well. The engine will eventually seize and require extensive and expensive repairs. When you suspect that the engine has run with a lack of sufficient lubrication, perform a compression test. The top cylinders normally suffer the most damage when oil is lacking or overheating has occurred. Disassemble and inspect the power head. A bluish tinge is normally present on crankshaft components when lubrication is lacking. The pistons and cylinder walls usually have scoring and scuffing in the areas near the exhaust ports (**Figure 130**). Crankshaft seals may also have a burned appearance. Take a sample of the fuel from the carburetor bowl on the premix models. Apply a small amount of the fuel to a white piece of cardboard and allow it to dry in a safe area (see Fuel Warning). Residual oil in the fuel sample will leave a blue stain on the cardboard indicating oil was present. On oil injected models, the *entire* oil injection system must be tested and inspected when power head failure has occurred and lack of sufficient lubrication is suspected as the cause.

Detonation

Detonation damage is the result of the heat and pressure in the combustion chamber becoming too great for the fuel that is used. Fuel normally burns at a controlled rate that produces the expanding gasses to drive the piston down. When conditions in the engine allow the heat and pressure to get too high, the fuel may explode violently. These violent explosions in the combustion chamber will cause serious damage to internal engine components. Carbon deposits, overheating, lean fuel conditions, over advanced timing and lugging are some of the conditions that may lead to damaging detonation. The octane rating of the fuel used in the engine must meet or exceed the octane requirements of the engine. Never use a fuel with a lower than recommended octane rating. It may cause detonation under normal operating conditions.

Combustion chamber pressure and temperature rise dramatically, creating severe shock waves in the engine when detonation occurs. This will cause severe engine damage. The engine will likely have a rough idle and may seize if the damage is great enough. A compression test will likely reveal one or more cylinders with low compression. Inspect the spark plug as you remove it to perform a compression test. The presence of aluminum deposits (**Figure 131**) indicates probable detonation damage. Complete power head repair is required when detonation has occurred.

Preignition

Preignition is the premature ignition of the air/fuel charge in the combustion chamber. Preignition is caused by hot spots in the combustion chamber. Wrong heat range, spark plugs, carbon deposits and inadequate cooling are some of the causes of preignition. Preignition will result in loss of power and eventually lead to severe damage to the internal engine components. The primary component that suffers is the piston. The damage is very similar to detonation, as the early ignition causes the heat and pressure to become too great for the fuel that is used. It will explode

violently causing a melted effect on the piston dome. It is not uncommon to have a hole form in the dome of the piston when preignition has occurred. Inspection of the spark plugs will likely reveal aluminum deposits (**Figure 131**) consistent with detonation failures.

Engine Seizure

The power head can seize at high speed, idle or any speed in between. Normally the engine will not seize up at high speed as the engine will gradually lose power and slow down. The primary reason for the seizure is an internal problem in the power head such as detonation or preignition. Always inspect the gearcase before removing the power head. Gearcase or jet pump failures will prevent the power head from rotating. Inspect the gearcase for metal contamination or the jet pump for a seized impeller or drive shaft. The gearcase can also be removed to check for gearcase seizure as instructed in Chapter Nine. Refer to Chapter Ten for jet pump repair information. Repair the gearcase or jet pump if the power head will turn over freely with the component removed.

Water Entering the Cylinder

Water can enter the cylinder from a number of areas. Water in the fuel, water entering the front of the carburetor, leaking exhaust covers/gaskets, leaking cylinder head and/or gaskets and cylinder block internal leaks are some

common causes. The typical symptom is rough running particularly at idle. The engine may run satisfactorily at higher speed. Water intrusion is usually discovered when the spark plugs are removed to perform a compression test. Water will likely be present on the spark plugs and a white deposit may be present. When the cylinder head is removed for further inspection the wet cylinder will usually have significantly less carbon deposit on the piston and cylinder dome. Continued operation with water intrusion will result in power head failure. Inspect the cylinder head gasket, cylinder head and exhaust cover gaskets. A black deposit over a sealing surface or damage to the gasket itself indicates the point of leakage. Leakage in the cylinder block can be difficult to find. Casting flaws, pinholes and cracks may or may not be visible. Replacement of the cylinder block is suggested when water is entering the cylinder and no visible gasket leakage can be found. Refer to Chapter Eight for power head repair procedures.

Puddle Fuel Drain System

During low-speed operation the air and fuel mixture tend to separate near the reed and reed block areas. The fuel will settle out of the air and form puddles in areas below the air stream. Fuel and oil may also settle out of the air and form

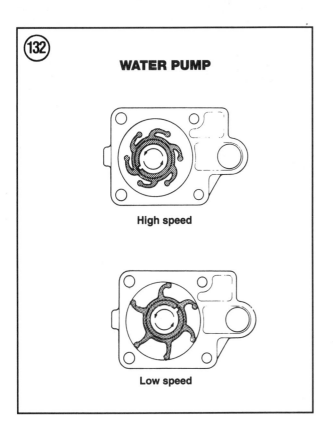

WATER PUMP

High speed

Low speed

puddles in some areas of the crankcase. The puddle fuel drain system uses existing crankcase pressure and vacuum to move this fuel and/or oil to a location where it can be used by a cylinder. Hoses, check valves and passages are used to route the fuel. At speeds above 2000 rpm, the volume and speed of the air moving to the cylinder will prevent fuel from puddling. When one of the hoses, check valves or passages is blocked, the typical symptom will be prevalent at low engine speed. The engine will idle well for a few minutes then begin to idle rough. The idle quality will continue to deteriorate and the engine may stall. When the operator attempts to accelerate, the puddled fuel may be picked up and flood the cylinder with excess fuel. The engine may bog or hesitate when this occurs. This condition is commonly called *loading up*. Check for improperly adjusted carburetor(s) or reed problems, as they may cause excessive fuel to puddle and exceed the capability of the puddle fuel system. Always check the routing of hoses before changing check valves or cleaning passages. Refer to the diagrams in Chapter Eight for hose routing.

COOLING SYSTEM

The cooling system for a Yamaha outboard is relatively simple. A water pump is mounted on the lower unit gearcase or jet pump (**Figure 132**). The pump supplies water to the exhaust area of the power head first, then to the cylinder block and head(s). The water exits the power head near the power head-mounting surface and travels out through the drive shaft housing. As the water travels through the power head, it absorbs heat and carries it away. If an overheating problem exists, the water is either not flowing through the power head in sufficient volume or is not absorbing the heat adequately. Most models are equipped with thermostats that help maintain a minimum power head temperature. They work by restricting exit water until a minimum water temperature is reached. A stream is visible at the rear of the motor lower cover when water is exiting the power head. The fitting for the stream will commonly become blocked with debris and cease flowing. Clean the passage with a small stiff wire. Inspect the cooling system if the water stream is still not present. V4 and V6 models are equipped with a water pressure control valve to provide adequate water pressure in the block at low speeds. Blockage in the valve will result in overheating at higher engine speeds.

Cooling System Inspection

When overheating is noticed on the gauge, the warning horn is sounding or the water stream is not present at the rear of the engine, check for a faulty water pump and repair as needed. Inspect and correct the water pump in the gearcase or jet pump. Refer to Chapter Nine for gearcase water pump repair and Chapter Ten for jet pump repair.

Inspect and test the thermostat (if so equipped) when overheating is occurring and the water pump is in good condition. Refer to *Thermostat Testing* in this section.

Inspect the cooling system for debris and deposit buildup when no faults can be found with the water pump and thermostat. Rocks, pieces of the water pump, sand, shells or other debris, may restrict the water.

Salt, calcium or other deposits can form in the cooling passages and can restrict water flow. A water pump is mounted on the lower unit gearcase or jet pump (**Figure 132**). The pump supplies water to the exhaust area of the power head first, then to the cylinder block and head(s). Use a cleaner specifically designed to dissolve cooling system deposits. Make sure that the cleaner is suitable for use on aluminum material. Always follow the manufacturer's instructions when using these products. These cleaners are usually available at marine specialty stores. Removal of water jackets will be necessary when inspecting cooling passages. Refer to Chapter Eight for water jacket removal and installation procedures.

Verifying Engine Temperature

When overheating is suspected, verify the actual temperature of the engine using Thermomelt sticks (**Figure 133**). Thermomelt sticks resemble crayons. They are designed to melt at a given temperature. Rub the sticks against the cylinder head, leaving marks near the temperature sender or switch. On the engines that do not have an overheat alarm, hold the stick near the spark plug mounting area. Try to check the temperature immediately after or during the suspected overheat condition. Use different temperature thermomelt sticks to determine the temperature range the engine is reaching. Stop the engine if the temperature exceeds 90° C (195° F) to avoid damage to the power head.

Perform this test with the engine in the water or use a test tank. Perform a complete cooling system inspection if overheating occurs. Test the temperature sender or switch if an alarm or gauge indicates overheating and the thermomelt sticks indicate normal temperature. Troubleshooting overheating problems with a flush/test attachment is difficult, as the water supplied through the hose will mask problems with the cooling system.

Thermostat Testing

Test the thermostat(s) if the engine is overheating or running too cool. A liquid thermometer, piece of string and container of water that can be heated are required to test a thermostat.

1. Remove the thermostats following the instructions provided in Chapter Eight.

2. Suspend the thermostat into the container of water with the string tied to the thermostat (**Figure 134**).

3. Place the liquid thermometer in the container and begin heating the water. Observe the temperature of the water and the thermostat. A correct thermostat will begin to open (**Figure 135**) at approximately 48-52° C (118-126° F).

4. Continue to heat the container while observing temperature and thermostat. A correct thermostat will be fully open (**Figure 135**) at approximately 60° C (140° F).

5. Replace the thermostat if it opens below or above the specified temperature.

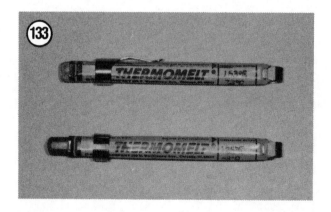

LOWER UNIT

Problems with the lower unit are generally related to two areas that include leakage and failed components. Troubleshooting the gearcase involves inspection of the gear lubricant when failed components are suspected. When

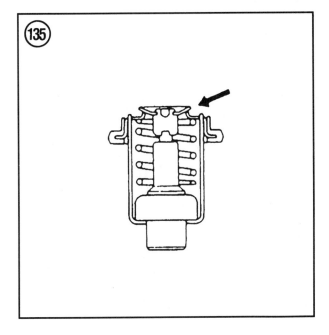

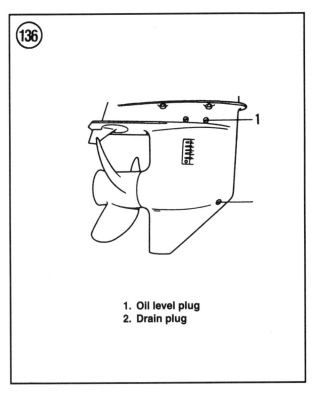

1. Oil level plug
2. Drain plug

leakage is suspected in the gearcase, perform a pressure test to determine if and where a leakage point exists. Maintenance procedure for the gearcase is located in Chapter Four. Gearcase repair procedures are located in Chapter Nine. Perform shift linkage adjustment if the gears do not engage properly. Refer to Chapter Five for adjustment procedures. Internal component inspection is required if adjustment fails to solve the problem.

Water in the Gearcase

Under certain conditions a small amount of water may be present in the gearcase lubricant. The conditions would involve a gearcase that has not received normal maintenance for several years and has been stored with the gearcase in the water. Pressure test the gearcase to determine the source of water intrusion if any water is found in the gearcase lubricant. Refer to *Pressure Testing* in this section. Failure to correct the leakage will eventually lead to extensive damage to the internal components or complete failure of the gearcase. Refer to Chapter Nine for gearcase repair procedures.

Lubricant Leakage

The presence of gearcase lubricant on the exterior or around the gearcase requires a pressure test to determine the source of the leakage. Refer to *Pressure Testing* in this section. Failure to correct the leakage will result in gear and bearing damage due to a lack of sufficient lubrication or a possible complete gearcase failure. Refer to Chapter Nine for gearcase repair procedures.

Pressure Testing

> *NOTE*
> *Gearcase pressure testers and other equipment can be purchased through tool suppliers.*

A suitable gearcase pressure tester is required to perform this test.

1. Place a suitable container below the gearcase. Position the gearcase so that the drain (2, **Figure 136**) is at the lowest point relative to the container. The unit may need to be tilted slightly. Remove the oil level plug (1, **Figure 136**) and drain plug (2, **Figure 136**) and allow the gearcase to drain completely.

2. Install the pressure tester in the upper threaded opening (1, **Figure 136**). Install the drain plug in the lower threaded opening (2, **Figure 136**).

3

3. Slowly apply air pressure to the gearcase (**Figure 137**) using the gearcase pressure tester. Push, pull and turn all shafts while observing the pressure gauge as the pressure is slowly increased. Stop increasing pressure when it reaches 100 kPa (14.2 psi).

4. Submerge the gearcase in water with the pressure applied if the unit will not hold this pressure for at least 10 seconds. Replace the seal and/or seal surface at the location that bubbles appear. Refer to Chapter Nine for repair procedures.

5. Bleed the air out of the gearcase and refill with lubricant as instructed in Chapter Four.

Metal Contamination in the Lubricant

Fine metal particles will form in the gearcase during normal usage. The gearcase lubricant may have a *metal flake* appearance when inspected during routine maintenance. The fine metal particles tend to cling to the end of the drain plug. Remove the drain plug and apply some of the material to your forefinger and thumb and rub them together. Inspect the gearcase if any of the material is large enough to feel as the finger and thumb are rubbed together. Removal of the bearing housing will allow a view of the internal components to determine if any major components have failed. Refer to Chapter Nine for removal, inspection and assembly procedures.

Gearcase Vibration or Noise

Gearcase noise does occur from normal usage. The normal noise is barely noticeable. A rough growling noise or a loud high-pitched whine is reason to suspect damaged or faulty components. On occasion, a knocking noise can emanate from the gearcase leading one to believe the power head has a failure. Inspect the gearcase lubricant for metal contamination. In most cases, the appearance of the gearcase lubricant will indicate when components have failed.

Knocking or grinding noise

When a knocking or grinding noise is coming from the gearcase, the cause is likely from damaged gears of other components in the gearcase. The damage will likely show a substantial amount of larger metal particles on the drain plug. The gears may have suffered damage as the result of underwater impact or high-speed shifting. Complete gearcase repair is required. Refer to Chapter Nine for procedures.

High-pitched whine

When a high-pitched whine is present, it normally indicates a bearing problem or, in some cases, the gears are running out of alignment. The only way to verify a problem is to disassemble and inspect the gearcase components. Refer to Chapter Nine for procedures.

Gearcase vibration

Vibration in the engine can and often does originate in the gearcase and often is due to a bent propshaft or damaged prop. A prop can appear perfect but really be out of balance. The best ways to determine this is to have the prop trued and balanced at a reputable prop repair station or simply try a different yet suitable prop for the engine. Always check for a bent propshaft when vibration is present. Follow the procedures provided in Chapter Nine. A bent propshaft is normally the result of impact with an underwater object. Other damage may be present in the gearcase. Never run the engine with severe vibration as added stress is then placed on the gears and bearings and other engine components. Excessive vibration can compromise the durability of the entire engine.

> **WARNING**
> *To avoid potential serious bodily injury or death, remove all spark plug leads and disconnect both battery cables before working around the propeller.*

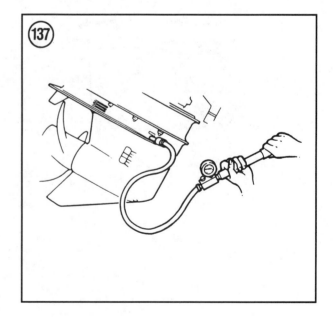

Prop Hub Slipping

The prop hub is installed within the propeller to cushion the shifting action and absorb minor impact damage. If the prop hub is spinning in its bore, the engine rpm will increase as the throttle is increased, yet the boat will not increase in speed. In most cases, the boat will not accelerate. Sometimes the operator believes that a problem exists with the gearcase. To check for prop hub slippage, make a reference mark on the propshaft that is aligned with a reference mark on the prop. Operate the boat and compare the reference marks after the engine is removed from the water. Have the prop repaired if the reference marks are not aligned after running the engine.

Shifting Difficulty

Hard shifting or difficulty engaging the gear is usually the result of improper shift cable adjustments. Refer to Chapter Five and adjust the shift cable and linkage as indicated. Gearcase removal, disassembly and inspection are required when shifting problems are not corrected with adjustments. Refer to Chapter Nine for gearcase repair procedures.

3

Table 1 STARTING SYSTEM TROUBLESHOOTING

Symptom	Cause	Corrective action
Engine will not crank	Weak or faulty battery	Fully charge and test battery
	Dirty or loose battery terminals	Clean and tighten battery terminals
	Blown fuse	Inspect fuse and wiring
	Faulty start circuit	Check and repair wiring/terminals
	Neutral switch activated	Shift into neutral
	Faulty or misadjusted switch	Check or replace neutral switch
	Faulty start switch	Check and/or replace start switch
	Faulty starter relay	Check and/or replace starter relay
	Low voltage at starter	Test wire connections/wires
	Defective starter motor	Test and inspect starter motor
	Seized or damaged gearcase	Inspect fluid in gearcase
	Seized or damaged powerhead	Inspect for damaged powerhead
Engine will not crank		
(rewind crank models)	Lockout activated	Shift into neutral
	Faulty or misadjusted lockout	Adjust or repair lockout
	Faulty rewind assembly	Clean and repair rewind assembly
	Seized powerhead	Inspect the powerhead
	Seized gearcase	Inspect for metal on drain plug
Engine cranks but will not start	Out of fuel	Check fuel supply
	Old or stale fuel	Supply with fresh fuel
	Lanyard switch activated	Switch to run position
	Faulty choke	Verify choke operation
	Faulty prime start pump	Inspect pump and hose connections
	Improper starting procedure	Verify correct procedure
	Faulty powerhead components	Test engine compression
	Weak or faulty battery	Fully charge and test battery
	Weak or lack of spark at plug	Refer to ignition troubleshooting
	Fuel system malfunction	Refer to fuel troubleshooting

Table 2 IGNITION SYSTEM TROUBLESHOOTING

Symptom	Cause	Corrective action
Engine cranks but will not start	Lanyard switch activated	Check lanyard switch position
	Shorted stop circuit	Check for shorted wire/switch
	Misadjusted ignition timing	Check and correct timing
	Loose connection	Check all external wire connections
	Faulty or wrong spark plugs	Check plug type and condition
	Improper spark plug gap	Check and correct plug gap
	Faulty spark plug lead	Check for damaged lead
	Faulty or incorrect electrical connections	Verify proper connections
	Faulty ignition charge coil	Check charge coil output/resistance
	Faulty secondary ignition coil	Check ignition coil resistance
	Faulty crank position sensor	Check crank sensor resistance
	Faulty pulser coil	Check pulser coil resistance/output
	Faulty CDI unit or microcomputer	Check for proper CDI unit operation
Rough engine operation	Faulty or wrong spark plugs	Check plug type and condition
	Improper spark plug gap	Check and correct plug gap
	Misadjusted ignition timing	Check and correct timing
	Low output from charge coil	Test charge coil resistance/output
	Faulty secondary ignition coil	Test ignition coil resistance
	Faulty pulser coil	Check pulser coil resistance/resistance
	Faulty crank position sensor	Check crank sensor resistance
	Improper synchronization	Adjust linkage and synchronization
	Misadjusted throttle position sensor	Correct throttle position sensor adjustment
	Faulty throttle position sensor	Test throttle position sensor
	Faulty secondary ignition leads	Check for damaged leads
	Faulty spark plug cap	Check for damaged cap
	Loose or dirty wire connections	Clean and inspect wire connections
	Faulty CDI unit or microcomputer	Check for proper CDI operation
Poor performance	Low oil level or overheating	Check low oil and thermoswitch
	Faulty or wrong spark plugs	Check plug condition and type
	Improper spark plug gap	Verify correct plug gap
	Misadjusted ignition timing	Check and correct timing
	Low output from charge coil	Test ignition charge coil
	Faulty secondary ignition coil	Test secondary coil resistance
	Faulty pulser coil	Test pulser coil
	Faulty crank position sensor	Test crank sensor resistance
	Faulty secondary ignition leads	Clean/inspect leads for damage
	Faulty spark plug cap	Inspect cap for damage
	Loose or dirty wire connections	Clean and inspect wires
	Faulty CDI unit or microcomputer	Check CDI unit operation

Table 3 FUEL SYSTEM TROUBLESHOOTING

Symptom	Cause	Corrective action
Engine cranks but will not start	Improper starting procedure	Verify correct procedure
	No fuel to the engine	Check fuel supply and fuel valve position
	Old or contaminated fuel	Supply engine with fresh fuel
	Loose fuel hoses	Tighten all clamps
	Air leak in fuel hoses	Check and correct hose condition
	Plugged fuel filter	Check fuel filter(s)
	Defective mechanical pump (EFI)	Remove and inspect fuel pump
	(continued)	

Table 3 FUEL SYSTEM TROUBLESHOOTING (continued)

3

Symptom	Cause	Corrective action
Engine cranks but will not start (continued)	Inoperative electric pump	Check fuel rail pressure
	Defective primer pump	Check connections and pump
	Faulty electrothermal valve	Clean an inspect the valve
	Faulty inlet valve	Clean and inspect carburetor(s)
	Plugged fuel passage	Clean and inspect carburetors
	No cold start enrichment	Faulty thermosensor
	Faulty injector driver circuit (EFI)	Check microcomputer operation
	Faulty resistor (EFI)	Check resistor
	Faulty or misadjusted throttle position sensor (EFI)	Check and adjust throttle position sensor
Rough idle	Incorrect pilot screw adjustment	Adjust pilot screw
	Idle speed too low	Adjust idle speed
	Improper ignition timing	Check and correct timing
	Faulty puddle fuel system	Check hoses and valves
	Plugged carburetor passage	Clean and inspect carburetor(s)
	Flooding carburetor	Check inlet valve operation
	Improper float level	Adjust float level
	Stuck Choke or enrichner	Check for proper operation
	Faulty prime start system	Clean and inspect
	Faulty thermosensor	Test thermosensor
	Faulty injector (EFI)	Test injector
	Misadjusted or faulty throttle position sensor	Test and adjust throttle position sensor
Bog or hesitation on acceleration	Improper pilot screw adjustment	Adjust pilot screw
	Improper linkage synchronization	Refer to Chapter Five
	Improper ignition timing	Check and correct timing
	Engine mounted too low	Check engine mounting height
	Exhaust relief holes under water	Idle with holes above water line
	Plugged puddle drain system	Clean and inspect valves/hoses
	Improper float level	Adjust float level
	Blockage in the carburetor(s)	Clean and inspect carburetor(s)
	Misadjusted or faulty throttle position sensor	Test and adjust throttle position sensor
	Binding throttle arm	Check for proper operation
	Old or contaminated fuel	Supply with fresh fuel
	Improper fuel/oil mixture (Oil injected models)	Supply with proper mixture Check oil injection pump adjustment
Poor performance	Restricted antisiphon valve	Check for plugged valve
	Choke or enrichner stuck	Check for proper operation
	Faulty fuel tank pickup	Check for loose connections
	Plugged fuel tank pickup	Clean and inspect pickup
	Defective primer bulb	Check for proper operation
	Leaking or blocked fuel line	Check all fuel hoses
	Air leaks at fuel line quick connect	Check connector for damage
	Blockage in fuel filter(s)	Check all filters
	Blockage in carburetor	Check all jets and passages
	Faulty diaphragm pump	Inspect fuel pump components.
	Wrong jets in the carburetors	Verify all jet locations
	Faulty electric fuel pump (EFI)	Check fuel pressure
	Faulty filter for electric fuel pump	Check filter in vapor tank
	Faulty fuel pressure regulator	Check fuel pressure
	Old or contaminated fuel	Supply with fresh fuel

Table 4 IGNITION CHARGE COIL RESISTANCE SPECIFICATIONS*

Model	Wire color	Ohms
2 hp	Brown-ground	316.8-387.2
3 hp	Brown-black	247.5-302.5
4 hp, 5 hp	Brown-black	248-303
6, 8 hp	Brown-black	81-99
9.9, 15 hp	Brown-blue	248-372
28 jet, 40-50 hp (except model E48)	Brown-blue	369-552
30	Brown-blue	164-296
C30	Brown-blue	401-490
C40,	Brown-ground	120.6-147.4
E48	Brown-black	81-99
60-70 hp (except model E60)	Brown-blue	136-204
E60	Brown-black	81-99
65 jet, 75-90 hp (except model E75)	Brown-red	191-288
	Blue-red	64-96
E75	Brown-red	48-72
	Red-blue	428-642

*Values at 20° C (68° F).

Table 5 PULSER COIL RESISTANCE SPECIFICATIONS*

Model	Wire color	Ohms
3 hp	Black-red/white	29.7-36.3
	Black-green/white	279-341
4, 5 hp	Black-white/red	30-36
	Black-white/green	279-341
6, 8 hp	Black-white/red	92-112
9.9, 15 hp	Black-white/red	352-528
28 jet, 35 jet, 40, 50 hp (exept model E48)	Black-white/red	168-252
	Black-white/black	168-252
	Black-white/green	168-252
30 hp	Black-white/red	276-415
	Black-white/black	276-415
	Black-white/green	276-415
C30	Black-white/red	311-381
	Black-white/black	311-381
C40	Black-white/red	12.6-15.4
E48	Black-white/red	92-112
60, 70 hp (except model E60)	White/red-white/black	240-360
E60	Black-white/red	117-143
	Black-white/ black	117-143
	Black-white/green	117-143
65 jet, 75-90 hp (except model E75)	White/red-white/black	241-362
E75	White/black-white/green	256-384
	White/red-white/yellow	256-384

*Values at 20° C (68° F).

Table 6 IGNITION COIL RESISTANCE SPECIFICATIONS*

Model	Primary coil (ohms)	Secondary coil (ohms)
2 hp	0.18-0.24	2700-3700
3 hp	0.08-0.12	2080-3120
4 MHR/MHS	0.17-0.25	2500-3700
4, 5 MHU	0.14-0.22	3200-4800

(continued)

Table 6 IGNITION COIL RESISTANCE SPECIFICATIONS* (continued)

Model	Primary coil (ohms)	Secondary coil (ohms)
6, 8 hp	0.25-0.35	6800-10,200
9.9, 15 hp	0.05-0.07	1680-2520
25, 30 hp three-cylinder	0.46-0.62	5360-7250
28 jet, C30, 35 jet, 40, 50 hp		
(except model E48)	0.18-0.24	2720-3680
C40	0.076-0.104	2970-4030
E48	0.12-0.18	4320-6480
60-90 hp		
(except model E60)	0.18-0.24	3260-4880
E60	0.18-0.26	3840-5760
*Values at 20° C (68° F).		

Table 7 PEAK VOLTAGE READINGS

Model	Cranking speed (volts)	1500 rpm (volts)	3500 rpm (volts)
Charge coil output			
20, 25 hp (two-cylinder)	125	125	–
28 jet, 35 jet, 30-50 hp	145	160	130
60-70 hp	150	160	120
65 jet, 75-90 hp			
(except model E75)	60 red-brown	170 red-brown	150 red-brown
	100 red-blue	135 red-blue	135 red-blue
E75	105 red-blue	135 red-blue	160 red-blue
	40 red-brown	145 red-brown	160 red-brown
80 jet, 115 hp	45 black/red-blue	165 black/red-blue	170 black/red-blue
	160 red-brown	165 red-brown	170 red-brown
130 hp	30 black/red-blue	160 black/red-blue	160 black/red-blue
	105 red-brown	160 red-brown	160 red-brown
150 hp-225 hp (90°)			
(except model C150)	55 black/red-blue	165 black/red-blue	165 black/red-blue
	160 red-brown	165 red-brown	165 red-brown
C150	30 black/red-blue	160 black/red-blue	170-black/redblue
	90 red-brown	165 red-brown	165 red-brown
200-250 hp (76°)	110 red-brown	150 red-brown	150 red-brown
	110 black-red/blue	150 black-red/blue	150 black red/blue
Pulser coil output			
20, 25hp two-cylinder	5.5 *	15*	–
28 jet, 35 jet, 40, 50 hp	3*	9*	15*
60-70 hp			
(except Model 65 jet)	2.5*	6.5*	10*
65 jet, 75-90 hp			
(except Model E75)	5*	14*	20*
E75	3.5*	8*	12*
80 jet, 115 hp	2.5*	7*	11*
130 hp	2.5*	8*	12*
150-200 hp (90° V)			
(except model C150)	2.0*	8.0*	14*
C150	2.0*	9.5*	16*
200-250 hp (76° V)	3.0*	16*	30*
CDI unit output			
20hp, 25 hp two-cylinder	105	110	–
28 jet, 35 jet, 40, 50 hp			
(except model E48)	125	140	110
60-70 hp			
(except model 65 jet)	105 cylinder No. 1, 3	145	105
	0 cylinder No. 2	145 cylinder No. 2	105 cylinder No. 2

(continued)

Table 7 PEAK VOLTAGE READINGS (continued)

Model	Cranking speed (volts)	1500 rpm (volts)	3,500 rpm (volts)
CDI unit output (continued)			
65 jet, 75-90 hp			
(except model E75)	130 cylinder No. 1, 3	155 cylinder No. 1, 3	130 cylinder No. 1, 3
	0 cylinder No. 2	155 cylinder No. 2	130 cylinder No. 2
E75	105	140	145
80 jet, 115 hp-130 hp			
(except C115)	125	140	145
C115	85	140	135
150 hp-225 hp (90° V)			
(except model C150)	130 cylinder No. 1, 3, 4, 6	145 cylinder No. 1, 3, 4, 6	145 cylinder No. 1, 3, 4, 6
	0 cylinder No. 2, 5	0 cylinder No. 2, 5	145 cylinder No. 2, 5
C150	65	140	135
200 hp-250 hp			
(76° V Models)	100 cylinder No.1, 3, 4, 6	150 cylinder No. 1, 3, 4, 6	130 cylinder No. 1, 3, 4, 6
	0 cylinder No. 2, 5	0 cylinder No. 2, 5	130 cylinder No. 2, 5

*These values represent the minimum peak voltage requirement.

Table 8 PRESSURE SENSOR SPECIFICATIONS

Pressure (kPa)	Volts
20	0.789-1.0
40	1.25-1.9
60	1.75-2.75
80	2.5-3.7
100	3.1-4.6

Table 9 AIR TEMP SENSOR SPECIFICATIONS

Temperature	Volts
-20° C (-4° F)	3.8-5.9
0° C (32° F)	2.75-5.7
20° C (68° F)	3.4-5.25
40° C (104° F)	2.75-4.5
60° C (140° F)	2.2-3.6
80° C (176° F)	1.5-2.5
100° C (212° F)	1.1-1.6

Table 10 CRANK POSITION SENSOR PEAK VOLTAGE SPECIFICATIONS

Model	RPM	Minimum peak voltage
60-70 hp	Cranking	5.0
	1500	20.0
	3500	16.0
75-90 hp	Cranking	5.5
	1500	25.0
	3500	20.0
150-225 hp (90° V)	Cranking	2.0
	1500	5.5
	3500	6.0
225-250 hp (76° V)	Cranking	0.5
	1500	3.0
	3500	4.0

Table 11 THERMOSWITCH RESISTANCE SPECIFICATIONS

Temperature	Ohms
5° C (41° F)	12,800
20° C (68° F)	5400-6900
100° C (212° F)	3120-3480

Table 12 THROTTLE POSITION SENSOR VOLTAGE SPECIFICATIONS

Output voltage (fully closed)	0.5-0.52 volts
Input voltage	4.75-5.25 volts

Table 13 OVERHEAT SWITCH SPECIFICATIONS

Model	Temperature
Switching ON	
20-50 hp (pink lead)	90-96° C (184-204° F)
40, 50 hp (orange lead)	38-52° C (100-126° F)
E48	77-83° C (171-181° F)
E60	87° C (189° F)
60-250 hp (except model E60)	84-90° C (183-194° F)
Switching OFF	
20-50 hp (pink lead)	76-90° C (168-194° F)
40, 50 hp (orange lead)	26-34° C (79-93° F)
E48	53-67° C (127-153° F)
60-250 hp (except model E60)	60-74° C (140-165° F)
E60	67° C (152° F)

Table 14 OXYGEN DENSITY SENSOR

Heater resistance	100 ohms maximum
Output voltage	0.3 volts minumum

Table 15 ELECTRONIC FUEL INJECTION SYSTEM

Resistor unit	0.54-0.56 ohms

Table 16 ENRICHMENT VALVE, ELECTROTHERMAL VALVE
AND CHOKE SOLENOID RESISTANCE SPECIFICATIONS*

	Ohms
Enrichment valve	
E75	3.7-4.0
80 jet-225 hp (90° V)	3.4-4.0
Electrothermal valve	
28 jet, 35 jet, 40 hp-50 hp	2.32-3.48
60 hp-90 hp (except 80 jet)	3.4-4.0
Choke solenoid	
E48,	3.6-4.4
*Values at 20° C (68° F).	

Table 17 LIGHTING/BATTERY CHARGING COIL SPECIFICATIONS*

Model	Resistance (ohms)
30	0.23-0.34
C30	0.31-0.37
C40	0.23-0.29
60-70 hp (except model 65 jet)	0.57-0.85
65 jet, 75 hp-90 hp	0.4-0.6
*Values at 20° C (68° F).	

Table 18 LIGHTING/CHARGE COIL OUTPUT

Model	Cranking speed volts	1500 rpm volts	3500 rpm volts
60 hp	8	25	25
65 jet, 70-90 hp	11	25	25
80 jet, 115 hp, 130 hp (except model C115)	7	35	85
C115	6	30	75
150 hp-225 hp (90° V) (except model C150)	5.5	35	85
C150	3	20	50
200-250 hp (76° V)	6	14	14

Table 19 HYDRAULIC TEST SPECIFICATIONS

Model	Up pressure	Down pressure
60-90 hp		
6H308*	35-45 kg/cm^2 (500-640 psi)	41-55 kg/cm^2 (583-782 psi)
6H1-15*	35-45 kg/cm^2 (500-640 psi)	22-38 kg/cm^2 (313-540 psi)
62F-02*	57-66 kg/cm^2 (299-526 psi)	21-37 kg/cm^2 (299-526 psi)
115-250 hp	100-120 kg/cm^2 (1422-1706 psi)	60-90 kg/cm^2 (853-1280 psi)
*Indicates the approved model code stamped on the serial number tag.		

Table 20 TRIM SENDER TEST RESISTANCE SPECIFICATIONS*

Model	Pink and black leads (ohms)	Orange and black leads (ohms)
40-90 hp	360-540	800-1200
115-130 hp	582-873	800-1200
150-200 (76° V) hp	582-873	800-1200
225 (model code 225G/V225)	582-873	800-1200
200 (76° V)-250 hp	494-742	800-1200
*Values at 20° C (68° F).		

Table 21 MODEL/SERIAL NUMBER/IDENTIFICATION INFORMATION

Hp	Model name	Model code	Serial No.	Characteristics
2	2MH	6A1	173931-on	Manual, tiller, premix
3	3MSH	6L5S	051884-on	Manual, tiller, premix
	3MLH	6L5L	310456-on	Long shaft model
4	4MSH	6EOS	143256-on	Manual, tiller, premix
	4MLH	6EOL	350748-on	Long shaft model
		(continued)		

Table 21 MODEL/SERIAL NUMBER/IDENTIFICATION INFORMATION (continued)

Hp	Model name	Model code	Serial No.	Characteristics
5	5MSH	6E3S	016331-on	Manual, tiller, premix
	5MLH	6E3L	311667-on	Long shaft model
6	6MSH	6H6S	030719-on	Manual, tiller, premix
	6MLH	6H6L	319248-on	Long shaft manual
8	8MSH	6G1S	056899-on	Manual, tiller, premix
	8MLH	6G1L	341213-on	Long shaft model
	9.9MSH	682CS	151247-on	Manual, tiller, premix
	9.9MLH	682CL	450357-on	Long shaft model
	–	–	850196-on	Extra long shaft model
	9.9ESH	682CS	700121-on	Electric, tiller, premix
	9.9ELH	682CL	600141-on	Long shaft model
	9.9ELR	682CL	690101-on	Remote, extra long shaft model
15	15MH	684C	405497-on	Manual, tiller, premix
	–	–	153352-on	Long shaft model
	–	–	830146-on	Extra long shaft model
	15EH	684C	300231-on	Electric, tiller, premix
	–	–	600511-on	Long shaft model
	–	–	900131-on	Extra long shaft model
20	20MH	6L3	003378-on	Manual, tiller, premix
	–	–	304074-on	Long shaft model
25	25MH2	6L2	111644-on	Manual, tiller, oil injected
	–	–	405543-on	Long shaft model
	25EH	6L2	253373-on	Electric, tiller, oil injected
	–	–	552726-on	Long shaft model
25	C25EL	695L	560182-on	Electric, long shaft, remote, premix
	C25ELH	595L	403121-on	Electric, long shaft, tiller, premix
	C25MLH	595L	332237-on	Manual, long shaft, tiller, premix
	C25MSH	595L	040683-on	Manual, short shaft, tiller, premix
25 (three-cylinder)	25MSH	6K9	200101-on	Manual, short shaft, tiller, premix, three-cylinder
	25 MLH	6K9	500101-on	Manual, long shaft, tiller, premix, three-cylinder
28 jet	40EJ	6H4	190601-on	Electric, jet drive, remote, oil injected
28 jet	40MJ	6H4	820151-on	Manual, tiller, oil injected
30	C30EL	61T	402011-on	Electric, long shaft, remote, premix
	30EL	6J8	760301-on	Electric, tiller, oil injected
	30ES	–	155465-on	Electric, remote, short, oil injected
	30ML	–	407006-on	Long shaft, manual, premix
	30MS	–	108356-on	Short shaft, manual, premix
35 jet	50EJ	6H5	090166-on	Electric, jet drive, remote, oil injected

(continued)

Table 21 MODEL/SERIAL NUMBER/IDENTIFICATION INFORMATION (continued)

Hp	Model name	Model code	Serial No.	Characteristics
40	C40MH	6H4	010262-on	Manual, tiller, premix,
	–	–	310801-on	Long shaft model
	40MH	6H4	191877-on	Manual, tiller, oil injected
	–	–	491566-on	Long shaft model
	C40ER	6H4	060285-on	Electric, remote, premix
	–	–	360173-on	Long shaft model
	40ER	6H4	110760-on	Electric, remote, oil injected
	–	–	842362-on	Long shaft model
	–	–	740146-on	Extra long shaft model
	P40TH	6H4	430386-on	Electric, tiller, trim, oil injected
	C40TR	6H4	921505-on	Electric, remote, trim, premix
	40TR	6H4	880367-on	Electric, remote, trim, oil injected
	–	–	544974-on	Long shaft model
	–	–	900196-on	Extra long shaft model
E48	E48C	670	010831-on	Manual, tiller, premix
	–	–	377728-on	Long shaft model
50	50ER	6H5	090431-on	Electric, remote, tilt, oil injected
	–	–	521079-on	Long shaft model
	C50TR	6H5	900101-on	Electric, remote, trim, premix
	50TR	6 H5	210142-on	Electric, remote, trim, oil injected
	–	–	444058-on	Long shaft model
	–	–	750216-on	Extra long shaft model
60	E60MH	6K5	001173-on	Manual, tiller, premix
	–	–	308948-on	Long shaft model
	E60EH	6K5	503128-on	Electric, tiller, premix
	P60TH	6H2	551724-on	Tiller, trim, oil injected
	C60TR	6H2	050464-on	Remote, trim, premix
	–	–	355433-on	Long shaft model
65 jet	90TJR	6H1	491185-on	Jet drive, remote, trim, oil injected
70	70TR	6H3	489951-on	Remote, trim, oil injected
	–	–	731192-on	Extra long shaft model
75	C75TR	6H0	000101-on	Remote, trim, premix
	P75TH	6H0	900266-on	Tiller, trim, oil injected
	E75MLH	692L	513499-on	Remote, trim, premix
80 jet	115TJR	6E5L	399422-on	Jet drive, remote, trim, oil injected
85	C85TLR	688L	431057-on	Remote , trim, premix
90	C90TR	6H1	352159-on	Remote, trim, premix
	90TR, B90TR	6H1	495876-on	Remote, trim, oil injected
	–	–	855646-on	Extra long shaft model
105 jet	150TJR	6G4I	350185-on	Jet drive, remote, trim, oil injected
115	C115TR	6E5	330577-on	Remote, trim, premix
	–	–	523095-on	Extra long shaft model
	S115TR	6E5	402128-on	Remote, trim, oil injected
	–	–	728224-on	Extra long shaft model
	B115TR	66Y	000101-on	Remote, trim, oil injected

(continued)

Table 21 MODEL/SERIAL NUMBER/IDENTIFICATION INFORMATION (continued)

Hp	Model name	Model code	Serial No.	Characteristics
130	S130TR	6L1	309624-on	Remote, trim, oil injected
	–	–	704831-on	Extra long shaft model
	L130TR	6L6	701785-on	Extra long shaft, counter
	–	–	–	rotation oil injected
150	C150TR	6G4	304508-on	Long shaft, oil injected
	–	–	703049-on	Extra long shaft model
150	150TR	6G4	351180-on	Long shaft, oil injected
	–	–	502676-on	Extra long shaft model
150	S150TR	6G4	351180-on	Saltwater series, oil injected
	–	–	502676-on	Extra long shaft model
	L150TR	6K0	350124-on	Counter rotation, oil injected
	–	–	500720-on	Extra long shaft model
	P150TR	6J9	501624-on	2.0 : 1 gear ratio, oil injected
	D150TR	6J9	600701-on	Twin. prop, oil injected
175	S175TR	6G5	500101-on	Saltwater series, oil injected
	–	–	500101-on	Extra long shaft model
	P175TR	62H	500101-on	Long shaft, oil injected
200	200TR	6G6	350108-on	90DEG. long shaft, oil injected
	–	–	503077-on	Extra long shaft model
	S200TR	6G6	500101-on	Saltwater series, oil injected
	–	–	500101-on	Extra long shaft model
	L200TR	6K1	501001-on	Counter rotation, oil injected
	–	–	5001019-on	90DEG. extra long shaft model
	P200TR	61H	500101-on	90DEG. long shaft, oil injected
	V200TLR	66X	NA	76° V long shaft EFI
225	V225TLR	66K	300101-on	VMAX long shaft
	225TLRU	6K7	450103-on	90° V long shaft
	S225TRW	62J	850171-on	76° V
	–	–	701202-on	Ultra long shaft model
	L225TRW	62K	700494-on	76° V counter rotation
	–	–	200121-on	Ultra long shaft model
	S225TXR	62J	100101-on	76° V EFI
	L225TXR	62K	100101-on	76° V EFI
	S225TUR	62J	200101-on	76° V X-long EFI
	L225TUR	62K	200101-on	76° V U-long EFI
250	S250TRW	61A	705034-on	76° V RH
	–	–	800596-on	Ultra long shaft model
	L250TRW	61B	702188-on	76° V LH
	–	–	800238-on	Ultra long shaft model
	S250TXR	61A	100101-on	Counter rotation X-long shaft EFI
	L250TXR	61B	100101-on	X-long shaft EFI
	S250TUR	61A	200101-on	Counter rotation U-long shaft EFI
	L250TUR	61B	200101-on	U-long EFI

Table 22 MICROCOMPUTER DIAGNOSTICS CODES

Code	Reason	Corrective action
1	Normal condition	None required
12	Ignition charge coil malfunction	Test ignition charge coil
13	Pulser coil malfunction	Test ignition pulser coil
	(continued)	

Table 22 MICROCOMPUTER DIAGNOSTICS CODES (continued)

Code	Reason	Corrective action
14	Crank position sensor malfunction	Test crank position sensor
15	Thermosensor malfunction	Test thermosensor
17	Knock sensor malfunction	Test knock sensor
18	Throttle position sensor malfunction	Adjust or/or test throttle position sensor
19	Low battery voltage	Check charging system and battery
21	Fuel enrichment valve malfunction	Test fuel enrichment valve
22	Pressure sensor malfunction	Test pressure sensor
23	Air temp sensor malfunction	Test air temp sensor
32	Shift cutout is functioning	Normal condition when shifting
33	Timing advancing during warm-up	Normal condition on cold engine
36	Knock retard is occurring	Correct causes of spark knock
41	Overspeed control is operating	Correct causes of overspeed condition
42	Speed reduction for overheat of low oil	Correct causes of overheat or low oil
43	Warning buzzer is activated	Check for overheat, low oil and overspeed
44	Lanyard switch is activated	Reset and or test lanyard switch

Table 23 MAXIMUM OPERATING SPEED

Model	Maximum recommended speed (rpm)
2 hp	4000-5000
3, 4, 5 hp	4500-5500
6 hp	4000-5000
8, 9.9, 15 hp	4500-5500
20, 25 (two-cylinder)	5000-6000
25 hp (three-cylinder)	5000-6000
30 hp	4500-5500
C30	4500-5500
C40	4500-5500
40, 50 hp	4500-5500
60 hp	4500-5500
70 hp	5000-6000
75-90 hp	4500-5500
115 hp	4500-5500
130 hp	5000-6000
150-250 hp	4500-5500

Table 24 OIL PUMP OUTPUT

Model	Correct quantity @1500 rpm
20	0.70-0.90 cc (0.027-0.035 oz.)
25 two-cylinder	0.70-0.90 cc (0.027-0.035 oz.)
25 three-cylinder	0.80-0.90 cc (0.029-0.035 oz.)
30	0.80-0.90 cc (0.029-0.035 oz.)
28 jet, 35 jet, 40, 50 hp	1.10-2.10 cc (0.037-0.071 oz.)
60, 70	1.70-2.70 cc (0.057-0.091 oz.)
65 jet, 90	2.4-3.8 cc (0.081-0.129 oz.)
80 jet, 115	2.5-3.9 cc (0.084-0.132 oz.)
130 hp	3.7-5.9 cc (0.125-0.199 oz.)
105 jet, 150-175	2.7-4.1 cc (0.091-0.139 oz.)
200, 225 (90° V)	3.7-5.9 cc (0.125-0.199 oz.)
200-250 (76° V)	5.3-7.9 cc (0.179-0.267 oz.)

Chapter Four

Lubrication, Maintenance and Tune-up

Performing regular maintenance and tune-ups is the key to getting the most out of your outboard. This chapter provides lubrication, maintenance and tune-up procedures for your Yamaha outboard.

Compared with outboards produced years ago, modern outboards deliver better performance, improved fuel economy, smoother operation and excellent reliability. The use of advanced engine control systems and excellent workmanship help provide these and other benefits for the boat owner.

Using the latest technology and the best quality control does not guarantee trouble free operation. The most effective way to ensure smooth running and trouble free performance is to perform regular maintenance and inspection. **Table 1** provides the maintenance intervals for your Yamaha outboard. Maintenance intervals are also listed in the Quick Reference Data near the front of the manual. **Table 2** and **Table 3** provide other information needed when performing tune-up and maintenance for your Yamaha outboard. **Tables 1-3** are located at the end of this chapter.

LUBRICATION

Lubrication is the most important maintenance item for any outboard. Your outboard simply will not operate without proper lubrication. Lubricant for the power head, gearcase and other areas helps prevent excessive component wear, guards against corrosion and provides smooth operation of turning or sliding surfaces (tilt tubes and swivel brackets). Power head, gearcase and jet pump lubrication procedures are provided in this section.

Power Head Lubrication

Two methods are used to lubricate the internal components of a two-stroke Yamaha outboard: premix and oil injection. Both methods introduce the lubricant into the internal engine components. The lubricant provides protection as it passes through the engine, and is eventually consumed with the fuel during the combustion process. Either system is only as reliable as the person operating the outboard. Make yourself familiar with proper fuel and oil mixing on premix models. Become familiar with the proper usage of Precision Blend oil injection and its warning systems.

During new engine break-in or after a power head repair, the engine must be provided with double the normal fuel/oil mixture. A 50:1 fuel/oil mixture should be used in the fuel tank for oil injected models in addition to the oil provided by the oil injection system. Mix the oil with the fuel at double the normal rate for premix models.

The premix method is used on 2-15 hp models. Some 20-150 hp models also use this method.

Precision Blend automatic oil injection is used on 175-250 hp models. It is also used on some 20-150 hp models.

Engine Oil Recommendation

Yamaha recommends the use of Yamalube Two-Cycle Outboard Oil. This oil meets or exceeds the TCW-3 standards set by the NMMA (National Marine Manufacturers Association). If Yamalube is not available, use a major engine manufacturer's oil that meets or exceeds the NMMA TC-W3 specification. Look for the NMMA logo on the container (**Figure 1**). If at all possible avoid mixing different brands as some oils may form a gel-like deposit in the oil reservoir on oil injected models.

> *CAUTION*
> *Never use an oil that is not specified for two-stroke water cooled engines. Do not use automotive motor oil. It will not provide adequate lubrication for the internal engine components. Operating the engine without adequate lubrication will result in severe power head damage or seizure.*

Premix Models

The oil is mixed into the fuel for the engine in the premix system. The fuel/oil mixture passes through the entire fuel system and into the engine for burning. Some of the oil tends to collect on the internal components and provide protection as it clings to the components. Residual oil will collect in certain areas of the power head where it is moved by the puddle drain system to other areas of the engine. The oil moves through the various passages and eventually passes out the exhaust.

When premix oiling is used, it must be mixed correctly for proper oil delivery. Using too little oil can result in insufficient lubrication and possible power head damage. Using too much oil will not decrease wear in the engine and may result in plug fouling, excessive smoke, lean fuel conditions and increased combustion chamber deposits.

Oil to fuel ratios vary by model and usage. For normal recreational usage, 2-15 hp and 20-40 hp premix models can operate on 100 parts fuel to 1 part oil or 100:1 (after break-in). For heavy commercial applications or heavy-duty usage, use a 50:1 fuel/oil ratio. 55-150 hp premix models use a 50:1 ratio for all conditions after break-in).

Thorough mixing of the oil and fuel is crucial for correct engine operation. If the oil is simply poured into the fuel, it will likely settle to the bottom of the tank. The engine may operate with a very rich oil mixture one-minute and a very lean oil mixture the next. The engine may run erratically until the oil thoroughly mixes with the fuel from wave action or movement of the vessel.

Proper mixing of oil into the fuel can be tricky. First determine the amount of fuel that will be needed. Then determine the amount of oil for the fuel. **Table 3** lists the amount of oil needed for an amount of fuel in both the 50:1 and 100:1 ratios.

> *NOTE*
> *Mix fuel and oil only when it will be used within a few weeks. Fuel has a relatively short shelf life. Fuel begins to lose some of its desirable characteristics in as little as 14 days. If left to sit for an extended period of time, the oil may settle to the bottom of the tank resulting in inconsistent fuel/oil delivery to the engine.*

If using a portable fuel tank, pour in the correct amount of oil for the amount of fuel needed and half of the fuel. Install the fill cap and shut the vent or valve. Carefully tip the tank onto its side and back to the upright position (**Figure 2**) several times to mix the oil. Remove the cap then add the other half of the fuel. Install the cap and repeat the mixing procedure. If the temperature is below 0° C (32°

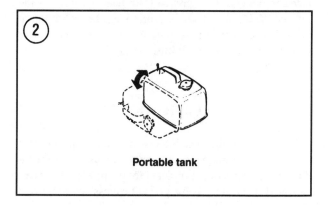

Portable tank

F) add the specified amount of oil to 1 gal. of fuel and mix as described. Add the remaining fuel and repeat the mixing process.

If using built in tanks, mix the required amount of oil for the fuel into a suitable container with 1 gal. of fuel. Carefully mix the oil into the fuel. Insert a large metal funnel

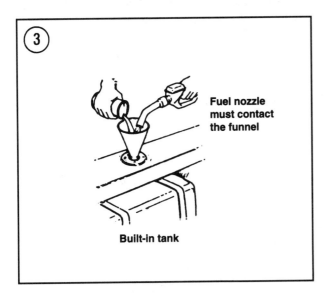

Fuel nozzle must contact the funnel

Built-in tank

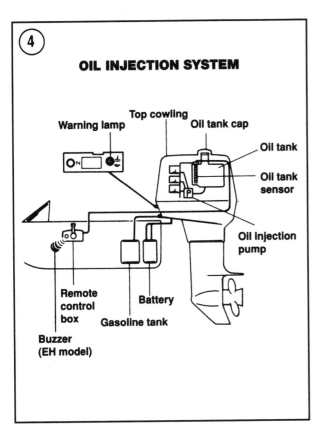

OIL INJECTION SYSTEM

Warning lamp
Top cowling
Oil tank cap
Oil tank
Oil tank sensor
Oil injection pump
Remote control box
Battery
Gasoline tank
Buzzer (EH model)

into the filler neck of the fuel tank and pour the mixture in as the fuel is added to the tank (**Figure 3**).

Oil-Injected Models

Oil injection eliminates the need to mix fuel and oil. A gear-driven variable rate oil pump delivers the correct amount of oil to the engine at all speeds. The oil is injected directly into the engine at the intake manifold (**Figure 4**). Air and fuel flowing into the engine disperses the oil throughout the power head. Oil is never introduced into the carburetor. This process significantly reduces the formation of deposits in the carburetor during extended storage. A warning system continuously monitors the oil level in the supply tank and provides adequate warning by horn and/or lamp when the supply tank needs to be filled. If the oil level drops below a critical level, the warning system will initiate power reduction to help prevent power head damage.

As trouble free as this system seems, it still requires some routine maintenance. The oil level should be checked and/or filled before operating the engine. The areas around the oil hoses and reservoir should be inspected for oil residue. Do this when performing routine inspection or anytime the engine cover is removed.

Check the oil pump control link (7, **Figure 5**)for free movement and proper adjustment. Oil pump control adjustment procedures are provided in Chapter Thirteen.

The water drain tube (1, **Figure 6**) should be inspected for the presence of water by removing the hose over a suitable container. Drain a few ounces from the reservoir. Completely drain and inspect the oil injection system when water or other contaminants are found in the oil. Oil injection disassembly Inspection and assembly procedures are provided in Chapter Thirteen.

Remove the oil level sensor (4, **Figure 6**) to gain access to the oil screen (3, **Figure 6**). Remove the screen and clean it with a soft brush and mild solvent. Dry solvents from the components before assembly. Removal and installation procedures for these and other oil injection components are provided in Chapter Thirteen.

Gearcase Lubrication

Change the gearcase lubricant after the first 10 hours of use on a new engine, new gearcase or after major gearcase repair. After the first 10 hours, change the gearcase lubricant at 50 hour intervals or once a season (whichever occurs first). Use Yamaha gearcase lubricant or a suitable outboard gearcase lubricant that meets GL5 specifications. Refer to the recommendations on the container as to proper

4

application. Check the gearcase lubricant level and condition at regular intervals. Correct problems before they lead to gearcase/component failure.

CAUTION
Never use automotive gear lubricant. These types of lubricants are not suitable for marine applications. They can lead to increased wear and corrosion of internal components.

Lubricant level and condition

Significant differences exist in gearcase appearance and size within the various models. The procedures listed are consistent with the majority of the models. Level and drain plug locations may vary from the illustration. Refer to Chapter Nine for specific information.

1. Position the engine in the upright position for at least two hours before checking the lubricant.

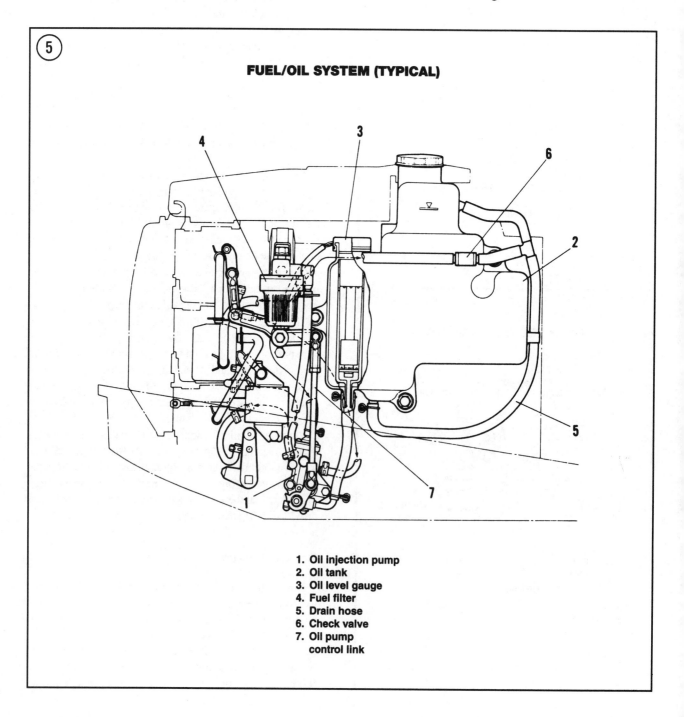

⑤

FUEL/OIL SYSTEM (TYPICAL)

1. Oil injection pump
2. Oil tank
3. Oil level gauge
4. Fuel filter
5. Drain hose
6. Check valve
7. Oil pump
   control link

2. Remove both battery cables at the battery terminals. Position a suitable container under the gearcase. Slowly remove the drain plug (**Figure 7**) and allow a small sample of fluid to drain from the gearcase. Quickly replace the drain plug and tighten securely. Pressure test to determine the source of leakage if water or a milky appearance was noted in the fluid sample.

3. Rub a small amount of the fluid sample between your finger and thumb. Disassembly and inspection of the gearcase is required if the sample feels contaminated or gritty. Refer to Chapter Nine for procedures.

4. Remove the oil level plug (**Figure 7**). The lubricant level should be even with the bottom of the threaded oil level plug opening. Add lubricant into the drain plug opening until full. If over an ounce is required to fill the unit, pressure test the unit as described in Chapter Three.

5. Allow the gearcase to sit in a shaded area for two hours and check the lubricant level again. Top off again if necessary.

6. Connect the battery cables to the proper terminals.

> *CAUTION*
> *Inspect the sealing washers on both gearcase plugs. Replace missing or damaged sealing washers to prevent water or lubricant from seeping past the threads.*

> *NOTE*
> *A small amount of very fine metal particles is usually present in the gear lubricant. These fine particles form during normal gearcase operation and their presence does not indicate a problem. Large particles, however, indicate a potential problem within the gearcase.*

Gearcase lubricant change

Significant differences exist within the various models as to gearcase appearance. Level and drain plug location may vary from the illustration. Refer to Chapter Nine for specific information.

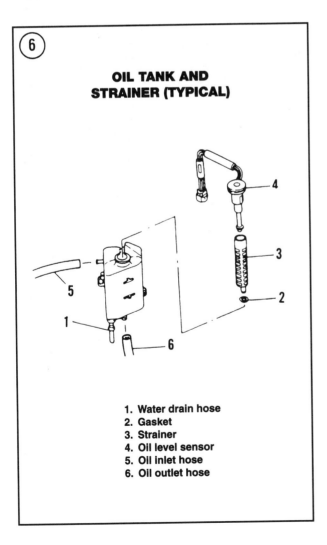

OIL TANK AND STRAINER (TYPICAL)

1. Water drain hose
2. Gasket
3. Strainer
4. Oil level sensor
5. Oil inlet hose
6. Oil outlet hose

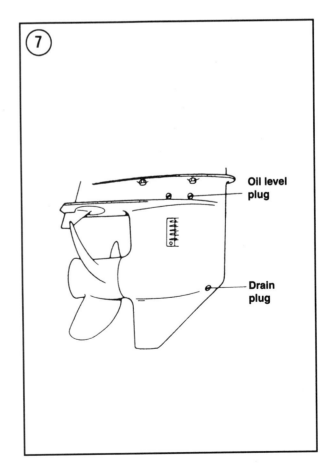

Oil level plug

Drain plug

1. Remove both battery cables at the battery terminals. Disconnect and ground the spark plug leads to prevent accidental starting.

2. Place a suitable container under the gearcase. Remove the drain plug (**Figure 7**) and oil level plug (**Figure 7**).

3. Take a small sample of the gearcase lubricant and inspect as described in *Lubricant Level and Condition*.

4. Allow the gearcase to drain completely. Tilt the engine slightly to ensure that the drain opening is at the lowest point.

5. Use a pump type dispenser and *slowly* pump Yamaha gearcase lubricant or a suitable substitute into the drain plug opening (**Figure 7**) until lubricant flows out the oil level opening. Without removing the pump from the drain opening, install the oil level plug (**Figure 7**) and tighten securely. Remove the pump from the drain opening and *quickly* install the drain plug (**Figure 7**). Tighten the drain plug securely.

6. Allow the engine to remain in the upright position for two hours in a shaded location and re-check the fluid level. Top off if necessary. Connect the spark plug leads and the battery cables to the proper terminals. Dispose of the drained gear lubricant in a suitable location.

Jet drive lubrication

The jet unit is attached to the drive shaft housing at the same location as the gearcase. Jet drive units require maintenance at frequent intervals. The drive shaft bearing must be lubricated after each operating period. Lubrication is also required after each 10 hours of usage and when preparing the engine for extended storage. Use Yamaha All-purpose Marine Grease or a grease that meets or exceeds NLGI No. 1 rating.

> *NOTE*
> *Slight discoloration of the expelled jet drive grease is normal during the break-in period. Inspection of the seals and internal components is required when the expelled grease is contaminated with metal filings, is dark gray in color or significant water is present.*

1. Locate the capped hose on the port side of the jet drive (**Figure 8**).

2. Disconnect the excess grease hose from the fitting. Connect a grease gun to the fitting on the jet drive and inject grease until grease exits the capped end of the disconnected hose.

3. Inspect the grease. Disassemble and inspect the seals and bearings if water or contaminants are noted in the expelled grease.

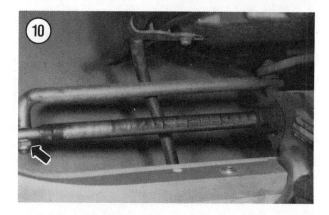

4. Wipe the expelled grease from the capped hose and connect the hose to the jet drive grease fitting (**Figure 8**).

Other lubrication points

Other lubrication points include throttle linkages, steering cables, shifting linkages, pivot shafts and tilt tubes. Maintenance is also required for the bearing carrier and propeller shaft. For frequency and description of lubrication points refer to **Table 1**.

Apply Yamaha All-purpose Marine Grease to the pivot points of the throttle linkage (**Figure 9**) to ensure smooth operation. A small amount of grease is required. Use just enough to lubricate the throttle connector.

Apply Yamaha All-purpose Marine Grease to the pivot points of the steering connection (**Figure 10**). Some steering cables are provided with a grease fitting. Regular lubrication of the steering cable will dramatically increase its life.

> *CAUTION*
> *The steering cable must be in the retracted position when grease is injected into the fitting. The cable can become hydro-locked when grease is injected with the cable extended. Refer to the cable manufacture's instructions for type and frequency of lubrication.*

Tiller control models require lubrication of the gears at the tiller handle pivot point (**Figure 11**). Pivot the handle to the up position and apply Yamaha All-purpose Marine Grease to the gears.

Grease fittings are provided under the protective cap on tilt tubes (**Figure 12**) and pivot shafts (A, **Figure 13**). Inject Yamaha All-purpose Marine Grease or its equivalent until it comes out of the joints.

Remove the bearing carrier (A, **Figure 14**) and clean all salt deposits and corrosion from the carrier and housing if the engine is frequently run in saltwater. The salt deposits can buildup at the carrier-to-housing contact area and eventually damage the housing. Install a new sealing O-ring (B, **Figure 14**) during assembly. Refer to Chapter Nine for bearing carrier removal and installation procedures.

Propeller Shaft and Propeller

Remove the propeller nut, attaching hardware and propeller. Inspect the propeller for damage and the propeller shaft for twisted splines or bent shaft. Replace the propeller shaft if bent shaft or twisted splines are noted. Refer to Chapter Nine for propeller shaft replacement. Have the propeller refinished by a reputable propeller repair shop if damage is noted. Clean all corrosion or deposits from the propeller shaft splines and the splined section of the pro-

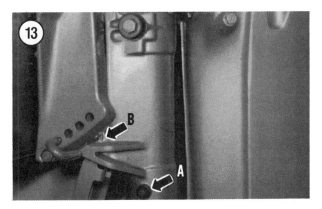

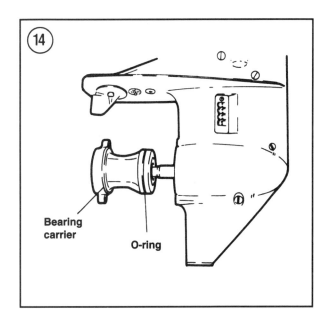

peller. Apply Yamaha All-purpose Marine Grease or its equivalent to the splines before installing the prop.

Cooling System Maintenance

Inspect the cooling system for proper operation every time the engine is run. A stream of water at the lower back area of the engine indicates that the water pump is operating. Never run the engine if it is overheating or you suspect the water pump is not operating at good efficiency. Inspect the water pump every 50 hours of operation, once a year or whenever the engine is running warmer than normal. Water pump inspection and repair procedures are provided in Chapter Nine.

Flush the cooling system at regular intervals to help prevent corrosion and deposit build-up in the cooling passages. Flush the cooling system after each operation when in salt or brackish water, polluted water or water that is laden with silt or sand. Frequent water pump inspection is required when operating the engine in these conditions. Use a standard flush/test adapter (**Figure 15**) or test tank for propeller drive models. Use a special jet flush adapter, Yamaha part No. 6EO-28193-00-94, to operate jet models on a water hose. The water pickup is located below the ventilation plate (**Figure 16**) on models with 9.9 hp or less. They will require a special adapter that can be purchased at most marine dealerships. Use full water pressure and never run the engine at high speed.

> *CAUTION*
> *Never run the engine without first providing cooling water. Use either a test tank or flush/test adapter. Remove the propeller before running the engine. Install a test propeller to run the engine in a test tank.*

> *WARNING*
> *Stay clear of the propeller shaft while running an engine on a flush/test adapter. The propeller should be removed before running the engine or performing a test to avoid rious bodily injury or death. Disconnect all spark plug leads and the battery connections before removing or installing a propeller.*

Flushing the cooling system

1. Use a test tank filled with clean water or a flushing attachment with a freshwater supply.
2. Attach a flush/test adapter to the gearcase (**Figure 15**) or jet drive when a test tank is not available.
3. Turn the water on. Make certain that the flush/test adapter is positioned over the water pickup area of the

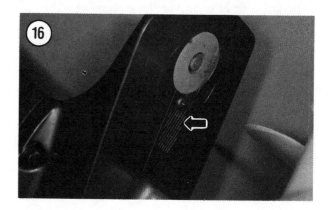

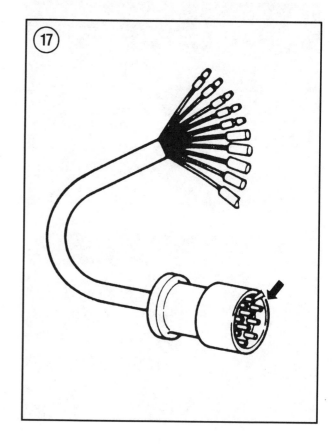

gearcase. Start the engine and run at a fast idle in neutral until the engine reaches full operating temperature.

4. Continue to run the engine until the water exiting the engine is clear and the engine has run for a minimum of 10 minutes. Monitor the engine temperature. Stop the engine if it begins to overheat.

5. Bring the engine back to idle for a few minutes and stop the engine. Remove the flush adapter or remove the engine from the test tank.

Electrical and Ignition

Many problems with a modern outboard are directly related to a lack of sufficient maintenance to the electrical systems. Components requiring maintenance include:

1. Cranking battery.
2. Wiring and electrical connections.
3. Starter motor.
4. Charging system.
5. Instruments.
6. Ignition system.

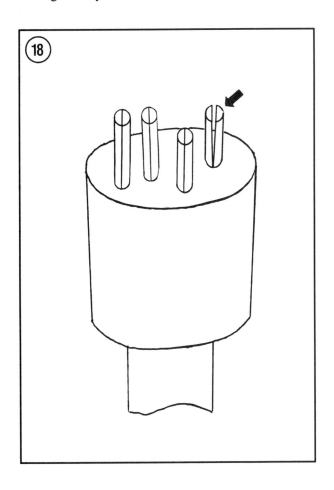

Battery Maintenance

The cranking battery requires more maintenance than any other component related to the engine. Unlike automobiles, boats may set idle for weeks or more without running. Without proper maintenance the battery will lose its charge and begin to deteriorate. Marine engines are exposed to a great deal more moisture than automobiles resulting in more corrosion forming at the battery terminals. Clean the terminals and charge the battery at no more than 30-day intervals when subjected to long-term storage. Refer to Chapter Seven for complete battery testing, maintenance and charging procedures.

Wiring and Connections

Periodically inspect the main harness connector (**Figure 17**) for corrosion or faulty pin connections. Carefully scrape corrosion from the contacts. Use Yamaha All-purpose Marine Grease on the main harness plug to seal out moisture and prevent corrosion.

> *CAUTION*
> *Use only enough grease to provide a light coating on the electrical contacts. The grease may seep into some electrical components such as relays and cause a malfunction.*

The male pins on the main engine connector tend to squeeze together and may not make good contact when connected to the female end. Use a very small screwdriver and slightly spread the pin apart to maintain a reliable connection (**Figure 18**). Disconnect and inspect the wire connectors for corrosion and loose (**Figure 19**) or bent terminals (**Figure 20**).

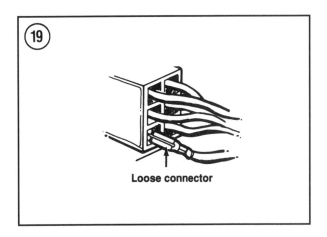

Loose connector

Starter Motor

Maintenance to the starter motor involves cleaning external electrical terminals, application of Yamaha All-purpose Marine Grease to the pinion gear (4, **Figure 21**), periodic cleaning and lubrication of internal components, and brushes (13, **Figure 21**) inspection. Refer to the procedures in Chapter Seven for starter motor removal, inspection and installation.

Preparing for Storage

The objective when preparing the engine for long-term storage is to prevent any corrosion or deterioration during the storage period. If done correctly the engine should operate properly when removed from storage. All major systems require some preparation before storing. Perform any maintenance that will come due during the storage period.

1. Check the gearcase lubricant level and condition, check and top off the fluid in the hydraulic tilt or trim system.
2. Lubricate the propeller shaft. Remove the battery and maintain it as described in Chapter Seven.
3. Check all electrical harnesses for corrosion or faulty connections and repair as required. Apply grease to the terminals as described in this chapter.
4. Lubricate all steering, throttle and control linkages.
5. Lubricate all pivot and swivel shafts.
6. Lubricate jet pumps when applicable.
7. Drain the fuel from the fuel tank and treat any residual fuel with an additive such as Sta-Bil.
8. Clean the exterior of the gearcase, drive shaft housing and swivel brackets to remove vegetation, dirt or deposit buildup.
9. Wipe down the components under the cover and apply a good corrosion preventative spray such as CR66 or its equivalent.
10. Change all fuel filters and clean the screens for the oil-injection system.
11. Flush the cooling system and treat the internal power head components with a storage sealing agent to prevent internal corrosion during the storage period.
12. Remove the silencer cover from the carburetors as described in Chapter Six.
13. Run the engine at idle speed in a test tank or on a flush/test adapter for 10 minutes or until the engine reaches operating temperature.
14. Raise the engine speed to 1500 rpm. Fill a squirt can with Yamalube two-cycle outboard oil or a storage sealing agent specified for outboard motors. Pump or spray the oil or agent into the carburetor inlets until the engine stalls out.
15. Remove the engine from the test tank or remove the flush/test adapter. Remove each spark plug and pour in

about 1 ounce of Yamalube two-cycle outboard oil into each spark plug hole. Crank the engine over a few times to distribute the oil.

16. Install the spark plugs and store the engine in the upright position.

17. Drain each carburetor float bowl orvapor separator on EFI models. Disconnect the fuel hose to the engine and slowly pump the primer bulb to move the residual fuel in the fuel hoses to the float bowl for drainage. Install the drain plugs and tighten securely. Connect the fuel hose to the engine. Place the engine in a protected area. Check all water drains to make sure they are clear.

Fitting Out

When the time comes to remove the outboard from storage, a few items need attention. Perform all required maintenance It is wise to service the water pump and replace the impeller as described in Chapter Nine. This vital component will deteriorate during extended storage. Change or correct all lubricant levels. Supply the engine with fresh fuel. Use a 50:1 fuel/oil mixture when the engine has been in storage for a year or longer or has been stored in a damp environment. Open the fuel valve or pump the primer bulb and check for a flooding carburetor. Refer to Chapter Three for instructions. Install the battery as instructed in Chapter Seven. Supply with cooling water and start the engine. Run the engine at low speeds for the first few minutes and avoid running at wide-open throttle for extended periods of time for the first few hours. Check for proper operation of the cooling electrical and oil injection systems and correct as required. Avoid continued operation when the engine is not operating properly. Refer to Chapter Three for troubleshooting and testing procedures.

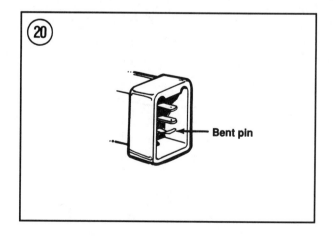

⑳

Bent pin

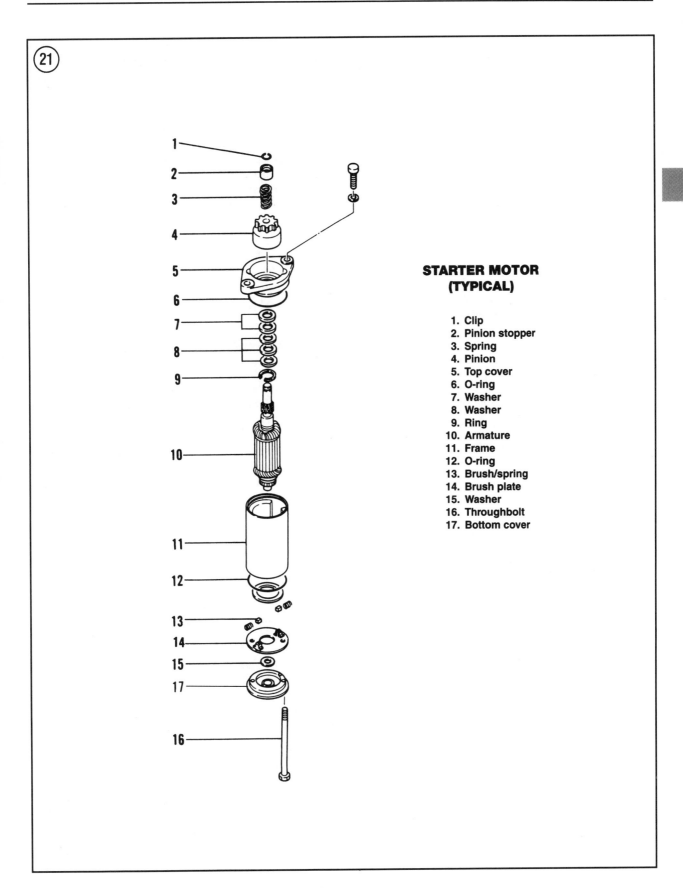

4

㉑

**STARTER MOTOR
(TYPICAL)**

1. Clip
2. Pinion stopper
3. Spring
4. Pinion
5. Top cover
6. O-ring
7. Washer
8. Washer
9. Ring
10. Armature
11. Frame
12. O-ring
13. Brush/spring
14. Brush plate
15. Washer
16. Throughbolt
17. Bottom cover

Corrosion Prevention

Corrosion prevention is an excellent way to increase the life and reliability of the engine.

Decrease corrosion in the power head cooling passages by flushing the cooling system as soon as possible after running the engine in salt, brackish or polluted water.

Clean and inspect the sacrificial anode (**Figure 22**) at the recommended intervals. Inspect and clean the anode more often if the engine is run or stored in salt, brackish or polluted water. Use a stiff brush to clean deposits and other material from the anode. Replace the anode when it has lost 40% or more of its material. Never paint or cover the anode with a protective coating. Doing so will dramatically decrease its ability to protect the underwater components. Clean the mounting area before installing a new anode to ensure a proper connection. Inspect the anode mounting area when corrosion is noted on engine components and the anode is not experiencing corrosion.

Complete Submersion

When the engine has been subjected to complete submersion, three factors need to be considered. Was the engine running when the submersion occurred? Was the engine submerged in salt, brackish or polluted water? How long has the engine been retrieved from the water?

Submerged while running

Complete disassembly and inspection of the power head is required if the engine was submerged when running. Internal damage to the power head (bent connecting rod) is likely when this occurs. Refer to Chapter Eight for power head repair procedures.

Submerged in salt, brackish or polluted water

Many components of the engine will suffer the corrosive effects of submersion in salt, brackish or polluted water. The symptoms may not occur for some time after the event. Salt crystals will form in many areas of the engine and will promote intense corrosion in that area. The wire harness and its connections are usually affected. It is difficult to remove all of the salt crystals from the harness connectors. Replace the wire harness and all connections to ensure a reliable repair. The starter motor, relays and any switch on the engine will likely fail if not thoroughly cleaned or replaced.

Retrieve and service the engine as soon as possible. Vigorously wash all debris from the engine with freshwater

upon retrieval. Complete power head disassembly and inspection is required when sand, silt or other gritty material is noted within the engine cover. Refer to Chapter Eight for power head repair procedures.

Service the engine to the point that it is running within two hours of retrieval. Clean the engine thoroughly and submerge in a barrel or tank of clean freshwater if the engine cannot be serviced within this two-hour time frame. This is especially important when the engine was submerged in salt, brackish or polluted water. This *protective submersion* will prevent exposure to air and decrease the potential for corrosion. This will not preserve the engine indefinitely. Service the engine within a few days of protective submersion.

You must completely disassemble and inspect the power head's internal components if the engine was retrieved, but not serviced in a timely manner.

Submerged engine servicing

1. Remove the engine cover and *vigorously* wash all material from the engine with freshwater. Completely disassemble and inspect the power head internal components if sand, silt or gritty material is present inside the engine cover.

2. Dry the exterior of the engine with compressed air or other means. Remove all spark plugs and ground all spark plug leads. Remove the propeller. Drain all water and residual fuel from the fuel system. Position the engine with the spark plug holes facing down.

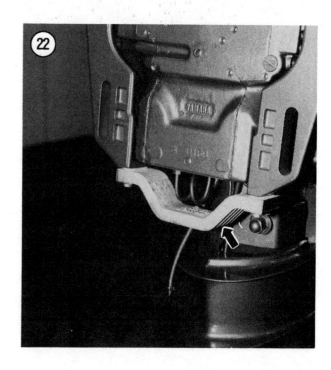

3. Slowly rotate the flywheel clockwise as viewed from the flywheel end by the recoil starter or manually on electric start models to force the water from the cylinder(s). Rotate the flywheel several times to note if the engine is turning over freely. Completely disassemble and inspect the internal components of the power head when interference or lack of smooth rotation is noted.

WARNING
Rubbing alcohol is extremely flammable. Never smoke when using rubbing alcohol. Never use rubbing alcohol around any flame or other source of ignition. Fire or explosion can occur and result in serious bodily injury or death and damage to property.

4. Position the power head with the spark plug holes facing down and pour common rubbing alcohol into the carburetor or throttle body openings. Allow the engine to set for a few minutes and rotate the flywheel one revolution.

5. Position the engine with the spark plug holes facing up and pour rubbing alcohol into the spark plug holes.

6. Slowly rotate the flywheel one full revolution. Position the engine with the spark plug holes down and drain the alcohol from the engine. Pour one teaspoon of Yamalube into each spark plug hole and into each carburetor or throttle body opening. Again rotate the flywheel one revolution.

7. Drain the entire oil injection system, clean all screens and filters and refill with the proper engine oil. Refer to Chapter Thirteen for oil injection servicing and air bleeding procedures.

8. Disconnect and air-dry all electrical connections. Remove, disassemble and inspect the electric starter motor following the procedures provided in Chapter Seven. Provide the engine with a fresh supply of fuel and oil mixed at a 50:1 ratio. Start the engine and run at low speed for at least one hour to remove any residual water. If the engine cannot be started refer to Chapter Three for troubleshooting procedures.

9. Perform all routine maintenance before putting the engine back into service. Install the propeller.

Fuel System

Topics covered in this section include fuel requirements, problems associated with old or stale fuel, fuel filter servicing, inspection of fuel hoses and clamps, and basic fuel system inspection. Refer to **Table 1** for required maintenance items and recommended intervals.

Fuel Requirements

Always use a major brand fuel from a facility that sells a large amount of fuel. As noted earlier, fuel has a relatively short shelf life and begins to lose some of its potency after as little as 14 days. This should be considered when purchasing fuel for your outboard.

Use a minimum average octane rating of 84 for 2-50 hp models. For 60-200 hp models, a minimum average octane rating should be at least 86. For 225 and 250 hp models, use a fuel with a minimum octane rating of 89. These fuels should meet the requirements for the engine when operated under normal conditions. Use a higher octane rating when the engine is used for commercial or heavy-duty service.

The use of premium brand fuel from a major supplier offers advantages. The higher octane rating provides added protection against damaging detonation. Major brands generally will have a high turnover of the fuel, helping to ensure fresh fuel for your engine. Premium fuel normally contains a high quality detergent that helps keep the internal components of the power head and fuel systems clean.

CAUTION
Never run your outboard on old or stale fuel. Severe power head damage could result from fuel that has deteriorated. Varnish-like deposits that form in the fuel system as fuel deteriorates can block fuel flow, resulting in lean fuel delivery. Severe power head damage can result from operation under a lean fuel condition. Dispose of fuel that has been stored for a considerable time without proper treatment. Fuel should not be stored for more that 60 days, even with proper treatment. Contact a local marine dealership or an automotive repair facility for information on disposal of old or stale fuel.

Fuel Additives

Use fuel additives such as Sta-Bil to help prevent the formation of gum or varnish-like deposits in the fuel system during a storage period. The use of additives to reduce the formation of combustion chamber deposits is recommended. Products such as Ring Free (produced by Yamaha) are commonly used and have shown to be effective. Using Ring Free along with Yamalube in your outboard will help reduce damaging carbon deposits in the piston rings. Use Ring Free additive on a continuous basis and mix 1 oz. (29.6 mL) to each 15 gal. (57 L) of fuel.

4

Fuel Filters

Clean, inspect or change fuel filters at the intervals listed in **Table 1**. Some of the low horsepower engines use an inline-type fuel filter (**Figure 23**) that is not serviceable. Visually inspect these filters and replace them if contaminants can be seen in them or the filter has become dark.

Most Yamaha engines use the serviceable canister-type fuel filter (**Figure 24**). Inspect and clean or replace the filter on a regular basis. This design of filter tends to collect water from the fuel system into the bottom of the canister. Inspect the fuel system components, including the fuel tanks, for contamination if water is found in the canister.

Some outboards are equipped with large spin-on type fuel filters that separate much of the water from the fuel. They are located between the primer bulb and fuel tank. Service these units when servicing other fuel filters on the engine.

1. Place a suitable container under the filter. While supporting the filter housing (5, **Figure 25**), carefully twist the canister, counterclockwise as viewed from the bottom, to remove the canister (1, **Figure 25**).

2. Remove and inspect the sealing O-ring (2, **Figure 25**) and replace if damaged. Remove the filter and upper seal (4, **Figure 25**) if so equipped.

3. Inspect the filter element (3, **Figure 25**) for deposits, debris or damage to the screen. Replace the filter element if it cannot be satisfactorily cleaned or if physical damage is evident. Inspect the other components of the fuel system for contamination if substantial deposits are present in the filter.

4. Clean the canister of any debris or deposits. Install the element into the canister and position the upper seal, if equipped, onto the top of the filter element. Install the O-ring onto the canister and carefully thread the canister onto the filter housing.

> *CAUTION*
> *Use caution when installing the canister onto the filter housing. Make certain that the canister threaded section is not cross-threaded during installation. A fuel leak may occur resulting in risk of fire or explosion. Always check the entire fuel system after servicing for fuel leaks and correct them before putting the engine into service.*

5. Tighten the canister securely by hand. Using other means to tighten the canister may crack or damage the component. Check the system for fuel leaks and correct them before putting the engine into service.

Fuel Hoses and Clamps

At the recommended intervals, check the entire fuel system for leaking hoses or connections. Check the condition of all fuel line clamps. Remove and replace plastic locking tie clamps when they appear old or have become brittle. They are relatively inexpensive and replacing them can avert trouble down the river. Carefully tug on the fuel lines to ensure a tight fit at the connection. Inspect the spring-type fuel clamps for corrosion or lack of spring tension. Replace any clamps that are in questionable condition.

Replace fuel lines that have become hard or brittle, are leaking or have a spongy feel. Use only the recommended hose available from a Yamaha dealership. Fuel hoses available at auto parts stores may not meet the demands placed upon these hoses or may not meet coast guard requirements.

Check the fuel cock (**Figure 26**) used on 2-5 hp models for proper operation and indication of leakage. Replace the fuel cock if its condition is questionable or appears to have leakage.

TUNE-UP

A tune-up is a series of tests, adjustments and inspections to put the engine back to factory specification. A properly tuned engine will perform better than one that has been neglected. A proper tune-up will often improve fuel economy and lower exhaust emissions. A properly adjusted engine is a longer lasting better performing engine.

This section will cover the required adjustments, inspections and spark plug replacement.

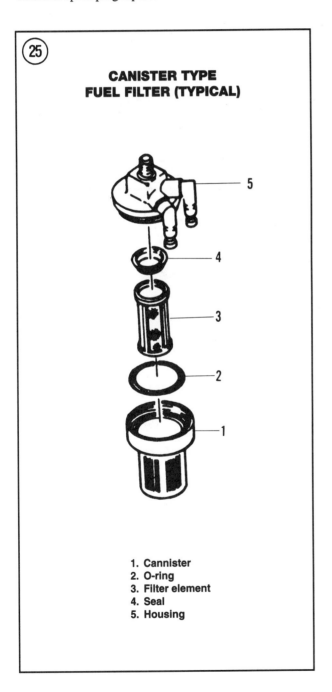

**CANISTER TYPE
FUEL FILTER (TYPICAL)**

1. Cannister
2. O-ring
3. Filter element
4. Seal
5. Housing

Compression Test

Perform a compression test (**Figure 27**) before beginning the tune-up. An engine with weak or unbalanced compression cannot be tuned properly. Refer to Chapter Three for compression testing procedures and recommendations.

Spark Plugs

No tune-up is complete without servicing the spark plug. Although spark plugs can be cleaned and gapped to restore performance, they will not last as long as new plugs. Spark plugs operate in a harsh environment. Replace spark plugs that are not in like-new condition. Both the standard type and surface gap spark plugs are used on Yamaha outboards. Remove the plugs and compare them to the plugs shown

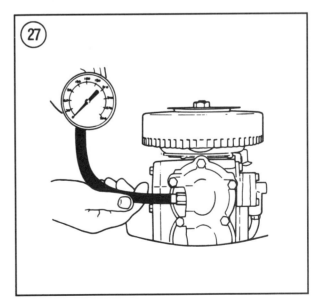

4

SPARK PLUG ANALYSIS
GAP TYPE PLUG

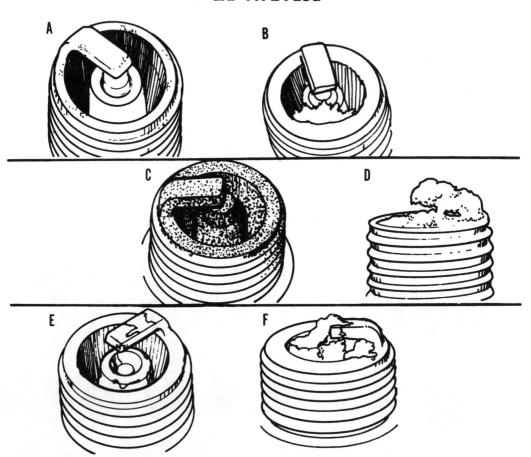

A. **Normal**—Light to tan gray color of insulator indicates correct heat range. Few deposits are present and the electrodes are not burned.

B. **Core bridging**—These defects are caused by excessive combustion chamber deposits striking and adhering to the firing end of the plug. In this case, they wedge or fuse between the electrode and core nose. They originate from the piston and cylinder head surfaces. Deposits are formed by one or more of the following:
   a. Excessive carbon in cylinder.
   b. Use of non-recommended oils.
   c. Immediate high-speed operation after prolonged trolling.
   d. Improper fuel-oil ratio.

C. **Wet fouling**—Damp or wet, black carbon coating over entire firing end of plug. Forms sludge in some engines. Caused by one or more of the following:
   a. Spark plug heat range too cold.
   b. Prolonged trolling.
   c. Low-speed carburetor adjustment too rich.

   d. Improper fuel-fuel oil ratio.
   e. Induction manifold bleed-off passage obstructed.
   f. Worn or defective breaker points.

D. **Gap bridging**—Similar to core bridging, except the combustion particles are wedged or fused between the electrodes. Causes are the same.

E. **Overheating**—Badly worn electrodes and premature gap wear are indicative of this problem, along with a gray or white "blistered" appearance on the insulator. Caused by one or more of the following:
   a. Spark plug heat range too hot.
   b. Incorrect propeller usage, causing engine to lug.
   c. Worn or defective water pump.
   d. Restricted water intake or restriction somewhere in the cooling system.

F. **Ash deposits or lead fouling**—Ash deposits are light brown to white in color and result from use of fuel or oil additives. Lead fouling produces a yellowish brown discoloration and can be avoided by using unleaded fuels.

in **Figure 28** for standard gap plugs or **Figure 29** for surface gap plugs. Spark plugs can give clear indication of problems within the engine, sometimes before the symptoms surface. Refer to the information provided in **Figure 28** and **Figure 29** for spark plug diagnosis.

Correct Spark Plug

Using the correct spark plug is vital to the performance and durability of your outboard. Refer to **Table 2** for the correct spark plug. Use the NGK part No. or, if necessary,

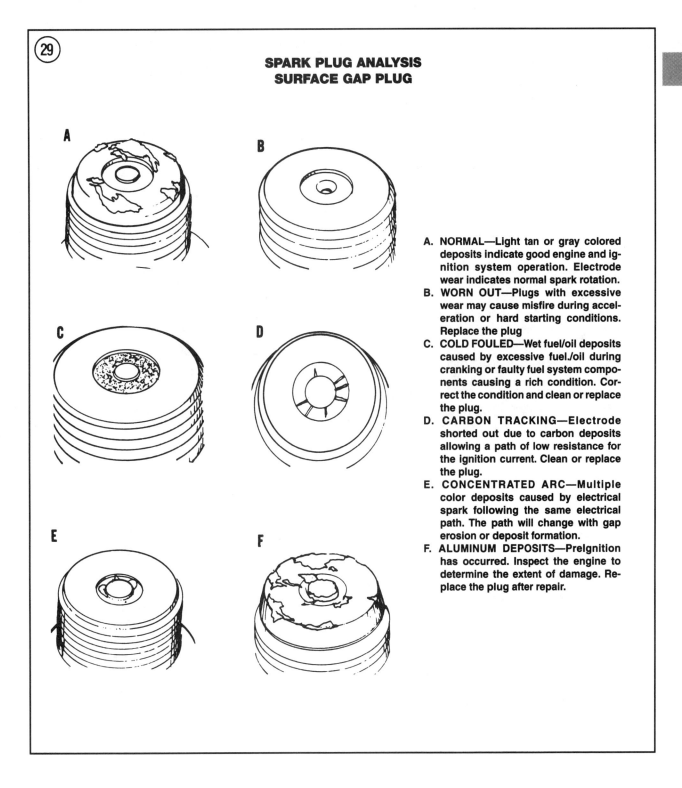

29

SPARK PLUG ANALYSIS
SURFACE GAP PLUG

4

A. **NORMAL**—Light tan or gray colored deposits indicate good engine and ignition system operation. Electrode wear indicates normal spark rotation.
B. **WORN OUT**—Plugs with excessive wear may cause misfire during acceleration or hard starting conditions. Replace the plug
C. **COLD FOULED**—Wet fuel/oil deposits caused by excessive fuel./oil during cranking or faulty fuel system components causing a rich condition. Correct the condition and clean or replace the plug.
D. **CARBON TRACKING**—Electrode shorted out due to carbon deposits allowing a path of low resistance for the ignition current. Clean or replace the plug.
E. **CONCENTRATED ARC**—Multiple color deposits caused by electrical spark following the same electrical path. The path will change with gap erosion or deposit formation.
F. **ALUMINUM DEPOSITS**—Preignition has occurred. Inspect the engine to determine the extent of damage. Replace the plug after repair.

the equivalent plug in a different brand. Alternate plugs are available for some models as listed. Use the standard plug for most applications. When used in very cold environments, the alternate plug may provide improved performance.

Spark plug removal

> **CAUTION**
> *Dirt or other foreign material surrounding the spark plug can fall into the cylinder when the spark plug is removed. Foreign material inside the cylinder can cause engine damage when the engine is started.*

1. Clean the area around the spark plug(s) using compressed air or a suitable brush.
2. Disconnect the spark plug lead(s) by twisting the boot back and forth on the spark plug while pulling outward. Pulling on the lead instead of the boot can cause internal damage to the lead.
3. Apply a penetrating oil to the threaded section and allow it to soak if the plug appears to have corrosion at the threaded connection.
3. Remove the spark plugs using correct size spark plug socket. Arrange the plugs in order of the cylinder from which they were removed.
4. Examine each spark plug and compare its condition with **Figure 28** for conventional gap plugs or **Figure 29** for surface gap plugs. Spark plug condition indicates engine condition and can warn of developing trouble.
5. Check each plug for make and heat range. All spark plugs must be identical.
6. Discard the plugs. Although they could be cleaned and reused if in good condition, they seldom last very long. New plugs are inexpensive and far more reliable.

Gapping conventional gap spark plugs

New spark plugs must be carefully gapped to ensure a reliable, consistent spark. Use a special spark plug gapping tool with wire gauges. **Figure 30** shows a common type of gapping tool.

1. Insert the appropriate size wire gauge (**Table 2**) between the electrodes (**Figure 31**). There will be a slight drag as the wire is pulled through if the gap is correct.

> **CAUTION**
> *Never attempt to close the gap by tapping the spark plug on a solid surface. This can damage the spark plug. Always use the gapping tool to open or close the gap.*

2. Carefully bend the side electrode with a gapping tool to adjust the gap. Measure the gap with the wire gauge.

Spark plug installation

1. Inspect the spark plug threads in the engine and clean with a thread chaser if necessary. Occasionally the alumi-

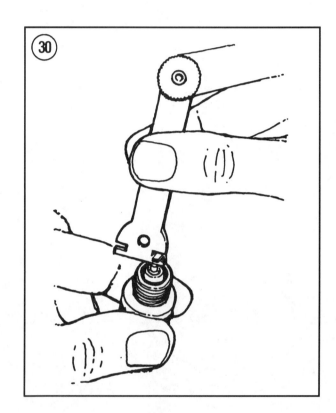

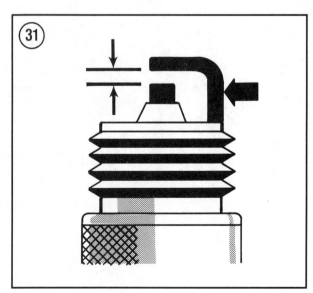

num threads from the cylinder head will come out with the spark plug. A threaded insert can be installed in the head to repair this situation. Have a repair shop perform this repair unless you are familiar with this operation and have access to the needed tools.

2. Make sure the gasket is installed on the spark plug.

3. Wipe the cylinder head seat clean before installing the new plug. Screw the plug in by hand until it seats. Very little effort is required. If force is necessary, the threads may be dirty or the plug may be cross-threaded. Unscrew the plug and try again.

4. Tighten the spark plug to 14-20 N•m (10-15 ft.-lb.). If a torque wrench is not available, seat the plugs finger-tight, then tighten an additional 1/4 turn with a wrench.

5. Inspect the spark plug lead before connecting it to its spark plug. If the insulation is damaged or deteriorated, install a new spark plug lead. Push the boot onto the plug terminal making sure it is fully seated.

Timing and Carburetor Adjustment

The final step in a tune-up is checking and adjusting the ignition timing. Timing adjustments can be made easily at low engine speeds. Checking the timing at higher speeds will generally require that the engine be test ran with a timing light installed.

Carburetor adjustments involve adjusting the idle mixture and idle speed for most models. Some models require adjustment to the pilot screw. Preliminary adjustments are provided in Chapter Six. Final adjustments are best made under actual running conditions. This will provide the smoothest and most efficient operation. *Carburetor Linkage Adjustments* must be performed when the carburetors are adjusted. Some models are equipped with a throttle position sensor that must be adjusted for proper engine operation.

Refer to Chapter Five for ignition timing and linkage adjustment procedures.

4

Table 1 MAINTENANCE SCHEDULE

After each use	Check for loose nuts, bolts, spark plugs
	Check propeller condition, fasteners and shear pin
	Check and correct oil reservoir level
	Flush the cooling system
	Grease jet drive bearings
	Check for and correct leaking fluids
	Wash the exterior of the gearcase and drive shaft housing
	Clean and touch and paint damage on the external surfaces
Before each use	Check the steering and controls for proper operation
	Fill oil reservoir
	Check for water proper cooling system water stream
Initial 10 hours or one month	Check throttle operation
	Check shift linkages for proper operation
	Check tightness of all accessible nuts and bolts.
	Check power trim or tilt operation
	Check choke lever operation
	Check fuel filter for contamination
	Check fuel hoses and connections for leaks
	Check or correct idle speed
	Check swivel bracket for damage or looseness
	Check spark plug condition
	Check oil injection pump adjustment and operation
	Check oil tank water drain for contaminants
	Check electrical wiring and connections
	Check for water leakage
	Check for exhaust leakage
	Check gearcase lubricant level and condition
	Check condition and charge level of battery
	Check carburetor adjustments and synchronization
	Check compression pressure
	Check propeller nut for tightness
	Check condition of sacrificial anode
	(continued)

Table 1 MAINTENANCE SCHEDULE (continued)

Initial 50 hours or three months	Check and adjust carburetor(s) Check and adjust carburetor(s) linkages Check fuel filter for contaminants Check spark plug condition and gap Check and correct ignition timing Check oil injection system operation Check oil tank water drain for contaminants Check wiring and connection Check for water leakage Check for exhaust leakage Inspect the water pump impeller Check all accessible nuts and bolts for tightness Check condition of sacrificial anode Check the condition of the propeller Check the propeller fasteners for tightness Check compression pressure
100 hours or six months	Adjust carburetor(s) Inspect fuel filters for contaminants Check for and correct fuel hose or fitting fuel leaks Check and adjust idle speed Check carburetor linkage and synchronization Check enrichner system operation Inspect spark plug condition and gap Check power trim or tilt operation Check manual tilt operation Inspect swivel bracket for damage or looseness Check the condition of sacrificial anode Check oil injection pump adjustment Check oil injection system for proper operation Check oil reservoir for contaminants Inspect wiring and connections Check for water leakage Check for exhaust leakage Inspect gearcase lubricant level and condition Check the condition and charge level of the battery Check propeller condition and fasteners for tightness Check compression pressure
200 hours or one year	Inspect fuel tank, hoses, filters for contamination Inspect for and correct any fuel system leakage Inspect wiring and connections Check throttle position sensor operation/adjustment Check fuel enrichner system filters and operation Check power trim or tilt system operation Check manual tilt system operation Check motor cover latch adjustment Check fuel cock for proper operation

Table 2 SPARK PLUG SPECIFICATIONS

Model	Spark plug type	Alternate plug	Spark plug gap
2MH	NGK B5HS	–	0.6-0.7 mm (0.024-0.028 in.)
3MHV	NGK B6HS-10	–	0.9-1.0 mm (0.035-0.039 in.)
4MH, 5MH	NGK B7HS	NGK BR7HS	0.6-0.7 mm (0.024-0.028 in.)
6, 8	NGKB7HS-10	NGK BR7HS-10	0.9-1.0 mm (0.035-0.039 in.)
9.9, 15, 20, 25 hp	NGKB7HS-10	–	0.9-1.0 mm (0.035-0.039 in.)
28 jet-50 hp	NGKB8HS-10	–	0.9-1.0 mm (0.035-0.039 in.)
30	NGK B7HS-10	–	1.0 mm (0.039 in.)
C30	NGK B8HS-10	–	1.0 mm (0.039 in.)
C40	NGK B7HS-10	–	1.0 mm (0.039 in.)
	(continued)		

Table 2 SPARK PLUG SPECIFICATIONS (continued)

Model	Spark plug type	Alternate plug	Spark plug gap
E48	NGK B7HS	NGK B8HS	0.6-0.7 mm (0.024-0.028 in.)
E75	NGK BR8HS-10	NGK B8HS-10	0.9-1.0 mm (0.035-0.039 in.)
E60, 60-90 hp	NGK B8HS	NGK BR8HS-10	0.9-1.0 mm (0.035-0.039 in.)
80 jet, 115 hp			
(except C115)	NGK BR8HS-10	–	0.9-1.0 mm (0.035-0.039 in.)
C115	NGK B8HS-10	–	0.9-1.0 mm (0.035-0.039 in.)
130hp	NGK BR9HS-10	–	0.9-1.0 mm (0.035-0.039 in.)
150-225 (90°)	NGK B8HS-10	–	0.9-1.0 mm (0.035-0.039 in.)
200-250 (76°)	NGK BR9HS-10	–	0.9-1.0 mm (0.035-0.039 in.)

4

Table 3 OIL AND FUEL MIXING RATES

Gallon(s) of fuel	Oil for 50:1 ratio	Oil for 100:1 ratio
3.79 L (1 gal.)	75.7 cc (2.56 oz.)	37.85 cc (1.23 oz.)
7.57 L (2 gal.)	141.41cc (5.02 oz.)	75.7 cc (2.56 oz.)
11.36 L (3 gal.)	227.12 cc (7.68 oz.)	113.56 cc (3.84 oz.)
15.04 L (4 gal.)	302.82 cc (10.24 oz.)	151.41 cc (5.02 oz.)
18.93 L (5 gal.)	378.54 cc (12.8 oz.)	189.27 cc (6.4 oz.)
22.71 L (6 gal.)	454.25 cc (15.36 oz.)	227.12 cc (7.68 oz.)
36.5 L (7 gal.)	529.96 cc (17.92 oz.)	264.98 cc (8.96 oz.)
30.28 L (8 gal.)	605.67 cc (20.48 oz.)	302.82 cc (10.24 oz.)
34.06 L (9 gal.)	681.37 cc (23.04 oz.)	340.68 cc (11.52 oz.)
37.85 L (10 gal.)	757.05 cc (25.6 oz.)	378.54 cc (12.8 oz.)
41.64 L (11 gal.)	832.79 cc (28.16 oz.)	416.4 cc (14.08 oz.)
45.42 L (12 gal.)	908.5 cc (30.72 oz.)	454.25 cc (15.36 oz.)

Chapter Five

Timing, Synchronization and Adjustments

Outboards now provide smoother running and better performance than those produced just a few years ago. To provide this high level of performance, the fuel and ignition systems must be precisely synchronized. This chapter provides the adjustment procedures to properly adjust and synchronize these systems. Perform all applicable adjustments in the order provided in this chapter. Adjustment procedures for the shifting and trim systems are provided as well. **Tables 1-6**, located at the end of the chapter, provide carburetor, timing and other adjustment specifications.

Ignition Timing

The burning of the fuel and air mixture in the combustion chamber produces the pressure to push the piston down and ultimately drive the propeller or impeller. Ideally, the pressure will peak just as the piston moves past the top dead

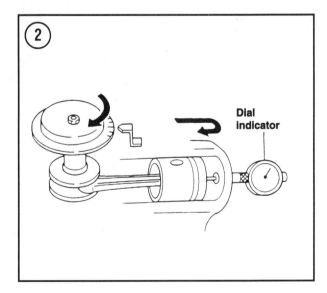

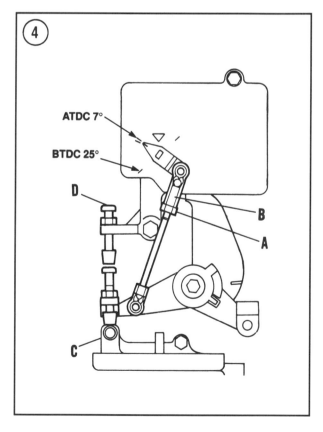

center position. This allows the expanding gasses to push the piston downward with the maximum force.

The fuel and air mixture, regardless of engine operating speed, in the combustion chamber burns at a relatively constant rate. To allow the pressure to peak at the proper time and produce maximum power, ignition must occur earlier at higher engine speeds. Proper timing and synchronization will ensure the spark occurs at precisely the right time for a given engine speed. Perform all applicable timing and synchronization adjustments anytime ignition components have been removed or replaced.

To check and adjust the timing, use a timing light (**Figure 1**) that is capable of attaching to a spark plug lead or use Yamaha part No. YU-33277-A. When checking the timing at a given engine speed, use an accurate shop tachometer that is capable of attaching to the spark plug lead or use Yamaha part No. YU-8036-A.

Timing pointer adjustments are required (on most models) after major powerhead repair or when the pointer has been disturbed. This adjustment matches the piston position (**Figure 2**) (relative to the cylinder head) and the pointer location to the timing marks on the flywheel. Perform this adjustment prior to performing other timing adjustments. With some models, the dial indicator must be used anytime the timing is adjusted. A dial indicator (**Figure 2**) and mounts are required to accurately adjust the pointer. Refer to *Timing Pointer Adjustment* in this chapter for procedures.

Throttle Position Sensor

On models so equipped, the microcomputer provides precise timing for the engine based upon engine temperature, engine speed and throttle position. Correct throttle position sensor adjustment is vital to correct microcomputer or YMIS operation. Poor performance, hard starting, and rough idle may occur if this sensor is misadjusted. On 76° V and some 90° V models the throttle position sensor is connected to one of the throttle shafts (**Figure 3**) on the carburetor or throttle body on EFI models. This allows rotation of the sensor along with the throttle shaft.

Three cylinder models with YMIS or microcomputer controlled ignition utilize a throttle position sensor mounted inside the CDI unit (**Figure 4**). Adjustable linkages allow movement of the sensor along with throttle movement. Proper adjustment of this linkage is vital to proper engine performance and durability. Perform this adjustment prior to performing carburetor adjustments.

Perform static timing adjustment (**Figure 5**) after major powerhead repair. Full retard and full advance timing adjustments are provided. The timing noted when running may be different than the timing noted during the static (not running) adjustments. Follow up by checking the full advance timing while running the engine. Always correct the timing to the running specification.

Fuel System

The carburetors, to realize a smooth idle and prompt throttle response, must be properly adjusted and synchronized to the ignition timing. Adjustments provided for the fuel system include pilot screw adjustment, idle speed adjustment, carburetor linkage adjustment, throttle pickup timing and throttle cable adjustment.

Perform all applicable adjustments when the carburetor/throttle body has been removed or any throttle linkages, cables or levers have been disturbed. Check these adjustments if poor idle and/or off idle conditions are noted. Check the throttle cable adjustment if rough and/or binding throttle operation is noted.

Pilot screw adjustment (**Figure 6**) allows the proper air to fuel ratio needed for efficient idle and off idle throttle response. Perform pilot screw adjustments after carburetor repair, replacement or when poor idle or off idle performance are noted. Refer to *Pilot Screw Adjustment* in this chapter for adjustment procedures.

Idle speed adjustment (**Figure 7**) provide the proper engine speed for shifting and the smoothest most consistent idle. To ensure accurate adjustments perform them with the engine at normal operating temperature and placed in the water at the normal water line height (**Figure 8**).

Use accurate shop tachometer that is capable of attaching to a spark plug lead or use Yamaha part No. YU-8036-A.

Perform the carburetor linkage adjustment if the carburetor or throttle linkages have been removed or disturbed. Adjustment is also required if a poor idle or off idle running condition is present. This adjustment ensures that all carburetors open at precisely the same time on multiple carburetor engines (**Figure 9**). Refer to *Carburetor Linkage Adjustment* in this chapter for adjustment procedures.

Throttle cable adjustment is required if the carburetor, throttle cables or other control system components have been removed. Perform these adjustments when inconsistent throttle control operation is noted. Refer to *Throttle Cable Adjustments* in this chapter for adjustment procedures. Procedures are included for both tiller and remote control models.

Pickup timing adjustment ensures the correct timing advancement when the throttle plate in the carburetor just begins to open. Rough off idle operation and/or a bog or

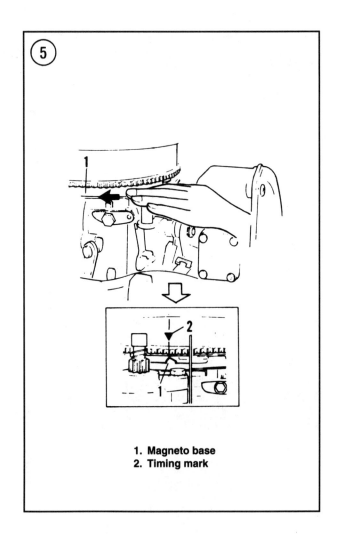

1. Magneto base
2. Timing mark

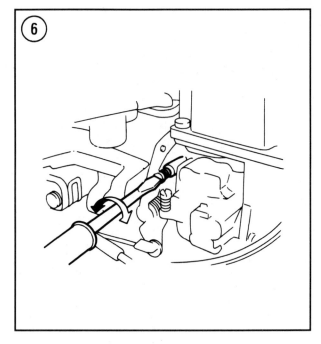

hesitation on acceleration is often noted when the pickup timing is out of adjustment. Perform this adjustment after the maximum timing and carburetor synchronization adjustments.

Trim Sender

Trim sender adjustment is required to ensure proper gauge readings on models equipped with a dash mounted trim position gauge. Perform this adjustment if the trim position sensor or gauge is removed or if improper gauge readings are noted.

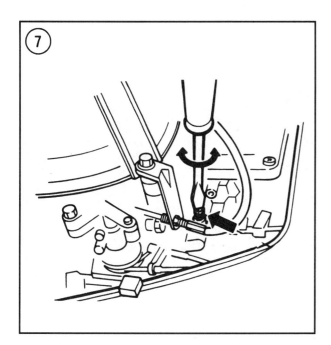

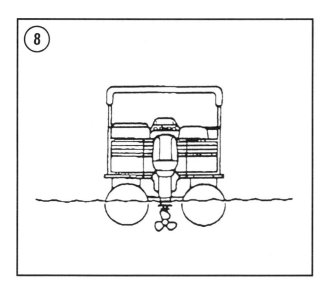

Shift Linkage

Shift linkage adjustment is required to ensure that the shifting of the gearcase is synchronized to the control system. Perform this adjustment any time the gearcase shifting linkage lever or other control component is removed or disturbed. Also perform the adjustment when improper or inconsistent shifting is noted. Procedures are provided for both tiller and remote control models. Refer to *Shift Adjustment* in this chapter for procedures.

5

TIMING POINTER ADJUSTMENT

WARNING
Batteries may contain explosive gases. Use extreme caution when removing or installing the battery cables. Refer to Chapter Four for instruction on the proper removal and installation of the battery terminals.

NOTE
All reference to the flywheel rotation is the rotation as viewed from the top of the flywheel.

A dial indicator Yamaha part No. YU-3097 and mount Yamaha part No. YU-1256 are required to accurately set the timing pointer.

2-5 hp Models

The timing is electronically controlled and timing pointer adjustment is not required.

6-8 hp and C40 Models

1. Disconnect both battery cables from the battery on electric start models. Remove the spark plugs from both cylinders. Shift the engine into neutral gear.
2. Attach the dial indicator mount to one of the head bolts. Install the dial indicator into the mount with the indicator stem inserted into the No. 1 spark plug hole and contacting the top of the piston (**Figure 10**).
3. Slowly rotate the flywheel in the clockwise direction while observing the dial indicator. Stop the flywheel when the piston reaches the top of its stroke (TDC). This is the point of rotation when the needle on the dial indicator just reverses its direction as the flywheel is rotated. Maintain this flywheel position while adjusting the pointer.
4. Refer to **Figure 11** for 6 and 8 hp models. Refer to **Figure 12** for 20 and 25 hp two-cylinder models. Refer to **Figure 13** for 25 hp three-cylinder, C30 and 30 hp three-cylinder models. Refer to **Figure 14** for C40 two-cylinder models. Loosen the fasteners and position the timing pointer to align with the TDC mark on the flywheel. Tighten the pointer fasteners securely after adjustment.
5. Remove the dial indicator and mount. Install the spark plugs. Connect the battery cables to the battery.

9.9 and 15 hp Models

A timing pointer is not used. Timing marks are verified during the static timing adjustment procedures.

28 Jet, 35 Jet, 40 and 50 hp Models

A timing pointer is not used. Timing marks are verified during the static timing adjustment.

E48 and E75 and 60-90 hp Models
(Except E60 Models)

1. Disconnect both battery cables from the battery. Shift the engine into neutral gear. Remove all spark plugs from the engine.

2. Thread the dial indicator and adapter into the No. 1 spark plug hole or use the mount to position the dial indicator directly over the No. 1 spark plug hole. The indicator stem must contact the top of the piston.

3. Slowly rotate the flywheel in the clockwise direction while observing the dial indicator. Stop the flywheel when the piston just reaches the top of its stroke or TDC. This is the point where the needle on the dial indicator just reverses its direction as the flywheel is rotated. Maintain this flywheel position while adjusting the pointer.

4. Locate the timing pointer. Loosen the timing pointer fasteners, then align the pointer to the TDC (**Figure 15**) mark on the flywheel. Tighten the pointer fasteners securely.

5. Remove the dial indicator and mount, then install the spark plugs. Connect the battery cables to the battery. Perform the other timing adjustments as indicated.

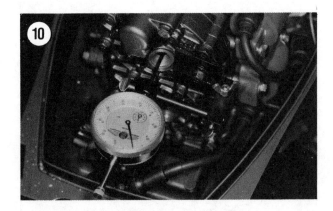

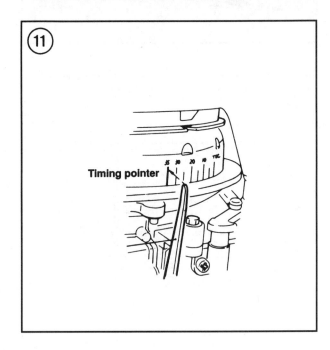

Timing pointer

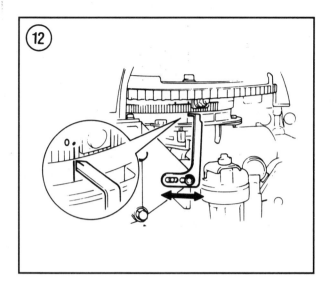

E60 models

Timing pointer adjustment is performed during the static timing adjustments.

115-225 hp 90° models

Timing pointer adjustment is performed during the static timing adjustments.

200-250 hp 76° V models

The timing is controlled by the microcomputer or YMIS and adjustment is not required.

THROTTLE POSITION SENSOR ADJUSTMENT

NOTE
Inaccurate readings may occur if the unused lead of the test harness makes contact with any portion of the engine. Isolate or tape over the unused lead to prevent accidental contact.

A digital multimeter and test harness Yamaha part No. YB-6443 are required to adjust the throttle position sensor.

200-250 hp V6 Models
(Equipped with a Throttle Position Sensor)

1. Refer to *Idle Speed Adjustment* in this chapter to locate the idle speed adjustment screw. Loosen the screw until the

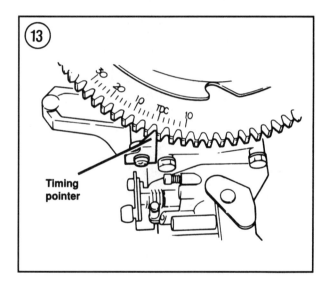

Timing
pointer

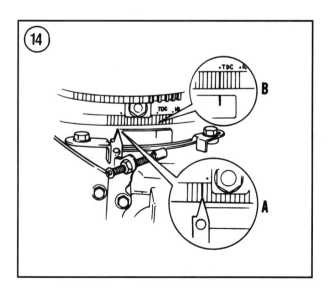

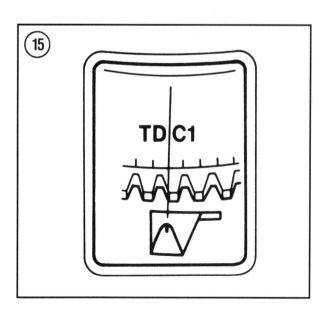

throttle plate next to the screw is completely closed (**Figure 16**).

2. Disconnect the three pin connector (**Figure 17**) from the throttle position sensor harness. Connect the test harness to each disconnected end of the throttle position sensor harness.

3. Connect the positive (**Figure 17**) test lead to the pink test harness lead. Connect the negative meter test lead to the orange test harness lead. Select the 1 or 2 volt scale on the meter.

4. Switch the key switch to the ON position. Do not run the engine. Turn the meter on. The correct meter reading is 0.49-0.51 volts at closed throttle. Go to Step 6 if correct readings are indicated.

5. To adjust the sensor, *loosen* the screw that retains the throttle position sensor. Slowly rotate the sensor as indicated in (**Figure 18**) until the correct reading is attained. Hold the sensor in position and securely tighten the retaining screws. Check the meter to ensure correct voltage readings. Readjust if required.

6. Turn the meter and key switch to the OFF position. Disconnect the test harness leads and connect the three-pin harness to the throttle position sensor harness.

STATIC TIMING ADJUSTMENT

NOTE
Flywheel rotation refers to the rotation as viewed from the top.

2-5 hp Models

The timing is electronically controlled and static timing adjustment is not required.

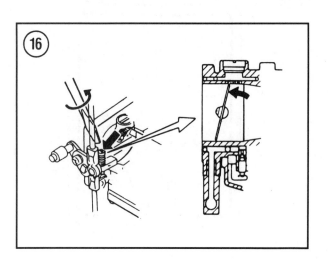

6 and 8 hp Models

1. Disconnect both battery cables from the battery on electric start models. Remove both spark plugs. Shift the engine into Neutral.

2. Use a screwdriver to carefully pry the ball joint loose, then disconnect the magneto linkage (**Figure 19**) from the throttle lever.

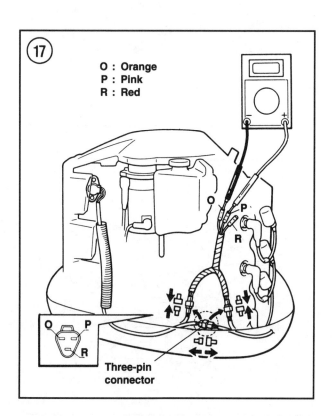

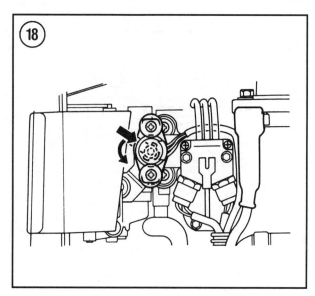

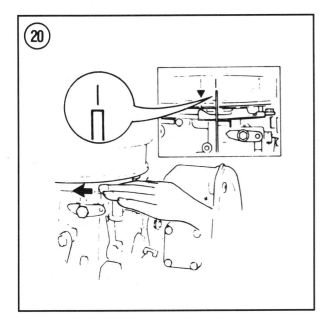

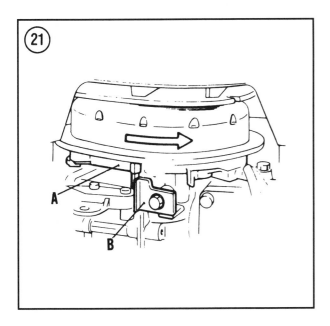

3. Observe the timing pointer as you slowly rotate the flywheel in the clockwise direction until the pointer is perfectly aligned with the 35° BTDC mark on the flywheel (**Figure 20**).

4. Move the magneto base (A, **Figure 21**) until the mark on the magneto base is aligned with the mark on the flywheel. Check for contact of the magneto base to the stopper plate (B, **Figure 21**) as the marks align. Go to Step 7 if adjustment checks correctly.

5. Perform the *Timing Pointer Adjustment* following the procedures listed in this chapter if the marks are not aligned as the magneto contacts the stopper plate. Perform Step 6.

6. Rotate the flywheel until the pointer is aligned with the 35° BTDC mark. Loosen the fastener for the stopper plate (B, Figure 21). Move the magneto (A, **Figure 21**) until the mark on the magneto base is aligned with the mark on the flywheel. Move the stopper plate (B, **Figure 21**) until it just touches the magneto base. Tighten the fasteners securely.

7. Attach the magneto linkage (**Figure 19**) to the throttle lever. Install both spark plugs. Connect both battery cables to the battery. Perform throttle linkage adjustments.

9.9 and 15 hp Models

1. Remove both spark plugs from the engine. Disconnect both battery cables from the battery on electric start models. Shift the engine into neutral.

2. Observe the mark on the rewind starter cover (A, **Figure 22**) and the timing marks on the flywheel (B, **Figure**

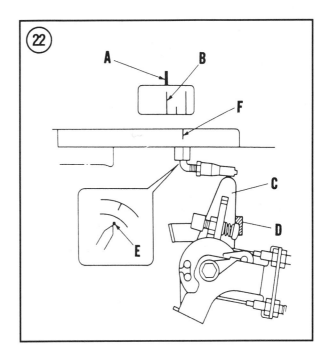

22) as you rotate the flywheel in the clockwise direction. Stop the flywheel when the 30° BTDC mark is aligned with the mark on the rewind starter cover (A, **Figure 21**).

3. Move the magneto advance lever (C, **Figure 22**) until it contacts the stopper (D, **Figure 22**). Check the alignment of the mark on the magneto base (E, **Figure 22**) and the mark on the flywheel (F, **Figure 22**). Go to Step 9 if the markings align properly. Perform Steps 4-8 if the marks are not aligned.

4. Loosen the jam nut (**Figure 23**), then disconnect the magneto linkage from the magneto lever (C, **Figure 22**). Attach the dial indicator mount to one of the head bolts or thread the dial indicator into the spark plug hole. Position the dial indicator stem to contact the top of the piston (**Figure 24**).

5. Observe the dial indicator while you rotate the flywheel in the clockwise direction. Stop the flywheel when the piston reaches the top of its stroke or TDC. This is the point where the needle on the dial indicator just reverses its direction as the flywheel is rotated.

6. Rotate the dial on the dial indicator until the needle is aligned with the 0 or TDC mark on the dial. Observe the dial indicator as you slowly rotate the flywheel in the counterclockwise direction. Stop the flywheel when the dial indicates the piston has moved down 4.22 mm (0.166 in.) BTDC. Maintain the flywheel in this position.

7. Position the magneto lever (C, **Figure 22**) against the stopper (D, **Figure 22**). Position the marking on the magneto base (E, **Figure 22**) with the marking on the flywheel (F, **Figure 22**).

8. Adjust the length of the magneto linkage until it can be attached to the magneto lever with all marks aligned. Tighten the jam nut. Remove the dial indicator from the cylinder head.

9. Rotate the flywheel until the marking on the rewind cover (A, **Figure 25**) is aligned with the 5° ATDC marking on the flywheel (B, **Figure 25**).

10. Move the magneto lever until the full retard screw cap (C, **Figure 25**) just touches the stopper (D, **Figure 25**). Check the alignment of the mark on the magneto base (E, **Figure 25**) with the mark on the flywheel (F, **Figure 25**). Go to Step 14 if the marks are properly aligned. Perform Steps 11-13 If the marks are not aligned.

11. Attach a dial indicator and position the flywheel at the TDC position as indicated in Steps 4 and 5.

12. Observe the dial indicator needle as you slowly rotate the flywheel in the RH direction. Stop the flywheel when the dial indicator needle indicates the piston has moved down 0.12 mm (0.005 in.) ATDC. Maintain the flywheel in this position.

13. Position the magneto lever until the full retard screw cap (C, **Figure 25**) just contacts the stopper (D, **Figure 25**). Hold the stopper screw cap in contact with the stopper.

Loosen the stopper screw jam nut then adjust the screw until the mark on the magneto base (E, **Figure 25**) is aligned with the mark on the flywheel (F, **Figure 25**). Tighten the jam nut securely.

14. Attach the magneto lever to the linkage. Install both spark plugs and leads. Connect both battery cables to the battery. Perform throttle linkage adjustments following the procedures listed in this chapter.

20 and 25 hp Models

1. Remove both spark plugs from the engine. Disconnect both battery cables from the battery on electric start models. Shift the engine into neutral.

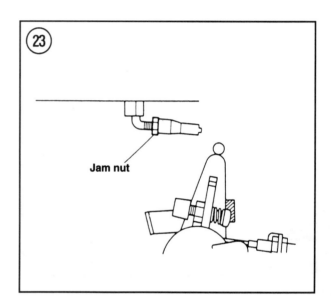

Jam nut

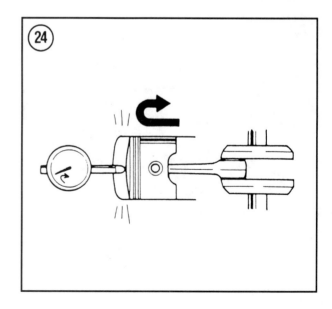

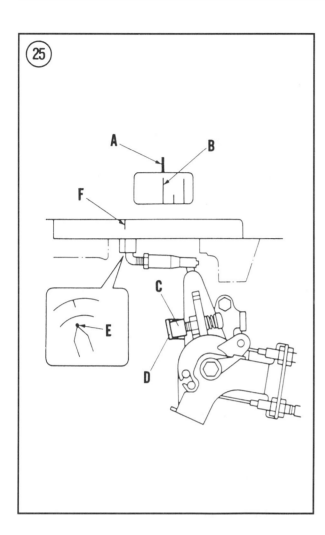

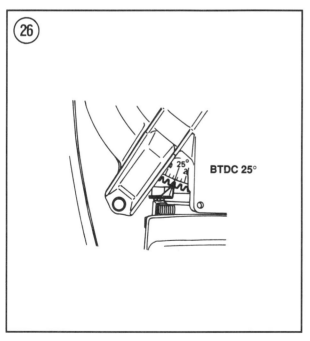

2. Observe the timing pointer and the timing marks on the flywheel as you rotate the flywheel in the clockwise direction. Stop the flywheel when the timing pointer is aligned with the 25°BTDC mark on the flywheel (**Figure 26**).

3. Move the magneto lever (A, **Figure 27**) until it just contacts the full advance stopper (B, **Figure 27**). Check the alignment of the mark on the magneto base with the mark on the flywheel (**Figure 27**). Go to Step 6 if the marks align properly. Perform Steps 3-5 if the marks are not aligned.

4. Loosen the jam nut on the magneto linkage (**Figure 27**) and carefully pry the linkage ball joint from the magneto lever (A, **Figure 27**). Attach the dial indicator mount to a head bolt or thread the dial indicator into the spark plug hole. The stem of the dial indicator must contact the top of the No. 1 piston.

5. Observe the needle on the dial indicator as you rotate the flywheel in the clockwise direction. Stop the flywheel when the piston reaches the top of its stroke (**Figure 24**). This is the point where the needle on the dial indicator just reverses its direction. Observe the dial indicator as you slowly rotate the flywheel in the counterclockwise direction. Stop the flywheel when the needle indicates the piston has moved down 3.34 mm, or 0.13 in. BTDC. Maintain the flywheel in this position.

6. Move the magneto lever until it contacts the full advance stopper (B, **Figure 27**). Make sure the marks on the flywheel and magneto base are aligned as well. Adjust the length of the magneto linkage so the linkage ball joint can be installed onto the magneto lever. Install the linkage to the lever and tighten the jam nut. Remove the dial indicator from the cylinder head.

7. Observe the timing pointer and flywheel markings as you slowly rotate the flywheel in the clockwise direction.

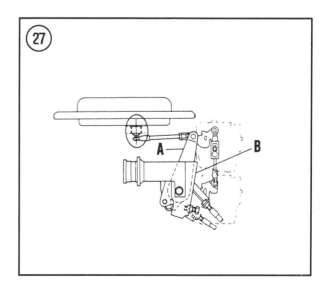

Stop the flywheel when the pointer is aligned with the 7° ATDC marking on the flywheel (**Figure 28**).

8. Move the magneto lever (A, **Figure 29**) until it just contacts the full retard stopper screw cap. Maintain the lever in constant contact with the stopper screw cap. Loosen the jam nut, then adjust the full retard stopper screw (B, **Figure 29**) until the mark on the magneto base aligns with the mark on the flywheel (C, **Figure 29**). Tighten the jam nut securely.

9. Install the spark plugs. Connect the battery cables to the battery.

C30 Two-Cylinder Models

1. Disconnect both battery cables from the battery on electric start models. Remove all spark plugs. Shift the engine into neutral.

2. Refer to *Timing Pointer Adjustment* to adjust the pointer as described.

3. Observe the timing pointer and the markings on the flywheel as you rotate the flywheel in the clockwise direction. Stop the flywheel when the pointer aligns with the 25° BTDC mark (**Figure 30**). Maintain the flywheel in this position.

4. Move the magneto base until its timing mark aligns with the mark on the flywheel (**Figure 31**). Check the magneto base stopper (A, **Figure 32**) for contact with the full advance stopper (B, **Figure 32**). Loosen the fasteners (**Figure 32**) and adjust the stopper until it just contacts the magneto stopper (with the timing marks aligned). Securely tighten the stopper plate fasteners.

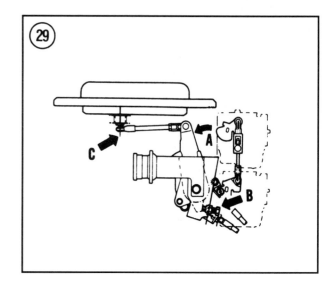

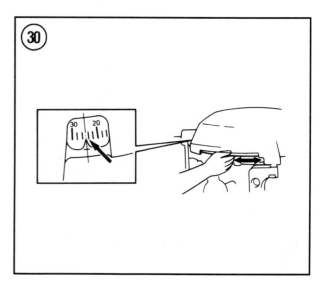

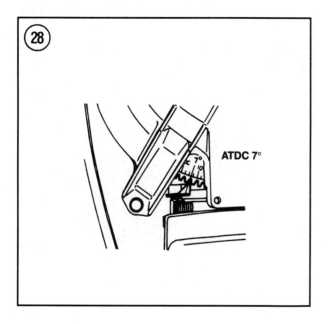

ATDC 7°

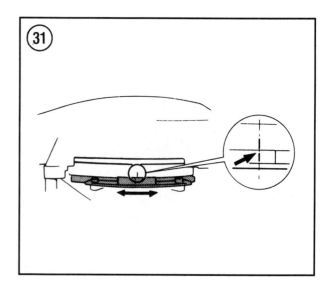

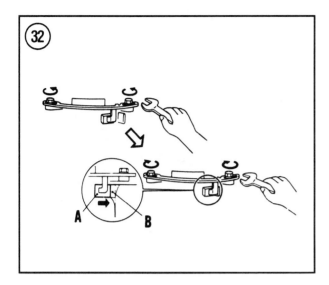

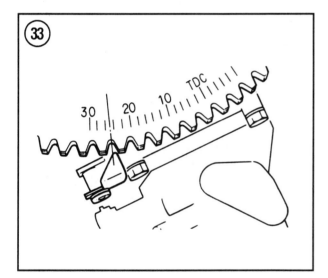

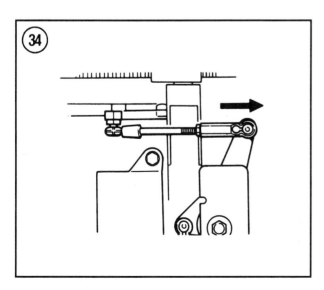

5. Install the spark plugs. Connect the battery cables to the battery.

30 hp Three-Cylinder Models

1. Disconnect both battery cables from the battery on electric start models. Remove all spark plugs. Shift the engine into neutral.

2. Refer to *Timing Pointer Adjustment* in this chapter and adjust the pointer as described.

3. Observe the timing pointer and flywheel markings as you rotate the flywheel in the clockwise direction. Stop the flywheel when the pointer aligns with the 25° BTDC marking (**Figure 33**) on the flywheel. Maintain the flywheel in this position.

4. Move the magneto lever to the right (**Figure 34**) until it contacts the full advance stopper. Observe the timing pointer and slowly rotate the flywheel in the clockwise direction. Stop the flywheel when the timing pointer aligns with the 5° ATDC mark on the flywheel (**Figure 35**).

5. Check the alignment of the marks on the magneto base and the flywheel (**Figure 36**). Go to Step 8 if the marks are

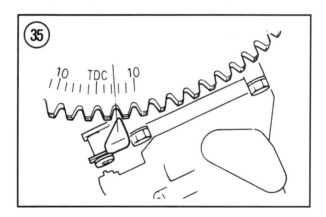

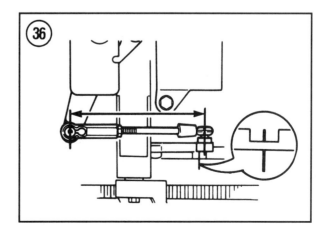

5

properly aligned. Perform Step 6 and Step 7 if they are not aligned.

6. Carefully pry the ball joint connector from the magneto lever. Loosen the jam nut on the linkage. Maintain the magneto in contact against the stop.

7. Adjust the length of the magneto linkage until it can be installed onto the magneto lever with the marks on the magneto base and flywheel perfectly aligned (**Figure 36**). Tighten the jam nut and carefully snap the magneto linkage onto the ball joint connector. Check the marks for proper alignment.

8. Install the spark plugs. Connect the battery cables to the battery.

C40 Two-Cylinder Models

1. Remove the spark plugs. Disconnect both battery cables from the battery on electric start models. Shift the engine into neutral. Disconnect the magneto linkage from the ball joint connector (**Figure 37**).

2. Refer to *Timing Pointer Adjustment* in this chapter and adjust the timing pointer as described.

3. Observe the timing pointer and markings on the flywheel as you rotate the flywheel in the counterclockwise direction. Stop the flywheel when the pointer aligns with the 22° BTDC marking on the flywheel (**Figure 38**). Maintain the flywheel in this position during the adjustment.

4. Align the mark on the magneto base with the TDC mark on the flywheel (**Figure 39**). Loosen the fasteners (**Figure 39**) for the full advance stopper on the left side of the bracket. Position the full advance stop against the full advance side of the magneto base stopper, then securely tighten the fasteners.

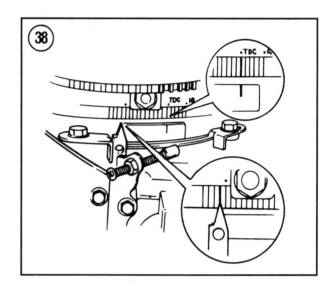

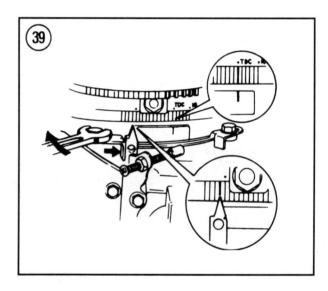

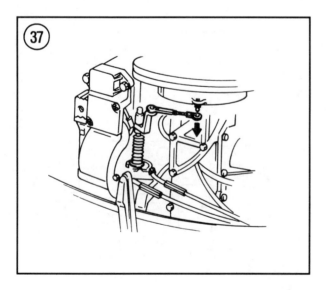

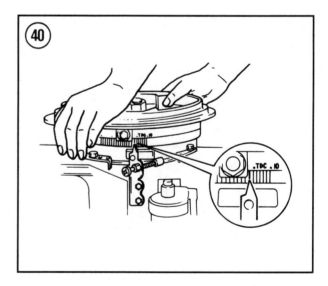

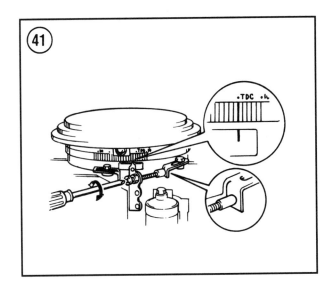

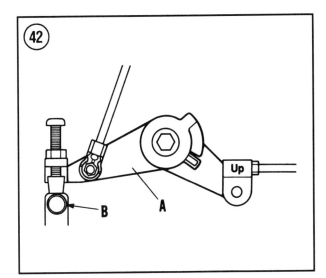

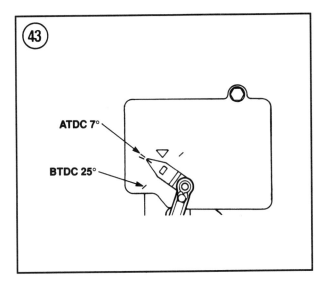

5. Observe the timing pointer and marks on the flywheel as you slowly rotate the flywheel in the clockwise direction. Stop the flywheel when the timing pointer aligns with the 2° BTDC mark on the flywheel. Maintain the flywheel in this position during the adjustment.

6. Align the mark on the magneto base with the TDC mark on the flywheel (**Figure 40**). Loosen the jam nut, then adjust the stopper screw (**Figure 41**) until the magneto base just touches the stopper. Securely tighten the jam nut.

7. Carefully snap the ball joint connector onto the magneto control lever. Install the spark plugs. Connect the battery cables to the battery. Refer to *Timing Check and Adjustment* in this chapter to check the timing under running conditions.

5

28 Jet, 35 Jet, 40 hp Three-Cylinder and 50 hp Models

1. Disconnect both battery cables from the battery. Shift the engine into neutral.

2. Move the magneto lever (A, **Figure 42**) until the adjusting screw cap just contacts the full retard stopper (B, **Figure 42**).

3. Locate the timing indicator on the CDI unit (**Figure 43**). Check the alignment of the indicator to the 7° ATDC mark as indicated. Go to Step 7 if the marks align properly. Perform Steps 4-6 if the marks are not aligned.

4. Loosen the jam nut on the full retard adjusting screw (**Figure 44**). Hold the magneto lever to maintain contact of the adjusting screw cap (B, **Figure 44**) with the stopper.

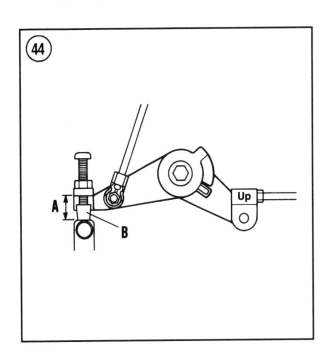

Adjust the stopper screw length (A, **Figure 44**) to 20.0 mm (0.79 in.). Securely tighten the jam nut.

5. Loosen the jam nut (A, **Figure 45**) on the indicator linkage. Carefully pry the linkage loose from the indicator lever (B, **Figure 45**).

6. Make sure the stopper screw cap is contacting the stopper (C, **Figure 45**) during the adjustment. Adjust the length of the indicator linkage until the mark on the indicator is properly aligned with the 7° ATDC mark (**Figure 45**) when the linkage is installed. Carefully snap the linkage onto the indicator.

7. Rotate the magneto lever until it just contacts the full advance screw (D, **Figure 45**) cap. Loosen the jam nut on the full advance screw (D, **Figure 45**).

8. Make sure the magneto lever is contacting the full advance stopper screw cap during the adjustment. Adjust the screw until the mark on the indicator aligns with the 25° BTDC mark on the CDI unit (**Figure 45**). Securely tighten the jam nut. Check for proper timing mark alignment. Connect both battery cables to the battery.

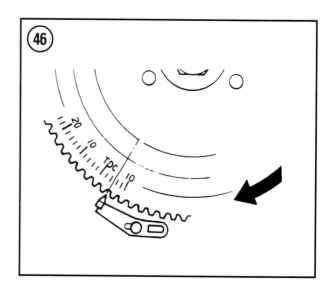

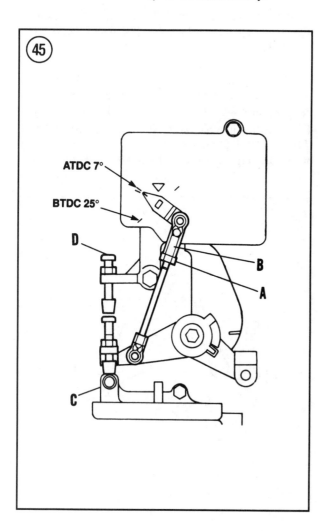

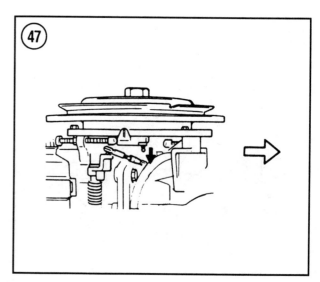

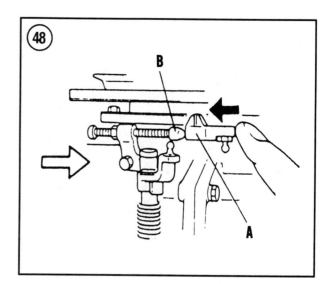

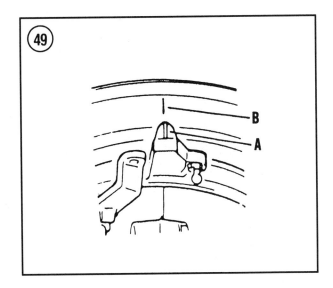

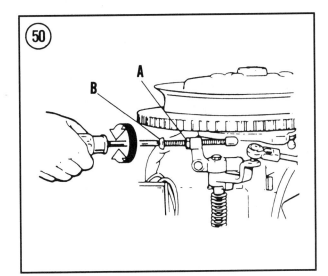

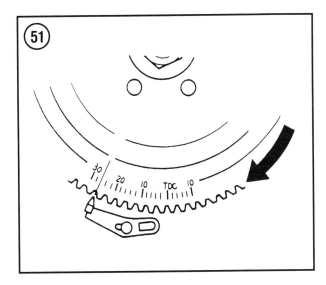

E48 Models

1. Disconnect both battery cables from the battery. Remove the spark plugs. Shift the engine into neutral.

2. Refer to *Timing Pointer Adjustment*, then adjust the pointer as described.

3. Observe the timing pointer and the markings on the flywheel as you slowly rotate the flywheel in the clockwise direction (**Figure 46**). Stop the flywheel when the pointer aligns with the 4° BTDC mark (**Figure 46**).

4. Use a screwdriver and carefully pry the ball joint connection loose from the magneto base (**Figure 47**). Move the magneto base (A, **Figure 48**) until it just contacts the cap (B, **Figure 48**) on the full retard adjustment screw.

5. Look under the flywheel to check the alignment of the mark on the magneto base (A, **Figure 49**) to the mark on the flywheel (B, **Figure 49**).

6. Maintain the magneto base in contact with the adjustment screw cap during the adjustment. Loosen the jam nut (A, **Figure 50**), then adjust the screw (B, **Figure 50**) until the marks on the magneto base and flywheel align (A and B, **Figure 49**). Securely tighten the jam nut and check the timing marks.

7. Observe the timing pointer and the timing marks on the flywheel as you slowly rotate the flywheel in the clockwise direction. Stop the flywheel when the timing pointer aligns with the 20° BTDC mark on the flywheel (**Figure 51**).

8. Move the magneto base (A, **Figure 52**) until it just contacts the cap (B, **Figure 52**) on the full advance adjust-

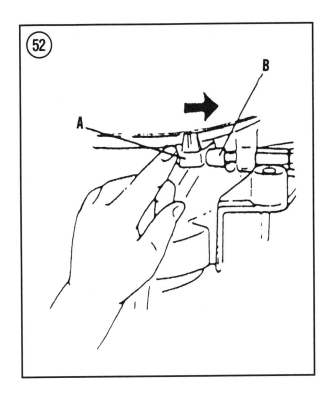

ment screw. Maintain the magneto in contact with the cap during the adjustment.

9. Look under the flywheel to check the alignment of the mark on the magneto base (A, **Figure 49**) to the mark on the flywheel (B, **Figure 49**). Loosen the jam nut (A, **Figure**

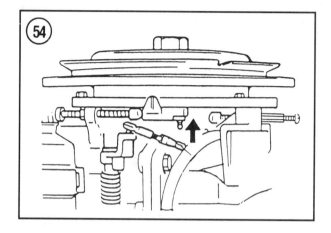

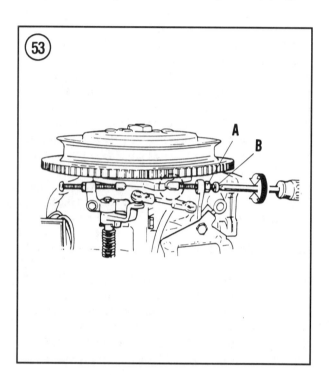

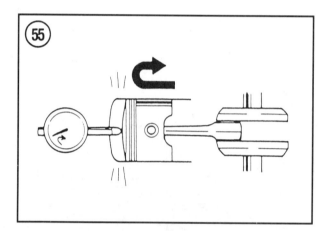

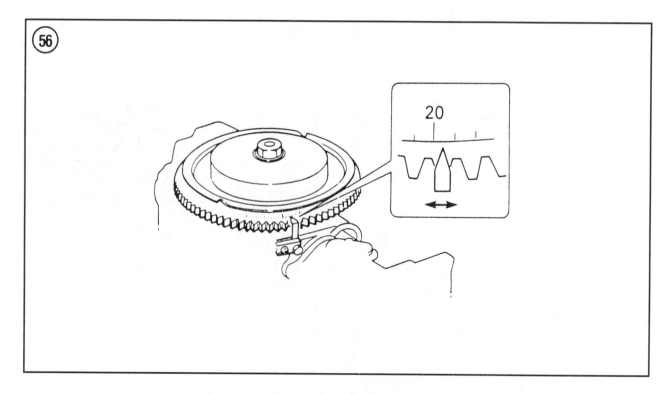

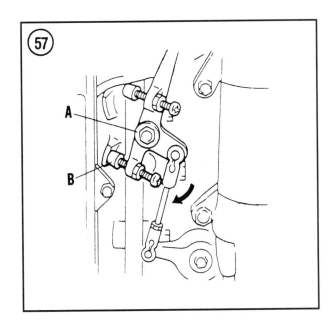

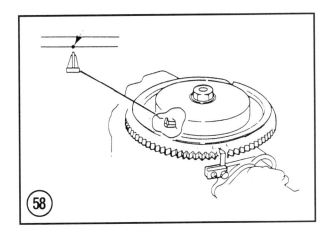

53). Adjust the full advance screw (B, **Figure 53**) until the marks on the magneto base and flywheel (A and B, **Figure 49**) align. Securely tighten the jam nut (A, **Figure 53**). Check the alignment of the timing marks.

10. Carefully snap the ball joint connector onto the magneto base (**Figure 54**). Install the spark plugs. Connect the battery cables to the battery.

E60 Models

1. Disconnect both battery cables from the battery on electric start models. Remove all spark plugs. Shift the engine into neutral.

2. Thread the dial indicator into the No. 1 spark plug hole. The stem of the pointer must contact the top of the piston.

3. Observe the needle on the dial indicator as you rotate the flywheel in the clockwise direction. Stop the flywheel when the piston reaches the upward limit of its stroke. This is the point where the needle on the dial indicator just changes direction (**Figure 55**). Rotate the dial to align the needle to the 0 mark or TDC mark on the dial indicator.

4. Observe the dial indicator as you slowly rotate the flywheel in the counterclockwise direction. Stop the flywheel when the dial indicator reading indicates the piston has moved down 2.42 mm (0.100 in.) BTDC. Maintain the flywheel in this position during adjustment.

5. Loosen the screw and position the timing pointer to align the pointer tip with the 19° BTDC mark on the flywheel (**Figure 56**). Securely tighten the fasteners for the pointer.

6. Move the magneto lever (A, **Figure 57**) until the cap on the full advance adjustment screw (B, **Figure 57**) just contacts the stopper.

7. Peer under the flywheel to check the alignment of the marks on magneto base and the flywheel (**Figure 58**). Maintain the adjustment screw cap in contact with the stopper during adjustment.

8. Loosen the jam nut on the full advance adjustment screw and rotate the screw until the marks on the magneto base and the flywheel align (**Figure 58**). Securely tighten the adjusting screw jam nut, then check the timing mark alignment.

9. Observe the timing pointer and the marks on the flywheel as you slowly rotate the flywheel in the clockwise direction. Stop the flywheel when the timing pointer aligns with the 2° ATDC mark on the flywheel. Maintain the flywheel in this position during the adjustment.

10. Move the magneto lever until the cap on the full retard adjustment screw just contacts the stop (**Figure 59**).

11. Look under the flywheel to check the alignment of the marks on the magneto base and the flywheel (**Figure 58**). Maintain the adjustment screw cap in contact with the stop during the adjustment.

12. Loosen the jam nut on the full retard adjustment screw. Rotate the screw (**Figure 60**) until the marks on the magneto base and the flywheel align (**Figure 58**).

13. Tighten the jam nut on the full retard adjusting screw. Check the alignment of the timing marks.

14. Install the spark plugs. Connect the battery cables to the battery.

E75 Models

1. Disconnect both battery cables from the battery. Remove all spark plugs. Shift the engine into neutral gear.

2. Observe the timing pointer as you rotate the flywheel in the clockwise direction. Stop the flywheel when the timing pointer aligns with the 22° BTDC mark (**Figure 61**) on the flywheel.

3. Look under the flywheel to check the alignment of the marks on the magneto base and the flywheel (**Figure 58**). Go to Step 9 if the marks are properly aligned. Perform Step 4-8 if the marks are not aligned.

4. Install the dial indicator into the No. 1 spark plug hole. Observe the dial indicator needle as you slowly rotate the flywheel in the clockwise direction. Stop the flywheel when the piston reaches the upper limit of its stroke. This is the point when the needle on the dial indicator just changes direction (**Figure 55**).

5. Rotate the dial on the indicator until the needle is aligned with the 0 or TDC marking. Observe the needle as you slowly rotate the flywheel in the counterclockwise direction. Stop the flywheel when the needle indicates the

piston has moved down 3.41 mm (0.13 in.) BTDC. Maintain the flywheel in this position during adjustment.

6. Loosen the fasteners for the timing pointer. Align the pointer tip to the 22° BTDC mark on the flywheel. Securely tighten fasteners for the pointer. Remove the dial indicator from the cylinder head.

7. Carefully pry the magneto linkage (E, **Figure 62**) from the magneto lever. Move the magneto base until its timing mark (A, **Figure 62**) is aligned with the mark on the flywheel (B, **Figure 62**). Loosen the jam nut and adjust the full advance stopper screw and cap until a length of 32.5 mm (1.29 in.) is measured (C, **Figure 62**). Securely tighten the jam nut.

8. Adjust the magneto linkage (E, **Figure 62**) to allow the magneto lever to contact the full advance adjustment screw cap. The timing marks (A and B, **Figure 62**) must align when the lever is installed. Carefully snap the linkage over the ball joint. Check the timing mark alignment. Correct the adjustment as required.

9. Observe the timing pointer and the marks on the flywheel as you slowly rotate the flywheel in the clockwise

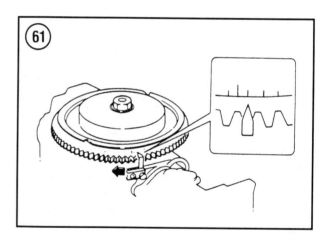

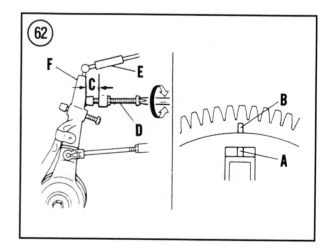

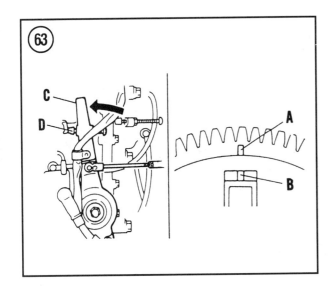

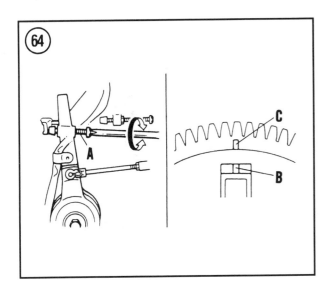

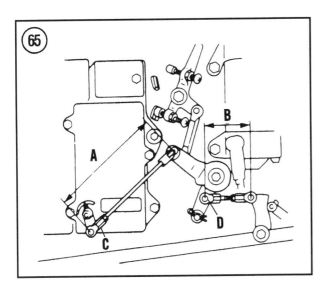

direction. Stop the flywheel when the timing pointer aligns with the 2° ATDC mark on the flywheel.

10. Move the magneto lever (C, **Figure 63**) until the adjustment screw cap just contacts the stopper (D, **Figure 63**).

11. Look under the flywheel to check the alignment of the timing marks on the magneto base and the flywheel (A and B, **Figure 63**).

12. Maintain the adjustment screw cap in contact with the stopper (D, **Figure 63**) during the adjustment.

13. Loosen the jam nut and rotate the adjustment screw (A, **Figure 64**) until the magneto base and flywheel timing marks (B and C, **Figure 64**) align. Securely tighten the jam nut.

14. Install the spark plugs. Connect the battery cables to the battery.

60-90 hp (Except 80 Jet Models)

1. Disconnect both battery cables from the battery. Remove all spark plugs. Shift the engine into neutral.

2. Refer to *Timing Pointer Adjustment* in this chapter and adjust the timing pointer as directed.

3. Carefully pry the throttle position sensor linkage ball joint from the indicator (C, **Figure 65**). Carefully pry the throttle linkage ball joint from the magneto lever (D, **Figure 65**).

4. On 60 and 70 hp models, Adjust the throttle position sensor linkage to a length of 129.0 mm (5.08 in.) as indicated (A, **Figure 65**). Adjust the throttle linkage to a length of 58.0 mm (2.28 in.) as indicated (B, **Figure 65**).

5. On 75-90 hp models (except E75 and 80 jet models) adjust the throttle position linkage to a length of 93.5 mm (3.68 in.) as indicated (A, **Figure 66**). Adjust the throttle

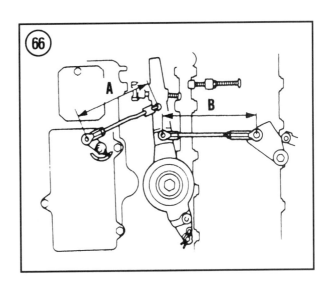

linkage to a length of 120.5 mm (4.74 in.) as indicated (B, **Figure 66**).

6. Connect the throttle position sensor and throttle linkages to their respective location. Snap the ball joint connectors onto the ball joints.

7. On 60 and 70 hp models, maintain contact of the full retard adjusting screw cap to the stop. Loosen the jam nut, then adjust the full retard screw (C, **Figure 67**) until the indicator (A, **Figure 67**) aligns with the mark (B, **Figure 67**) on the CDI unit. Securely tighten the jam nut.

8. On 75-90 hp models, maintain contact of the full retard adjusting screw cap to the stop. Loosen the jam nut, then adjust the full retard screw (C, **Figure 68**) until the indicator (A, **Figure 68**) aligns with the mark (B, **Figure 68**) on the CDI unit. Securely tighten the jam nut.

9. Install the spark plugs. Connect the battery cables to the battery terminals.

10. On 60 and 70 hp models, Position the cap on the full advance adjusting screw (D, **Figure 69**) against the stop. Maintain this position during the adjustment. Loosen the jam nut. Adjust the screw until the indicator (A, **Figure 69**) aligns with the mark for the selected model. Use the mark shown in B, **Figure 69** for 60 hp models. Use the mark shown in C, **Figure 69** for 70 hp models. Securely tighten the jam nut.

11. On 75-90 hp models, position the magneto lever against the cap on the full advance adjusting screw (D, **Figure 70**). Maintain this position during the adjustment. Loosen the jam nut and adjust the screw until the indicator (A, **Figure 70**) aligns with the mark for the selected model. Use the mark indicated (B, **Figure 70**) for 75 and 80 hp

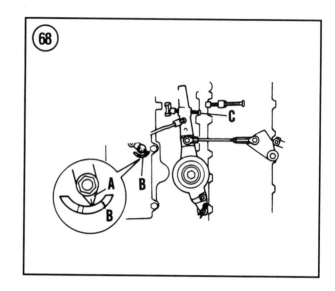

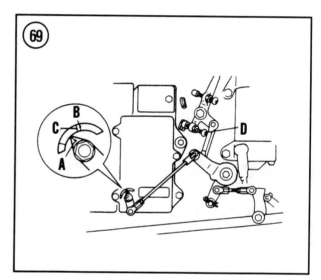

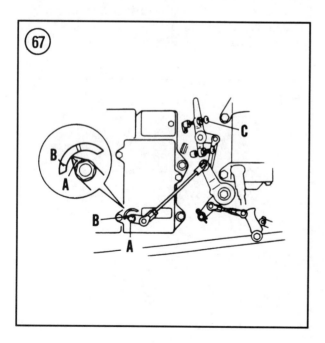

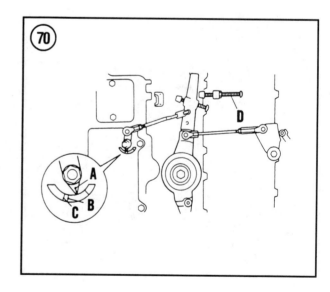

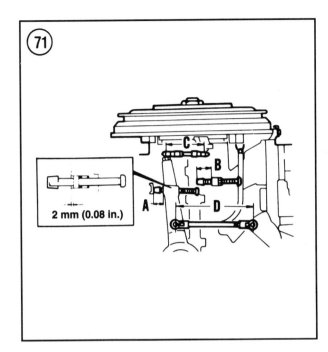

2 mm (0.08 in.)

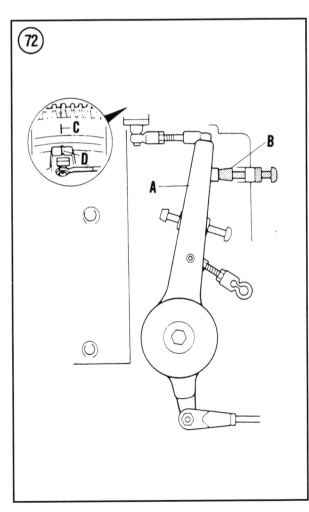

models. Use the mark indicated (C, **Figure70**) for 65 jet and 90 hp models. Securely tighten the jam nut. Install the spark plugs. Connect the battery cables to the battery.

C75 and C85 Models

1. Disconnect both battery cables from the battery. Remove the spark plugs. Shift the engine into neutral.

2. Refer to *Timing Pointer Adjustment* and adjust the timing pointer as described.

3. Loosen the jam nuts or connectors and adjust the length of the adjustment screws or linkage (**Figure 71**) to the dimensions indicated:

    a. 13.0 mm (0.51 in.).
    b. 35.0 mm (1.38 in.).
    c. 74.0 mm (2.91 in.).
    d. 124.0 mm (4.88 in.).

4. Perform the remaining adjustments under running conditions. Refer to *Timing Check and Adjustment* in this chapter. Tighten the jam nuts after adjustments.

80 Jet, 105 Jet and
115-225 hp 90° V Models

1. Disconnect both battery cables from the battery. Remove all spark plugs. Shift the engine into neutral.

2. Observe the timing pointer and marks on the flywheel as you slowly rotate the flywheel in the clockwise direction. Stop the flywheel when the pointer aligns with the full advance timing mark indicated.

    a. For 115 hp models, use the 25° BTDC mark.
    b. For 130 hp models, use the 22° BTDC mark.
    c. For C150, D150 and P150 models, use the 19° BTDC mark.
    d. For 150TR and S175TR models, use the 22° BTDC mark.
    e. For P175TR and P200 TR models, use the 23° BTDC mark.
    f. For L200TR models, use the 20° BTDC mark.
    g. For 200TR and 225 models, use the 21° BTDC mark.

3. Maintain the flywheel in this position. Move the magneto lever (A, **Figure 72**) until it just contacts the cap on the full advance adjustment screw (B, **Figure 72**). Look under the flywheel to check the alignment of the marks on the magneto base (D, **Figure 72**) and the flywheel (C, **Figure 72**). Go to Step 11 if the marks are aligned. Perform Steps 4-10 if the marks are not aligned.

4. Install the dial indicator into the No. 1 spark plug hole. Observe the dial indicator as you slowly rotate the flywheel in the clockwise direction. Stop the flywheel when the piston reaches the top of its stroke (**Figure 73**). This is the

point when the needle on the dial indicator just changes direction.

5. Rotate the dial on the dial indicator until the needle aligns with the 0 or the TDC mark. Observe the needle as you slowly rotate the flywheel in the LH direction. Stop the flywheel when the needle indicates the piston has reached the proper point down from the top of its stroke (BTDC).

   a. For 80 jet and 115 hp models, stop the flywheel at 3.91 mm (0.15 in.).

   b. For 130 hp models, stop the flywheel at 3.05 mm (0.12 in.).

   c. For 105 jet, C150, D150 and P150 models, stop the flywheel at 2.28 mm (0.09 in.).

   d. For 150TR and S175TR models, stop the flywheel at 3.05 mm (0.12 in.).

   e. For P175TR and P200TR models, stop the flywheel at 3.33 mm (0.13 in.).

   f. For L200TR models, stop the flywheel at 2.53 mm (0.10 in.).

   g. For 200TR and 225 models, stop the flywheel at 2.78 mm (0.11 in.).

6. Loosen the fasteners for the timing pointer (B, **Figure 74**). Position the pointer to the full advance marking on the flywheel (A, **Figure 74**) indicated in Step 2. Securely tighten the fasteners for the timing indicator. Remove the dial indicator from the cylinder head.

7. Adjust the full advance adjusting screw length (A, **Figure 75**) to the dimension indicated:

   a. For C115 models, adjust to 22.0 mm (0.87 in.).

   b. For 80 jet and 115 hp models, adjust to 26.0 mm (1.02 in.).

   c. For 130 hp models, adjust to 29.0 mm (1.14 in.).

   d. For C150 and D150 models, adjust to 41.2 mm (1.62 in.).

   e. For 105 jet and P150 models, adjust to 43.5 mm (1.71in.).

   f. For L150TR and S175TR models, adjust to 21.5 mm (0.85 in.).

   g. For L200TR models, adjust to 24.0 mm (0.94 in.).

   h. For P175TR and P200TR models, adjust to 40.0 mm (1.57 in.).

   i. For 200TR and 225 models, adjust to 42.5 mm (1.67 in.).

8. Carefully disconnect the magneto linkage (C, **Figure 75**) from the magneto lever (B, **Figure 75**). Loosen the jam nut on the magneto linkage.

9. The magneto lever (B, **Figure 75**) must touch the cap on the full advance adjustment screw during the adjustment. Adjust the length of the linkage until it can be connected to the magneto lever without disturbing the alignment of the timing marks (D and E, **Figure 75**) on the

magneto base and the flywheel. Connect the magneto linkage.

10. Observe the timing pointer and the markings on the flywheel as you rotate the flywheel in the clockwise direction.

   a. For 80 jet and 115 and 130 hp models, stop the flywheel when the timing pointer is aligned with the 5° ATDC mark.

   b. For 105 jet and 150-200 hp models, stop the flywheel when the pointer is aligned with the 7°ATDC mark.

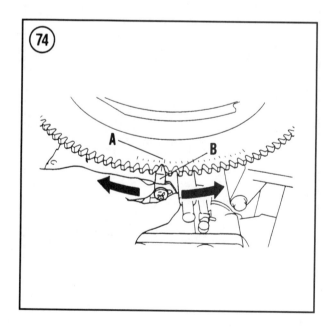

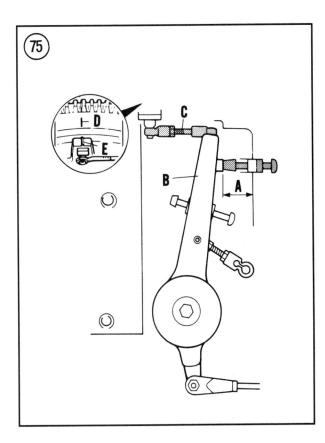

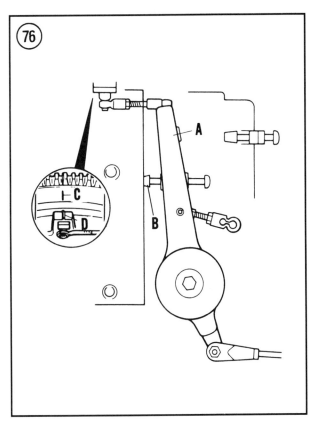

c. For 225 hp models, stop the flywheel when the pointer is aligned with the 6° ATDC mark.

11. Move the magneto lever until the cap on the full retard adjusting screw (B, **Figure 76**) just contacts the stop. Maintain the lever in contact with the stop during the adjustment.

12. Loosen the jam nut, then adjust the full retard screw until the marks (C and D, **Figure 76**) on the magneto base and the flywheel align. Securely tighten the jam nut.

13. Install the spark plugs. Connect the battery cables to the battery.

200-250 hp 76° V Models

The timing on these models is controlled by the microcomputer or YMIS. Timing adjustment is not required.

THROTTLE LINKAGE ADJUSTMENTS

NOTE
Disconnect the oil pump control link on oil injected models prior to performing linkage adjustments. Incorrect linkage adjustment may result if the oil pump lever interferes with linkage movement. Connect the oil pump control link after linkage adjustment is completed. Install the oil pump control link after adjustments. Refer to Chapter Thirteen for removal, installation and adjustment procedures.

2 hp Models

The throttle lever is connected directly to the carburetor and linkage adjustment is not required.

3-5 hp Models

The throttle cable is connected directly to the carburetor throttle shaft and linkage adjustment is not required. Refer to *Throttle Cable Adjustment* in this chapter.

6-15 hp Models

Refer to *Throttle Cable Adjustment* in this chapter for adjustments procedure.

20 and 25 hp Models

1. Remove the front cover/silencer from the engine as instructed in Chapter Six. Loosen the throttle linkage screw (B, **Figure 77**).

2. Look into the carburetor opening as you rotate the idle speed screw (A, **Figure 77**). Adjust the screw until the throttle plate in the carburetor next to the screw just reaches the closed position.

3. Loosen the carburetor lever screw(s) (1, **Figure 78**) to allow all throttle plates to completely close.

4. Securely tighten the carburetor lever screw(s). Gently hold the throttle linkage in a position to ensure the throttle plates are closed, then securely tighten the linkage screw (2, **Figure 78**).

5. Observe the throttle plates as you turn the idle speed screw (A, **Figure 77**) in the clockwise direction. Stop when both throttle plates just start to move.

6. Install the silencer/cover as instructed in Chapter Six. Perform the idle speed adjustment following the procedure listed in this chapter.

C30 Models

1. Remove the front cover/silencer from the engine as instructed in Chapter Six. Loosen the carburetor lever screw (A, **Figure 79**).

2. Align the idle speed screw to the middle of its adjusting range. Position the throttle lever to contact the idle speed adjusting screw or tip as indicated (**Figure 79**).

3. Look into the carburetor opening. With the throttle plate completely closed, securely tighten the carburetor lever screw (A, **Figure 79**).

4. Turn the idle speed screw in the clockwise direction until the throttle plate just starts to move open.

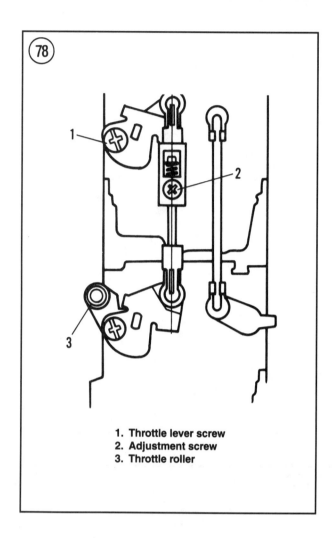

1. Throttle lever screw
2. Adjustment screw
3. Throttle roller

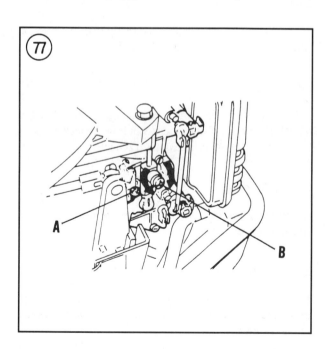

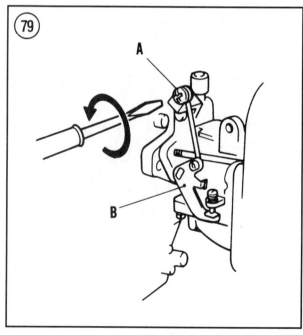

5. Attach the silencer/cover to the front of the carburetor as instructed in Chapter Six.

30 hp Three-Cylinder Models

Refer to *Throttle Cable Adjustment* in this chapter for adjustment procedure.

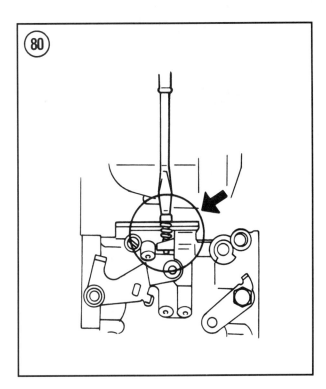

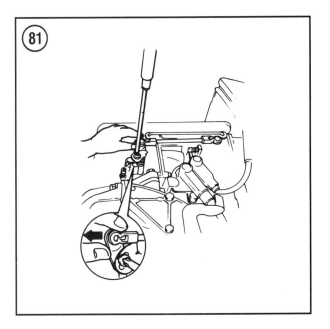

C40 Two-Cylinder Models

1. Remove the cover/silencer from the carburetor openings as instructed in Chapter Six.

2. Locate the idle speed adjusting screw (**Figure 80**). Look into the lower carburetor opening as you loosen the idle speed screw. Stop when the throttle plate just reaches the closed position.

3. Loosen the upper carburetor lever screw (**Figure 81**). Gently pull up on the linkage, then securely tighten the carburetor lever screw (**Figure 81**).

4. Move the throttle several times from idle to full advance. Position the throttle at the idle position. Inspect both throttle plates for a fully closed position. Repeat this step if either plate is open.

5. Disconnect the magneto linkage from the magneto lever. Move the magneto lever to contact the full advance stop.

6. Position the throttle cam to contact the throttle roller as indicated (**Figure 82**). Make sure the magneto lever is contacting the full advance stop.

7. Adjust the length of the throttle cam linkage to align with the ball joint connector when the roller just contacts the cam. Carefully snap the linkage over the ball joint (**Figure 82**).

8. Adjust the idle speed screw until the throttle plates just start to move open. Install the silencer/cover as instructed in Chapter Six.

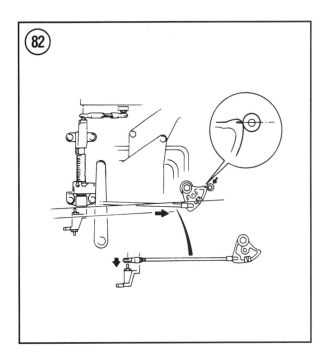

28 Jet, 35 Jet, 40 Three-Cylinder and 50 hp Models

1. Position the throttle at the full advance position. Inspect the carburetor lever (**Figure 83**).

2. The carburetor lever must contact the throttle stop (**Figure 83**).

3. Perform Steps 4-6 if the lever is *not* contacting the stop

4. Position the throttle control to the idle or closed throttle position. Loosen the jam nut (A, **Figure 84**), then remove the pin (B, **Figure 84**) from the throttle linkage connector.

5. Disconnect the throttle linkage from the magneto lever (A, **Figure 85**). Position the magneto lever against the full retard stop (B, **Figure 85**). Adjust the throttle linkage length to fit its attaching points and install onto the throttle lever. Be sure the UP mark on the linkage connector faces upward.

6. Adjust the length of the carburetor linkage to ensure the throttle reaches full advance. Refer to *Static Timing Adjustment* and check timing adjustment.

E60 Models

1. Position the throttle at the full advance position. Inspect the carburetor lever (**Figure 83**).

2. The carburetor lever must contact the throttle stop (**Figure 83**).

3. If the lever is *not* contacting the stop perform Steps 4-6.

4. Remove the silencer/cover as instructed in Chapter Six. Look into the No. 2 carburetor opening and adjust the idle speed screw (A, **Figure 86**) until the throttle plate just reaches the closed position. Make sure the magneto lever is against the full retard stop. Refer to *Static Timing Adjustment* if necessary.

5. Loosen the carburetor lever screws (B, **Figure 86**). Make sure each of the throttle plates is at the fully closed position. Support the linkage and securely tighten the carburetor lever screws (B, **Figure 86**).

6. Adjust the idle speed screw until the throttle plates just begin to open. Move the throttle plates several times to ensure correct operation. All plates must move at the same time and return to the same partially open position.

7. Install the silencer/cover as instructed in Chapter Six. Perform the idle speed adjustment as instructed in this chapter.

60-90 hp (Excludes 80 Jet) Models

1. Remove the silencer/cover as instructed in Chapter Six. Position the throttle at the idle or closed throttle position. Make sure the magneto lever is against the full retard stop.

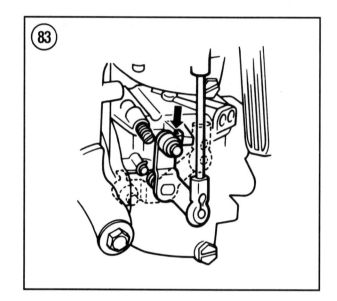

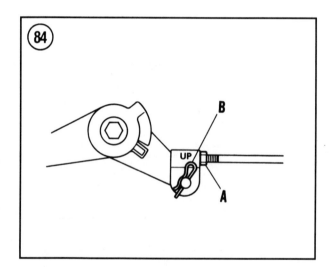

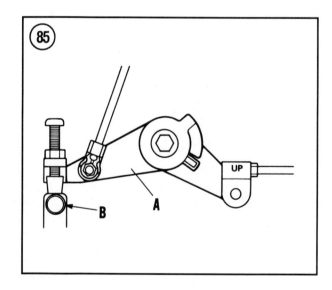

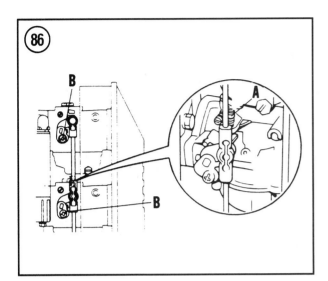

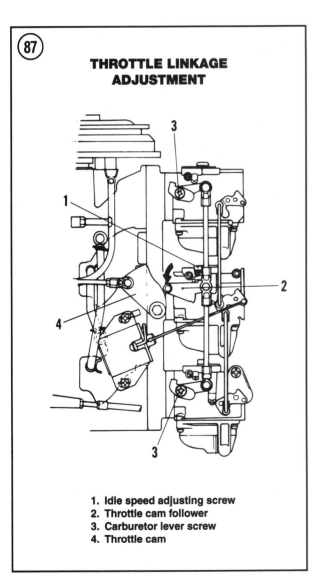

THROTTLE LINKAGE ADJUSTMENT

1. Idle speed adjusting screw
2. Throttle cam follower
3. Carburetor lever screw
4. Throttle cam

Refer to *Static Timing Adjustment* for component identification.

2. Look into the opening of the No. 2 carburetor as you loosen the idle speed screw (**Figure 87**). Stop when the throttle plate just reaches the closed position. Loosen the screw on the throttle roller lever.

3. Loosen the carburetor lever screws (**Figure 87**). Inspect the throttle plates in all three carburetors. They must all be in the closed position. Check for tight or binding linkages if any plates are open.

4. Align the roller to contact the throttle cam (**Figure 87**). Tighten the screw for the throttle roller lever. Pull the throttle linkage lightly in the UP direction. Support the throttle linkage as you securely tighten the carburetor lever screws.

5. Look into the carburetor openings. Tighten the idle speed screw until the throttle plates just begin to move in the open direction. Move the throttle several times to check for proper operation. All throttle plates must move at the same time and return to the same partially open position when closed.

6. Install the silencer cover as instructed in Chapter Six. Perform the idle speed adjustment as instructed in this chapter.

80 Jet and 115-225 hp (90° V) Models

1. Remove the silencer/cover as instructed in Chapter Six. Position the throttle at the idle or closed throttle position. Make sure the magneto lever is against the full retard stop. Refer to *Static Timing Adjustment* for component identification.

2. Look into the opening of the No. 2 carburetor as you slowly loosen the idle speed screw (A, **Figure 88**). Stop when the throttle plate just reaches the fully closed position. Loosen the throttle roller lever screw.

3. Loosen the carburetor lever screws (C, **Figure 88**). Inspect all throttle plates to ensure they are fully closed.

4. Lightly pull UP on the throttle linkage. Support the throttle linkage and securely tighten the carburetor lever screws (C, **Figure 88**). Move the throttle roller until it just contacts the throttle cam, then tighten its screw.

5. Peer into the carburetor opening as you slowly turn the idle speed screw (A, **Figure 88**). Stop when the throttle plates just begin to move in the open direction.

6. Operate the throttle several times to check for proper operation. All throttle plates must move at the same time and return to the same partially open position when closed.

7. Install the silencer cover as instructed in Chapter Six. Perform the idle speed adjustments as instructed in this chapter.

225-250 hp (76°) Carbureted Models

To assist with component identification and orientation refer to **Figure 89** during the adjustment procedure.

Follow Steps 1-9 to adjust the throttle linkage.

1. Position the throttle in idle or fully closed position. Remove the silencer/cover from the carburetors as instructed in Chapter Six.

2. Loosen the throttle roller adjusting screw. Turn the idle adjustment screw until it no longer contract the carburetor lever.

3. Disconnect the accelerator link from the throttle cam and between the carburetors. Disconnect the joint link and adjust to a dimension of 141.5 mm (5.571 in.). Connect the accelerator links.

4. Loosen the throttle synchronization screw on both outer banks. Make sure that all throttle plates are completely closed. Support the throttle linkages as you securely tighten the throttle valve synchronization screws.

5. Loosen the throttle valve synchronization screw located between the banks, then lightly push down on the linkage to remove the slack. Securely tighten the synchronization screw.

6. Observe the throttle plate nearest the idle adjustment screw. Turn the screw until the throttle plate just begins to open. Turn the screw an additional 1 1/2 turns.

7. Position the throttle roller in light contact with the throttle cam, then tighten the throttle roller screw.

8. Operate the throttle several times as you observe the throttle plates. All throttle plates must move at the same time and return to the same partially open position when closed.

9. Install the silencer/covers as instructed in Chapter Six. Refer to *Idle Speed Adjustment*, then perform the idle speed adjustments as instructed.

200-250 hp 76° EFI Models

Throttle linkage adjustments are not required on these models. Refer to *Throttle Pickup Timing* in this chapter for required adjustment.

TIMING CHECK AND ADJUSTMENT

NOTE
On 90° models, the engine model name is used to identify the maximum timing specifications. Locate the serial number tag and identify the model name of the engine before checking the ignition timing.

2 hp Models

The timing is not adjustable and ignition timing check is not required.

3-5 hp Models

The timing on these models is not adjustable. Check the timing while running to ensure proper ignition system operation.

1. Place the engine in a suitable test tank. Install a test propeller (Yamaha part No. 90890-06130) as instructed in Chapter Nine.

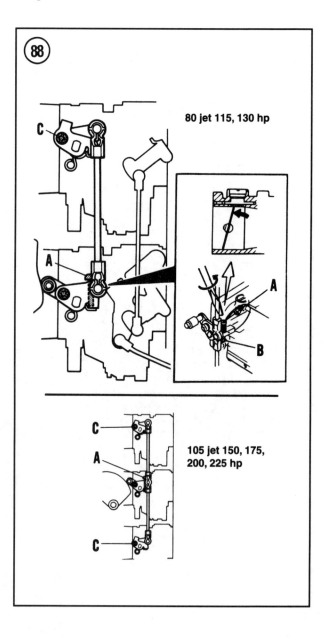

88

80 jet 115, 130 hp

C

A

B

105 jet 150, 175, 200, 225 hp

C

A

C

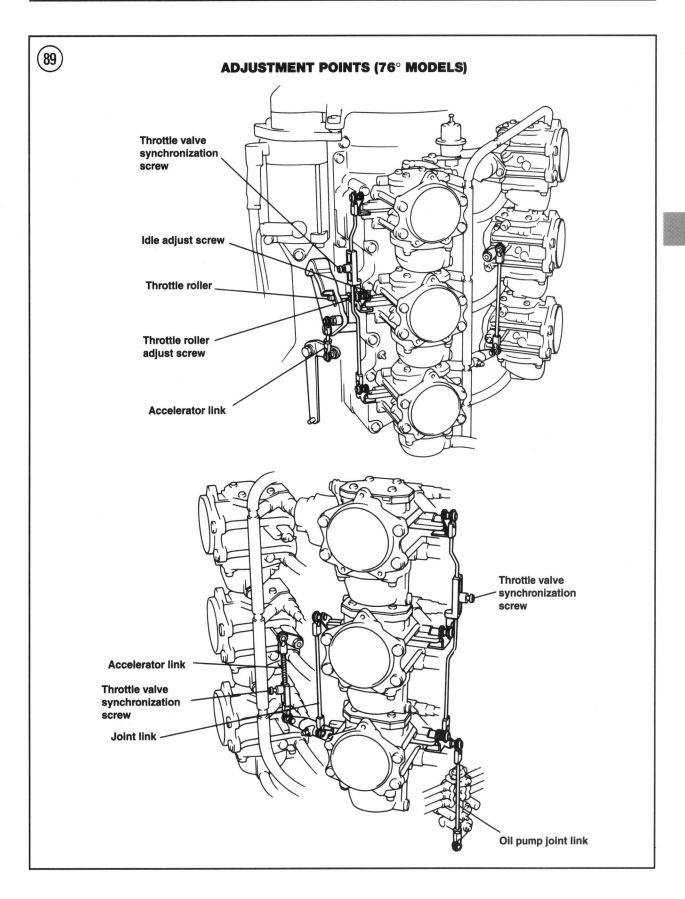

89

ADJUSTMENT POINTS (76° MODELS)

Throttle valve synchronization screw

Idle adjust screw

Throttle roller

Throttle roller adjust screw

Accelerator link

Throttle valve synchronization screw

Accelerator link

Throttle valve synchronization screw

Joint link

Oil pump joint link

5

2. Install a suitable tachometer and timing light (Yamaha part No. YM-33277) to the spark plug lead (**Figure 90**).

3. Start the engine and allow it to run for a few minutes. Refer to **Table 3** for the correct timing and rpm specifications. Point the timing light at the timing indicator windows (**Figure 91**). The timing mark should appear in the *left* window at idle speed. Shift the engine into forward gear. Have an assistant hold the tiller handle while you check the timing.

4. Slowly advance the throttle until the engine reaches the rpm specified in **Table 2**. The timing mark should appear in the *Right* window (**Figure 91**) at the specified rpm.

5. Check the pulsar coils and/or replace the CDI unit if the timing mark does not appear at the specified speed. Switch the engine off and remove the engine from the test tank. Install the correct propeller as instructed in Chapter Nine.

NOTE
Some small engine models are not provided with a timing pointer or timing marks on the flywheel. Checking the timing under running conditions is not required on these models. Refer to Static Timing Adjustment in this chapter for timing adjustment procedures.

6-225 hp 90° V Models
(Except C75 and C85)

The timing is checked to verify proper timing adjustment. Use a test propeller on 6-175 hp models. Refer to **Table 6** for the test propeller part number. Check maximum timing with the motor in a suitable test tank or with the boat and motor in the water. For 200-225 hp models, check the timing under actual running conditions. Use the standard propeller used with the boat and engine combination.

1. On 6-175 hp models, install the test propeller (**Figure 92**) listed in **Table 6** as instructed in Chapter Nine.

2. On 200-225 (90° V) models, use the standard propeller. Have an assistant operate the boat as you check the timing.

3. Connect a suitable timing light to the No. 1 spark plug lead. Follow the manufacturer's instructions for connecting the timing light leads. Connect a suitable tachometer to one of the spark plug leads. follow the manufacturer's instructions for connecting the tachometer leads.

4. Locate the timing pointer and the timing marks on the flywheel (**Figure 93**). Start the engine and allow it to run at low speed for 10 minutes. This will allow the engine to reach operating temperature.

5. Refer to **Table 3** for the maximum timing or full advance specification and the proper speed. Shift the engine into forward gear.

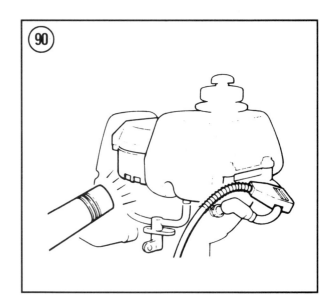

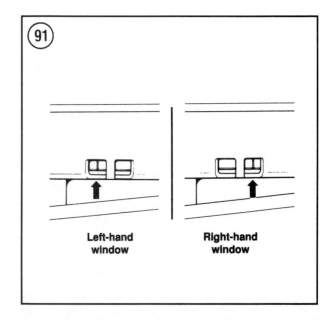

Left-hand window   Right-hand window

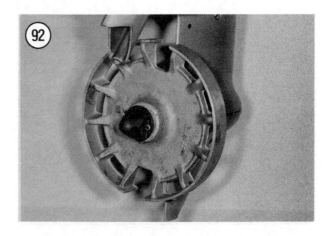

6. Observe the timing pointer (**Figure 94**) and tachometer as you slowly advance the throttle until the engine reaches the specified rpm. Verify correct timing at the specified rpm. Return the engine to idle rpm.

7. Refer to *Static Timing Adjustments* in this chapter and adjust the timing if it is incorrect. Adjust as required until the proper timing is indicated while running.

8. Refer to *Pickup Timing* in this chapter for instructions and check the pickup timing. Adjust as required.

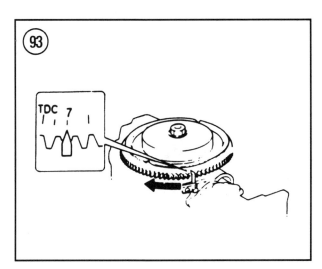

9. Install the correct propeller as instructed in Chapter Nine. Remove the timing light and tachometer. Perform throttle linkage adjustments following the procedures listed in this chapter.

C75 and C85 Models

Refer to *Timing Pointer Adjustment* in this chapter for instructions. Adjust the timing pointer prior to performing the timing adjustments.

1. Refer to **Table 6** for test propeller part number. Install a test propeller (**Figure 92**), and then place the motor in a suitable test tank.

2. Connect a suitable timing light to the No. 1 spark plug lead. Connect a suitable tachometer to one of the spark plug leads. Follow the manufacturer's instructions when connecting the timing light and tachometer to the engine.

3. Locate the timing pointer and timing marks on the flywheel (**Figure 93**).

4. Start the engine and allow it to run at low speed for 10 minutes. This will allow the engine to reach normal operating temperature. Shift the engine into neutral.

5. Use a timing light to observe the timing pointer and timing marks on the flywheel (**Figure 94**) as you manually

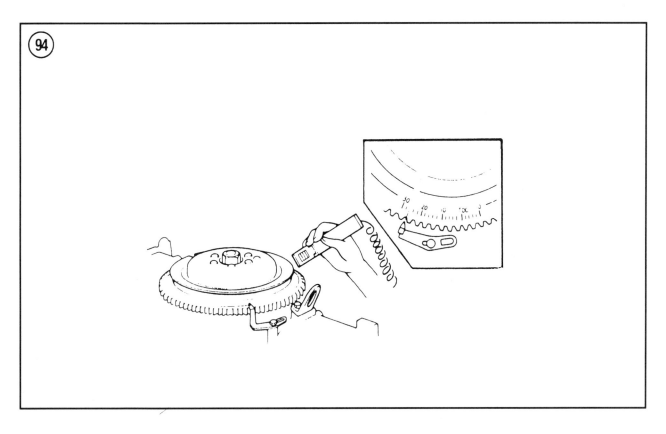

move the magneto lever to the full retard position (**Figure 95**). The lever must remain in contact with the cap on the full retard adjusting screw during the adjustment.

6. Loosen the jam nut and adjust the full retard screw (**Figure 96**) until the timing pointer aligns with the 2° ATDC mark on the flywheel. Securely tighten the jam nut, then check the timing with the timing light to verify correct adjustment.

7. Shift the engine into forward gear. Refer to **Table 3** for the maximum timing, specification and the proper rpm. Observe the timing pointer and the timing marks on the flywheel as you move the magneto lever to the full advance position (**Figure 97**).

8. Maintain the magneto lever in contact with the cap on the full advance adjusting screw during the adjustment. Read the timing when the engine reaches the specified speed. Loosen the jam nut and adjust the screw (**Figure 98**) until the timing pointer aligns with the specified mark on the flywheel. Securely tighten the jam nut. Return the engine to idle speed.

9. Refer to *Pickup Timing* in this chapter for instructions and check the pickup timing. Adjust as required.

10. Install the correct propeller as instructed in Chapter Nine. Remove the timing light and tachometer. Perform the linkage adjustment following the procedure listed in this chapter.

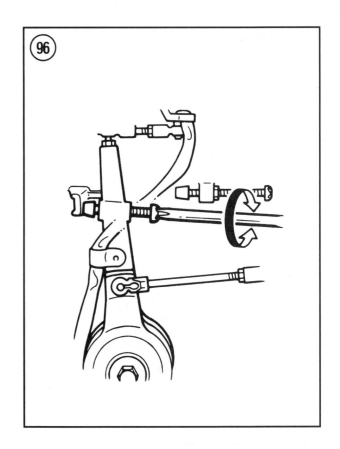

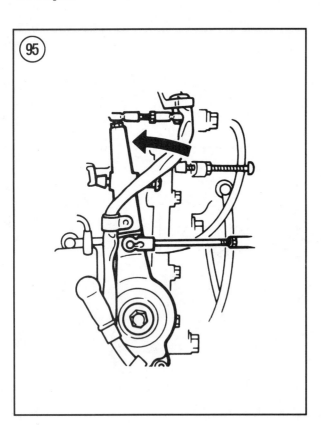

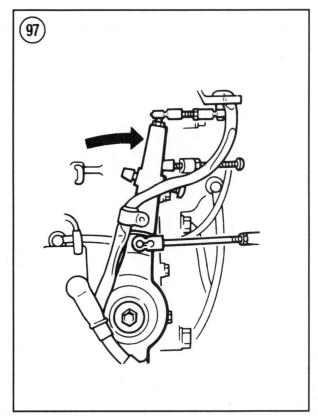

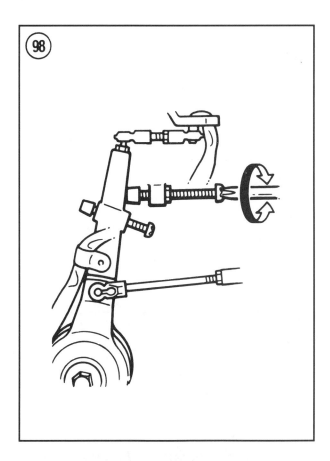

200-250 hp 76° V Models

The timing is controlled by the microcomputer or YMIS on these models. Timing checks and adjustments are not required.

CAUTION
The throttle roller adjusting screw is a left-hand thread on some models. Use care when loosening the screw. Try turning the screw in the clockwise direction to loosen if it does not turn easily in the counterclockwise direction.

THROTTLE PICKUP TIMING (CHECK AND ADJUSTMENT)

Throttle pickup is the point in throttle advancement that the magneto lever just starts to open the carburetor or throttle body on EFI models. A throttle cam (A, **Figure 99** typical) contacts a throttle roller (B, **Figure 99**) that is connected to the throttle linkage. Proper adjustment allows the throttle cam to contact the roller at the proper ignition timing specification. Changing the length of the control linkage (**Figure 100**, typical) moves the roller in relation to the throttle linkage.

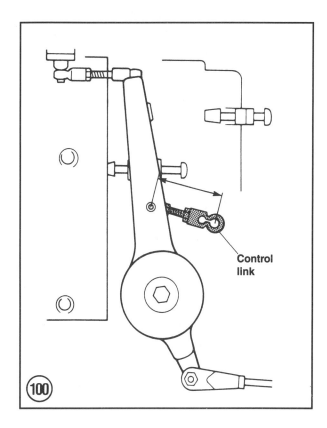

Control link

Refer to the applicable illustration (**Figure 101-110**) during the adjustment procedure.

For 2-5 hp models, the timing is electronically controlled and pickup timing adjustment is not required. For 6-15 hp, 28 jet, 35 jet, 40 hp (three-cylinder) and 50 hp models, pickup timing adjustment is not required.

For 20 and 25 hp models, refer to **Figure 101**.

For C30 models, refer to **Figure 102**.

For 40 hp (three-cylinder) models, refer to **Figure 103**.

For E48 models, refer to **Figure 104**.

For E60, 60 and 70 hp models, refer to **Figure 105**.

For C75 and C85 models, refer to **Figure 106**.

For 65 jet and 75-90 hp models (except 80 jet), refer to **Figure 107**.

For 80 jet and 115-200 hp, 90° V models, refer to **Figure 108**.

For 225-250 hp 76° carbureted models, refer to **Figure 109**.

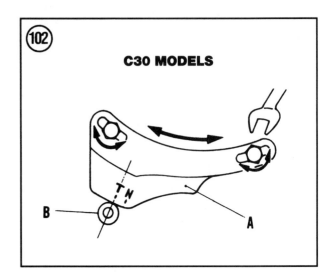

(102)

C30 MODELS

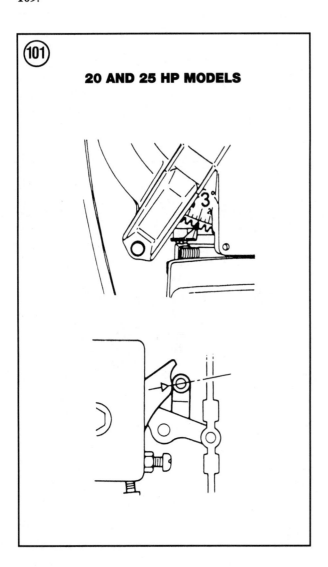

(101)

20 AND 25 HP MODELS

(103)

40 HP (THREE-CYLINDER) MODELS

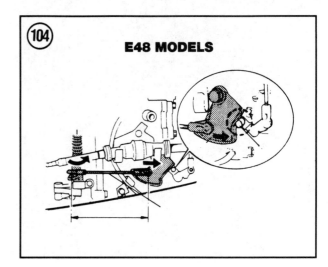

(104)

E48 MODELS

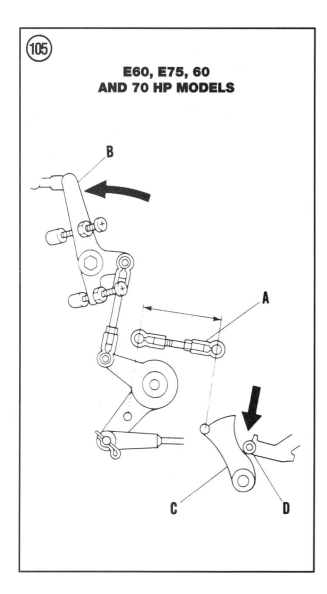

105

**E60, E75, 60
AND 70 HP MODELS**

B

A

C

D

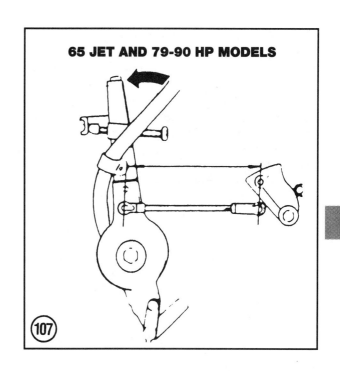

65 JET AND 79-90 HP MODELS

107

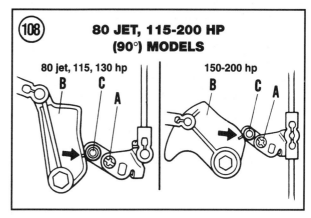

108

**80 JET, 115-200 HP
(90°) MODELS**

80 jet, 115, 130 hp

B C A

150-200 hp

B C A

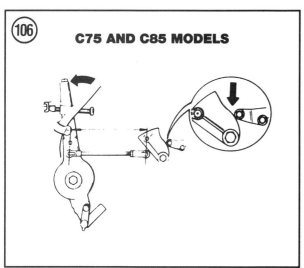

106

C75 AND C85 MODELS

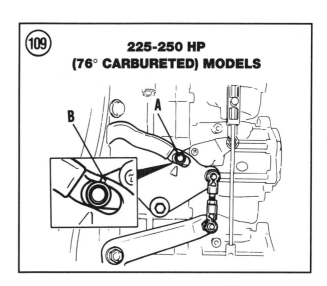

109

**225-250 HP
(76° CARBURETED) MODELS**

B

A

5

For 200-250 hp 76° EFI models, refer to **Figure 110**.

1. Refer to *Timing Check and Adjustment* to prepare the engine for running timing check. Refer to **Table 2** for the pickup timing specification.

2. Observe the timing pointer and the marks on the flywheel as you slowly advance the throttle. Note the ignition timing at the point that the throttle cam just makes contact with the throttle roller. Also note the point of contact on the throttle cam.

3. Adjust the length of the throttle link or adjust the throttle roller to allow the roller to contact the cam at the proper timing specification. Follow the instruction for the indicated model.

   a. On 20 and 25 hp models, loosen the adjusting screw and pivot the roller to contact the cam. Change the length of the cam linkage until the roller contacts the cam at the specified timing. Align the center of the roller with the mark on the cam. Tighten the roller pivot screw.

   b. On C30 models, turn the engine OFF then position the throttle at full advance. Adjust the cam plate to align the roller to the T mark on the plate (B, **Figure 102**). Observe the cam plate and roller as you slowly operate the throttle from idle to full advance. The roller should align with the marking (A, **Figure 102**) as it contacts the cam plate.

   c. On 30 hp models, loosen the No. 2 carburetor throttle roller (**Figure 103**). Move the roller so it just con-

tacts the throttle cam at the specified timing, then tighten the roller pivot screw.

   d. On E48 models, adjust the length of the throttle cam linkage (**Figure 104**) until the throttle roller just contacts the throttle cam at the specified timing.

   e. On E60, 60 hp, 70 hp and E75 models, position the magneto lever against the full retard stop (B, **Figure 105**). Adjust the length of the throttle cam linkage

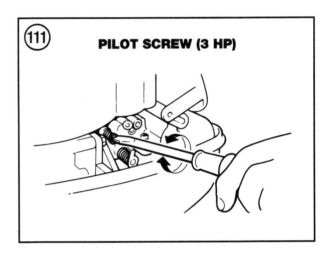

(111)   **PILOT SCREW (3 HP)**

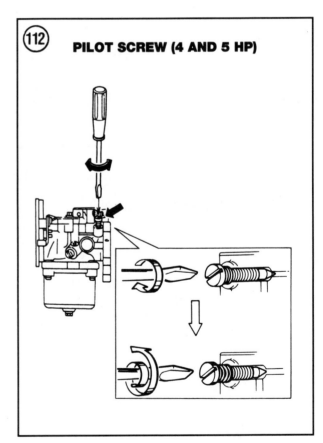

(112)   **PILOT SCREW (4 AND 5 HP)**

(110)   **225-250 HP (76° EFI) MODELS**

(A, **Figure 105**) until the throttle cam (C, **Figure 105**) just contacts the throttle roller (D, **Figure 105**).

f. On C75 and C85 models, position the magneto lever to the full retard stop. Adjust the length of the throttle cam linkage (**Figure 106**) until the cam just contacts the throttle roller.

g. On 75-90 hp models, change the length of the throttle cam linkage (**Figure 107**) until the cam just makes contact with the throttle roller at the specified timing.

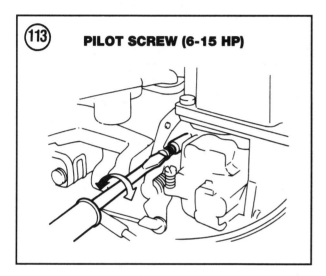

h. On 80 jet and 115-225 hp 90° models, loosen the screw (A, **Figure 108**). Adjust the length of the throttle cam linkage until the cam (B, **Figure 108**) just contacts the roller (C, **Figure 108**) at the specified timing. Ensure that the roller contacts at the mark on the cam. Pivot the roller lever if necessary. Securely tighten the screw (A, **Figure 108**).

i. On 225-250 hp 76° carbureted models, adjustment to a specified timing is not required. Roller-to-cam alignment adjustment is required. Position the throttle plates in the closed position. Loosen the roller lever screw. Adjust the length of the cam linkage until the roller (A, **Figure 109**) just contacts the cam at the indicated mark (B, **Figure 109**). Securely tighten the roller lever screw.

j. On 200-250 hp 76° EFI models, adjustment to a specified timing is not required. Adjust the roller as follows. Loosen the roller lever screw (B, **Figure 110**). Adjust the length of the throttle cam linkage until the throttle roller (A, **Figure 110**) aligns with the throttle cam as indicated (D, **Figure 110**). Tighten the roller lever screw.

4. Securely tighten all jam nuts and check all throttle linkages for sufficient engagement into the connectors.

5. Observe the roller and throttle cam as you slowly advance the throttle to ensure proper cam and roller contact. Check for proper operation of the engine.

PILOT SCREW ADJUSTMENT

> *NOTE*
> *Many models have multiple carburetors. Adjust the pilot screw to the same position on all carburetors unless different settings are recommended.*

> *CAUTION*
> *Use extreme caution when seating the pilot screw prior to adjustment. The tapered seat will be permanently damaged if excessive force is used. Turn the screw with very light force and stop the instant resistance is felt.*

> *NOTE*
> *Pilot screw adjustment is not required on 2 hp models as the carburetor does not use an adjustable pilot jet.*

To assist with the pilot screw location, refer to the illustration for your model.

a. For 3 hp models, refer to **Figure 111**.

b. For 4 and 5 hp models, refer to **Figure 112**.

c. For 6-15 hp models, refer to **Figure 113**.

d. For 20 and 25 hp models, refer to **Figure 114**.

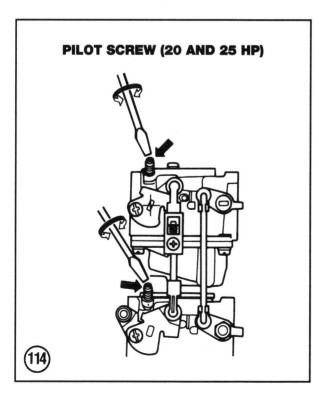

(115) **PILOT SCREW (C30)**

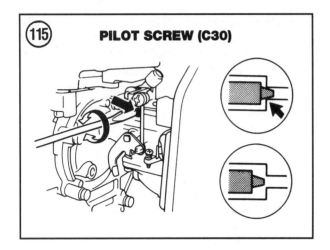

(116) **PILOT SCREW
(30 HP THREE-CYLINDER)**

(117) **PILOT SCREW (C40)**

(118) **PILOT SCREW
(28 JET, 35 JET, 40 HP
[THREE-CYLINDER], AND 50 HP)**

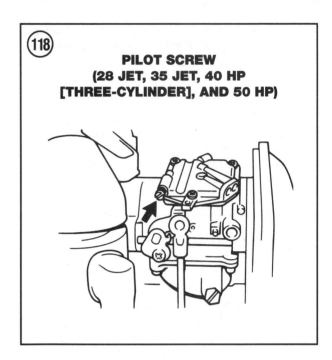

(119) **PILOT SCREW (E48)**

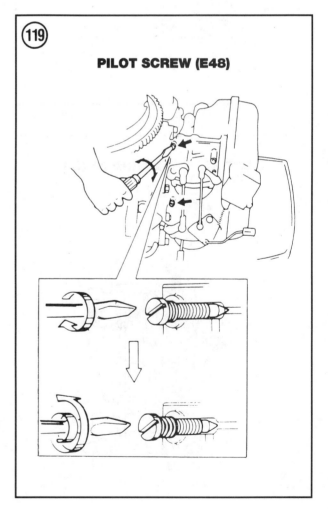

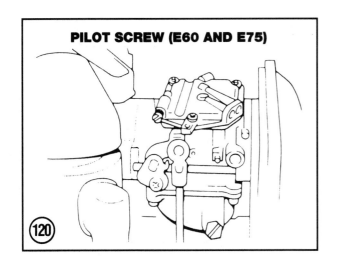

PILOT SCREW (E60 AND E75)

⑫⓪

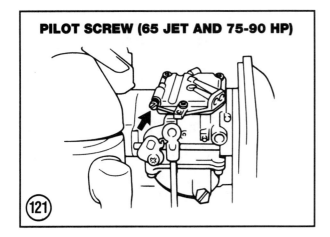

PILOT SCREW (65 JET AND 75-90 HP)

⑫①

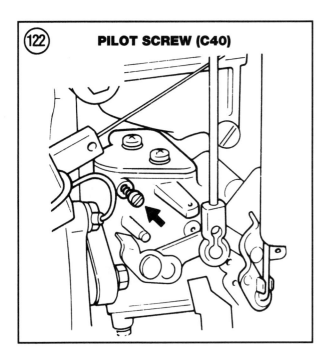

⑫② **PILOT SCREW (C40)**

e. For C30 models, refer to **Figure 115**.

f. For 30 hp (three-cylinder) models, refer to **Figure 116**.

g.

h. For C40 models, refer to **Figure 117**.

i. For 28 jet, 35 jet, 40 three-cylinder and 50 hp models, refer to **Figure 118**.

j. For E48 models, refer to **Figure 119**.

k. For E60 and E75 models, refer to **Figure 120**.

l. For 65 jet and 75-90 hp models, refer to **Figure 121**.

m. For C75 and C85 models, refer to **Figure 122**.

n. For 80 jet and 115-225 hp 90° models, refer to **Figure 123**.

o. For 225-250 hp 76° models, refer to **Figure 124**.

5

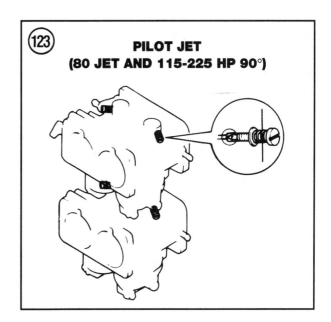

⑫③ **PILOT JET (80 JET AND 115-225 HP 90°)**

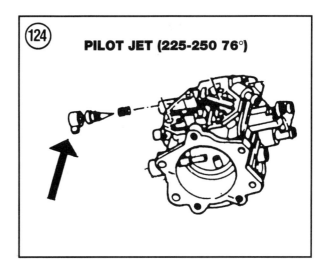

⑫④ **PILOT JET (225-250 76°)**

Use a screwdriver and carefully turn the pilot screw in clockwise until lightly seated. Refer to **Table 4** for adjustment specifications. Turn the pilot screw out counterclockwise to the middle of the specified range.

Prepare the engine for running in a test tank or on the boat as instructed in *Timing Check and Adjustment* in this chapter. Start and run the engine at low speed for about 10 minutes. This will allow the engine to reach operating temperature.

Advance the throttle rapidly from idle and check for proper throttle response. Adjust the pilot screw to a slightly richer, turn counterclockwise, or leaner, turn clockwise, setting if a bog or hesitation is noted when the throttle is increased. Perform the adjustments in 1/8 turn increments, then check the throttle response. Reverse the screw adjustment direction if the bog or hesitation worsens. Adjust all screws to the same settings on multiple carburetor engines. The pilot screw setting must remain within the specification listed in **Table 4**. Refer to *Idle Speed Adjustment* in this chapter for instructions and adjust the idle speed as indicated.

> *WARNING*
> *Use extreme caution when working around a running engine. You can become entangled in the flywheel or the propeller. Stay clear of the flywheel and the propeller shaft.*

> *CAUTION*
> *Never run an outboard without first providing cooling water. The water pump will suffer damage within a few seconds if ran dry. A damaged water pump will result in insufficient water for proper cooling of the powerhead. The engine will overheat and/or suffer*

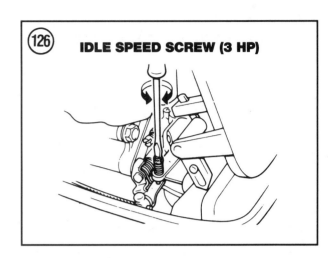

IDLE SPEED SCREW (3 HP)

IDLE SPEED SCREW (4 AND 5 HP)

IDLE SPEED SCREW (6 AND 8 HP)

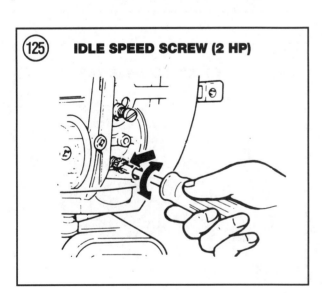

IDLE SPEED SCREW (2 HP)

serious damage if ran without sufficient cooling water.

IDLE SPEED ADJUSTMENT

Refer to *Timing Check and Adjustment* in this chapter for instructions to prepare the engine for running adjustments.

Refer to *Pilot Screw Adjustment* in this chapter then perform the pilot screw adjustment prior to adjusting the idle speed.

For assistance with locating the idle speed screw, refer to the applicable illustration for the your model.

  a. For 2 hp models, refer to **Figure 125**.
  b. For 3 hp models, refer to **Figure 126**.
  c. For 4 and 5 hp models, refer to **Figure 127**.
  d. For 6 and 8 hp models, refer to **Figure 128**.
  e. For 9.9 and 15 hp models, refer to **Figure 129**.
  f. For 20 and 25 hp models, refer to **Figure 130**.
  g. For C30 models, refer to **Figure 131**.
  h. For 30 hp (three-cylinder) models, refer to **Figure 132**.

5

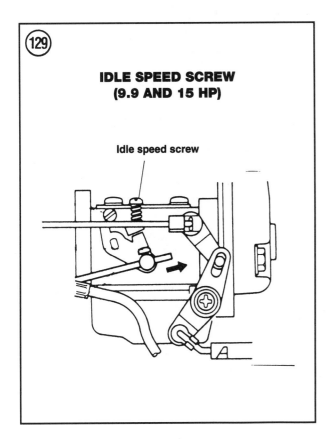

IDLE SPEED SCREW (9.9 AND 15 HP)

Idle speed screw

IDLE SPEED SCREW (C30)

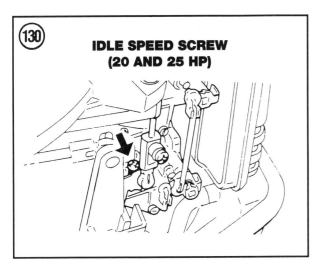

IDLE SPEED SCREW (20 AND 25 HP)

IDLE SPEED SCREW (30 HP THREE-CYLINDER)

i. For C40 models, refer to **Figure 133**.
j. For 28 jet, 35 jet, 40 (three-cylinder) and 50 hp models, refer to **Figure 134** and **Figure 135**.
k. For E48 models, refer to **Figure 136**.
l. For E60 and E75 models, refer to **Figure 137**.
m. For 60 and 70 hp models (except E60), refer to **Figure 138**.
n. For 65 jet and 75-90 hp models (except E75 and 80 jet), refer to **Figure 139**.
o. For C75 and C85 models, refer to **Figure 140**.
p. For 80 jet and 115-225 hp, 90° models, refer to **Figure 141**.

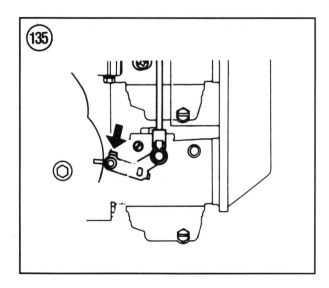

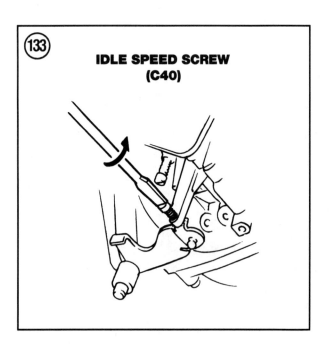

IDLE SPEED SCREW (C40)

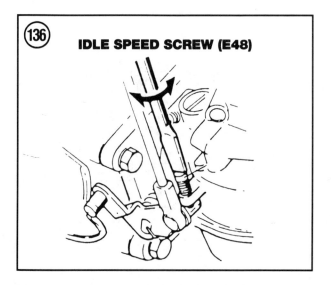

IDLE SPEED SCREW (E48)

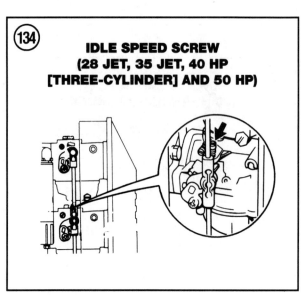

IDLE SPEED SCREW (28 JET, 35 JET, 40 HP [THREE-CYLINDER] AND 50 HP)

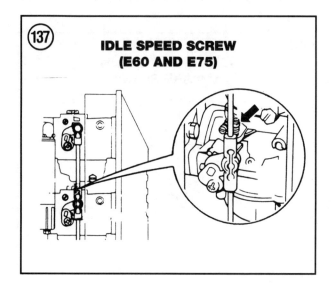

IDLE SPEED SCREW (E60 AND E75)

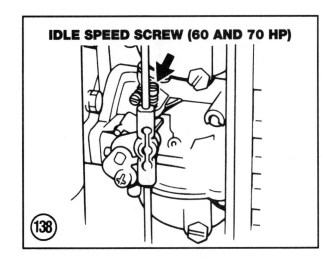

IDLE SPEED SCREW (60 AND 70 HP)

(138)

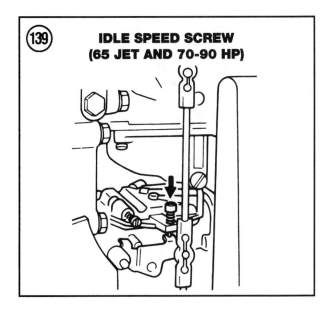

IDLE SPEED SCREW
(65 JET AND 70-90 HP)

(139)

IDLE SPEED SCREW (C75 AND C85)

(140)

q. For 225-250 hp, 76°, carbureted models, refer to **Figure 142**.

r. For 200-250 hp, 76°, EFI models, refer to **Figure 143**.

1. Install a suitable tachometer to one of the spark plug leads. Follow the manufacturer's instructions when connecting the leads.

2. Run the engine for 10 minutes at low speed to bring the engine to normal operating temperature.

3. Check the throttle lever or magneto lever to ensure they are at the full retard or idle stop. Refer to *Throttle Linkage*

5

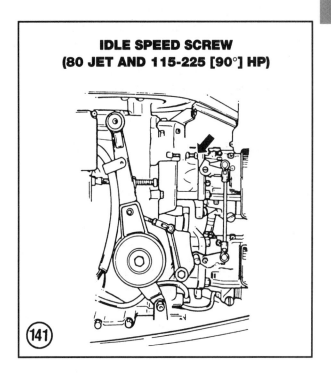

IDLE SPEED SCREW
(80 JET AND 115-225 [90°] HP)

(141)

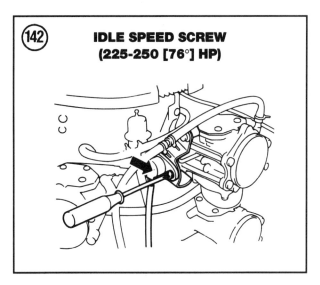

(142) **IDLE SPEED SCREW**
(225-250 [76°] HP)

Adjustment in this chapter if necessary. Place the throttle at the idle position.

4. Refer to **Table 5** for the correct idle speed for the selected model.

5. Locate the idle speed adjusting screw. Observe the idle speed on the tachometer as you adjust the screw. Stop when the idle speed is within the middle of the range listed in **Table 5**.

6. Slowly advance the throttle, then bring it back down to the idle position. Check for binding linkage and/or readjust the idle speed screw if the idle speed does not return to the specified range within 30-40 seconds.

7. Shift the engine into forward gear and read the idle speed. Additional adjustment may be necessary if the speed is not within the specified range. Make sure the neutral rpm reading remains within the specified range.

8. Securely tighten all jam nuts. Remove the tachometer and test prop from the engine as instructed in *Timing Check and Adjustment.*

ENRICHMENT VALVE ADJUSTMENT

Adjust the enrichment valve in its mount (**Figure 144**) or adjust the linkage length to ensure that the choke valve(s) covers the carburetor opening when activated.

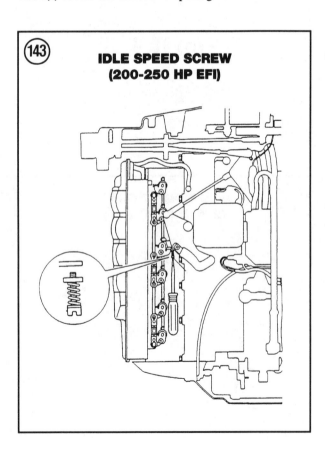

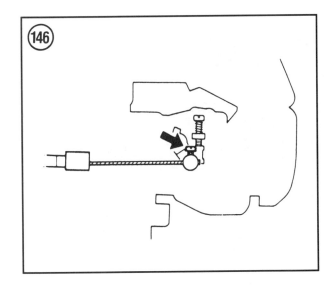

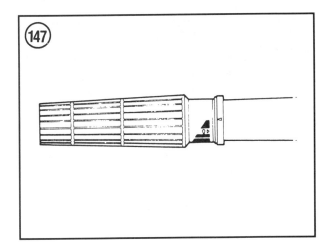

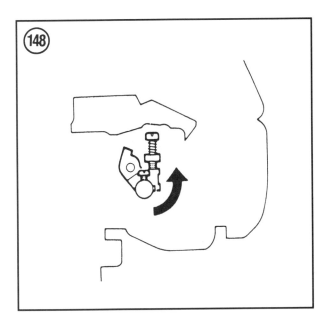

Make sure the choke valve(s) are fully open (**Figure 145**) when the valve is not activated.

THROTTLE CABLE/LINKAGE ADJUSTMENT

Tiller Models

2 hp models

The throttle lever is attached directly to the carburetor and adjustment is not required.

3 hp models

Perform idle speed adjustment prior to adjusting the throttle cable.

1. Loosen the throttle cable anchor screw (**Figure 146**).

2. Place the throttle handle in the idle or lowest speed setting (**Figure 147**).

3. Place the carburetor throttle lever in the idle position (**Figure 148**).

4. Without disturbing the throttle handle setting, lightly pull the cable into the anchor to remove any slack in the cable.

5. Support the carburetor throttle lever and securely tighten the cable anchor screw (**Figure 146**).

6. Rotate the throttle handle to ensure the throttle reaches full throttle (**Figure 149**) and returns to the idle position. Repeat the adjustment steps if required.

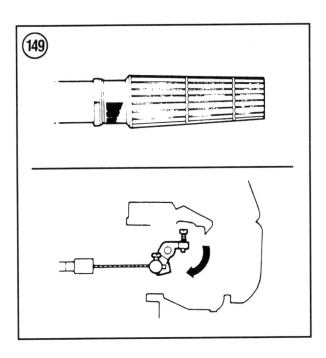

5

4 and 5 hp models

Perform the idle speed adjustment prior to adjusting the throttle cable.

1. Remove the two screws and silencer cover from the carburetor (**Figure 150**).

2. Place the throttle handle in the lowest speed setting (A, **Figure 151**).

3. Loosen the cable anchor screw (D, **Figure 151**) several turns.

4. Position the carburetor throttle lever (C, **Figure 151**) in the idle or closed throttle position.

5. Make sure the cable (F, **Figure 151**) is properly positioned in the cable jacket retainer (G, **Figure 151**).

6. Without disturbing the throttle handle setting or carburetor throttle lever position, lightly pull the cable wire (B, **Figure 151**) to remove the slack from the cable. Securely tighten the cable anchor screw (D, **Figure 151**).

7. Operate the throttle several times to ensure the throttle reaches the full throttle position (E, **Figure 151**) with the throttle lever slightly away from the stopper, and returns to the idle position. Repeat the adjustment steps if required.

8. Install the silencer cover and check for proper operation before putting the engine into service.

6-60 hp models

Adjust the tiller throttle cables to ensure that the idle and full throttle positions are reached. Refer to *STATIC TIMING ADJUSTMENT* in this chapter to identify the full advance and full retard stops. All adjustments are made with the engine off and the spark plugs removed. Disconnect both battery cables during the adjustment.

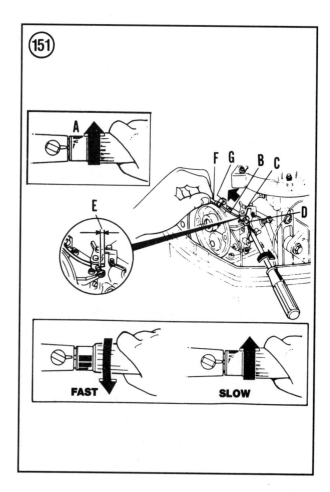

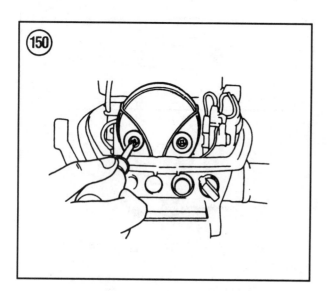

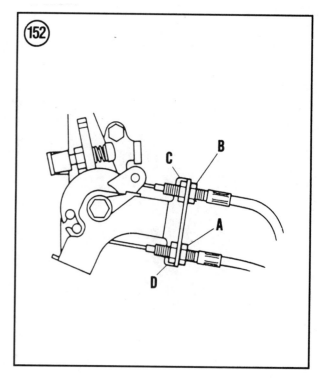

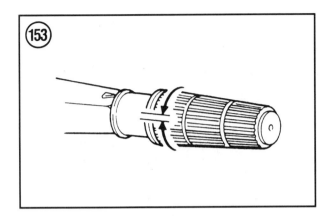

1. Position the throttle handle in the idle speed setting. Loosen the jam nuts (A and B, **Figure 152**).

2. Adjust the nuts (C and D, **Figure 152**) until the throttle returns to the full retard stop each time the throttle handle reaches the idle or slow position.

3. Adjust the nuts (C and D, **Figure 152**) until the magneto just reaches the full advance stop each time the throttle is moved to the full throttle or fast position.

4. Check the amount of slack or free movement in the handle (**Figure 153**). Adjust both nuts (C and D, **Figure 152**) until a slight amount of free play or slack is felt.

5. Securely tighten the jam nuts (A and B, **Figure 152**).

Remote Control Models

Variations exist among the models as to type and location of the throttle cable connection. This section provides a typical cable adjustment.

1. Remove both battery cables and all spark plugs from the engine.

2. Locate the throttle cable connection on the engine (A, **Figure 154**). The shift cable (B, **Figure 154**) will move before the throttle cable when the shift handle is moved.

3. Position the remote control in the idle and neutral position. Disconnect the throttle cable from the attaching point (**Figure 155**, typical).

5

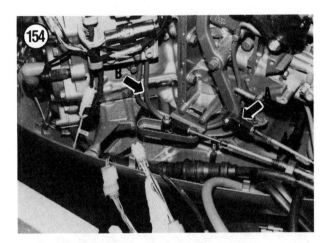

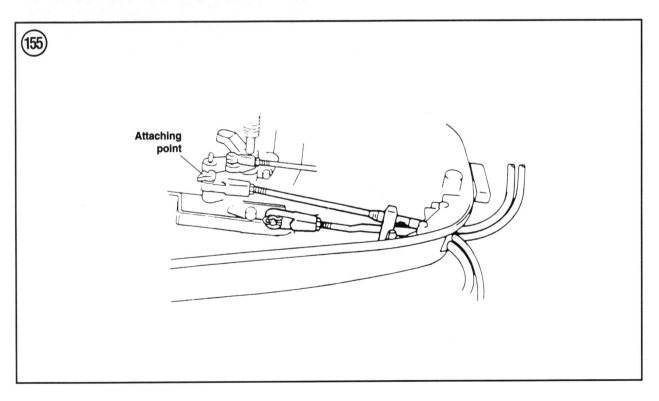

Attaching point

4. Lift the cable from the attaching point. Loosen the jam nut (A, **Figure 156**) at the cable end. Position the remote control and the magneto lever in the closed throttle and full retard position. Adjust the cable end (B, **Figure 156**) until the cable will slide over the attaching post without moving the lever.

5. Check the cable end for adequate thread engagement (C, **Figure 156**). A minimum of 8 mm (0.31 in.) of engagement is required (**Figure 156**). Properly engage the cable fasteners.

6. Move the throttle cable from idle to full throttle several times. Make sure the magneto lever just reaches the full advance stop and returns to the full retard stop each time without binding or a loose feel. Check the control box and repeat the adjustment steps if a problem is noted. Securely tighten the jam nut on the cable end.

7. Install the spark plugs. Connect the battery cables to the battery.

SHIFT ADJUSTMENT

WARNING
Avoid serious bodily injury or death. Remove all spark plug leads and both battery cables prior to removing the propeller.

Tiller Models

2 hp models

Shift adjustment is not required as these models use a non-shifting gearcase.

3-30 hp models

Shift adjustment is made at the upper-to-lower shift shaft connector (**Figure 157** typical). This section provides a typical shift adjustment.

1. Remove all spark plugs and disconnect both battery cables at the battery.

2. Refer to Chapter Nine for procedures to access the shift shaft connector.

3. Remove the propeller from the gearcase as instructed in Chapter Nine.

4. Loosen the connector bolt until both shift shafts are just free to move. Position the shift handle in the neutral position (**Figure 158**).

5. Move the lower shift shaft down it is in the neutral position. The propeller shaft can be rotated both directions when neutral is selected.

6. Ensure that both shift shafts are fully engaged in the connector (**Figure 159** typical). Tighten the shift shaft connector. Look for additional adjustment points along the

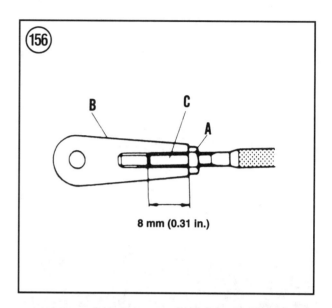

8 mm (0.31 in.)

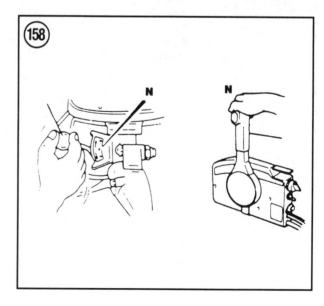

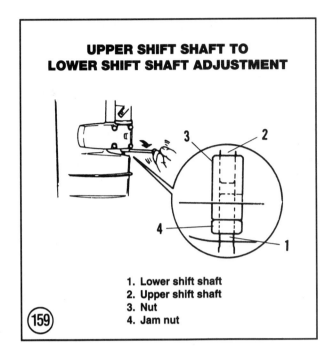

UPPER SHIFT SHAFT TO LOWER SHIFT SHAFT ADJUSTMENT

1. Lower shift shaft
2. Upper shift shaft
3. Nut
4. Jam nut

(159)

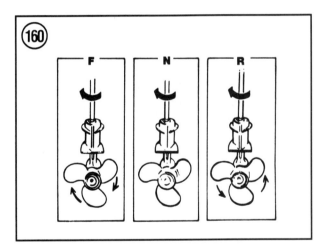

(160)

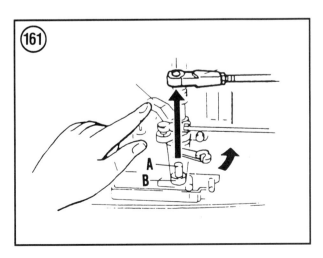

(161)

linkage if you are unable to properly engaged in the connector with proper shift engagements.

7. Install the propeller, then check for proper shift operation (**Figure 160**).

8. Install the spark plugs. Connect the battery cables to the battery.

40-60 hp models

Variations exist among the models as to the type and location of the shift cable connection. This section provides typical adjustment procedures.

1. Remove the spark plugs and disconnect both battery cables at the battery.

2. Shift the tiller handle control to the neutral position (**Figure 158**).

3. Locate the shift cable connection on the engine. Loosen the cable fastener or pin, and lift the cable end from the attaching point (A, **Figure 161**). Note the location and orientation of any washer or spacer at the attaching point (B, **Figure 161**).

4. On models with a shift lever that resembles the type in **Figure 161** perform Step 5. On models with the shift lever that resembles the type in **Figure 162** perform Step 6.

5. Move the engine mounted, not the tiller, shift lever (**Figure 161**) to determine the center of the neutral detent. This is the midpoint between the forward and the reverse gear shift points. Place the lever in the middle of the neutral range. Go to Step 7.

6. Move the shift attaching point to the center of the slide (B, **Figure 162**) and align with the marking. Position the shift handle to the neutral position (A, **Figure 162**).

7. For both types of connection, loosen the jam nut (D, **Figure 162**). Adjust the shift cable to allow the cable end to slide over its attaching point without moving the lever. Securely tighten the jam nut. Be sure to provide adequate engagement of the threaded end into the cable end. A minimum of 8.0 mm (0.31 in.) is required.

8. Securely attach all fasteners, spacers and washers. Check for proper operation of the shift (**Figure 160**). Install the spark plugs. Connect the battery cables to the battery.

Remote Control Models

Variation exists between the models as to the type and location of the shift cable connection (**Figure 163**). This section provides a typical adjustment procedure.

1. Remove the spark plugs. Disconnect both battery cables from the battery.

2. Shift the remote control into neutral gear (**Figure 158**).

3. Locate the shift cable attaching points on the engine. Remove the shift cable fasteners at the attaching points. Note the location and orientation of the fasteners, washers and spacers prior to removal.

4. On models with a connection that resembles the type in **Figure 161** perform Step 5. On models with a connection that resembles the type in **Figure 162** go to Step 6. For V4 and V6 models go to Step 7.

5. Move the shift lever (**Figure 161**) to determine the center of the neutral detent. This is the midpoint between the forward and reverse gear shift points. Place the shift lever in the middle of the neutral range. Go to Step 8.

6. Move the shift cable attaching point to the center of the slide (B, **Figure 162**) and align with the marking. Go to Step 8.

7. Move the shift lever to align the pin (A, **Figure 164**) with the marking on the lower engine cover (B, **Figure 164**).

8. Loosen the jam nut on the cable end (B, **Figure 165**). Adjust the cable end to allow the cable to slide over its attaching point without moving the shift linkage or lever. Be sure to provide adequate engagement of the threaded end of the cable into the connector. A minimum of 8.0 mm (0.31 in.) is required.

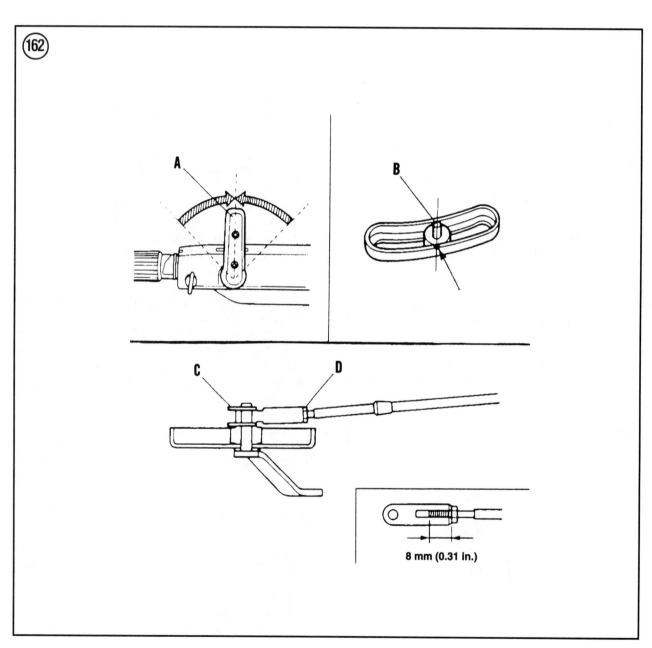

8 mm (0.31 in.)

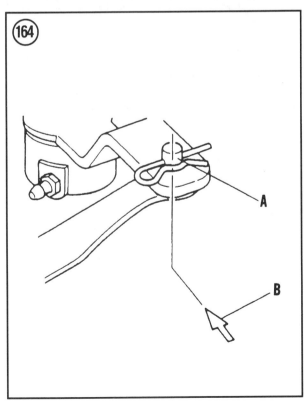

9. Install all fasteners, washers and spacers (A, **Figure 165**). Securely tighten the jam nut (B, **Figure 165**) and the cable fasteners. Check for proper operation as indicated (**Figure 160**). Counter rotation models are the opposite of what is indicated in **Figure 160**.

Jet Models

> *NOTE*
> *The linkage that connects the scoop lever to the cable pivot bracket must attach to the lower hole on the scoop lever.*

On jet drive models the shift cable is connected directly to the jet drive unit. Proper adjustment of the jet drive unit will allow the reverse scoop to completely clear the discharge nozzle when in forward (**Figure 166**). The reverse

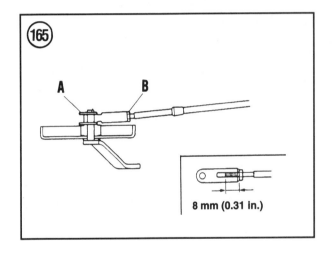

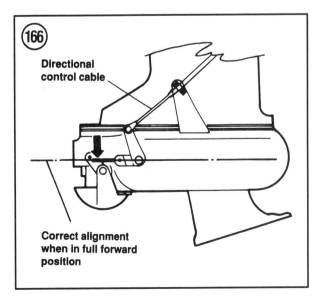

scoop must completely cover the discharge nozzle when in reverse. Neutral adjustment will position the scoop half-way between these points.

To adjust the jet drive, first position the control in forward. Adjust the cable until the cable pivot bracket is aligned with the linkage that connects the cable bracket to the scoop arm (**Figure 166**). The scoop should contact the rubber pad on the bottom of the jet drive.

Position the shift handle to the neutral position. Loosen the nut (**Figure 167**) and move the stop to contact the scoop lever. Securely tighten the nut (**Figure 167**). Check for proper directional control before putting the engine into service.

TRIM SENDER ADJUSTMENT

Adjustment to the trim sender involves moving the sender within the limits of the adjusting slot until the trim gauge reads correctly.

For models with the analog gauge (**Figure 168**), check the reading on the gauge when the engine reaches the full down position. The needle should reach the down mark (A, **Figure 168**) at the same time the engine reaches its down limit.

For models with the digital gauge (**Figure 169**), check the reading when the engine reaches the full down position. One segment on the gauge should be displayed with the engine in the full down position.

When an adjustment is required, raise the engine to the full tilt position. Block the engine to prevent it from falling. Loosen the screws until the sender will barely move on the mount. Remove the block and position the engine in the

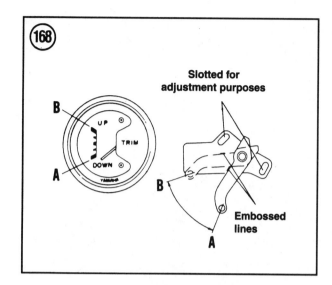

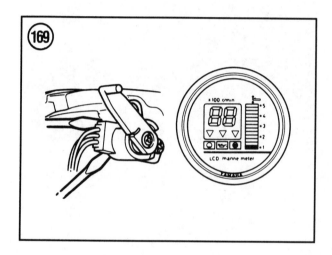

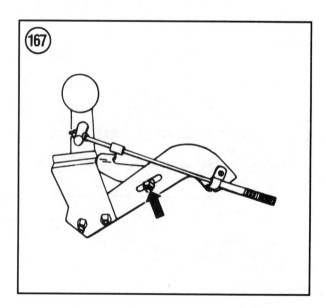

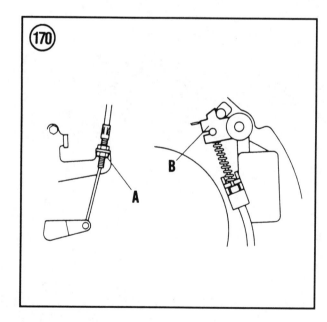

full down position. Use a screwdriver to move the sender slightly within the adjusting slot (**Figure 169**) until a correct reading is indicated on the gauge. Raise the engine to access the screws and block the engine. Securely tighten the sender retaining screws. Remove the blocks, then operate the trim to the up and down limits to check for proper gauge readings.

START IN GEAR
PROTECTION ADJUSTMENT

This section will provide the procedures to adjust the start in gear protection cable.

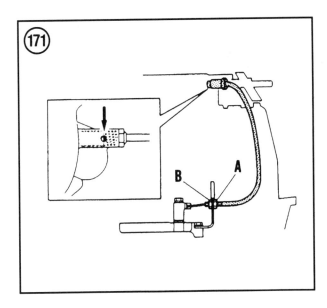

9.9 and 15 hp Models

1. Shift the engine to neutral. Remove the spark plugs. Disconnect both battery cables on electric start models.
2. Loosen the jam nut on the cable (A, **Figure 170**).
3. Adjust the other cable nut until the marking on the rewind housing is aligned with the end of the plunger (B, **Figure 170**)
4. Securely tighten the jam nut (A, **Figure 170**). Shift the engine to forward then pull the rewind starter. Shift the engine to reverse then pull the rewind starter.
5. Repeat the adjustments and check for worn or damaged components if the rewind starter will activate in either forward or reverse. Replace worn or damaged components then adjust the cable.
6. Install the spark plugs. Connect the battery cables to the battery.

6, 8 and 20-50 hp Models

1. Shift the engine to neutral. Remove the spark plugs. Disconnect both battery cables on electric start models.
2. Loosen the jam nut (A, **Figure 171**). Adjust the nut (B, **Figure 171**) until the plunger is aligned with the center of the alignment hole in the rewind housing.
3. Securely tighten the jam nut (A, **Figure 171**). Shift the engine into forward, then pull the rewind starter. Shift the engine to reverse then pull the rewind starter.
4. Repeat the adjustments and check for worn or damaged components if the rewind starter will activate in either forward or reverse. Replace worn or damaged components, then adjust the cable.
5. Install the spark plugs. Connect the battery cables to the battery.

Model	Full retard	Full advance
Table 1 PISTON POSITION (TIMING POINTER ADJUSTMENT)		
Model	**Full retard**	**Full advance**
2 hp	*	*
3 hp	*	*
4, 5 hp	*	*
6, 8 hp	0.04-0.12 mm (0.0015-0.0047 in.) BTDC	4.53-5.05 mm (0.179-0.199 in.) BTDC
9.9, 15 hp	0.08-0.16 mm (0.003-0.007 in.) ATDC	3.95-4.50 mm (0.155-0.177 in.) BTDC
20, 25 hp (two-cylinder)	*	3.34 mm (0.13 in.)
E48	0.06-0.18 mm (0.003-0.007 in.) BTDC	2.56-3.10 mm (0.100-0.122 in.) BTDC
60 hp	*	3.23 mm (0.127 in.) BTDC
E60	0.03 (0.001in.) ATDC	2.42 mm (0.095 in.) BTDC
70 hp	*	2.68 mm (0.106 in.) BTDC
E75	0.03 (0.001 in.) ATDC	3.41 mm (0.134 in.) BTDC
75-80 (except E75, 80 jet)	*	2.83 mm (0.111 in.) BTDC
	(continued)	

Table 1 PISTON POSITION (TIMING POINTER ADJUSTMENT) (continued)

Model	Full retard	Full advance
65 jet and 90 hp	*	3.41 mm (0.134 in.) BTDC
C75	*	*
C85	*	*
80 jet, 115	*	3.91 mm (0.150 in.) BTDC
130hp	*	3.05 mm (0.120 in.) BTDC
105 jet, C150,	*	2.28 mm (0.009 in.) BTDC
D150, P150	–	–
150TR, S175TR	*	3.05 mm (0.120 in.) BTDC
P175TR, P200TR	*	3.33 mm (0.130 in.) BTDC
L200TR	*	2.53 mm (0.100 in.) BTDC
200TR, 225	*	2.78 mm (0.110 in.) BTDC
200-250 (76°)	*	*

*Timing is adjusted by means other than piston position.

Table 2 PICKUP TIMING SPECIFICATIONS

Model	Timing
3-5 hp	6° BTDC
6, 8 hp	4° BTDC
9.9, 15 hp	5° ATDC
20, 25 hp (two-cylinder)	3° ATDC
C25 (two-cylinder)	2° ATDC
25 hp (three-cylinder)	2° ATDC
C30 (two-cylinder)	–
30 hp (three-cylinder)	5° ATDC
28 jet, 35 jet, 40, 50 hp	7° ATDC
E48	3-5° BTDC
E60	2° ATDC
E75	2° BTDC
60 and 70 hp (except E60)	6-8° ATDC
65 jet and 75-90 hp (except 80 jet)	7-9° ATDC
80 jet, 115 and 130 hp	5° ATDC
150-200 hp (90° V)	7° ATDC
225 hp (90° V)	6° ATDC

Table 3 MAXIMUM TIMING

Model	Maximum timing	Maximum timing speed
2 hp	16-20° BTDC	5000
3 hp	Visible in right window	5000
4, 5 hp	Visible in right window	5500
6 hp	34-36° BTDC	4700
8 hp	34-36° BTDC	5500
9.9, 15 hp	30° BTDC	5500
20 hp	25° BTDC	5000
25 hp (two-cylinder)	25° BTDC	5000
25 hp (three-cylinder)	23-27° BTDC	5000
C30 (two-cylinder)	23-27° BTDC	5000
30 hp (three-cylinder)	25° BTDC	5000

(continued)

Table 3 MAXIMUM TIMING (continued)

Model	Maximum timing	Maximum timing speed
C40 (two-cylinder)	22° BTDC	5000
40, 50 hp (three-cylinder)	25° BTDC	5500
E48	19-21° BTDC	5000
E60	19-21° BTDC	5000
E75	22° BTDC	5000
60	22° BTDC	5000
70-80 hp (except E75)	19-21° BTDC	5000
65 jet and 90 hp	21-23° BTDC	5000
80 jet, 115	25° BTDC	5000
130 hp	22° BTDC	5000
105 jet, C150, D150, P150	19° BTDC	5000
150TR and S175TR	22° BTDC	5000
P175TR and P200TR	23° BTDC	5000
L200TR	20° BTDC	5000
200TR and 225 (90°)	21° BTDC	5000

5

Table 4 PILOT SCREW ADJUSTMENT

Model	Turns out
3 hp	1-1 1/2
4 hp	1 1/2-2
5 hp	1 1/4-1 3/4
6 hp	7/8-1 3/8
8 hp	7/8-1 3/8
9.9, 15 hp	1 1/4-1 3/4
20 hp	1 3/4-3 1/4
25 hp (two-cylinder)	1 1/4-2 3/4
25 hp (three-cylinder)	1 3/4-2 1/4
C30 (two-cylinder)	1 1/4-1 3/4
30 hp (three-cylinder)	
Top carburetor	5/8-7/8
Middle carburetor	1 1/2-2
Bottom carburetor	7/8-1 1/8
C40 (two-cylinder)	1 1/2-2
40 hp (three-cylinder)	1 1/4-1 3/4
50 hp (three-cylinder) manual start	1 3/8-1 7/8
50 hp (three-cylinder) electric start	1 1/8-1 5/8
E48	1 1/8-1 5/8
E60	1 1/4-1 3/4
E75	1-1 1/2
60 hp (except E60)	1 1/4-1 3/4
70 hp	1-1 1/2
80 hp	1 1/8-1 5/8
65 jet and 90 hp	1-1 1/2
C75	1-1 1/2
C85	1-1 1/4
80 jet, 115 hp	3/8-7/8
130 hp	5/8-1 1/8
C150	3/4-1 1/4
S150TR, L150	1-1 1/2
P150, D150	
Starboard side screws	1 5/16-1 3/4
Port side screws	13/16-1 5/16
S175TR	13/16-1 5/16

(continued)

Table 4 PILOT SCREW ADJUSTMENT (continued)

Model	Turns out
P175TR	
Starboard side screws	1 3/8-1 7/8
Port side screws	7/8-1/3/8
200TR	7/8-1/3/8
S200TR	
Starboard side screws	7/8-1 3/8
Port side screws	3/8-7/8
L200TR	
Starboard side screws	7/8-1 3/8
Port side screws	3/8-7/8
P200TR	
Starboard side screws	1-1 1/2
Port side screws	1/2-1
225 hp (90°)	1-1 1/4
225, 250 hp (76°)	1/2-3/4

TABLE 5 ENGINE IDLE SPEED

Model	Idle rpm (neutral)	Idle speed (in gear)
2 hp	–	1100-1200
3 hp	1150-1250	1050
4, 5 hp	1100-1200	1000
6, 8 hp	850-950	700-800
9.9, 15 hp	700-800	650-750
20, 25 hp (two-cylinder)	700-800	600
C25	950	850
25 hp (three-cylinder)	750	600
C30 (two-cylinder)	1150	950
30 (three-cylinder)	750	650
C40 (two-cylinder)	1150	950
40, 50 hp (three-cylinder)	750-850	600-700
E48	1200-1300	1000-1100
E60	950-1050	800-900
E75	750-850	600-700
60-90 (except E60, 80 jet)	750-850	600-700
80 jet, 115, 130	700-800	600-700
105 jet, 150, 175 hp	675-725	550-600
200TR, S200TR, L200TR	675-725	550-600
P200TR	675-725	575-625
225 hp (90°)	725-775	575-625
225, 250 hp (76°)		
(except EFI models)	675-725	600-650
200-250 (76° EFI)	700-760	600-660

Table 6 TEST PROPELLERS

Model	Propeller part No.
4, 5 hp	90890-01630
6, 8 hp	90890-01625
9.9, 15 hp	YB-1619
20, 25 and 30 hp (three-cylinder)	YB-1621
	(continued)

Table 6 TEST PROPELLERS (continued)

Model	Propeller part No.
C30	YB-1629
40-90 hp (except C75, C85)	YB-1611
C75, C85	YB-1620
115-130 hp	YB-1624
150-175 hp	YB-1626

5

Chapter Six

Fuel System

This chapter provides instructions for removal, repair and installation of fuel system components. Fuel system components covered include fuel tanks, fuel hoses, connectors, and fuel pumps. In addition, carburetors, enrichment valves, reed valves and EFI fuel delivery components are covered.

Diagrams are provided to assist with fuel hose routing and identifying component mounting locations. Refer to these when removing and installing components. Drawings are also provided for the various carburetors and fuel system components. Refer to these drawings when disassembling or assembling components.

Specifications for fuel system components are provided in **Tables 1-5**. They are located at the end of this chapter.

> *WARNING*
> *Use caution when working with the fuel system to avoid damage to property, potential bodily injury or death. Never smoke around fuel of fuel vapor. Make sure that no flame or source of ignition is present in the work area. Flame or sparks can ignite fuel or vapor resulting in fire or explosion.*

Use eye protection and work in a well-ventilated area when repairing the fuel system. Take all necessary Precautions against fire or explosion. Always disconnect the battery cables *before* servicing any outboard. Pay close attention when removing and installing components, especially carburetors, to avoid installing them in the wrong location. Mark them if necessary.

When disassembling carburetors, pay very close attention to location and orientation of the internal parts. Jets will normally have a jet number stamped on the side or opening end. Replacement jets can be purchased at a Yamaha dealership or carburetor specialty shop. Replacement jets must have the same size and shape of opening as the original jets. Engines used at higher altitudes or in extreme environments may require alternate jets to be installed. Contact a Yamaha dealership for information if the engine will be used in these environments.

Use great care and patience when removing jets and other threaded or pressed-in components. Clean the passage without removing the jet if it cannot be easily removed. Carburetor jets are easily damaged if the screwdriver slips in the slot. Never install a damaged jet in the carburetor as the fuel or air flow characteristics may be altered. Altering the fuel and air flow can cause performance problems or potentially serious engine damage.

To avoid fuel or air leakage, replace all gaskets, seals or O-rings anytime a fuel system component is disassembled.

The most important step in carburetor repair is the cleaning process. Use a good quality solvent to remove the varnish-like deposits that commonly occur in fuel systems. Spray-type carburetor cleaners available at auto parts stores are effective in removing most stubborn deposits. Avoid using any solvent that is not suitable for aluminum. Remove all plastic or rubber components from the fuel pump, carburetor or filter assembly before cleaning them with solvent. Gently scrape away gasket material with a razor scraper. To prevent leakage, avoid removing any of the material from the components. Use a stiff brush and solvent to remove deposits from the carburetor bowl. Never use a wire brush as delicate surfaces can be quickly damaged. Use compressed air to blow out all passages and orifices. A piece of straw from a broom works well to clean out small passages. Never use stiff wire for this purpose as the wire may enlarge the size of the passage and alter the carburetor calibration. Allow the component to soak in the solvent if the deposits are particularly difficult to remove. Never compromise proper cleaning in the repair process. Continue to clean until deposits and debris are removed.

Fuel Tank and Fuel Hose Components

Three types of fuel tanks are used with Yamaha outboards. These types are integral tanks, portable remote tanks and vessel mounted tanks. Integral tanks (**Figure 1**) are mounted on 2-5 hp models. An optional valve that allows either the use of a remote or the integral tank is available for 4 and 5 hp models.

Portable remote tanks (**Figure 2**) are used on 6-250 hp models. Portable fuel tanks are manufactured by several companies. Go to a marine repair shop or marine dealership when purchasing parts for the tank. The cleaning and repair procedures are consistent for all brands.

Vessel mounted fuel tanks are used on some 6-250 hp models. They are sometimes difficult to access. Removable panels are used in some boats to provide access to the fitting and sender assembly. The major components requiring service include the fuel pickup, fuel level sender, fuel fill fitting and the antisiphon device.

6

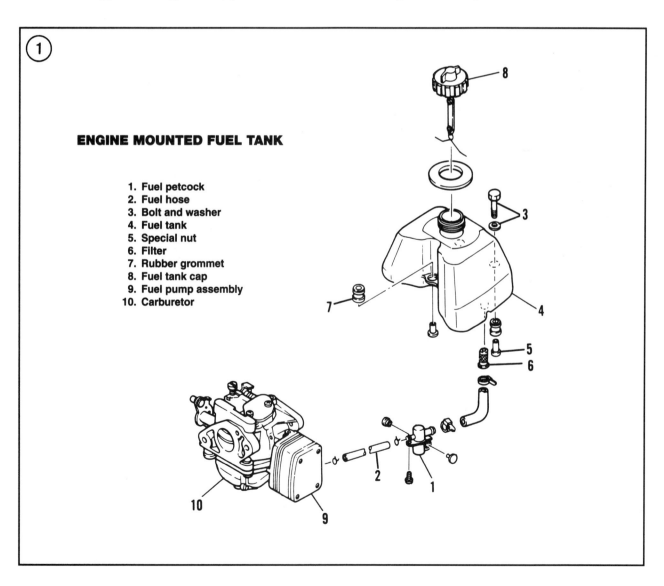

(1)

ENGINE MOUNTED FUEL TANK

1. Fuel petcock
2. Fuel hose
3. Bolt and washer
4. Fuel tank
5. Special nut
6. Filter
7. Rubber grommet
8. Fuel tank cap
9. Fuel pump assembly
10. Carburetor

Integral Fuel Tank Removal and Inspection

1. Turn the fuel petcock to the OFF position. Drain any residual fuel from the fuel hose and carburetor.

2. For 3-5 hp models, carefully disconnect the fuel hose clamp and remove the fuel hose that connects the carburetor to the fuel petcock (**Figure 1**). Use a shop towel for any residual fuel that spills from the fuel hose. Remove the tank mounting bolt and washer located at the rear of the fuel tank (**Figure 1**). The bolt is located on the lower motor cover and under the fuel tank on 4 and 5 hp models.

3. For 2 hp models, carefully disconnect the fuel hose clamp and remove the fuel hose at the petcock fitting. Use a shop towel for any residual fuel that spills from the hose. Remove the bolt and grommet (1, **Figure 3**) located at the rear of the rewind housing. Remove the tank mounting bolt and washers (2-4, **Figure 3**) located at the rear of the fuel tank.

4. Carefully remove the tank from the engine.

5. Operate the fuel petcock and check for proper operation. Replace if necessary.

6. Remove the fill cap from the tank. Empty the fuel into a suitable container for proper disposal. Put a small amount of solvent in the fuel tank and shake it for a few minutes, then empty the tank. Inspect the tank mounted filter for blockage or damage. Replace if required. Thoroughly drain the tank and dry it with compressed air. Inspect the tank for contaminants. Repeat the cleaning process until the tank is completely clean. Inspect the tank for cracks or other physical damage and replace the tank if any defects are noted.

7. The installation is the reverse of removal. Be sure to inspect all fuel hoses and clamps. Replace any fuel hose that has cracks, holes or possible leaks. Replace any fuel hose clamp that is physically damaged, corroded or lacks spring tension. Tighten all fasteners securely. Check for and correct all fuel leakage.

Portable Fuel Tank

Portable remote fuel tanks may require periodic cleaning and inspection. If water is present in the tank, be sure to inspect the remainder of the fuel system for potential contamination.

1. Remove the fuel hose connector and fuel tank cap (**Figure 2**). Drain the fuel into a suitable container for proper disposal.

2. Remove the screws that retain the fuel metering assembly. Carefully remove the fuel metering assembly from the tank. Never force the assembly or damage may occur to the assembly. Remove and discard the gasket that is between the fuel metering assembly and the fuel tank.

3. Check for free movement of the float arm on the fuel metering assembly. Replace the assembly if binding cannot be corrected by bending the float arm into the correct position. Inspect the float. Replace the float if any physical damage is noted or if it appears to be saturated with fuel.

4. Add a small amount of solvent to the fuel tank. Block the fuel metering assembly opening with a shop towel. Install the fuel tank cap. Shake the tank for a few minutes. Drain the solvent and blow dry with compressed air.

5. Inspect the tank's internal surfaces for the presence of rust corrosion or debris. Replace the tank if internal or

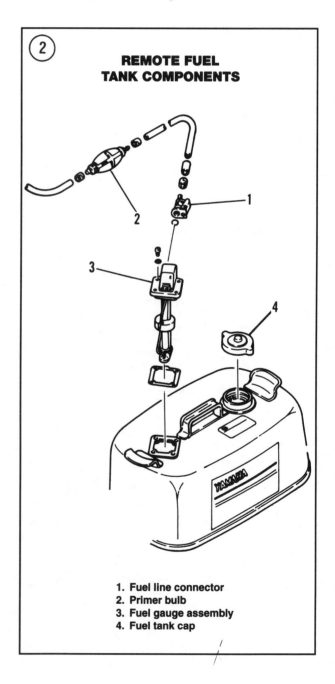

REMOTE FUEL TANK COMPONENTS

1. Fuel line connector
2. Primer bulb
3. Fuel gauge assembly
4. Fuel tank cap

external rust or corrosion is present or if physical damage is evident. Replace the tank if fuel leakage is present or suspected. Repeat Step 4 if residual deposits or debris are found in the tank.

6. Install the fuel metering assembly to the tank with a new gasket (**Figure 2**). Tighten all fasteners securely. Check for and correct all fuel leaks.

Vessel Mounted Fuel Tank

The only components that can be serviced without major disassembly of the boat include the fuel pickup, fuel fill,

fuel level sender and antisiphon device. These components are available from many different suppliers. Removal and inspection procedures vary by model and brand. Contact the tank manufacturer or boat manufacturer for specific instructions.

Primer Bulb

The primer bulb is located between the fuel tank and the engine. See **Figure 2**. A hand operated pressure pump is required to properly inspect this component.

1. Disconnect the hose that connects the fuel tank to the engine. Drain the fuel from the hose into a suitable container for proper disposal. Remove the fuel hose clamps at both fuel hose connections to the primer bulb and discard them.

2. Squeeze the primer bulb until fully collapsed. Replace the bulb if it does not freely expand when released or sticks in the collapsed position. Replace the bulb if it appears weathered, has surface cracks or is hard to squeeze.

3. Connect a hand operated pressure pump hose to the fitting on the fuel tank side of the primer bulb. As the pressure pump is operated, air must exit on the fitting on the engine side of the primer bulb. Replace the primer bulb if air does not exit the fitting.

4. Connect the pressure pump to the fitting on the engine side of the primer bulb. Air must not exit the fitting on the fuel tank side of the primer bulb as the pump is operated. Replace the bulb if air exits the fitting.

5. Connect the fuel hose to the bulb. Install new fuel hose clamps. Note the direction of flow (**Figure 4**) as the new bulb is installed onto the fuel hose. Arrows are present on the new bulb for correct orientation.

Fuel Hoses

Fuel hoses vary by model. Refer to the illustrations for correct connections and routing. Use only Yamaha replace-

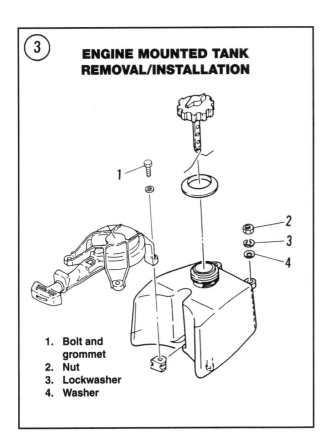

(3)

ENGINE MOUNTED TANK REMOVAL/INSTALLATION

1. Bolt and grommet
2. Nut
3. Lockwasher
4. Washer

6

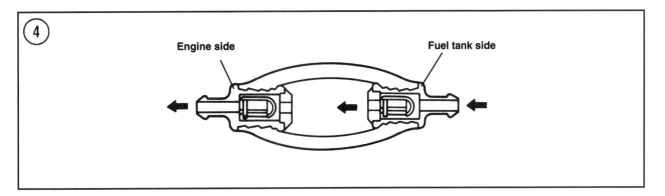

(4)

Engine side   Fuel tank side

ment hoses or hose that meets US Coast Guard requirements for marine applications. Never install a fuel hose that is smaller in diameter than the original hose. Replace all fuel hoses at the same time unless unusual circumstances create the need to replace only one fuel hose. When one hose fails, other hoses are suspect.

Replace hoses that feel sticky to the touch, feel spongy, are hard and brittle or have surface cracks. Replace a hose that has split on the end instead of cutting the end off and reattaching the hose. The hose will likely split again. To avoid hose failure or interference with other components,

never cut the replacement hose shorter or longer than the original.

Fuel Hose Connectors

Connectors used on fuel hoses include the quick connect type (1, **Figure 2**), spring type hose clamp (5, **Figure 5**) and plastic locking tie type of clamp. The plastic locking tie type of clamp must be cut to be removed. Replace them with the correct Yamaha part. Some plastic locking ties are not suitable for the application and may fail. Use the same

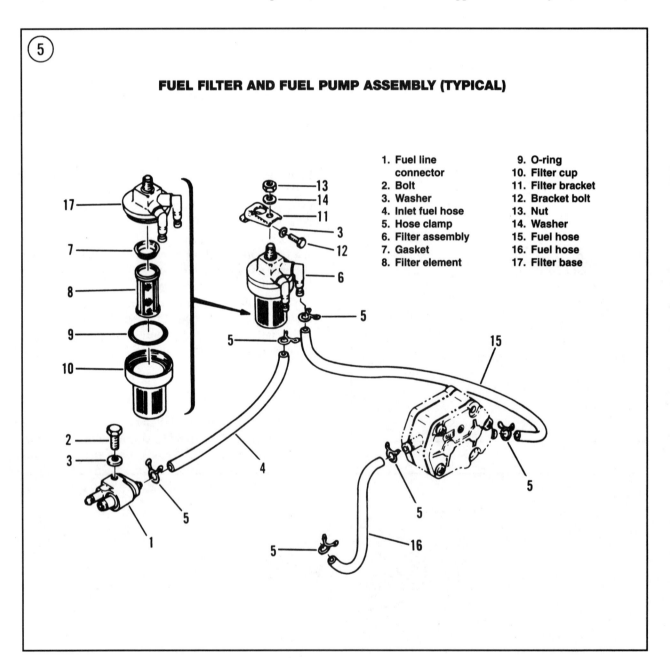

FUEL FILTER AND FUEL PUMP ASSEMBLY (TYPICAL)

1. Fuel line connector
2. Bolt
3. Washer
4. Inlet fuel hose
5. Hose clamp
6. Filter assembly
7. Gasket
8. Filter element
9. O-ring
10. Filter cup
11. Filter bracket
12. Bracket bolt
13. Nut
14. Washer
15. Fuel hose
16. Fuel hose
17. Filter base

width as the removed plastic locking tie. Pull the end through the clamp until the hose is securely fastened and will not rotate on the fitting. Avoid pulling the clamp too tight as the clamp may fail or be damaged and loosen.

The quick connect clamp should be inspected by squeezing the primer bulb while checking for leakage at the engine side quick connector. Replace the connector(s) if leakage is observed at the engine or fuel tank end.

The spring type clamps are removed by squeezing the ends together with a pair of pliers while carefully moving the clamp away from the fitting. Replace the clamp if corroded, bent, deformed or if it has lost spring tension.

WARNING
Fuel leakage can lead to fire or explosion with potential bodily injury, death or destruction of property. Always check for and correct fuel leaks after any repair is made to the fuel system.

Fuel Pump

Two types of fuel pumps are used on Yamaha outboards. A gravity fuel delivery system is used on 2 hp models. A carburetor mounted fuel pump (**Figure 6**) is used on 3-30

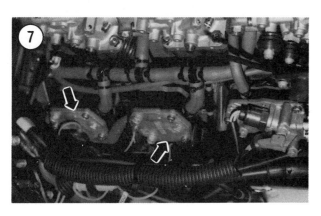

hp models (except 28 jet). One or more powerhead-mounted fuel pump(s) (**Figure 7**) are used on 28 jet and 40-250 hp models. Illustrations are provided to help ensure proper fuel hose routing and connections. Replace all gaskets, diaphragms, check valves and seals when servicing the fuel pump(s). Check for proper operation and correct fuel leakage after the repair is complete.

Carburetor-Mounted Pump

Repair of carburetor mounted fuel pumps is possible without removing the carburetor. However, the carburetor also is likely in need of cleaning and repair if debris, varnish deposits or brittle gaskets are the cause of fuel pump failure. Repair only the fuel pump if you are certain that the carburetor is in good condition. Refer to the diagram for the model requiring service, to help locate the components. Mark all components during disassembly to ensure proper orientation during assembly.

    a. For 3, 6 and 8 hp models, refer to **Figure 8**.

    b. For 4 and 5 hp models, refer to **Figure 9**.

    c. For 9.9 and 15 hp models, refer to **Figure 10**.

    d. For 20 and 25 hp models, refer to **Figure 11**.

    e. For 30 hp model, refer to **Figure 12**.

1. Remove the carburetor cover and carburetor. Refer to *Carburetor removal* for the required model.

2. Remove the four screws and carefully remove the fuel pump cover, outer gasket and outer diaphragm, if so equipped. Discard the gasket and diaphragm.

3. Carefully remove the fuel pump body from the carburetor. Remove the check valve screws and check valves from the body. Remove the boost spring and plate on 4 and 5 hp models.

4. Remove the inner diaphragm and gasket from the fuel pump mounting point.

5. Clean all components with a suitable solvent. Carefully scrape gasket material from the carburetor, fuel pump cover and fuel pump body. Never scratch or damage the gasket mating surfaces. Inspect the check valves and contact area on the fuel pump body. Replace the body and/or check valves if either surface is damaged or deteriorated.

6. Replace all gaskets, diaphragms and seals when assembling the fuel pump. Refer to the diagram for proper orientation of components. Handle the diaphragm with care to avoid tearing the areas where the fasteners pass through. Tighten all fasteners securely. Install the carburetor as instructed. Check for and correct all fuel leaks before putting the engine into service. Refer to Chapter Five for carburetor and linkage adjustments.

⑧

**CARBURETOR MOUNTED FUEL PUMP
(3, 6 AND 8 HP MODELS)**

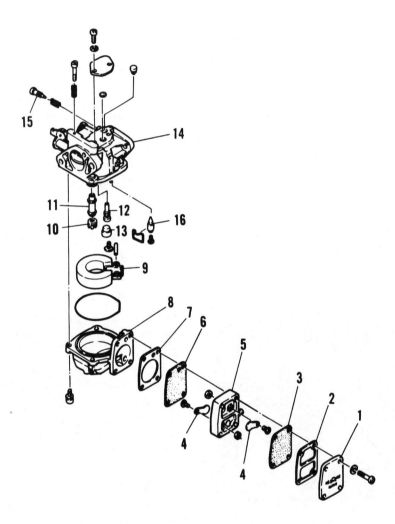

1. Pump cover
2. Gasket
3. Diaphragm
4. Check valve
5. Fuel pump body
6. Diaphragm
7. Gasket
8. Float bowl
9. Float
10. Main jet
11. Main nozzle
12. Idle jet
13. Seal
14. Caruretor body
15. Idle mixture screw
16. Inlet needle

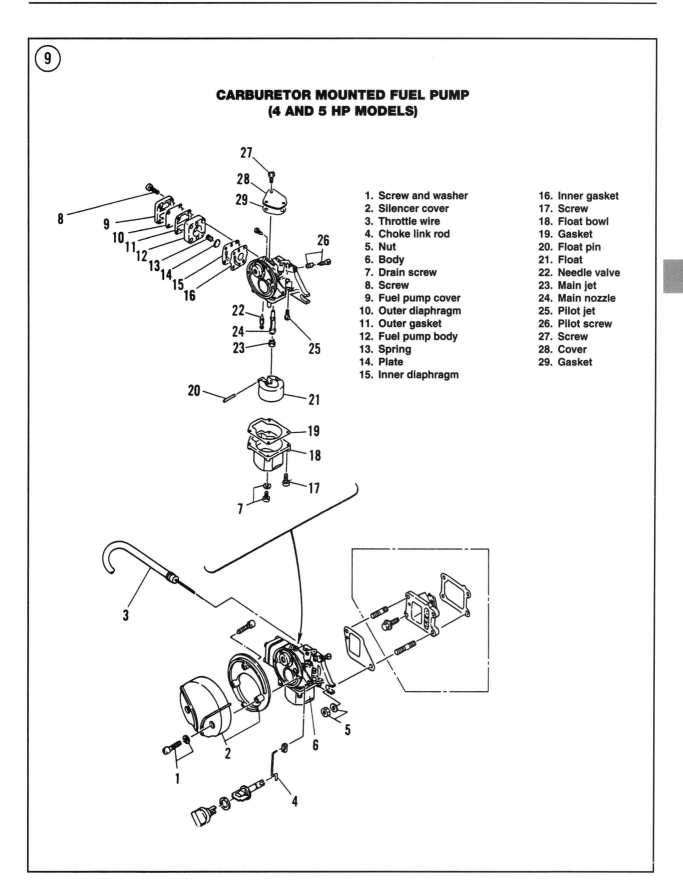

**CARBURETOR MOUNTED FUEL PUMP
(4 AND 5 HP MODELS)**

1. Screw and washer
2. Silencer cover
3. Throttle wire
4. Choke link rod
5. Nut
6. Body
7. Drain screw
8. Screw
9. Fuel pump cover
10. Outer diaphragm
11. Outer gasket
12. Fuel pump body
13. Spring
14. Plate
15. Inner diaphragm
16. Inner gasket
17. Screw
18. Float bowl
19. Gasket
20. Float pin
21. Float
22. Needle valve
23. Main jet
24. Main nozzle
25. Pilot jet
26. Pilot screw
27. Screw
28. Cover
29. Gasket

6

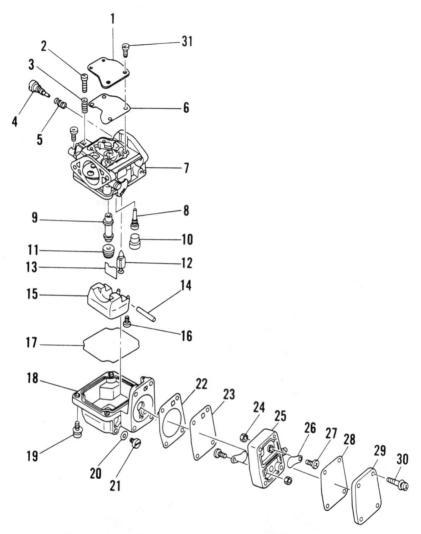

**CARBURETOR MOUNTED FUEL PUMP
(9.9 AND 15 HP MODELS)**

1. Cover
2. Idle speed screw
3. Spring
4. Pilot screw
5. Spring
6. Gasket
7. Body
8. Pilot jet
9. Main nozzle
10. Plug
11. Main jet
12. Inlet needle
13. Clip
14. Float pin
15. Float
16. Float pin screw
17. Seal
18. Float bowl
19. Screw
20. Gasket
21. Drain plug
22. Inner gasket
23. Inner diaphragm
24. Nut
25. Fuel pump body
26. Check valve
27. Screw
28. Outer diaphragm
29. Fuel pump cover
30. Screw
31. Screw

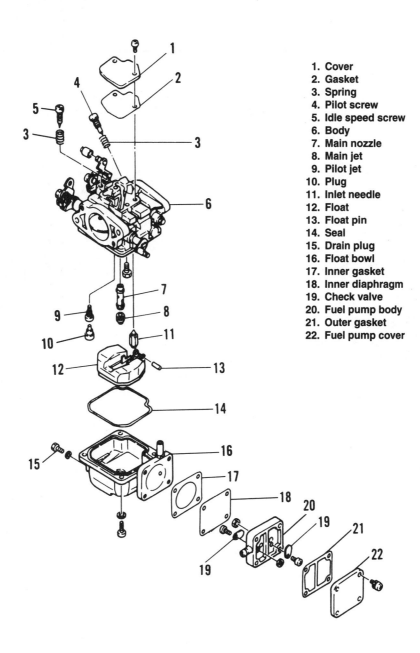

⑪

**CARBURETOR MOUNTED FUEL PUMP
(20 AND 25 HP [TWO-CYLINDER] MODELS)**

1. Cover
2. Gasket
3. Spring
4. Pilot screw
5. Idle speed screw
6. Body
7. Main nozzle
8. Main jet
9. Pilot jet
10. Plug
11. Inlet needle
12. Float
13. Float pin
14. Seal
15. Drain plug
16. Float bowl
17. Inner gasket
18. Inner diaphragm
19. Check valve
20. Fuel pump body
21. Outer gasket
22. Fuel pump cover

6

Powerhead-mounted diaphragm type pump

Deformed or damaged diaphragms, brittle gaskets and faulty check valves are some common causes of failure for diaphragm type pumps. Inspect all the fuel pumps on engines with multiple fuel pumps and repair as needed. Mark all components during disassembly to ensure proper orientation during assembly. To assist with fuel pump mounting locations and fuel hose routing, refer to the diagrams for the model requiring service. A pressure/vacuum tester (Miti-Vac or Yamaha part No. YB-35956/90890-06756) is required for testing the pump when assembly is complete.

   a. For 28 jet, 35 jet and 40-50 hp models (except Model E48), refer to **Figure 13**.

   b. For model E48, refer to **Figure 14**.

**CARBURETOR MOUNTED FUEL PUMP
(30 HP MODELS)**

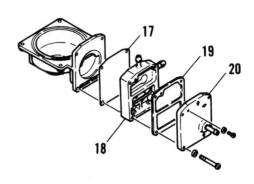

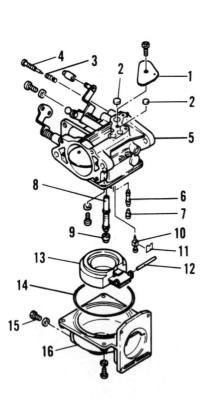

1. Cover
2. Seal
3. Spring
4. Pilot screw
5. Body
6. Pilot jet
7. Plug
8. Main nozzle
9. Main jet
10. Inlet needle
11. Clip
12. Float pin
13. Float
14. Seal
15. Bowl drain
16. Float bowl
17. Inner diaphragm
18. Fuel pump body
19. Outer gasket
20. Fuel pump cover

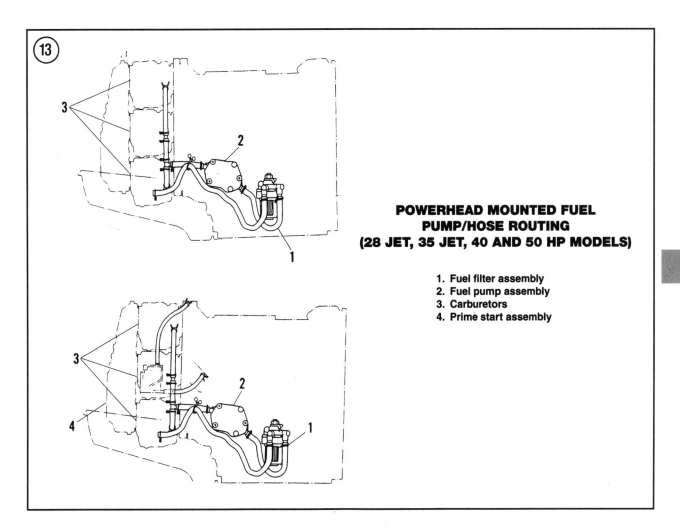

POWERHEAD MOUNTED FUEL PUMP/HOSE ROUTING (28 JET, 35 JET, 40 AND 50 HP MODELS)

1. Fuel filter assembly
2. Fuel pump assembly
3. Carburetors
4. Prime start assembly

6

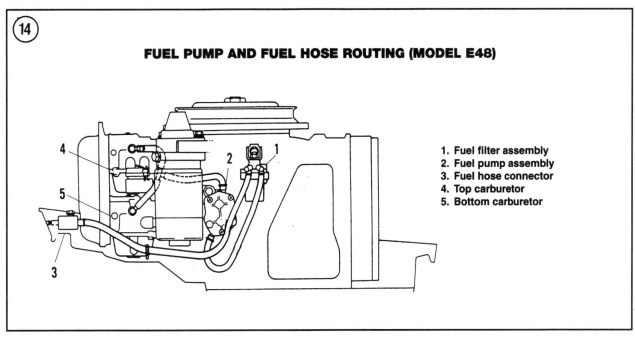

FUEL PUMP AND FUEL HOSE ROUTING (MODEL E48)

1. Fuel filter assembly
2. Fuel pump assembly
3. Fuel hose connector
4. Top carburetor
5. Bottom carburetor

c. For 60-90 hp models (except Models E60 and E75), refer to **Figure 15**.

d. For E60 and E75 models, refer to **Figure 16**.

e. For 80 jet and 115-130 hp models, refer to **Figure 17**.

f. For 105 jet and 150-225 hp, (90°) models, refer to **Figure 18**.

g. For 1996 225 and 250 hp, 76° engines equipped with carburetors, refer to **Figure 19**.

h. For 1997 and 1998 200-250 hp, (76°) engines equipped with EFI, refer to **Figure 20**.

1. Use a shop towel and a suitable container to collect any residual fuel that spills out of the disconnected hoses. Locate the hose connection at the inlet and outlet on the fuel pump(s). Cut and dispose of plastic locking ties used on the hoses for some models. Remove spring type hose clamps by squeezing the ends together.

2. Position a suitable container below the hose connection to the fuel pump and carefully remove the inlet and outlet

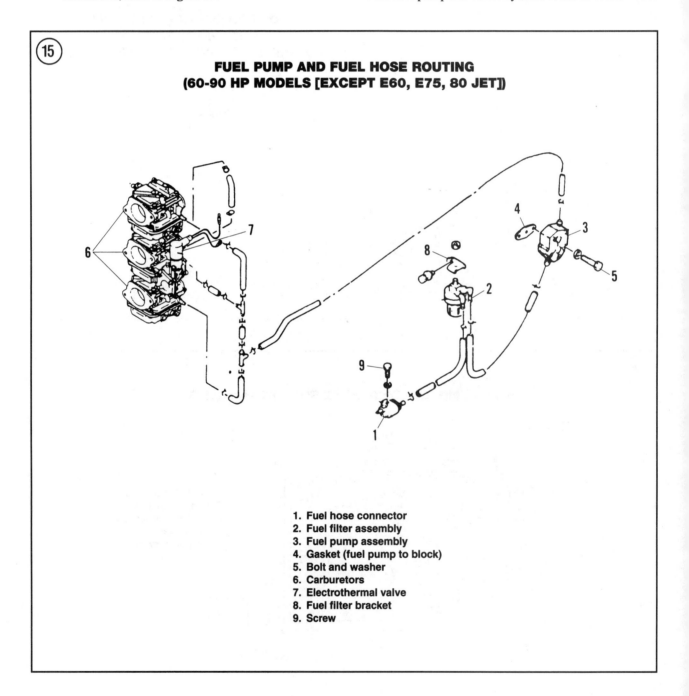

(15)

**FUEL PUMP AND FUEL HOSE ROUTING
(60-90 HP MODELS [EXCEPT E60, E75, 80 JET])**

1. Fuel hose connector
2. Fuel filter assembly
3. Fuel pump assembly
4. Gasket (fuel pump to block)
5. Bolt and washer
6. Carburetors
7. Electrothermal valve
8. Fuel filter bracket
9. Screw

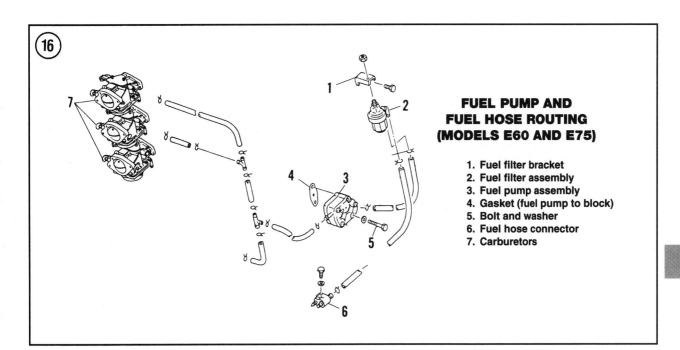

FUEL PUMP AND FUEL HOSE ROUTING (MODELS E60 AND E75)

1. Fuel filter bracket
2. Fuel filter assembly
3. Fuel pump assembly
4. Gasket (fuel pump to block)
5. Bolt and washer
6. Fuel hose connector
7. Carburetors

6

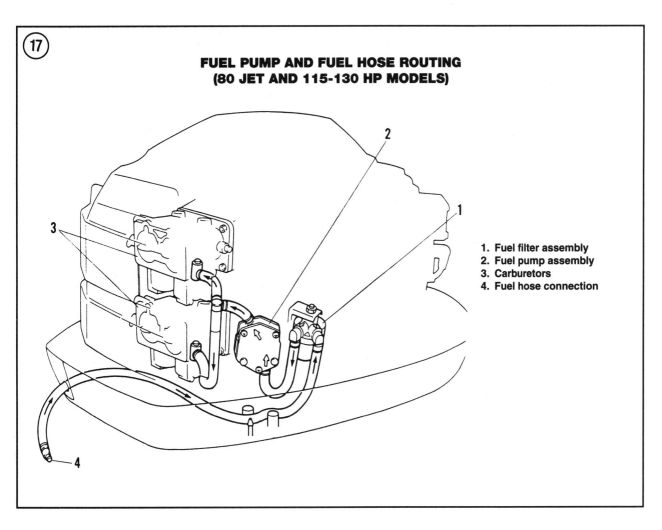

FUEL PUMP AND FUEL HOSE ROUTING (80 JET AND 115-130 HP MODELS)

1. Fuel filter assembly
2. Fuel pump assembly
3. Carburetors
4. Fuel hose connection

⑱

**FUEL PUMP AND FUEL HOSE ROUTING
(105 JET AND 150-225 HP MODELS [90°])**

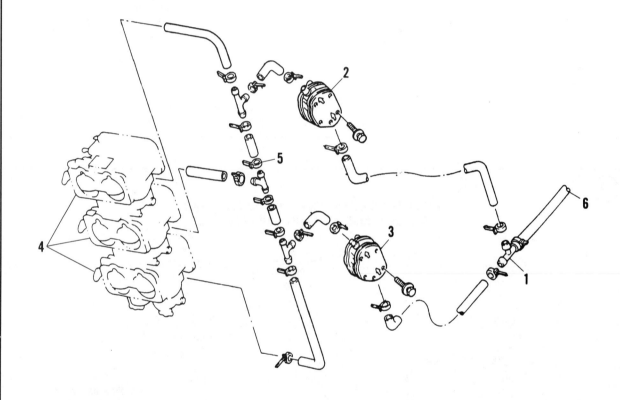

1. Fuel hose T-connector
2. Top fuel pump assembly
3. Bottom fuel pump assembly
4. Carburetors
5. Plastic locking tie clamps
6. Inlet fuel hose

⑲

FUEL PUMP AND FUEL HOSE ROUTING
(225 AND 250 HP MODELS [76°])

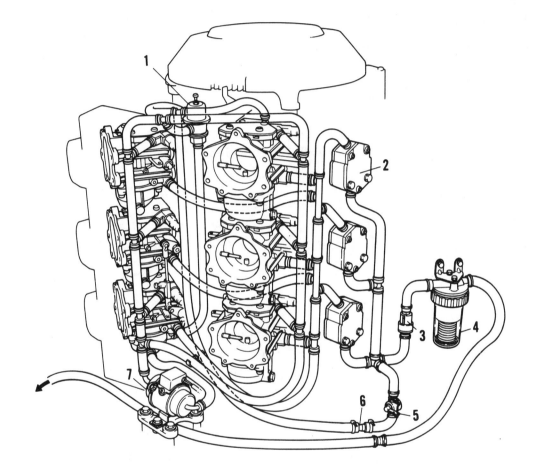

1. Fuel pressure regulator
2. Fuel pump
3. Fuel check valve
4. Fuel filter
5. Manual enrichment valve
6. Breather
7. Enrichner feed pump

6

hose for each fuel pump. Pull or twist the hose to free it from the fuel pump. Manipulate the hose carefully to avoid bending or breaking the fuel pump fittings. Cut, remove and replace hoses that have become hard or brittle. When cutting the hose, avoid damaging the fuel pump fittings. Inspect spring clamps for corrosion or lack of spring tension and replace any faulty or questionable hose clamp.

3. Remove both fuel pump mounting screws. Carefully remove the pump from the powerhead. Remove the fuel pump mounting gasket. Remove the three screws that hold the fuel pump assembly together. Being careful to avoid damaging gasket surfaces, pry the fuel pump cover from

the fuel pump body (**Figure 21**). Remove the outer gasket and diaphragm. Be extremely careful when the gasket must be scraped for removal, to avoid damaging gasket surfaces. Discard all gaskets and diaphragms.

4. Using the same procedures, remove the back cover, gasket(s) and diaphragm from the fuel pump body (**Figure 21**). Remove the boost spring and plate. Inspect the spring for a bent or rusted condition. Replace if necessary. Discard all gaskets and diaphragms.

5. Remove the screws and nuts that retain the check valves. Inspect the check valves for a bent, cracked or broken condition. Check the valve contact surfaces for

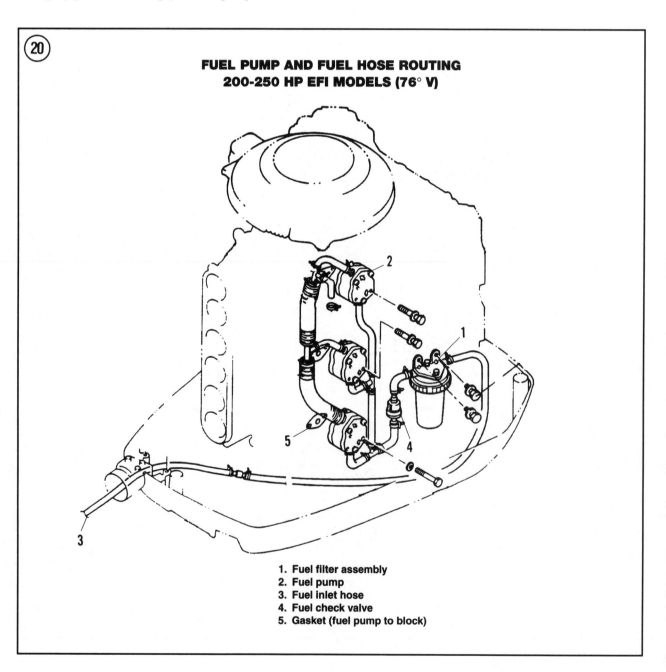

**FUEL PUMP AND FUEL HOSE ROUTING
200-250 HP EFI MODELS (76° V)**

1. Fuel filter assembly
2. Fuel pump
3. Fuel inlet hose
4. Fuel check valve
5. Gasket (fuel pump to block)

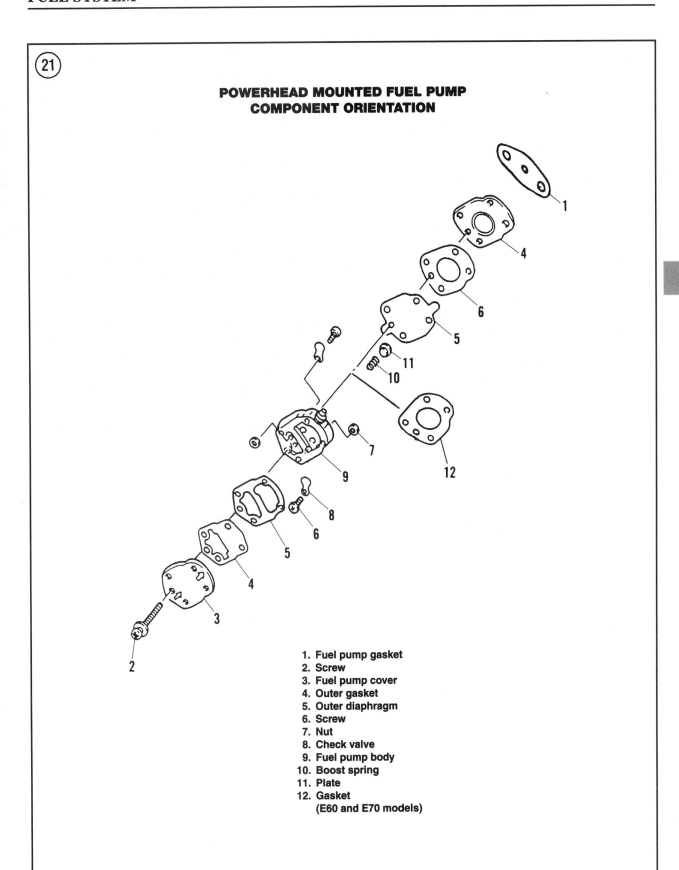

**POWERHEAD MOUNTED FUEL PUMP
COMPONENT ORIENTATION**

1. Fuel pump gasket
2. Screw
3. Fuel pump cover
4. Outer gasket
5. Outer diaphragm
6. Screw
7. Nut
8. Check valve
9. Fuel pump body
10. Boost spring
11. Plate
12. Gasket
   (E60 and E70 models)

6

corrosion or deterioration. Replace any faulty or questionable components.

6. Use a straightedge to inspect the fuel pump body, fuel pump cover and back fuel pump cover for warped surfaces. Inspect gasket surfaces for scratches, voids or any irregularities. Inspect the fuel pump body for cracks. Inspect the check valve mounting surfaces for scratches, nicks or deteriorated surfaces. Replace any components that are found to be warped or have questionable gasket or sealing surfaces.

7. Install new gaskets and diaphragms during assembly. Use screw hole locations in the gaskets and diaphragms for proper orientation. Carefully position the diaphragm over the boost spring and plate. Align the screw openings as the components are held together. Tighten all fasteners securely.

8. Pressure test the pump before installation onto the powerhead. Refer to the illustrations during pump installation for correct hose connections and routing. Use new hose clamps when required. Check for any fuel leaks and correct them before putting the engine into service.

Pressure test

> *NOTE*
> *A small amount of fuel must be put into the fuel pump fitting immediately before performing this test to ensure accurate test results. Use only enough fuel to wet the inner components and surfaces.*

Connect a hand operated vacuum/pressure tester to the *inlet side* of the pump. Block the *outlet side* of the pump with a finger (A, **Figure 22**). Slowly apply pressure until reaching 50 kPa (7.2 psi). Faulty gaskets or incorrect assembly is indicated if the test pressure cannot be attained.

1. Connect the vacuum/pressure tester to the *inlet side* hose fitting (B, **Figure 22**). Do not block the *outlet side* hose fitting. Apply a vacuum until reaching 30 kPa (8.9 in. Hg). The check valve is faulty if the test vacuum cannot be attained.

2. Connect the vacuum/pressure tester to the *outlet side* hose fitting (C, **Figure 22**). Slowly apply pressure until reaching 50 kPa (7.2 psi). The check valve is faulty if the test pressure cannot be attained.

3. Disassemble, inspect and assemble the pump if failure is noted in Step 1. Disassemble and inspect the check valves and/or pump body if a failure is noted in Step 2 or Step 3. Replace the check valves if necessary. Install a new pump if the pump body is faulty.

Prime Start Pump

The prime start system (**Figure 23**) provides extra fuel to the engine during cold starting/operation. It is controlled by the CDI unit or microcomputer.

1. Disconnect both battery connections before proceeding.

2. Mark all hose connections prior to removal. Cut and discard plastic locking ties when used and remove all hose clamps. To remove spring type clamps, squeeze clamp ends together. Inspect spring type clamps for corrosion or lost tension and replace as required.

3. Remove hoses and plug the disconnected ends to prevent fuel leakage and contamination. Disconnect all electrical connectors. Remove the bolts (3, **Figure 23**) and washers that retain the pump.

4. Remove and discard the mounting gasket (4, **Figure 23**). Remove the electromagnetic valve(s) (6, **Figure 23**) from the unit. Discard the sealing O-ring (7, **Figure 23**).

5. Remove the three screws at the rear and two screws at the front of the pump and carefully remove the rear cover. Remove all gaskets and diaphragms and discard them.

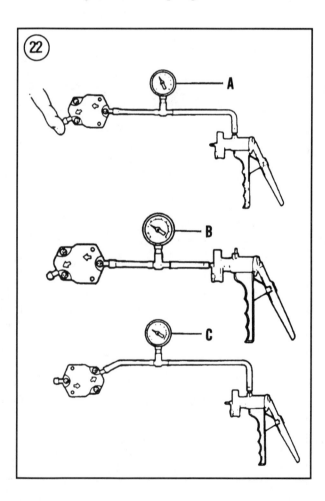

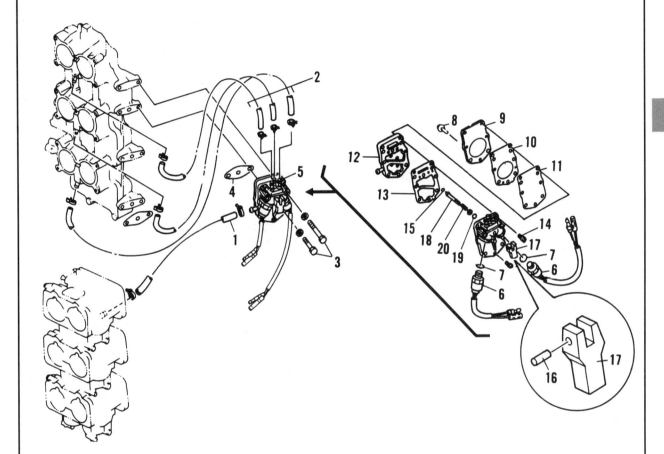

**PRIME START ASSEMBLY
(225 AND 250 HP CARBURETOR EQUIPPED MODELS [76°])**

1. Vacuum hose
2. Fuel delivery hose
3. Bolt
4. Gasket
5. Prime start assembly
6. Electromagnetic valve
7. O-ring
8. Screw
9. Back cover
10. Gasket
11. Diaphragm
12. Pump body
13. Gasket
14. Screw
15. O-ring
16. Pin
17. Lever
18. Valve
19. O-ring
20. Spring

6

Inspect all surfaces for warped or damaged areas. Replace if required.

6. Replace all gaskets and diaphragms along with new O-rings on the electromagnetic valve(s) during assembly.

Fuel Filter

Several versions of fuel filters are used on Yamaha outboards. Some small engines use a nonserviceable in-line style fuel filter (**Figure 24**). All other engines use a serviceable filter with a spin on canister (**Figure 25**). The canister-type filter has a feature that traps small amounts of water in the bottom of the filter cup. The water can be easily drained by removing the filter cup from the fuel filter assembly. Inspect all fuel hoses and the fuel tank if significant amounts of debris or deposits are found in the fuel filter. Inspect the *carburetor(s) and fuel pump* if a significant amount of varnish deposits is found in the fuel filter. Service the fuel filters following the listed procedures. Use a suitable container to capture the fuel from the components during disassembly.

Inline fuel filter

1. Cut and remove plastic locking tie clamps at the hose-to-filter connections. Squeeze the ends of spring type hose clamps to remove them from the fuel filter fitting. Replace corroded or weak hose clamps. Carefully twist or pull the hose to remove it from the filter. Cut stubborn hoses to remove them and replace them with the correct type of fuel hose. Discard the fuel filter.

2. Refer to the fuel hose illustrations (**Figures 8-12**) to determine the correct fuel flow direction for the model specified. Observe the arrow on the side of the filter (**Figure 24**) to determine the direction of fuel flow, then push the fuel hoses fully onto each end of the *new* fuel filter.

3. Install new plastic locking tie or spring type hose clamp onto each hose connection for the filter. Ensure that all connections are secure and will not interfere with any

components on the engine. Run the engine and check for proper operation. Check for any fuel leaks and correct them before putting the engine into service.

Canister fuel filter

1. Position a suitable container under the filter cup (**Figure 26**). While grasping the filter assembly, twist the filter cup in the clockwise direction as viewed from the top and remove it from the filter assembly. Remove the O-ring and gasket (**Figure 26**) and discard them.

2. Clean the filter cup in a suitable solvent. Inspect the filter element for holes, tears or other imperfections. Carefully clean or replace the filter element. Replace any cracked or damaged components.

3. Install a new O-ring onto the fuel filter cup (**Figure 26**). Position the new or cleaned filter element into the filter cup with a new gasket installed at the top end of the element. Carefully thread the filter cup into the filter assembly. Make sure the filter gasket is in proper position. While grasping the filter assemble securely tighten the filter cup into position.

4. Run the engine and check for proper operation. Check for any fuel leaks and correct them before putting the engine into service.

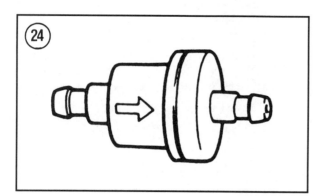

Silencer Cover and Carburetor

Numerous mounting variations exist for the silencer cover and carburetor. Refer to the following illustrations for the required model during the removal and installation procedures. Use a suitable container to capture the residual fuel from the components as the fuel hose is removed. Perform the step by step procedures for the required model. Refer to Chapter Five when the assembly is complete for carburetor and linkage adjustments. Always run the engine to check for proper operation. Check for any fuel leaks and correct them before putting the engine into service.

a. For 2 hp models, refer to **Figure 27**.
b. For 3 hp models, refer to **Figure 28**.
c. For 4 and 5 hp models, refer to **Figure 29**.
d. For 6-15 hp models, refer to **Figure 30**.
e. For 20-30 hp (two-cylinder models), refer to **Figure 31**.
f. For 28 jet, 35 jet and 40-50 hp models, refer to **Figure 32**.
g. For Model E48, refer to **Figure 33**.
h. For Model E60, refer to **Figure 34**.
i. For Model E75, refer to **Figure 35**.
j. For 60 and 70 hp models, refer to **Figure 36**.
k. For 65 jet and 75-90 hp models (except 80 jet), refer to **Figure 37**.
l. For 80 jet and 115-130 hp models, refer to **Figure 38**.
m. For 105 jet and 150-225 hp 90° models, refer to **Figure 39**.
n. For 1996 225-250 hp 76° models, refer to **Figure 40**.
o. For 1997-on 200-250 hp 76° EFI models, refer to **Figure 41**.

2 hp models

1. Remove the screw and throttle lever knob. Remove the stop switch white lead and bracket. Pull the stop switch from the cover. Pull the choke knob and O-ring from the choke valve shaft.
2. Remove the two screws (8, **Figure 27**) and the front cover. Close the fuel cock and remove the fuel hose clamp and hose from the carburetor. Remove the top screw, washer and throttle lever link.
3. Remove the screw, spring and plate from the side of the throttle lever. Remove the circlip, pin and throttle lever from the top of the carburetor.
4. Remove the screw, washer, nut and clamp from the back of the carburetor. Remove the O-ring seal as the carburetor is pulled from the reed housing and discard it.
5. Replace the O-ring at the carburetor to reed housing mating surface during installation. Inspect the spring type hose clamp for corrosion or inadequate spring tension. Replace if required. Apply a light coating of Yamaha water resistant grease or its equivalent to all throttle linkage pivot points and choke valve shaft. Tighten all fasteners securely.

3 hp models

1. Close the fuel petcock. Cut the plastic locking tie and remove the fuel hose from the carburetor.

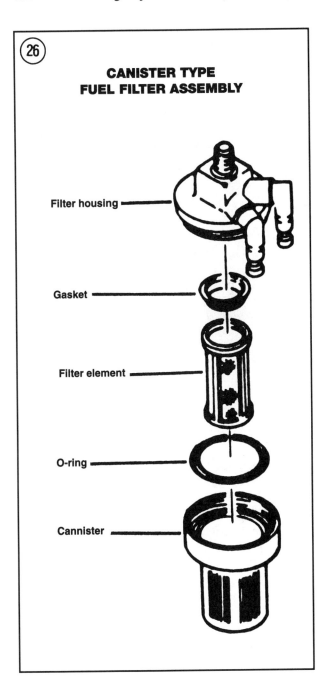

(26)

CANISTER TYPE FUEL FILTER ASSEMBLY

Filter housing

Gasket

Filter element

O-ring

Cannister

6

㉗

COVER/SILENCER (2 HP MODELS)

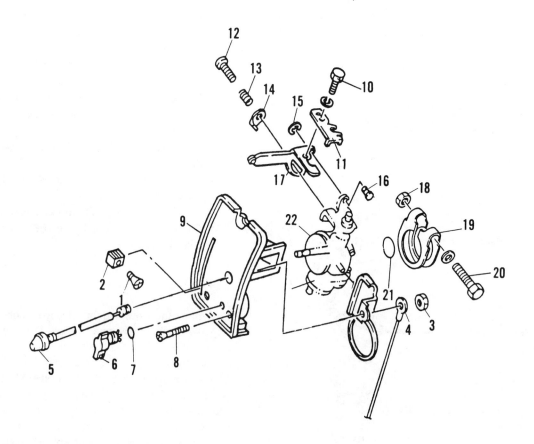

1. Screw	12. Screw
2. Throttle lever knob	13. Spring
3. Nut	14. Plate
4. Stop switch lead	15. Lock ring
5. Stop switch	16. Pivot
6. Choke knob	17. Throttle lever
7. O-ring	18. Nut
8. Screw	19. Clamp
9. Cover	20. Bolt
10. Screw	21. O-ring
11. Throttle lever linkage	22. Carburetor

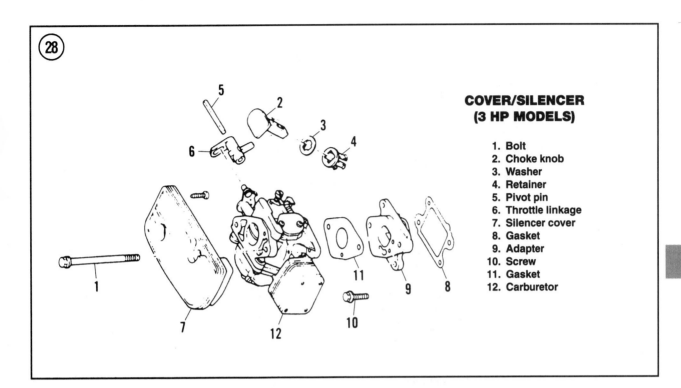

**COVER/SILENCER
(3 HP MODELS)**

1. Bolt
2. Choke knob
3. Washer
4. Retainer
5. Pivot pin
6. Throttle linkage
7. Silencer cover
8. Gasket
9. Adapter
10. Screw
11. Gasket
12. Carburetor

6

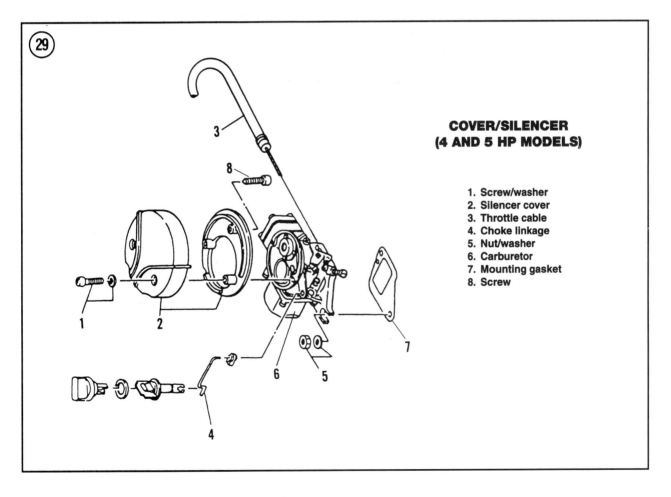

**COVER/SILENCER
(4 AND 5 HP MODELS)**

1. Screw/washer
2. Silencer cover
3. Throttle cable
4. Choke linkage
5. Nut/washer
6. Carburetor
7. Mounting gasket
8. Screw

(30)

COVER/SILENCER (6-15 HP MODELS)

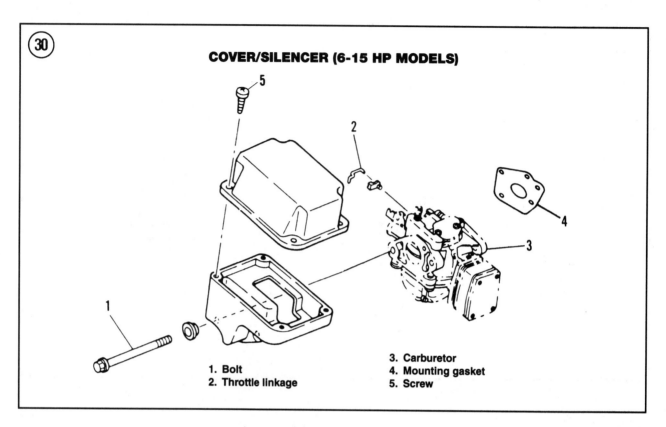

1. Bolt
2. Throttle linkage
3. Carburetor
4. Mounting gasket
5. Screw

(31)

COVER/SILENCER (20-30 HP MODELS [TYPICAL])

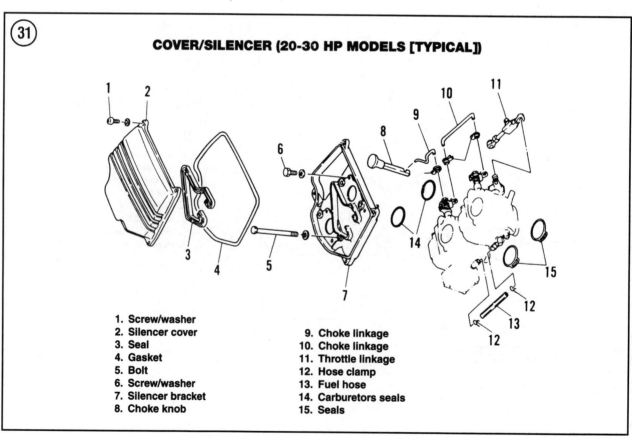

1. Screw/washer
2. Silencer cover
3. Seal
4. Gasket
5. Bolt
6. Screw/washer
7. Silencer bracket
8. Choke knob
9. Choke linkage
10. Choke linkage
11. Throttle linkage
12. Hose clamp
13. Fuel hose
14. Carburetors seals
15. Seals

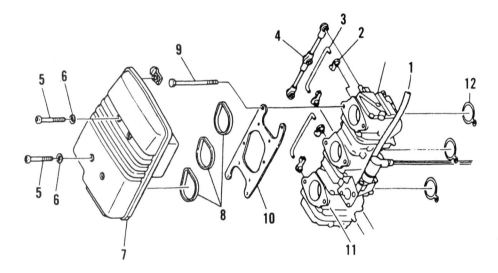

**COVER/SILENCER
(28 JET, 35 JET, 40 AND 50 HP MODELS)**

1. Fuel inlet hose
2. Linkage connector
3. Choke linkage
4. Throttle linkage
5. Bolt
6. Washer
7. Silencer cover
8. Seal
9. Bolt
10. Silencer bracket
11. Carburetors
12. Seals

6

(33)

COVER/SILENCER (MODEL E48)

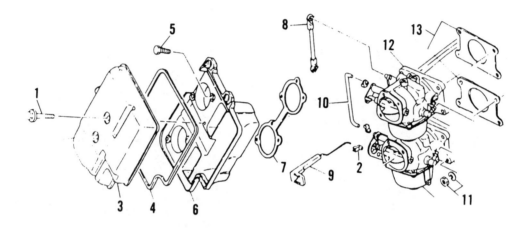

1. Bolt
2. Linkage connector
3. Silencer cover
4. Gasket
5. Screw
6. Silencer assembly
7. Gasket
8. Throttle linkage
9. Choke lever
10. Choke linkage
11. Nut/washer
12. Carburetors
13. Mounting gaskets

COVER/SILENCER (MODEL E60)

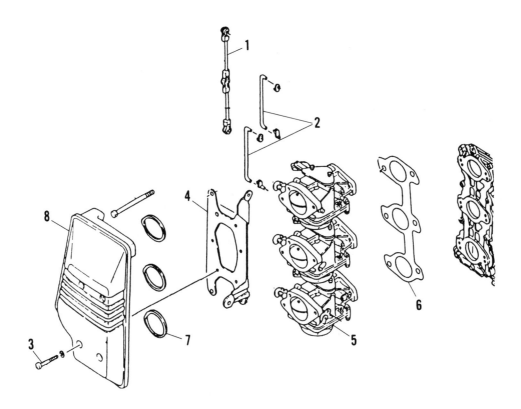

6

1. Throttle linkage
2. Choke linkage
3. Bolt/washer
4. Silencer/cover bracket
5. Carburetors
6. Mounting gasket
7. Seals
8. Silencer/cover

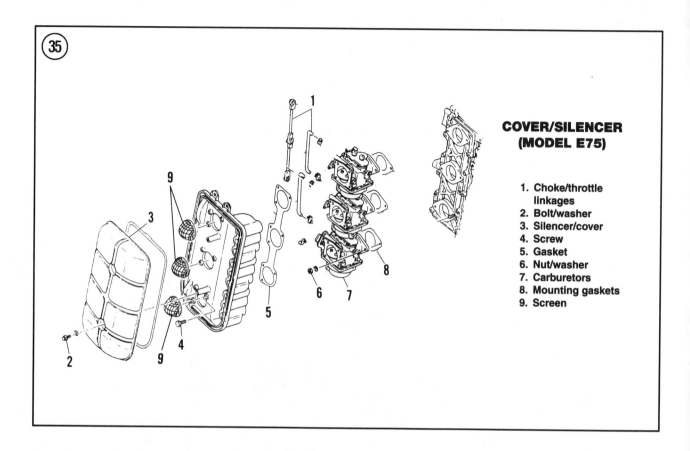

COVER/SILENCER (MODEL E75)

1. Choke/throttle linkages
2. Bolt/washer
3. Silencer/cover
4. Screw
5. Gasket
6. Nut/washer
7. Carburetors
8. Mounting gaskets
9. Screen

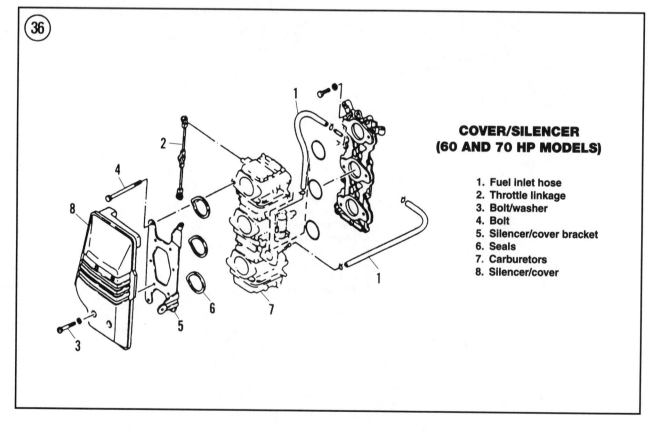

COVER/SILENCER (60 AND 70 HP MODELS)

1. Fuel inlet hose
2. Throttle linkage
3. Bolt/washer
4. Bolt
5. Silencer/cover bracket
6. Seals
7. Carburetors
8. Silencer/cover

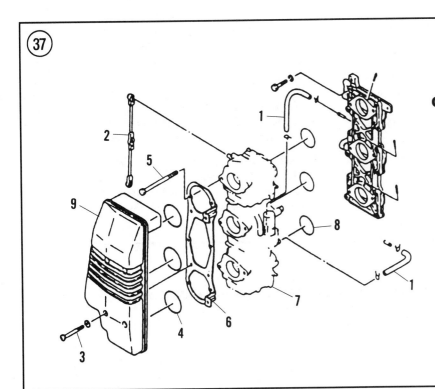

COVER/SILENCER (65 JET AND 75-90 HP MODELS [EXCEPT 80 JET])

1. Fuel inlet hose
2. Throttle linkage
3. Bolt/washer
4. Seals
5. Bolt
6. Silencer/cover bracket
7. Carburetors
8. Seals
9. Silencer/cover

6

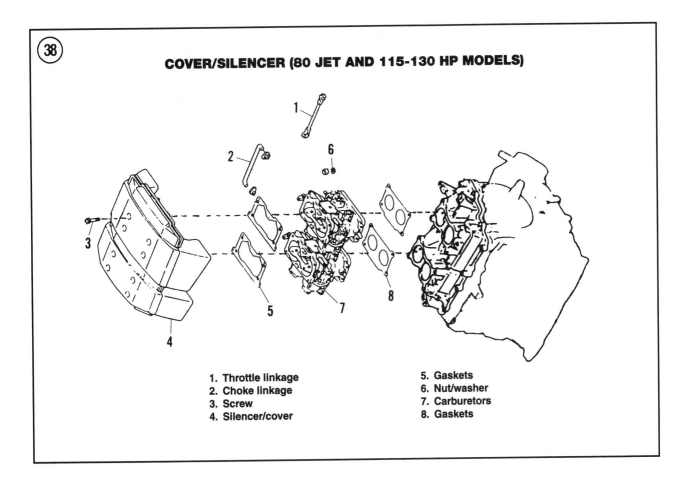

COVER/SILENCER (80 JET AND 115-130 HP MODELS)

1. Throttle linkage
2. Choke linkage
3. Screw
4. Silencer/cover
5. Gaskets
6. Nut/washer
7. Carburetors
8. Gaskets

2. Disconnect the throttle cable connection from the carburetor throttle shaft.

3. Remove the screw(s) that retain the silencer cover to the front of the carburetor. Remove the two screws that retain the carburetor to the reed housing. Remove the roll pin and choke linkage from the carburetor.

4. Remove the carburetor from the reed housing. Discard the mounting gasket.

5. Replace the mounting gasket and fuel hose clamp during installation. Apply a light coating of Yamaha water resistant grease or its equivalent to the choke linkage on assembly.

4 and 5 hp models

1. Close the fuel cock. Remove the fuel hose clamp and fuel hose from the carburetor.

2. Remove the two screws, washers and silencer cover (1 and 2, **Figure 29**) from the carburetor. Loosen the locking screw and remove the throttle cable from the carburetor.

3. Remove the choke link rod and clip (4, **Figure 29**) by carefully prying it loose with a screwdriver. Remove the nuts and washers (5, **Figure 29**). Remove the carburetor. Remove the mounting gasket (7, **Figure 29**) and discard

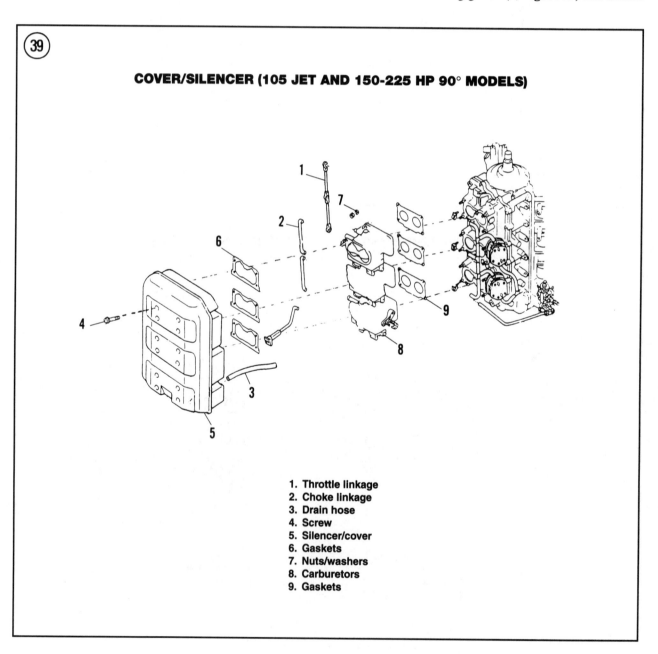

(39)

COVER/SILENCER (105 JET AND 150-225 HP 90° MODELS)

1. Throttle linkage
2. Choke linkage
3. Drain hose
4. Screw
5. Silencer/cover
6. Gaskets
7. Nuts/washers
8. Carburetors
9. Gaskets

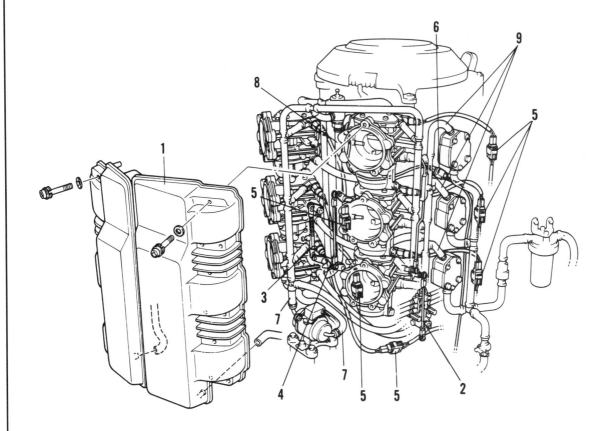

**COVER/SILENCER
(225 AND 250 HP 76° CARBURETOR EQUIPPED)**

1. Intake silencer
2. Oil pump joint link
3. Accelerator linkage
4. Joint linkage
5. Fuel enrichment
   valve connector
6. Throttle position
   sensor connector
7. Feed pump fuel hose
8. Fuel regulator hose
9. Fuel pump hose

6

it. Remove the screw (8, **Figure 29**) and back cover from the silencer cover.

4. Installation is the reverse of removal. Inspect the fuel hose clamp and replace if necessary. Install a new carburetor mount gasket. Tighten all fasteners securely.

6-15 hp models

1. Remove the clamp and fuel hose from the carburetor fitting. Remove the two screws retaining the silencer cover to the carburetor.

2. Remove the choke link rod and clip from the choke valve shaft. Disconnect the throttle linkage from the throttle shaft. Remove the two nuts and washers at the carburetor mounting base.

3. Carefully remove the carburetor from the engine. Remove the carburetor mount gasket and discard it. Remove the four screws and the top of the silencer cover (except 9.9 and 15 hp models).

4. Installation is the reverse of removal. Replace the carburetor mount gasket during installation. Inspect the fuel hose clamp and replace if necessary. Tighten all fasteners securely.

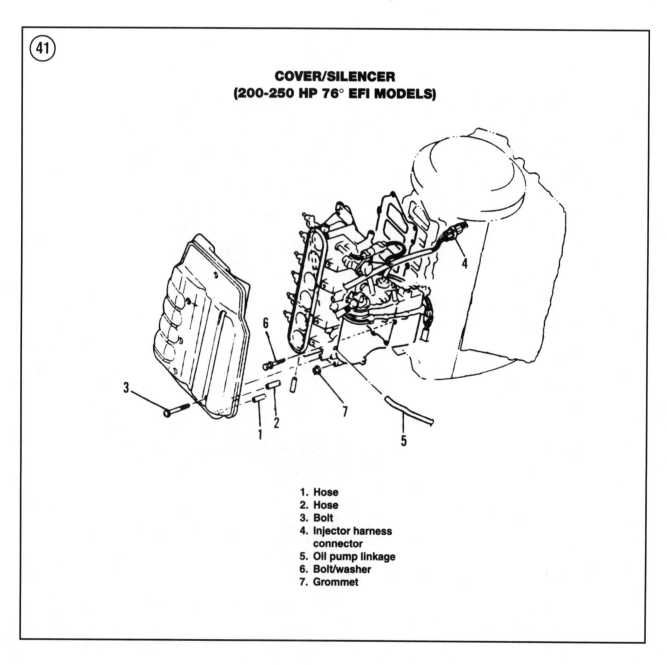

**COVER/SILENCER
(200-250 HP 76° EFI MODELS)**

1. Hose
2. Hose
3. Bolt
4. Injector harness connector
5. Oil pump linkage
6. Bolt/washer
7. Grommet

20-30 hp models

1. Remove the screws, washers and front cover from the silencer cover. Remove the packing, seal, fasteners and rear cover of the silencer cover. Retain the O-ring seal, or gasket for three-cylinder models, from the carburetor mount for later use.

2. Disconnect the fuel hoses from the carburetor mounted fuel pump and the carburetor(s). Inspect the hose clamp for corrosion and inadequate spring tension. Replace if necessary.

3. Disconnect the choke and throttle linkage from both carburetors. Remove the nuts and washers that retain the carburetors to the intake. Carefully remove the carburetors. Remove the seals at the carburetor mount and discard them.

4. Inspect all seals and packing and replace if damaged. Installation is the reverse of removal. Replace both seals at the carburetor mount during installation. Tighten all fasteners securely.

28 jet, 35 jet and 40-50 hp models
(except model E48)

1. Disconnect clamps and fuel hoses from the carburetors. Inspect the hose clamps for corrosion and inadequate spring tension. Replace if necessary. Disconnect the choke and throttle linkages (**Figure 32**) from the carburetors.

2. Remove the four screws and washers that retain the cover silencer to the bracket (**Figure 32**). Remove the bolts that retain the bracket. Inspect the seals and replace if damaged.

3. Remove the bracket, seals and carburetors. Discard the carburetor mount seals (**Figure 32**).

4. Installation is the reverse of removal. Replace the seals at the carburetor mount during installation. Tighten all fasteners securely.

Model E48

1. Remove the two screws and washers from the silencer cover. Remove the front cover and seal. Remove the screws and rear portion of the cover assembly. Remove the gasket and discard it.

2. Disconnect the fuel hose clamps and fuel hoses from all carburetors. Disconnect the throttle and choke linkage from the carburetors.

3. Remove the nuts and washers that retain the carburetors to the intake. Carefully remove the carburetors. Remove the carburetor mount gaskets and discard it.

4. Installation is the reverse of removal. Replace the carburetor mount gaskets and the silencer cover-to-carburetor gasket during installation. Apply Loctite 242 to the screws

that retain the silencer cover to the front of the carburetors (5, **Figure 33**). Tighten all fasteners securely.

Model E60

1. Remove the fuel hose clamps and fuel hoses from all carburetors. Disconnect the throttle and choke linkages from the carburetors.

2. Completely loosen the six bolts that retain the silencer cover, bracket and carburetors to the intake. Carefully remove all components as one assembly from the intake. Separate the cover and bracket from the carburetors.

3. Remove the carburetor mount gaskets and discard them. Inspect the seals at the rear of the silencer cover and replace if damaged.

4. Installation is the reverse of removal. Replace the carburetor mount gaskets during installation. Ensure the mount gaskets are aligned properly as the carburetors are installed onto the intake.

Model E75

1. Remove the fuel hose clamps and fuel hoses from all carburetors. Disconnect the throttle and choke linkages from the carburetors.

2. Remove the two screws and washers from the front of the cover silencer. Remove the front cover seal and carefully remove the three screens from the air openings. Remove the three bolts that retain the rear portion of the cover silencer, and remove it from the carburetors. Remove the silencer cover-to-carburetor gasket and discard it.

3. Remove the nuts and washers from the mount of the carburetors. Carefully remove the carburetors from the intake. Remove the carburetor mount gaskets and discard them.

4. Installation is the reverse of removal. Replace the carburetor mount and silencer cover gaskets during installation. Tighten all fasteners securely.

60 hp models (except model E60)

1. Remove the fuel hose clamps and fuel hoses from all carburetors. Disconnect the throttle linkages from the carburetors.

2. Remove the retaining bolts and remove the silencer cover. Completely loosen the bolts that retain the bracket and carburetors to the intake. Remove these components as an assembly. See **Figure 35**.

3. Remove the O-ring seals from the carburetor mount and discard them. Inspect the seals at the cover silencer to carburetor mating surface. Replace if damaged.

6

4. Installation is the reverse of removal. Replace the O-ring seals at the carburetor mount during installation. Tighten the bolts that retain the cover silencer and carburetors to 2 N.m (17 in. lb.). Tighten other fasteners securely.

65 jet and 75-90 hp models

1. Remove the fuel hose clamps and fuel hoses from all carburetors. Disconnect the throttle linkages from the carburetors.

2. Remove the two screws and the silencer cover. Inspect the O-ring seals and replace if damaged.

3. Completely loosen the six bolts that retain the bracket and carburetors to the intake. Remove these components and separate as shown in **Figure 37**. Remove the O-ring seals from the carburetor mount and discard them.

4. Installation is the reverse of removal. Replace the O-ring seals at the carburetor mount during installation. Tighten the silencer cover screws to 2 N.m (17 in. lbs.). Tighten other fasteners securely.

80 jet and 115-130 hp models

1. Remove the fuel hose clamps and fuel hoses from the carburetors. Disconnect the throttle and choke linkages from the carburetors.

2. Remove the eight bolts that retain the cover silencer to the carburetors. Remove the cover silencer and discard the gaskets.

3. Remove the nuts and washers that retain the carburetors to the intake. Carefully remove the carburetors from the intake. Remove the carburetor mount gaskets and discard them.

4. Installation is the reverse of removal. Replace the carburetor-to-cover silencer and carburetor-to-intake gaskets during installation. Tighten all fasteners securely.

105 jet and 150-225 hp 90° V models

1. Cut the plastic locking tie fuel hose clamps and remove all fuel hoses from the carburetors. Disconnect the throttle and choke linkages from the carburetors.

2. Disconnect the drain hose at the lower end of the silencer cover. Remove the twelve screws from the front of the silencer cover. Remove the silencer cover from the carburetors. Discard the silencer cover gasket.

3. Remove the nuts and washers that retain the carburetors to the intake. Carefully remove the carburetors. Discard the carburetor mounting gaskets.

4. Installation is the reverse of removal. Replace the carburetor mount gaskets and the silencer cover gasket during

installation. Install new plastic locking ties onto the fuel hose connections. Tighten all fasteners securely.

225-250 hp 76° models (1996)

1. Remove the 18 screws that retain the silencer cover to the carburetors. Remove the drain hoses from the lower end of the silencer cover. Remove the silencer cover from the carburetors.

2. Cut the plastic locking tie clamps and remove the fuel hoses from the six carburetor assemblies. Disconnect the throttle linkages from the carburetors.

3. Remove the carburetors from the intake. Discard the carburetor mounting gaskets.

4. Installation is the reverse of removal. Install new plastic locking ties at fuel hose fittings and tighten securely. Replace carburetor mounting gaskets during installation. Tighten all fasteners securely.

200-250 76° models (1997-on)

1. Remove the breather tube connecting the silencer cover and throttle body.

2. Remove the breather tube connecting the silencer cover and engine oil tank.

3. Remove the six screws from the front of the silencer cover and remove it from the throttle body.

4. Installation is the reverse of removal. Tighten all fasteners securely.

CARBURETOR

A clean work environment is essential to perform successful carburetor repairs. Mark all hose connections during removal and refer to the supplied illustrations to ensure correct hose routing and orientation. On multiple-carburetor engines (**Figure 42**), match each carburetor to its respective cylinder and repair *one* carburetor at a time. On some models, the fuel and air jet sizes are calibrated for the cylinder to which they supply fuel, and their sizes vary depending on the position of the cylinder within the engine. On V-model engines, note on which side of the engine the carburetor is located. Carburetor jet specifications often refer to *port and starboard* for correct jet placement in the carburetors. **Table 2** and **Table 3** provide jet sizes

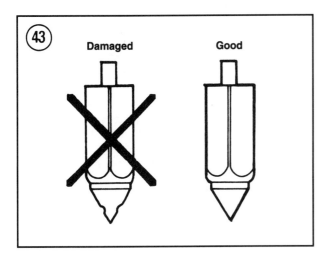

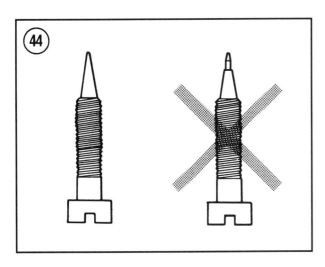

for all carburetors. Carburetor and linkage adjustment instructions are provided in Chapter Five.

> *CAUTION*
> *Make certain that all jets are installed into the correct location in the carburetor. Improper fuel calibration can result if jets are incorrectly installed or installed in the wrong location. Severe powerhead damage can occur from improper fuel calibration.*

Place all components on a clean surface as they are removed from the carburetor and cleaned. Arrange these components in a manner consistent with the provided illustrations. This will save time and help ensure a proper repair.

Using a suitable solvent, clean all deposits from the carburetor passages, jets, orifices and fuel bowl. Use compressed air and blow through the passages to remove contaminants. Carefully remove the jets from the carburetor to avoid damaging them. If the jets cannot be easily removed, soak the carburetor in solvent before attempting to remove them. Clean the carburetor without removing the jets if they are especially difficult to remove or if the carburetor has a significant amount of corrosion or deposits. Replace the jets if they are damaged during removal.

> *CAUTION*
> *Never use stiff steel wire to clean carburetor passages. Material can be removed from the inner diameter of the orifice, disturbing the fuel calibration. Carburetor replacement may be required if passages are damaged during the cleaning process.*

> *NOTE*
> *Never compromise the cleaning process for the carburetor(s). Residual debris or deposits in the carburetor may break free at a later time and block passages. Use compressed air and blow through all passages to ensure they are completely clear.*

> *CAUTION*
> *Always replace damaged carburetor jets. Seemingly insignificant damage to a jet can have a profound effect on fuel delivery and adversely affect performance and durability.*

Inspect the fuel valve needle for damaged sealing surfaces (**Figure 43**). Inspect the valve seat for pitting, worn or irregular surfaces. Replace worn or damaged components.

Inspect mixture adjusting screws for worn or damaged surfaces (**Figure 44**) and replace if required.

6

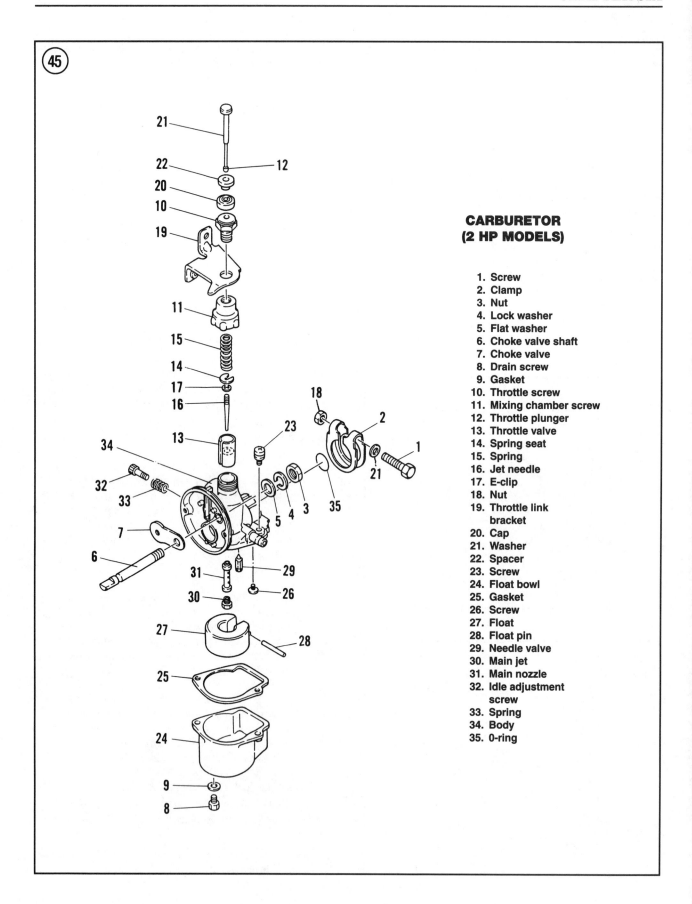

45

CARBURETOR (2 HP MODELS)

1. Screw
2. Clamp
3. Nut
4. Lock washer
5. Flat washer
6. Choke valve shaft
7. Choke valve
8. Drain screw
9. Gasket
10. Throttle screw
11. Mixing chamber screw
12. Throttle plunger
13. Throttle valve
14. Spring seat
15. Spring
16. Jet needle
17. E-clip
18. Nut
19. Throttle link bracket
20. Cap
21. Washer
22. Spacer
23. Screw
24. Float bowl
25. Gasket
26. Screw
27. Float
28. Float pin
29. Needle valve
30. Main jet
31. Main nozzle
32. Idle adjustment screw
33. Spring
34. Body
35. 0-ring

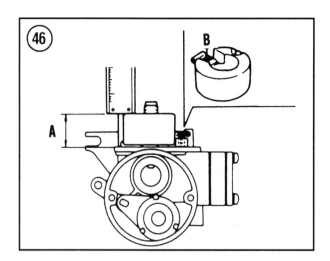

Use a suitable ruler or measuring device to check the float level and drop settings. Set the float exactly as specified to ensure proper performance and durability. Float specifications are provided in **Table 1**. Replace the float valve if it does not move freely on the pivot pin.

Refer to *Silencer cover and carburetor* in this chapter for the carburetor removal and installation procedure. Locate the illustration for the required model and follow the instructions provided to disassemble, inspect and assemble the carburetor. Drain any residual fuel from the carburetor prior to disassembly.

a. For 2 hp models, refer to **Figure 45** and **Figure 46**.

b. For 3, 6 and 8 hp models, refer to **Figure 47** and **Figure 48**.

6

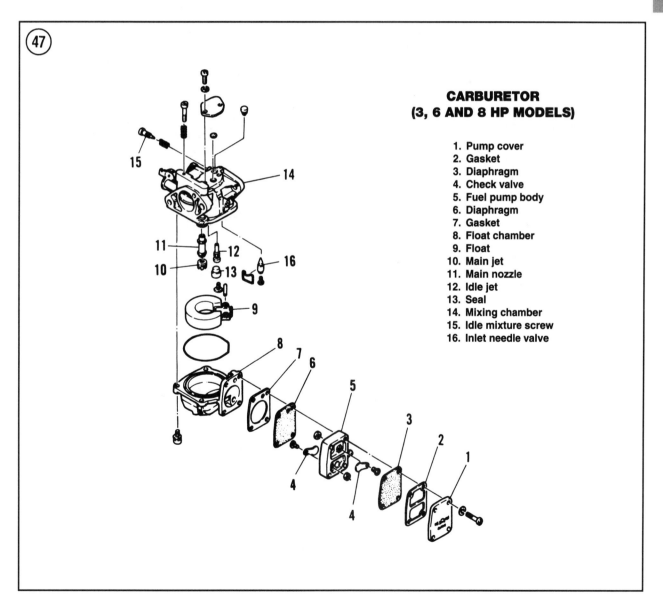

CARBURETOR
(3, 6 AND 8 HP MODELS)

1. Pump cover
2. Gasket
3. Diaphragm
4. Check valve
5. Fuel pump body
6. Diaphragm
7. Gasket
8. Float chamber
9. Float
10. Main jet
11. Main nozzle
12. Idle jet
13. Seal
14. Mixing chamber
15. Idle mixture screw
16. Inlet needle valve

c. For 4 and 5 hp models, refer to **Figure 49**.

d. For 9.9 and 15 hp models, refer to **Figure 50** and **Figure 51**.

e. For 20 and 25 hp two-cylinder models, refer to **Figure 52**.

f. For 25 and 30 hp three-cylinder models, refer to **Figure 53**.

g. For 28 jet, 35 jet, 65 jet and 40-90 hp models with prime start, refer to **Figure 54** and **Figure 55**.

h. For 60-90 hp models with a choke valve, refer to **Figure 56**.

i. For 115-225 hp 90° models, refer to **Figure 57-60**.

j. For 225-250 hp 76° models, refer to **Figure 61**.

2 hp Throttle Plunger Carburetor

1. Refer to *Silencer cover and carburetor* for the carburetor removal and installation procedure. Refer to **Figure 45** during the disassembly and assembly process. Remove the nut, lockwasher and plain washer from the choke valve shaft. Remove the shaft and choke valve. Remove the drain screw and gasket (8 and 9, **Figure 45**) and drain the fuel into a suitable container. Discard the drain screw gasket.

2. Remove the throttle screw, throttle link bracket, cap, spacer and throttle plunger from the carburetor (**Figure 45**). Note the E-clip position on the plunger. Remove the jet needle, spring seat, E-clip, spring and throttle plunger from the mixing chamber screw (14-17, **Figure 45**). Carefully remove the throttle valve (13, **Figure 45**) from the throttle valve bore.

3. Remove the two float bowl retaining screws. Remove the float bowl and gasket. Discard the float bowl gasket. Remove the float pin, float and needle valve (27-29, **Figure 45**).

4. Remove the screw (26, **Figure 45**), main nozzle (31) and main jet (30). Remove the idle adjusting screw and spring.

5. Assembly is the reverse of disassembly. Clean all passages completely. Inspect all components for cracked or worn areas and replace if required. Inspect the float for cracks or any indication of leakage and replace if required. Replace the float bowl gasket and drain screw gasket. Apply Loctite 242 to the threads of the throttle screw (10, **Figure 45**). Apply water-resistant grease to the choke shaft (6, **Figure 45**) and idle adjusting screw spring (33, **Figure 45**). Adjust the float as indicated in Step 6. Tighten all fasteners securely.

6. Float specifications are provided in **Table 1**. With the float gently resting on the needle valve, measure the float height as shown in A, **Figure 46**. Remove the float and gently bend the adjusting tab (B, **Figure 46**) until the float measurement is correct.

Carburetor (3, 6 and 8 hp) Disassembly/Assembly

1. Refer to *Silencer cover and carburetor* for the carburetor removal and installation procedure. Refer to **Figure 47** during the disassembly and assembly process. Refer to *Carburetor mounted fuel pump* in this chapter for fuel pump repair procedures.

2. Remove the four screws, float chamber and O-ring from the carburetor. Discard the O-ring. Remove the float pivot pin, float and inlet needle valve (**Figure 47**).

3. Remove the main jet and nozzle (10 and 11, **Figure 47**). Remove the idle jet and seal (12 and 13, **Figure 47**) along with other components in the float chamber. Note the location for all removed components.

4. Remove the idle mixture screw and spring (15, **Figure 47**). Remove the two screws and the top cover and gasket from the carburetor. Discard the top cover gasket.

5. Assembly is the reverse of disassembly. Clean all passages completely. Inspect all components for cracked or worn areas and replace if required. Inspect the float for cracks or any indication of leakage. Replace if required. Replace the float chamber O-ring and top cover gasket. Adjust the float as indicated in Step 6. Tighten all fasteners securely.

6. Float specifications are provided in **Table 1**. With the float gently resting on the inlet needle valve, measure the float height at the point shown in **Figure 48**. Remove the float and gently bend the adjusting tab until float height is correct.

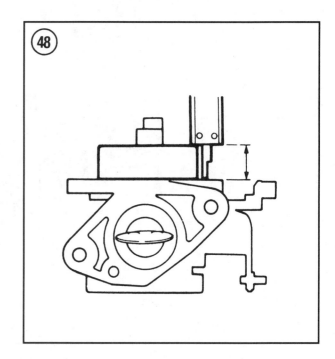

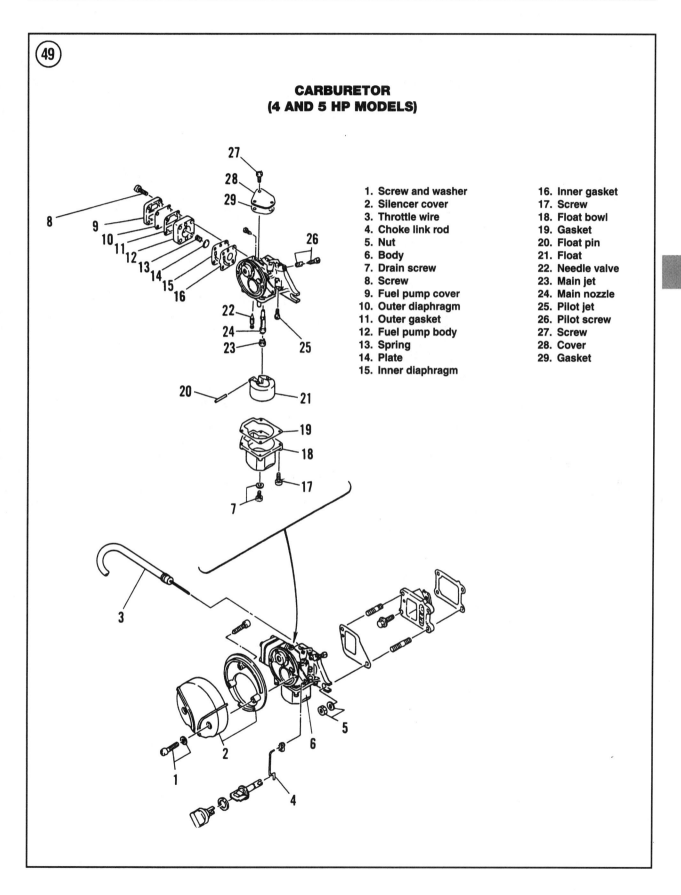

**CARBURETOR
(4 AND 5 HP MODELS)**

1. Screw and washer
2. Silencer cover
3. Throttle wire
4. Choke link rod
5. Nut
6. Body
7. Drain screw
8. Screw
9. Fuel pump cover
10. Outer diaphragm
11. Outer gasket
12. Fuel pump body
13. Spring
14. Plate
15. Inner diaphragm
16. Inner gasket
17. Screw
18. Float bowl
19. Gasket
20. Float pin
21. Float
22. Needle valve
23. Main jet
24. Main nozzle
25. Pilot jet
26. Pilot screw
27. Screw
28. Cover
29. Gasket

6

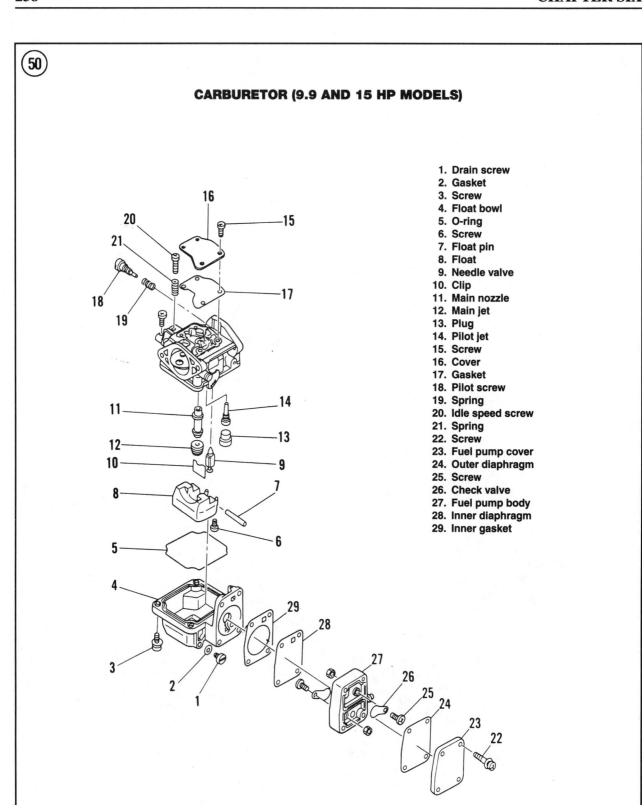

⑤⓪

CARBURETOR (9.9 AND 15 HP MODELS)

1. Drain screw
2. Gasket
3. Screw
4. Float bowl
5. O-ring
6. Screw
7. Float pin
8. Float
9. Needle valve
10. Clip
11. Main nozzle
12. Main jet
13. Plug
14. Pilot jet
15. Screw
16. Cover
17. Gasket
18. Pilot screw
19. Spring
20. Idle speed screw
21. Spring
22. Screw
23. Fuel pump cover
24. Outer diaphragm
25. Screw
26. Check valve
27. Fuel pump body
28. Inner diaphragm
29. Inner gasket

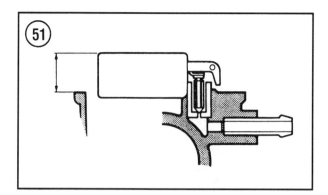

**Carburetor Disassembly/Assembly
(4 and 5 hp Carburetor)**

1. Refer to *Silencer cover and carburetor* for carburetor removal and installation procedures. Refer to **Figure 49** during the disassembly and assembly process. Refer to *Carburetor mounted pumps* for fuel pump repair procedures.

2. Remove the drain screw and gasket (7, **Figure 49**) from the float bowl (18, **Figure 49**) and drain the residual fuel into a suitable container. Remove the four screws, float

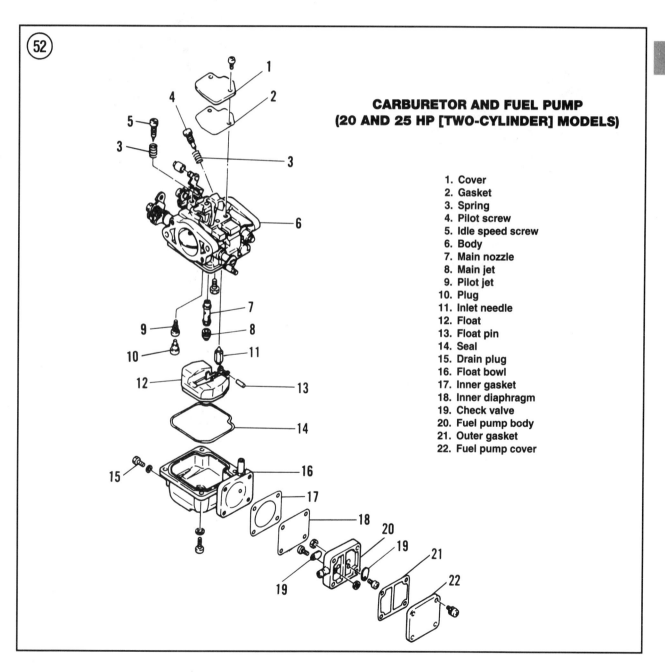

**CARBURETOR AND FUEL PUMP
(20 AND 25 HP [TWO-CYLINDER] MODELS)**

1. Cover
2. Gasket
3. Spring
4. Pilot screw
5. Idle speed screw
6. Body
7. Main nozzle
8. Main jet
9. Pilot jet
10. Plug
11. Inlet needle
12. Float
13. Float pin
14. Seal
15. Drain plug
16. Float bowl
17. Inner gasket
18. Inner diaphragm
19. Check valve
20. Fuel pump body
21. Outer gasket
22. Fuel pump cover

6

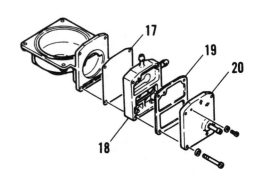

**CARBURETOR
(25 AND 30 HP [THREE-CYLINDER] MODELS)**

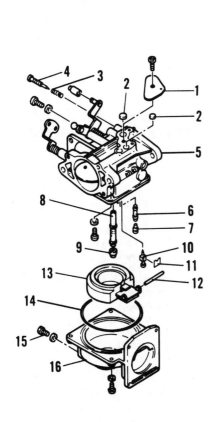

1. Cover
2. Gasket
3. Spring
4. Idle mixture
   screw
5. Body
6. Idle jet
7. Plug

8. Main nozzle
9. Main jet
10. Inlet needle valve
11. Clip
12. Float pin
13. Float
14. Seal
15. Drain plug
16. Float bowl
17. Diaphragm
18. Fuel pump body
19. Gasket
20. Fuel pump cover

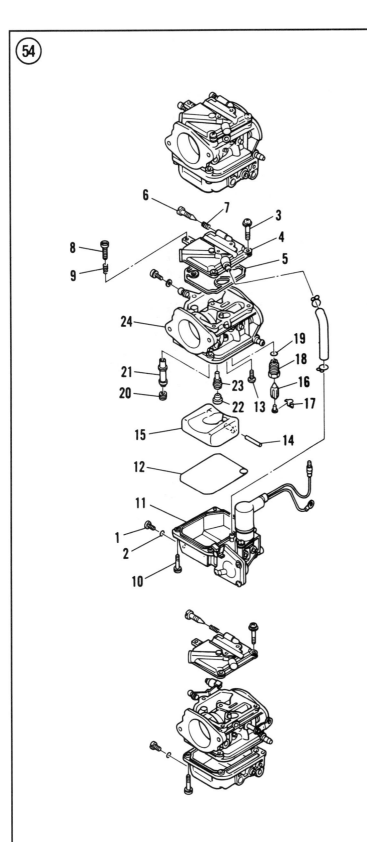

(54)

CARBURETOR (28 JET, 35 JET, 65 JET AND 40-90 HP MODELS WITH PRIME START)

1. Drain screw
2. O-ring
3. Screw/washer
4. Cover
5. Gasket
6. Pilot screw
7. Spring
8. Idle speed screw
9. Spring
10. Screw/washer
11. Float bowl
12. Gasket
13. Screw
14. Float pin
15. Float
16. Inlet needle valve
17. Clip
18. Inlet valve seat
19. Gasket
20. Main jet
21. Main nozzle
22. Plug
23. Pilot jet
24. Body

6

bowl and gasket from the carburetor. Discard the float bowl gasket and drain screw gasket.

3. Remove the float pin (20, **Figure 49**,) float (21, **Figure 49**) and needle valve (22, **Figure 49**). Remove the pilot jet (25, **Figure 49**), main nozzle (24, **Figure 49**) and main jet (23, **Figure 49**).

4. Remove the pilot screw and spring (26, **Figure 49**). Remove the three screws cover and gasket from the carburetor. Discard the top cover gasket.

5. Assembly is the reverse of disassembly. Clean all passages completely. Inspect all components for cracked or worn areas and replace if required. Inspect the float for cracks or any indication of leakage and replace if required. Replace the float chamber gasket, top cover gasket and drain screw gasket. Adjust the float as indicated in Step 6. Tighten all fasteners securely.

6. Float specifications are provided in **Table 1**. With the float gently resting on the needle valve, measure the float height at the points shown in **Figure 46**. Remove the float and gently bend the adjusting tab (B, **Figure 46**) until float height is correct.

Carburetor Disassembly/Assembly (9.9 and 15 hp)

1. Refer to *Silencer cover and carburetor* for carburetor removal and installation instructions. Refer to *Carburetor mounted pumps* for fuel pump repair procedures. Refer to **Figure 50** during the disassembly and assembly process.

2. Remove the drain screw and gasket (1 and 2, **Figure 50**) and drain the residual fuel into a suitable container. Remove the four screws, float bowl (4, **Figure 50**) and O-ring (5, **Figure 50**). Discard the O-ring and drain screw gasket.

3. Remove the screw and float pin (6 and 7, **Figure 50**), float (8, **Figure 50**) and needle valve (9, **Figure 50**). Turn

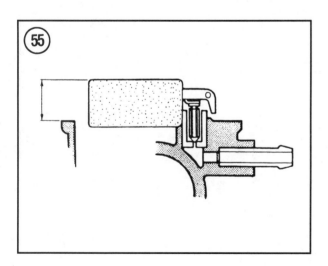

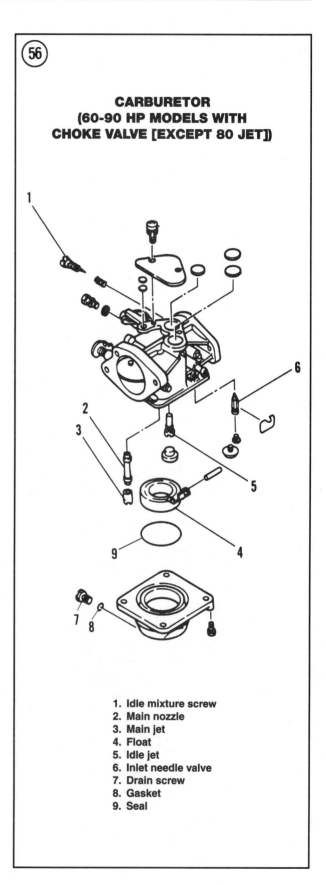

CARBURETOR (60-90 HP MODELS WITH CHOKE VALVE [EXCEPT 80 JET])

1. Idle mixture screw
2. Main nozzle
3. Main jet
4. Float
5. Idle jet
6. Inlet needle valve
7. Drain screw
8. Gasket
9. Seal

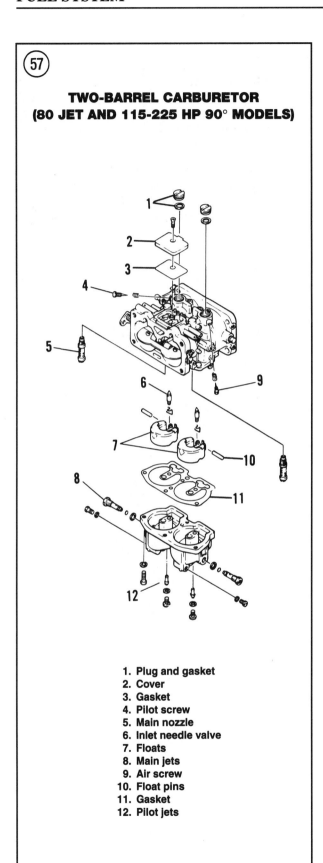

**TWO-BARREL CARBURETOR
(80 JET AND 115-225 HP 90° MODELS)**

1. Plug and gasket
2. Cover
3. Gasket
4. Pilot screw
5. Main nozzle
6. Inlet needle valve
7. Floats
8. Main jets
9. Air screw
10. Float pins
11. Gasket
12. Pilot jets

the main nozzle and main jet (11 and 12, **Figure 50**) counterclockwise and remove them along with the plug and pilot jet (13 and 14, **Figure 50**). Remove any other components of the float chamber noting the location.

4. Remove the four screws, top cover (15, **Figure 50**) and gasket (17, **Figure 50**). Remove the pilot screw and spring (18 and 19, **Figure 50**) along with the idle speed screw and spring (20 and 21, **Figure 50**).

5. Assembly is the reverse of disassembly. Clean all passages completely. Inspect all components for cracks or worn areas and replace if required. Inspect the float for cracks or any indication of leakage. Replace if required. Replace the float chamber O-ring, top cover gasket and drain screw gasket. Adjust the float as indicated in Step 6. Tighten all fasteners securely.

6. Float specifications are provided in **Table 1**. With the float gently resting on the needle valve, measure the float height as shown in **Figure 51**. Replace the float if the measurement is not within the specification.

6

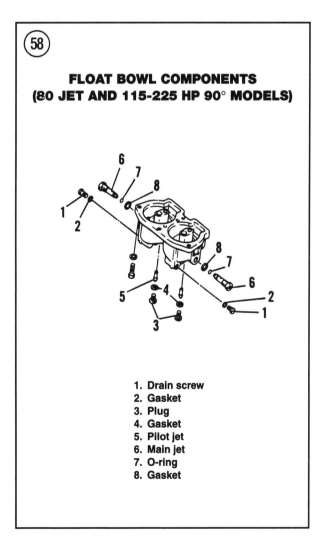

**FLOAT BOWL COMPONENTS
(80 JET AND 115-225 HP 90° MODELS)**

1. Drain screw
2. Gasket
3. Plug
4. Gasket
5. Pilot jet
6. Main jet
7. O-ring
8. Gasket

**Carburetor Disassembly/Assembly
(20 and 25 hp [Two-Cylinder] Models)**

1. Refer to *Silencer cover and carburetor* for carburetor removal and installation procedures. Refer to *Carburetor mounted pumps* for fuel pump repair procedures. Refer to **Figure 52** during the disassembly and assembly process.

2. Use a suitable container to capture the residual fuel. Remove the drain screw and gasket (15, **Figure 52**). Remove the four screws, float bowl and seal (16 and 14, **Figure 52**). Discard the drain screw gasket and float bowl seal.

3. Remove the pin (13, **Figure 52**), float (12, **Figure 52**) and inlet needle valve (11, **Figure 52**). Remove the main nozzle and main jet (7 and 8, **Figure 52**) along with the plug and idle jet (9 and 10, **Figure 52**).

4. Remove the two screws, cover and gasket (1 and 2 **Figure 52**). Remove the idle mixture screw and spring (3 and 4, **Figure 52**) along with the idle speed screw and spring (5, **Figure 52**).

5. Assembly is the reverse is disassembly. Clean all passages completely. Inspect all components for cracked or worn areas and replace if required. Inspect the float for cracks or any indication of leakage and replace if required. Replace the float bowl seal, top cover gasket and drain screw gasket. Adjust the float as indicated in Step 5-6. Tighten all fasteners securely.

6. Float specifications are provided in **Table 1**. With the float gently resting on the inlet needle valve, measure the float height as shown in **Figure 51**. Remove the float and gently bend the adjusting tab until the float height is correct.

**Carburetor Disassembly/Assembly
(25 and 30 hp [Three-Cylinder] Models)**

1. Refer to *Silencer cover and carburetor* for carburetor removal and installation procedures. Refer to *Carburetor mounted pumps* for repair of the fuel pump mounted on the No. 2 carburetor. Refer to **Figure 53** during the disassembly and assembly process.

2. Use a suitable container to capture the residual fuel. Remove the drain plug and gasket (15, **Figure 53**). Discard the drain plug gasket. Remove the four screws, float bowl and seal (14 and 16, **Figure 53**). Discard the seal.

3. Remove the pin and float (12 and 13, **Figure 53**) along with the clip and inlet needle valve (10 and 11, **Figure 53**). Carefully remove the main nozzle and main jet (8 and 9, **Figure 53**) along with the idle jet and plug (6 and 7, **Figure 53**).

4. Remove the screw, top cover and two gaskets (1 and 2, **Figure 53**). Remove the idle mixture screw and spring (3 and 4, **Figure 53**).

5. Assembly is the reverse of disassembly. Clean all passages completely. Inspect all components for cracks or worn areas and replace if required. Inspect the float for cracks or any indication of leakage and replace if required. Replace the float bowl seal, drain screw gasket and top cover gaskets. Adjust the float as indicated in Step 6. Tighten all fasteners securely.

6. Float specifications are provided in **Table 1**. With the float gently resting on the inlet needle valve, measure the float height as shown in **Figure 51**. Remove the float and carefully bend the adjusting tab until the float height is correct.

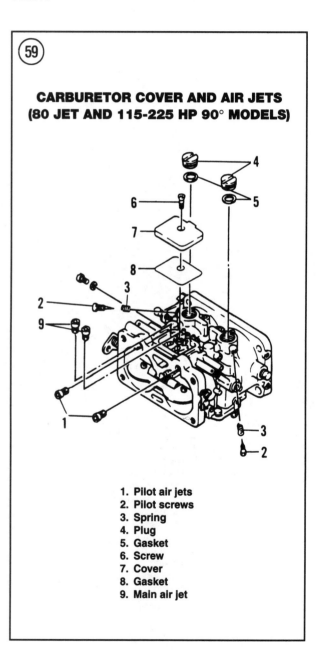

**CARBURETOR COVER AND AIR JETS
(80 JET AND 115-225 HP 90° MODELS)**

1. Pilot air jets
2. Pilot screws
3. Spring
4. Plug
5. Gasket
6. Screw
7. Cover
8. Gasket
9. Main air jet

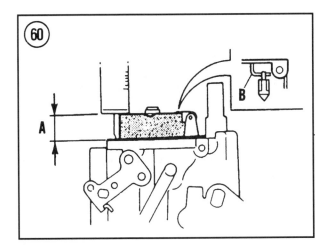

Carburetor Disassembly/Assembly
(40-90 hp Models Equipped with Prime Start)

1. Refer to *Silencer cover and carburetor* for carburetor removal and installation procedures. Refer to *Electrothermal valve* for primer pump and thermal valve replacement procedures. Refer to **Figure 54** during the disassembly and assembly process.

2. Use a suitable container to capture the residual fuel, then remove the drain screw and gasket (1 and 2, **Figure 54**). Remove the four screws and washers (10, **Figure 54**), float chamber and gasket (11 and 12, **Figure 54**) from the carburetor. Discard the drain screw gasket and the float chamber gasket.

6

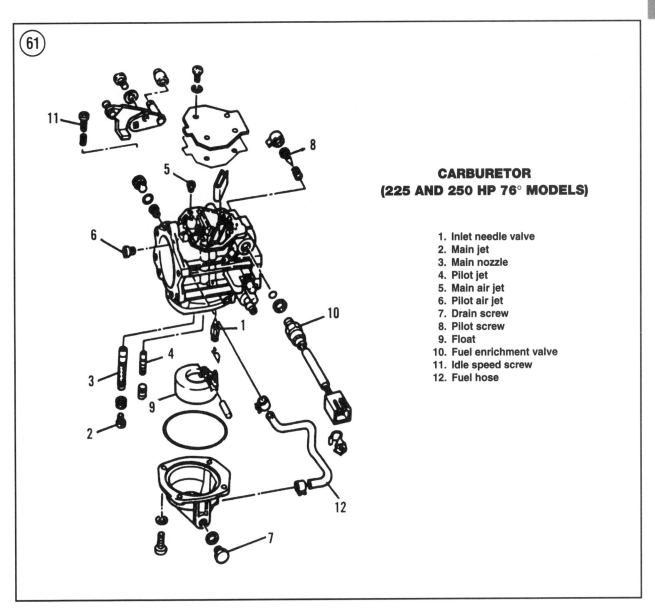

CARBURETOR
(225 AND 250 HP 76° MODELS)

1. Inlet needle valve
2. Main jet
3. Main nozzle
4. Pilot jet
5. Main air jet
6. Pilot air jet
7. Drain screw
8. Pilot screw
9. Float
10. Fuel enrichment valve
11. Idle speed screw
12. Fuel hose

3. Remove the pivot pin and float (14 and 15, **Figure 54**) along with the needle valve and clip (16 and 17, **Figure 54**). Remove the valve seat and gasket (18 and 19, **Figure 54**). Carefully remove the main nozzle and main jet (20 and 21, **Figure 54**) along with the plug and pilot jet (22 and 23, **Figure 54**).

4. Remove the four screws, cover and gasket (4 and 5, **Figure 54**). Discard the gasket. Remove the idle speed screw and spring (8 and 9, **Figure 54**) along with the pilot screw and spring (6 and 7, **Figure 54**).

5. Assembly is the reverse of disassembly. Clean all passages completely. Inspect all components for cracks or worn areas and replace if required. Inspect the float for cracks or any indication of leakage and replace if required. Replace the float chamber gasket, top cover gasket and drain screw gasket. Adjust the float as indicated in Step 6. Tighten all fasteners securely.

6. Float specifications are provided in **Table 1**. With the float gently resting on the needle valve, measure the float height as shown in **Figure 55**. Remove the float and carefully bend the adjusting tab until the float height is correct or replace the float if necessary to correct the float height.

**Carburetor Disassembly/Assembly
(60-90 hp Models Equipped with Choke Valve)**

1. Refer to *Silencer cover and carburetor* for carburetor removal and installation procedures. Refer to **Figure 56** during the disassembly and assembly process. Use a suitable container to capture the residual fuel, then remove the drain screw and gasket. Discard the drain screw gasket.

2. Remove the four screws, float bowl and seal. Discard the float bowl seal (9, **Figure 56**). Remove the pivot pin, float (4, **Figure 56**), clip and needle valve (6, **Figure 56**). Remove the idle jet (5, **Figure 56**) and sealing plug.

3. Remove the two screws top cover and gaskets. Discard the gaskets. Remove the idle mixture screw (1, **Figure 56**) along with the stop screw.

4. Assembly is the reverse of disassembly. Clean all passages completely. Inspect all components for cracked or worn areas and replace if required. Inspect the float for cracks or any indication of leakage and replace if required.

5. Replace the float bowl seal, drain screw gasket and top cover gaskets. Adjust the float as indicated in Step 6. Tighten all fasteners securely.

6. Float specifications are provided in **Table 1**. With the float gently resting on the needle valve, measure the float height as shown in **Figure 55**. Remove the float and carefully bend the adjusting tab until the float height is correct.

**Two-Barrel Carburetor Disassembly/Assembly
(115-225 hp 90° Models)**

1. Refer to *Silencer cover and carburetor* for carburetor removal and installation procedures. Refer to **Figure 57** during the disassembly and assembly process.

2. Use a suitable container to capture the residual fuel, then remove the drain screw and gasket (1 and 2, **Figure 58**) from the float bowl. Remove the four screws and washers, float bowl and gasket (11, **Figure 57**). Discard the gasket.

3. Carefully remove the pivot pin and float (7 and 10, **Figure 57**) along with the needle valve (6, **Figure 57**). Remove the main nozzle (5, **Figure 57**).

4. Remove the main jets (6, **Figure 58**), O-rings and gaskets (7 and 8, **Figure 58**) from the float bowl. Discard the gasket and O-ring. Remove the plug (3, **Figure 58**), gaskets and pilot jets (4 and 5, **Figure 58**) from the float bowl. Discard the plug gaskets.

5. Remove the screw (6, **Figure 59**), cover and gasket (7 and 8, **Figure 59**). Discard the gasket. Remove the pilot screw and spring (2 and 3, **Figure 59**). Remove the pilot air jets (1, **Figure 59**) and main air jets (9, **Figure 59**) from the carburetor body.

6. Assembly is the reverse of disassembly. Clean all passages completely. Inspect all components for cracks or worn areas and replace if required. Inspect the floats for cracks or any indication of leakage and replace if required. Replace the float bowl gasket, drain plug gaskets, pilot plug gaskets, cover gasket and main jet O-rings. Adjust the floats as instructed in Step 7. Tighten all fasteners securely.

7. Float specifications are provided in **Table 1**. With the float gently resting on the needle valve, measure the points indicated (A, **Figure 60**). Remove the float and carefully bend the adjusting tab (B, **Figure 60**) until the float height is correct.

**Carburetor Disassembly/Assembly
(225-250 hp 76° Models)**

1. Refer to *Silencer cover and carburetor* for carburetor removal and installation procedures. Refer to **Figure 61** during the disassembly and assembly process. Remove the drain screw and gasket (7, **Figure 61**) along with the four screws and washers for float bowl. *Discard* the drain screw gasket.

2. Remove the float bowl and seal. Discard the seal. Remove the pivot pin, float, clip and needle valve (9 and 1, **Figure 61**). Remove the pilot jet and seal (4, **Figure 61**) along with the main nozzle and main jet (2 and 3, **Figure 61**).

3. Remove the four screws and washers, top cover and gasket. Discard the gasket. Remove the main air jets and

pilot air jets (5 and 6, **Figure 61**) along with the idle adjustment screw and pilot screw (11 and 8, **Figure 61**).

4. Remove the fuel enrichment valve, gasket and O-ring (10, **Figure 61**).

5. Assembly is the reverse of disassembly. Clean all passages completely. Inspect all components for cracks or worn areas and replace if required. Inspect the float for cracks or any indication of leakage and replace if required. Replace all gaskets and seals in the carburetor. Adjust the float as instructed in Step 6. Tighten all fasteners securely.

6. Float specifications are provided in **Table 1**. With the float gently resting on the needle valve, measure the points indicated (A, **Figure 60**). Remove the float and carefully bend the adjusting tab (B, **Figure 60**) until the float height is correct.

Electrothermal Valve/Fuel Enrichment Pump

Electrothermal valve removal/installation

1. Disconnect both leads from the valve.

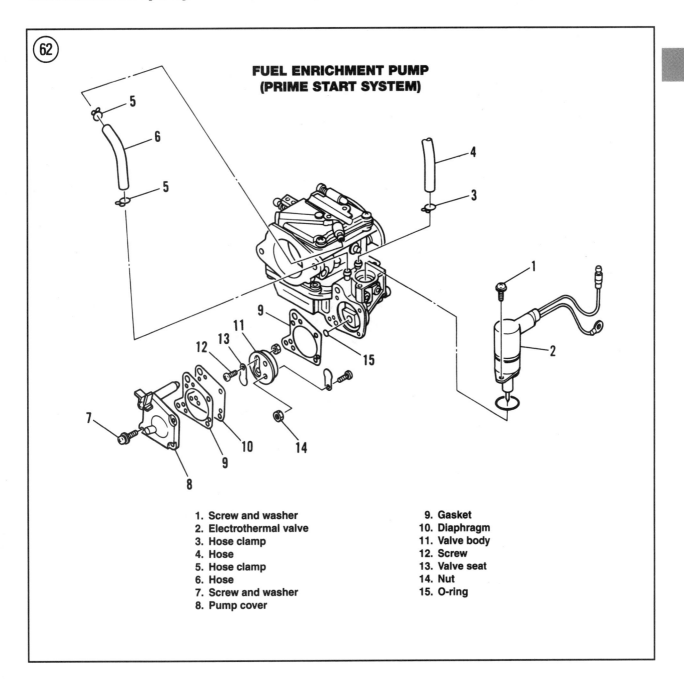

FUEL ENRICHMENT PUMP (PRIME START SYSTEM)

1. Screw and washer
2. Electrothermal valve
3. Hose clamp
4. Hose
5. Hose clamp
6. Hose
7. Screw and washer
8. Pump cover
9. Gasket
10. Diaphragm
11. Valve body
12. Screw
13. Valve seat
14. Nut
15. O-ring

2. Remove the retaining screw (1, **Figure 62**).

3. Remove the electrothermal valve (2, **Figure 62**) and O-ring. Discard the O-ring.

4. Install a new O-ring on the electrothermal valve. Carefully install the electothermal valve into position.

5. Install the retaining screws and tighten securely. Connect the leads to the proper location.

Fuel enrichment pump removal/installation

1. Remove the three screws and washers (7, **Figure 62**). Remove the pump cover (8, **Figure 2**) along with the gaskets and diaphragm (9 and 10, **Figure 62**). Discard the gaskets and diaphragm.

2. Remove the valve body and O-ring (11 and 15, **Figure 62**) from the carburetor. Discard the O-ring. Remove the screws and nuts (12 and 14, **Figure 62**) from the valve body. Remove the valves (13, **Figure 62**) from the valve body.

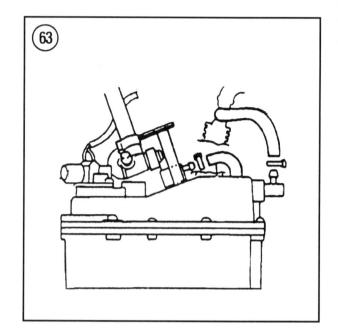

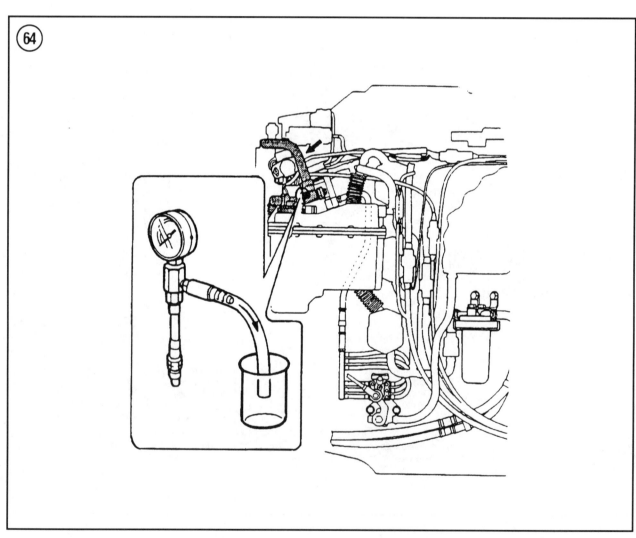

3. Assembly is the reverse of disassembly. Inspect the valves for bent or broken components and replace if required. Inspect the valve seat at the valve body for worn or damaged surfaces and replace if required. Replace gaskets, diaphragm and O-ring on assembly. Tighten all fasteners securely.

EFI COMPONENTS

Vapor Separator Tank Disassembly/Assembly

1. Prior to removal, mark all hose connections on the vapor separator tank (**Figure 63**). Connect a fuel pressure gauge and bleed-off tube to the schrader valve connection (**Figure 64**). Using a suitable container relieve the system pressure. Use a suitable container when removing hoses and components to capture residual fuel that will likely spill from the disconnected hoses and components.

2. Remove the screw and pressure hose fitting (1 and 2, **Figure 65**). Remove and discard the O-rings. Disconnect the fuel pump leads (3, **Figure 65**) from the main harness. Remove the bolt (4, **Figure 65**) and washers from the lower support. Remove the grommet and sleeve (8 and 9, **Figure 65**) from the vapor separator tank.

3. Remove the two screws (1, **Figure 66**) along with the plate and seat (2 and 3, **Figure 66**). Disconnect the vacuum hose and remove the fuel pressure regulator and sleeves (4

6

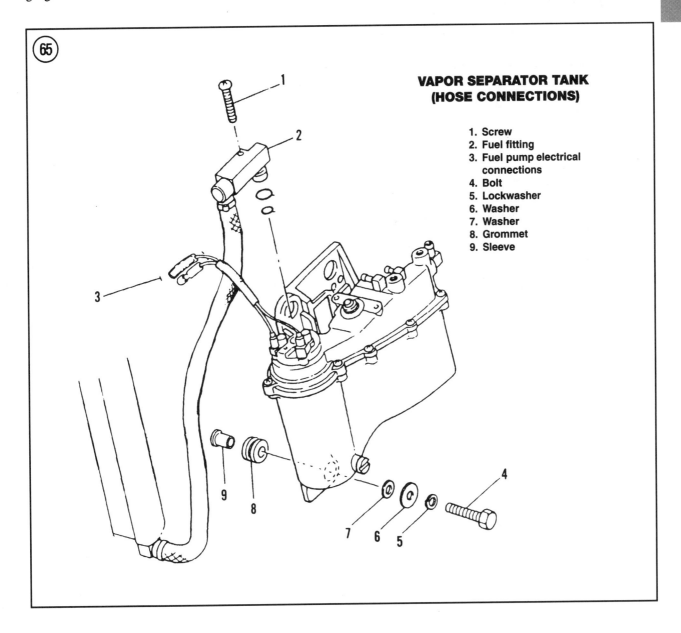

(65)

**VAPOR SEPARATOR TANK
(HOSE CONNECTIONS)**

1. Screw
2. Fuel fitting
3. Fuel pump electrical
   connections
4. Bolt
5. Lockwasher
6. Washer
7. Washer
8. Grommet
9. Sleeve

and 5, **Figure 66**). Remove and discard the O-ring (6, **Figure 66**).

4. Remove the oil hose fitting and O-ring (7 and 8, **Figure 66**). Discard the O-ring. Remove the two screws (9, **Figure 66**) and separate the return hose fitting (10, **Figure 66**) from the fuel pressure regulator. Remove the screen and O-ring (11 and 12, **Figure 66**). Discard the O-ring.

5. Use a suitable container to capture the residual fuel, then remove the drain screw and gasket (2 and 3, **Figure 67**). Carefully remove the screws (4, **Figure 67**). Remove the top cover and O-ring (5 and 6, **Figure 67**). Discard the O-ring.

> *CAUTION*
> *Considerable effort may be required when removing the screws from the top cover. Avoid the use of an impact driver as the top cover or tank may be damaged. Drill out and replace the screws as necessary.*

6. Carefully twist the filter (7, **Figure 67**) in a clockwise direction as viewed from the bottom and remove the filter. Gently clean the filter with a soft brush in suitable solvent. Avoid the use of strong compressed air as the filter may be damaged. Replace the filter when it cannot be easily or completely cleaned.

7. Remove the retainer and insulator (8 and 9, **Figure 67**) from the electric fuel pump.

8. Remove the pivot pin (1, **Figure 68**), float and needle valve (2 and 3, **Figure 68**). Mark the location for future reference and carefully remove the insulating caps (4, **Figure 68**). Replace the caps if they are damaged during the removal process.

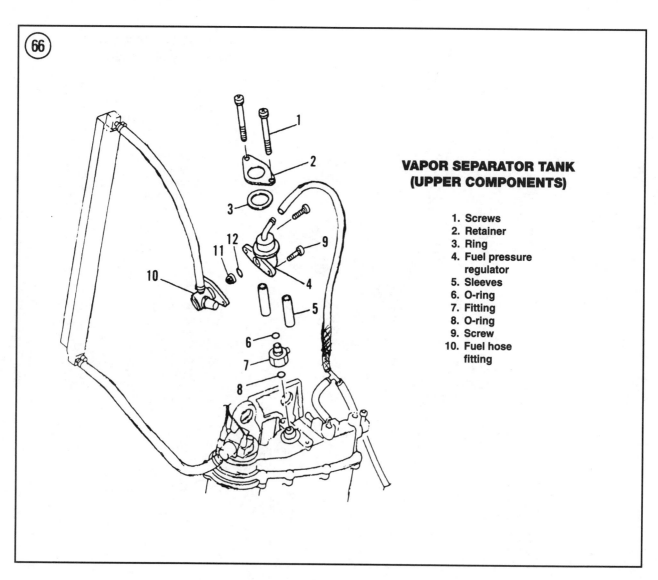

66

VAPOR SEPARATOR TANK (UPPER COMPONENTS)

1. Screws
2. Retainer
3. Ring
4. Fuel pressure regulator
5. Sleeves
6. O-ring
7. Fitting
8. O-ring
9. Screw
10. Fuel hose fitting

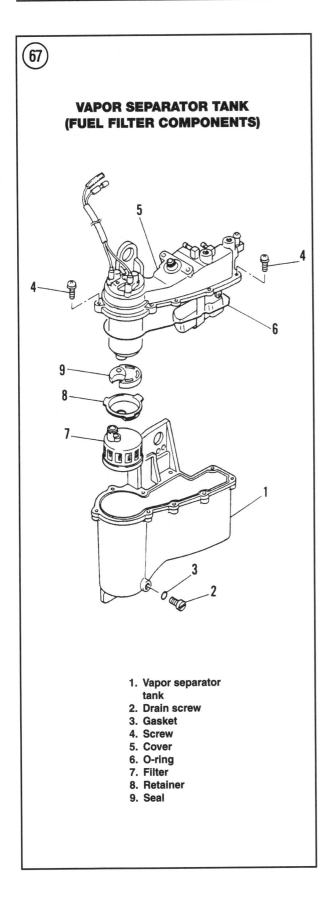

67

VAPOR SEPARATOR TANK (FUEL FILTER COMPONENTS)

1. Vapor separator tank
2. Drain screw
3. Gasket
4. Screw
5. Cover
6. O-ring
7. Filter
8. Retainer
9. Seal

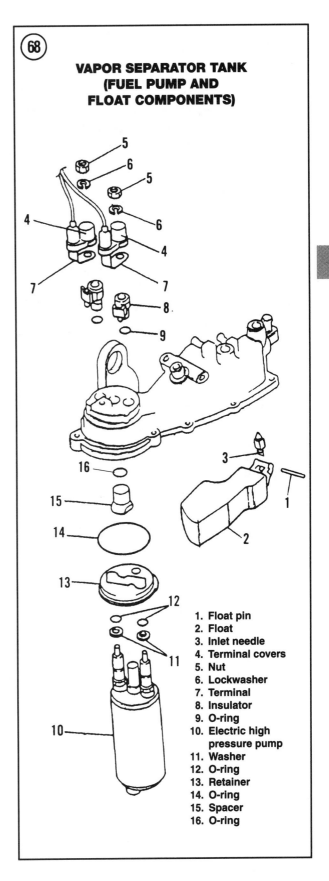

68

VAPOR SEPARATOR TANK (FUEL PUMP AND FLOAT COMPONENTS)

1. Float pin
2. Float
3. Inlet needle
4. Terminal covers
5. Nut
6. Lockwasher
7. Terminal
8. Insulator
9. O-ring
10. Electric high pressure pump
11. Washer
12. O-ring
13. Retainer
14. O-ring
15. Spacer
16. O-ring

6

9. Mark the fuel pump orientation for future reference. While supporting the fuel pump, remove the nuts and washers (5 and 6, **Figure 68**) from the terminals. Mark the location of the lead connections and remove them(7, **Figure 68**)from the terminals.

10. Remove the insulators and O-rings (8 and 9, **Figure 68**) from the top cover. Inspect them for cracks or damage and replace as required. Discard the O-rings. Carefully slide the fuel pump (10, **Figure 68**) from the top cover. Remove the white washers and O-rings (11 and 12, **Figure 68**). Discard the O-rings.

11. Remove the alignment plate and O-ring (13 and 14, **Figure 68**). Slide the O-ring and spacer (15, **Figure 68**) from the fuel pump.

12. Clean all components completely in a suitable solvent. Inspect all components for cracks or worn areas and replace if required. Inspect the float for cracks or any indication of leakage and replace if required. Replace the drain screw gasket and *all* O-rings during assembly. Assembly procedures are the reverse of disassembly. Tighten all fasteners securely. Check for any fuel leaks and correct them before putting the engine into service.

Fuel Rail and Injectors Removal/Installation

> *CAUTION*
> *Remove fuel hose clamps as indicated in Step 1. The fuel hoses may be damaged if the clamps are removed by twisting. Always relieve the fuel system pressure before attempting any repairs.*

1. Use sharp cutters to cut and remove all fuel hose clamps (A, **Figure 69**) as indicated. Use a suitable container to capture residual fuel that will likely spill during hose removal. Carefully remove the hoses (2, **Figure 70**) from the high pressure fitting (3, **Figure 70**), return hose fitting (4, **Figure 70**) and fuel rail fittings (5, **Figure 70**). Use a common valve stem tool to remove the schrader valve from the return hose fitting.

2. Remove the four bolts and washers (1 and 2, **Figure 71**) from the fuel rail. Working carefully to avoid disturbing the fuel injectors, remove the fuel rail (3, **Figure 71**) from the throttle body. Remove both alignment pins (4, **Figure 71**). Carefully remove each injector connection and remove the injectors (5, **Figure 71**) from the throttle body.

3. Remove and discard the O-ring (1, **Figure 72**) along with the seal and collar (2 and 3, **Figure 72**) from the injector.

> *CAUTION*
> *Be careful when installing the injectors into the throttle body and when installing the fuel rail onto the injector connection. Never force*

the fuel rail into position. The O-rings may become damaged and result in a fuel leak.

4. Assembly is the reverse of disassembly. Replace all O-rings in this assembly. Inspect the hoses for damaged areas, brittle condition or sponge-like feel and replace if required. Replace all hose clamps by positioning them properly over the hose and fitting. Use cutters and securely clamp as shown (B, **Figure 69**). *Do not use excessive force* when installing the clamps as they may be damaged.

5. Lubricate all O-rings, seals and grommets with Yamalube 2 cycle outboard oil or its equivalent during assembly. Tighten all fasteners securely. Check for any fuel

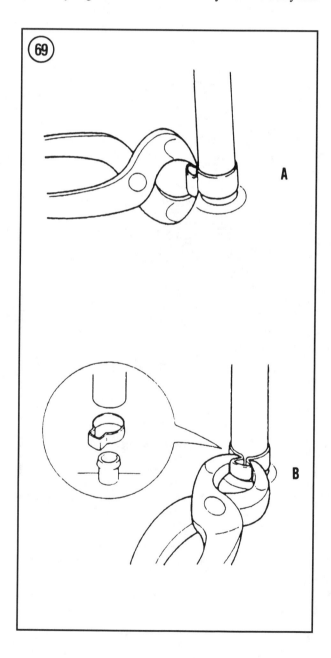

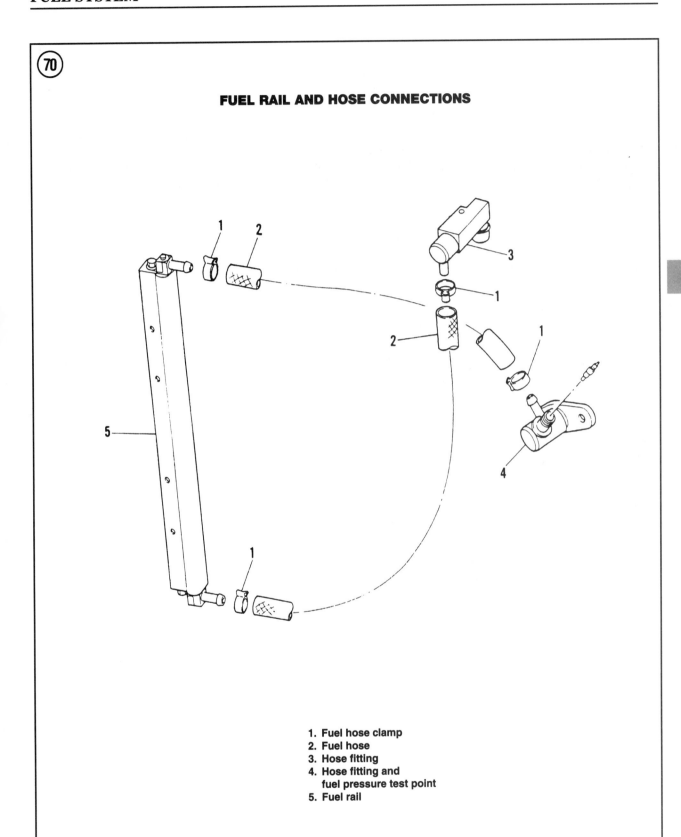

FUEL RAIL AND HOSE CONNECTIONS

70

6

1. Fuel hose clamp
2. Fuel hose
3. Hose fitting
4. Hose fitting and
   fuel pressure test point
5. Fuel rail

leaks and correct them before putting the engine into service.

Throttle Position Indicator Removal/Installation

1. Disconnect the harness to lead coupler and remove the screws (6, **Figure 71**). Remove the throttle position indicator (9, **Figure 71**).

2. Remove both screws and washers (7 and 8, **Figure 71**) along with the bracket (10, **Figure 71**).

3. Remove the grommet and sleeves (11 and 12, **Figure 71**) along with the coupler and spring (13 and 14, **Figure 71**).

4. Assembly is the reverse of disassembly. Inspect and replace any worn or damaged components. Throttle position indicator adjustment procedures are provided in Chapter Five. Tighten all fasteners securely.

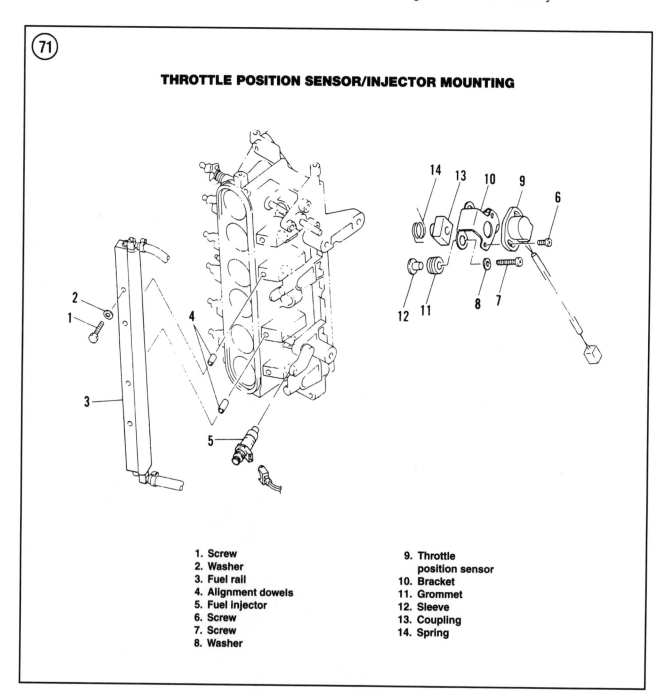

(71)

THROTTLE POSITION SENSOR/INJECTOR MOUNTING

1. Screw
2. Washer
3. Fuel rail
4. Alignment dowels
5. Fuel injector
6. Screw
7. Screw
8. Washer
9. Throttle position sensor
10. Bracket
11. Grommet
12. Sleeve
13. Coupling
14. Spring

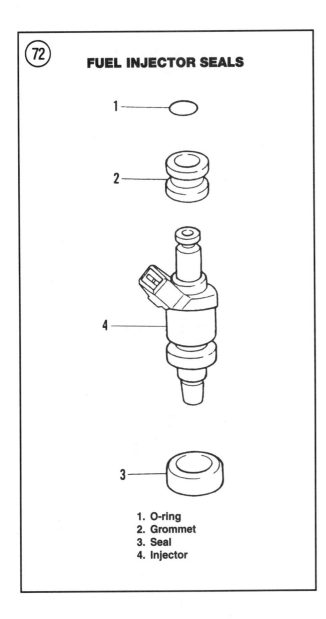

FUEL INJECTOR SEALS

1. O-ring
2. Grommet
3. Seal
4. Injector

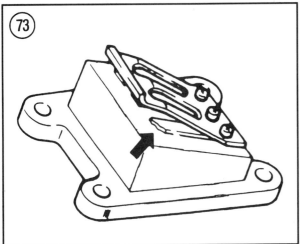

REED VALVE

Inspect the reed valves for bent, cracked or missing sections (**Figure 73**). Measure reed tip (A, **Figure 74**) and reed stop (B) opening during inspection and after installing the reed valves. Reed valve specifications are provided in **Table 4**.

Reed valve design and mounting configurations vary by model. Refer to the appropriate illustration during the removal, disassembly, assembly and installation process.

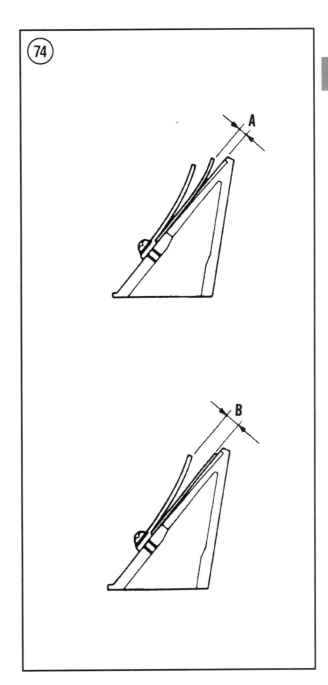

6

Variations in component appearance in the illustration may occur. Use a comparable illustration to determine component configuration and location. Tighten all fasteners to the values provided in **Table 5**. Apply Loctite 242 to reed valves/reed stop fasteners.

    a. For 2 hp models, refer to **Figure 75**.
    b. For 3 hp models, refer to **Figure 76**.
    c. For 4 and 5 hp models, refer to **Figure 77**.
    d. For 6 and 8 hp models, refer to **Figure 78**.
    e. For 9.9 and 15 hp models, refer to **Figure 79**.
    f. For 20-30 hp models, refer to **Figure 80**.
    g. For 28 jet, 35 jet and 40-50 hp models (except model E48), refer to **Figure 81**.
    h. For E48 models, refer to **Figure 82**.
    i. For 60-90 hp models (excluding E60 and E75), refer to **Figure 83**.

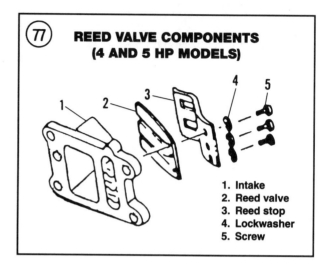

(77)

**REED VALVE COMPONENTS
(4 AND 5 HP MODELS)**

1. Intake
2. Reed valve
3. Reed stop
4. Lockwasher
5. Screw

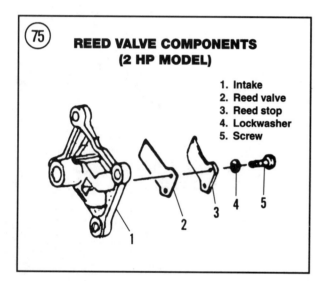

(75)

**REED VALVE COMPONENTS
(2 HP MODEL)**

1. Intake
2. Reed valve
3. Reed stop
4. Lockwasher
5. Screw

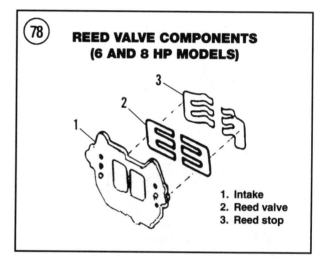

(78)

**REED VALVE COMPONENTS
(6 AND 8 HP MODELS)**

1. Intake
2. Reed valve
3. Reed stop

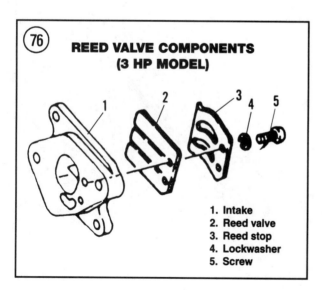

(76)

**REED VALVE COMPONENTS
(3 HP MODEL)**

1. Intake
2. Reed valve
3. Reed stop
4. Lockwasher
5. Screw

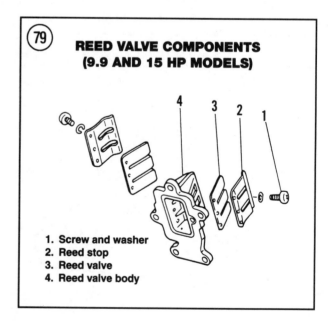

(79)

**REED VALVE COMPONENTS
(9.9 AND 15 HP MODELS)**

1. Screw and washer
2. Reed stop
3. Reed valve
4. Reed valve body

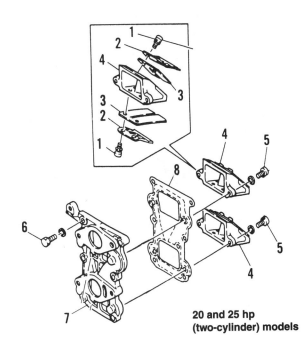

20 and 25 hp
(two-cylinder) models

**REED VALVE/HOUSING
COMPONENTS (20 AND 25 HP
[TWO-CYLINDER] MODELS, 25 AND
30 HP [THREE-CYLINDER] MODELS)**

1. Screw
2. Reed stop
3. Reed valve
4. Reed valve
   assembly
5. Screw/washer
6. Screw/washer
7. Intake manifold
8. Gasket

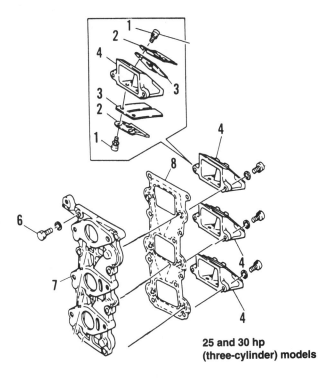

25 and 30 hp
(three-cylinder) models

6

j. For E60 and E75 models, refer to **Figure 84**.

k. For 80 jet and 115-130 hp models, refer to **Figure 85**.

l. For 105 jet and 150-225 hp 90° models, refer to **Figure 86**.

m. For 200-250 hp 76° models, refer to **Figure 87**.

Refer to *Silencer cover and carburetor* for carburetor and related component removal.

1. Remove the fasteners for the reed housing/intake and remove the intake. Remove and discard housing gaskets and seals.

2. Remove the fasteners attaching the reed block to the intake. Remove and discard reed block-to-intake gaskets when present.

3. Remove the fasteners attaching the reed stops and reed valves to the reed block.

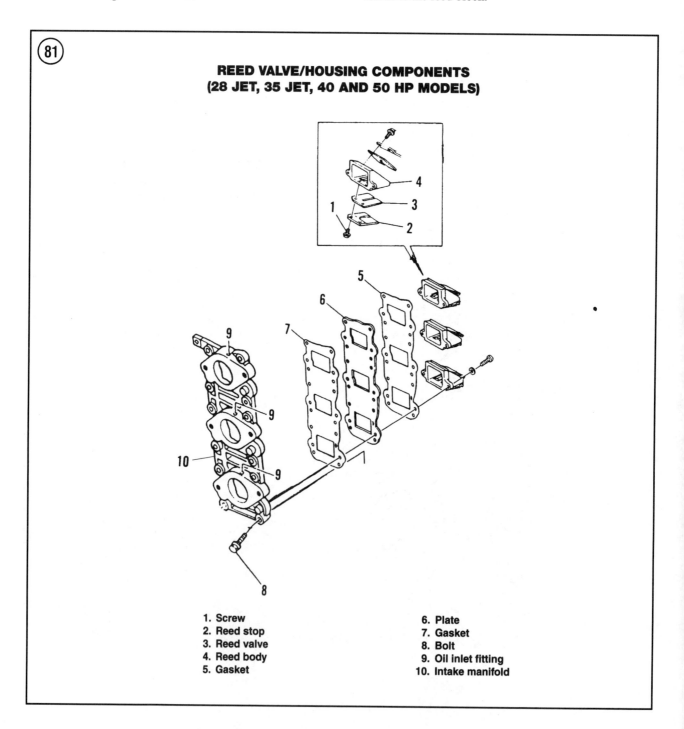

(81)

**REED VALVE/HOUSING COMPONENTS
(28 JET, 35 JET, 40 AND 50 HP MODELS)**

1. Screw
2. Reed stop
3. Reed valve
4. Reed body
5. Gasket
6. Plate
7. Gasket
8. Bolt
9. Oil inlet fitting
10. Intake manifold

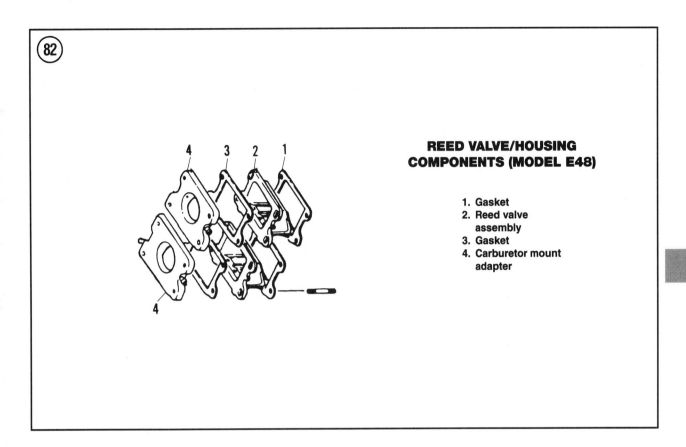

82

REED VALVE/HOUSING COMPONENTS (MODEL E48)

1. Gasket
2. Reed valve assembly
3. Gasket
4. Carburetor mount adapter

6

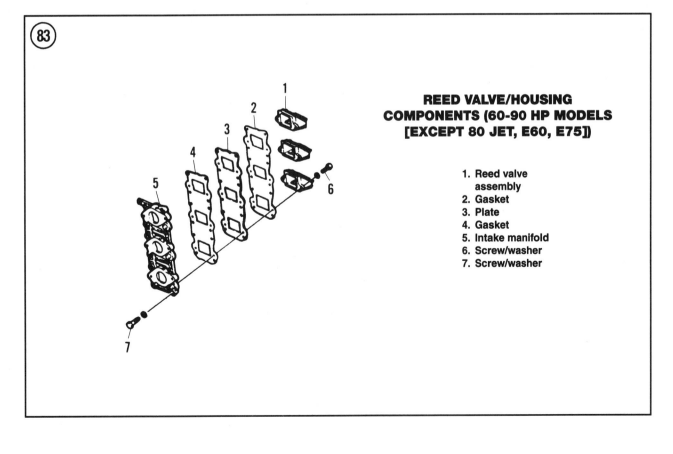

83

REED VALVE/HOUSING COMPONENTS (60-90 HP MODELS [EXCEPT 80 JET, E60, E75])

1. Reed valve assembly
2. Gasket
3. Plate
4. Gasket
5. Intake manifold
6. Screw/washer
7. Screw/washer

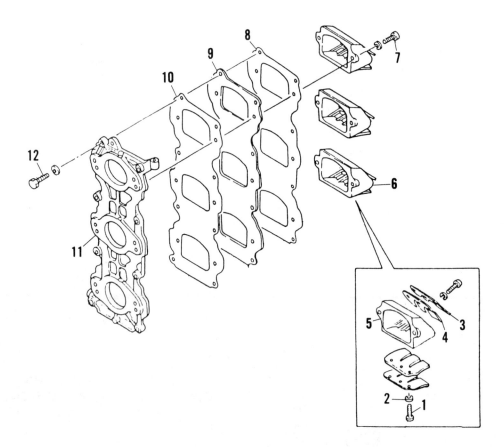

**REED VALVE/HOUSING COMPONENTS
(MODELS E60 AND E75)**

1. Screw
2. Washer
3. Reed stop
4. Reed valve
5. Reed body
6. Reed valve assembly
7. Screw/washer
8. Gasket
9. Plate
10. Gasket
11. Intake manifold
12. Bolt/washer

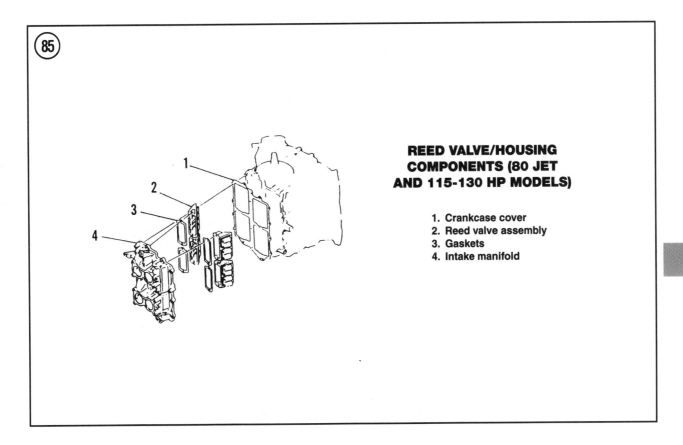

85

REED VALVE/HOUSING COMPONENTS (80 JET AND 115-130 HP MODELS)

1. Crankcase cover
2. Reed valve assembly
3. Gaskets
4. Intake manifold

6

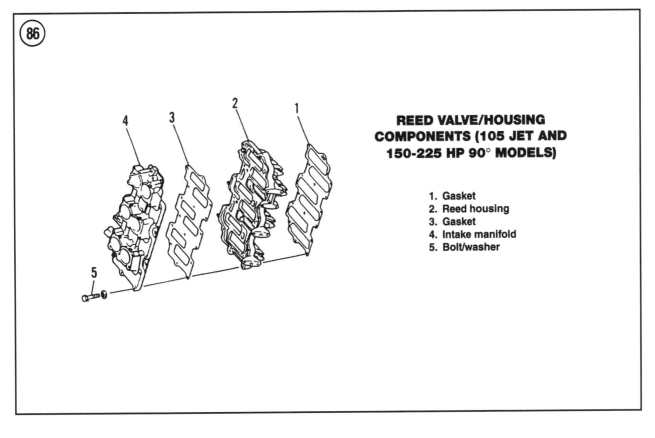

86

REED VALVE/HOUSING COMPONENTS (105 JET AND 150-225 HP 90° MODELS)

1. Gasket
2. Reed housing
3. Gasket
4. Intake manifold
5. Bolt/washer

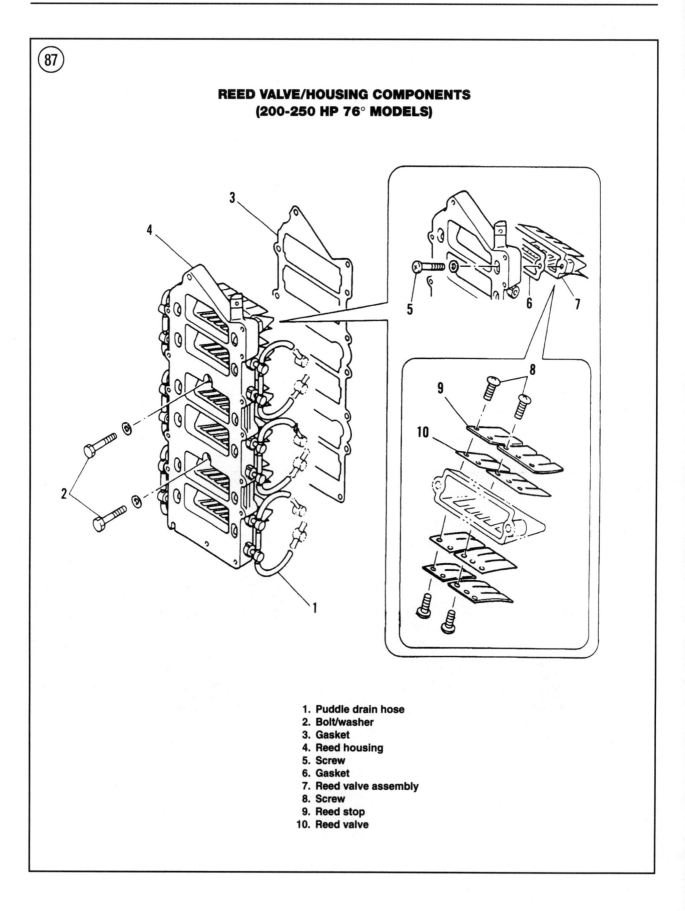

**REED VALVE/HOUSING COMPONENTS
(200-250 HP 76° MODELS)**

1. Puddle drain hose
2. Bolt/washer
3. Gasket
4. Reed housing
5. Screw
6. Gasket
7. Reed valve assembly
8. Screw
9. Reed stop
10. Reed valve

4. Inspect the reed valves, reed valve contact surfaces and reed stops for cracked or worn areas and replace if required.

5. Assembly is the reverse of disassembly. Replace all gaskets and seals for the reed housing, intake and reed blocks. Measure the reed and reed stop openings at the points indicated (**Figure 74**). Replace components that are not within the specifications listed in **Table 5**.

6. Torque all fasteners to the specifications listed in **Table 5**. Use Loctite 242 or 271 on the reed/reed stop fasteners and intake manifold fasteners. Use a two-step method when tightening intake fasteners. Torque fasteners in sequence percent of the specified value, then torque to full value. Tightening sequence steps are provided in Chapter Eight.

Table 1 FLOAT HEIGHT

Model	
2 hp	16.8-17.8 mm (0.66-0.60 in.)
3, 6 and 8 hp	12.0-16.0 mm (0.47-0.63 in.)
4 and 5 hp	21.5-22.5 mm (0.85-0.89 in.)
9.9 and 15 hp	12.5-15.5 mm (0.49-0.61 in.)
20 and 25 hp two-cylinder	14.0-15.0 mm (0.55-0.59 in.)
25 and 30 hp three-cylinder	14.4-15.5 mm (0.59-0.61 in.)
C30	14.5-15.5 mm (0.59-0.61 in.)
C40	16.5-22.5 mm (0.65-0.89 in.)
28 jet, 35 jet and 40-50 hp	14.0-16.0 mm (0.55-0.63 in.)
60-70 (except 65 jet)	13.0-15.0 mm (0.51-0.59 in.)
C75, C80 and C85	16.5-22.5 mm (0.65-0.89 in.)
65 jet and 90 hp	13.0-15.0 mm (0.51-0.59 in.)
80 jet and 115-130 hp	15.5-16.5 mm (0.61-0.63 in.)
105 jet and 150-225 (90°)	15.5-16.5 mm (0.61-0.63 in.)
225-250 hp (76°)	15.0-16.0 mm (0.61-0.65 in.)

Table 2 CARBURETOR JET SIZES

Model	Main jet size	Pilot jet	Pilot air jet
2 hp	No. 96	–	–
3 hp	No. 68	No. 40	No. 70
4 hp	No. 80	No. 46	1.4 mm (0.055 in.)
5 hp	No. 80	No. 52	1.2 mm (0.047 in.)
6 hp	No. 98	No. 45	–
9.9 and 15 hp	No. 110	No. 48	No. 75
20 and 25 hp two-cylinder	No. 125	No. 60	–
30 hp (except C30)	No. 102	No. 50	No. 140 carb No. 1 and 2 No. 120 carb No. 3
C30	No. 130	No. 64	0.8 mm (0.031 in.)
C40	No. 170	No. 75	No. 100
40 electric	No. 115	No. 60	No. 75
40 manual	No. 118	No. 60	No. 75
50 electric	No. 130	No. 62	No. 80
50 manual	No. 125	No. 62	No. 90
C60	No. 140	No. 70	No. 80
60 hp	No. 140	No. 65	No. 75
70 hp	No. 150	No. 75	No. 70
C75	No. 160	No. 80	No. 75
75, 80 hp	No. 160	No. 78	No. 80
(continued)			

Table 2 CARBURETOR JET SIZES (continued)

Model	Main jet size	Pilot jet	Pilot air jet
65 jet and 90 hp	No. 160	No. 78	No. 70
80 jet and 115 hp	No. 176	No. 78	No. 60
130 hp	No. 180	No. 82	No. 60
150TR, P150TR,	No. 150 cylinder 1, 3, 5	No. 84	No. 60
D150TR	No. 154 cylinder 2, 4	–	–
	No. 158 cylinder 6	–	–
S150TR, S175TR,	No. 142	No. 84	No. 60
L150TR	–	–	–
P175TR	No. 152 cylinder 1, 3, 5	No. 80	No. 60
	No. 154 cylinder 2, 4	–	–
	No. 158 cylinder 6	–	–
S200TR, L200TR	No. 146	No. 84	No. 60
200TR	No. 150 cylinder 1, 3	No. 84	–
	No. 152 cylinder 5	–	–
	No. 154 cylinder 2, 4	–	–
	No. 158 cylinder 6	–	–
P200TR	No. 150 cylinder 1, 3, 5	No. 80	No. 60
	No. 154 cylinder 2, 4	–	–
	No. 158 cylinder 6	–	–
225 (76°)	No. 150 cylinder 1, 2, 3, 4, 5	No. 94	No. 70
	No. 155 cylinder 6	–	–
250 (76°)	No. 155 cylinder 1, 2, 3, 4	No. 102	No. 6
	No. 165 cylinder 5, 6	–	–

Table 3 MAIN NOZZLE AND MAIN AIR JET SIZES

Model	Main Nozzle	Main Air Jet
6 hp	2.2 mm (0.087 in.)	–
8 hp	2.4 mm (0.094 in.)	–
9.9 and 15 hp	3.0 mm (0.12 in.)	–
30 hp (except C30)	–	No. cylinder 1, 2
		No. cylinder 3
C30	–	0.8 mm (0.031 in.)
C40	–	No. 180
40	–	No. 160
40 electric	–	No. 140
50 manual	–	No. 130
C60	–	No. 180
60	–	No. 175
70	–	No. 160
75 and 80 hp	–	No. 180
65 jet and 90 hp	–	No. 175
80 jet and 115 hp	3.6 mm (0.14 in.)	No. 270
130 hp	3.6 mm (0.14 in.)	No. 240
150TR, D150TR,	4.2 mm (0.17 in.)	No. 310
P150TR	–	–
S150TR, L150TR	4.0 mm (0.16 in.)	No. 310
S175TR	–	–
P175TR	4.2 mm (0.17 in.)	No. 280
200TR	4.5 mm (0.18 in.)	No. 270
L200TR, S200TR	4.0 mm (0.16 in.)	No. 310
P200TR	4.5 mm (0.18 in.)	No. 260
225 (76°)	–	No. 230 cylinder 1, 2
		No. 240 cylinder 3, 4, 5
		No. 200 cylinder 6
250 (76°)	–	No. 220 cylinder 1, 2, 3, 5
		No. 200 cylinder 4, 6

Table 4 REED VALVE SPECIFICATIONS

Model	Reed stop opening	Reed valve warp limit
2 hp	5.8-6.2 mm (0.23-.025 in.)	0.3 mm (0.01 in.)
3 hp	3.8-4.2 mm (0.152-0.168 in.)	0.2 mm (0.008 in.)
4, 5 hp	6.8-7.2 mm (0.272-0.288 in.)	0.2 mm (0.008 in.)
6, 8 hp	4.3-4.7 mm (0.172-0.185 in.)	0.2 mm (0.008 in.)
9.9 hp	0.6-0.8 mm (0.026-0.034 in.)	0.2 mm (0.008 in.)
15 hp	5.9-6.1 mm (0.236-0.244 in.)	0.2 mm (0.008 in.)
20-25	5.8-6.2 mm (0.228-0.256 in.)	0.2 mm (0.008 in.)
30 hp, C30 models	2.5-2.9 mm (0.098-0.114 in.)	0.2 mm (0.008 in.)
28 jet, 35 jet and 40-50 hp models (except model E48)	5.8-6.2 mm (0.23-0.25 in.)	0.2 mm (0.008 in.)
C40	4.8-5.2 mm (0.19-0.21 in.)	0.2 mm (0.008 in.)
E48	2.8-3.2 mm (0.112-0.128 in.)	0.2 mm (0.008 in.)
60 hp (except model E60)	2.8-3.2 mm (0.112-0.128 in.)	0.2 mm (0.008 in.)
E60	2.8-3.2 mm (0.112-0.128 in.)	0.2 mm (0.008 in.)
65 jet and 70-90 hp (except E75)	9.7-10.1 mm (0.38-0.40 in.)	0.2 mm (0.008 in.)
E75	9.7-10.1 mm (0.38-.040 in.)	0.2 mm (0.008 in.)
80 jet and 115-130 hp	6.2-6.8 mm (0.244-0.268 in.)	0.2 mm (0.008 in.)
150-225 (90°)	6.2-6.8 mm (0.25-0.25 in.)	0.2 mm (0.008 in.)
225 (76°) (except 225 G/V)	7.6-8.2 mm (0.30-0.32 in.)	0.2 mm (0.008 in.)
225G,225V, 250 (76°)	8.7-9.3 mm (0.34-0.36 in.)	0.2 mm (0.008 in.)

6

Table 5 TIGHTENING TORQUE

	Torque
Reed valve/reed stop to housing	
All models	1 N•m (8.8 in.-lb.)
Intake to cylinder block	
2 hp	10 N•m (88 in.-lb.)
4, 5 hp	12 N•m (106 in.-lb.)
6, 8 hp	11 N•m (97 in.-lb.)
9.9, 15 hp	11 N•m (97 in.-lb.)
20-30 hp (except 28 jet)	11 N•m (97 in.-lb.)
28 jet, 35 jet and 40, 50 hp	8 N•m (71 in.-lb.)
E48	Securely tightened
60-90 hp (except E60, E75, 80 jet)	8 N•m (71 in.-lb.)
E60	8 N•m (71 in.-lb.)
E75	12 N•m (106 in.-lb.)
80 jet and 115-130 hp	8 N•m (71 in.-lb.)
105 jet and 150-225 (90°)	8 N•m (71 in.-lb.)
200-250 (76°)	10 N•m (88 in.-lb.)
Reed block to intake housing	
20-30 hp (except 28 jet)	4 N•m (35 in.-lb.)
All other models	Tighten securely

Chapter Seven

Electrical and Ignition

This chapter provides removal, inspection and installation procedures for the following:

1. Starting system.
2. Charging system.
3. Warning system.
4. Ignition system.

In addition, battery maintenance and testing procedures are provided in this chapter.

Tables 1-3, located at the end of this chapter, provide starter motor specifications, correct tightening torque for electrical and ignition components and battery maintenance information.

STARTING SYSTEM COMPONENTS

This section will provide removal, inspection and installation for the following components:

1. Starter relay.
2. Key ignition switch.
3. Start switch.
4. Neutral start switches.
5. Starter motor.

In addition, starter motor repair procedures are provided in this chapter.

Starter Relay Removal/Installation

Use the wiring diagrams located at the back of the manual to identify the starter relay (**Figure 1**) wire colors. Trace the wires to the component on the engine. It may be

necessary to remove the electrical component cover (**Figure 2**) to access the starter relay. The relay and electrical cover appearance will vary by model. Removal and installation procedures are similar. Refer to **Table 1** for applicable tightening torque.

1. Disconnect both battery cables from the cranking battery.

2. Remove the fasteners (**Figure 2**) and carefully pull the electrical component cover away from the relay mounting plate.

3. Mark the terminal connections to ensure correct connection on installation.

4. Remove the nuts, washers and large wire connectors from the starter relay. Clean corrosion and contaminants from the connectors.

5. Remove the two small connectors and wires from the relay. Clean corrosion and contaminants from the wire connectors.

6. Remove the mounting hardware and the relay. Remove the separate grounding lead from the relay when present and install onto the replacement relay. Install the replacement relay and relay attaching hardware. Tighten the fasteners securely.

7. Install the electrical component cover if removed. Connect the battery cables to the proper terminals. Check for proper starter relay operation.

Key Switch Removal/Installation

1. Disconnect both battery cables from the battery terminals. Remove the remote control from its mounting location.

2. *Remote control*—Use a small screwdriver and carefully pry the lower cover (**Figure 3**) from the control. Remove the screws and both back covers (**Figure 4**).

3. Use the wire charts located near the back of the manual to locate the key switch wires. Identify the wire colors and trace them to the key switch. Mark the wire attachment locations. Disconnect the key switch wires from the wire harness (A, **Figure 5**).

4. Loosen and remove the key switch retaining nut (B, **Figure 5**). Remove the key switch.

5. Install the key switch to its mounting location. Tighten the retaining nut securely.

6. Attach the key switch wires to the correct harness connector.

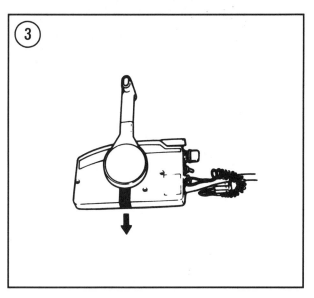

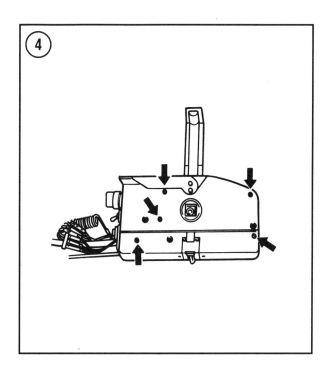

7

7. *Remote control*—Assemble the back covers (**Figure 4**) to the control along with the lower cover (**Figure 3**) and install the control to its mounting location.

8. Attach the battery cables to the correct terminals. Check for proper starter operation.

Start Switch Removal/Installation
(Tiller Control Models)

Refer to the proper illustration for the mounting location of the start switch for tiller models. Removal of other components may be required for access.

    a. For 6-15 hp models, refer to **Figure 6**.

    b. For 20-30 hp models (except 28 jet), refer to **Figure 7**.

    c. For E60 and E75 models, refer to **Figure 8**.

    d. For 40-90 hp models (excluding E48, E75), refer to **Figure 9**.

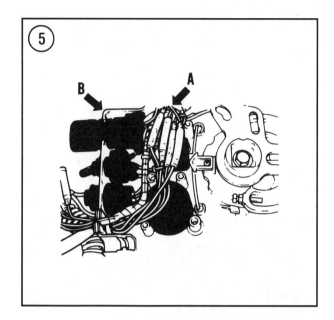

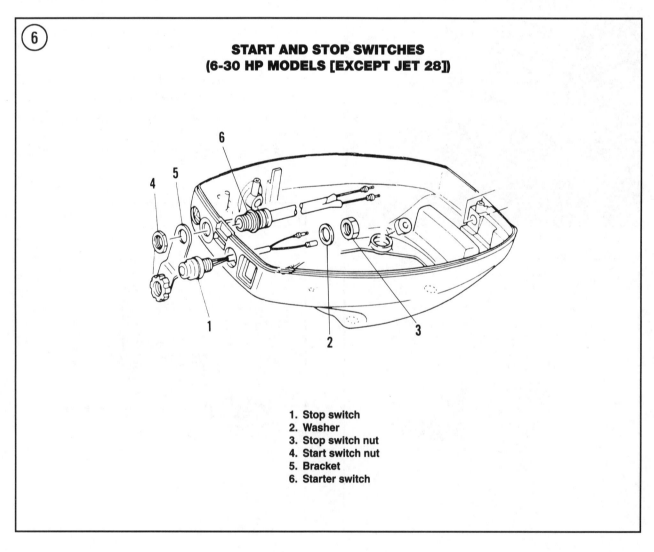

**START AND STOP SWITCHES
(6-30 HP MODELS [EXCEPT JET 28])**

1. Stop switch
2. Washer
3. Stop switch nut
4. Start switch nut
5. Bracket
6. Starter switch

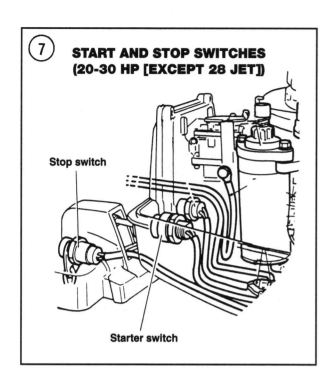

⑦ **START AND STOP SWITCHES
(20-30 HP [EXCEPT 28 JET])**

Stop switch

Starter switch

NOTE
Use the wire charts to determine the switch wire colors, then trace them to locate the switch. Switch location may differ slightly from the illustration.

6-30 hp models

1. Disconnect both battery cables from the battery terminals.

2. Loosen and remove the starter switch retaining nut along with the bracket used on some models.

3. Disconnect the starter switch leads from the main engine harness. Remove the starter switch.

4. Install the replacement switch, bracket and nut in the lower motor cover.

5. Tighten the nut to the specification listed in **Table 1**. Connect the switch leads to the harness.

6. Connect the battery cables to the proper terminals. Check for proper switch operation.

7

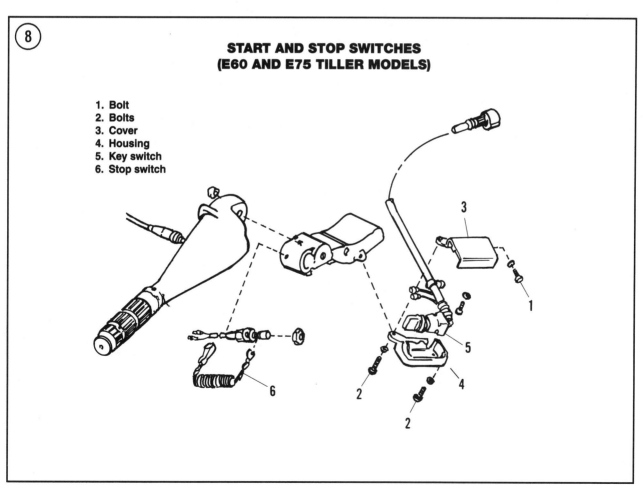

⑧ **START AND STOP SWITCHES
(E60 AND E75 TILLER MODELS)**

1. Bolt
2. Bolts
3. Cover
4. Housing
5. Key switch
6. Stop switch

⑨
START AND STOP SWITCHES
(40-90 TILLER MODELS [EXCEPT MODELS E60 AND E75])

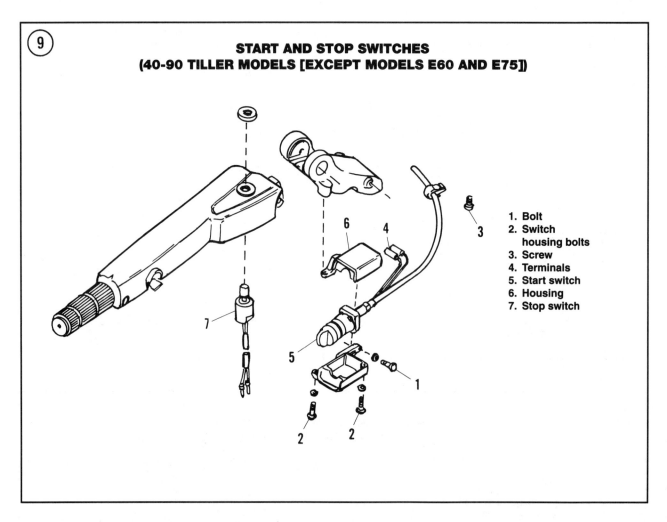

1. Bolt
2. Switch housing bolts
3. Screw
4. Terminals
5. Start switch
6. Housing
7. Stop switch

⑩
REMOTE CONTROL MOUNTED NEUTRAL SWITCH

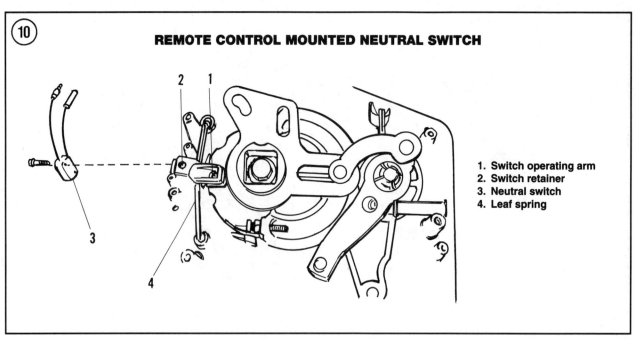

1. Switch operating arm
2. Switch retainer
3. Neutral switch
4. Leaf spring

40-90 hp models

1. Disconnect both battery cables from the battery terminals.

2. Remove the bolts that retain the switch housing to the tiller bracket.

3. Remove the bolts that retain the cover to the switch housing. Disconnect the wire terminals from the main engine harness. Remove the wire retainer and pull the start switch harness from the engine.

4. Position the replacement switch in the switch housing. Route the switch leads to the main harness connection and attach the leads. Install the wire retainer and screw. Tighten the screw securely.

5. Position the cover onto the switch housing. Avoid pinching the wires and install the bolts into the housing cover and tighten them securely. Position the switch housing assembly to the tiller bracket. Install the retaining bolt and tighten securely.

6. Connect the battery cables to the correct terminals. Check for proper starter switch operation.

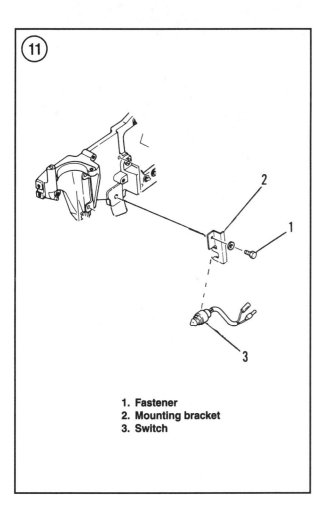

1. **Fastener**
2. **Mounting bracket**
3. **Switch**

Neutral Start Switch Removal/Installation (Remote Control Models)

NOTE
Some Yamaha outboards are not equipped with Yamaha controls. Contact the manufacturer of the controls or a reputable marine dealership for repair information.

1. Remove the control from its mounting location.

2. Use a small screwdriver to carefully pry the lower cover from the control (**Figure 3**).

3. Remove the screws and both back covers from the control (**Figure 4**).

4. Locate the yellow and pink wires for the neutral switch and disconnect the wires from the main harness.

5. Remove the screw and switch retainer then the neutral switch.

6. Inspect the switch operating arm (1, **Figure 10**) and leaf spring (4, **Figure 10**) for cracks or worn areas. Replace if required.

7. Position the replacement switch and install the screw and retainer.

8. Connect the pink and yellow wires to the main harness.

9. Install the back cover and screws and tighten securely. Install the control.

10. Connect both battery cables to the correct terminals. Check for proper switch operation.

Neutral Start Switch Removal/Installation (Tiller Control Models)

Neutral switch location and means of mounting vary by model. Refer to the wire charts near the back of the manual to identify the wire color used for the required model. Trace the wires to locate the neutral switch.

1. Disconnect both battery cables from the battery terminals.

2. Disconnect the neutral switch wires from the harness connection.

3. Remove the fasteners and mounting bracket (1 and 2, **Figure 11**). Remove the switch (3, **Figure 11**) from the bracket.

4. Position the switch (3, **Figure 11**) in the mounting bracket (2, **Figure 11**). Install the bracket and switch to the mounting location. Tighten the fasteners securely.

5. Connect the switch wires to the main harness connection. Use plastic locking tie clamps to secure wiring. Connect both battery cables to the proper terminal.

6. Check for proper neutral switch operation.

7

Starter Motor Removal/Installation

NOTE
Starter motor appearance and the method for mounting vary by model. The illustrations may not exactly resemble the model. The procedures for removal and replacement are similar.

1. Disconnect both battery cables from the battery. Locate the starter motor on the engine (**Figure 12**).
2. Remove the fasteners and pinion cover if so equipped.
3. Remove the terminal insulator and the terminal bolt from the starter motor (**Figure 13**). Clean corrosion and contaminants from the cable terminal. Remove the bolts or nuts that retain the starter to the cylinder block. Clean and inspect the mounting location for cracks or damage.
4. Install the replacement starter motor and tighten the fasteners to the specification listed in **Table 1**.
5. Attach the cable terminal to the starter motor and tighten the fastener securely. Install the pinion cover and fasteners if so equipped.
6. Connect the battery cables to the correct terminal. Check for proper starter motor operation.

Starter Motor Repair

This section provides complete disassembly, inspection and assembly instructions for a typical starter motor. The starter motor and the internal components vary by model. The procedures indicate when a model specific procedure is required.

    a. For 6-25 (two-cylinder) models, refer to **Figure 14**.
    b. For 28 jet, 25 hp (three-cylinder) and 30-50 hp models, refer to **Figure 15**.
    c. For E48 and 60-70 hp models (except 65 jet), refer to **Figure 16**.
    d. For 65 jet and 75-90 hp models (except 80 jet), refer to **Figure 17**.
    e. For 80 jet, 105 jet and 115-250 hp models, refer to **Figure 18**.

CAUTION
Never strike the frame of the starter motor with a hard object. The permanent magnets will crack or break and result in starter motor failure.

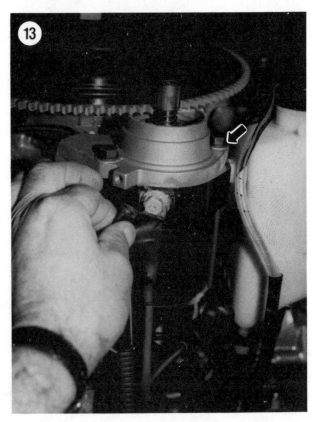

Starter motor disassembly

1. Remove the starter as described in this chapter.
2. With the starter carefully mounted in a vise, grasp the starter pinion drive and stopper (2 and 3, **Figure 19**) and pull it towards the starter to expose the locking clip.

Carefully pry the locking clip from the armature shaft. Remove the locking clip and stopper.

3. Turn the pinion drive counterclockwise to remove it from the armature shaft.

4. Mark the mating locations for the top and bottom covers to the frame. While supporting both ends of the starter motor, remove both throughbolts.

5. Remove the top cover from the frame assembly. If necessary, lightly tap on the top cover with a plastic mallet. Remove and discard the O-ring, if so equipped.

6. With the frame assembly placed on its side, lightly tap the exposed end of the armature shaft with a plastic mallet to remove the armature and lower cover from the frame.

7. Note the orientation of the composite and metal washers on the armature shaft. Wire them together to insure they are installed in exactly the same order and position.

8. Carefully pull the lower cover from the armature. Remove and discard the O-ring, if so equipped. Mark the brush plate to ensure correct orientation to the lower cover during assembly. Remove the fasteners, starter terminal

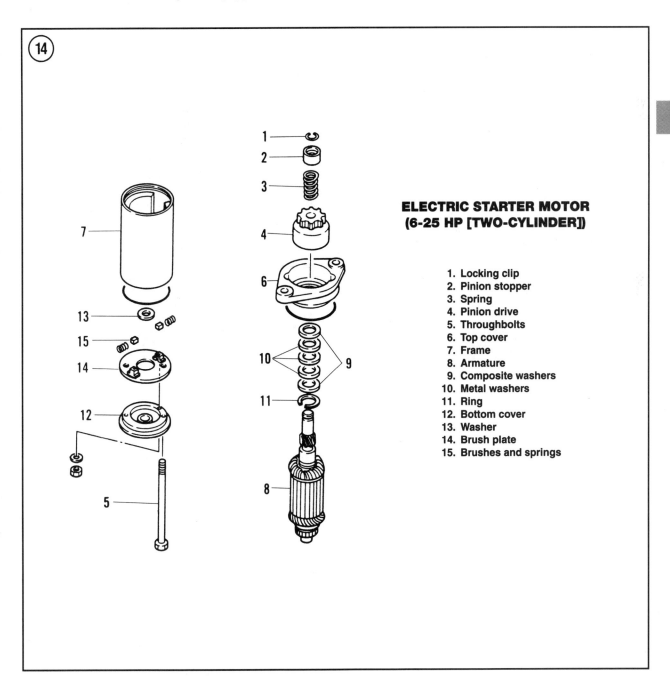

ELECTRIC STARTER MOTOR (6-25 HP [TWO-CYLINDER])

1. Locking clip
2. Pinion stopper
3. Spring
4. Pinion drive
5. Throughbolts
6. Top cover
7. Frame
8. Armature
9. Composite washers
10. Metal washers
11. Ring
12. Bottom cover
13. Washer
14. Brush plate
15. Brushes and springs

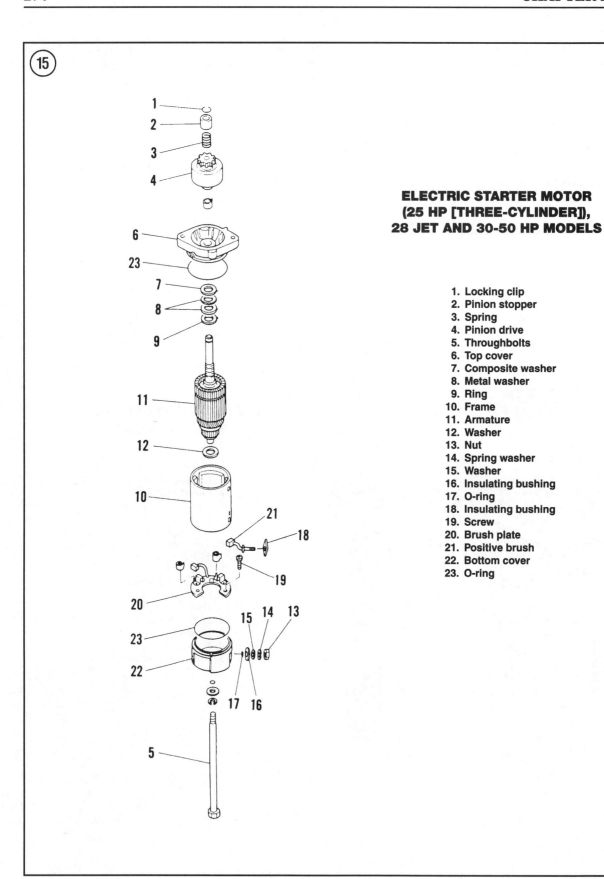

**ELECTRIC STARTER MOTOR
(25 HP [THREE-CYLINDER]),
28 JET AND 30-50 HP MODELS**

1. Locking clip
2. Pinion stopper
3. Spring
4. Pinion drive
5. Throughbolts
6. Top cover
7. Composite washer
8. Metal washer
9. Ring
10. Frame
11. Armature
12. Washer
13. Nut
14. Spring washer
15. Washer
16. Insulating bushing
17. O-ring
18. Insulating bushing
19. Screw
20. Brush plate
21. Positive brush
22. Bottom cover
23. O-ring

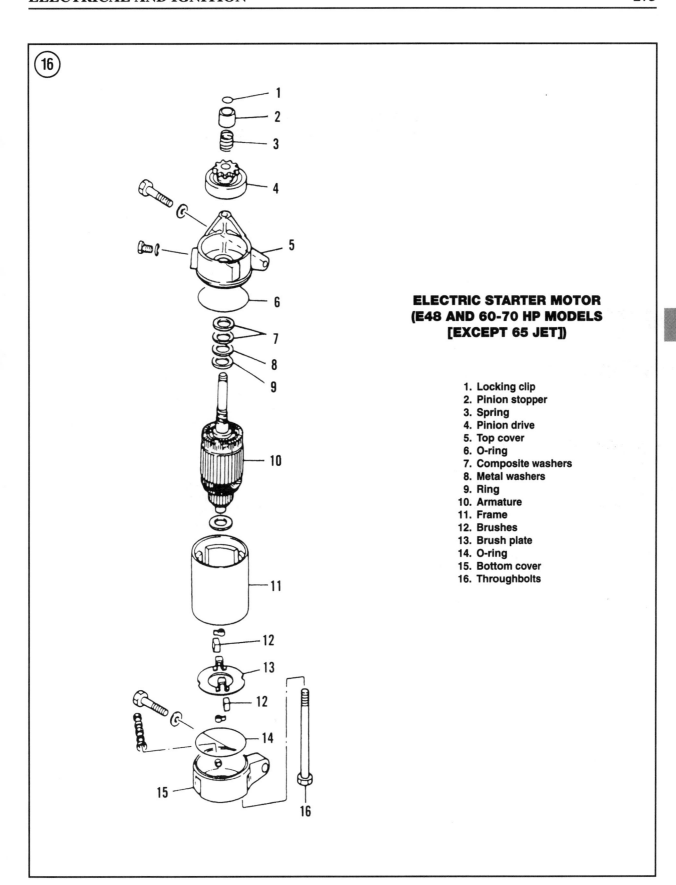

16

**ELECTRIC STARTER MOTOR
(E48 AND 60-70 HP MODELS
[EXCEPT 65 JET])**

7

1. Locking clip
2. Pinion stopper
3. Spring
4. Pinion drive
5. Top cover
6. O-ring
7. Composite washers
8. Metal washers
9. Ring
10. Armature
11. Frame
12. Brushes
13. Brush plate
14. O-ring
15. Bottom cover
16. Throughbolts

⑰

ELECTRIC STARTER MOTOR
(65 JET AND 75-90 HP MODELS)

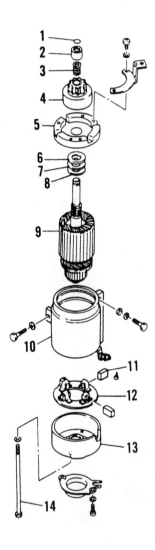

1. Locking clip
2. Pinion stopper
3. Spring
4. Pinion drive
5. Top cover
6. Composite washer
7. Metal washer
8. Ring
9. Armature
10. Frame
11. Brushes
12. Brush plate
13. Bottom cover
14. Throughbolts

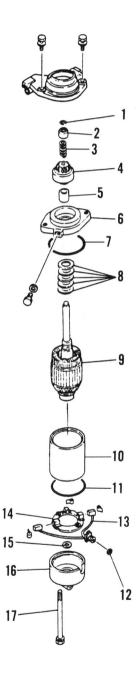

**ELECTRIC STARTER MOTOR
(80 JET, 105 JET AND
115-250 HP MODELS)**

1. Locking clip
2. Pinion stopper
3. Spring
4. Pinion drive
5. Collar
6. Top cover
7. O-ring
8. Washers
9. Armature
10. Frame
11. O-ring
12. Nut
13. Brushes
14. Brush plate
15. Washer
16. Bottom cover
17. Throughbolt

7

nuts and insulators when used along with the brush plate. Use compressed air to blow debris from the components. Use a mild solvent to clean contaminants from the components (except the brush plate and brushes).

Starter motor inspection

1. Place the pinion drive on a flat surface. Attempt to rotate the pinion in the clockwise and counterclockwise directions (**Figure 20**). Replace the pinion drive if it does not *turn freely* when rotated in the clockwise direction and *lock* when rotated in the counterclockwise direction.

2. Inspect the pinion for chipped, cracked or worn teeth (**Figure 21**). Replace the pinion drive if these conditions are noted. Inspect the helical splines at the pinion end of the armature. Replace the armature if chipped areas are noted or the pinion drive will not thread smoothly onto the shaft.

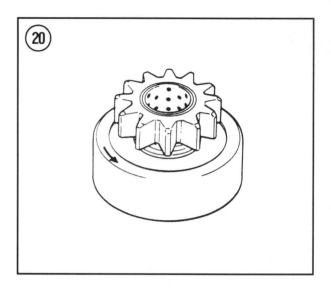

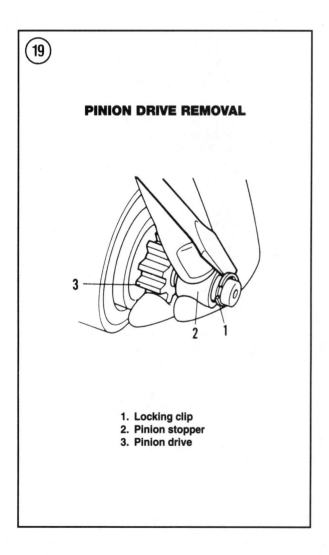

PINION DRIVE REMOVAL

1. Locking clip
2. Pinion stopper
3. Pinion drive

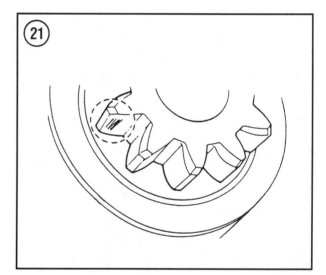

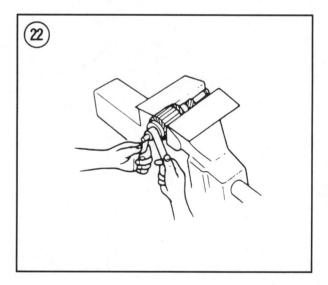

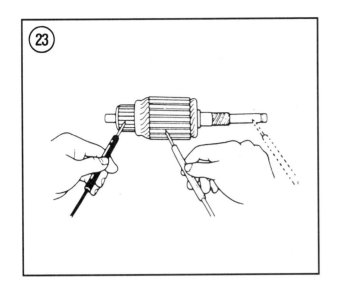

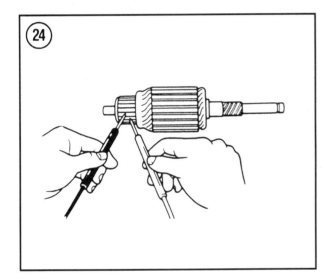

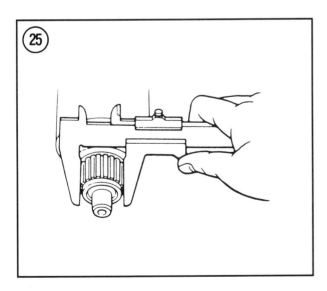

3. Carefully secure the armature in a vise with soft jaws. Tighten the vise only enough to secure the armature. Use 600 grit carburundum (wet or dry polishing cloth) to remove corrosion deposits and glazed surfaces from the commutator area of the armature (**Figure 22**). Work the area enough to clean the surfaces. Avoid removing too much material. Rotate the armature often to polish the surfaces evenly.

4. Select the ohms or resistance scale on a multimeter. Select the 1 ohm scale. Connect the meter negative test lead to one of the commutator contacts and the positive test lead to the laminated section of the armature (**Figure 23**). The correct reading is an open circuit or very high resistance.

5. Connect the meter negative test lead to one of the commutator contacts and the positive meter test lead to the armature shaft (**Figure 23**). The correct reading is an open circuit or very high resistance.

6. Connect the meter negative test lead to one of the commutator contacts and the meter positive test lead to each of the remaining commutator contacts (**Figure 24**). Note the meter reading for each selected contact. The correct reading is a closed circuit or very low resistance.

7. Replace the armature if an incorrect meter reading is noted.

8. Measure the diameter of the commutator (**Figure 25**). Compare the measurement with the specification listed in **Table 2**. Replace the armature if commutator diameter is less than minimum specification.

9. Use a disposable nail file or a suitable small file (**Figure 26**) and remove the metal and mica particles from the undercut, or area between and below the commutator contacts.

10. Blow away any particles with compressed air and use a depth micrometer to measure the depth of the undercut

7

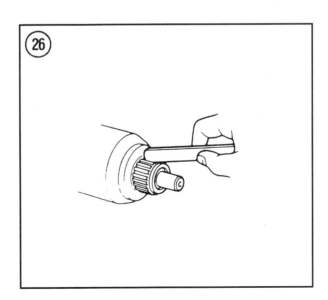

(**Figure 27**). Compare the measurement with the specification listed in **Table 2**.

11. Support the armature on V blocks or other suitable supports. Position a dial indicator to measure the armature for shaft deflection (**Figure 28**). Rotate the armature and read the deflection on the dial indicator. Compare the measurement with the specification listed in **Table 2**. Replace the armature if the deflection exceeds the specifications.

12. Measure the brush length as shown in **Figure 29**. Compare the measurement with the minimum and standard length listed in **Table 2**. Replace brushes if any one brush length is less than the minimum specification in **Table 2**. Replace the brushes if corrosion or contaminants are present or any chipping or irregular surfaces are noted.

13. Inspect the magnets in the frame assembly for corrosion or other contaminants and clean if required. Inspect the frame assemble for cracked or loose magnets. Replace the frame assembly if it cannot be adequately cleaned or if damaged magnets are noted.

14. Inspect the bearing surfaces on the armature and the bushings for discoloration and excessive or uneven wear. Replace any questionable bushings using a suitable pulling tool and driver. Replace the armature when rough or uneven surfaces are present on bearing surfaces.

Starter motor assembly

1. Align the orientation marks and install the brush plate on the lower starter cover. Tighten all fasteners securely. Refer to the illustrations for insulator and terminal orientation.

2. Wipe a small amount of Yamaha water resistant grease on the bottom cover bushing. Install the washer over the lower end of the armature shaft. Manually hold the brushes away and carefully slide the armature into position. Release the brushes and inspect for correct installation (**Figure 30**).

3. Fabricate a brush retaining tool to assist with the armature installation. Bend a stiff piece of thin rod into a U shape and position it between the brushes (**Figure 31**). Install the armature and carefully remove the tool.

4. Install a new O-ring onto the lower cover (**Figure 32**). While holding the armature firmly in position in the lower cover, install the frame assembly over the armature. Align reference marks and antirotation structures (**Figure 32**). Install the stack of washers over the upper end of the armature shaft in exactly the same orientation as removed.

5. Install a new O-ring onto the upper cover. Wipe a small amount of Yamaha water resistant grease onto the bearing surface in the upper cover. Align the reference marks and install the upper cover. Install the throughbolts and tighten to standard torque specification listed in **Table 1**.

6. Thread the pinion drive onto the armature shaft. Install the spring (1, **Figure 33**) and pinion stopper (2, **Figure 33**) onto the shaft. Push the pinion stopper toward the starter and position the locking clip (3, **Figure 33**) into the groove on the armature shaft (**Figure 33**). Use pliers to form the locking clip if distorted during installation. Release the pinion stopper and inspect to ensure proper installation.

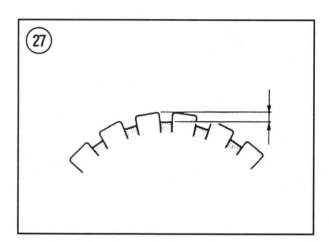

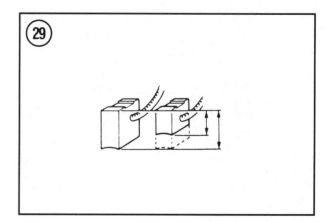

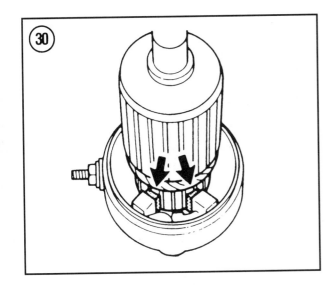

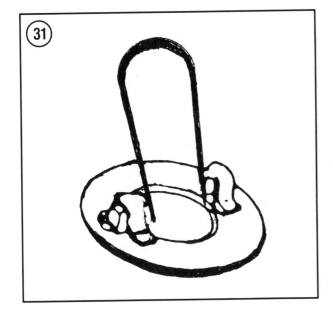

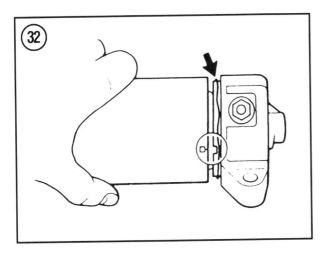

7. Install the starter as described in this chapter. Check for proper starter operation.

CHARGING SYSTEM COMPONENTS

This section provides removal, inspection and installation procedures for the battery charge/lighting coil, rectifier regulator unit and rectifier.

Battery Charge/Lighting Coil Removal/Installation

Battery charge/lighting coil appearance and mounting arrangements vary by model. The recoil starter assembly must be removed on some models. Flywheel removal is required on all models. Refer to Chapter Eight for flywheel removal and installation. Prior to component removal, make a drawing or take a photograph of the wire routing. This important step will help ensure proper routing during assembly.

On 6-50 hp models, the battery charge/lighting coil is fastened to a mounting base alongside the ignition charge

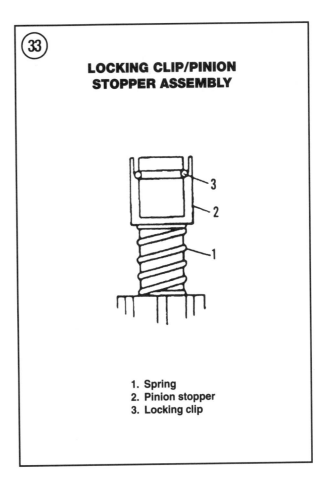

LOCKING CLIP/PINION STOPPER ASSEMBLY

1. Spring
2. Pinion stopper
3. Locking clip

7

coils (**Figure 34**). Refer to the wire charts located at the end of the manual to identify the wire colors for the battery charge/lighting coil. Trace the wires to the component. Note the size and location of any plastic tie clamps.

The battery charge/lighting coil and ignition charge coil are integrated into a single stator assembly on 60-250 hp models (**Figure 35**).

1. Disconnect the battery cables from the battery terminals on electric start models. Remove the recoil starter, if equipped, as instructed in Chapter Eleven. Remove the flywheel as instructed in Chapter Eight.

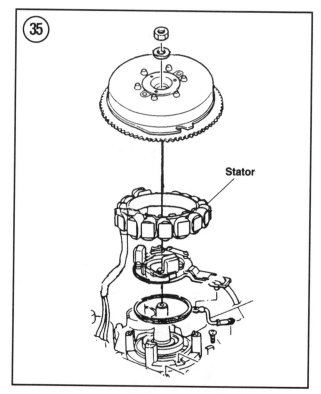

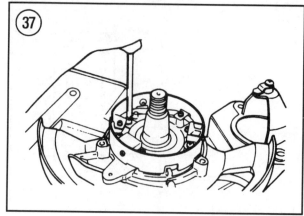

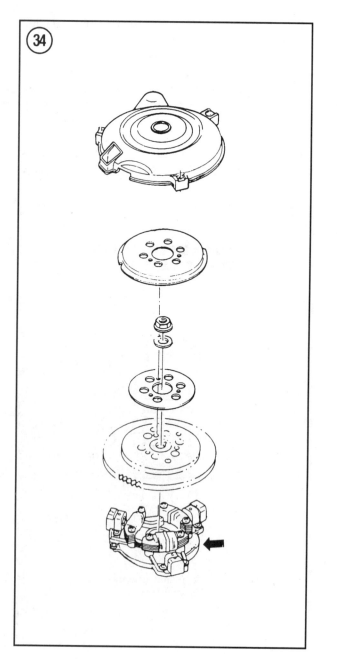

2. On 6-50 hp models, identify the proper wire connections. Mark these wires to ensure proper connections on assembly. Disconnect the battery charge/lighting coil wires from the rectifier/regulator, rectifier or terminal block (**Figure 36**). On 60-250 hp models, disconnect all wires leading to the battery charge and ignition charge coil assembly.

> *CAUTION*
> *It may be necessary to use an impact driver to remove the battery charge/lighting and ignition charge coil mounting screws. Work carefully and avoid the use of excessive force. The magneto base and possibly the cylinder block can sustain considerable damage if excessive force is used.*

3 Note the screw locations prior to removal. Remove the screws (**Figure 37**) for the battery charge/lighting coil only on the 6-50 hp models. On 60-250 hp models, remove all screws (**Figure 38**) that retain the battery charge and ignition charge coil assembly to the magneto base.

4. Mark the orientation of the coil relative to its mounting location and remove the component from the engine. Care-

fully guide the coil wires during removal. Make note of the wire routing prior to removal. Clean the coil mounting location of corrosion and other debris or contaminants. Inspect, clean and repair, if necessary, the threads for the coil mounting location.

5. Carefully route the coil wires and place the coil on the mounting location. Check and correct the orientation of the coil. Make certain that the coil is properly seated on the magneto base. Install the screws, spacers and washers in the original locations and tighten them securely.

6. Clean and inspect all terminals. Connect the battery charge/lighting coil wires to the proper terminals. Install the flywheel and recoil starter, if so equipped, following the procedures listed in Chapter Eight and Chapter Eleven.

7. Connect the battery cables to the proper terminals on electric start models. Check for proper charging and ignition system operation.

Rectifier/Regulator Unit Removal/Installation

Rectifier/regulator unit appearance and mounting locations vary by model. Use the wire charts located at the back of the manual to identify the wire colors used for the rectifier/regulator. Trace the wires to the component on the engine (**Figure 39**). Note the size and location of plastic locking tie clamps that must be removed and replace them.

1. Disconnect both battery cables from the battery terminals. Remove the electrical component cover (**Figure 40**) if necessary to access the rectifier/regulator.

2. Mark the wire connections to the rectifier/regulator to ensure proper connections on assembly. Disconnect the wires.

3. Remove the screws that retain the rectifier/regulator unit to its mounting location (**Figure 41**). Carefully route the disconnected wires and remove the component from the engine.

4. Clean, inspect and repair, if necessary, the threads in the mounting location. Clean all corrosion and contaminants from the mounting location.

5. Carefully route the rectifier/regulator unit leads and install the component to its mounting location. Tighten the retaining screws securely.

6. Clean all terminals and connect the wires to the proper terminals. Install the electrical component cover if used.

Connect the battery cables to the proper terminals. Check for proper charging system operation.

Rectifier Removal/Installation

Use the wire charts located at the back of the manual to identify the wire color used for the rectifier. Trace the wires to the component. Note the size and location of plastic locking tie clamps that must be removed and replace them.

1. Disconnect both battery cables from the battery terminals. Remove the electrical component cover (**Figure 40**). Locate and mark the wire connections to ensure proper connections during assembly. Disconnect all wires leading

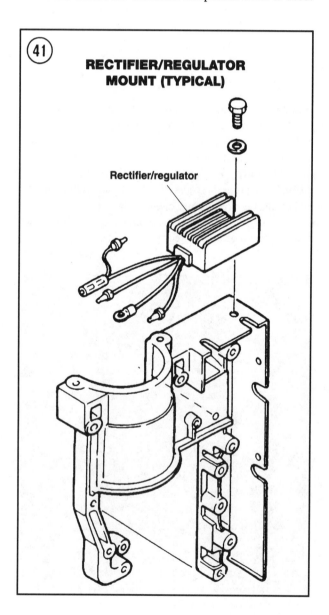

RECTIFIER/REGULATOR MOUNT (TYPICAL)

Rectifier/regulator

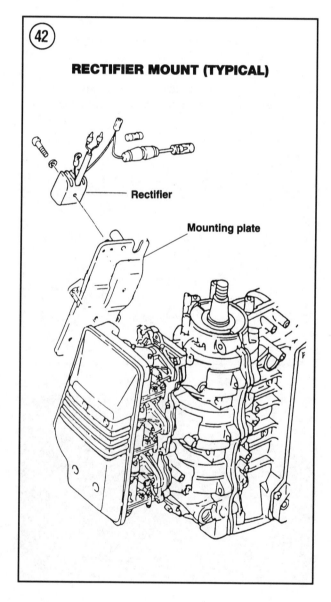

RECTIFIER MOUNT (TYPICAL)

Rectifier

Mounting plate

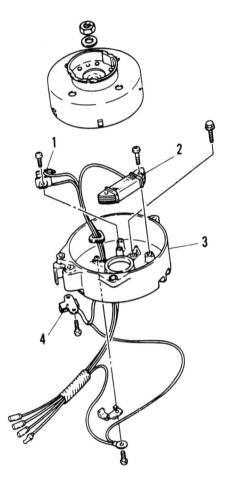

IGNITION CHARGE/PULSER COIL (3 HP MODEL)

1. Pulser coil No. 1
2. Ignition charge coil
3. Magneto base
4. Pulser coil No. 2

to the rectifier. Inspect the condition of the fuse and replace if necessary.

2. Remove the screw, washer and rectifier (**Figure 42**). Clean, inspect and repair, if necessary, the threads on the rectifier mount. Clean all corrosion and contaminants from the rectifier mount.

3. Carefully route the wires to the correct location. Install the rectifier, washer and screw. Tighten the screw securely.

4. Clean and inspect all terminals. Attach all wires to the proper terminals. Install the electrical component cover. Connect the battery cables to the proper terminals. Check for proper charging system operation.

IGNITION SYSTEM

This section will provide removal, inspection and installation procedures for the *ignition charge coil, pulser coil, CDI unit and the ignition coil*.

Ignition Charge Coil
Removal/Installation

The ignition charge coil appearance and mounting locations vary by model. Use the wire charts located near the back of the manual to identify the wire color for the *ignition charge coil*. Trace the wires to the component on the engine. Note the size and location of plastic locking tie clamps that must be removed and replace them.

Follow steps 1-7 under *Battery Charge/Lighting Coil Removal/Installation* to replace the ignition charge coil. On 2-50 hp models, be sure to identify and replace the ignition charge coil instead of the battery charge/lighting coil. The battery charge/lighting coil and ignition charge coil are integrated into a single component on 60-250 hp models. Refer to the illustrations provided in **Figure 43-50** during the removal and installation procedure.

NOTE
The battery charge and ignition charge coils are almost identical on some 6-50 hp models. Use the wire colors and illustrations to identify the proper coil.

Pulser Coil

Pulser coil appearance and mounting locations vary by model. Refer to the charts located near the back of the manual to identify the wire color for the pulser coil(s). Trace the wire to the component on the engine. Note the size and location of any plastic tie clamps that must be removed for reference during assembly. The first sequence of steps will cover the E60 and 3-70 hp models (excluding

7

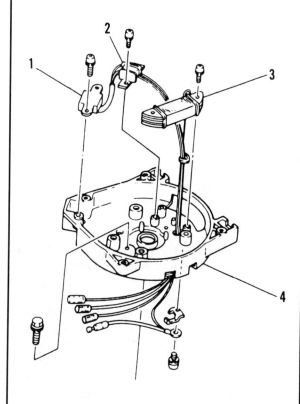

**IGNITION CHARGE/PULSER COIL
(4 AND 5 HP MODELS)**

1. Pulser coil No. 1
2. Pulser coil No. 2
3. Ignition charge coil
4. Magneto base

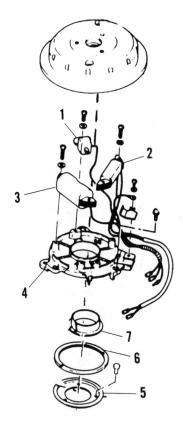

**IGNITION CHARGE/PULSER/
LIGHTING COIL (6 AND 8 HP MODELS)**

1. Pulser coil
2. Lighting coil
3. Ignition charge coil
4. Magneto base
5. Base plate
6. Retainer
7. Bushing

(46)

IGNITION CHARGE/PULSER/LIGHTING COIL (9.9 AND 15 HP MODELS)

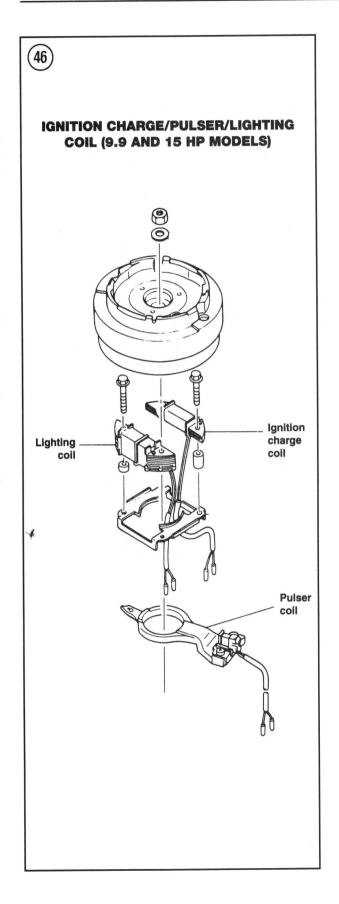

Lighting coil

Ignition charge coil

Pulser coil

(47)

IGNITION CHARGE/PULSER/ LIGHTING COIL (20 AND 25 HP [TWO-CYLINDER] MODELS)

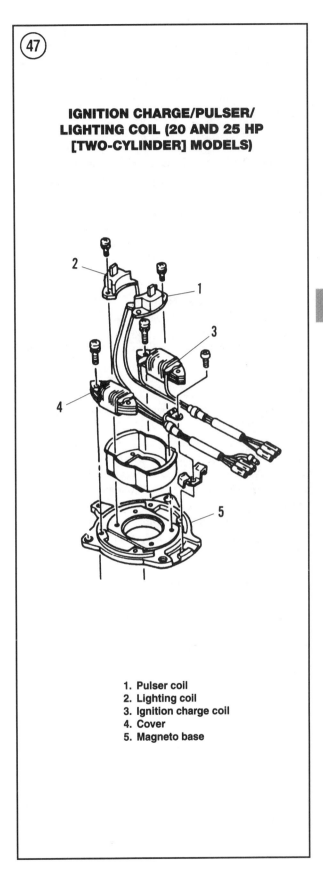

1. Pulser coil
2. Lighting coil
3. Ignition charge coil
4. Cover
5. Magneto base

65 jet). The second sequence of steps will cover 65 jet and 75-250 hp models. The pulser coils for 65 jet and 75-250 hp models are located in one assembly. Replace the assembly if one coil is faulty. Refer to the illustrations during the removal and installation procedure.

    a. For 3 hp models, refer to **Figure 43**.
    b. For 4 and 5 hp models, refer to **Figure 44**.
    c. For 6 and 8 hp models, refer to **Figure 45**.
    d. For 9.9 and 15 hp models, refer to **Figure 46**.
    e. For 20-25 hp (two-cylinder) models, refer to **Figure 47**.
    f. For 25 hp (three-cylinder) and 30-70 hp models, except Models E48 and 65 jet, refer to **Figure 48**.
    g. For Model E48, refer to **Figure 49**.
    h. For Model E60, refer to **Figure 50**.

Pulser coil removal/installation (E60 and 3-70 hp [except 65 jet])

1. Disconnect both battery cables from the battery terminals.

2. Remove the recoil starter, if present, as instructed in Chapter Eleven.

3. Remove the flywheel following the procedures listed in Chapter Eight.

4. Refer to the illustrations and wire colors to identify the pulser coil. Mark or make note of wire routing and connection points. Disconnect the wires that lead from the pulser coil to the harness or other components.

5. On 3 hp models, a second pulser coil is mounted under the magneto base. To access this coil remove the two screws that retain the magneto base to the crankcase halves. Lift the magneto base from the powerhead.

6. Remove the screws that retain the pulser coil to the magneto base. Remove the pulser coil. Lift the base enough to gain access to the sliding surfaces located under the magneto base on 6-50 hp and E60 models only. Apply a small amount of Yamaha all-purpose grease to the surfaces that contact the magneto base (pulser coil assembly) and the surfaces below the magneto base.

7. Install the pulser coil to the magneto base or the correct mounting location. Tighten the screws and other fasteners securely. Clean and inspect all leads before connecting them. Install clamps as required.

8. On 3 hp models, install the magneto assembly to the crankcase halves and tighten the two screws securely.

9. Install the flywheel and recoil starter, if so equipped, following the procedures listed in Chapter Eight. Connect the battery cables to the proper terminals. Install the electrical component cover if removed.

10. Check and correct the ignition timing and synchronization following the procedures listed in Chapter Five.

Check for proper engine operation before putting it back in service.

Pulser coil removal/installation (65 jet and 75-250 hp)

1. Disconnect both battery cables from the battery terminals.

2. Remove the flywheel as described in Chapter Eight. Remove the recoil starter, if so equipped, as described in Chapter Eleven.

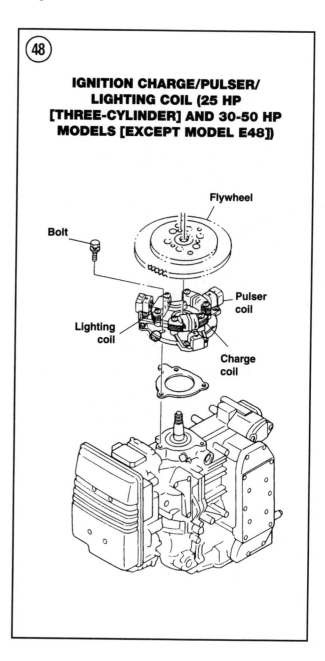

(48)

IGNITION CHARGE/PULSER/ LIGHTING COIL (25 HP [THREE-CYLINDER] AND 30-50 HP MODELS [EXCEPT MODEL E48])

49

IGNITION CHARGE/PULSER/ LIGHTING COIL (MODEL E48)

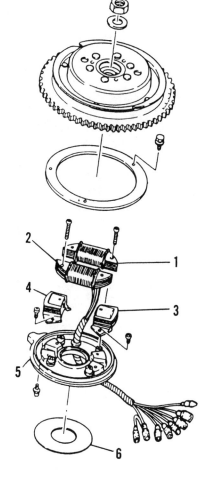

1. Lighting coil
2. Ignition charge coil
3. Pulser coil No. 1
4. Pulser coil No. 2
5. Magneto base
6. Washer

50

IGNITION CHARGE/PULSER/ LIGHTING COIL (MODEL E60)

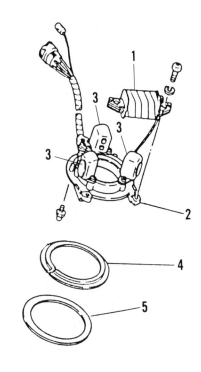

1. Ignition charge coil
2. Magneto base
3. Pulser coils
4. Base retainer
5. Washer

7

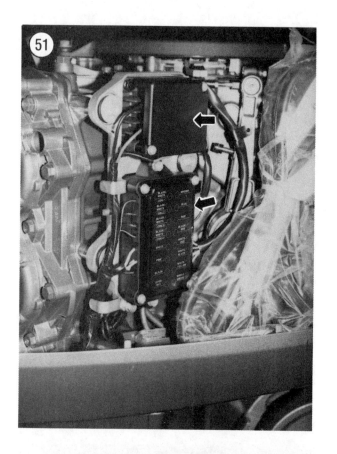

3. Remove the electrical component cover(s) to access the terminal connections. Refer to **Figure 51** or **Figure 52** for inline engines and **Figure 53** for V models.

4. Mark or make note of the wire routing and connection points to ensure proper connections on assembly. See **Figure 54**. Disconnect the leads from the pulser coil assembly to the harness or other components.

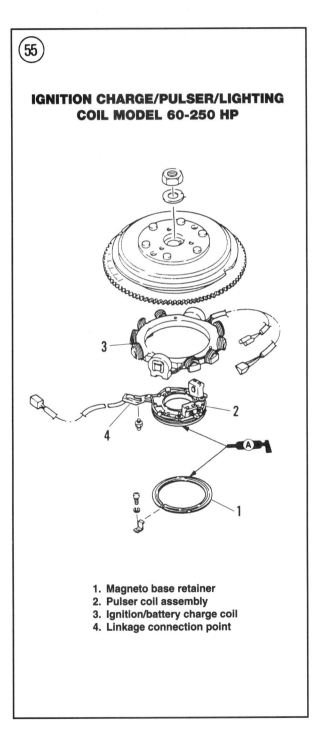

IGNITION CHARGE/PULSER/LIGHTING
COIL MODEL 60-250 HP

1. Magneto base retainer
2. Pulser coil assembly
3. Ignition/battery charge coil
4. Linkage connection point

5. Mark the orientation of the pulser coil relative to its mounting location. Disconnect the linkage from the pulser coil assembly (4, **Figure 55**) and remove the pulser coil (2, **Figure 55**) from the engine.

6. Clean corrosion and contaminants from the pulser coil assembly mounting area. Apply a small amount of Yamaha all-purpose grease to the sliding surfaces where the pulser coil assembly contacts the magneto base retainer (1, **Figure 55**).

7. Position the pulser coil on the engine. Rotate it slightly to ensure free movement. Connect the linkage. Clean and inspect all wire terminals. Repair if required. Connect all leads to the proper terminal.

8. Install the electrical component covers(s). Install the flywheel and recoil starter, if so equipped, as instructed in Chapter Eight and Chapter Eleven. Connect the battery cables to the proper terminals.

9. Perform the timing and synchronization procedures listed in Chapter Five. Check the engine for proper operation.

CDI Unit Removal/Installation

CDI unit (**Figure 56**) appearance and mounting locations vary by model. Refer to the wire charts located near the end of the manual to identify the wire colors leading to the CDI unit. Trace the wires to the component on the engine. Note the size and location of any plastic tie clamps that must be removed.

1. Disconnect the battery cables from the battery terminals. Remove the electrical component cover (**Figure 52** or **Figure 53**) to access the terminals. Refer to **Figure 54** for inline engine terminal locations and **Figure 57** for V models. Some models do not use an electrical component cover.

7

2. Mark all wire attaching points and routing to ensure proper connections on assembly. Disconnect all wires connected to the CDI unit. Remove the linkage connection, if used.

3. Locate and remove the screws that retain the CDI unit to its attaching point. Make note of any ground wires connected at these points (A, **Figure 57**). Make sure they are properly connected on assembly.

4. Remove the CDI unit. Clean any corrosion and contaminants from the CDI mounting location. Clean inspect and repair, if necessary, the threads on the mounting location.

5. Install the CDI unit and tighten all fasteners securely. Check all grounding wires for proper connections. Take care when routing all wires. They must not interfere with other components (B, **Figure 57**). Connect the linkage, if so equipped, to the CDI unit.

6. Clean, inspect and attach all wires to the correct terminal connections.

7. Install the electrical component cover if removed. Connect the battery cables to the proper terminals. Perform the timing and synchronization procedures listed in Chapter Five. Check the engine for proper operation before putting it into service.

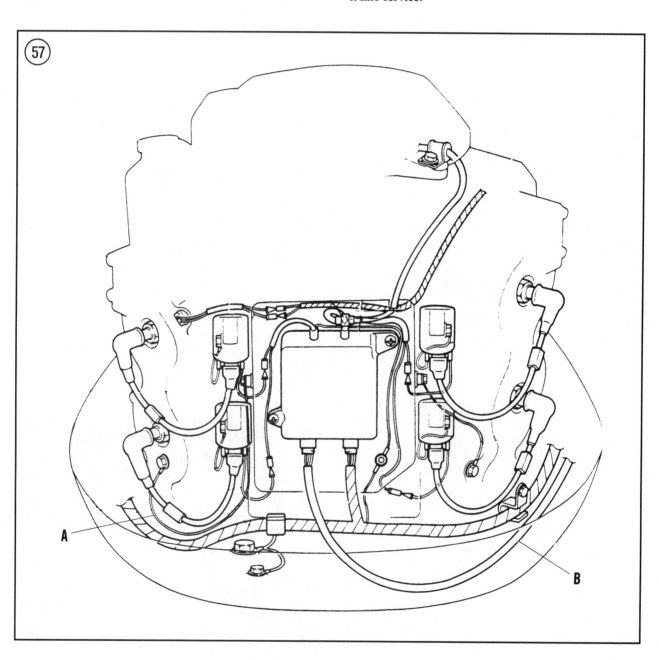

Ignition Coil Removal/Installation

Ignition coil appearance and mounting locations vary by model. Refer to the wire charts located at the back of the manual to determine the wire color for the coil. Trace the wire to the coil needing replacement. Note the size and location of any plastic tie clamps for reference during installation.

Follow Steps 1-5 to replace the ignition coil.

1. Disconnect the battery cables from the battery terminals. Remove the electrical component cover when required. Locate the proper ignition coil (**Figure 58**).

2. Mark the coil wires to ensure correct connections on installation. Disconnect the coil wires and the spark plug lead from the coil.

3. Remove the mounting hardware and the coil. Clean and inspect the wire connections, fastener threads and the mounting locations. Apply *RTV sealant* to the threads of the ground wire fastener.

4. Install the coil and mounting hardware. Attach the coil ground wire to one of the fasteners. Tighten the fasteners securely. Install the electrical component cover.

5. Connect the battery cables to the proper terminals. Check the engine for proper engine operation.

YAMAHA MICROCOMPUTER IGNITION SYSTEM COMPONENTS

This section provides removal, inspection and installation procedures for the following:

1. YMIS microcomputer.
2. Coolant temperature sensor.
3. Crank position sensor.
4. Oxygen density sensor.
5. Pressure sensor.
6. Air temperature sensor.
7. Spark knock sensor.
8. Resistor.
9. Shift cutoff switch.
10. Injection system relay.

Microcomputer Removal/Installation

Be careful when handling the microcomputer. This component is easily damaged if handled roughly.

Note the size and location of any plastic tie clamps.

1. Disconnect both battery cables from the battery terminals. Remove the electrical component cover (**Figure 59**) to access the microcomputer.

2. Mark all electrical connections to ensure correct connections on assembly.

7

3. Disconnect, inspect and clean all connectors to the microcomputer. Remove the four screws that retain the microcomputer to the mounting bracket. Note the ground wire attached to one of the fasteners (**Figure 60**).

4. Clean any corrosion and contaminants from the mounting location and threaded screw holes. Position the microcomputer on the bracket. Apply RTV sealant to the threads of the ground wire fastener, then install the ground wire. Tighten all fasteners securely.

5. Connect all leads and connectors to the proper location.

6. Install the electrical component cover. Connect the battery cables to the correct battery terminals. Adjust the throttle position indicator following the procedures in Chapter Five.

Coolant Temperature Sensor
Removal/Installation

The appearance and mounting locations of the coolant temperature sensor (**Figure 61**) vary by model. Proper identification is important as the sensor's appearance is almost identical to the thermoswitch. Refer to the wire charts located near the back of the manual to identify the temperature sensor wire color. Trace the wire to the correct component on the engine. Note the size and location of plastic locking tie clamps that must be removed and replace them.

1. Disconnect both battery cables at the battery terminals. Carefully disconnect the plug for the coolant temperature sensor. Clean and inspect the terminals in the connectors.

2. Remove the coolant temperature sensor and sealing washer from the engine. Use the proper thread chaser or tap to remove corrosion and contaminants from the threaded opening.

3. Install the replacement coolant temperature sensor and use a crows foot adapter to torque the sensor to the specification listed in **Table 3**.

4. Connect the sensor lead to the main harness. Connect the battery cables to the proper terminals. Check for proper operation before putting the engine into service.

Crank Position Sensor
Removal/Installation

The crank position sensor is positioned next to the flywheel (**Figure 62**). An opening is provided in the flywheel cover for the sensor. Air gap adjustment is not required. However, the sensor must not contact the fly-

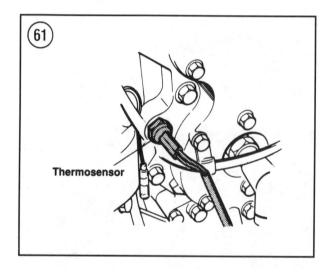

Thermosensor

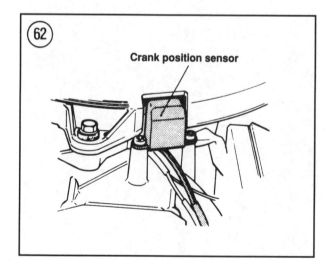

Crank position sensor

wheel at any point of rotation. Check for and correct the fastener orientation if the sensor is contacting the flywheel.

Refer to the wire charts located at the back of the manual to identify the wire color for the crank position sensor. Trace the wire to the component on the engine. Note the size and location of plastic locking tie clamps that must be removed and replace them.

1. Disconnect both battery cables from the battery terminals. Disconnect the sensor wires from the harness. Clean and inspect the harness and sensor terminals.

2. Note the orientation of the screws and washers that retain the sensor to the mounting location. Remove the sensor.

3. Clean corrosion and contaminants from the sensor mounting location. Clean and inspect the threaded holes for the sensor mounting screws.

4. Position the replacement sensor on the mount. Install the fasteners and tighten securely. Manually rotate the

flywheel while checking for adequate clearance between the flywheel and sensor. Correct as required.

5. Connect the battery cables to the proper terminals. Check for proper engine operation.

Oxygen Density Sensor
Removal/Installation

This sensor is mounted to a bracket located near the starboard cylinder head. Refer to the wire charts located near the back of the manual to identify the sensor wire color. Trace the wire to the component on the engine. Note the size and location of plastic locking tie clamps that must be removed and replace them.

1. Disconnect both battery cables from the battery terminals. Disconnect the sensor connector from the main harness.

2. Remove the two screws (2, **Figure 63**) that retain the cover (3, **Figure 63**) to the mounting location.

7

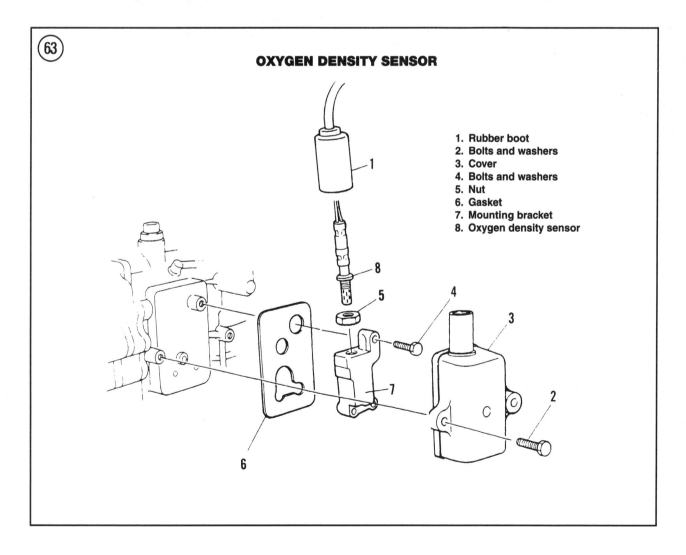

63

OXYGEN DENSITY SENSOR

1. Rubber boot
2. Bolts and washers
3. Cover
4. Bolts and washers
5. Nut
6. Gasket
7. Mounting bracket
8. Oxygen density sensor

3. Remove the screws (4, **Figure 63**) and pull the sensor assembly and mounting bracket from the mounting location. Remove and discard the gasket (6, **Figure 63**).

4. Remove the sensor assembly from the cover. Pull the rubber cap (1, **Figure 63**) away from the sensor. Loosen the nut (5, **Figure 63**) and remove the sensor (8, **Figure 63**) from the assembly.

5. Installation is the reverse of removal. Install a new gasket (6, **Figure 63**). Torque the retaining nut (5, **Figure 63**) and the mounting bracket screws (4, **Figure 63**) to the specifications listed in **Table 3**.

Pressure Sensor Removal/Installation

The pressure sensor is mounted to the junction box assembly on the starboard side of the powerhead (**Figure 64**). Refer to the wire charts located at the back of the manual to identify the wire color for the pressure sensor. Trace the wire to the component on the engine. Note the size and location of any plastic tie clamps.

1. Disconnect the harness connection plug (1, **Figure 65**) from the pressure sensor. Clean and inspect the connector terminals.

2. Remove the two screws that attach the pressure sensor (3, **Figure 65**) to the junction box.

3. Clean any debris from the pocket and passage at the pressure sensor mount.

4. Install the replacement pressure sensor and screws. Tighten the fasteners securely. Properly attach the connector. Check the engine for proper operation.

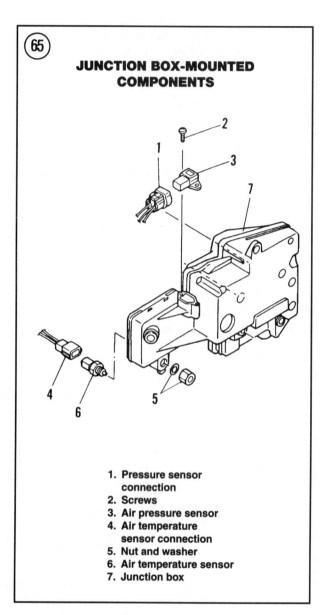

JUNCTION BOX-MOUNTED COMPONENTS

1. Pressure sensor connection
2. Screws
3. Air pressure sensor
4. Air temperature sensor connection
5. Nut and washer
6. Air temperature sensor
7. Junction box

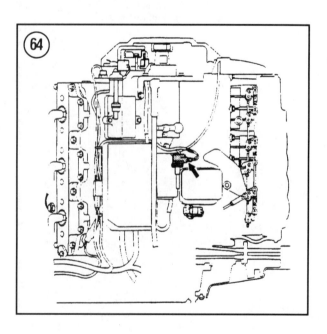

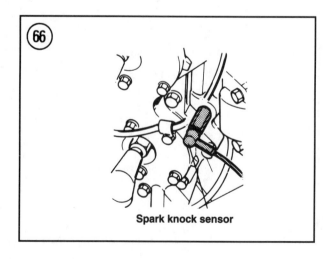

Spark knock sensor

Air Temperature Sensor
Removal/Installation

The air temperature sensor is located at the lower inside area of the junction box (**Figure 65**). Refer to the wire charts located at the back of the manual to identify the wire color for the air temperature sensor. Trace the wire to the component on the engine. Note the size and location of any plastic tie clamps.

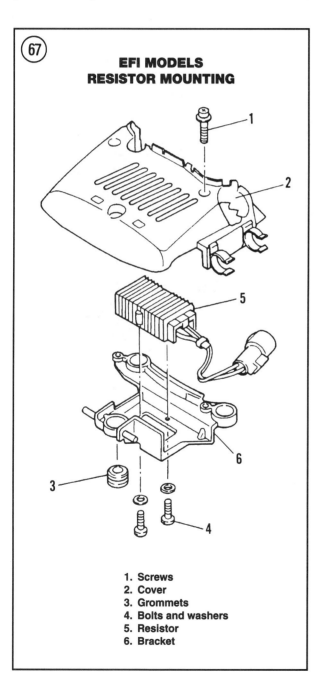

67

EFI MODELS
RESISTOR MOUNTING

1. Screws
2. Cover
3. Grommets
4. Bolts and washers
5. Resistor
6. Bracket

1. Disconnect the harness connector (4, **Figure 65**) from the air temperature sensor. Clean and inspect the harness terminals. Remove the nut and washer (5, **Figure 65**) from the air temperature sensor.
2. Remove the air temperature sensor from the junction box. Clean any debris or contaminants from the air temperature sensor mounting area and the passages leading into the junction box.
3. Install the air temperature sensor into the junction box. Install the washer and nut (5, **Figure 65**) onto the air temperature sensor and tighten securely.
4. Connect the harness connector to the air temperature sensor. Check the engine for proper operation.

Spark Knock Sensor
Removal/Installation

Appearance and mounting locations for the spark knock sensor vary by model. It will always be located on one of the cylinder heads (**Figure 66**). Refer to the wire charts located at the back of the manual to identify the wire color for the spark knock sensor. Trace the wire to the component on the engine. Note the size and location of any plastic tie clamps and replace them during installation.
1. Disconnect both battery cables from the battery terminals. Remove the rubber boot and disconnect the wire from the spark knock sensor.
2. Remove the spark knock sensor from the cylinder head using a suitable wrench. Clean and inspect the threaded hole for the spark knock sensor.
3. Install the replacement spark knock sensor into the threaded hole (finger tight only). Use a torque wrench to tighten the spark knock sensor to the specification listed in **Table 1**.
4. Connect the spark knock sensor lead to the sensor and slide the boot over the terminal. Connect the battery cables to the proper terminal. Check for proper engine operation.

EFI Resistor Removal/Installation

The resistor is located forward of the flywheel and above the throttle body. Refer to the wire charts located at the back of the manual to identify the wire color for the resistor. Trace the wire to the component on the engine. Note the size and location of any plastic tie clamps and replace them during installation.
1. Disconnect both battery cables from the battery terminals. Remove the three screws (1, **Figure 67**) that retain the cover (2, **Figure 67**) to the mounting bracket.
2. Remove the three grommets (3, **Figure 67**) from the bracket. Disconnect the resistor plug-type connector from the main harness. Clean and inspect the harness terminals.

7

3. Remove the two bolts and washers (4, **Figure 67**) from the bottom of the bracket and lift the resistor from the bracket. Clean corrosion and contaminants from the bracket.

4. Installation is the reverse of removal. Tighten all fasteners securely.

5. Connect the battery cables to the correct terminals. Check the engine for proper operation.

Shift Cutoff Switch
Removal/Installation

The shift cutoff switch is mounted to a bracket located on the lower starboard side of the powerhead. Refer to the wire charts located at the back of the manual to identify the wire color for the switch. Trace the wire to the component on the engine. Note the size and location of plastic tie clamps and replace them during installation.

1. Disconnect both battery cables from the battery terminals.

2. Remove the shift cable and fasteners from the switch assembly.

3. Remove the two bolts (2, **Figure 68**) that retain the switch assembly to the power head. Remove the bolt, bushing and actuator bracket (4, **Figure 68**) from the assembly.

4. Remove the spring, bushing and collar from the assembly.

5. Remove the two screws (9, **Figure 68**) and cover. Carefully lift the switch (10, **Figure 68**) from the mounting bracket.

6. Installation is the reverse of removal. Apply a coating of Yamaha all-purpose grease or its equivalent to the bushings and collars during assembly. Tighten all fasteners securely.

7. Connect the battery cables to the proper terminals. Perform *Shift Cable Adjustment* as described in Chapter Five. Check for proper engine operation.

Injection System Relay
Removal/Installation

The injection system relay is mounted to the junction box (**Figure 65**). Refer to the wire charts located at the end of the manual to identify the wire color for the relay. Trace the wire to the component on the engine. Note the size and location of any plastic tie clamps and replace them during installation.

NOTE
The injection system relay is located very close to the starter relay. Check the wire

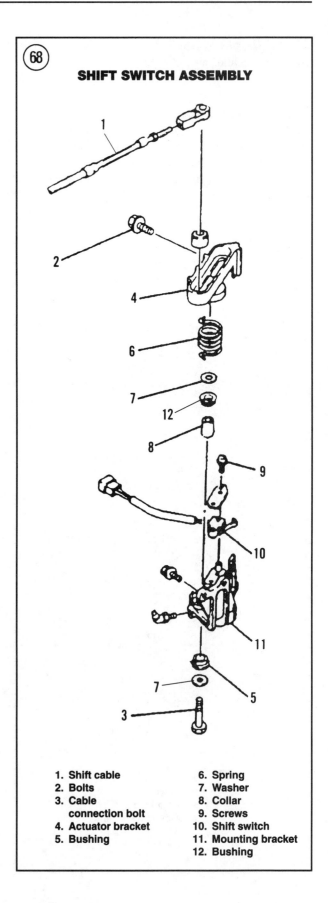

68

SHIFT SWITCH ASSEMBLY

1. **Shift cable**	6. **Spring**
2. **Bolts**	7. **Washer**
3. **Cable**	8. **Collar**
connection bolt	9. **Screws**
4. **Actuator bracket**	10. **Shift switch**
5. **Bushing**	11. **Mounting bracket**
	12. **Bushing**

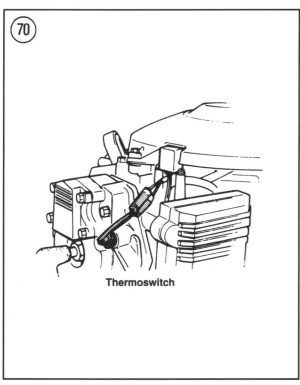

Thermoswitch

color and verify that the proper component has been identified.

1. Disconnect both battery cables from the battery terminals. Disconnect the yellow and black wire connection plug from the relay. Clean and inspect the connector terminals. Disconnect the red/yellow and red bullet-style connectors from the relay. Clean and inspect the terminals.

2. Remove the retaining screw and relay from the junction box. Inspect the black wire to the connection plug for a clean and tight connection to the engine ground.

3. Installation is the reverse of removal. Tighten the screw securely.

4. Connect the battery cables to the proper terminals. Check the engine for proper operation.

Warning System Components

This section will provide identification, removal and installation procedures for the thermoswitch, warning horn and emergency switch.

Thermoswitch removal/installation

The thermoswitch and thermosensor are similar in appearance and mounting location. Refer to the wire charts located near the back of the manual to identify the wire color for the thermoswitch. Trace the wire to the component on the engine. The thermoswitch is fastened to the upper end of the cylinder head (**Figure 69**). A thermoswitch is used on both cylinder heads on 200-250 hp 76° models.

To replace the switch, disconnect the switch wires from the main harness. Pull the switch from its bore in the cylinder head (**Figure 70**). Insert and fully seat the new switch in the cylinder head. Connect the leads.

Warning horn removal/installation

Refer to *Neutral switch* in this chapter for the control box mounted warning horn. The warning horn is mounted under the dash on some applications. If the warning horn is mounted inside the motor cover refer to the wire charts located at the back of the manual. Identify the wire color for the warning horn and trace it to the component. The replacement procedures are similar regardless of the mounting location. Disconnect the terminals and clean them. Remove any fasteners for the horn. Install the replacement horn and connect the wire terminals.

7

Emergency switch removal/installation

The emergency switch is located near the electrical component cover (**Figure 71**). Refer to the wire charts located near the end of the manual to identify the wire color for the switch. Check the wire color at the switch before removal. Note the direction the switch will toggle and position the replacement switch to retain the same switch toggle direction.

1. Remove the electrical component cover to gain access to the switch. Disconnect, clean and inspect the switch terminal connectors.

2. Remove the retaining nut from the toggle end of the switch and remove the switch from its mount.

3. Install the replacement switch and tighten the retainer securely. Connect the leads and install the electrical component cover.

BATTERY MAINTENANCE AND TESTING

Battery Requirements

Batteries used in marine applications are subjected to far more vibration and pounding action than automotive applications. Always use a battery that is designated for marine applications (**Figure 72**). These batteries are constructed with thicker cases and plates than typical automotive batteries.

Use a battery that meets or preferably exceeds the cold cranking amperage requirements for the engine. Refer to the *Quick Reference Data* for the battery requirements. Some marine batteries will list *Marine/Deep Cycle* on the label. Deep cycle batteries are constructed to allow repeated discharge and charge cycles. These batteries are an excellent power source for accessories such as trolling motors. Always charge deep cycle batteries at a low amperage rate. They are not generally designed to be charged or discharged at a rapid rate. **Table 3** provides the usage hours (capacity) for both 80 and 105 amp-hour batteries. Approximate recharge times are listed as well. Compare the amperage draw of the accessory with the information provided in **Table 3**. Deep cycle batteries can be used as the starting battery providing they meet the cold cranking amperage requirements for the engine.

Cable Connections

Insufficient or dirty cable connections cause many problems in marine applications. Use cable connectors that are securely crimped or molded to the cable. Avoid the use of temporary or emergency clamps for normal usage. They

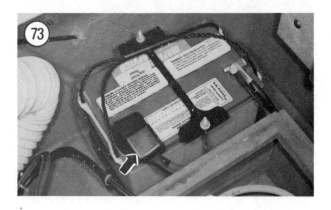

are prone to corrosion and do not meet the coast guard requirements for terminal connections.

Use a cover on the positive terminal post (**Figure 73**). They are available at marine dealerships. Use either the around-the-post connector or the spade-type clamp that attaches to the top of the post.

Battery Mounting Requirements

Make sure the battery is securely mounted in the boat to avoid dangerous acid spills or electrical arcing that can cause a fire. The most common type of battery mounting is the bracket mounted to the floor of the boat and the support across the top of the battery (**Figure 73**). The other common type of battery mounting is the battery case and cover that encloses the battery and secures it to the boat

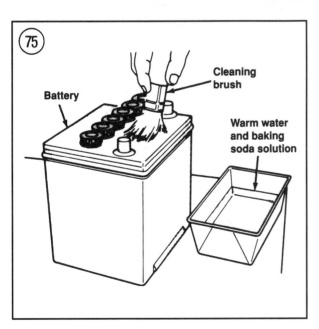

structure (**Figure 74**). When properly installed, either of these will provide secure mounting and protection for the terminals.

Mount the battery in a location that allows easy access for maintenance. Ensure that the battery terminals are not able to contact any component in the mounting area.

> *WARNING*
> *When mounting a battery in a boat constructed of aluminum, ensure that the battery is securely mounted to eliminate the possibility of the battery contacting metal components. Electrical arcing can result in fire or explosion if a fuel source is present. Bodily injury, death or damage to property can occur. Batteries produce explosive gases that can ignite if arcing is present.*

Battery Case Inspection and Maintenance

> *WARNING*
> *Always wear gloves and protective eyewear when working with batteries to avoid injury. Batteries contain a corrosive acid solution. Never smoke or allow any source of ignition to be near a battery. Batteries produce explosive gases that can ignite and result in battery explosion if a source of ignition is present.*

> *CAUTION*
> *Never allow the water and baking soda solution to enter the battery solution through the vent caps. The acid solution will become neutralized and cause permanent damage to the battery.*

The battery case should be inspected for cracks, leakage, abrasion points and other damage when the battery is removed for charging. Replace the battery when any questionable condition exists. A corrosive deposit will form on the top of the battery during normal usage. These deposits may allow the battery to discharge at a rapid rate as current can travel through the deposits from one post to the other.

Make sure the battery caps are properly installed. Remove the battery from the boat and carefully wash loose material from the top of the battery with clean water. Use a solution of warm water and baking soda along with a soft bristled brush to clean the deposits from the battery (**Figure 75**). Wash the battery again with clean water to remove all of the baking soda solution from the battery case.

> *WARNING*
> *Be careful when lifting or transporting the battery. With age, the carry strap can become*

7

weak or brittle and break. If the battery is dropped, the case may break and release a dangerous acid solution. Use other suitable means to lift and transport the battery.

NOTE
Never overfill the battery. The electrolyte may expand with the heat created from charging and overflow from the battery.

Check the battery solution level on a regular basis. Heavy usage or usage in warm climates will increase the frequency that water needs to be added to the battery. Carefully remove the vent caps (**Figure 76**) and inspect the electrolyte level in each cell. The electrolyte level should be approximately 5 mm (3/16 in.) above the plates, yet below the bottom of the vent well (**Figure 76**). Use distilled water to fill the cells to the proper level. Never use battery acid to correct the electrolyte level. The acidic solution will become too strong and lead to damage or deteriorated plates.

Battery Terminal Maintenance

Cleaning the terminals

Clean the battery terminals at regular intervals and any-time the terminal has been removed. Use a battery cleaning tool available at most automotive parts stores. Remove the terminal and clean the post as indicated (**Figure 77**). Avoid removing too much material from the post, or the terminal may not attach properly. Rotate the tool on the post until the post is cleaned of corrosion.

Use the other end of the tool to clean the cable end terminal. Clean flat spade-type connectors and the attaching nuts with the wire brush end of the tool (**Figure 78**).

Attaching the terminals

Apply a coating of petroleum gel or other corrosion preventative agent on the battery post and cable terminal. Tighten the fasteners securely. Avoid using excessive force when tightening these terminals as the battery can sustain considerable damage.

Battery Testing

Two methods are commonly used to test batteries. One method involves measuring the battery voltage as an electrical load is applied to the battery. The load is applied either by cranking the engine with the starter motor or by a special load tester or carbon pile. The other method involves the use of a hydrometer to measure the specific

gravity of the battery electrolyte. Both methods give an accurate reading of the charge level of the battery.

Hydrometer testing

On batteries with removable vent caps, using a hydrometer to check the specific gravity of the electrolyte is the best method to check battery condition. Use a hydrometer with numbered graduations from 1.100-1.300 points rather than one with color-coded bands.

NOTE
Inaccurate readings will result if the specific gravity is checked immediately after adding

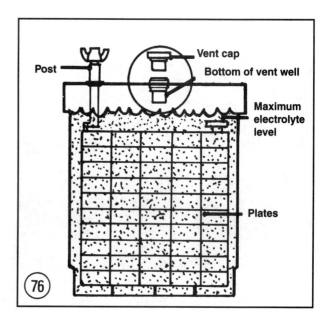

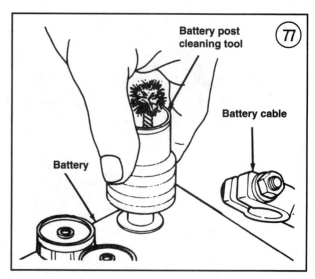

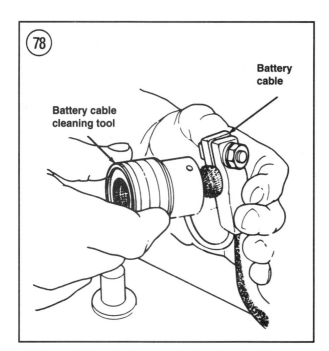

Figure 78. Battery cable cleaning tool, Battery cable

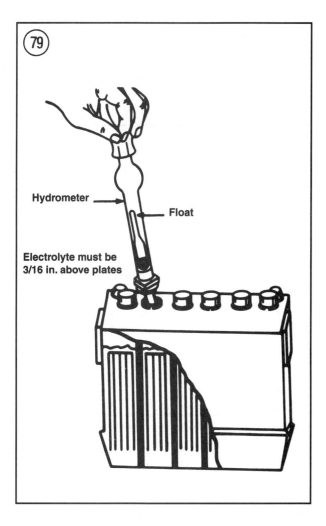

Figure 79. Hydrometer, Float, Electrolyte must be 3/16 in. above plates

water to the battery. To ensure accuracy, charge the battery for 15-20 minutes after adding water.

To use the hydrometer, remove the battery vent cap, squeeze the rubber bulb and insert the tip of the hydrometer into the vent opening. Release the bulb to draw electrolyte into the hydrometer (**Figure 79**). Hold the hydrometer upright and note the number on the float that is even with the surface of the electrolyte (**Figure 80**). This number is the specific gravity for the cell. Discharge the electrolyte

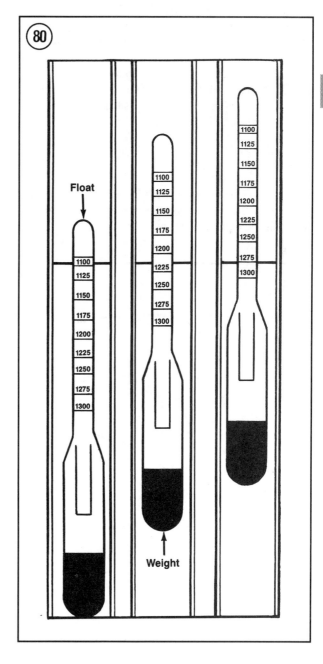

Figure 80. Float, Weight

7

into the cell from which it came. Measure the specific gravity of each cell. If using a temperature-compensated hydrometer, take several readings in each cell to allow the thermometer to adjust to the electrolyte temperature.

NOTE
If a temperature-compensated hydrometer is not used, add 0.004 to the reading for every 10° above 25° C (80° F). Subtract 0.004 from the reading for every 10° below 25° C (80° F).

The specific gravity of a cell indicates the cell's state of charge. A specific gravity reading of 1.260 or higher indicates a fully charged battery. Compare the hydrometer readings with the information provided in **Table 3** to determine the level of charge. Charge the battery and recheck the specific gravity if readings vary more than 0.050 from one cell to another. If 0.050 variation remains between cells after charging, the battery has failed and must be replaced.

Load testing

Perform the load test to check the ability of the battery to maintain the starting system's minimum required voltage while cranking the engine.

1. Connect the voltmeter positive test lead to the battery positive terminal. Connect the voltmeter negative test lead to a suitable engine ground.
2. Remove the spark plug leads and ground them to the engine to prevent accidental starting.
3. Measure the voltage while cranking the engine (**Figure 81**).
4. The battery is discharged or defective if the voltage drops below 9.6 volts while cranking. Fully charge the battery, then test the cranking voltage again. Replace the battery if the voltage is not 9.6 volts or higher after a complete charge.

Battery Storage

Batteries slowly discharge during storage. The rate of discharge will increase in a warm environment. Store the battery in a cool dry location to minimize the loss of charge. Check the specific gravity every 30 days of non-use and charge the battery if required. Perform the maintenance on the battery case and terminals as described in this section. Refer to *Battery charging* for battery charging times.

WARNING
Batteries produce explosive hydrogen gas. Charge the battery in a well ventilated area.

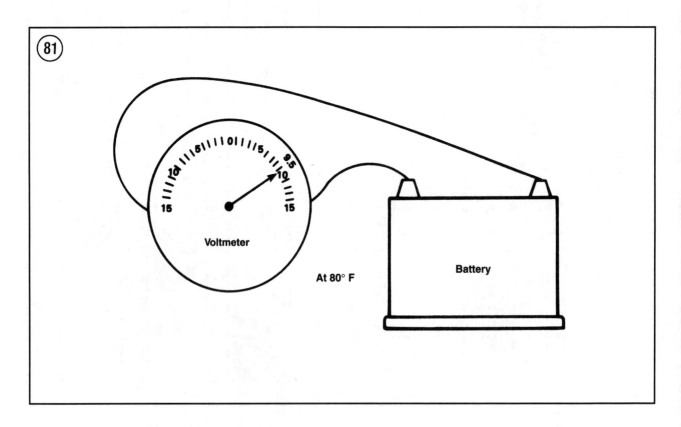

Wear protective eyewear and suitable gloves when working around batteries. Never smoke or allow any source of ignition in the area where batteries are stored or charged. Never allow any conductive components to contact the battery terminals as arcing can occur and ignite the hydrogen gas. The battery can explode, resulting in serious bodily injury, death or damage to property.

Battery Charging

Although it is not necessary, remove the battery from the boat when charging. Batteries give off explosive hydrogen gas. Because many boats have limited ventilation, these explosive gases may remain in the area for a fair amount of time. In addition to the hazards of explosion, the gases will cause accelerated corrosion of components in the battery compartment. Never attempt to charge a battery that is frozen. On batteries with removable vent caps, check the electrolyte level before charging the battery. Maintain the correct electrolyte level throughout the charging process.

WARNING
Use extreme caution when connecting any wires to the battery terminals. Avoid making the last connection at the battery terminal. Explosive hydrogen gas in and around the

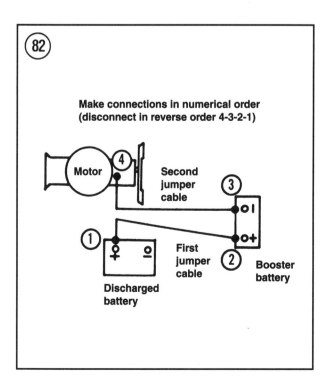

Make connections in numerical order (disconnect in reverse order 4-3-2-1)

Motor 4 Second jumper cable 3

1 First jumper cable 2 Booster battery

Discharged battery

battery may ignite and lead to an explosion, resulting in severe bodily injury, death or damage to property.

Connecting the charger

Make the connections to the battery before plugging the charger in or switching the charger on to help avoid arcing at the terminals. Connect the battery charger cables to the proper terminals on the battery. Plug the charger into its power supply and select the 12 volt battery setting.

Charging rate and charging times

It is preferable to charge a battery slowly at low amp settings, approximately 4 amps, rather than quickly at high amp settings. If the battery is severely discharged, it may be necessary to charge the battery at a higher amperage rate for a few minutes before starting the lower rate charge.

Refer to **Table 3** for battery charging times. Severely discharged batteries may require as long as 8 hours to recharge. On batteries with removable vent caps, check the specific gravity often and halt the charging process when the battery is fully charged. Halt the charging process if the temperature of the electrolyte reaches or exceeds 53° C (125° F).

Jump Starting Procedure

If the battery becomes severely discharged, it is possible to start the engine by jump starting it from another battery. However, jump starting can be dangerous if correct procedures are not followed. Never attempt to jump start a frozen battery. Check and correct the electrolyte level in the discharged battery before making any connections. Jump starting a battery with a low electrolyte level can cause the battery to become extremely overheated and possibly explode. Keep the jumper cable clamps separated from any metallic or conductive material. Never allow the clamps to contact other clamps.

1. Connect a jumper cable clamp to the positive terminal of the discharged battery (1, **Figure 82**).

2. Connect the same jumper cable's remaining clamp to the positive terminal of the fully charged battery (2, **Figure 82**).

3. Connect the second jumper cable clamp to the negative terminal of the fully charged battery (3, **Figure 82**).

4. Connect the second jumper cable's remaining clamp to a good engine ground such as the starter ground cable (4, **Figure 82**).

7

5. Make sure the cables and clamps are positioned so that they will not become trapped or interfere with moving components.

6. Start the engine and run it at a moderate speed. Remove the cables in exactly the reverse of the connection order (Steps 4-1).

Wiring for 12 and 24 Volt Electric Trolling Motors

Many fishing boats are equipped with an electric trolling motor that requires 24 volts to operate. Two or more batteries must be connected in series to provide the required voltage.

A series connection (**Figure 83**) will provide the approximate total voltage of the two 12-volt batteries, or 24 volts. The amperage provided is the approximate average of the two batteries.

If the trolling motor requires 12 volts to operate, a parallel connection (**Figure 84**) will provide the approximate average voltage of the two 12-volt batteries, or 12 volts. The amperage provided will be the approximate total of the two batteries.

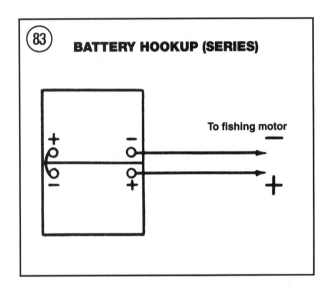

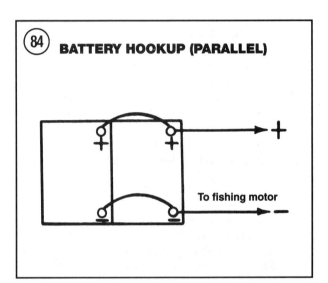

Table 1 TIGHTENING TORQUE

Fastener	Torque
Starter mounting bolts	32 N•m (23 ft.-lb.)
Starter switch retainer	5 N•m (44 in.-lb.)
Starter cable to starter relay	9 N•m (79 in.-lb.)
Starter cable to engine ground	7 N•m (62 in.-lb.)
Engine temperature sensor	15 N•m (11 ft.-lb.)
Spark knock sensor	28 N•m (20 ft.-lb.)
Oxygen density sensor nut	49 N•m (36 ft.-lb.)
Oxygen density sensor bracket	8 N•m (70 in.-lb.)
Standard torque by fastener size	
M5 bolt or 8 mm nut	5 N•m (44 in.-lb.)*
M6 bolt or 10 mm nut	8 N•m (70 in.-lb.)*
M8 bolt or 12 mm nut	18 N•m (13 ft.-lb.)*
M10 bolt or 14 mm nut	36 N•m (26 ft.-lb.)*
M12 bolt or 17 mm nut	42 N•m (30 ft.-lb.)*

*These values apply to fasteners with threads that are dry and clean and measured at room temperature.

Table 2 STARTER MOTOR SPECIFICATIONS

Armature deflection	
Maximum deflection	
All Models	0.05 mm (0.002 in.)
Commutator diameter	
6-8 hp	
Minimum	19.4 mm (0.76 in.)
Standard	20.0 mm (0.79 in.)
9.9-25 hp	
Minimum	19.4 mm (0.76 in.)
30-70 hp (excludes 65 jet)	
Minimum	29.0 mm (1.14 in.)
Standard	30.0 mm (1.18 in.)
65 jet and 75-90 hp models (except 80 jet)	
Minimum	31.0 mm (1.22 in.)
Standard	33.0 mm (1.30 in.)
80 jet and 115-130 hp	
Minimum	32.0 mm (1.26 in.)
105 jet and 150-250	
Minimum	31.0 mm (1.22 in.)
Mica undercut depth	
30-70 hp (except 65 jet)	
Minimum undercut	0.2 mm (0.01 in.)
Maximum undercut	0.8 mm (0.03 in.)
65 jet and 75-90 hp models (except 80 jet)	
Minimum undercut	0.5 mm (0.02 in.)
Maximum undercut	1.0 mm (0.04 in.)
80,105 jet and 115-250 hp	
Minimum undercut	0.2 mm (0.01 in.)
Brush length	
6-8 hp	
Minimum	4.5 mm (0.18 in.)
Standard	7.5 mm (0.30 in.)
9.9-25 hp	
Minimum	4.5 mm (0.18 in.)
30-70 hp (except 65 jet)	
Minimum	9.0 mm (0.35 in.)
Standard	12.5 mm (0.49 in.)
65 jet and 75-90 hp models (except 80 jet)	
Minimum	12.0 mm (0.47 in.)
Standard	16.0 mm (0.63 in.)
80 jet and 115-130 hp	
Minimum	10.0 mm (0.39 in.)
105 jet and 150-250 hp	
Minimum	12.0 mm (0.47 in.)

7

Table 3 BATTERY CAPACITY (HOURS OF USE)

Amperage draw	Hours of usage with 80 amp-hour battery	Hours of usage with 105 amp-hour battery	Recharge time (approximate)
5 amps	13.5 hours	15.8 hours	16 hours
15 amps	3.5 hours	4.2 hours	13 hours
25 amps	1.8 hours	2.4 hours	12 hours

Table 4 STATE OF CHARGE

Specific gravity reading	Percentage of charge remaining
1.120-1.140	0
1.135-1.155	10
	(continued)

Table 4 STATE OF CHARGE (continued)

Specific gravity reading	Percentage of charge remaining
1.150-1.170	20
1.160-1.180	30
1.175-1.195	40
1.190-1.210	50
1.205-1.225	60
1.215-1.235	70
1.230-1.250	80
1.245-1.265	90
1.260-1.280	100

Chapter Eight

Power Head

Power head repair can be as simple as replacing a gasket to stop an external water leak or as complicated as a complete power head rebuild. This chapter provides complete power head rebuild procedures. When replacing external or easily accessible components complete power head disassembly is not required. Follow the step-by-step disassembly procedure until the required component is accessible. Reverse the disassembly steps to install the required component(s). Follow all steps for complete power head repairs.

The major topics in this chapter include power head removal, flywheel removal/installation, power head disassembly, component inspection, power head assembly, power head installation and break-in procedures. Significant variations in the procedures exist from one model to the next. The procedures are tailored to the unique requirements of the various model groups.

Virtually all components attached to the power head must be removed to perform a complete power head repair. References will be made to other chapters in this manual for component removal and installation procedures. When performing minor repairs or removal of external power head components, remove only the components necessary to access the faulty component(s). Refer to the provided illustrations to determine which components must be removed to gain the required access.

Tables 1-12 are located at the end of this chapter. **Table 1** provides tightening torque specifications for power head

fasteners and standard tightening torque specifications. Refer to the standard tightening torque specification in **Table 2** if a specific tightening torque value is not listed for a component. **Tables 2-12** provide component tolerances and dimensions.

If you decide not to attempt a major power head disassembly or repair, it may be financially beneficial to perform certain preliminary operations yourself. Consider separating the power head from the outboard motor and removing the fuel, ignition and electrical system components, taking only the basic power head to the dealership for the major repair or overhaul.

Many marine dealerships have a backlog of service work during the boating season. Often your repairs can be scheduled and performed much quicker if you have done much of the preliminary work. Always discuss your options with the servicing dealer before appearing at the dealership with a disassembled engine. The dealer will often want to install, adjust and test run the engine after completing the overhaul or repair.

If you will be performing the entire repair, contact your local Yamaha dealership to purchase the required parts and special service tools. Some dealerships will rent or loan special tools. Secure all special tools before attempting any repair. The use of makeshift tools may result in damaged power head components. The cost of the damage caused by using a substitute tool can far exceed the cost of the special service tool. Use a reputable machine shop for boring, honing and measurements if required.

POWER HEAD REMOVAL

Preparation for Removal

Visually inspect the engine to locate the fuel supply hose and battery connections. Virtually all hoses and wire connections must be removed when performing a complete power head repair. Many of the hoses are much more accessible after the power head has been removed from the engine. Disconnect only the hoses and wires necessary to remove the power head from the engine. The other wires and hoses can be removed after the power head is removed.

Diagrams of the fuel and electrical systems are provided throughout this manual. Use them to assist with hose and wire routing. To speed up the installation of the power head and ensure correct connections take pictures or make note of all wire and hose connections *before* beginning the power head removal process.

Secure the proper lifting equipment before attempting to remove the power head. It is not exceedingly difficult to manually lift a 20 hp and smaller power head provided you have some assistance. Large bore two-cylinder engines (E48) and all three-cylinder and larger engines require an overhead hoist. A complete power head may weigh nearly 300 lb. (136 kg). Use assistance when lifting or moving any power head. Use the lifting hook (**Figure 1**) located at the top of the engine when lifting all 30-225 hp (90°) power heads. Use the special lifting hook (**Figure 2**) part No. YB 6117/90890-6202 when lifting all 200-250 hp models (76°). This hook mounts to the threaded end of the crankshaft.

NOTE
Power head mounting fastener location and quantity varies within the models. Refer to the illustrations for assistance in locating the mounting fasteners. Variations also exist within the models as to which components must be removed prior to removing the power head. Make sure all required fasteners and components are removed before attempting to lift the power head from the mid-section.

CAUTION
Avoid damage to the power head mounting machined surfaces. Check for overlooked

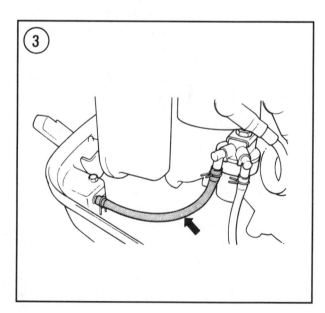

fasteners before attempting to pry the power head from the mid-section. Corrosion may prevent easy removal of the power head. Apply a penetrating oil to the mating surface and allow it to soak in before attempting power head removal.

WARNING
The power head may abruptly separate from the mid-section during removal with an overhead hoist causing bodily injury or property damage. Avoid using excessive force when lifting the power head with an overhead hoist. Carefully use pry bars to separate the power head from its mount before lifting with a hoist.

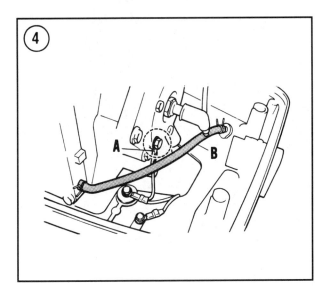

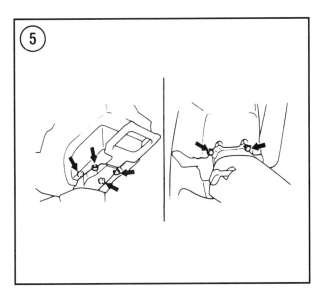

Removal (2-15 hp)

NOTE
Many variations exist within the models as to wire and hose routing as well as shift and throttle linkages. Mark or make notes of all wire routing, hose routing and linkage orientation before beginning the power head removal procedure.

1. Disconnect both cable connections from the battery terminals on electric start models.

2. Disconnect the fuel supply hose (**Figure 3**) from the hose connector (remote tank models).

3. Drain all fuel from the engine mounted fuel tank, carburetor, filters and fuel hoses.

4. Disconnect the ground lead (A, **Figure 4**) and water stream hose (B, **Figure 4**) from the power head.

5. Note the location and orientation then disconnect the throttle and shift linkages from the carburetor/lever.

6. Remove the battery leads from the starter relay and ground terminal on electric start models. Unplug the main engine harness from the remote control harness on remote control models.

7. Mark or make note of the lead connections, then remove the start and stop switch leads from the main harness.

8. Remove the lockout assembly cable at the flywheel end, if so equipped.

9. Inspect the power head for attached wires or hoses and remove them if necessary for power head removal.

10. Locate and remove the power head mounting bolts. For 2-5 hp models, refer to **Figure 5**. For 6-15 hp models, refer to **Figure 6**.

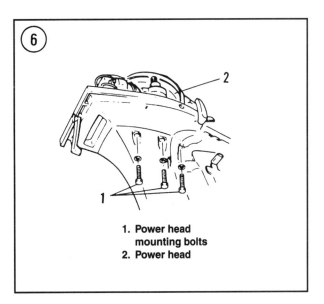

1. Power head mounting bolts
2. Power head

11. Carefully lift the power head from the mid-section. Put the power head assembly on a stable work surface.

12. Remove and discard the power head mounting gasket (2, **Figure 7**). Clean then inspect the power head mounting surfaces for deep pitting or extensive corrosive damage. Replace the housing if defects are noted. Inspect the locating pins (1, **Figure 7**) for damaged or missing pins. Inspect the pin holes for elongation or cracked areas and replace the component if defects are noted. Remove the pins from the power head and position them into the mid-section pin holes if they remained with the power head base.

Removal (20-250 hp)

1. Disconnect both cable connections from the battery terminals on electric start models.

2. Unplug the main engine harness from the remote control harness (A, **Figure 8**).

3. Disconnect the battery leads from the starter relay and ground connection (**Figure 9**)

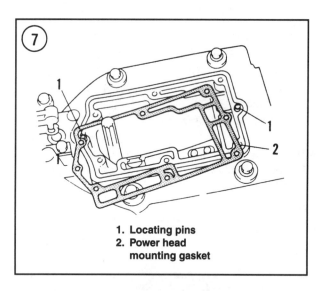

1. Locating pins
2. Power head mounting gasket

4. Remove the oil supply hose from the oil supply tank. Refer to Chapter Thirteen to identify the proper hose. Plug the disconnected hoses to prevent leakage. Remove the retainer (B, **Figure 8**) and route the hoses and wires out and away from the power head.

5. Remove the flywheel cover (A, **Figure 10**) if so equipped. Remove the fasteners, then remove the front (B,

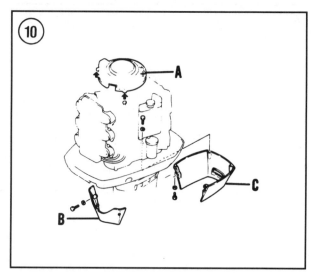

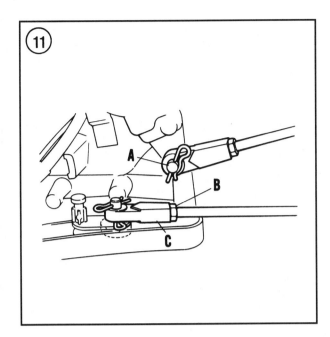

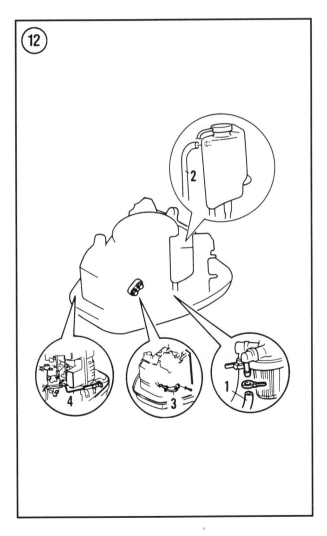

Figure 10) and rear (C, **Figure 10**) lower motor cover, if so equipped.

6. Remove the retaining pin (A, **Figure 11**). Do not loosen the jam nut (B, **Figure 11**). Lift the cable ends (C, **Figure 11**) from the throttle and shift linkages.

7. Disconnect the fuel supply hose and drain the fuel from the carburetor bowls. Refer to Chapter Six for instructions

8. Visually inspect the power head to ensure that the required fasteners, hoses, wires and linkages are removed before proceeding with power head removal (**Figure 12**).

9. Position the engine in the upright position. Remove the mounting bolts (**Figure 13**).

10. On the 200-250 hp (76°) models, install the lifting hook (part No. YB 6202) onto the crankshaft threads (**Figure 14**). Ensure that the hook is fully threaded onto the crankshaft threads.

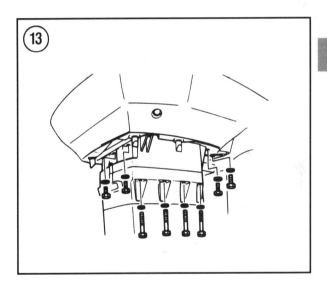

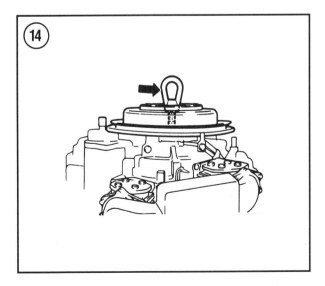

8

11. Attach an overhead hoist to the lifting hook and provide enough force to take all slack from the lifting cable or chain.

12. Remove the lower engine cover if necessary to gain access to the mating surfaces. Locate an area that allows a pry bar to be inserted between the power head and mid-section. Carefully lift and rock the power head to separate it from the mid-section (**Figure 15**). Work carefully to avoid damaging the power head to mid-section mating surfaces.

CAUTION
Lift the power head slowly and maintain support to ensure that the power head is lifted straight off the mid-section. The drive shaft and other components may be damaged if the power head is lifted or lowered at an angle.

13. Slowly lift the power head from the mid-section. Provide support (**Figure 16**) while lifting to prevent the power head from tilting back while lifting.

14. Mount the power head assembly to a suitable engine stand or stable work surface (**Figure 17**). A proper power head repair is difficult if the power head is not securely mounted.

15. Inspect the power head mounting surface for damaged or missing locating pins (A, **Figure 18**). Remove any pins from the power head base and install into the correct location on the mid-section. Replace pins that are bent or damaged. Inspect the pin holes in the block and adapter for cracks or elongation and replace the components as required.

16. Remove and discard the power head mounting gasket. Inspect the machined mating surfaces (B, **Figure 18**) for cracks, pitting or damaged areas. Replace the adapter or drive shaft housing if defects cannot be corrected.

FLYWHEEL REMOVAL/INSTALLATION

CAUTION
Use only the appropriate tools and procedures to remove the flywheel. Never strike the flywheel with a hard object. The magnets may break and result in poor ignition system

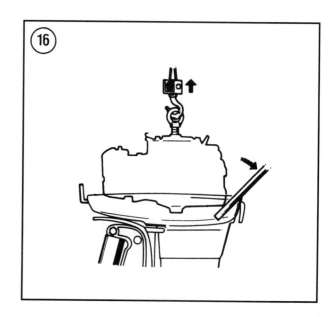

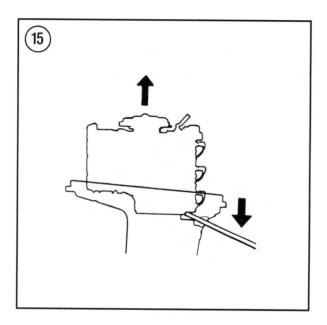

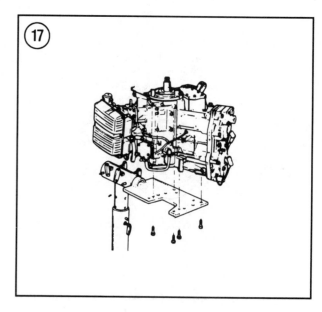

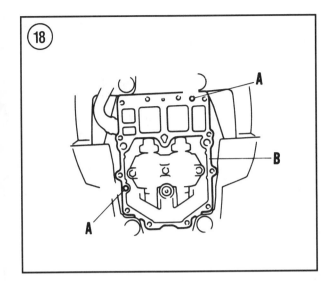

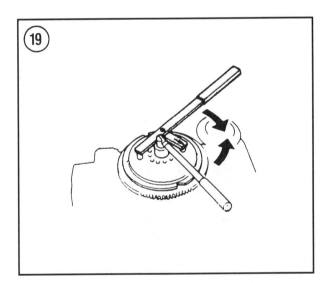

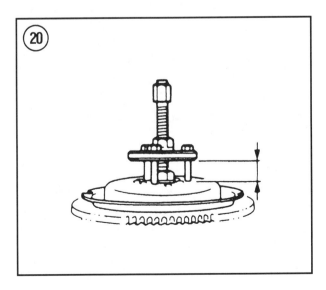

performance or potential damage to other engine components.

WARNING
Wear safety glasses when removing or installing the flywheel or other components of the engine. Never use a hammer or other tools without using safety glasses.

Ensure that the engine or power head is securely mounted before attempting to remove the flywheel. A suitable flywheel holder such as Yamaha part No. YB 01639-90890-06522 and a flywheel removing tool such as Yamaha part No. YB 6117/90890-6521 are required to remove and install the flywheel.

1. Disconnect both battery cables from the battery terminals. Mark the cylinder number and disconnect all spark plug leads.

2. Position the flywheel holding tool into the holes in the flywheel (**Figure 19**). Use a hinged handle and appropriate size socket to loosen the flywheel nut.

3. Remove nut until the top edge is flush or slightly above the threads of the crankshaft. Position the flywheel removing tool onto the flywheel. Make sure the puller bolts are threaded several turns into the flywheel and the puller is parallel with the flywheel surface (**Figure 20**). Check to make sure that the puller bolt is contacting the top end of the crankshaft and not the flywheel nut.

4. Use the flywheel holder to ensure that the flywheel will not rotate. Turn the puller bolt in a clockwise direction until the bolt is difficult to turn (**Figure 21**).

8

5. Provide support for the flywheel and lightly tap the puller bolt (**Figure 22**). Tighten the bolt and tap it again if the flywheel will not pop free from the crankshaft. Repeat this step if necessary.

6. Remove the flywheel puller. Remove and discard the flywheel nut and washer. Remove the woodruff key from the slot in the crankshaft taper (**Figure 23**). Retrieve the woodruff key from the ignition coils or flywheel magnets if not found in the slot. Inspect the woodruff key for corrosion, bent or marked surfaces and replace if not in excellent condition.

7. Clean debris and contaminants from the crankshaft threads, key slot and tapered area. Use compressed air to remove contaminants or debris from the flywheel magnets and other surfaces. Inspect the flywheel for cracks or damaged magnets and replace if any defects are noted.

8. Place the woodruff key into the key slot as shown in **Figure 23**. Position the flywheel onto the crankshaft. While providing support, slowly rotate the flywheel to align the slot in the flywheel with the woodruff key. When the flywheel drops onto the taper, rotate it while observing the threaded end of the crankshaft. Remove the flywheel and check the position of the woodruff key if the crankshaft does rotate with the flywheel.

9. Apply a light coating of Yamalube 2-cycle outboard oil or its equivalent to the threads on the crankshaft. Place a new flywheel washer over the crankshaft and onto the flywheel. Thread the new flywheel nut onto the crankshaft threads. Use the flywheel holding tool part No. YB 01639-90890-06522, socket and a suitable torque wrench to tighten the flywheel to the specification listed in **Table 1**.

10. Connect all spark plug leads to the correct spark plug(s). Connect the battery cables to the correct terminals.

Check and correct engine timing and synchronization as described in Chapter Five.

POWER HEAD DISASSEMBLY

Always make notes, drawings or photographs of all externally mounted power head components indicating the

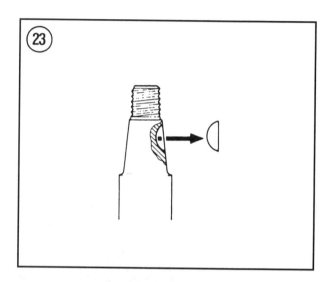

location and orientation *before* beginning power head disassembly. Although illustrations are provided throughout this manual making notes, drawings and photographs will save a great deal of time during the assembly process. Correct hose and wire routing is important for proper engine operation (**Figure 24**). An incorrectly routed hose or wire may interfere with linkage movement and result in a dangerous lack of throttle control. Hoses or wires may chafe and short circuit or leak when allowed to contact sharp or moving parts. Other components such as fuel pumps can be mounted in two or more positions. Mark or make note of the top and forward direction before removing components. If possible, remove a cluster of components that share common wires or hoses. This will reduce the time required to disassemble and assemble the power head and reduce the chance of improper connection on assembly.

Bearings and some other internal components of the power head (**Figure 25**) can be removed and reused if in good condition. The component inspection section of this

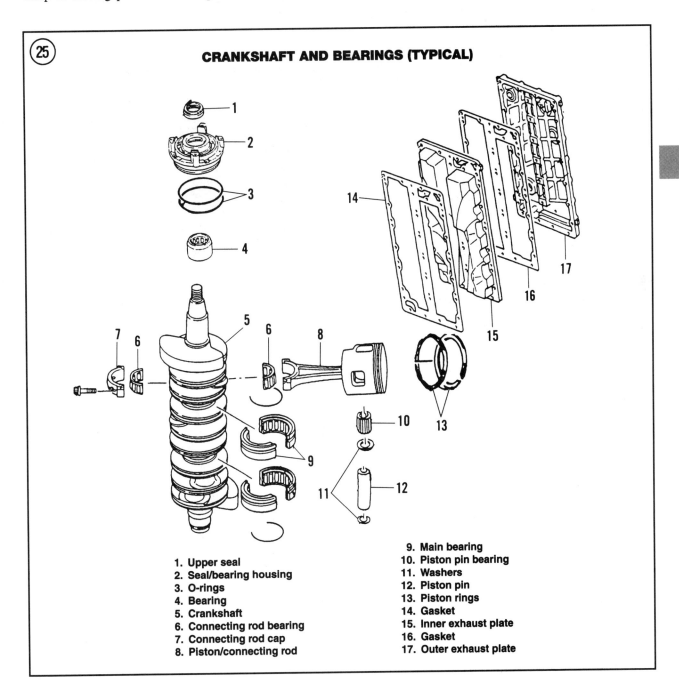

CRANKSHAFT AND BEARINGS (TYPICAL)

1. Upper seal
2. Seal/bearing housing
3. O-rings
4. Bearing
5. Crankshaft
6. Connecting rod bearing
7. Connecting rod cap
8. Piston/connecting rod
9. Main bearing
10. Piston pin bearing
11. Washers
12. Piston pin
13. Piston rings
14. Gasket
15. Inner exhaust plate
16. Gasket
17. Outer exhaust plate

8

chapter will indicate which components must be replaced. It is a good practice to replace all needle bearings, piston rings, seals, connecting rod bolts, gaskets and piston pin lock rings on assembly. If needle bearings must be reused, make certain that they remain in the same location on assembly. Piston rings must be replaced and cylinder bores honed when the piston is removed. The cost of these components is small compared with the damage that can result to other components should they fail.

Use muffin tins or egg cartons to organize the fasteners as they are removed. Use a tag with the fasteners to mark the correct installation location.

Never use corroded or damaged fasteners. Replace self-locking type nuts if they are not in excellent condition. Never use locking type fasteners more than twice without replacement.

External Component Removal

1. Remove the flywheel as instructed in this chapter.

2. Make note of connections and mounting locations and remove all electrical and ignition components. Refer to Chapter Seven for removal procedures.

3. Make note of all hose, wire and linkage connections and remove all fuel system components. Refer to Chapter Six for removal procedures.

4. Drain the oil from the supply tank and remove all oil injection components. Refer to Chapter Thirteen for component removal procedures.

5. Ensure that all throttle linkages are disconnected then loosen the bolt (A, **Figure 26**) for the throttle control arm. Remove the bolts and carefully remove the throttle control arm as an assembly (B, **Figure 26**) from the power head.

> *CAUTION*
> *Remove the control arm carefully and do not allow the upper and lower arms to separate. A spring is located within the upper and lower control arms pivot. Tape or wire the control arm assembly together, then remove the tape or wire after it is assembled onto the power head.*

> *NOTE*
> *Not all engines use a throttle control arm as part of the throttle linkage. On models without the arm, make note of the linkage orientation, then remove the linkage from the power head. If possible, allow the linkage to remain connected to other components that are removed from the power head.*

6. On 3, 6 and 8 hp models, remove the fasteners and the exhaust tuner/manifold (**Figure 27**) from the bottom of the cylinder block.

7. On 4-15 hp models, remove the bolt and washer (1 and 2, **Figure 28**) from the oil seal housing. Carefully pull the housing from the power head. The housing can be removed later if necessary. Remove and discard the 0-ring (5, **Figure 28**) from the housing. Pry the seal (4, **Figure 28**) from the oil seal housing. Be careful not to nick or scratch the housing surface during this operation. Retrieve the spacer (6, **Figure 28**) from the oil seal recess in the power head. On some V6 models, the oil seal housing must be pressed

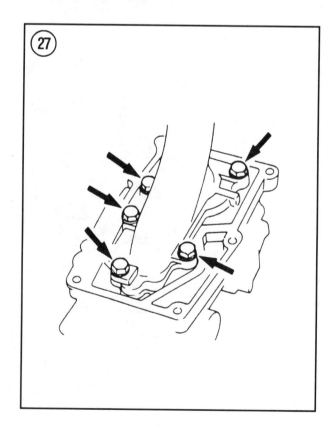

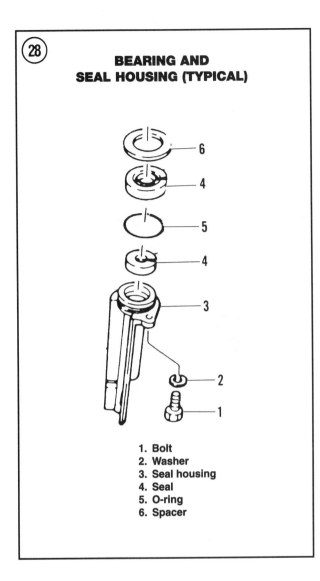

(28)

**BEARING AND
SEAL HOUSING (TYPICAL)**

1. Bolt
2. Washer
3. Seal housing
4. Seal
5. O-ring
6. Spacer

from the crankshaft after it is removed from the cylinder block.

8. Remove the reed housing/intake manifold (**Figure 29**) from the power head assembly as instructed in Chapter Six. Inspect the reed valves as described. Replace components if required.

Model Variations

Many variations exist within the models as to number of cylinders, crankshaft/rod arrangements, exhaust covers and water jacket covers. Refer to the figure indicated for your model during the component removal procedures. This will help you determine if a particular component is used and where it is located.

    a. For 2 hp models, refer to **Figure 30**.

    b. For 3 hp models, refer to **Figure 31**.

    c. For 4 and 5 hp models, refer to **Figure 32**.

    d. For 6 and 8 hp models, refer to **Figure 33**.

    e. For 9.9 and 15 hp models, refer to **Figure 34**.

    f. For 20 and 25 hp (2-cylinder) models, refer to **Figure 35**.

    g. For 25 (3-cylinder) and 30 hp models, refer to **Figure 36**.

    h. For 28 jet, 35 jet, 40 and 50 hp models, refer to **Figure 37**.

    i. For Model E48, refer to **Figure 38**.

    j. For E60, 60 and 70 hp models, refer to **Figure 39**.

    k. For E75 and 75-90 hp models (except 80 jet) refer to **Figure 40**.

    l. For 80 jet and 115-130 hp models, refer to **Figure 41**.

    m. For 105 jet and 150-225 hp (90°) models, refer to **Figure 42**.

    n. For 200-250 hp (76°) models, refer to **Figure 43**.

8

Water Jacket, Exhaust Cover, Thermostat and Bearing/Seal Housing Removal

Outboard engines are normally exposed to a corrosive operating environment. Corrosion will be more prevalent if the engine is operated in saltwater. Corroded fasteners can be difficult to remove. Refer to Chapter Two in this manual for useful tips on removing stubborn fasteners.

Loosen water jacket bolts or exhaust cover bolts gradually in a crossing pattern to help prevent plate warpage. Use caution when it is necessary to pry a component loose. Avoid using any sharp object that may damage the mating surfaces of the components. Castings or pry points are usually present that allow you to pry the components apart without risking damage to mating surfaces.

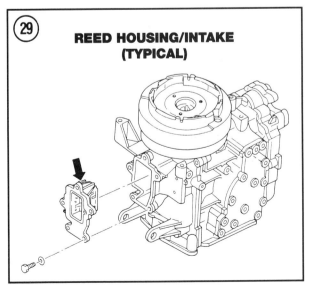

(29)

**REED HOUSING/INTAKE
(TYPICAL)**

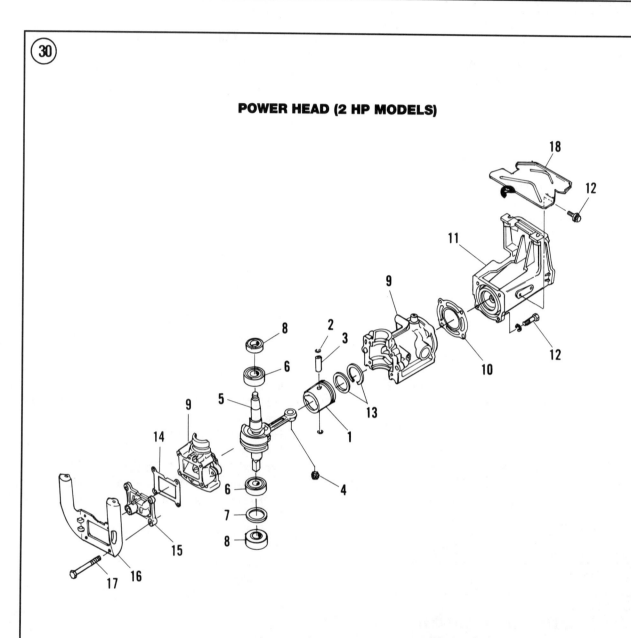

POWER HEAD (2 HP MODELS)

1. Piston
2. Lockring
3. Piston pin
4. Piston pin bearing
5. Crankshaft/rod
   assembly
6. Main bearing
7. Spacer
8. Seal
9. Cylinder block/
   crankcase cover
10. Head gasket
11. Cylinder head
12. Bolt
13. Piston rings
14. Intake gasket
15. Reed housing/intake
16. Bracket
17. Bolt
18. Fuel tank mount

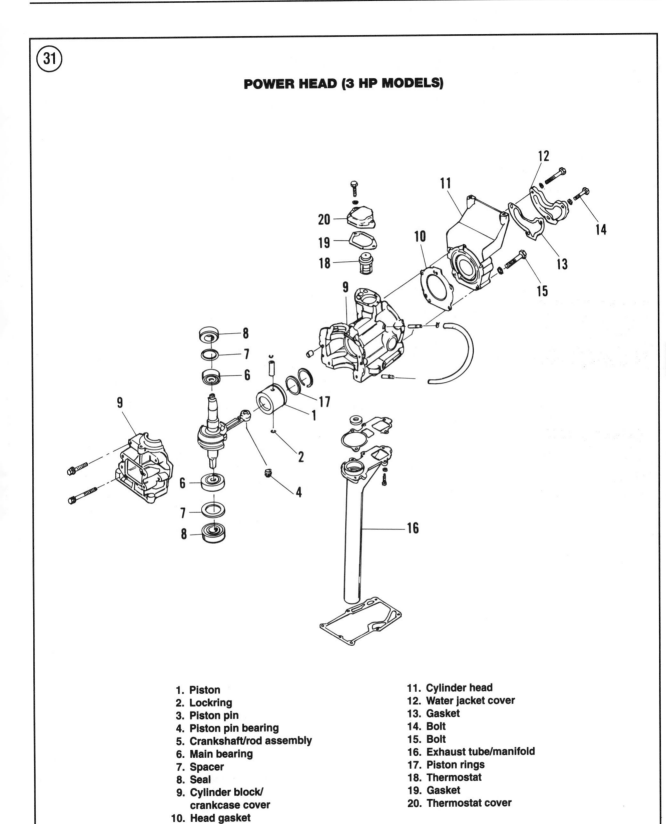

③①

POWER HEAD (3 HP MODELS)

1. Piston
2. Lockring
3. Piston pin
4. Piston pin bearing
5. Crankshaft/rod assembly
6. Main bearing
7. Spacer
8. Seal
9. Cylinder block/
   crankcase cover
10. Head gasket

11. Cylinder head
12. Water jacket cover
13. Gasket
14. Bolt
15. Bolt
16. Exhaust tube/manifold
17. Piston rings
18. Thermostat
19. Gasket
20. Thermostat cover

8

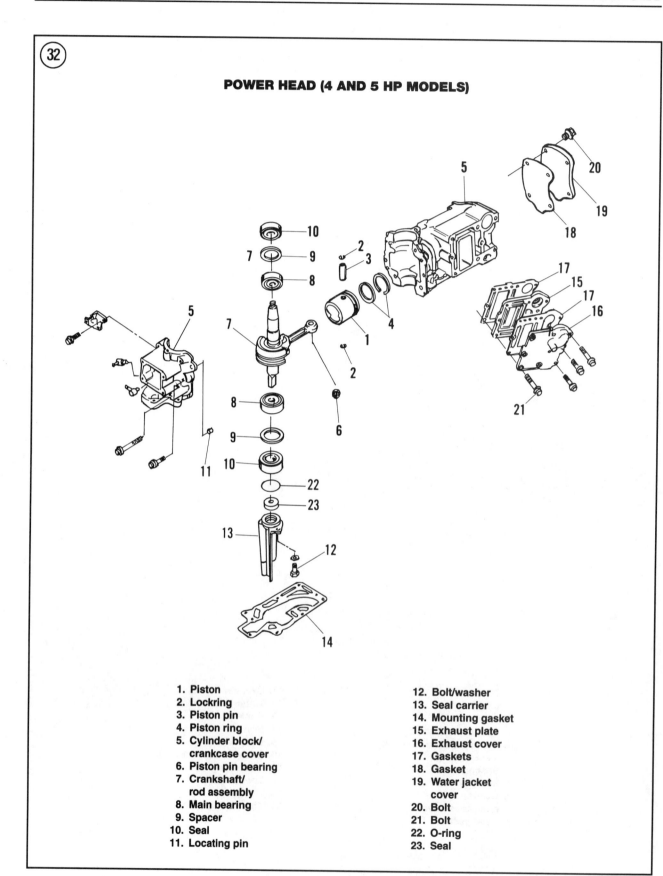

POWER HEAD (4 AND 5 HP MODELS)

1. Piston
2. Lockring
3. Piston pin
4. Piston ring
5. Cylinder block/
   crankcase cover
6. Piston pin bearing
7. Crankshaft/
   rod assembly
8. Main bearing
9. Spacer
10. Seal
11. Locating pin
12. Bolt/washer
13. Seal carrier
14. Mounting gasket
15. Exhaust plate
16. Exhaust cover
17. Gaskets
18. Gasket
19. Water jacket
    cover
20. Bolt
21. Bolt
22. O-ring
23. Seal

㉝

POWER HEAD (6 AND 8 HP MODELS)

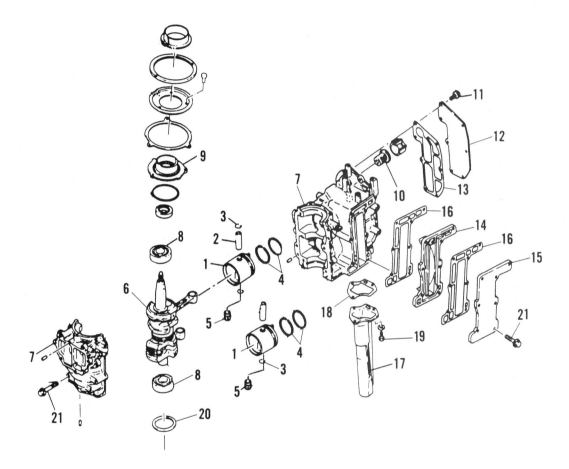

8

1. Piston	11. Bolt
2. Piston pin	12. Water jacket cover
3. Lockring	13. Gasket
4. Piston rings	14. Exhaust plate
5. Piston pin bearing	15. Exhaust cover
6. Crankshaft/	16. Gasket
rod assembly	17. Exhaust
7. Cylinder block/	tube tuner
crankcase cover	18. Gasket
8. Main bearing	19. Bolt
9. Top cover	20. Seal
10. Thermostat	21. Bolt

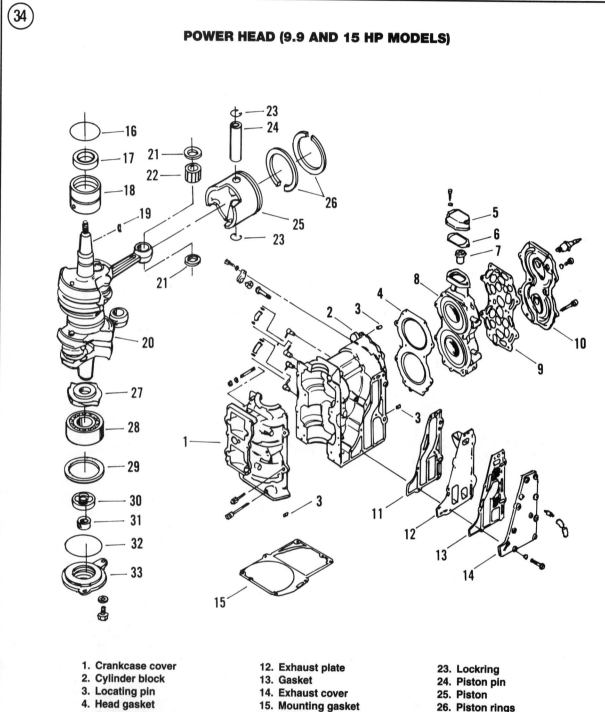

POWER HEAD (9.9 AND 15 HP MODELS)

1. Crankcase cover
2. Cylinder block
3. Locating pin
4. Head gasket
5. Thermostat cover
6. Gasket
7. Thermostat
8. Cylinder head
9. Gasket
10. Water jacket cover
11. Gasket
12. Exhaust plate
13. Gasket
14. Exhaust cover
15. Mounting gasket
16. O-ring
17. Seal
18. Upper bearing
19. Key
20. Crankshaft/rod assembly
21. Thrust washer
22. Piston pin bearing
23. Lockring
24. Piston pin
25. Piston
26. Piston rings
27. Spacer
28. Main bearing
29. Spacer
30. Seal
31. Seal
32. O-ring
33. Lower seal carrier

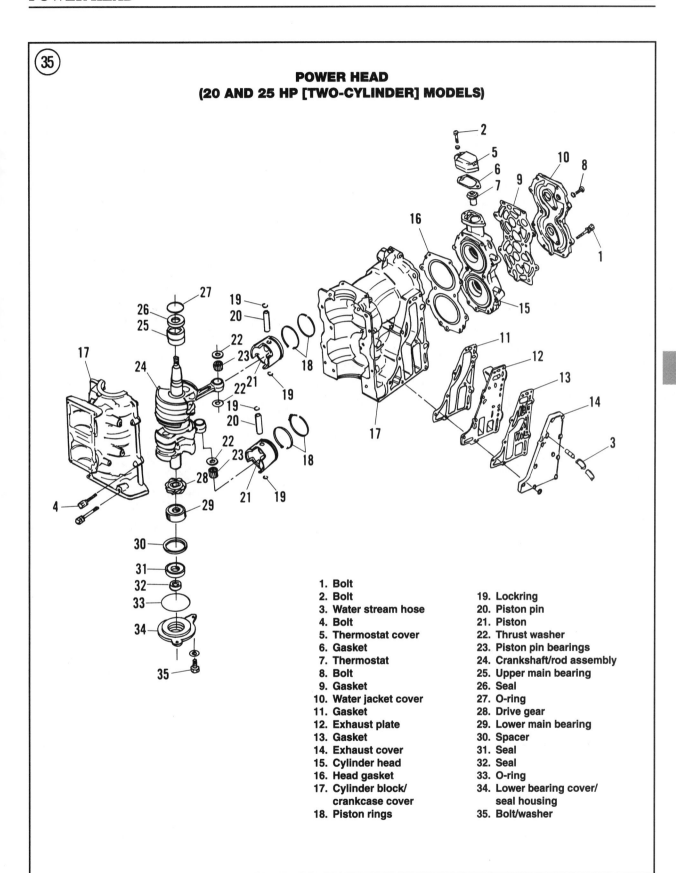

③⑤

**POWER HEAD
(20 AND 25 HP [TWO-CYLINDER] MODELS)**

8

1. Bolt
2. Bolt
3. Water stream hose
4. Bolt
5. Thermostat cover
6. Gasket
7. Thermostat
8. Bolt
9. Gasket
10. Water jacket cover
11. Gasket
12. Exhaust plate
13. Gasket
14. Exhaust cover
15. Cylinder head
16. Head gasket
17. Cylinder block/
    crankcase cover
18. Piston rings

19. Lockring
20. Piston pin
21. Piston
22. Thrust washer
23. Piston pin bearings
24. Crankshaft/rod assembly
25. Upper main bearing
26. Seal
27. O-ring
28. Drive gear
29. Lower main bearing
30. Spacer
31. Seal
32. Seal
33. O-ring
34. Lower bearing cover/
    seal housing
35. Bolt/washer

(36)

**POWER HEAD
(25 HP [THREE-CYLINDER] AND 30 HP MODELS)**

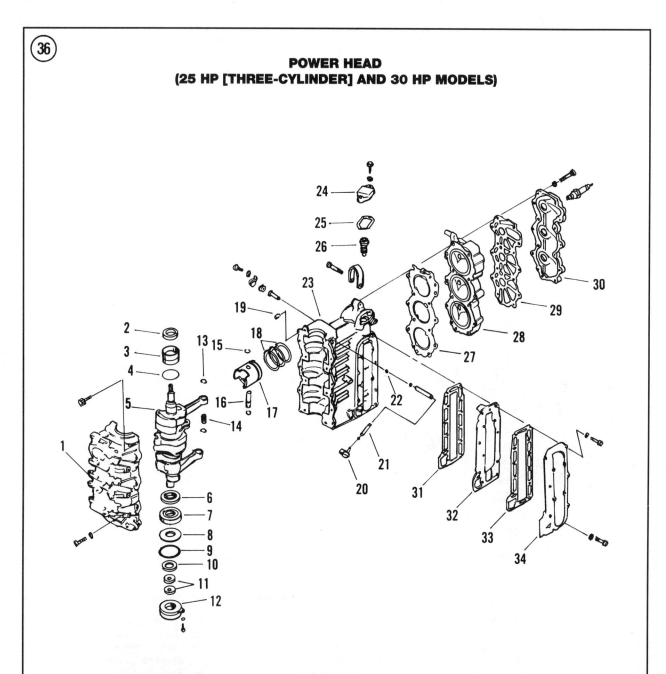

1. Crankcase cover	12. Lower bearing	23. Cylinder block
2. Seal	cover/seal housing	24. Thermostat cover
3. Bearing	13. Washer	25. Gasket
4. O-ring	14. Piston pin bearings	26. Thermostat
5. Crankshaft/rod	15. Lockring	27. Head gasket
assembly	16. Piston pin	28. Cylinder head
6. Drive gear	17. Piston	29. Gasket
7. Bearing	18. Piston rings	30. Water jacket cover
8. Washer	19. Locating pin	31. Gasket
9. O-ring	20. Fitting	32. Exhaust plate
10. Seal	21. Hose	33. Gasket
11. Seal	22. O-ring	34. Exhaust cover

POWER HEAD
(28 JET, 35 JET, 40 AND 50 HP MODELS)

1. Crankcase cover
2. Bearing cover/
   seal housing
3. Gasket
4. Seal
5. Main bearing
6. Crankshaft/
   rod assembly
7. Drive gear
8. Main bearing
9. Washer
10. Seal
11. Seal
12. O-ring
13. Bearing cover/
    seal housing
14. Thrust washer
15. Piston pin bearing

16. Piston
17. Lockring
18. Piston pin
19. Piston rings
20. Cylinder block
21. Locating pin
22. Thermostat
23. Gasket
24. Thermostat cover
25. Gasket
26. Cylinder head
27. Gasket
28. Water jacket cover
29. Gasket
30. Exhaust plate
31. Gasket
32. Exhaust cover

8

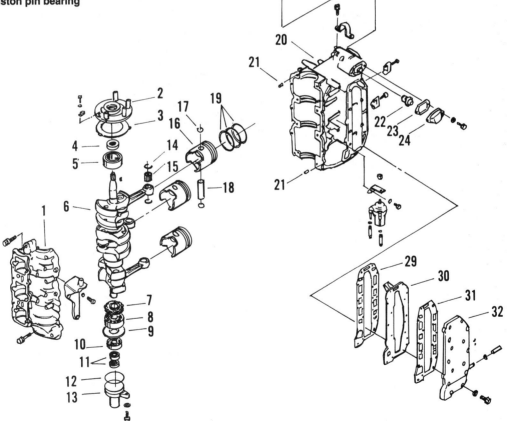

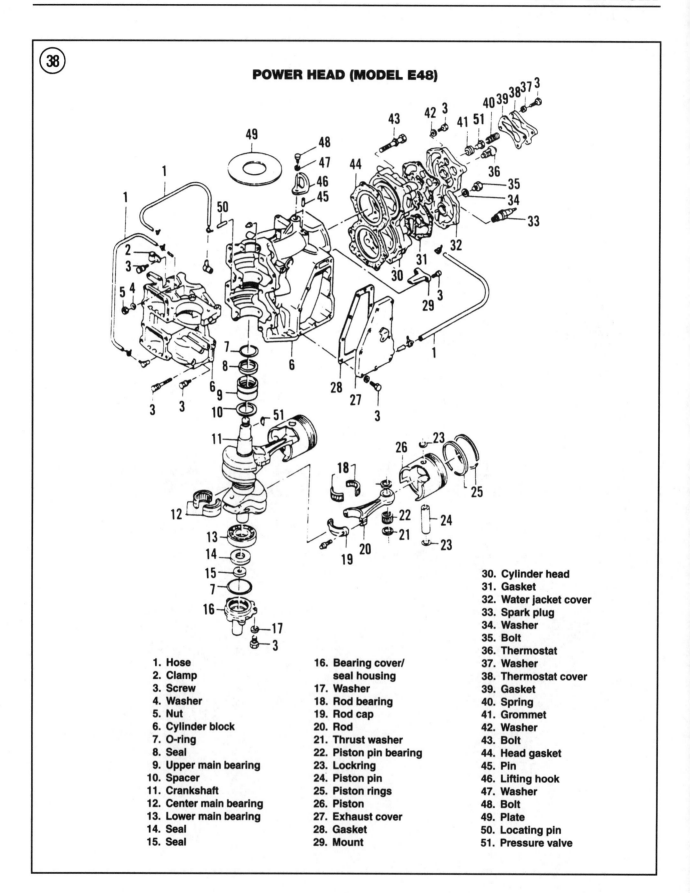

POWER HEAD (MODEL E48)

1. Hose
2. Clamp
3. Screw
4. Washer
5. Nut
6. Cylinder block
7. O-ring
8. Seal
9. Upper main bearing
10. Spacer
11. Crankshaft
12. Center main bearing
13. Lower main bearing
14. Seal
15. Seal
16. Bearing cover/
    seal housing
17. Washer
18. Rod bearing
19. Rod cap
20. Rod
21. Thrust washer
22. Piston pin bearing
23. Lockring
24. Piston pin
25. Piston rings
26. Piston
27. Exhaust cover
28. Gasket
29. Mount
30. Cylinder head
31. Gasket
32. Water jacket cover
33. Spark plug
34. Washer
35. Bolt
36. Thermostat
37. Washer
38. Thermostat cover
39. Gasket
40. Spring
41. Grommet
42. Washer
43. Bolt
44. Head gasket
45. Pin
46. Lifting hook
47. Washer
48. Bolt
49. Plate
50. Locating pin
51. Pressure valve

POWER HEAD (E60, 60 AND 70 HP MODELS)

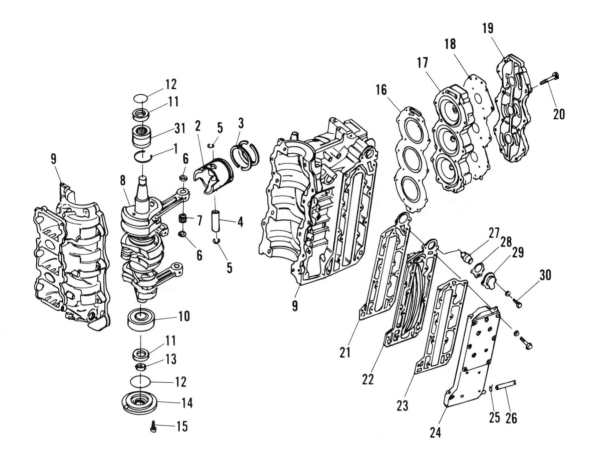

8

1. Retaining ring	15. Bolt
2. Piston	16. Head gasket
3. Piston rings	17. Cylinder head
4. Piston pin	18. Gasket
5. Lockring	19. Water jacket cover
6. Thrust washer	20. Bolt
7. Piston pin bearing	21. Gasket
8. Crankshaft/rod assembly	22. Exhaust plate
9. Cylinder block/ crankcase cover	23. Gasket
10. Lower main bearing	24. Exhaust cover
11. Seal	25. Clamp
12. O-ring	26. Hose
13. Seal	27. Thermostat
14. Lower bearing cover/seal housing	28. Gasket
	29. Thermostat cover
	30. Bolt
	31. Upper main bearing

40

POWER HEAD (65 JET, E75 AND 75-90 HP MODELS [EXCEPT 80 JET])

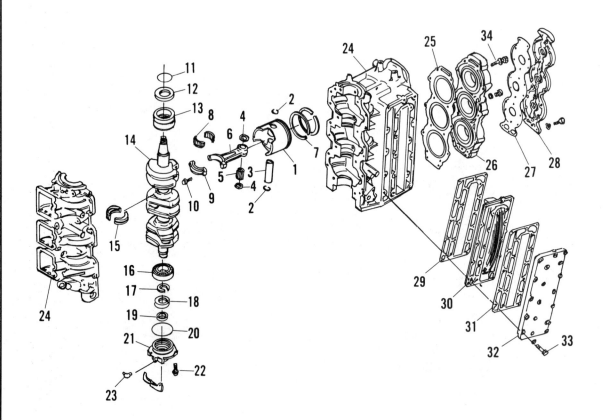

1. Piston	19. Seal
2. Lockring	20. O-ring
3. Piston pin	21. Lower bearing cover/
4. Thrust washer	seal housing
5. Piston pin bearing	22. Bolt
6. Rod	23. Fitting
7. Piston rings	24. Cylinder block/
8. Bearing set	crankcase cover
9. Rod cap	25. Head gasket
10. Rod bolt	26. Cylinder head
11. O-ring	27. Gasket
12. Seal	28. Water jacket cover
13. Upper main bearing	29. Gasket
14. Crankshaft	30. Exhaust plate
15. Center main bearing	31. Gasket
16. Lower main bearing	32. Exhaust cover
17. Circlip	33. Bolt
18. Seal	

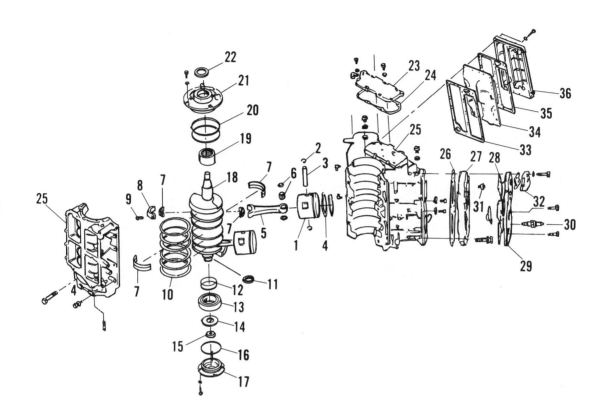

**POWER HEAD
(80 JET AND 115-130 HP MODELS)**

1. Piston
2. Lockring
3. Piston pin
4. Piston rings
5. Rod
6. Bearing/washers
7. Bearing set
8. Rod cap
9. Rod bolt
10. Sealing rings
11. Circlip
12. Gear
13. Lower main bearing
14. Seal
15. Seal
16. O-ring
17. Lower bearing
cover/seal housing
18. Crankshaft
19. Upper main bearing
20. O-rings
21. Upper bearing
cover/seal housing
22. Seal
23. Water jacket cover
24. Gasket
25. Cylinder block/
crankcase cover
26. Head gasket
27. Cylinder head
28. Gasket
29. Water jacket cover
30. Spark plug
31. Thermostat
32. Thermostat cover
33. Gasket
34. Exhaust plate
35. Gasket
36. Exhaust cover

8

42

POWER HEAD
(105 JET AND 150-225 HP MODELS)

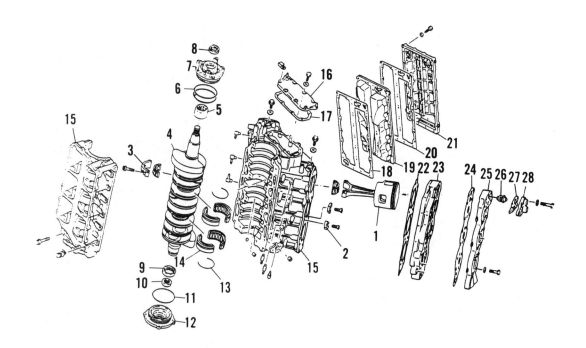

1. Piston/rod assembly
2. Anode
3. Rod cap
4. Crankshaft
5. Upper main bearing
6. O-rings
7. Upper bearing
   cover/seal housing
8. Seal
9. Drive gear
10. Seal
11. O-ring
12. Lower bearing
    cover/seal housing
13. Retainer
14. Center main bearing
15. Cylinder block/
    crankcase cover
16. Water jacket cover
17. Gasket
18. Gasket
19. Exhaust plate
20. Gasket
21. Exhaust cover
22. Head gasket
23. Cylinder head
24. Gasket
25. Water jacket cover
26. Thermostat
27. Gasket
28. Thermostat cover

POWER HEAD (200-250 HP 76° MODELS)

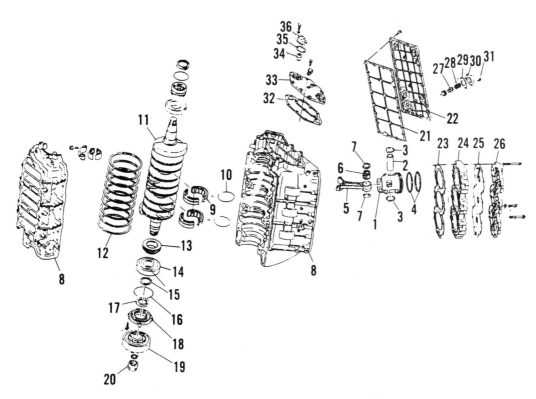

8

1. Piston
2. Piston pin
3. Lockring
4. Piston rings
5. Rod
6. Piston pin bearing
7. Thrust washer
8. Cylinder block/
   crankcase cover
9. Center main bearing
10. Retainer
11. Crankshaft
12. Sealing rings
13. Drive gear
14. Lower main bearing
15. Circlip

16. O-ring
17. Seal
18. Lower bearing
    cover/seal housing
19. Torsional damper
20. Nut
21. Gasket
22. Exhaust cover
23. Head gasket
24. Cylinder head
25. Gasket
26. Water jacket cover
27. Water pressure valve
28. Spring
29. Gasket
30. Cover
31. Bolt
32. Gasket
33. Water jacket cover
34. Thermostat
35. Gasket
36. Cover

1. Loosen and remove the exhaust cover bolts. Remove the exhaust cover, exhaust plate and gaskets from the side of the power head (**Figure 44**). Use care if it is necessary to pry the components from the block. Remove and discard all gaskets and seals.

2. Loosen and remove the cylinder head bolts and remove the cylinder head/water jacket cover assembly (**Figure 45**) from the block. Use care if it is necessary to pry the cylinder head from the block. Tap lightly on the end of the cylinder head with a plastic mallet to break the contact. Remove the cylinder head and discard the gasket.

3. On 200-250 hp models, remove the torsional dampener. A flywheel holding tool Yamaha part No. YB 01639-90890-06522 and a universal puller tool Yamaha part No. YB 6117/90890-06521 are required.

   a. Install flywheel holding tool (A, **Figure 46**) into holes in the torsional dampener. Hold the flywheel tool securely and turn the nut in the direction indicated with a suitable tool (B, **Figure 46**).

   b. Place a pad on the block and thread the three bolts of the puller tool fully into the torsional dampener until the tool is seated against the pad (**Figure 47**).

Tighten the puller bolt to remove the torsional dampener from the power head.

4. Remove the fasteners for the upper and lower bearing cover/seal housings (**Figure 48**). Removal of the housings is not necessary at this time.

5. Remove the bolts, locate a pry point (**Figure 49**) and carefully pry the water jacket cover, if so equipped, from

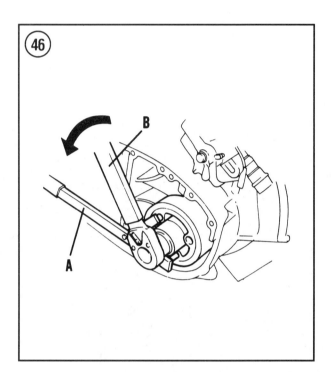

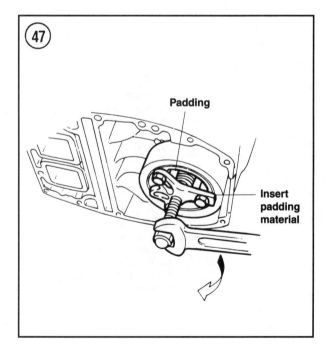

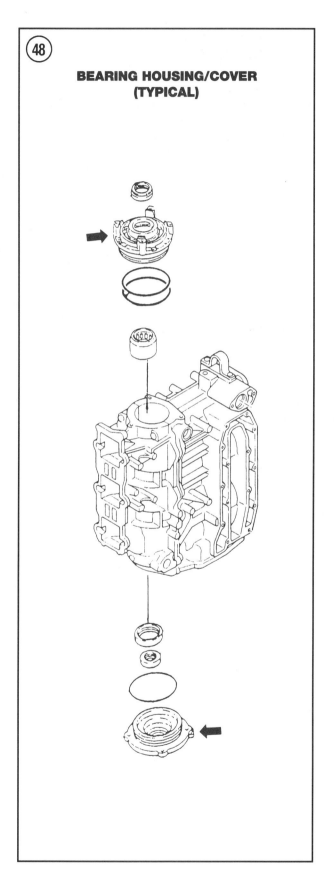

the cylinder head. Remove any other water jackets (**Figure 50**) remaining on the power head.

6. Locate and remove the thermostat housing (**Figure 51**) if so equipped. Use pliers to pull the thermostat from the housing. Remove and discard the housing gasket.

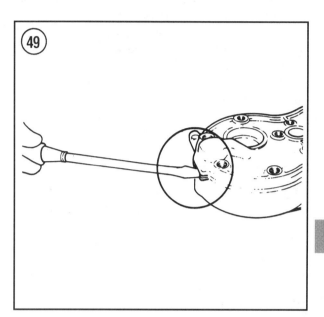

8

7. Locate and remove the water pressure valve cover (1, **Figure 52**) along with the gasket, spring and valve (2-4, **Figure 52**) if so equipped. Use needlenose pliers to remove the seat (5, **Figure 52**) from the recess. Discard the gasket.

8. Locate and remove all fasteners for the crankcase cover. Locate suitable pry points (**Figure 53**) and carefully pry the crankcase cover from the cylinder block.

9. Grasp the flywheel end of the crankshaft to hold it in the cylinder block, then lift the crankcase cover from the cylinder block (**Figure 54**).

10. Remove the upper and lower bearing/seal housings from the crankshaft. Pry the seals from the housing with a blunt tip screwdriver. *Do not* allow the screwdriver to damage the housing. Discard the seals.

Crankshaft, Piston and Connecting Rod Removal

Always keep components organized when removed. The piston/rod and other components must be installed into the same cylinder as removed unless the component is replaced. Mark the cylinder number on the pistons and rods as they are removed. Use an ink marker that can withstand solvent cleaning or a scratch awl to mark the components. On inline engines, the number one cylinder is the top cylinder. On V models the number one cylinder is the top starboard cylinder as viewed from the cylinder head. Even numbered cylinders are located on the port side cylinder bank. The connecting rod cap is matched to the connecting

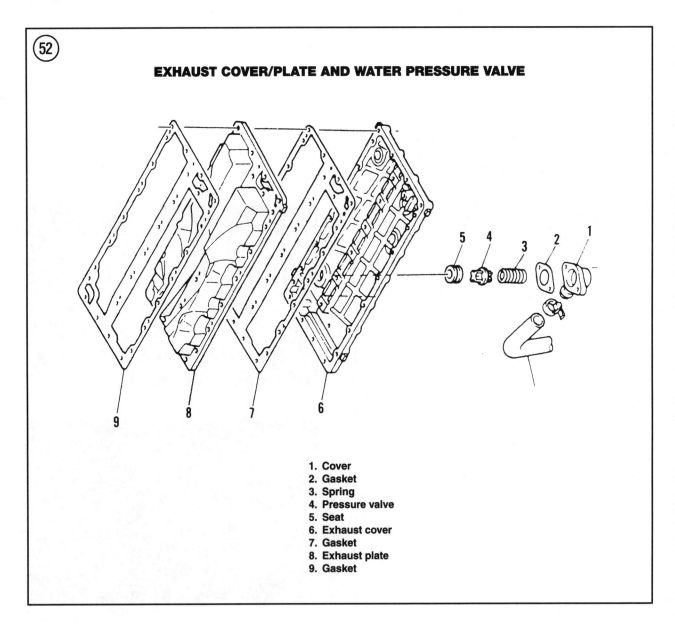

52

EXHAUST COVER/PLATE AND WATER PRESSURE VALVE

1. Cover
2. Gasket
3. Spring
4. Pressure valve
5. Seat
6. Exhaust cover
7. Gasket
8. Exhaust plate
9. Gasket

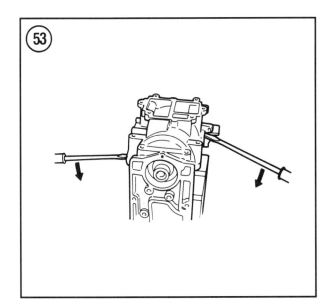

rod. Install the cap onto the rod in the proper position. DO NOT allow the rod cap to become switched with another rod.

NOTE
Not all models use an upper seal/bearing housing. The bearing and seal are assembled as one component that is retained by the crankcase halves.

WARNING
Wear safety glasses when working with the power head. Piston lockrings and other components may spring free and result in serious bodily injury.

CAUTION
Avoid using excessive force when removing the crankshaft from the cylinder block. The use of excessive force may dislodge or damage the main bearing locating pins or damage the cylinder block.

1. On 2-70 hp models (except 65 jet and E48), support the cylinder block and carefully tap the threaded end of the crankshaft (**Figure 55**) with a *plastic mallet* until the crankshaft moves slightly away from the cylinder block. Gently rock the crankshaft as the crankshaft, pistons and rods are removed as an assembly from the cylinder block.

2. On Models E48, 65 jet and 75-250 hp models, rotate the crankshaft until the number one cylinder is at the bottom of its stroke. Remove in steps the two bolts for the rod caps (**Figure 56**). Gently tap the rod cap to loosen the cap.

8

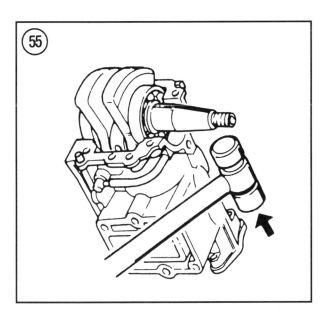

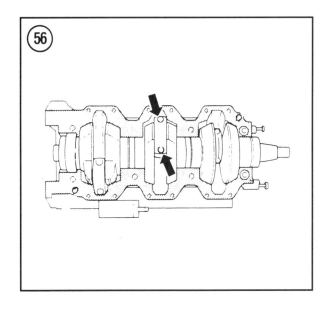

3. Mark the flywheel side of the rod cap (2, **Figure 57**) and remove the cap. Mark or note the top side orientation of the bearings if they must be reused. Remove the needle bearings or assembly (3, **Figure 57**) from the crankshaft.

4. Use a large wooden dowel or hammer handle to push the piston/rod assembly (4 and 5, **Figure 57**) out of the cylinder head side of the block. Provide continuous sup-

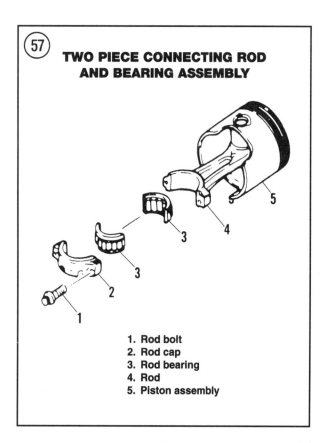

57

TWO PIECE CONNECTING ROD AND BEARING ASSEMBLY

1. Rod bolt
2. Rod cap
3. Rod bearing
4. Rod
5. Piston assembly

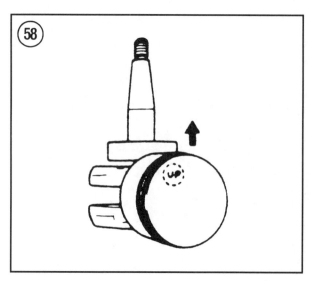

58

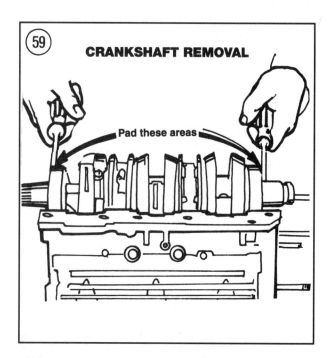

59

CRANKSHAFT REMOVAL

Pad these areas

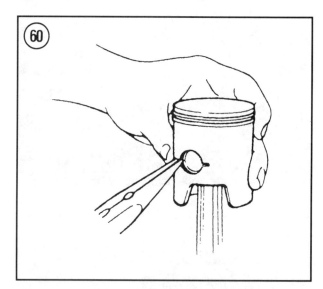

60

61

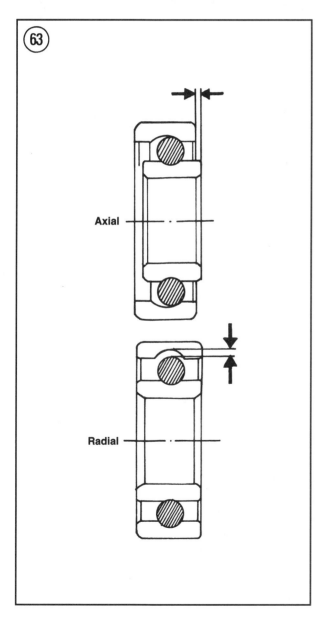

port for the piston (5, **Figure 57**) during the removal process. Note the UP mark on the piston dome (**Figure 58**) when removed .

5. Position the rod cap on the rod with the up side correctly orientated. Install the rod bolts and thread in until hand tight only. Mark the cylinder with the cylinder number. Mark the inside of the piston skirt or the I-beam portion of the rod with the cylinder number. Repeat Steps 2-5 for the remaining cylinders.

6. Use cloth or wooden pads (**Figure 59**) to protect the cylinder block and crankshaft, then carefully pry the crankshaft from the cylinder block. Avoid using excessive force.

7. Position the crankshaft on a suitable stand or mount to a vise using soft jaws. Verify that the piston(s) and rod(s) are marked with the cylinder number and the up or flywheel side.

8. Use needlenose pliers (**Figure 60**) or a small screwdriver to remove both lockrings from the piston(s). Place a shop towel over the lockring and hold a finger or thumb against the lockring opening during removal to prevent the ring from springing free upon removal. Work carefully to avoid damaging the lockring groove. Avoid any unnecessary tool contact with the piston surfaces. Discard the lockrings after removal.

9. Use a suitable steel rod or socket to push the piston pin from the piston. The tool used must be slightly smaller than the pin in the piston. Refer to **Table 5** for piston pin diameter.

NOTE
If piston pin removal is difficult, heat the piston to approximately 60° C (140° F). The piston bore will expand, allowing the pin to be easily removed.

10. Pull the piston from the rod when the pin has cleared the rod (**Figure 61**). Retain the caged or loose needle bearings and thrust washers (**Figure 62**) from the piston pin. Locate all missing needles. The number of needles should be the same in all pistons. Repeat Steps 8-10 for the remaining pistons.

NOTE
Remove the ball-type bearings from the crankshaft only if necessary to remove the oil injection drive gear or if excessive play or rough operation is noted. The removal process will likely damage the bearing. Replace the bearing if removed.

11. Slide the upper bearing from the crankshaft on 9.9-30, E48 and 60-250 hp models. For other models or to remove the lower ball-type bearing, go to step 12.

12. Grasp the bearing and move it to check for axial and radial play (**Figure 63**). Rotate the bearing while applying

axial and radial load. Remove and replace the bearing if play or rough operation is noted. Otherwise leave the bearing on the crankshaft.

13. If bearing removal is necessary, remove the snap ring (**Figure 64**) from the crankshaft.

14. Install a universal puller plate (**Figure 65**). Tighten the bolts on the puller plate until just snug. Position the plate so that the sharp edge contacts between the crankshaft and bearing (**Figure 66**).

15. Use a piece of hard plastic or wood to protect the crankshaft surface from the press. Support the crankshaft and operate the press to push the crankshaft from the bearing. Repeat the process for the upper bearing if so equipped.

16. Mark the center main bearing location and flywheel end reference. Remove the retaining ring from the center main bearings with an awl or small screwdriver (**Figure 67**). Be prepared to capture the bearing rollers, then separate the halves of the bearing cage and remove it from the crankshaft.

17. Mark the top or bottom location of the piston rings. Avoid scratching or damaging the pistons while removing the rings. Spread the rings (**Figure 68**) just enough to clear the ring grooves and slide them from the piston.

18. Carefully spread and remove the crankshaft sealing rings (V4 and V6 models) from the grooves on the crankshaft (**Figure 69**). Replace the sealing rings if any wear is noted or steps have formed on the surfaces. Slide the oil injection drive gear from the bottom end of the crankshaft.

COMPONENT INSPECTION

This section includes component cleaning procedures, inspecting for defects, and measuring the components. Variations exist within the models as to component appearance and location. To assist with component identification and orientation refer to **Figure 30-43**.

Take all precautions necessary to maintain the marks indicating the original position of each component. All components must be installed into the same cylinder or position they were in when removed unless the components are replaced. Wear patterns will form on any contact

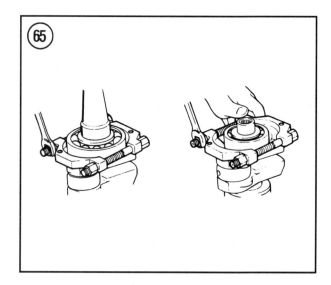

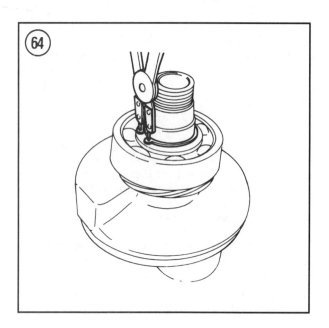

surfaces with use. Maintaining the wear patterns will help ensure a durable and reliable repair.

Component Cleaning

Use compressed air to blow any loose debris from the components. Solvent wash all components, except the cylinder block, one at a time and make sure that their identifying markings are present after washing. Mark the cylinder number on the component again if needed. Allow the solvent to drain for a few minutes and use compressed air to remove any remaining solvent. Never allow bearings to spin while blowing them dry with compressed air. The bearing will suffer damage within a few seconds. Hold the bearing still while drying. Cover the components with shop towels to protect them from dust contamination.

Cleaning the cylinder block

Use hot soapy water to clean the cylinder block, exhaust covers and cylinder heads. Clean the block with pressurized water. Dry the cylinder block, covers and cylinder heads with compressed air. Apply Yamalube 2-cycle outboard oil to the cylinder walls immediately after the walls are dry to prevent corrosion. Aluminum deposits will be present on the cylinder walls when piston failure has occurred. Use a blunt tip of a screwdriver to carefully pry the aluminum particles from the cylinder walls. Minor deposits will be removed during the honing or boring process.

> *CAUTION*
> *Never use a wire brush to remove carbon from the piston. Small particles of steel may become imbedded in the piston surface. These small particles glow when hot and result in preignition or detonation damage to the piston.*

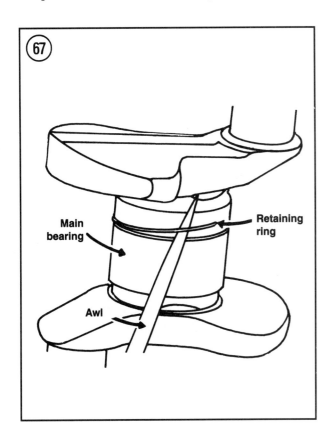

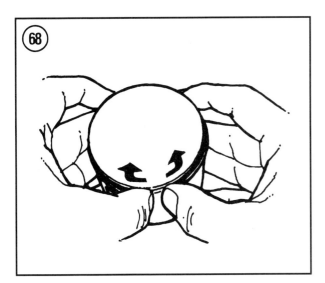

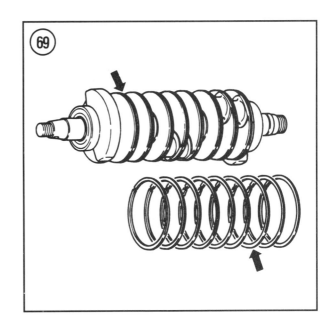

Cleaning the piston

Use a dull chisel or blunt screwdriver to remove carbon deposits from the top of the piston (**Figure 70**). Use very light force to help prevent gouging or scratching of the piston. Use a scotchbrite pad and mild solvent to remove remaining carbon deposits from the piston.

> *CAUTION*
> *The locating pin in the ring grooves may become loosened within its bore if care is not taken when cleaning the ring grooves. If loosened, the pin may dislodge while the engine is running and result in power head failure. Use solvent and a small brush to remove carbon from the locating pin areas.*

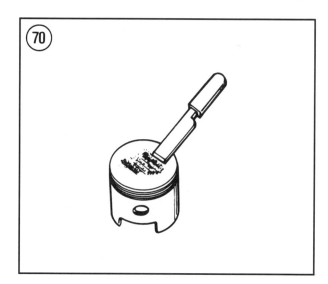

Use a broken piece of the piston ring from the piston to remove carbon from the ring grooves (**Figure 71**). Work carefully and avoid any contact with the locating pin in the ring groove. Use a top ring for the top ring groove and bottom ring for the bottom ring groove. Using the wrong type of piston ring can result in damage to the ring groove. Use enough force to remove the carbon only. Never allow the ring to scrape aluminum material from the groove. Use a brush and solvent to remove remaining carbon deposits. Keep the connecting rod, rod cap and pin with the piston.

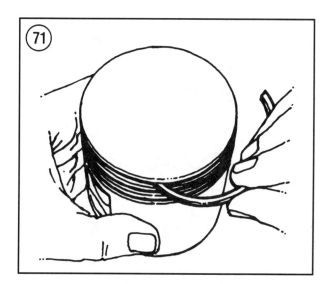

Cleaning the cylinder head

Use a blunt scraper to remove carbon deposits from the combustion chamber portion of the cylinder head (**Figure 72**). Avoid scraping aluminum material from the cylinder head.

Use a scraper to remove deposits and remaining gasket material from the exhaust plates, covers and the mating surfaces of the cylinder block. Work carefully and avoid scratching or damaging any mating surfaces.

Inspection

Cylinder block and crankcase cover

Inspect the cylinder bores for cracks or deep grooves. Replace the cylinder block or have a sleeve installed in the cylinder block if the cracks or grooves cannot be removed by boring the cylinder. Contact a reputable marine dealership to locate a source for block sleeving.

Inspect the mounting surfaces for the power head, exhaust cover, water jacket cover and crankcase cover for cracks or damage. Replace the cylinder block if cracks or extensive damage such, as corrosion or scratches, is noted.

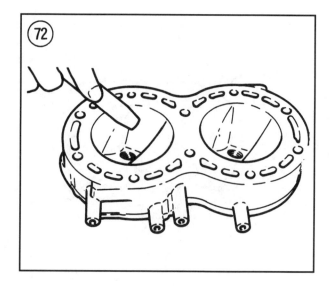

Inspect the areas near the exhaust ports for signs of cracks if the engine has experienced overheating.

White powder-like deposits in the combustion chamber usually indicate that water is entering the combustion chamber. Inspect the cylinder walls and cylinder head dome thoroughly for cracks if this type of deposit is noted. Inspect the oil injection gear bushing on V4 and V6 models (**Figure 73**). Remove and replace the bushing if discoloration, wear, damage or corrosion is noted. Mark the depth at which the bushing is installed in the block. Carefully thread a properly sized lag bolt into the bushing and pull to remove the bushing. Use a properly sized bushing driver

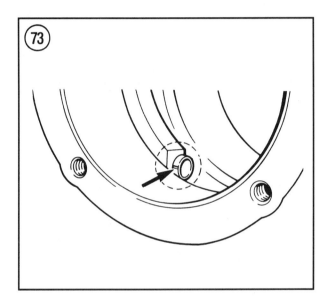

to install the new bushing into the block. Measure to ensure that the new bushing is installed to the same depth as the removed bushing.

Inspect all bolt holes for cracks, corrosion or damaged threads. Use a thread chaser to clean the threads. Pay particular attention to the cylinder head bolt holes.

> *NOTE*
> *The cylinder block and crankcase are a matched assembly. Replace the assembly if either portion is damaged.*

Pistons and connecting rods

Inspect the piston for eroded surfaces at the edge of the dome, cracks near the ring grooves, cracks or missing portions in the piston dome, erosion in the ring groove and scoring or scuffing on the piston skirt (**Figure 74**). Replace the piston if any of these defects are noted.

Insert the piston pin into the pin bore about the depth of the width of the pin. Move the pin in the direction indicated (**Figure 75**). Replace the piston if any wobble is noted.

On 65 jet, E48 and 75-250 hp models, inspect both connecting rod bearing surfaces for corrosion etching, chatter marks, bluing or discolored appearance or any surface defects. Replace the connecting rod if any defects are noted.

On 2-70 hp models (except 65 jet and E48), inspect the piston pin bearing surface for bluing or discolored appearance, corrosion etching, chatter marks or any surface defects. Manipulate the rod in the direction indicated (**Figure**

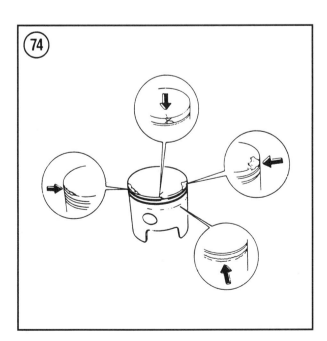

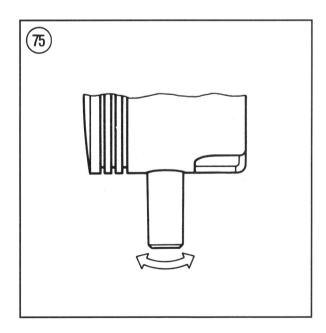

76) to check for bearing wear or bearing failure. Rotate the rod to check for smooth bearing movement. Replace the crank and rod assembly if defects or bearing wear are noted.

> *NOTE*
> *Normal bearing surface coloration is a silver surface with very fine lines in the surface. Discolored surfaces occur when excessive heat is applied. Chatter marks may occur where needle bearing contacts the bearing surface. The bearing surface will resemble the surface of a washboard.*

> *NOTE*
> *Some minor surface corrosion, glaze-like deposits or minor scratches can be removed with crocus cloth or 320 grit carburundum. Polish the surfaces only enough to remove the deposits. Excessive polishing can remove a considerable amount of material from the rod and crank surfaces.*

Crankshaft

Inspect the crankshaft bearing surfaces for cracks, corrosion etching, chatter marks, bluing or discolored appearance, rough or irregular surfaces or transferred bearing material. Replace the crankshaft if defects are noted. The hardening process used does not allow for machining of the crankshaft.

Puddle fuel valves and fittings

Inspect the check valves for proper operation as indicated in Chapter Three. Inspect the fittings for blockage and proper fit into the intake and cylinder location. Replace any fitting if damage or loose fit is noted.

Measuring the Components

Refer to **Figure 30-43** for the model you are working with to assist with component identification and orientation. A considerable amount of measuring equipment is required to perform the measurements. If you do not have access to the proper equipment or are unfamiliar with these types of measuring devices, have a reputable marine repair shop or machine shop perform the measurements. All components must be clean and dry before measuring. Keep the components at room temperature for several hours before measuring them.

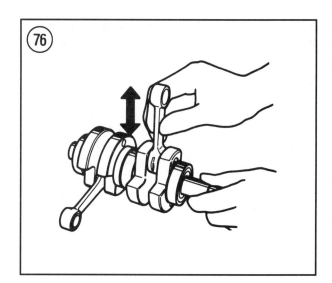

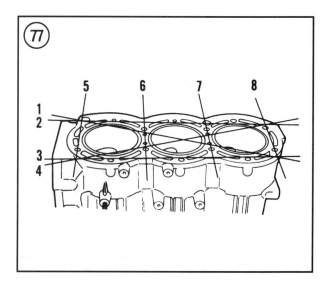

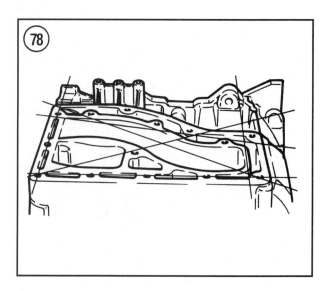

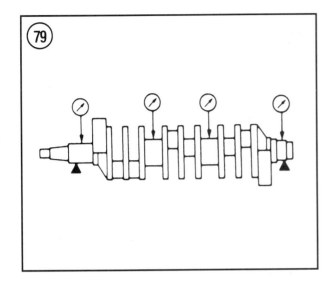

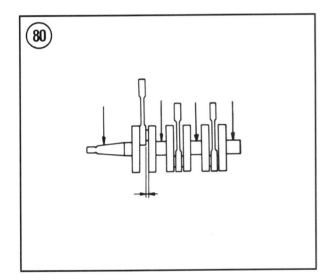

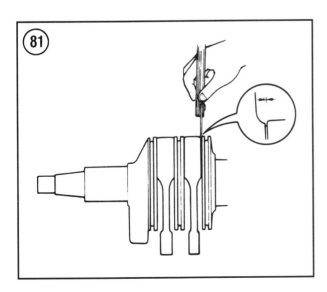

Cylinder block mating surfaces

Use a straightedge to measure the amount of surface variation at the cylinder head (**Figure 77**) and exhaust cover areas (**Figure 78**). Lay the straightedge at multiple locations on the clean and dry surface. Hold the straightedge firmly against the surface and use a feeler gauge to check for a gap at the midpoint of the straightedge. Compare the gap width with the specification listed in **Table 11**. Replace the cylinder block if the gap exceeds the specification.

Crankshaft

> *NOTE*
> *Crankshaft bearing surface diameters are not provided. Replace the crankshaft if these surfaces are damaged, have transferred bearing material or are discolored. The hardening process used does not allow for machining of the crankshaft or the use of undersized bearings.*

Use V-blocks or other means to support the crankshaft when checking crankshaft runout (**Figure 79**). Position a dial indicator at the bearing surfaces and measure deflection at the points indicated (**Figure 79**). Slowly rotate the crankshaft as you observe the needle on the dial indicator. The needle movement will indicate the amount of crankshaft runout. On 2-70 hp models (except E48 and 65 jet) the measurements must be made with the rods on the crankshaft (**Figure 80**). Position the supports as indicated (**Figure 80**) and measure the deflection at the points indicated (**Figure 80**). Compare the measurements with the specification listed in **Table 9**. Replace the crankshaft if not within the specification.

Use feeler gauges to measure the rod to journal side clearance (**Figure 81**) on 2-70 hp models (except E48 and 65 jet). Insert the gauges as indicated until one of them will fit into the gap with a slight drag when removed. The clearance is indicated when a selected feeler gauge can be inserted with only a slight drag or resistance. Compare the measured rod to journal side clearance with the specification listed in **Table 10**. Replace the crank/rod assembly if not within the listed specification.

On E48, 65 jet and 75-250 hp models, individually install each rod and needle bearing assembly onto the correct crankshaft journal. Use the original rod bolts and refer to *rod alignment* for specific instructions. Tighten the rod bolts to the tightening torque specification listed in **Table 1**. Measure the rod to journal side clearance at the point indicated for each cylinder. Compare the measurements with the specification listed in **Table 10**. Replace the rod and bearing if the clearance is not within the specification listed in **Table 10** and measure again. Replace the crankcase if the clearance is still not within the specification.

Use an inside micrometer to measure the diameter of the piston pin opening in the rod. Compare the measurement with the small end diameter specifications listed in **Table 10**. Replace the rod on E48, 65 jet and 75-225 hp models if not within the listed specification. Replace the crankshaft/rod assembly if not within the listed specifications for all other models.

Make sure that the rod remains assembled to the crankshaft. Secure the crankshaft in a horizontal position. Position a dial indicator to measure axial play (**Figure 82**). Observe the needle movement while moving the rod in the direction indicated. Compare the measurement with the axial play specification listed in **Table 10**. On 2-70 hp models (excluding E48, 65 jet) replace the crankshaft if not within the specification listed. On E48, 65 jet and 75-250 hp models, replace the rod and bearing if the measurement is not within the specification listed and measure again. Replace the crankshaft if measurement is still not within the specification.

On 2-70 hp models (except E48 and 65 jet) use an accurate caliper to measure the outside single journal width (A, **Figure 83**). Take the measurement at several measuring points. Repeat the measurement for each journal. Compare the measurements with the specification listed in **Table 9**. Replace the crankshaft/rod assembly if not within the listed specification. Measure the distance between the journals (B, **Figure 83**) on 28 jet, 35 jet, E60, 9.9-25 hp (2-cylinder)and 40-50 hp models. Take the measurement at several points. Compare the measurement with the between journal specification listed in **Table 9**. Replace the crankshaft/rod assembly if the measurement is not within the specification.

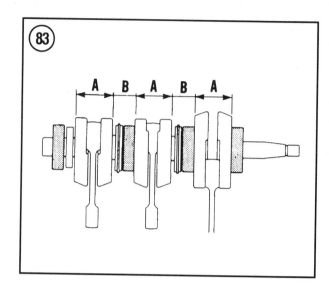

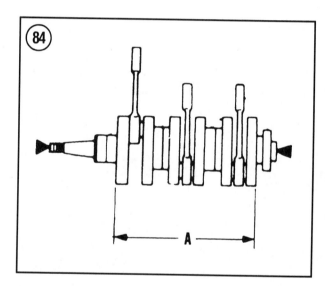

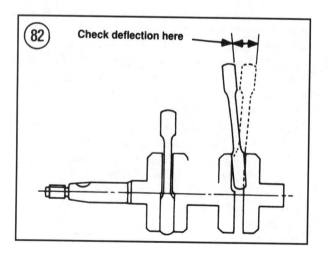

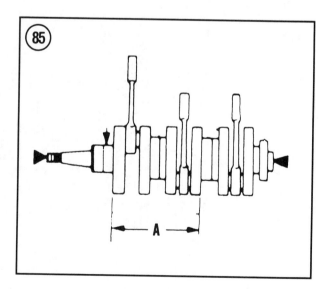

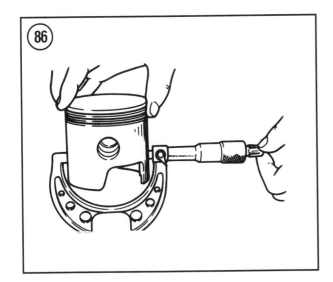

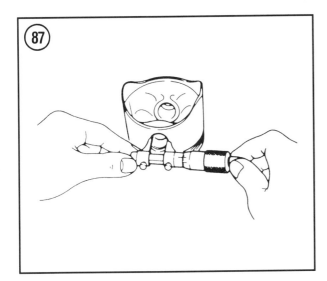

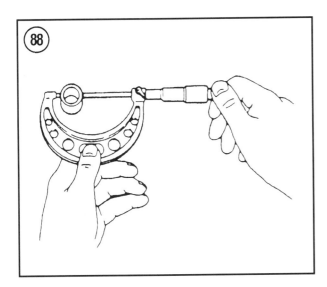

On 6, 8, E48, and 60-90 hp models (except 80 jet), measure the distance outside all journals (**Figure 84**). Take the measurements at several locations. On 60 and 70 hp models, measure the dimension between the outside edges of journals 1 and 2 (**Figure 85**). Compare all measurements with the specification listed in **Table 9**. Replace the crankshaft/rod assembly on 6-70 hp models (except 65 jet). Replace the crankshaft on 65 jet and 75-90 hp models (except 80 jet) if the measurement is not within the listed specification.

Piston and piston pin

Measure the diameter of the piston at a point 10.0 mm (0.40 in.) up from the bottom of the skirt at a 90° angle to the piston pin bore (**Figure 86**). Compare the measurement with the specification listed in **Table 6** for a standard size piston or **Table 12** for an oversize piston. Replace the piston if not within the listed specification. Measure all pistons in the power head.

Use an inside micrometer to measure the pin bore diameter at both sides of the piston as indicated in (**Figure 87**). Compare the measurements with the specification listed in **Table 5**.

Measure the pin diameter at the piston and rod contact areas as indicated in **Figure 88**. Compare the measurement with the specifications listed in **Table 5**. Replace the piston and pin if either component is not within the listed specifications.

Note the shape of the rings and the ring groove in the piston (**Figure 89**). Carefully spread and install new rings

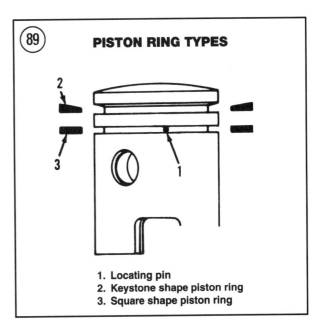

PISTON RING TYPES

1. Locating pin
2. Keystone shape piston ring
3. Square shape piston ring

onto the piston (**Figure 90**). Make sure that properly shaped rings are used in the ring grooves. Align the ring gap with the locating pin as indicated in **Figure 91**. Measure the piston ring side clearance with a feeler gauge as indicated in **Figure 92**. Measure the clearance on the top and bottom rings. The feeler gauge must be inserted at the square side of the ring as indicated in **Figure 93**. Remove the piston rings from the pistons. Compare the measurements with the specifications listed in **Table 8**. Replace the piston if the clearance is not within the listed specification.

Cylinder bore

Clean the cylinder block as described in *Cylinder block cleaning*. Use either a dial type cylinder bore gauge (**Figure 94**) or a telescoping type gauge (**Figure 95**) and micrometer to measure the cylinder bore. Take three sets of measurements: at the top, middle and bottom of the ring travel area (**Figure 96**). Take two measurements 90° apart at each location (**Figure 97**).

1. Take the first measurement at the top of the ring travel area with the gauge aligned with the crankshaft centerline. Record the reading. Turn the gauge 90° to the crankshaft and take another reading (**Figure 97**). The difference between the two readings is the cylinder out-of-round. The out-of-round dimension must not exceed the specified wear limit (**Table 3**).

2. Take a second set of measurements at the midpoint of the ring travel just above the ports. Record the readings. The difference between the two readings indicates the out-of-round measurement. Compare the measurement with the specified wear limit (**Table 3**).

3. Take a third set of measurements at the bottom of the ring travel just below the ports. Record the readings. Cal-

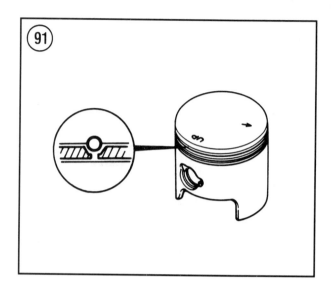

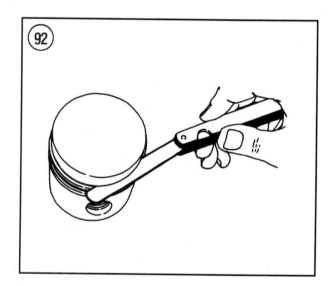

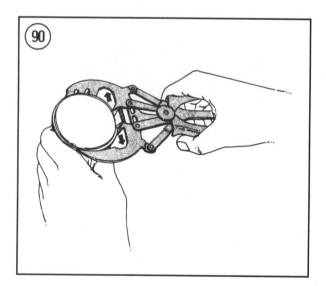

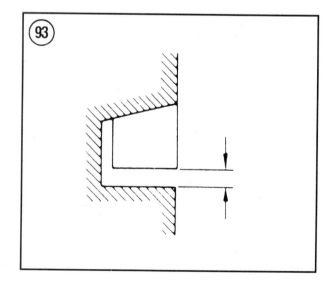

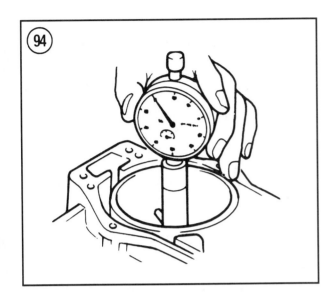

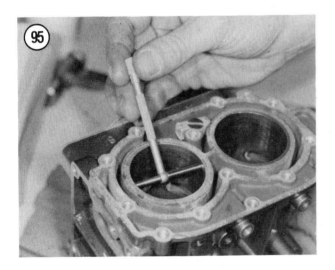

culate the cylinder out-of-round by determining the difference between the two readings. The out-of-round dimension must not exceed the specified wear limit (**Table 3**).

4. To determine the cylinder taper, subtract the smallest reading taken at the bottom of the ring travel from the largest reading taken at the top of the ring travel. The difference in the two readings is the cylinder taper. The taper must not exceed the wear limit specified in **Table 3**.

5. Bore the cylinder to fit an oversize piston or replace the cylinder block if the taper or out-of-round measurements are not within the listed specifications. Refer to **Table 12** for oversize piston specifications.

6. Subtract the piston diameter measurement from the smallest cylinder bore measurement to determine the piston-to-cylinder clearance (**Figure 98**). Compare the clearance with the specification listed in **Table 4**. Bore the

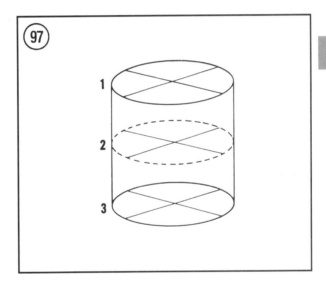

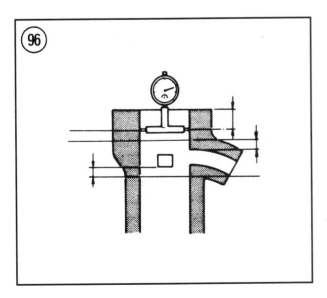

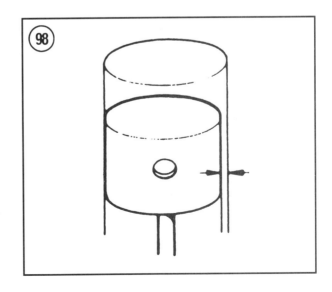

cylinder to fit an oversize piston if the piston-to-cylinder clearance exceeds the listed specification.

7. Inspect the sacrificial anode located in the water jacket between the cylinders (**Figure 99**) or under a cylinder block cover (**Figure 100**). Refer to **Figure 30-43** for additional cylinder block anode locations if not present in these two locations. Replace the anode if a dark gray deposit is present on it or if it has deteriorated 30% or more.

8. Measure the ring gap for all rings and cylinders after the cylinder bore and piston diameter are confirmed to be correct. Carefully compress and install the ring into the top of the bore. Use a piston without rings and slowly push the *new* ring to the proper depth (**Figure 101**). Refer to **Table 7** for the ring depth specifications. Use a feeler gauge to measure the ring end gap (**Figure 102**). Compare the feeler gauge measurement with the specification listed in **Table 7**. For some models a normal ring gap is listed along with a limit. Try a different ring if the measurement is not within the specifications. Repeat the cylinder bore measurements and/or verify that the correct rings are used if the measurements are still incorrect. Make certain that the rings are tagged or marked to ensure that they are installed onto the correct piston and into the proper cylinder bore on assembly.

POWER HEAD ASSEMBLY

Cylinder Block

Clean the cylinder block thoroughly after boring or honing to remove any contaminants. Use hot soapy water under pressure. *Do not* use solvent. Use compressed air to dry the cylinder block. Wipe the cylinder bores with a white shop towel. The cleaning process is complete when the towel is clean and white after wiping the cylinder bores. Thoroughly coat the inside of all cylinder bores with

Yamalube 2-cycle outboard oil or its equivalent immediately after the cleaning process to prevent corrosion.

Piston and Rod Assembly

Variations exist within the models as to component appearance and the type of bearing used on the piston pin. Refer to **Figure 30-43** to determine the components used and orientation for a particular model.

Coat the piston pin, pin bore and the needle bearings with Yamalube 2-cycle outboard oil or its equivalent. Use

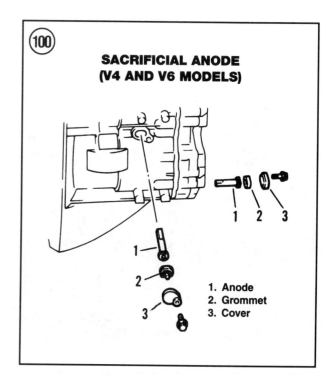

SACRIFICIAL ANODE (V4 AND V6 MODELS)

1. Anode
2. Grommet
3. Cover

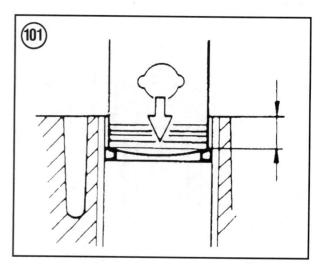

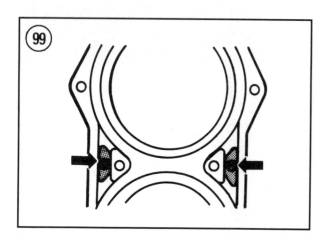

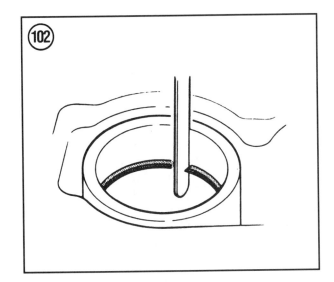

(102)

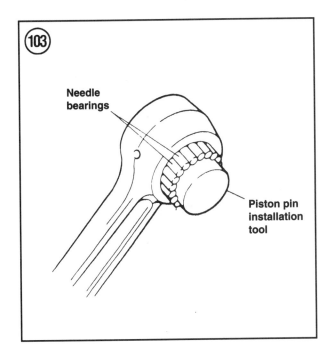

(103)

Needle
bearings

Piston pin
installation
tool

(104)

the recommended piston pin installation tool (**Figure 103**) or a short piece of an appropriately sized rod or tubing to retain the needle bearings (**Figure 103**) in position during assembly. A tool is not required on 80 jet, 105 jet, 2-8 hp and 115-250 hp models as a caged bearing assembly is used.

The Yamaha recommended pin tools are listed following:

    a. For 9.9 and 15 hp models, use part No. YB-06104-90890-06543.

    b. For 20 and 25 hp models, use part No. YB-06107/90890-06526.

    c. For 28 jet, 35 jet, 40 and 50 hp models, use part No. YB-06106/90890-06526.

    d. For E48, E60, 60 and 70 hp models, use part No. YB-6287-1, 90890-06527.

    e. For 65 jet and 75-90 hp models (except 80 jet), use part No. YB-06107/90890-06527.

Note the orientation of the numbers or Yamaha name cast into the rod. On assembly the numbers or Yamaha name must face the up or flywheel side of the crankshaft.

1. Insert the piston pin tool into the small end of the rod as indicated in **Figure 104**.

2. Insert the new or original needle bearings into the rod between the tool and the rod. If loose needle bearings are used, the quantity used should be the same as noted on disassembly.

3. Position the piston on the connecting rod with the *UP* mark on the piston and the numbers or Yamaha name cast into the rod facing in the same direction (**Figure 105**).

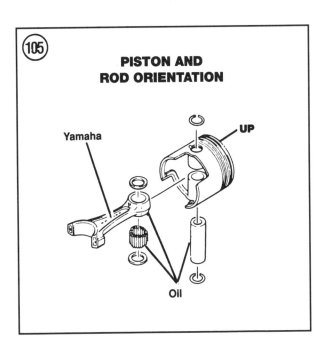

(105)

**PISTON AND
ROD ORIENTATION**

Yamaha

UP

Oil

8

4. Position the thrust washers (1, **Figure 106**) onto the piston and rod with the convex side facing the piston (2, **Figure 106**). Align the piston pin bore (3, **Figure 106**) with the piston pin tool (or bearing assembly) and rod bore.

5. Use an appropriately sized socket or section of tubing to push the piston pin into the rod bore without disturbing the bearings. Push the piston pin in enough to expose the groove for the lockring (4, **Figure 106**). The piston pin tool will exit from the other side as the piston pin is inserted.

6. Use needle nose pliers to insert the lockring into the groove in the piston pin bore (**Figure 107**). On 80 jet, 105 jet and 115-250 hp models, rotate the lockring so that the tang is positioned into the tang recess in the groove (**Figure 108**).

7. Repeat Step 6 to install the lockring into the other side of the piston. Push the piston pin into the bore enough to fully expose the lockring groove. Inspect the piston to ensure that the lockrings are fully seated into the groove and the locking tab is properly positioned.

Piston Ring Installation

Various types of rings are used. A rectangular ring (2, **Figure 109**) or keystone ring (3, **Figure 109**) may be used. The piston may use one style only or both styles. Inspect the ring and ring groove on the piston to ensure that the proper ring is installed. Mark the ring after inspection. Most rings will have a mark or symbol on the ring indicating the up direction (4, **Figure 109**).

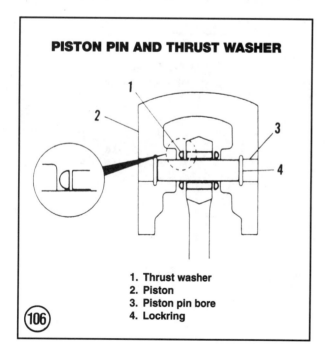

PISTON PIN AND THRUST WASHER

1. Thrust washer
2. Piston
3. Piston pin bore
4. Lockring

106

CAUTION
Use care when spreading the rings for installation onto the piston. Spread the gap ends only enough to allow the rings to slide over the piston. The ring will break or crack if spread too much on installation.

Use a ring expander to spread the bottom ring open enough to clear the top of the piston. Avoid scratching the piston. Slide the ring over the piston and release the ring into position on the ring groove. Repeat these instructions for the top ring. Install the rings onto all the pistons. Apply a coating of Yamalube 2-cycle outboard oil or its equivalent to the rings and piston prior to installation into the cylinder block.

Center Main Bearing Installation

Center main bearing installation is required on Models E48, 65 jet and 75-250 hp Models. Coat the bearing and crankshaft surfaces with Yamalube 2-cycle outboard oil and install the bearings and race onto the crankshaft.

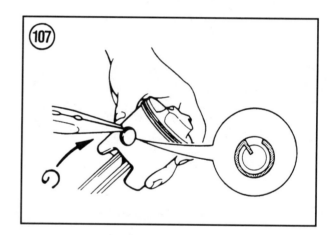

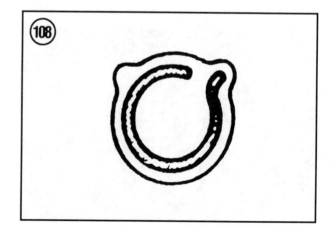

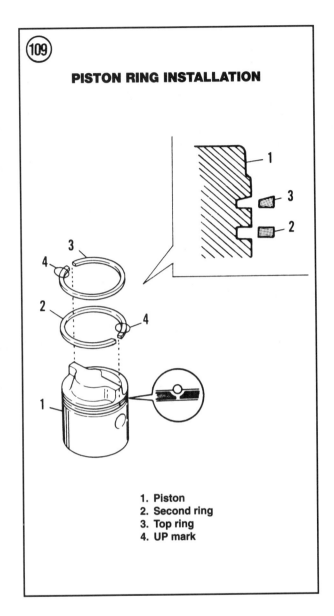

PISTON RING INSTALLATION

1. Piston
2. Second ring
3. Top ring
4. UP mark

Spread the retaining ring enough to slip it over the bearing race. Position the retaining ring onto the groove on the outside of the bearing race (**Figure 110**).

**Top Bearing/Seal Assembly
(9.9-30 hp [Except 28 Jet],
E48 and 60-90 hp Models)**

1. Remove the seal (A, **Figure 111**) with a blunt screwdriver if still installed. Do not allow the screwdriver to contact the bearing surfaces. Clean all debris and contaminants from the seal bore. Refer to **Figure 111** and note that the seal lip must face down or away from the flywheel side of the crankshaft.

**CENTER MAIN
BEARING INSTALLATION**

8

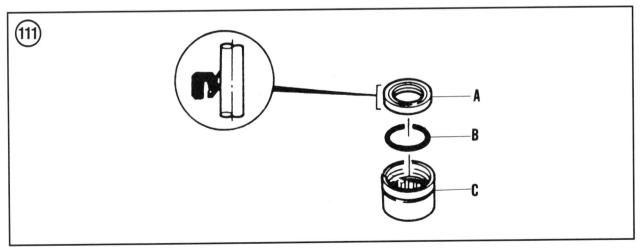

2. Use an appropriately sized socket or tubing to push the new seal (A, **Figure 111**) into the recess in the top bearing. Use just enough force to seat the seal in position.

3. Lubricate the seal lip with Yamaha all-purpose grease or its equivalent.

4. Lubricate the inner and outer surfaces of the bearing with Yamalube 2 cycle outboard oil or its equivalent.

5. Install a new O-ring (B, **Figure 111**) onto the groove on the bearing (C, **Figure 111**).

6. Carefully slide the bearing onto the crankshaft and seat in position. Do not allow the bearing to slip from the crankshaft during other operations.

> *CAUTION*
> *Do not allow the tool to contact the threaded end of the crankshaft while pressing the top and lower bearing onto the crankshaft. Use a tool with sufficient length and of a diameter that it will contact only the inner bearing race.*

Top Bearing/Seal Assembly
(2-8 hp, 28 Jet, 35 Jet and 40-50 hp Models)

1. Use a blunt tip screwdriver to carefully pry the seal from the top cover. Clean all debris and contaminants from the seal bore.

2. Coat the bore with a light coat of Yamalube 2-cycle outboard oil. Note the position of the seal lips as indicated

in **Figure 112**. The seal lip must face down or away from the flywheel when the top cap is installed on the power head.

3. Use an appropriately sized socket or bushing tool to press the seal (A, **Figure 112**) into position.

4. Lubricate and install new O-rings, if so equipped, onto the top cover assembly.

5. Lubricate the seal lips with Yamaha all-purpose grease and the bearing bore with Yamalube 2-cycle outboard oil.

6. Lubricate bearing contact areas of the crankshaft. Position the tapered side of the bearing diameter toward the crankshaft. Press the bearing onto the crankshaft using a piece of heavy tubing or other appropriately sized tool as indicated (**Figure 113**).

Lower Crankshaft Bearing/Oil Injection
Gear Installation

Installation of the oil injection drive gear and lower main bearing is similar for all models. Variation exists as to the size, appearance and usage of the lower bearing components. Oil-injected and some non oil-injected models use

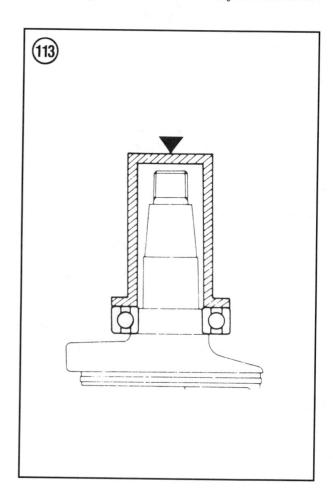

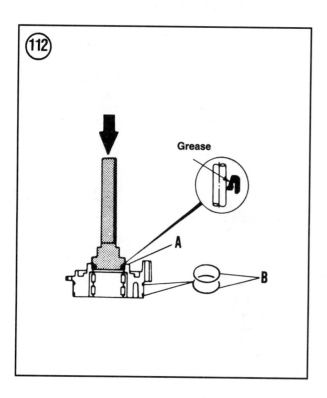

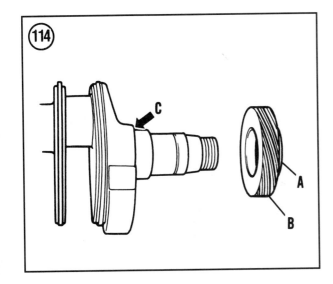

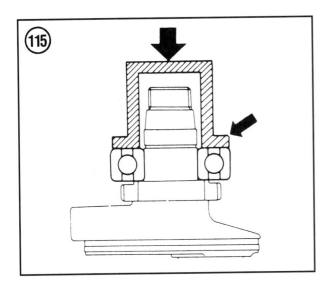

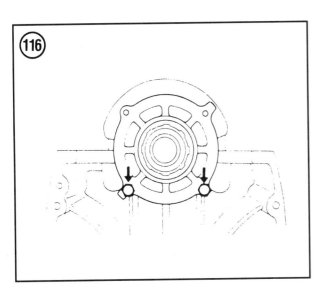

an oil injection drive gear. Note the position of the step on the gear (A, **Figure 114**) and install the gear (B, **Figure 114**) onto the crankshaft. Ensure that the gear is fully seated on the crankshaft (C, **Figure 114**). Lightly press the gear in position if necessary.

Position the tapered inner diameter of the bearing toward the crankshaft. Use an appropriately sized tubing or tool to press the bearing onto the crankshaft (**Figure 115**). The tool used must contact the inner race of the bearing only and not contact the crankshaft at any time. Ensure that the bearing is fully seated onto the step of the crankshaft. Install the circlip if so equipped. Make certain that the circlip is seated into the groove on the crankshaft.

Piston and Crankshaft Installation
(2-70 hp models [Except E48 and 65 jet])

On these models, the crankshaft, pistons and rods are installed into the cylinder block as an assembly. Work carefully and patiently to avoid breaking piston rings or damaging other components. A taper in the crankcase near the bottom of the bore will help compress the piston rings.

1. Apply a generous coat of Yamalube 2-cycle outboard oil to the cylinder bores, pistons, rings, and bearings.

2. Position the ring gap over the locating pin as indicated in **Figure 109**.

3. On 28 jet, 35 jet, 40 and 50 hp models, install the sealing rings onto the grooves on the crankshaft.

4. Position the crankshaft over the crankcase with the flywheel taper end facing the top of the block. Carefully lower the crankshaft and insert the piston into the bore.

5. Guide the piston into the bore as you carefully and gently rock the piston to compress the rings. Do not rotate the piston within the bore. Remove the assembly and inspect the ring gap position if the piston will not enter the bore.

6. Guide the other piston into the bore as the crankshaft is lowered into the crankcase.

7. Carefully rotate and manipulate the main and end bearings to allow the bearing locating pins to align with the recess in the block or bearing. Continue to work with the bearings until the crankshaft is fully seated in the crankcase.

8. Temporarily install the lower bearing cover and rotate the cover to align the bolt holes for the cylinder block (**Figure 116**). Install the bolts and hand tighten them to help retain the crankshaft.

9. Look into the exhaust opening and slowly rotate the crankshaft until the piston rings span the exhaust port (**Figure 117**). Use a screwdriver and carefully press *in* on each ring. The ring must spring back when the screwdriver

8

is pulled back. Note any cylinder with rings that do not spring back.

10. Remove the crankshaft, rod and piston assembly and inspect the pistons for broken or cracked rings if any rings fail to spring back.

Piston and Crankshaft Installation (E48, 65 Jet and 75-250 hp Models)

On these models, the crankshaft and supporting bearings are installed into the cylinder block prior to installation of the rod and piston assembly. The individual piston and rod assemblies are installed onto the crankshaft through the cylinder openings. Use a suitable automotive style ring compressor to ease piston installation.

1. Apply a generous coat of Yamalube 2-cycle outboard oil to the cylinder bores, pistons, rings and bearings.

2. On 80 jet, 105 jet and 115-250 hp models, spread the crankshaft sealing rings just enough to pass them over the crankshaft ends and position them into the sealing ring grooves on the crankshaft.

3. Position the crankshaft assembly with the flywheel taper end toward the top of the cylinder block.

4. On 80 jet, 105 jet and 15-250 hp models, rotate the sealing rings so that all end gaps face away from the crankcase and cylinder block mating surface and are aligned with the crankshaft (**Figure 118**).

5. Carefully lower the crankshaft into position in the crankcase.

6. Carefully rotate or manipulate the main bearings to align the locating pins for the bearings with the pin recess in the bearing or cylinder block. Continue to work with the bearing until the crankshaft is fully seated in the crankcase.

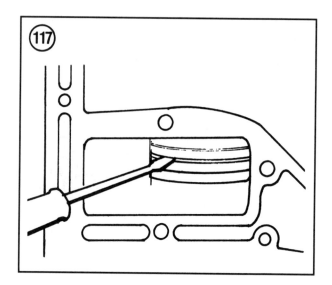

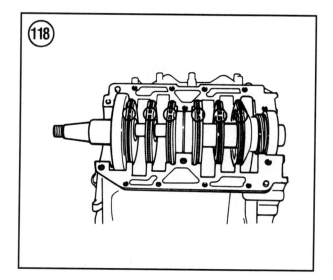

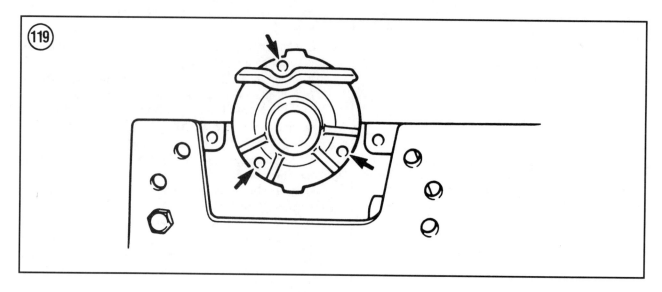

7. Temporarily install the lower bearing cover onto the crankshaft. Rotate the cover until the bolt holes for the cover to cylinder block align (**Figure 119**). Install the bolts and hand tighten them to help retain the crankshaft.

8. Slowly rotate the crankshaft within the cylinder block. Remove the crankshaft and inspect all bearings and align-ment pins for damage if any binding or rough operation is noted.

9. Rotate the crankshaft until Number 1 crank journal is at the bottom of the stroke.

10. Position the piston ring gaps over the locating pins as indicated in **Figure 109**.

11. Select the piston, rings and rod assembly for No. 1 cylinder. No. 1 is the top cylinder on inline cylinder con-figuration engines. Refer to **Figure 120** for V4 and V6 engines to determine the cylinder number locations.

12. Use a ring compressor to retain the rings in position. Position the UP marking on the piston toward the top of the cylinder block.

13. On V models, the *arrow* must face the exhaust side of the cylinder (**Figure 121**). Port and starboard locations are indicated by the *P or S* marking on the piston dome. Mark the rod cap for orientation and remove it from the rod.

14. Position the piston skirt into the bore at the cylinder head mating surface. Hold the ring compressor firmly against the block. To avoid damaging the block, crank or rod, guide the rod into position on the crankshaft as the piston is installed into the cylinder block. Use a large wooden dowel to carefully push the piston into the bore (**Figure 122**).

CAUTION
DO NOT force the piston into the bore. Light force is required to slide the piston into the bore. Piston rings and other components will

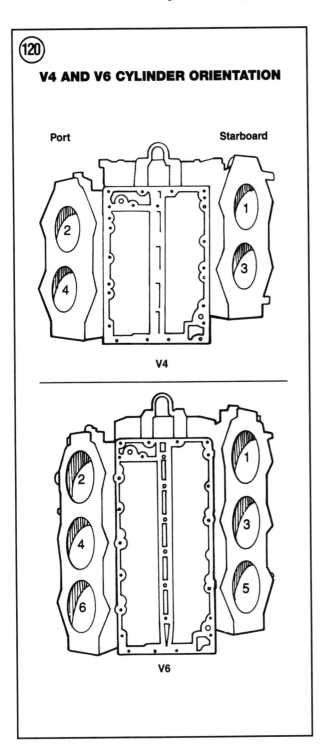

8

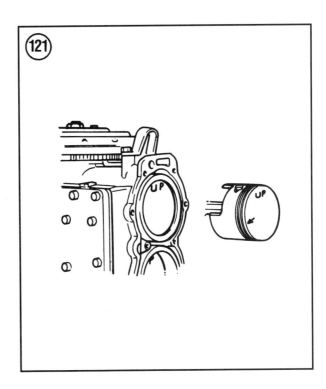

be damaged if the piston is forced into the bore with any interference present.Remove the piston and check the ring gap alignments and ring compressor fit if the piston will not slide into the bore

15. Apply Yamalube 2-cycle outboard oil to the bearing and install both halves onto the crankshaft. Install the rod cap onto the rod. Ensure that the rod cap is orientated correctly and install the used rod bolts. Torque the bolts in two steps to the specification listed in **Table 1**.

16. Check the alignment as indicated in **Figure 123**. Pass a sharp pencil point or another sharp pointed object across the rod and cap mating surface. If the pencil point catches an edge, it indicates that the rod is not aligned properly.

17. If visual misalignment or the sharp point indicated misalignment, remove the rod cap and inspect for debris or contaminants. Carefully align the rod cap and repeat Steps 15 and 16. Replace the rod if misalignment is still detected.

18. Loosen and remove one of the rod bolts. Install a new rod bolt and torque in two steps to the specification listed in **Table 1**. Remove and replace the other bolt as well.

19. Rotate the crankshaft several revolutions. Remove the rod and inspect the bearing if binding or rough operation is noted. Rotate the crankshaft to position the Number 2 cylinder at the bottom of its stroke.

20. Repeat Steps 12-19 for the remaining cylinders.

Crankcase Cover Installation

1. On V4 and V6 models use bearing installation tools YB 06205/89890-06663 and 90890-06606 to install the roller bearing into the upper bearing cover as indicated in **Figure**

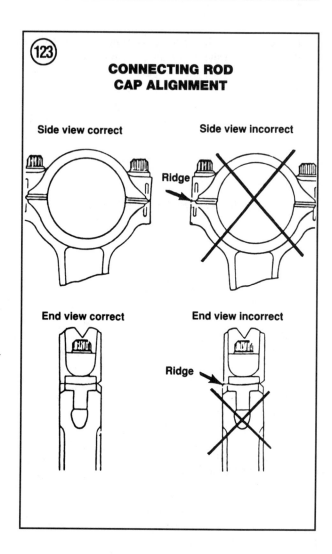

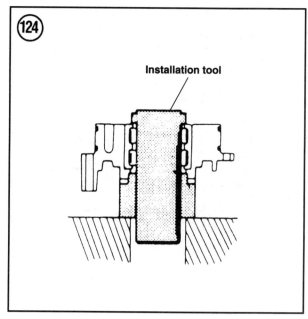

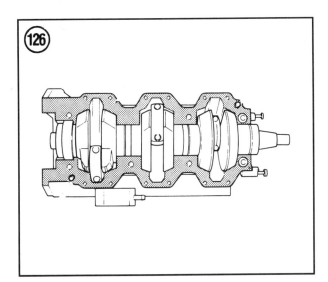

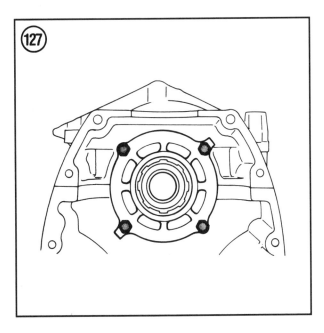

124. Use the same tool to install the upper seal. The seal lip must face away from the flywheel end when the cover is installed.

2. Coat the seal lips with Yamaha all-purpose grease.

3. Install a new O-ring into position on the lower housing.

4. Temporarily install the cover over the crankshaft.

5. Remove the lower cover from the cylinder block. Lubricate the seals and install a new O-ring onto the cover. Lubricate the contact surfaces and install the cover into position on the crankshaft.

6. Apply a light bead of a liquid gasket maker compound to the mating surface of the cylinder block (**Figure 125**).

7. Make sure that the alignment pins (**Figure 126**) fit into the recess. Install the crankcase cover onto the cylinder block. The surface must be cleaned and a new coating of gasket maker applied if the cover is removed. Inspect the upper and lower covers (**Figure 127**) to ensure that the bolt holes are properly aligned. Install the bolts and hand tighten them. Make sure that the mating surfaces are in contact. Rotate the crankshaft. Remove the cover and inspect the bearing locating pins for proper seating if binding or rough operation is noted.

8. Install the cover bolts and tighten in a crossing pattern to the specification listed in **Table 1**.

9. Tighten the upper, if so equipped, and lower bearing cover or seal housing to the specification listed in **Table 1**.

10. On 200-250 hp 76° models install the torsional dampener into the dampener bore. Tighten the nut using the tools used for removal. Torque the nut to 98.0 N•m (72 ft. lb.).

Cylinder Head/Water Jacket/Exhaust Cover Installation

Use a straightedge to measure cylinder head warpage at the points indicated in **Figure 128**. Hold the straightedge firmly against the head and use a feeler gauge to check the gap at the midpoint in the straightedge. Compare the

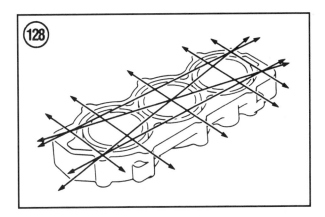

8

thickness of the feeler gauge that can be passed under the straightedge (**Figure 129**) with the warpage limit listed in **Table 11**. Minor warpage can be trued by placing a sheet of 600 grit wet or dry abrasive paper on a surfacing plate. Use slight downward pressure and move the cylinder head in a figure 8 motion as indicated (**Figure 130**). Stop periodically and check the warpage with a straightedge. Remove only the material necessary to remove the excess warpage. Thoroughly clean the cylinder head with hot soapy water and dry with compressed air when finished.

Install the anodes into the cylinder water jacket if removed. Position a new head gasket and the cylinder head onto the cylinder block. Install a new gasket and the water jacket cover onto the cylinder head if the cylinder head bolts pass through it. Sealant or adhesives are not required on these gaskets. Coat the threads of the cylinder head bolts with Yamalube 2-cycle outboard oil or its equivalent. Install all head bolts and hand tighten. Check the alignment of the mating surfaces. Tighten the head bolts in steps in a crossing pattern to the tightening torque specification listed in **Table 1**.

Install new gaskets and install the exhaust and water jacket covers and plates. Sealant or adhesives are not required on these gaskets. Apply Loctite 572 to the threads of the bolts. Tighten the bolts in steps to the specification listed in **Table 1**.

After the engine has run enough to reach normal operating temperature, the bolt torque should be checked. Stop the engine and allow it to cool for 30 minutes. Loosen the bolts 1/4 turn one at a time and tighten to the correct tightening torque as listed in **Table 1**. Use the standard tightening torque specification if a specific torque value is not listed.

External Component Installation

This section provides the instructions for component installation. Refer to the proper chapter in the manual for installation of the intake manifold, fuel system, electrical and ignition system. Refer to Chapter Thirteen and install the oil injection system. Install the wiring harness using the drawings and wiring charts located near the back of the manual. This section will provide hose routing information for puddle fuel system hose and the throttle arm installation.

Refer to Chapter Six for reed housing assembly instructions and/or intake manifold installation. Torque sequences are not provided for all models. Use a crossing pattern starting from the middle and working outward for models without a specified sequence. Tightening torque specifications are provided in **Table 1**.

a. For 80 jet and 115-30 hp models, refer to **Figure 131**.

b. For 105 jet and 150-200 hp (90°) models, refer to **Figure 132**.

c. For 225 hp (90°) models, refer to **Figure 133.**

Refer to Chapter Six and install all components of the fuel system.

Install the throttle arm components. Apply Yamaha all-purpose grease onto all springs, bushings and sliding surfaces. Refer to **Figures 134-141** to assist throttle arm assembly and linkage installation. Refer to Chapter Six for instructions on models not listed. Refer to Chapter Five after power head assembly is complete for synchronization, timing, and linkage adjustments.

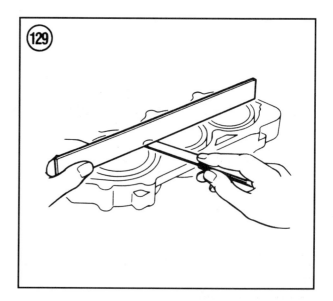

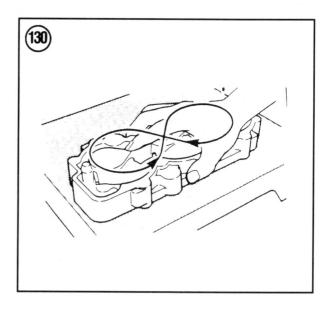

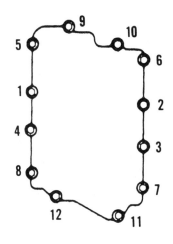

131

INTAKE MANIFOLD
TIGHTENING SEQUENCE
(80 JET AND 115-130 HP MODELS)

a. For 20 and 25 hp (two-cylinder) models, refer to **Figure 134**.
b. For 40-50 hp models (except E48), refer to **Figure 135**.
c. For Model E48, refer to **Figure 136**.
d. For 60 and 70 hp models (except E60), refer to **Figure 137**.
e. For Model E60, refer to **Figure 138**.
f. For Model E75, refer to **Figure 139**.
g. For 65 jet and 75-90 hp models (except E75 and 80 jet), refer to **Figure 140**.
h. For 80 jet, 105 jet and 115-225 hp (90°) models, refer to **Figure 141**.

Install all components of the oil injection system as instructed in Chapter Thirteen.

Install all electrical and ignition system components onto the power head as instructed in Chapter Seven.

Install the Flywheel onto the crankshaft as instructed in this chapter.

Inspect all puddle fuel hoses for tears, leaks or deterioration. Install all hoses to the fitting on the original loca-

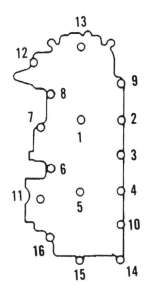

132

INTAKE MANIFOLD
TIGHTENING SEQUENCE (105 JET
AND 150-200 HP [90°] MODELS)

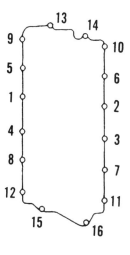

133

INTAKE MANIFOLD
TIGHTENING SEQUENCE
(225 HP [90°] MODELS)

8

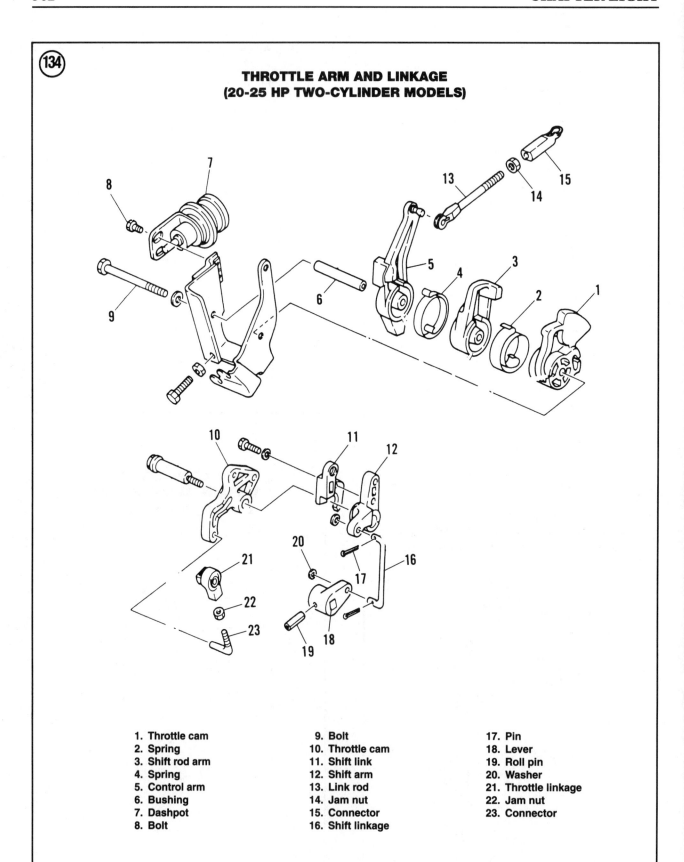

(134)

**THROTTLE ARM AND LINKAGE
(20-25 HP TWO-CYLINDER MODELS)**

1. Throttle cam	9. Bolt	17. Pin
2. Spring	10. Throttle cam	18. Lever
3. Shift rod arm	11. Shift link	19. Roll pin
4. Spring	12. Shift arm	20. Washer
5. Control arm	13. Link rod	21. Throttle linkage
6. Bushing	14. Jam nut	22. Jam nut
7. Dashpot	15. Connector	23. Connector
8. Bolt	16. Shift linkage	

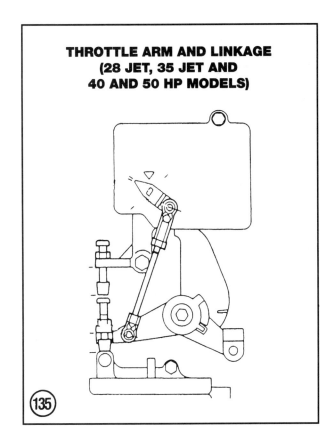

**THROTTLE ARM AND LINKAGE
(28 JET, 35 JET AND
40 AND 50 HP MODELS)**

(135)

tions. For assistance with hose installation, refer to **Figure 142-150**. Puddle fuel system routing illustrations are not provided for all models. Many models have a single hose or short sections of hose that are simple to route. Route the hose to the fittings noted when the hose was removed.

  a. For 4 and 5 hp models, refer to **Figure 142**.

  b. For 28 jet, 35 jet and 40 hp models, refer to **Figure 143**.

  c. For Model E48, refer to **Figure 144**.

  d. For 60 and 70 hp models, refer to **Figure 145**.

  e. For 65 jet and 75-90 hp models (except E65 and 80 jet), refer to **Figure 146**.

  f. For 80 jet and 115-130 hp models, refer to **Figure 147**.

  g. For 105 jet and 150-225 hp (90°) models, refer to **Figure 148**.

  h. For 225 and 250 hp (76°) carbureted models, refer to **Figure 149**.

  i. For 200-250 hp (76°) EFI models, refer to **Figure 150**.

POWER HEAD INSTALLATION

Power head installation is the reverse of removal. Use a sufficient overhead hoist if necessary to lift and lower the

8

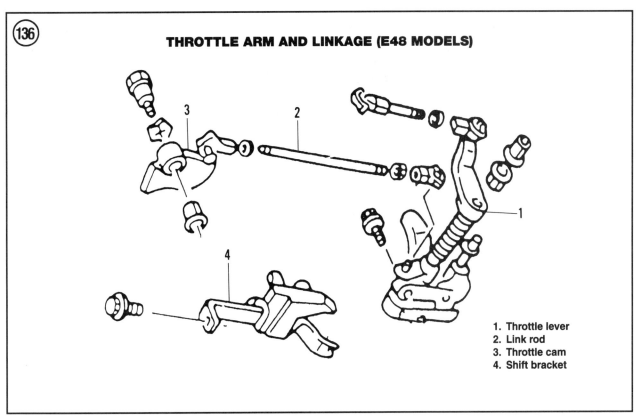

(136)

THROTTLE ARM AND LINKAGE (E48 MODELS)

1. Throttle lever
2. Link rod
3. Throttle cam
4. Shift bracket

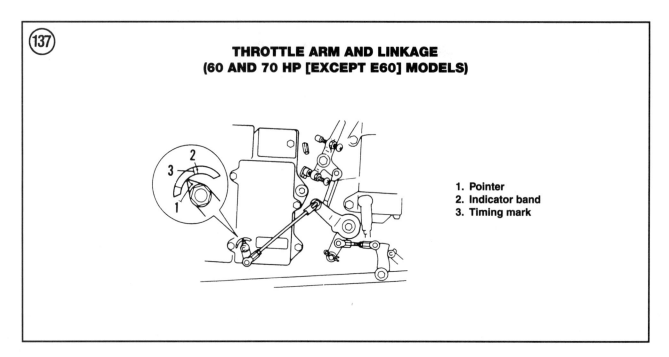

(137)

**THROTTLE ARM AND LINKAGE
(60 AND 70 HP [EXCEPT E60] MODELS)**

1. Pointer
2. Indicator band
3. Timing mark

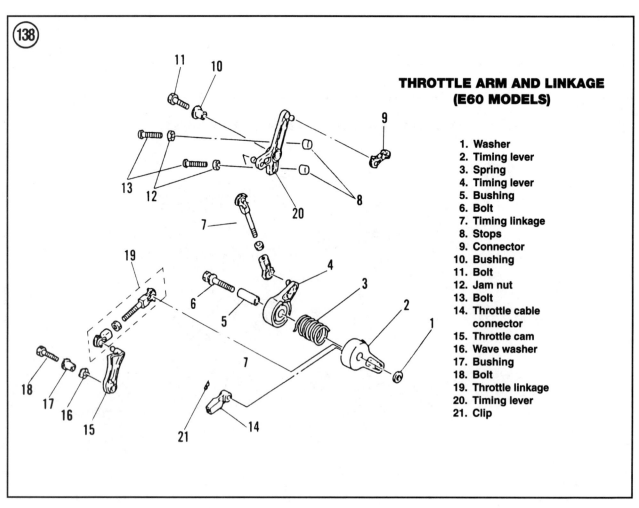

(138)

**THROTTLE ARM AND LINKAGE
(E60 MODELS)**

1. Washer
2. Timing lever
3. Spring
4. Timing lever
5. Bushing
6. Bolt
7. Timing linkage
8. Stops
9. Connector
10. Bushing
11. Bolt
12. Jam nut
13. Bolt
14. Throttle cable
    connector
15. Throttle cam
16. Wave washer
17. Bushing
18. Bolt
19. Throttle linkage
20. Timing lever
21. Clip

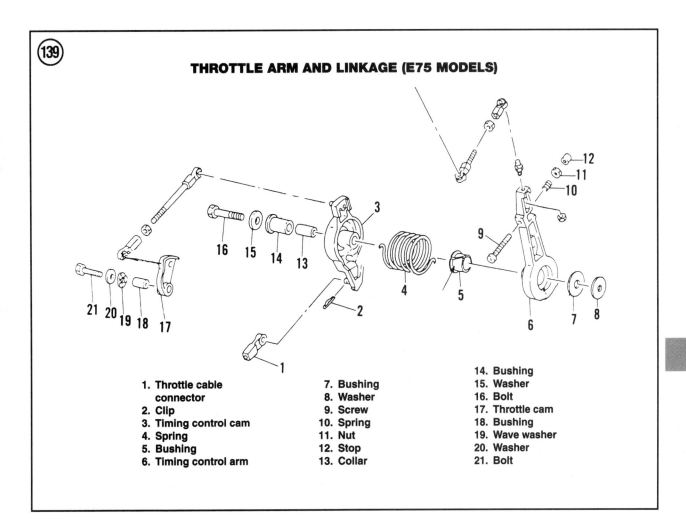

139

THROTTLE ARM AND LINKAGE (E75 MODELS)

1. Throttle cable connector	9. Screw
2. Clip	10. Spring
3. Timing control cam	11. Nut
4. Spring	12. Stop
5. Bushing	13. Collar
6. Timing control arm	14. Bushing
7. Bushing	15. Washer
8. Washer	16. Bolt
	17. Throttle cam
	18. Bushing
	19. Wave washer
	20. Washer
	21. Bolt

8

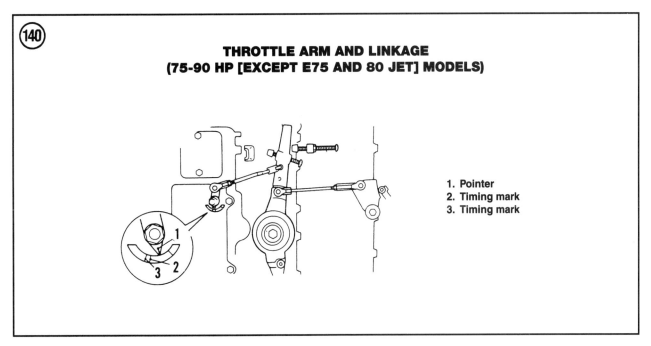

140

THROTTLE ARM AND LINKAGE
(75-90 HP [EXCEPT E75 AND 80 JET] MODELS)

1. Pointer
2. Timing mark
3. Timing mark

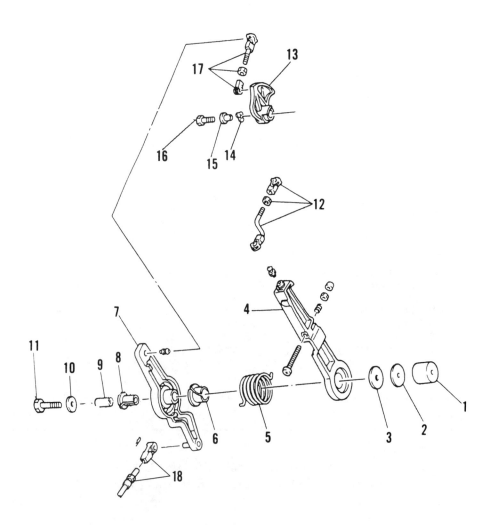

THROTTLE ARM AND LINKAGE
(80 JET, 105 JET AND 115-225 HP [90°] MODELS)

1. Bushing
2. Washer
3. Washer
4. Throttle arm
5. Spring
6. Bushing
7. Throttle arm
8. Bushing
9. Collar
10. Washer
11. Bolt
12. Throttle linkage
13. Throttle cam
14. Wave washer
15. Bushing
16. Bolt
17. Throttle cam linkage
18. Throttle cable connector

142

FUEL SYSTEM HOSE ROUTING (4 AND 5 HP MODELS)

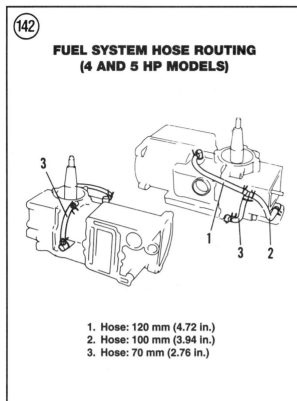

1. Hose: 120 mm (4.72 in.)
2. Hose: 100 mm (3.94 in.)
3. Hose: 70 mm (2.76 in.)

143

PUDDLE FUEL SYSTEM HOSE ROUTING (28 JET, 35 JET, 40 AND 50 HP MODELS)

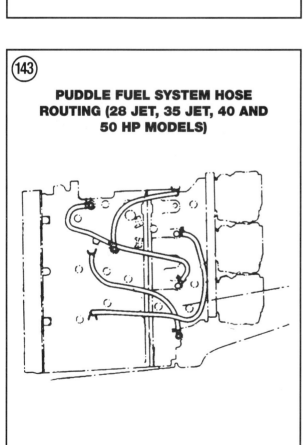

144

PUDDLE FUEL SYSTEM HOSE ROUTING (MODEL E48)

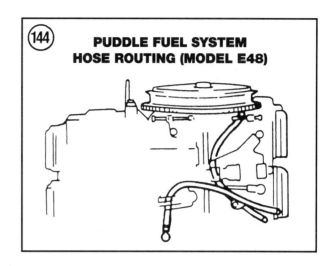

145

PUDDLE FUEL SYSTEM HOSE ROUTING (60 AND 70 HP MODELS)

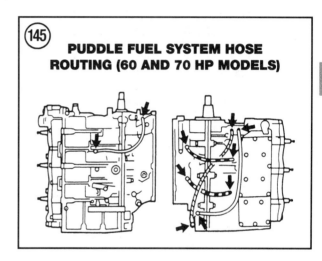

8

146

PUDDLE FUEL SYSTEM HOSE ROUTING (65 JET AND 75-90 HP [EXCEPT 80 JET] MODELS)

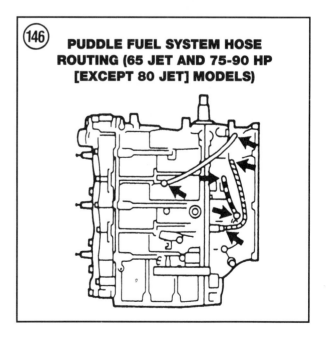

PUDDLE FUEL SYSTEM HOSE ROUTING (80 JET AND 115-130 HP)

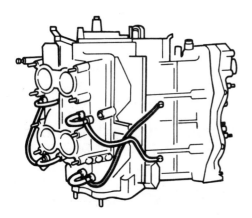

Port side

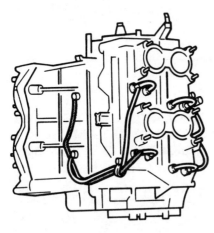

Starboard side

PUDDLE FUEL SYSTEM HOSE ROUTING (105 JET AND 150-225 HP [90°] MODELS)

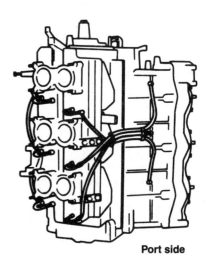

Port side

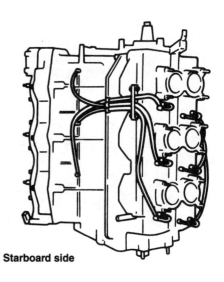

Starboard side

power head. Work carefully and make sure that hoses, wires, and linkages are clear before lowering the power head into position.

1. Install the exhaust tuner/manifold on the models so equipped. Refer to **Table 1** and tighten the fasteners to the listed specification.

2. Install a new power head mounting gasket onto the adapter or drive shaft housing surface.

3. Coat the lower seal with Yamaha all-purpose grease or its equivalent. Lubricate the drive shaft splines prior to installation.

4. Slowly lower the power head onto the midsection. Keep the flywheel as level as possible to avoid damaging the drive shaft, gasket or mating surfaces. Rotate the flywheel to align the splines and lower the power head to the mounting surface.

5. Install all power head mounting fasteners and torque to the specifications listed in Table 1. Refer to the standard tightening torque if a specific value is not listed.

6. Install all hoses, wires, cables and control linkages to the power head.

7. Properly gap and install new spark plugs. Refer to Chapter Four for specification.

8. Install the rewind starter, if so equipped, as instructed in Chapter Eleven.

9. Connect the battery terminals to the proper terminals on electric start models.

10. Perform the synchronization, timing and linkage adjustments following the procedures in Chapter Five.

11. Refer to *Break-in Procedure* in this chapter.

BREAK-IN PROCEDURE

During the first few hours of running, many of the internal engine components should not be subjected to continuous full-load conditions until wear patterns are established. To ensure a reliable and durable repair, perform the break-in procedure anytime internal components of the power head are replaced. Use a 25 to 1 fuel/oil mixture on premix models during the first 10 hours of operation. On oil injected models, use a 50 to 1 fuel/oil mixture in the fuel tank in addition to the normal oil injection. This will provide additional lubrication required for break-in.

Operate the engine at a fast idle, approximately 1500 rpm, in neutral for the first 10 minutes of engine operation. During the next 50 minutes of operation, avoid full-throttle operation, except to quickly plane the boat, and change the

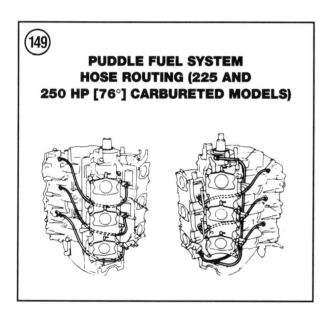

(149)

PUDDLE FUEL SYSTEM HOSE ROUTING (225 AND 250 HP [76°] CARBURETED MODELS)

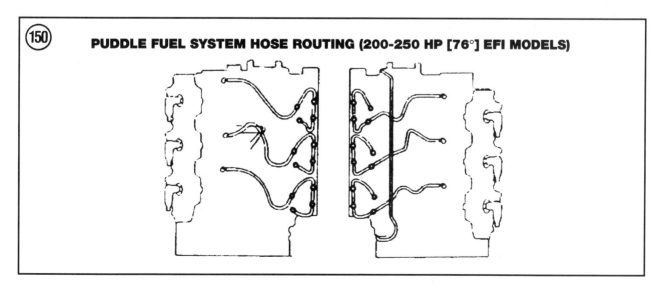

(150) **PUDDLE FUEL SYSTEM HOSE ROUTING (200-250 HP [76°] EFI MODELS)**

8

engine speed frequently. Do not exceed 3000 rpm. During the second hour of running, use full throttle to plane the boat, then reduce the throttle setting to maximum of 3/4 open. Frequently vary the throttle setting. During the third hour of operation, run the engine at varying throttle openings. Occasionally advance the throttle to wide open for a short period of time, up to 5 minutes, then reduce the throttle setting to 3/4 open to allow the power head to cool. During the remaining seven hours of the 10 hour break-in period, avoid continuous full-throttle operation and do not operate the engine at any one throttle setting for more than 15 minutes. After the 10 hour break-in period, use the standard fuel/oil mixture recommended in Chapter Four. The engine can be operated as desired within the normal operating guidelines.

NOTE
During the first 10 hours of operation, do not run EFI models for more than 1 hour at speeds below 2000 rpm. During extended running at low speeds, the additional oil used for break-in may interfere with the oxygen sensor operation. Never use leaded fuel with a Yamaha EFI engine.

Table 1 TIGHTENING TORQUE

	First torque	Final torque
Flywheel nut		
2 hp	–	45 N•m (33 ft.-lb.)
3 hp	–	45 N•m (33 ft.-lb.)
4 and 5 hp	–	45 N•m (33 ft.-lb.)
6 and 8 hp	–	45 N•m (33 ft.-lb.)
9.9 and 15 hp	–	105 N•m (77 ft.-lb.)
20 and 25 hp (two-cylinder)	–	100 N•m (73 ft.-lb.)
25 (three-cylinder) and 30 hp	–	110 N•m (81 ft.-lb.)
C30	–	140 N•m (103 ft.-lb.)
C40	–	160 N•m (118 ft.-lb.)
28 jet, 35 jet and 40-50 hp	–	110 N•m (81 ft.-lb.)
E48	–	160 N•m (118 ft.-lb.)
60-90 hp (except E60, E75 and 80 jet)	–	160 N•m (118 ft.-lb.)
E60	–	160 N•m (118 ft.-lb.)
E75	–	160 N•m (118 ft.-lb.)
80 jet and 115-130 hp	–	190 N•m (140 ft.-lb.)
105 jet and 150-225 hp (90°)	–	190 N•m (140 ft.-lb.)
200-250 hp (76°)	–	186 N•m (137 ft.-lb.)
Cylinder head		
3 hp	5 N•m (44 in.-lb.)	11 N•m (97 in.-lb.)
9.9 and 15 hp	8 N•m (70 in.-lb.)	17 N•m (12 ft.-lb.)
20 and 25 (two-cylinder) hp	15 N•m (11 ft.-lb.)	28 N•m (20 ft.-lb.)
25 (three-cylinder) and 30 hp	15 N•m (11 ft.-lb.)	28 N•m (20 ft.-lb.)
C30	15 N•m (11 ft.-lb.)	27 N•m (20 ft.-lb.)
28 jet, 35 jet, 40 and 50 hp	15 N•m (11 ft.-lb.)	28 N•m (20 ft.-lb.)
C40	15 N•m (11 ft.-lb.)	28 N•m (20 ft.-lb.)
E48	15 N•m (11 ft.-lb.)	30 N•m (22 ft.-lb.)
60-70 hp (except E60)	15 N•m (11 ft.-lb.)	32 N•m (23 ft.-lb.)
E60	15 N•m (11 ft.-lb.)	32 N•m (23 ft.-lb.)
65 jet	15 N•m (11 ft.-lb.)	32 N•m (23 ft.-lb.)
75-90 (except E75 and 80 jet)	15 N•m (11 ft.-lb.)	30 N•m (22 ft.-lb.)
E75	15 N•m (11 ft.-lb.)	30 N•m (22 ft.-lb.)
80 jet and 115-130 hp	15 N•m (11 ft.-lb.)	30 N•m (22 ft.-lb.)
105 jet and 150-225 hp (90°)	15 N•m (11 ft.-lb.)	30 N•m (22 ft.-lb.)
200-250 hp (76°)	15 N•m (11 ft.-lb.)	27 N•m (20 ft.-lb.)
Cylinder head water jacket cover		
2 hp	5 N•m (44 in.-lb.)	10 N•m (87 in.-lb.)
4 and 5 hp	3 N•m (26 in.-lb.)	9 N•m (78 in.-lb.)
C30	15 N•m (11 ft.-lb.)	27 N•m (20 ft.-lb.)
C40	15 N•m (11 ft.-lb.)	30 N•m (22 ft.-lb.)
E48, E75	4 N•m (35 in.-lb.)	8 N•m (70 in.-lb.)
80 jet, 105 jet and 115-250 hp	4 N•m (35 in.-lb.)	8 N•m (70 in.-lb.)
	(continued)	

Table 1 TIGHTENING TORQUE (continued)

	First torque	Final torque
Exhaust cover/water jacket		
3 hp	3 N•m (26 in.-lb.)	8 N•m (70 in.-lb.)
4 and 5 hp	3 N•m (26 in.-lb.)	9 N•m (79 in.-lb.)
6 and 8 hp	4 N•m (35 in.-lb.)	8 N•m (70 in.-lb.)
9.9 and 15 hp	6 N•m (53 in.-lb.)	12 N•m (106 in.-lb.)
20-25 hp (two-cylinder)	3 N•m (26 in.-lb.)	8 N•m (70 in.-lb.)
25 hp (three-cylinder)	4 N•m (35 in.-lb.)	8 N•m (70 in.-lb.)
28 jet, 35 jet and 30-50	4 N•m (35 in.-lb.)	8 N•m (70 in.-lb.)
60, E60 and 70 hp	3 N•m (26 in.-lb.)	8 N•m (70 in.-lb.)
E75	9 N•m (84 in.-lb.)	18 N•m (13 ft.-lb.)
65 jet and 75-90 hp (except E75, 80 jet)	9 N•m (79 in.-lb.)	18 N•m (13 ft.-lb.)
80 jet and 115-250 hp	4 N•m (35 in.-lb.)	8 N•m (70 in.-lb.)
Bypass cover		
80 jet and 115-225 hp	4 N•m (35 in.-lb.)	8 N•m (70 in.-lb.)
Connecting rod		
E48	17 N•m (150 in.-lb.)	32 N•m (23 ft.-lb.)
E75	17 N•m (150 in.-lb.)	35 N•m (26 ft.-lb.)
60-90 (except E60, E75 and 80 jet)	12 N•m (106 in.-lb.)	35 N•m (26 ft.-lb.)
80 jet and 115-130 hp	17. N•m (12 ft.-lb.)	37 N•m (27 ft.-lb.)
105 jet and 150-225 hp (90°)	19 N•m (14 ft.-lb.)	37 N•m (27 ft.-lb.)
200-250 hp (76°)	20 N•m (15 ft.-lb.)	44 N•m (32 ft.-lb.)
Crankcase Cover		
2 hp	5 N•m (44 in.-lb.)	10 N•m (88 in.-lb.)
3 hp	5 N•m (44 in.-lb.)	11 N•m (97 in.-lb.)
4 and 5 hp	6 N•m (53 in.-lb.)	12 N•m (106 in.-lb.)
6 and 8 hp	6 N•m (53 in.-lb.)	11 N•m (97 in.-lb.)
9.9 and 15 hp	15 N•m (11 ft.-lb.)	30 N•m (22 ft.-lb.)
20 and 25 hp (two-cylinder)		
(M6 bolts)	5 N•m (44 in.-lb.)	11 N•m (97 in.-lb.)
(M8 bolts)	15 N•m (11 ft.-lb.)	28 N•m (21 ft.-lb.)
C30	15 N•m (11 ft.-lb.)	27 N•m (20 ft.-lb.)
C40		
(M6 bolts)	5 N•m (44 in.-lb.)	11 N•m (97 in.-lb.)
(M10 bolts)	20 N•m (15 ft.-lb.)	40 N•m (29 ft.-lb.)
28 jet, 35 jet and 30-50 (except E48)		
(M6 bolts)	5 N•m (44 in.-lb.)	11 N•m (96 in.-lb.)
(M8 bolts)	15 N•m (11 ft.-lb.)	28 N•m (20 ft.-lb.)
E48		
(M10 bolts)	20 N•m (15 ft.-lb.)	40 N•m (29 ft.-lb.)
(M6 bolts)	6 N•m (53 in.-lb.)	12 N•m (106 in.-lb.)
60 and 70 hp (except E60)		
(M8 bolts)	10 N•m (86 in.-lb.)	20 N•m (14 ft.-lb.)
(M10 bolts)	20 N•m (15 ft.-lb.)	40 N•m (29 ft.-lb.)
E60	20 N•m (15 ft.-lb.)	40 N•m (29 ft.-lb.)
E75		
(M10 bolts)	20 N•m (15 ft.-lb.	40 N•m (29 ft.-lb.)
(M6 bolts)	6 N•m (53 in.-lb.)	12 N•m (106 in.-lb.)
65 jet and 75-90 hp (except E75, 80 jet)		
(M6 bolts)	4 N•m (35 in.-lb.)	12 N•m (106 in.-lb.)
(M10 bolts)	20 N•m (15 ft.-lb.)	40 N•m (29 ft.-lb.)
80 jet, 105 jet and 115-225 hp (90°)		
(M10 bolts)	20 N•m (15 ft.-lb.)	40 N•m (29 ft.-lb.)
(M8 bolts)	10 N•m (88 in.-lb.)	18 N•m (13 ft.-lb.)
200-250 hp (76°)		
(M10 bolts)	20 N•m (15 ft.-lb.)	39 N•m (28 ft.-lb.)
(M8 bolts)	4 N•m (35 in.-lb.)	8 N•m (70 in.-lb.)

(continued)

8

Table 1 TIGHTENING TORQUE (continued)

	First torque	Final torque
Powerhead mounting fasteners		
2 and 3 hp	8 N•m (70 in.-lb.)	16 N•m (11 ft.-lb.)
4 and 5 hp	3 N•m (26 in.-lb.)	8 N•m (70 in.-lb.)
20-30 hp (except 28 jet)	10 N•m (88 in.-lb.)	21 N•m (15 ft.-lb.)
40-50 hp (except E48)*	–	–
E48, E60 and E75	10 N•m (88 in.-lb.)	21 N•m (15 ft.-lb.)
60-90 hp (except E60, E75, 80 jet)	10 N•m (88 in.-lb.)	21 N•m (15 ft.-lb.)
80 jet, 105 jet and 115-250 hp	10 N•m (88 in.-lb.)	21 N•m (15 ft.-lb.)

*Specification is not available. Refer to Table 2.

Table 2 STANDARD TIGHTENING TORQUE

Fastener Size	Torque Specification
8 mm bolt, M5 nut	5 N•m (44 in.-lb.)
10 mm bolt, M6 bolt	8 N•m (70 in.-lb.)
12 mm bolt, M8 bolt	18 N•m (13 ft.-lb.)
14 mm bolt, M10 bolt	36 N•m (26 ft.-lb.)
17 mm bolt, M12 bolt	43 N•m (31 ft.-lb.)

Table 3 CYLINDER BORE SPECIFICATIONS

Model	
Cylinder bore diameter	
2 hp	39.00-39.10 mm (1.535 -1.540 in.)
3 hp	46.00-46.10 mm (1.811-1.815 in.)
4 hp	50.00-50.10 mm (1.969-1.972 in.)
5 hp	54.00-54.10 mm (2.126-2.130 in.)
6 and 8 hp	50.00-50.10 mm (1.969-1.972 in.)
9.9 and 15 hp	56.00-56.10 mm (2.205-2.210 in.)
20, 25 hp (two-cylinder)	67.00-67.10 mm (2.638-2.642 in.)
25 hp (three-cylinder) and 30 hp	59.50-59.52 mm (2.343-2.344 in.)
C30	72.00-72.02 mm (2.8346-2.8354 in.)
C40	75.00-75.02 mm (2.953-2.954 in.)
28 jet, 35 jet, 40 and 50 hp	67.00-67.10 mm (2.638-2.642 in.)
E48	82.00-82.00 mm (3.228-3.230 in.)
60-70 hp (except 65 jet and E60)	70.00-72.02 mm (2.834-2.835 in.)
E60	72.00-72.10 mm (2.835-2.838 in.)
E75	82.00-82.10 mm (3.228-3.230 in.)
65 jet, 75-90 (except 80 jet and E75)	80.00-82.02 mm (3.228-3.229 in.)
80 jet and 115-250 hp	90.00-90.10 mm (3.543-3.550 in.)
Maximum taper	
2-250 hp	0.08 mm (0.003 in.)
Maximum out-of-round	
2-250 hp	0.05 mm (0.002 in.)

Table 4 PISTON TO CYLINDER CLEARANCE

Model	Specifications
2 hp	0.030-0.085 mm (0.0012-0.003 in.)
3, 4, 5 hp	0.030-0.035 mm (0.0012-0.0014 in.)
6, 8 hp	0.040-0.045 mm (0.0016-0.0018 in.)
9.9, 15	0.035-0.040 mm (0.0014-0.0016 in.)
	(continued)

Table 4 PISTON TO CYLINDER CLEARANCE (continued)

Model	Specifications
20-30 hp (except 28 jet)	0.040-0.045 mm (0.0016-0.0018 in.)
C30	0.060-0.065 mm (0.0024-0.0025 in.)
C40	0.050-0.055 mm (0.0020-0.0022 in.)
28 jet, 35 jet, 40, 50	0.060-0.065 mm (0.0024-0.0026 in.)
E48	0.065-0.120 mm (0.0026-0.0047 in.)
60-70 hp (except 65 jet and E60)	0.050-0.055 mm (0.0020-0.0022 in.)
E60	0.055-0.060 mm (0.0022-0.0024 in.)
65 jet, 75-90 hp (except 80 jet and E75)	0.060-0.065 mm (0.0024-0.0026 in.)
E75	0.065-0.070 mm (0.0026-0.0028 in.)
80 jet and 115-130 hp	0.020-0.060 mm (0.0010-0.0020 in.)
105 jet and 150-250 hp	0.100-0.106 mm (0.0039-0.0042 in.)

Table 5 PISTON PIN SPECIFICATIONS

	Specifications
Pin bore diameter	
2 hp	10.004-10-015 mm (0.3939-0.3943 in.)
3 hp*	–
4-8 hp	12.004-12.015 mm (0.4726-0.4730 in.)
9.9 and 15 hp	14.004-14.015 mm (0.5513-0.5518 in.)
20 and 25 hp (two-cylinder)	18.004-18.015 mm (0.7093-0.9088in.)
25 hp (three-cylinder) and 30 hp*	–
28 jet, 35 jet and 40-50 hp	18.008-18.015 mm (0.7090-0.7093 in.)
60-90 hp* (except 80 jet, 65 jet, E60 and E75)	–
E48, E60 and E75	19.904-19.915 mm (0.7836-0.7841 in.)
80 jet and 115-225 hp	23.074-23.085 mm (0.9084-0.9089 in.)
(90°)	–
200-250 hp (76°)	26.004-26.015 mm (1.0238-1.0242 in.)
Pin diameter	
2 hp	9.996-10.000 mm (0.3935-0.3937 in.)
3 hp*	–
4-8 hp	11.996-12.000 mm (0.4723-0.4724 in.)
9.9 and 15 hp	13.996-14.000 mm (0.5510-0.5512 in.)
20 and 25 hp (two-cylinder)	17.995-18.000 mm (0.7085-0.7093 in.)
25 hp (three-cylinder) and 30hp*	–
28 jet, 35 jet and 40-50 hp	17.995-18.000 mm (0.7085-0.7087 in.)
60-90* hp (except 80 jet, E60 and E75)	–
E48, E60 and E75	19.895-19.900 mm (0.7833-0.7835 in.)
80 jet and 115-225 hp	23.065-23.070 mm (0.9081-0.9083 in.)
(90°)	–
200-250 hp	25.995-26.000mm (1.0234-1.0236 in.)
(76°)	–

*Measurement is not required on these models

Table 6 STANDARD PISTON DIAMETER

Model	Piston diameter
2 hp	38.967-38.986 mm (1.5341-1.5349 in.)
3 hp	45.965-45.990 mm (1.8096-1.8106 in.)
4 hp	49.970-50.000 mm (1.9673-1.9685 in.)
	(continued)

Table 6 STANDARD PISTON DIAMETER (continued)

Model	Piston diameter
5 hp	53.973-54.000 mm (2.124802.1268 in.)
6 and 8 hp	49.995-49.980 mm (1.9667-1.9677 in.)
9.9 and 15 hp	55.940-55.985 mm (2.2024-2.2041 in.)
20 and 25 hp (two-cylinder)	66.995-66.980 mm (2.636-2.637 in.)
C30	71.94-71.96 mm (2.8323-2.8331 in.)
C40	74.945-74.970 mm (2.9506-2.9516 in.)
25 hp (three-cylinder) and 30 hp	59.460-59.480 mm (2.341-2.241 in.)
28 jet, 35 jet, 40 and 50 hp	66.940-67000 mm (2.6354-2.6378 in.)
E48	81.935-81.955 mm (3.2259-3.2266 in.)
60 and 70 hp (except E60)	71.945-71.970 mm (2.8325-2.8335 in.)
E60	71.940-71.965 mm (2.8230-2.8333 in.)
75-90 hp (except E75 and 80 jet)	81.935-81.960 mm (3.2258-3.2268 in.)
E75	81.935-81.955 mm (3.2258-3.2266 in.)
80 jet and 115-130	89.920-89.935 mm (3.5402-3.5407 in.)
105 jet and 150-225 hp (90°)	89.895-89.915 mm (3.5392-3.5400 in.)
200-250 hp (76°)	89.840-89.860 mm (3.5370-3.5378 in.)

Table 7 PISTON RING END GAP

Model	Normal gap	Limit	Measuring depth
2 and 3 hp	0.10-0.30 mm (0.004-0.012 in.)	—	20.0 mm 0.80 in.)
4 and 5 hp	0.15-0.35 mm (0.006-0.014 in.)	—	70.0 mm (2.76 in.)
6 and 8 hp	0.15-0.35 mm (0.006-0.014 in.)	—	60.0 mm (2.36 in.)
9.9 and 15 hp	0.15-0.35 mm (0.006-0.014 in.)	0.55 mm (0.022 in.)	20.0 mm (0.80 in.)
20 and 25 hp (two-cylinder)	0.40-0.60 mm (0.016-0.024 in.)	0.80 mm (0.031 in.)	20.0 mm (0.80 in.)
30 hp	0.15-0.30 mm (0.006-0.012 in.)	—	20.0 mm (0.80 in.)
C30	0.20-0.35 mm (0.008-0.014 in.)	—	20.0 mm (0.80 in.)
C40	0.30-0.50 mm (0.012-0.020 in.)	—	20.0 mm (0.80 in.)
40, 50 hp	0.40-0.60 mm (0.016-0.024 in.)	0.80 mm (0.31 in.)	20.0 mm (0.80 in.)
E48	0.40-0.60 mm (0.016-0.024 in.)	—	20.0 mm (0.80 in.)
60 and 70 hp (except E60)	0.30-0.50 mm (0.012-0.020 in.)	—	20.0 mm (0.80 in.)
E60	0.30-0.50 mm (0.012-0.020 in.)	0.70 mm (0.028 in.)	20.0 mm (0.80 in.)
75-90 hp (except E75 and 80 jet)	0.40-0.60 mm (0.016-0.024 in.)	—	20.0 mm (0.80 in.)
E75	0.40-0.60 mm (0.016-0.024 in.)	0.80 mm (0.031 in.)	20.0 mm (0.80 in.)
80 jet and 115-250 hp	0.30-0.40 mm (0.012-0.016 in.)	0.60 mm (0.024 in.)	20.0 mm (0.80 in.)

Table 8 PISTON RING SIDE CLEARANCE

Model	Clearance
2 hp	
Top and second ring	0.030-0.070 mm (0.001-0.003 in.)
3-8 hp	
Top ring	0.020-0.060 mm (0.001-0.002 in.)
Second ring	0.030-0.070 mm (0.0012-0.0028 in.)
9.9 and 15 hp	
Top ring	0.020-0.060 mm (0.001-0.002 in.)
Second ring	0.040-0.080 mm (0.002-0.003 in.)
20 and 25 hp (two-cylinder)	
Top ring	0.020-0.060 mm (0.001-0.002 in.)
Second ring	0.030-0.070 mm (0.001-0.003 in.)
	(continued)

Table 8 PISTON RING SIDE CLEARANCE (continued)

Model	Clearance
25 hp (three-cylinder) and 30 hp	
Top and second ring	0.050-0.090 mm (0.002-0.004 in.)
28 jet, 35 jet, 40 and 50 hp	
Top ring	0.040-0.080 mm (0.002-0.003 in.)
Second ring	0.030-0.070 mm (0.001-0.003 in.)
E48	
Top and second ring	0.065-0.070 mm (0.0026-0.0028 in.)
60 and 70 hp (includes E60)	
Top and second ring	0.030-0.070 mm (0.0012-0.0028 in.)
75-90 hp (except E75 and 80 jet)	
Top and second ring	0.030-0.060 mm (0.0012-0.0024 in.)
E75	
Top and second ring	0.030-0.060 mm (0.0012-0.0024 in.)
80 jet and 115-250 hp	
Top ring	0.020-0.060 mm (0.001-0.002 in.)

Table 9 CRANKSHAFT SPECIFICATIONS

	Specification
Outside single journal	
2 hp	27.90-27.95 mm (1.098-1.100 in.)
4-8 hp	39.90-39.95 mm (1.571-1.573 in.)
9.9, 15 hp	46.90-46.95 mm (1.846-1.848 in.)
20-30 hp (except 28 jet)	49.90-49.95 mm (1.965-1.967 in.)
C30	56.90-56.95 mm (2.240-2.242 in.)
C40	60.25-60.50 mm (2.372-2.382 in.)
28 jet, 35 jet, 40 and 50 hp	53.90-53.95 mm (2.122-2.124 in.)
E48	61.9-62.5 mm (2.44-2.46 in.)
E60	57.90-57.95 mm (2.280-2.281 in.)
60 and 70 hp	57.90-57.95 mm (2.280-2.281 in.)
Outside all journals	
6 and 8 hp	101.7-102.0 mm (4.004-4.016 in.)
E48	163.8-164.2 mm (6.45-6.46 in.)
60 and 70 hp	245.5-246.1 mm (9.67.9.69 in.)
(outside journal 1-2)	151.7-152.0 mm (5.972-5.984 in.)
65 jet and 75-90 hp (except 80 jet)	284.2-284.8 mm (11.19-11.21 in.)
Between journal	
9.9 and 15 hp	25.90-26.10 mm (1.020-1.028 in.)
20 and 25 hp (two-cylinder)	38.90-39.10 mm (1.531-1.539 in.)
26 jet, 35 jet, 40 and 50 hp	32.88-33.10 mm (1.294-1.303 in.)
E60	35.90-36.10 mm (1.413-1.421 in.)
Maximum crankshaft runout	
2 hp	0.02 mm (0.008 in.)
3-50 hp (except E48)	0.03 mm (0.0012 in.)
E48	0.05 mm (0.002 in.)
E60	0.03 mm (0.0012 in.)
E75	0.05 mm (0.002 in.)
60 and 70 hp	0.03 mm (0.0012 in.)
65 jet, 85 jet and 115-250 hp	0.05 mm (0.0012 in.)

Table 10 CONNECTING ROD SPECIFICATIONS

	Specification
Rod-to-journal side clearance	
2, 3 hp	0.30-0.60 mm (0.012-0.024 in.)
4-8 hp	0.20-0.70 mm (0.008-0.027 in.)
9.9 and 15	0.30-0.80 mm (0.012-0.031 in.)
	(continued)

8

Table 10 CONNECTING ROD SPECIFICATIONS (continued)

	Specification
Rod-to-journal side clearance (continued)	
20-50 hp (except E48)	0.20-0.70 mm (0.008-0.027 in.)
E48	0.12-0.26 mm (0.005-0.010 in.)
60, E60 and 70 hp	0.20-0.70 mm (0.008-0.027 in.)
E75	0.12-0.26 mm (0.005-0.010 in.)
65 jet and 90-250 hp	0.12-0.26 mm (0.005-0.010 in.)
Maximum axial play	
2-250 hp	2.0 mm (0.08 in.)
Small end diameter	
2 hp	14.000-14.011 mm (0.5512-0.5516 in.)
4 and 5 hp	15.000-15.011 mm (0.5906-0.5910 in.)
9.9 and 15 hp	18.000-18.011 mm (0.7087-0.7091 in.)
20 and 25 hp (two-cylinder)	22.024-22.035 mm (0.8671-0.8675 in.)
28 jet, 35 jet, 40 and 50 hp	22.005-22.008 mm (0.8663-0.8665 in.)
E48, E60 and E75	24.900-24.912 mm (0.9803-0.9808 in.)
200-250 hp (76°)	31.000-31.012 mm (1.2205-1.2209 in.)

Table 11 MATING SURFACES WARPAGE LIMIT

	Warpage limit
Cylinder head, water jacket, exhaust cover mating surface	
All models	0.1 mm (0.004 in.)

Table 12 OVERSIZE PISTON DIAMETERS

Model	First oversize	Second oversize
2 hp[1]	39.50 mm (1.555 in.)	–
3 hp[1]	46.50 mm (1.831 in.)	–
4 and 5 hp[2]	–	–
6 and 8 hp[1]	50.50 mm (1.988 in.)	–
9.9 and 15 hp[1]	56.50 mm (2.224 in.)	–
20 and 25 hp (two-cylinder)	67.25 mm (2.648 in.)	67.50 mm (2.657 in.)
25 hp (three-cylinder) and 30 hp	59.75 mm (2.352 in.)	60.00 mm (2.362 in.)
C30	72.25 mm (2.844 in.)	72.50 mm (2.854 in.)
C40[1]	75.50 mm (2.972 in.)	–
28 jet, 35 jet, 40 and 50 hp	67.25 mm (2.648 in.)	67.50 mm (2.657 in.)
50-60 hp	72.25 mm (2.844 in.)	72.50 mm (2.854 in.)
E48, 65 jet and 75-90 hp (except 80 jet)	82.25 mm (3.238 in.)	82.50 mm (3.248 in.)
80 jet and 115-130[1]	90.50 mm (3.563 in.)	–
105 jet and 150-225 hp (90°)[1]	90.40 mm (3.549 in.)	–
200-250 hp (76°)	90.15 mm (3.549 in.)	90.40 mm (3.559 in.)

1. Second oversize pistons are not available for this model.
2. Oversize pistons are not available for this model.

Chapter Nine

Gearcase Repair

This chapter provides removal and installation, disassembly, inspection and assembly procedures for Yamaha gearcases. Special tools and accurate measuring devices are required to repair many components within the gearcase. Contact a Yamaha dealership to purchase the required tools. Some dealerships will rent or loan the required tools.

Use only the required tools. The use of makeshift tools may result in extensive damage to the housing or internal components of the gearcase.

The major sections covered in this chapter include gearcase operation, gearcase removal and installation, water pump servicing and complete gearcase repair. Follow the step by step instructions for the required section.

Tables 1-7, located at the back of this chapter, provide tightening torque specifications and other gearcase specifications.

Repair or maintenance involving the gearcase can be as simple as servicing the water pump or as complicated as a complete gearcase rebuild. Normal maintenance procedures are described in Chapter Four.

Shims are used to provide the precise alignment of the drive and driven gears necessary for durability and quiet operation. Special tools, gauges and meters are used to measure and compute the shim thickness required to prop-

erly position the gears. The durability of the gearcase is substantially reduced if the gears are improperly positioned. Shimming procedures must be performed if replacing gears, bearings, shafts or housings. Refer to *Shim selection* in this chapter for instructions.

Allow a reputable marine repair shop to perform the repairs if you do not have access to the required tools or are uncomfortable with the repair procedures. Improper repairs can result in extensive and expensive damage to the gearcase.

GEARCASE OPERATION

The gearcase provides a means to transfer the rotation of a vertical drive shaft (A, **Figure 1**) to a horizontal propeller shaft (B, **Figure 1**). Bevel gears (**Figure 2**) attached to each shaft are used to transfer the rotational force to the propeller shaft.

A sliding clutch (**Figure 3**) that is splined to the propeller shaft provides a neutral gear position on 3-250 hp models and neutral, forward and reverse on 4-250 hp models.

The remote control, tiller mounted or engine mounted selector is used for gear selection. Shafts, linkage and/or cables move the clutch. A nonshifting direct drive is used for 2 hp models.

Nonshifting Units

The drive and driven gears rotate anytime the engine is running. On 2 hp models, the propeller shaft maintains a constant connection to the driven gear. This provides for continuous clockwise rotation of the propeller shaft when the engine is running. To provide reverse thrust, the entire engine is pivoted so that the propeller thrust is directed under the boat. If neutral is desired, the engine is simply switched OFF.

Forward and Reverse Shifting Units

A propeller shaft mounted sliding clutch is used on 3 hp models to provide either neutral or engaged thrust. Both the drive and driven gear rotate anytime the engine is running. When neutral is selected the clutch is positioned away from the rotating driven gear. The propeller shaft is allowed to freewheel or remain stationary as the gears rotate. When forward or reverse thrust is desired, the clutch is moved by the shift mechanism to engage the driven gear. The propeller shaft will rotate in the direction of the driven gear as the clutch dogs (raised bosses) connect with the dogs on the driven gear.

When reverse thrust is desired, pivot the entire engine to direct the propeller thrust under the boat.

NOTE
Models with an L in the model designation have a left-hand rotation gearcase. The gearcase is designed to provide forward thrust when the propeller shaft is rotated in the left-hand, or counterclockwise, direction (as viewed from the rear). A left-hand propeller must be used.

Neutral, Forward and Reverse Shifting Units

Neutral, forward and reverse operations are provided on all 4-250 hp models. The drive gear and both driven gears are in constant mesh and rotate anytime the engine is running. A sliding clutch that is splined to the propeller shaft is used to select the neutral, forward or reverse operation.

When neutral is desired (**Figure 4**), the clutch is positioned away from, or disengaged, from the driven gears. The propeller shaft is allowed to freewheel or remain

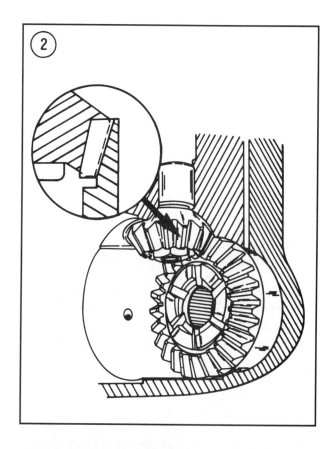

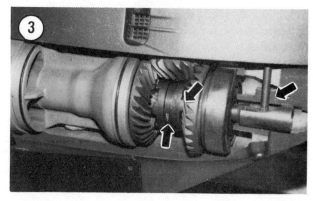

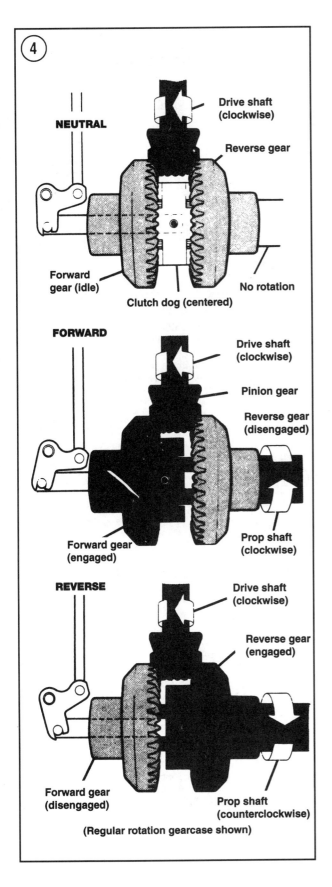

NEUTRAL

Drive shaft (clockwise)

Reverse gear

Forward gear (idle)

No rotation

Clutch dog (centered)

FORWARD

Drive shaft (clockwise)

Pinion gear

Reverse gear (disengaged)

Forward gear (engaged)

Prop shaft (clockwise)

REVERSE

Drive shaft (clockwise)

Reverse gear (engaged)

Forward gear (disengaged)

Prop shaft (counterclockwise)

(Regular rotation gearcase shown)

stationary as the gears rotate. No propeller thrust is delivered.

When forward thrust is desired (**Figure 4**), the sliding clutch is moved with the shift mechanism to engage the front mounted driven gear on right-hand rotation models. The propeller shaft will rotate in the same direction (clockwise as viewed from the propeller end) as the front driven gear when the clutch dogs (or lugs) connect with the lugs on the driven gear. This provides the rotational direction to the propeller shaft necessary for forward thrust.

When reverse thrust is desired (**Figure 4**), the sliding clutch is moved with the shift mechanism to engage the rear mounted driven gear. The propeller shaft will rotate in the same direction (counterclockwise as viewed from the propeller end) as the rear driven gear. This provides the rotational direction to the propeller shaft necessary for reverse thrust.

Left-Hand Rotation Gearcases

Left-hand, or counterclockwise, propeller shaft rotation is used for forward thrust on models with an *L* in the model. Left-hand units are used along with a right-hand unit on dual engine applications. The use of the left-hand unit allows for balanced propeller torque from the two engines. The propeller shaft rotation is selected as described in *Neutral, Forward and Reverse Shifting Units*. A control box is used that provides the opposite direction of shift cable movement versus the units. When forward thrust is desired, the rear mounted gear is engeaged to drive the propeller shaft. When reverse thrust is desired, the front mounted gear is engaged to drive the propeller shaft.

> *CAUTION*
> *Never use a left-hand rotation gearcase with a right-hand propeller. Also, never use a right-hand gearcase with a left-hand propeller. Gearcase component failure may result from continued operation in the wrong direction for forward thrust.*

Twin Prop Units

Twin counter-rotating propellers are used on 150 hp models with a D in the model. The use of two propellers and one engine provides balanced propeller torque and improved performance. Both propellers are used for forward thrust and one propeller is used for reverse thrust.

9

Propeller Removal/Installation

Two methods are used for absorbing shock and mounting of the propeller. A shear pin design is used on 2-5 hp models. A thrust hub design is used on 6-250 hp models.

With the shear pin design, the propeller is held onto the propeller shaft with the propeller nut (2, **Figure 5**) and cotter pin (1, **Figure 5**). A shear pin (4, **Figure 5**) is positioned in its hole in the propeller shaft (5, **Figure 5**). The shear pin engages and drives the propeller. The shear pin is designed to break in the event of underwater impact and provides some protection for the gearcase components.

With the thrust hub design, the propeller is driven via a splined connection of the propeller shaft to the rubber thrust hub. The rubber thrust hub is pressed into a bore in the propeller and provides a cushion effect when shifting. It also provides some protection for the gearcase components in the event of underwater impact. The propeller is held onto the propeller shaft with the propeller nut (5, **Figure 6**) and cotter pin (6, **Figure 6**). A forward mounted spacer (1, **Figure 6**) directs the propeller thrust to a tapered area of the propeller shaft.

> *CAUTION*
> *Use light force if necessary to remove the propeller from the propeller shaft. The use of excessive force will result in damage to the propeller, propeller shaft and internal components of the gearcase. If you are unable to remove the propeller by normal means, have a reputable marine repair shop or propeller repair shop remove the propeller.*

Shear pin design

Always replace the cotter pin and shear pin during installation. Purchase the replacement pins at a marine dealership and select the proper size and material. The cotter pin is made with stainless steel. Use a shear pin designated for the correct model to ensure it will shear at the required load.

1. Remove all spark plug leads and disconnect both battery cables from the battery terminals on electric start models.

2. Use pliers to straighten and remove the cotter pin. To prevent propeller rotation, place a block of wood between the propeller and the gearcase above the propeller.

3. Use a suitable wrench and turn the propeller nut counterclockwise to remove the nut.

4. Pull the propeller from the propeller shaft. Use a block of wood for a cushion and carefully drive the propeller rearward if necessary for removal. Inspect the propeller for

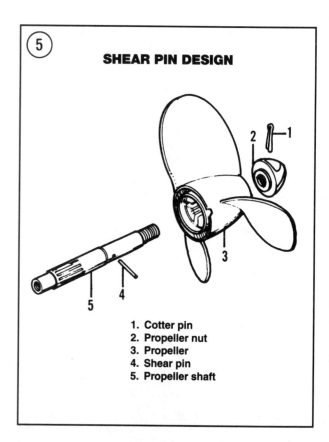

(5)

SHEAR PIN DESIGN

1. Cotter pin
2. Propeller nut
3. Propeller
4. Shear pin
5. Propeller shaft

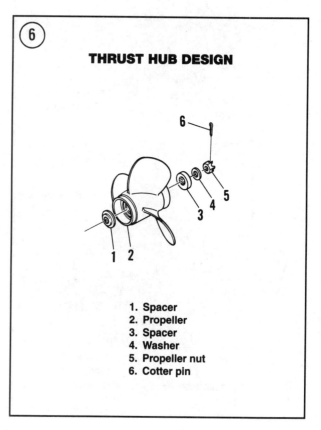

(6)

THRUST HUB DESIGN

1. Spacer
2. Propeller
3. Spacer
4. Washer
5. Propeller nut
6. Cotter pin

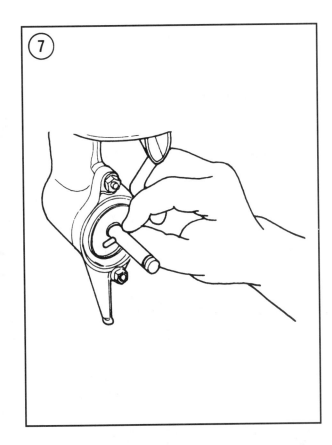

damaged or eroded surfaces. Repair or replace the propeller if defects are noted.

5. Use pliers to straighten the shear pin if necessary. Gently drive the shear pin until flush on one side of the propeller shaft. Use pliers to twist and pull the shear pin from the propeller shaft.

6. Inspect the shear pin hole for burrs or elongation. Dress burrs down with a file. Attempt to fit the new shear pin into the shear pin hole. Check the pin for correct size if the pin fits loosely. Propeller shaft replacement is required to correct a loose fit when the correct shear pin is installed.

7. Clean all surfaces of the propeller shaft and propeller bore for the shaft. Inspect the shear pin engagement slot in the propeller for damage or wear. Replace the propeller if defects are noted in these areas.

8. Position a new shear pin into the shear pin hole (**Figure 7**). Use a small hammer and gently drive the pin into the propeller shaft until the same amount of the pin protrudes from each side of the propeller shaft.

9. Apply a light coating of Yamaha all-purpose grease or its equivalent to shear pin and propeller shaft threads. Apply grease to the propeller shaft and the bore in the propeller. Slide the propeller onto the propeller shaft. Rotate the propeller while pushing forward until the shear pin engages the slot in the propeller.

10. Install the propeller nut until hand tight. Position a block of wood between the propeller and housing to prevent rotation. Tighten the propeller nut to the specification listed in **Table 1**. Align the hole in the propeller nut with the hole in the threaded section of the propeller shaft. Install a new cotter pin and bend the ends over. Connect all spark plug leads. Connect the battery cables to the battery terminals.

Thrust hub design

Always install a new cotter pin (**Figure 8**) when the propeller is removed from the propeller shaft. Make sure the pin is the correct size and material. Inspect the propeller for the presence of black rubber material in the drive hub area. Have the hub inspected or replaced at a propeller repair facility if this material is noted. It normally indicates that the propeller hub has spun in the propeller bore. Satisfactory performance is not possible with a spun propeller hub.

1. Disconnect all spark plug leads and both battery cables (electric start models) at the battery terminals.

2. Use pliers to straighten and remove the cotter pin (1, **Figure 9**) from the propeller nut.

3. Position a block of wood between the propeller and the housing to prevent propeller rotation. Use a suitable wrench to loosen and remove the propeller nut. Note the

9

orientation and remove the plain washer and splined washer (3 and 4, **Figure 9**) from the propeller shaft.

4. Pull the propeller from the propeller shaft. Use a block of wood as a cushion and carefully drive the propeller from the shaft if necessary. Use light force only to avoid damaging the propeller or gearcase components.

5. Note the orientation and remove the front spacer (6, **Figure 9**) from the propeller shaft. Tap the spacer lightly if it is seized to the propeller shaft.

6. Clean all debris and contaminates from the propeller shaft. Inspect the propeller shaft for twisted splines or excessively worn areas. Rotate the propeller shaft while observing for shaft deflection. Remove and replace the propeller shaft if excessively worn areas, twisted splines or a bent shaft is noted. Refer to gearcase disassembly in this chapter for procedures.

7. Apply a light coating of Yamaha all-purpose grease or its equivalent to all surfaces of the propeller shaft. Clean then install the inner spacer. The tapered side of the inner spacer and propeller shaft must contact at the tapered surfaces.

8. Install the propeller onto the propeller shaft. Rotate the propeller to align the splines and slide the propeller fully against the inner spacer. Install the splined washer (4, **Figure 9**) and plain washer (3, **Figure 9**) onto the propeller shaft.

9. Place a block of wood between the propeller and housing to prevent propeller rotation. Install the propeller nut onto the propeller shaft with the cotter pins facing out. Tighten the propeller nut to the specification listed in **Table 1**. Align the cotter pin hole in the propeller shaft with one of the slots in the propeller nut. Install a new cotter pin and use pliers to bend the ends over.

10. Connect all spark plug leads. Connect the battery cables to the battery terminals on electric start models.

Twin propeller

Refer to the section *Special Procedures for Twin Propeller Models* in this chapter for instruction when removing or installing the propellers on these models.

GEARCASE REMOVAL/INSTALLATION

Always remove the propeller prior to removing the gearcase. Refer to *Propeller Removal/Installation* in this chapter for the removal procedure.

Always disconnect all spark plug leads and both battery cables from the battery terminals prior to gearcase removal.

Drain the gearcase prior to removal if the gearcase will require disassembly. Refill the gearcase after installation. Refer to Chapter Four for procedures.

Gearcase removal procedures vary by model. Refer to the section that relates to your model for removal procedures.

NOTE
Use caution if using a pry bar to separate the housings. Always ensure that all fasteners are removed before attempting to pry the gearcase from the drive shaft housing. Use a blunt tip pry bar and locate a pry point near the front and rear mating surfaces. Apply moderate heat to the gearcase and drive shaft housing if corrosion prevents easy removal.

CAUTION
Never apply grease to the top of the drive shaft or fill the connection at the crankshaft. The grease may cause a hydraulic lock on the shaft that can cause failure of the power head, gearcase or both. Use a light coating

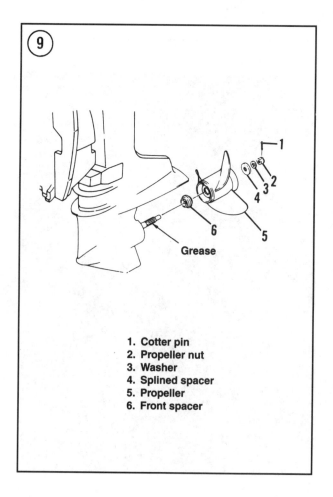

1. Cotter pin
2. Propeller nut
3. Washer
4. Splined spacer
5. Propeller
6. Front spacer

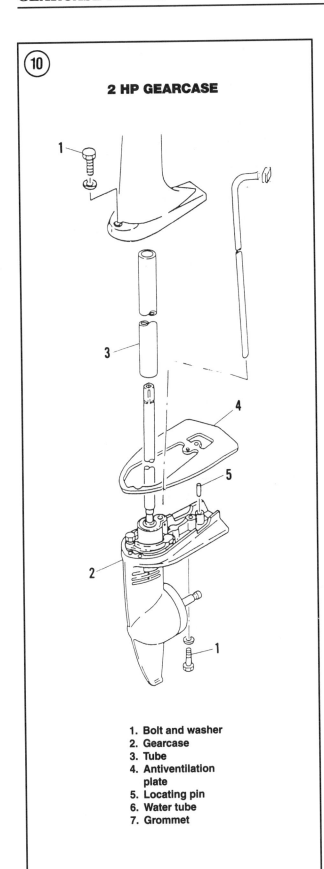

⑩

2 HP GEARCASE

1

3

4

5

2

1

1. **Bolt and washer**
2. **Gearcase**
3. **Tube**
4. **Antiventilation plate**
5. **Locating pin**
6. **Water tube**
7. **Grommet**

of Yamaha all-purpose grease or its equivalent on the sides or splined upper end of the drive shaft.

CAUTION
Work carefully when installing the upper end of the drive shaft into the crankshaft. The lower seal on the crankshaft may be dislodged or damaged by the drive shaft. Never force the drive shaft into position. Rotate the drive shaft and attempt to install the gearcase again if there is difficulty.

Gearcase Removal (2 hp Models)

1. Disconnect the spark plug lead. Remove the bolt and washer located above the propeller shaft.

2. Support the gearcase (2, **Figure 10**) and remove the bolt and washer (1, **Figure 10**) located on the drive shaft housing.

3. Carefully tug or pry the gearcase from the drive shaft housing. Remove the lower plate (4, **Figure 10**) and tube (3, **Figure 10**) from the gearcase and/or drive shaft housing. Install the water tube and grommet seal (6 and 7, **Figure 10**) into the drive shaft housing if they were dislodged during removal of the gearcase.

4. Retrieve the locating pin (5, **Figure 10**). Install the pin in the hole provided in the gearcase. Clean contaminants and debris from upper end of the drive shaft.

Gearcase Installation (2 hp Models)

1. Apply a very light coating of Yamaha all-purpose grease or its equivalent to the locating pin and upper end of the drive shaft. Position the plate (4, **Figure 10**) over the locating pin and onto the gearcase.

2. Install the pipe over the drive shaft, then carefully guide the drive shaft into the drive shaft housing. Make sure that the water tube (6, **Figure 10**) is aligned with the grommet on the water pump. Lower the gearcase and rotate the drive shaft clockwise as viewed from the top slightly until the drive shaft square connection engages with the crankshaft connection. When properly aligned, the housing will contact the drive shaft housing and slip into position. Align the water tube with the grommet each time installation is attempted. Make sure the locating pin is positioned into its hole in the drive shaft housing.

3. Apply Loctite 572 to the threads of the bolts (1, **Figure 10**). With the gearcase held in position, install both bolts and washers. Tighten the bolts to the specification listed in **Table 1**. Attach all spark plug leads. Run the engine and check for correct cooling system operation.

9

Gearcase Removal (3-8 hp Models)

1. Remove all spark plug leads. Disconnect both battery cables from the battery terminals on electric start models.
2. Locate the shift lever on the side of the lower cover or tiller arm. Shift the engine into reverse on 5-8 hp models or forward on 3 hp models.
3. On 3-5 hp models, use a screwdriver to pry out and remove the rubber grommet from the port side of the drive shaft housing. This will allow access to the shift shaft connector (**Figure 11**). Use a marker to scribe the connector position on both the upper and lower shift shafts. This will assist you a great deal during shift adjustment. Loosen the bolt (2, **Figure 12**) on the shift shaft connector three turns.
4. On 6 and 8 hp models, trace the shift shaft up to the shift shaft connector (B, **Figure 13**). Scribe or mark the connector position on the upper and lower shift shafts to assist with shift adjustments. Remove the bolt (A, **Figure 13**) and remove the shift shaft connector from the upper and lower shift shafts.
5. Support the gearcase and remove the four bolts on 3, 6 and 8 hp models and two bolts on 4 and 5 hp models (**Figure 14**). Loosen the shift shaft connector bolt on 3-5 hp models to separate the shift shafts after the gearcase drops down.
6. If necessary, carefully tug or pry the gearcase from the drive shaft housing. Reposition the water tube and sealing grommet if they were dislodged during removal of the gearcase.

Gearcase Installation (3-8 hp Models)

1. Clean debris and contaminants from the drive shaft, shift shafts and gearcase. Apply Yamaha all-purpose grease or its equivalent to the upper end (splines only) of the drive shaft. Inspect the grommet that connects the water tube to the water pump for damage or deterioration. Replace the grommet if required. Apply grease to the grommet. Make sure that the dowel or locating pin is properly positioned in the gearcase.

> *CAUTION*
> *Never rotate the propeller shaft to align the drive shaft to the crankshaft. The water pump impeller can suffer damage that leads to overheating of the engine.*

2. Carefully insert the drive shaft into the drive shaft housing. Guide the water tube into the grommet on the water pump each time you attempt to install the gearcase.

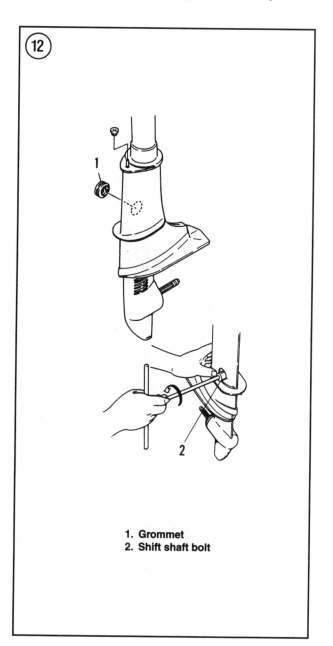

1. Grommet
2. Shift shaft bolt

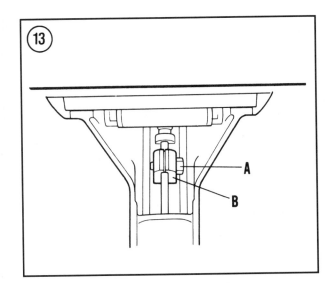

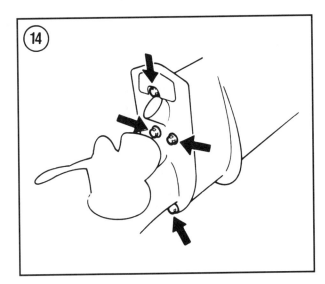

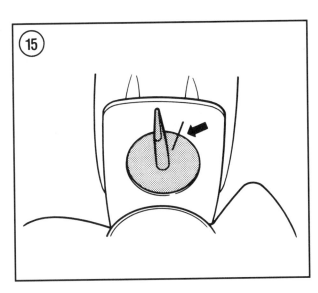

If installation is difficult, lower the gearcase and slightly rotate the drive shaft clockwise as viewed from the top to align the drive shaft with the connection at the crankshaft. Repeat until the drive shaft enters the connection and the gearcase mates with the drive shaft housing.

3. Make sure that the shift shafts are aligned with the shift shaft connector. Apply Loctite 572 to the threads of the mounting bolts. Install the mounting bolts and tighten to the specification listed in **Table 1**. Position the shift shaft connector onto the shift shaft and align it with the markings made prior to removal. Rotate the propeller to ensure that the gearcase is in the same gear as the shift selector. Tighten the shift shaft connector bolt to the specification listed in **Table 1** or the standard tightening torque. Install the grommet into the port side of the drive shaft housing.

4. Adjust the shift linkages as instructed in Chapter Five. Connect the spark plug leads. Connect the battery cables to the battery terminals on electric start models. Check for proper shift and cooling system operation before putting the engine into service.

Gearcase Removal (9.9-50 hp [Except E48] Models)

1. Position the shift selector in reverse gear. Disconnect all spark plug leads. Disconnect both battery cables from the battery terminals.

2. Use a marker to reference the trim tab setting (**Figure 15**). Do not use a scribe as it will promote corrosion where the paint was scratched. Locate and remove the bolt access cover (A, **Figure 16**). Use a socket and extension to remove the trim tab bolt and trim tab. Disconnect the

9

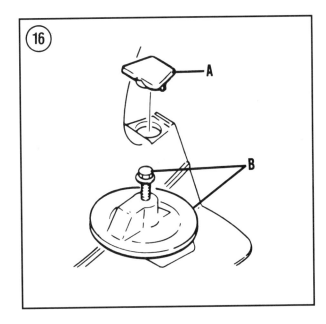

speedometer connection. Cut the hose as close to the connector as possible (1, **Figure 17**).

3. Locate the shift shaft connection (**Figure 18**). Loosen the jam nut (A, **Figure 18**). Mark the position of the connector nut or count the number of turns as you loosen and remove the nut (B, **Figure 18**) from the lower shift shaft. Counting the turns will provide a great deal of help when the shift linkage is adjusted.

4. Note the location and type of all washers during removal. Support the gearcase to prevent it from dropping. Remove the bolts on the side of the gearcase (**Figure 19**) and the bolt(s) located above the propeller shaft (3, **Figure 17**). On the 20 and 25 hp models, remove the reverse lock connector from the shift shaft connection (**Figure 20**).

5. Shake or carefully pry the gearcase from the drive shaft housing. Pry at the points located near the front and rear of the gearcase. Install the water tube into position in the drive shaft housing if dislodged during removal of the gearcase.

Gearcase Installation
(9.9-50 hp [Except E48] Models)

1. Clean debris and contaminants from the drive shaft and shift shaft connector. Apply Yamaha all-purpose grease or its equivalent to the splined connection of the drive shaft and the water tube grommet in the water pump housing (**Figure 21**). Make sure that the dowel or locating pin is properly positioned in the gearcase.

2. Place the shift selector into reverse. Make sure that the shift shaft enters the proper opening. Guide the water tube into the water pump grommet (**Figure 21**) and insert the drive shaft into the splined crankshaft connection. Lower the gearcase and slightly rotate the drive shaft clockwise as viewed from the top if the gearcase and drive shaft housing will not mate. Repeat this until the splined connections align and the housing will mate. Make sure that the water tube enters the water pump grommet each time you attempt to install the gearcase.

3. Apply Loctite 572 to the threads of the attaching bolts. Secure the gearcase in position, then install the fasteners. Tighten the fasteners to the specification provided in **Table 1**. Slightly heat the end of the speedometer hose and install it over the fitting. Do not pull on the hose until cooled.

4. Align the upper and lower shift shafts as indicated in **Figure 22**. Thread the upper shift shaft nut (3, **Figure 22**) onto the lower shift shaft the recorded number of turns or to the marking made prior to removal. Make sure that the nut makes several turns of engagement onto the lower shift shaft. Hold the upper shift shaft nut with a wrench and tighten the jam nut until firmly contacted and locked to the upper shift shaft nut.

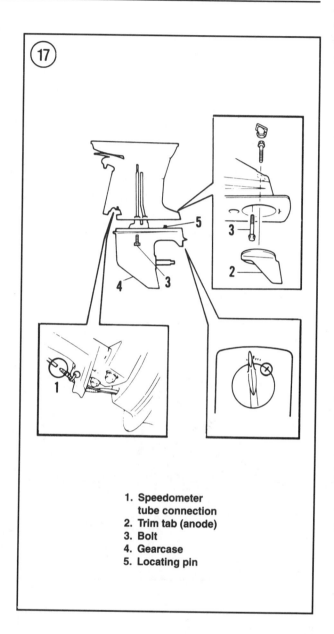

1. Speedometer
   tube connection
2. Trim tab (anode)
3. Bolt
4. Gearcase
5. Locating pin

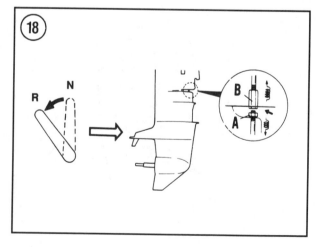

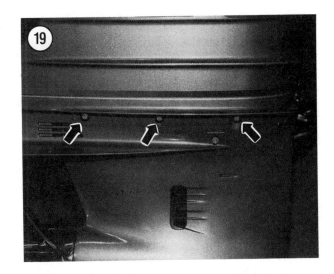

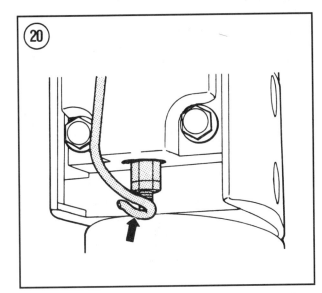

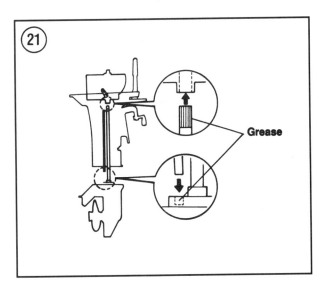

Grease

5. Install the trim tab and bolt. Align the reference marks and tighten the bolt securely. Adjust the shift linkage and/or cables as instructed in Chapter Five. Connect all spark plug leads. Clean then connect the battery cables to the proper battery terminals. Run the engine to check for proper shift and cooling system operation before putting the engine into service.

Gearcase Removal
(E48 and 60-250 hp Models)

1. Disconnect spark plug leads. Disconnect both battery cables from the battery terminals. Position the shift selector into neutral.

2. Use a marker to reference the trim tab position (**Figure 15**). Do not use a scribe as it will promote corrosion where the paint was scratched. Remove the speedometer hose from the fitting. Cut the hose as close as possible to the fitting.

3. Note the type and location of all washers during removal of the mounting bolts. Support the gearcase to prevent it from falling. Locate and remove the bolts (3, **Figure 17**) on the side of the gearcase and above the propeller shaft.

4. Shake or carefully pry the gearcase from the drive shaft housing. Pry at points located near the front and rear of the gearcase. Install the water tube and sealing grommet into position in the drive shaft housing if dislodged during the removal of the gearcase.

9

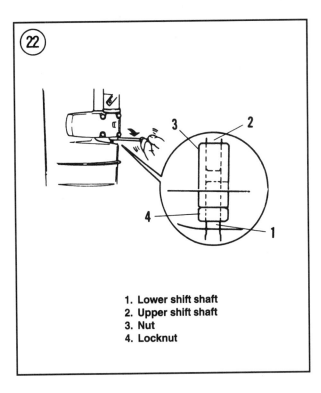

1. **Lower shift shaft**
2. **Upper shift shaft**
3. **Nut**
4. **Locknut**

Gearcase Installation (E48 and 60-250 hp Models)

1. Apply a light coating of Yamaha all-purpose grease or its equivalent to the splined portion of the drive shaft, water tube grommet and locating pins. Position the shift selector in neutral.

2. Install the shift handle (Yamaha part No. YB-6052) onto the lower shift shaft (**Figure 23**).

3. Rotate the drive shaft in the right-hand or clockwise direction while noting the propeller shaft direction (**Figure 23**). Move the shift handle while rotating the drive shaft and mark or make note of the handle position when forward and reverse directions are engaged. Position the shift handle at the point midway between forward and reverse positions (**Figure 23**). Rotate the drive shaft to ensure that the gearcase is in the neutral position. Remove the tool and apply a light coating of grease onto the splines of the lower shift shaft.

4. Guide the water tube into position while inserting the drive shaft into the crankshaft connection. Lower the gearcase and rotate the drive shaft clockwise as viewed from the top if the drive shaft will not engage the crankshaft. Repeat until the shafts align and the gearcase and drive shaft housing will mate. If difficulty is encountered with lower and upper shift shaft alignment, have an assistant slightly toggle the shift selector to align the shift shaft splines. Never force the gearcase into position. This could result in damage to the shift shaft and drive shaft seal.

5. Apply Loctite 572 to the threads of the mounting bolts. Install the bolts and tighten to the specification listed in **Table 1**. Slighty heat the end of the speedometer hose and slide it over the speedometer fitting. Do not pull on the hose until cooled.

6. Attach all spark plug leads. Connect the battery cables to the proper battery terminals. Adjust the shift cable as instructed in Chapter Five. Run the engine and check for proper shift and cooling system operation.

WATER PUMP SERVICING

The water pump must be serviced if the engine is running warmer than normal. Always service the water pump at the intervals listed in Chapter Four.

Replace the impeller, seals, O-rings and all gaskets anytime the water pump is serviced. Never compromise

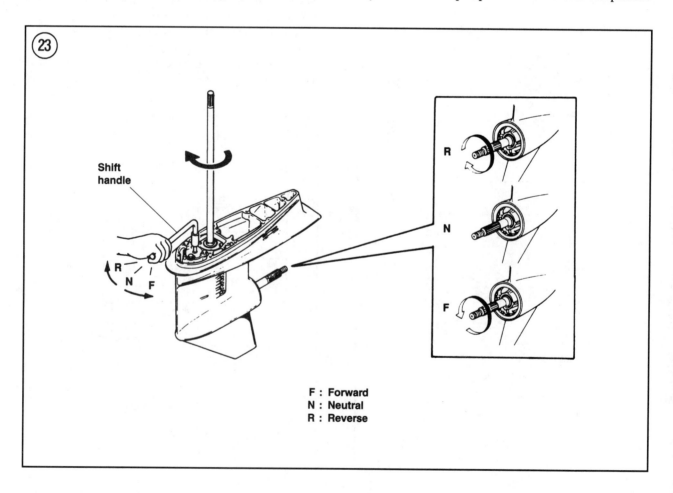

F : Forward
N : Neutral
R : Reverse

the operation of these vital components. Overheating and extensive power head damage can result from a faulty water pump.

Water Pump Disassembly

Component appearances and mounting arrangements vary by model. To assist with component identification and orientation, refer to the illustration that applies to your model during the disassembly procedure. The appearance of the components may differ slightly from the illustration. Four different designs of water pumps are used. Repair procedures are very similar among all the models.

    a. For 2 hp models, refer to **Figure 24**.

    b. For 3-50 hp models (except Model E48), refer to **Figure 25**.

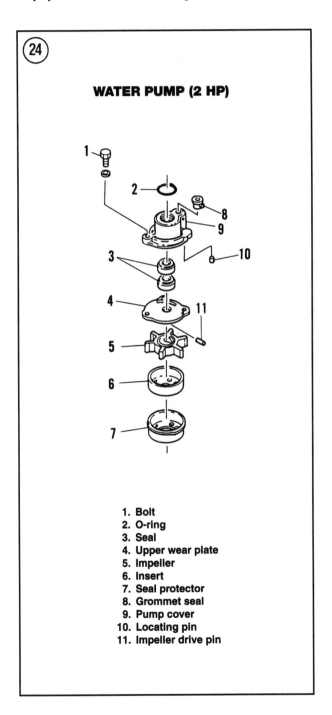

(24)

WATER PUMP (2 HP)

1. Bolt
2. O-ring
3. Seal
4. Upper wear plate
5. Impeller
6. Insert
7. Seal protector
8. Grommet seal
9. Pump cover
10. Locating pin
11. Impeller drive pin

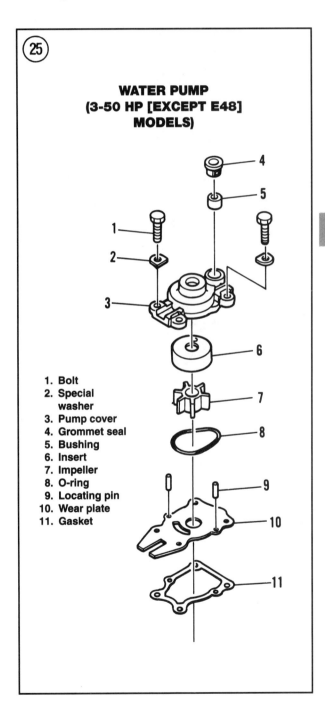

(25)

**WATER PUMP
(3-50 HP [EXCEPT E48]
MODELS)**

1. Bolt
2. Special washer
3. Pump cover
4. Grommet seal
5. Bushing
6. Insert
7. Impeller
8. O-ring
9. Locating pin
10. Wear plate
11. Gasket

9

WATER PUMP (E48, E60, E75 AND 60-90 HP MODELS)

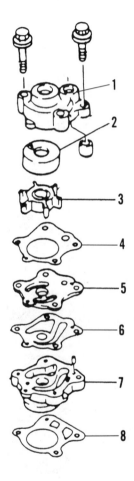

1. Pump cover
2. Insert
3. Impeller
4. Gasket
5. Wear plate
6. Gasket
7. Pump base
8. Gasket

WATER PUMP COMPONENTS (115-250 HP MODELS)

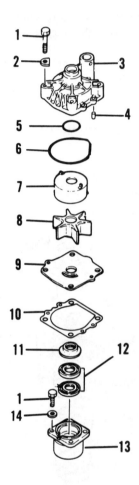

1. Bolt
2. Special washer
3. Pump housing
4. Locating pin
5. O-ring
6. O-ring
7. Insert
8. Impeller
9. Wear plate
10. Gasket
11. Seal protector
12. Upper seal
13. Bearing and seal housing
14. Washer

c. For Model E48 and 60-90 hp models, refer to **Figure 26**.

d. For all V4 and V6, models refer to **Figure 27**.

1. Refer to *Gearcase Removal* in this chapter and remove the gearcase from the engine.

2. Remove the water tube sealing grommet and all fasteners that retain the water pump cover to the water pump base. Remove the plates on 3-20 hp models.

3. Use two screwdrivers to carefully pry the cover from the water pump. Remove and discard the sealing O-ring or gasket that seals the water pump cover to the water pump base. Remove the cover plate on the 2 hp models.

4. Mark the *up* side of the impeller if it must be reused. Remove the water pump impeller from the water pump insert in the cover or base.

5. Drive shaft stabilizing washers are used on 115-225 hp 90° models (except premix models) to reduce gearcase noise. Note the orientation prior to removal of the washers to ensure proper assembly.

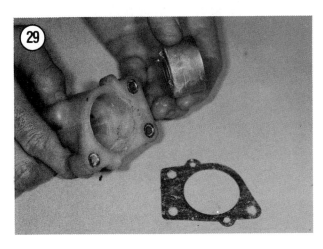

6. Remove the impeller if it remained on the drive shaft when the cover was removed. Use a chisel and carefully break the inner hub of the impeller if it is seized to the drive shaft. Do not allow the chisel to contact or mar the drive shaft. Retain the drive key from the impeller or slot on the drive shaft.

7. On 2 hp models, use a small screwdriver to carefully pry the insert from the gearcase. On 3-250 hp models, *do not* remove the insert from the water pump body unless it must be replaced.

8. On 3-250 hp models, remove the plate from the water pump base. Do not remove the water pump base unless access to drive shaft seals is required.

Water Pump
Component Inspection

Inspect the impeller (**Figure 28**) for brittle, missing or burnt vanes. Squeeze the vanes toward the hub and release the vanes. The vanes should spring back to the extended position. Replace the impeller if damaged, burnt, brittle or stiff vanes are noted. Replace the impeller if vanes are curled.

Inspect the water pump insert for worn or damaged surfaces. Remove and replace the insert if any defect is noted (**Figure 29**). Inspect the water pump cover for melted plastic or indications of impeller material on the insert. Replace the cover and the water pump base if either defect is noted. Refer to *Gearcase Disassembly* for procedures. Inspect the water tube sealing grommet for cracks or brittle material and replace as required.

Inspect the water pump base plate for worn or damaged areas. Replace the base plate if a groove is worn in the plate at the impeller contact area.

Clean all debris or contaminants from the drive shaft. The impeller must slide freely into position on the drive shaft.

Water Pump Assembly

To assist with component identification and orientation, refer to the illustrations that apply to your model during the assembly procedure.

1. Install the water pump base assembly if removed. Refer to *Gearcase Assembly*.

2. On 2 hp models, install the water pump insert into the gearcase if removed. On 3-250 hp models, push the insert into the pump cover if removed. Make sure that the tab on the insert fits into the slot in the pump cover.

9

3. On 25 hp (3-cylinder) and 30 hp models, install a new gasket onto the water pump base. On 3-250 hp models, install the plate onto the pump base (**Figure 30**). Make sure the base fits over the locating pins (A, **Figure 30**). Apply a light coating of Yamaha all-purpose grease or its equivalent into the slot and install the impeller drive key (B, **Figure 30**).

4. On 2 hp models, apply grease to the inner surfaces of the insert. Place the insert into the oil seal protector. Apply grease to the impeller drive key then install it into the slot on the drive shaft. Slide the new impeller over the drive shaft until it contacts the insert. Rotate the drive shaft in the clockwise direction as viewed from the top as you push lightly down on the impeller. Rotate the drive shaft until the impeller has completely entered the insert.

5. On 3-250 hp models, slide the impeller over the drive shaft and position it onto the drive key. Install the collars and washers onto the drive shaft on models so equipped (**Figure 31**).

6. On 3-250 hp models, apply Yamaha all-purpose grease or its equivalent to the surfaces of the insert in the water pump cover. Install a new gasket or O-ring onto the water pump cover. Use a very light coat of 3M Weather-strip Adhesive to hold the gasket or O-ring in position. Slide the cover over the drive shaft and allow it to rest on the impeller vanes.

7. On 3-250 hp models, rotate the drive shaft in the right-hand or clockwise direction as viewed from the top (**Figure 32**) while lightly pressing down on the water pump cover. Continue to rotate the drive shaft while pressing down on the cover until the impeller enters the water pump cover and the cover seats on the base plate.

8. On 2 hp models, apply grease to the impeller contact surfaces and install the plate over the drive shaft and onto the insert. Install the water pump cover into position.

9. For all models, install the fasteners and tighten to the standard tightening torque specifications listed in **Table 1**. Use a crossing pattern and torque in two or more steps. Apply grease and install the water tube sealing grommet into position in the water pump cover. Ensure that the tip on the insert enters the locating hole in the water pump cover.

10. Refer to *Gearcase Installation* and install the gearcase. Run the engine and check for proper operation of the cooling system.

GEARCASE DISASSEMBLY/INSPECTION/ASSEMBLY

This section will provide disassembly, inspection and assembly procedures for the internal components of the gearcase. Gearcases covered include the standard or right-hand rotation gearcase, counter rotation or left-hand gearcase and the twin propeller gearcase. Refer to the procedures for the type of gearcase used.

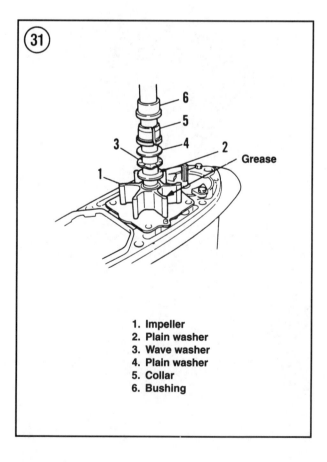

1. Impeller
2. Plain washer
3. Wave washer
4. Plain washer
5. Collar
6. Bushing

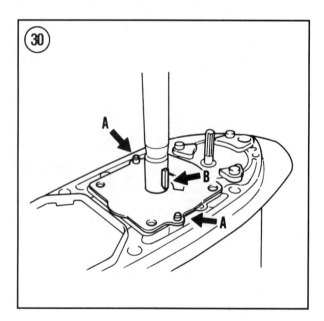

When replacing the propeller shaft seals, refer to the gearcase cap/bearing carrier for procedures to access the seals.

When replacing the seals on the drive shaft, refer to *Water pump servicing* and *Seal/bearing housing* for procedures to access the seals. Drive shaft removal may be required with some models. Refer to *Gearcase disassembly* for procedures when required.

NOTE
Refer to the serial number tag for the type of gearcase used on the engine. Models with an L in the model number use a left-hand or counter-rotation gearcase. Models with a D in the model number use a twin propeller gearcase. Other models will use the standard or right-hand gearcase.

Standard Rotation Gearcase

This section provides complete disassembly, inspection and assembly procedures for the internal components of standard right-hand gearcases.

Procedures unique to counter rotation (left-hand) and D models (twin props) are provided at the end of this section.

When complete disassembly is not required, follow the procedure until the required component is accessible. Reverse the disassembly procedures to install the components. Make notes of the location and orientation of all components prior to removal.

When the repair involves the replacement of gears, bearings, drive shaft or housing, the entire repair and shimming procedures must be followed. This is necessary to ensure that the gears are properly aligned on assembly.

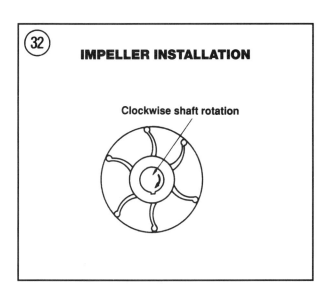

(32)

IMPELLER INSTALLATION

Clockwise shaft rotation

This important step will help maintain wear pattern on moving or sliding surfaces.

The appearance and orientation of the internal components varies by model. Refer to the illustration that applies to your model during the disassembly and assembly procedure.

  a. For 2 hp models, refer to **Figure 33**.
  b. For 3 hp models, refer to **Figure 34**.
  c. For 4 and 5 hp models, refer to **Figure 35**.
  d. For 6 and 8 hp models, refer to **Figure 36**.
  e. For 9.9 and 15 hp models, refer to **Figure 37**.
  f. For 20, 25 hp (2-cylinder) and C30 models, refer to **Figure 38**.
  g. For 25 hp (2-cylinder) and 30 hp models, refer to **Figure 39**.
  h. For Model C40 (2-cylinder), refer to **Figure 40**.
  i. For 40 (3 cylinder) and 50 hp models, refer to **Figure 41**.
  j. For E48 and 60-90 hp models, refer to **Figure 42**.
  k. For 115-225 hp (90°) models, refer to **Figure 43**.
  l. For 200-250 hp (76°) models, refer to **Figure 44**.

Gearcase Disassembly

Remove the gearcase from the engine and remove the components of the water pump from the gearcase before beginning the disassembly process. Refer to *Gearcase Removal and Installation* and *Water Pump Servicing*.

Mount the gearcase in a suitable holding fixture or a sturdy vise with wooden blocks to protect the surfaces of the gearcase. Clamp the gearcase on the skeg (lower fin) when using a vise.

Note the location and thickness of all shims (**Figure 45**) in the gearcase. Use a micrometer to measure and record each shim or spacer in a location. Make sure that all shims are removed before cleaning the gear case. Wire the shims together or place them in an envelope with the location noted on the cover.

Use pressurized water to thoroughly clean all debris from the gearcase prior to disassembly. Pay particular attention to the bearing carrier area. This will help prevent debris from contaminating the bearings during the disassembly process.

The procedures listed will not apply to all models. Refer to **Figure 33-44** to determine if a component described is used on the selected model.

1. Remove the water pump assembly. Refer to *Water Pump*.

2. Drain all gear lubricant from the gearcase. Refer to Chapter Four for procedure.

3A. On 2 and 3 hp models, remove the two bolts and washers that retain the gearcase cap. Use a blunt tip

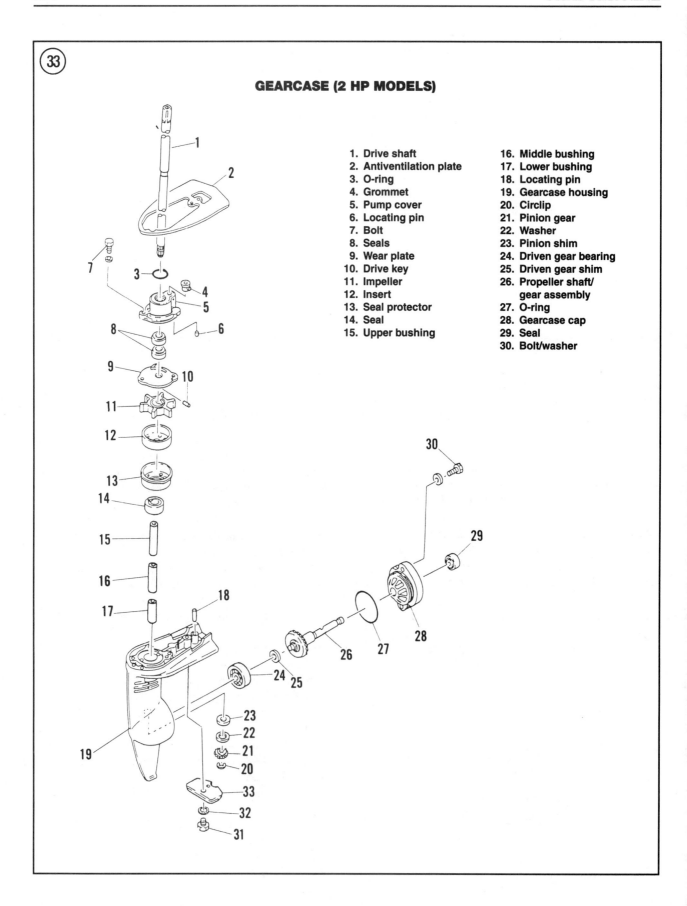

GEARCASE (2 HP MODELS)

1. Drive shaft
2. Antiventilation plate
3. O-ring
4. Grommet
5. Pump cover
6. Locating pin
7. Bolt
8. Seals
9. Wear plate
10. Drive key
11. Impeller
12. Insert
13. Seal protector
14. Seal
15. Upper bushing
16. Middle bushing
17. Lower bushing
18. Locating pin
19. Gearcase housing
20. Circlip
21. Pinion gear
22. Washer
23. Pinion shim
24. Driven gear bearing
25. Driven gear shim
26. Propeller shaft/
    gear assembly
27. O-ring
28. Gearcase cap
29. Seal
30. Bolt/washer

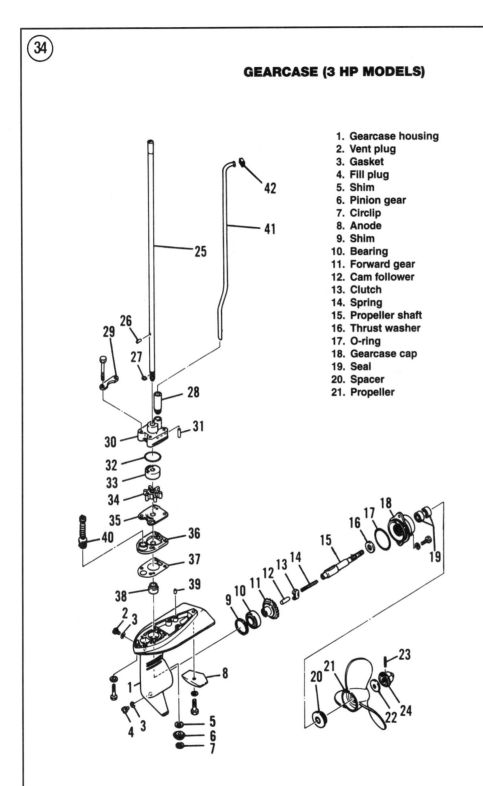

GEARCASE (3 HP MODELS)

1. Gearcase housing
2. Vent plug
3. Gasket
4. Fill plug
5. Shim
6. Pinion gear
7. Circlip
8. Anode
9. Shim
10. Bearing
11. Forward gear
12. Cam follower
13. Clutch
14. Spring
15. Propeller shaft
16. Thrust washer
17. O-ring
18. Gearcase cap
19. Seal
20. Spacer
21. Propeller
22. Washer
23. Shear pin
24. Propeller nut
25. Drive shaft
26. Drive key
27. Clip
28. Water tube seal
29. Plate
30. Pump cover
    (housing)
31. Locating pin
32. O-ring
33. Insert
34. Impeller
35. Wear plate
36. Water pump base
37. Gasket
38. Seal
39. Locating pin
40. Shift shaft bellows
41. Water tube
42. Grommet

9

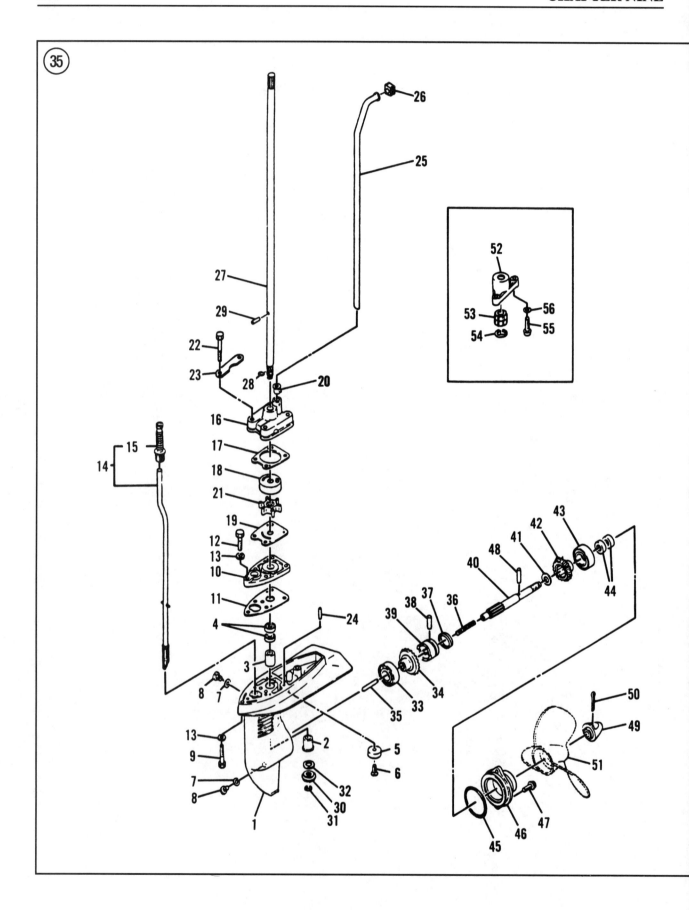

GEARCASE (4 AND 5 HP MODELS)

1. Gearcase housing
2. Bushing
3. Bushing
4. Seals
5. Anode
6. Bolt
7. Gasket
8. Plug
9. Bolt
10. Water pump base
11. Gasket
12. Bolt
13. Lockwasher
14. Shift shaft assembly
15. Shift shaft bellows
16. Pump cover
17. Gasket
18. Insert
19. Wear plate
20. Grommet seal
21. Impeller
22. Bolt
23. Plate
24. Locating pin
25. Water tube
26. Grommet
27. Drive shaft
28. Clip
29. Drive key
30. Pinion gear
31. Circlip
32. Shim
33. Forward gear bearing
34. Forward gear
35. Cam follower
36. Spring
37. Spring
38. Cross pin
39. Clutch
40. Propeller shaft
41. Thrust washer
42. Reverse gear
43. Reverse gear bearing
44. Propeller shaft seals
45. O-ring
46. Gearcase cap
47. Bolt
48. Shear pin
49. Propeller nut
50. Cotter pin
51. Propeller
52. Bushing housing (long shaft models)
53. Bushing (long shaft models)
54. Clip (long shaft models)
55. Bolt (long shaft models)
56. Washer (long shaft models)

9

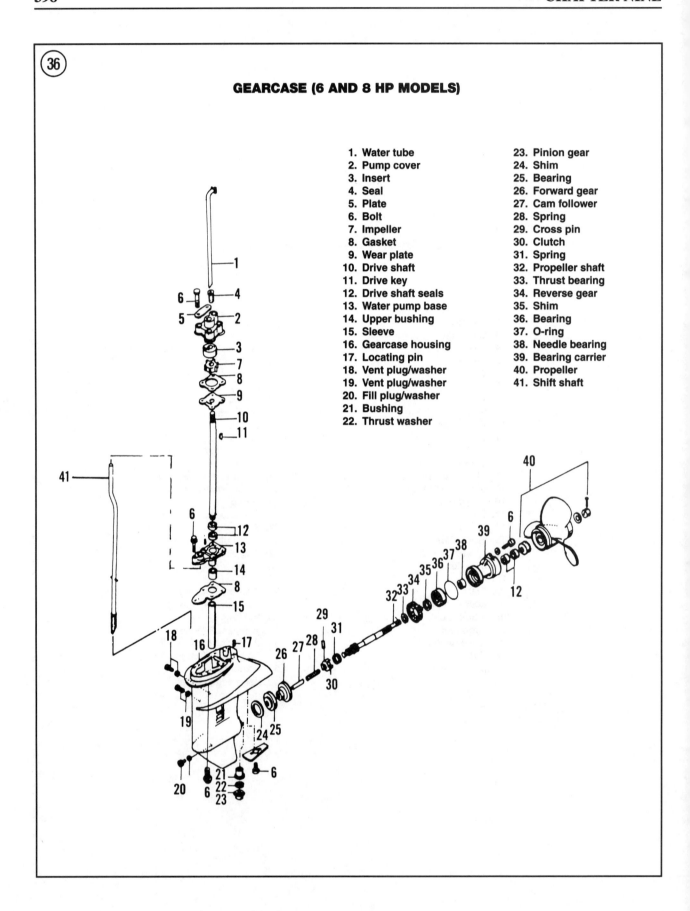

GEARCASE (6 AND 8 HP MODELS)

1. Water tube
2. Pump cover
3. Insert
4. Seal
5. Plate
6. Bolt
7. Impeller
8. Gasket
9. Wear plate
10. Drive shaft
11. Drive key
12. Drive shaft seals
13. Water pump base
14. Upper bushing
15. Sleeve
16. Gearcase housing
17. Locating pin
18. Vent plug/washer
19. Vent plug/washer
20. Fill plug/washer
21. Bushing
22. Thrust washer
23. Pinion gear
24. Shim
25. Bearing
26. Forward gear
27. Cam follower
28. Spring
29. Cross pin
30. Clutch
31. Spring
32. Propeller shaft
33. Thrust bearing
34. Reverse gear
35. Shim
36. Bearing
37. O-ring
38. Needle bearing
39. Bearing carrier
40. Propeller
41. Shift shaft

GEARCASE (9.9 AND 15 HP MODELS)

1. Drive shaft
2. Bolt
3. Plate
4. Grommet seal
5. Pump cover
6. Impeller
7. O-ring
8. Locating pin
9. Drive shaft seals
10. Bushing
11. Gasket
12. Lubrication sleeve
13. Shift shaft
14. Water inlet
15. Nut
16. Bearing
17. Shim
18. Pinion gear
19. Pinion nut
20. Bolt/washer
21. Propeller shaft seals
22. Needle bearing
23. O-ring
24. Spacer
25. Reverse gear bearing
26. Shim
27. Reverse gear
28. Propeller shaft
29. Spring
30. Follower
31. Spring
32. Clutch
33. Cross pin
34. Forward gear
35. Forward gear bearing
36. Bearing race
37. Shim
38. Water inlet
39. Bolt
40. Washer
41. Bolt
42. Anode
43. Bolt
44. Wear plate
45. Water pump base
46. Bearing carrier

9

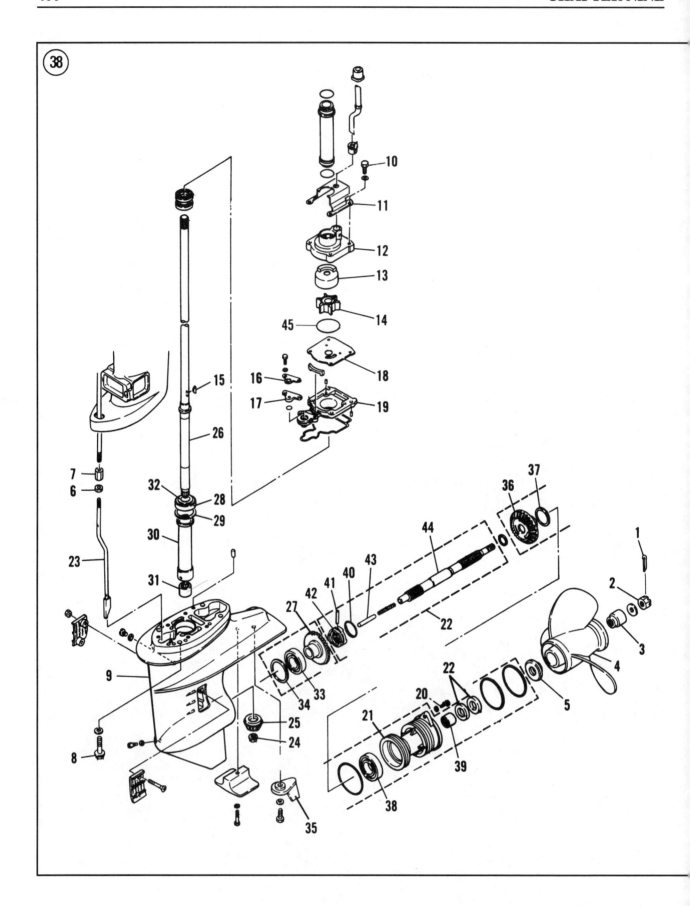

**GEARCASE (20 AND 25 HP [TWO-CYLINDER]
AND C30 MODELS)**

1. Cotter pin
2. Propeller nut
3. Bushing
4. Propeller
5. Forward spacer
6. Nut
7. Connector
8. Bolt/washer
9. Gearcase housing
10. Bolt/washer
11. Cover
12. Water pump body
13. Insert
14. Impeller
15. Drive key
16. Plate
17. Cover
18. Wear plate
19. Water pump base
20. Bolt/washer
21. Bearing carrier
22. Seals
23. Shift shaft/cam assembly

24. Pinion nut
25. Pinion gear
26. Drive shaft
27. Forward gear
28. Bearing race
29. Shim
30. Lubrication sleeve
31. Needle bearing
32. Bearing
33. Bearing
34. Shim
35. Trim tab
36. Reverse gear
37. Shim
38. Bearing
39. Needle bearing
40. Spring
41. Cross pin
42. Clutch
43. Follower
44. Propeller shaft
45. O-ring

9

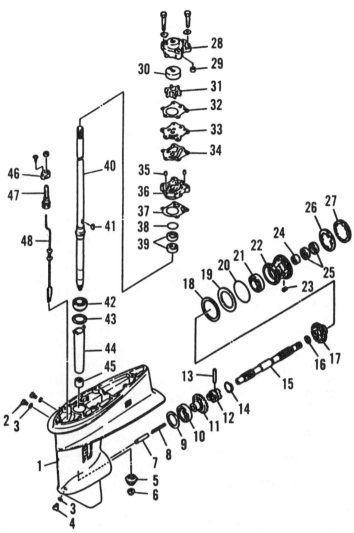

**GEARCASE
(25 AND 30 HP [THREE-CYLINDER] MODELS)**

1. Gearcase housing
2. Vent plug
3. Gasket
4. Fill plug
5. Pinion gear
6. Pinion nut
7. Follower
8. Spring
9. Shim
10. Forward gear bearing
11. Forward gear
12. Clutch
13. Cross pin
14. Spring
15. Propeller shaft
16. Thrust washer

17. Reverse gear
18. Shim
19. Thrust washer
20. O-ring
21. Reverse gear bearing
22. Bearing carrier
23. Locating key
24. Needle bearing
25. Propeller shaft seals
26. Locking tab washer
27. Cover nut
28. Pump cover
29. Grommet
30. Insert
31. Impeller
32. Gasket

33. Wear plate
34. Gasket
35. Locating pin
36. Water pump base
37. Gasket
38. O-ring
39. Drive shaft seals
40. Drive shaft
41. Drive key
42. Drive shaft bearing
43. Shim
44. Lubrication sleeve
45. Drive shaft
    lower bearing
46. Retainer
47. Shift shaft bellows
48. Shift shaft

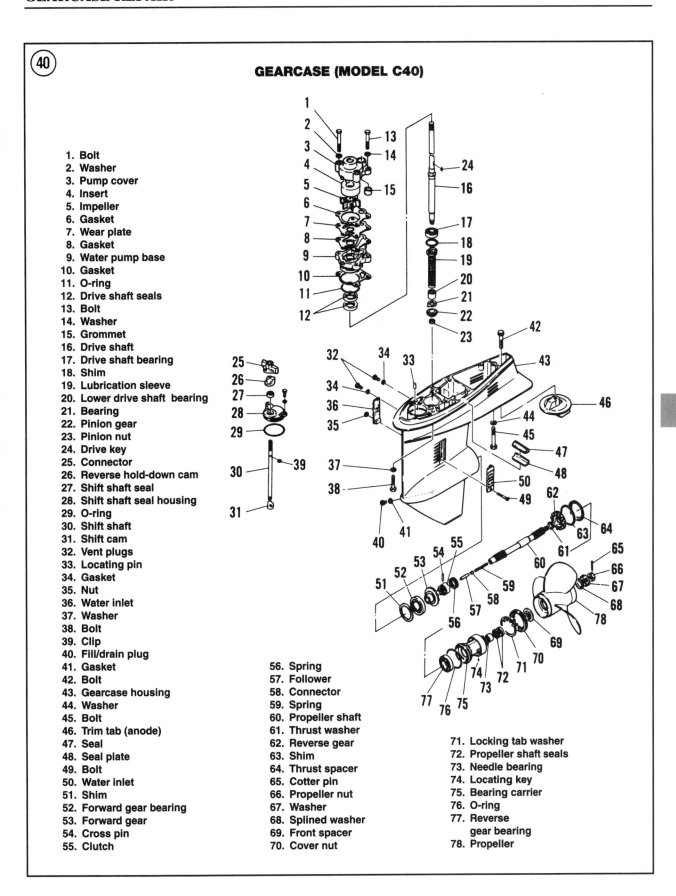

GEARCASE (MODEL C40)

1. Bolt
2. Washer
3. Pump cover
4. Insert
5. Impeller
6. Gasket
7. Wear plate
8. Gasket
9. Water pump base
10. Gasket
11. O-ring
12. Drive shaft seals
13. Bolt
14. Washer
15. Grommet
16. Drive shaft
17. Drive shaft bearing
18. Shim
19. Lubrication sleeve
20. Lower drive shaft bearing
21. Bearing
22. Pinion gear
23. Pinion nut
24. Drive key
25. Connector
26. Reverse hold-down cam
27. Shift shaft seal
28. Shift shaft seal housing
29. O-ring
30. Shift shaft
31. Shift cam
32. Vent plugs
33. Locating pin
34. Gasket
35. Nut
36. Water inlet
37. Washer
38. Bolt
39. Clip
40. Fill/drain plug
41. Gasket
42. Bolt
43. Gearcase housing
44. Washer
45. Bolt
46. Trim tab (anode)
47. Seal
48. Seal plate
49. Bolt
50. Water inlet
51. Shim
52. Forward gear bearing
53. Forward gear
54. Cross pin
55. Clutch

56. Spring
57. Follower
58. Connector
59. Spring
60. Propeller shaft
61. Thrust washer
62. Reverse gear
63. Shim
64. Thrust spacer
65. Cotter pin
66. Propeller nut
67. Washer
68. Splined washer
69. Front spacer
70. Cover nut

71. Locking tab washer
72. Propeller shaft seals
73. Needle bearing
74. Locating key
75. Bearing carrier
76. O-ring
77. Reverse
 gear bearing
78. Propeller

9

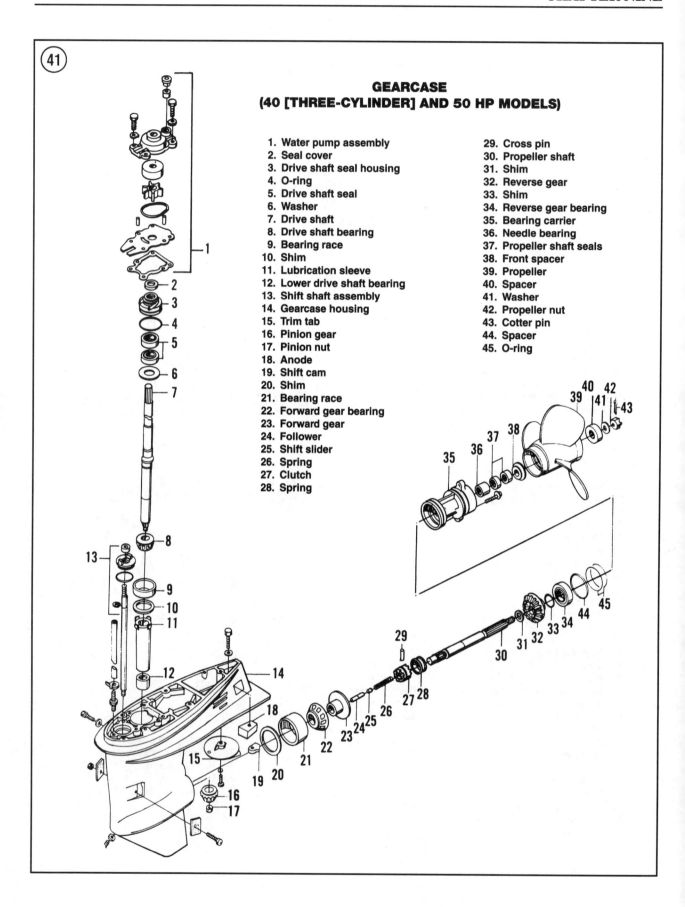

**GEARCASE
(40 [THREE-CYLINDER] AND 50 HP MODELS)**

1. Water pump assembly
2. Seal cover
3. Drive shaft seal housing
4. O-ring
5. Drive shaft seal
6. Washer
7. Drive shaft
8. Drive shaft bearing
9. Bearing race
10. Shim
11. Lubrication sleeve
12. Lower drive shaft bearing
13. Shift shaft assembly
14. Gearcase housing
15. Trim tab
16. Pinion gear
17. Pinion nut
18. Anode
19. Shift cam
20. Shim
21. Bearing race
22. Forward gear bearing
23. Forward gear
24. Follower
25. Shift slider
26. Spring
27. Clutch
28. Spring
29. Cross pin
30. Propeller shaft
31. Shim
32. Reverse gear
33. Shim
34. Reverse gear bearing
35. Bearing carrier
36. Needle bearing
37. Propeller shaft seals
38. Front spacer
39. Propeller
40. Spacer
41. Washer
42. Propeller nut
43. Cotter pin
44. Spacer
45. O-ring

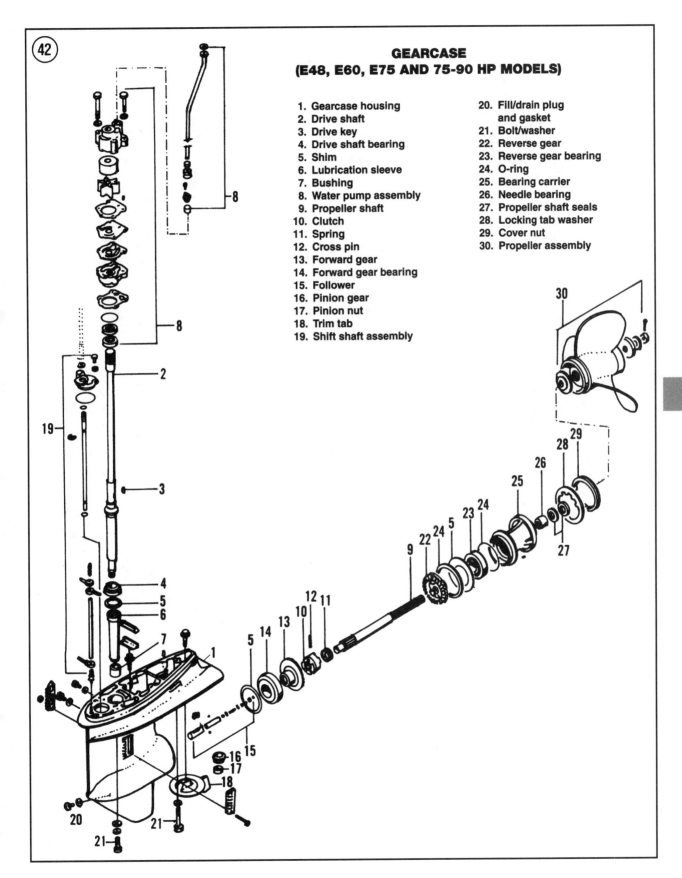

42

GEARCASE
(E48, E60, E75 AND 75-90 HP MODELS)

1. Gearcase housing
2. Drive shaft
3. Drive key
4. Drive shaft bearing
5. Shim
6. Lubrication sleeve
7. Bushing
8. Water pump assembly
9. Propeller shaft
10. Clutch
11. Spring
12. Cross pin
13. Forward gear
14. Forward gear bearing
15. Follower
16. Pinion gear
17. Pinion nut
18. Trim tab
19. Shift shaft assembly

20. Fill/drain plug
    and gasket
21. Bolt/washer
22. Reverse gear
23. Reverse gear bearing
24. O-ring
25. Bearing carrier
26. Needle bearing
27. Propeller shaft seals
28. Locking tab washer
29. Cover nut
30. Propeller assembly

9

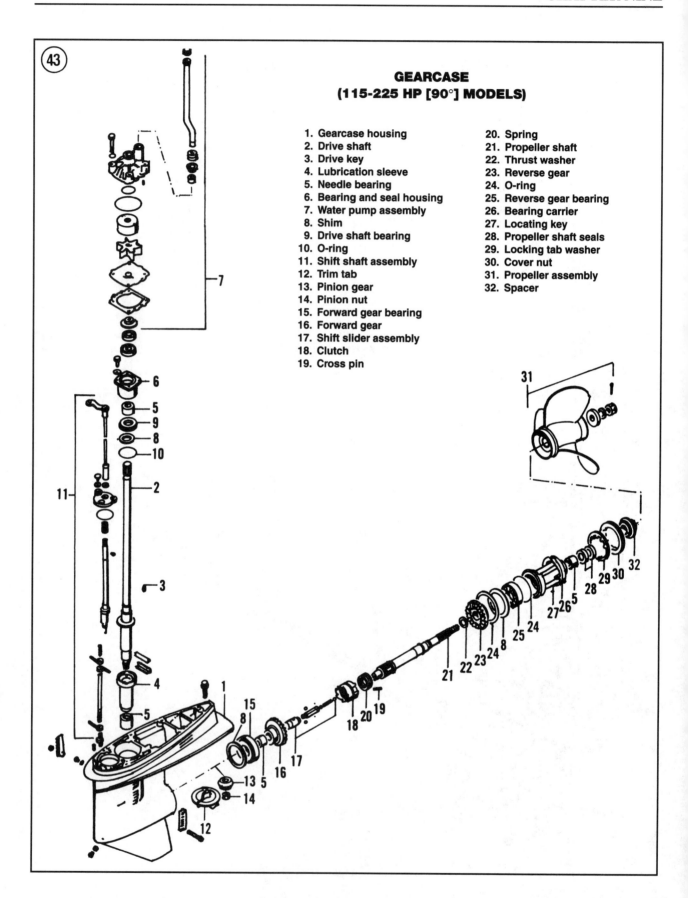

**GEARCASE
(115-225 HP [90°] MODELS)**

1. Gearcase housing
2. Drive shaft
3. Drive key
4. Lubrication sleeve
5. Needle bearing
6. Bearing and seal housing
7. Water pump assembly
8. Shim
9. Drive shaft bearing
10. O-ring
11. Shift shaft assembly
12. Trim tab
13. Pinion gear
14. Pinion nut
15. Forward gear bearing
16. Forward gear
17. Shift slider assembly
18. Clutch
19. Cross pin
20. Spring
21. Propeller shaft
22. Thrust washer
23. Reverse gear
24. O-ring
25. Reverse gear bearing
26. Bearing carrier
27. Locating key
28. Propeller shaft seals
29. Locking tab washer
30. Cover nut
31. Propeller assembly
32. Spacer

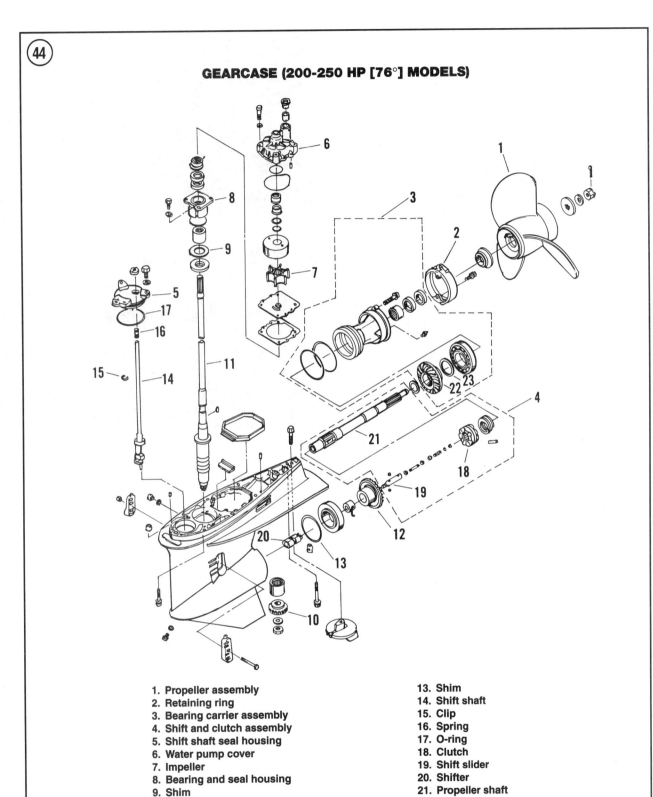

GEARCASE (200-250 HP [76°] MODELS)

1. Propeller assembly
2. Retaining ring
3. Bearing carrier assembly
4. Shift and clutch assembly
5. Shift shaft seal housing
6. Water pump cover
7. Impeller
8. Bearing and seal housing
9. Shim
10. Pinion gear
11. Drive shaft
12. Forward gear
13. Shim
14. Shift shaft
15. Clip
16. Spring
17. O-ring
18. Clutch
19. Shift slider
20. Shifter
21. Propeller shaft
22. Reverse gear
23. Shim

9

screwdriver and carefully pry the case from the housing. Remove the O-ring located between the gearcase and cap and discard it.

3B. On 4-25 (two-cylinder), 40 and 50 models, remove the two bolts and washers from the bearing carrier (**Figure 46**). Use a blunt tip screwdriver to carefully pry the bearing carrier assembly slightly away from the mating surface. Hold the propeller shaft into the housing with a thumb and pull the bearing carrier from the gearcase (**Figure 47**). Remove the large O-ring from the bearing carrier and discard it. Place the bearing carrier assembly, gear side up, in a safe area to prevent damage to the reverse gear.

NOTE
To assist with the removal of the gearcase cap or bearing carrier, use a torch to apply heat to the gearcase near the gearcase-to-cap mating surface.

CAUTION
Never heat the housing to the point that the finish is burned. Continually move the flame around the mating surface to apply heat evenly. Excessive use of heat can distort or melt the gearcase.

4. On 25 hp (three-cylinder), 30, C40, E48 and all 60-225 hp (90°) models, use a screwdriver to bend the tabs on the locking tab washer (2, **Figure 48**) away from the cover nut (1, **Figure 48**). Use the correct cover nut tool and turn it counterclockwise to remove the cover nut.

   a. For 25 hp (3-cylinder) and 30 hp models, use cover nut tool part No. YB-06075/90890-06510.

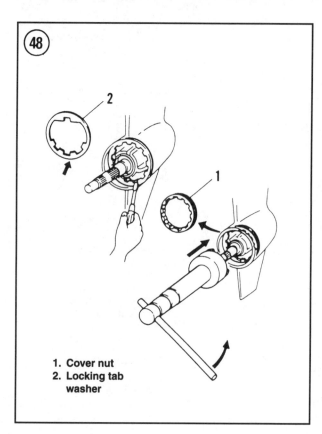

1. Cover nut
2. Locking tab washer

b. For models E48 and C40, use cover nut tool part No. YB-06048/90890-6510.

c. For 60-130 hp models, use cover nut tool part No. YB-34447/90890-06511.

d. For 150-225 hp (90°) models, use cover nut tool part No. YB-34447/90890-06512.

NOTE
Apply heat if necessary to assist with the removal of the cover nut on models so equipped. If corrosion prevents rotation and

removal of the cover nut, drill two holes approximately 25 mm (1 in.) apart into the surface of the cover nut. Drill the holes to the depth of the cover nut thickness. Use a chisel to break a small section from the cover nut at the drilled holes. Remove the cover nut with the cover nut tool as indicated.

5. On the models listed in Step 4, use the universal puller (part No. YB-6117). Use puller claws (part No. YB-6234 for 25-40 hp models) to remove the bearing carrier as indicated in (**Figure 49**). Use puller claws (part No. YB-6207) for 60-225 hp models. Remove the large O-ring from the bearing carrier.

6. On 200-250 hp (76°) models, remove the two bolts (A, **Figure 50**) from the ring (B, **Figure 50**). Remove the ring (B, **Figure 50**) from the gearcase. Remove the two bolts (A, **Figure 51**) from the bearing carrier (B, **Figure 51**). Use the puller (part No. YB-6117) and puller claws (part No. YB-6207) to pull the bearing carrier and gear assembly from the gearcase as indicated in **Figure 52**. Remove the large O-ring from the bearing carrier and discard it. Ensure that the bearing carrier locating key is retrieved from the

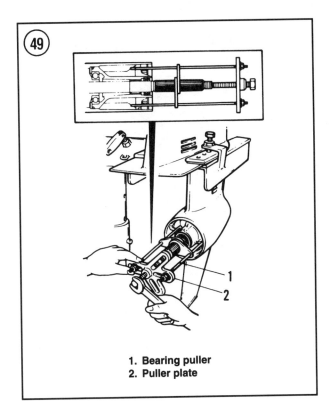

49

1. Bearing puller
2. Puller plate

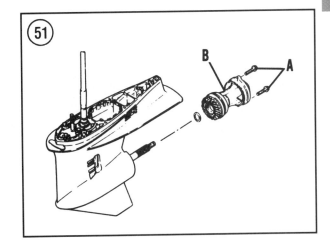

51

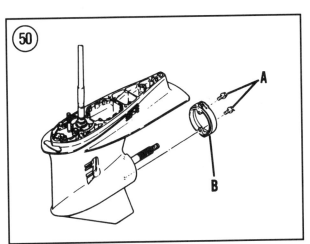

50

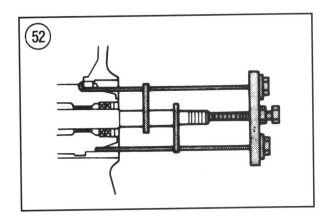

52

9

bearing carrier (**Figure 53**) or gearcase on removal. Refer to **Figures 33-44** to determine if a locating key is used on your model.

7. Manipulate the shift shaft and rotate the drive shaft clockwise, as viewed from the top, until neutral is obtained (no propeller shaft rotation). On 4-25 hp (two-cylinder) models, the water pump base must be removed prior to removing the shift shaft. Remove the bolts and cover for

the shift shaft (**Figure 54** or **Figure 55**). Remove the reverse lock cam, if so equipped, and any seals or couplings on the shift shaft. Carefully pull the shift shaft from the gearcase. Do not rotate the shift shaft or propeller shaft during removal of the shift shaft.

8. On 2 hp models, use needlenose pliers to pull the circlip from the pinion gear/drive shaft connection (**Figure 56**). Pull up on the drive shaft and remove the pinion gear, shim

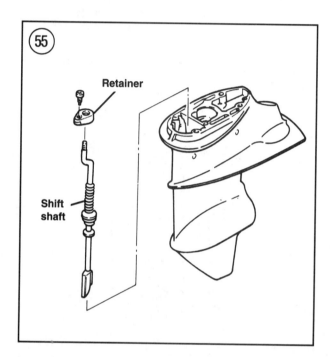

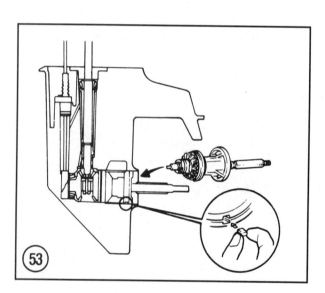

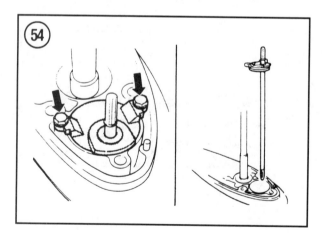

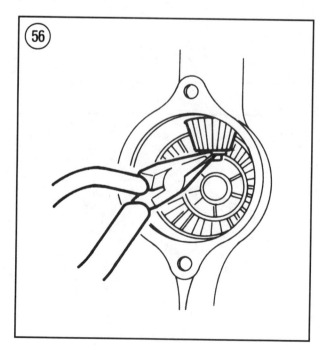

and washer. Pull the drive shaft from the gearcase. Pull the propeller shaft and driven gear assembly from the gear-case.

9. Use care to avoid rotating the propeller shaft during removal. Pull the propeller shaft (C, **Figure 57**) from the gearcase. Place the propeller shaft assembly on a stable work surface. Make sure that the shaft cannot roll off the surface. On 40-70 hp models, reach into the gearcase and

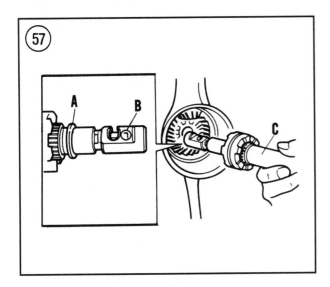

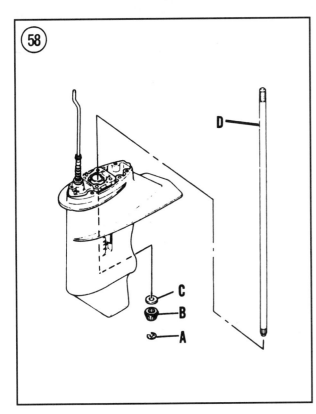

remove the shift cam from the forward end of the gearcase. Use long needlenose pliers if necessary.

10. On 3-8 hp models, use needlenose pliers (**Figure 56**) to remove the circlip from the pinion gear/drive shaft connection. Prior to removal, note the orientation of the washers, shims or spacers on the pinion gear and drive shaft. Pull the drive shaft in the up direction to remove the pinion gear, related washers and shims (A-C, **Figure 58**). Pull the drive shaft (D, **Figure 58**) from the housing.

11. On 9.9-250 hp models, select the correct splined drive shaft adapter indicated for your model.

    a. For 9.9-15 hp models, use adapter part No. YB-6228.

    b. For 20 and 25 hp (two-cylinder) models, use adapter part No. YB-6238.

    c. For 25 hp (three-cylinder) and 30-50 hp models (except Model E48), use adapter part No. YB-6079.

    d. For E60, 60 and 70 hp models, use adapter part No. YB-6049.

    e. For Model E48 and 75-90 hp models, use adapter part No. YB-6151.

    f. For 115-250 hp models, use adapter part No. YB-6201.

NOTE
Prior to removal, note the location and ori-entation of the pinion nut, washers, shims or spacers on the pinion gear or drive shaft.

12. On 9.9-250 hp models, use a suitable socket wrench to properly engage the pinion nut. Use shop towels to protect the inner surfaces of the gearcase from damage. Attach a socket and hinge handle to the splined drive shaft adapter. Place the adapter onto the splined section of the drive shaft (**Figure 59**). Make sure that the socket is properly engaged to the pinion nut, then rotate the drive shaft in the left-hand

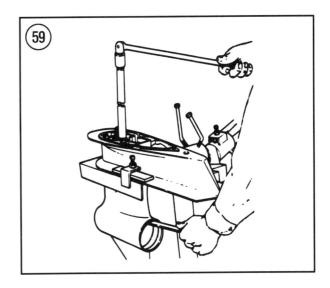

9

or counterclockwise direction to loosen and remove the pinion nut.

13. On 115-250 hp models, remove the four bolts that retain the bearing and seal housing to the gearcase (**Figure 60**). On 40 and 50 hp models, use two screwdrivers to carefully pry the oil seal carrier from the gearcase.

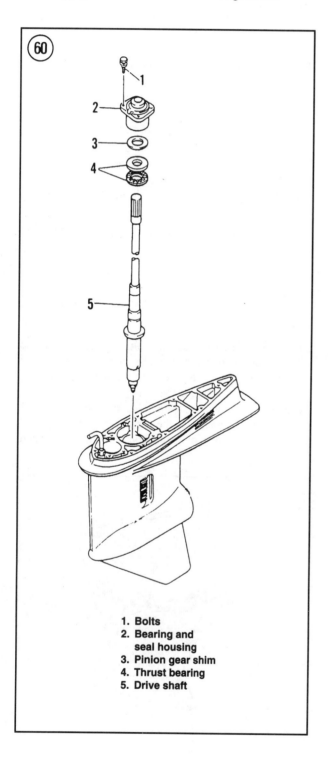

1. Bolts
2. Bearing and seal housing
3. Pinion gear shim
4. Thrust bearing
5. Drive shaft

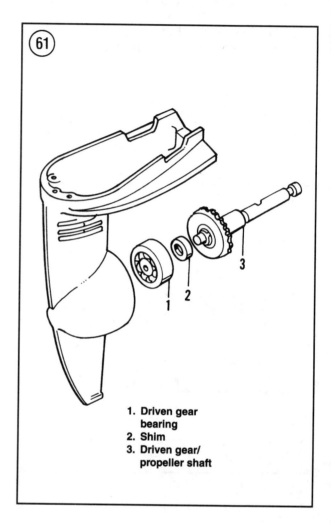

1. Driven gear bearing
2. Shim
3. Driven gear/ propeller shaft

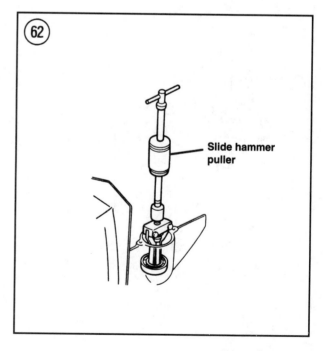

Slide hammer puller

14. On 9.9-250 hp models, note the location and orientation of the pinion gear, then remove the gear along with all related washers, shims and spacers. Pull the drive shaft from the gearcase. On 115-250 hp models, note the location and orientation of the shim and thrust bearing, then remove them from the drive shaft. Measure and record the thickness of the shim. Drive shaft removal can be difficult. When necessary, clamp the drive shaft in a soft-jawed vise. Place a large sponge in the gearcase opening to prevent components from falling from the housing. Support the gearcase and use a block of wood for a cushion to carefully drive the gearcase from the shaft.

15. For all models, pull the forward driven gear from the gearcase. Use a slide hammer (part No. YB-6096) and puller assembly (part No. 90890-06535) to remove the gear when it cannot be easily pulled from the gearcase.

16. On 3-5 hp models, reach into the gearcase and rotate the ball bearing (1, **Figure 61**). Leave the bearing in the gearcase unless the gear lubricant is contaminated with debris or the bearing feels rough or loose when rotated. Use the slide hammer and puller assembly listed in Step 15 to remove the bearing from the gearcase as indicated (**Figure 62**).

17. Use a slide hammer and puller assembly (**Figure 63**) to remove the bearing race (A, **Figure 63**) and shims (B, **Figure 63**) from the gearcase. Refer to Step 15 for the part numbers of the tools. Use a micrometer to measure each shim thickness individually. Record the total shim thickness.

18. On 2-5 hp models equipped with drive shaft seals installed into the gearcase (A, **Figure 64**), use a depth micrometer to measure the distance from the gearcase surface to the top of the outer seal (B, **Figure 64**). Working carefully to avoid damaging the gearcase, pry the seals from the gearcase with a blunt tip screwdriver or suitable pry bar.

19. On 25 hp (3-cylinder)-90 hp models with the tapered bearing race located in the housing, remove the race and shims with a slide hammer and puller assembly as indicated (**Figure 65**). For the tool part number refer to Step

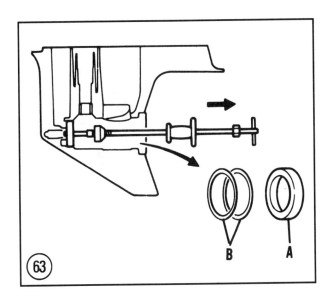

63

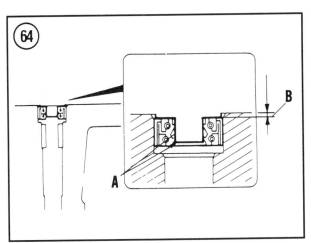

64

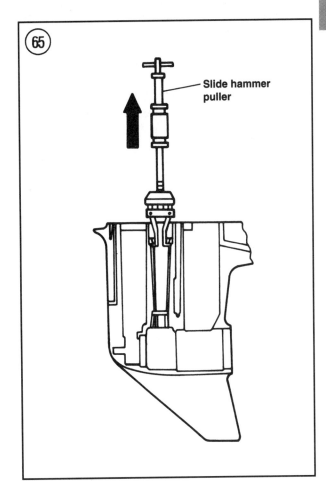

65 — Slide hammer puller

9

15. Measure each shim individually and record the total shim thickness.

Gearcase Cap/Bearing Carrier Disassembly

Disassembly of the gearcase cap/bearing carrier assembly involves the removal of the support bearing or the seals for the propeller shaft.

Always measure the depth of the propeller shaft seals prior to removal. This is necessary to ensure that the seals are positioned properly on assembly. Use a depth micrometer to measure the seal depth at the points indicated. Refer to **Figure 66** for 2-5 hp models. Refer to **Figure 67** for all other models. Record the seal depth measurement.

1. On 6-250 hp models, remove the seals along with the propeller shaft support bearing when bearing removal is required. Remove the seals using the following method when bearing removal is not required. Use a blunt tip screwdriver or suitable pry bar to remove the seals from the assembly. Work carefully and pad any contact surfaces to prevent damage to the seal bore. Discard both oil seals.

2. On 4-250 hp models, grasp and spin the reverse gear. Note the presence of rough operation or a loose feel to the bearing. Replace the bearing if either of these conditions is noted. Refer to component inspection to determine if gear replacement is required. Remove the reverse gear and ball bearing assembly only if replacement is required. Remove the reverse gear and bearing as follows:

    a. On 6-15 hp models, use two flat tip screwdrivers and carefully pry the reverse gear from the bearing (**Figure 68**).

    b. On 20-250 hp models, use a slide hammer (part No. YB-6096) and puller assembly (part No. YB-90890-06536) to remove the reverse gear from the bearing carrier. Clamp the bearing carrier firmly into a vise using soft jaws. Engage the puller jaws into the inner bore of the gear (**Figure 69**). Slide the hammer against the stop until the gear or gear and bearing slide from the bearing carrier.

    c. Remove the ball bearing from the bearing carrier using a slide hammer and puller assembly. Refer to Step 2 for the part numbers of the tools. Clamp the bearing carrier firmly into a vise using soft jaws. Engage the jaws of the puller into the bore of the

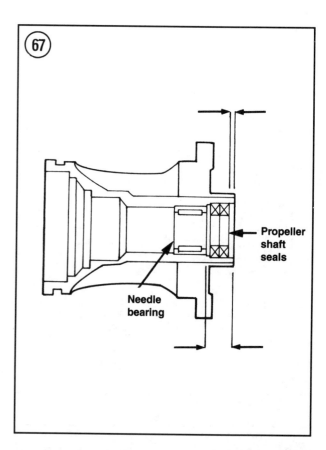

Propeller shaft seals

Needle bearing

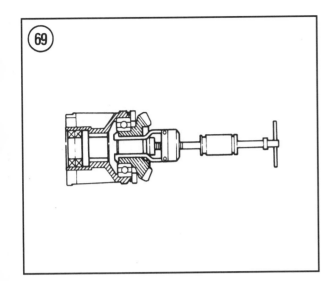

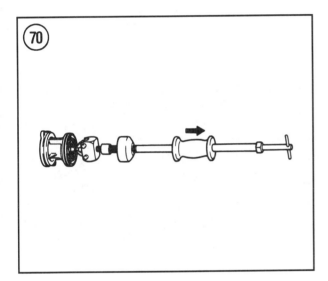

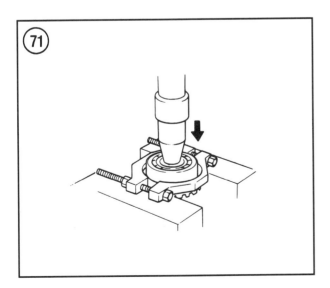

bearing (**Figure 70**). Slide the hammer against the stop until the bearing slides from the bore. Discard the bearing after removal.

    d. In some instances, the bearing will remain on the reverse gear when removed from the bearing carrier. Clamp a bearing separator plate (part No. YB-6219-90890) onto the ball bearing (**Figure 71**). Select a piece of rod or pipe slightly smaller than the bore of the bearing to press the hub of the reverse gear from the bearing. Discard the bearing after removal.

3. Remove the propeller shaft support bearing only if replacement is required. Refer to *Component Inspection* to determine if replacement is required. Use a depth micrometer to measure the depth of the bearing within the bore prior to removal. This is necessary to ensure that the bearing will contact the propeller shaft at the proper location when assembled. Measure the depth at the point indicated (B, **Figure 67**). Record the measurement. Remove the propeller shaft support bearing as follows:

    a. Place the bearing carrier with the seals facing down over an open area. The opening must allow for the removal of the seals and bearings (**Figure 72**).

    b. Select an appropriately sized socket, pipe or rod to drive the bearing and seals from the bearing carrier. The rod, pipe or socket used must be slightly larger than the inner bore of the bearing yet not large enough in diameter to contact the bearing bore within the bearing carrier.

    c. Use an extension bar and carefully tap the bearing and seals from the bearing carrier (**Figure 72**).

    d. Discard the seals and bearing.

9

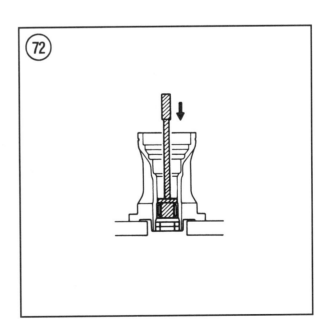

Propeller shaft disassembly

The propeller shaft is integral with the driven gear on 2 hp models.

1A. On 3 hp models, press the cam follower (1, **Figure 73**) inward to collapse the spring (3, **Figure 73**) and move the sliding clutch (2, **Figure 73**) rearward in the slot. Slide the clutch from the slot while the spring is collapsed. Remove the cam follower and spring (1 and 3, **Figure 73**) from the propeller shaft.

1B. On 4-70 hp and E75 models, a spring-loaded follower is used to move the clutch (1, **Figure 74**). The cross pin retaining spring (5, **Figure 74**) is wrapped around the dog clutch to retain the cross pin (6, **Figure 74**). Disassemble the propeller shaft as follows:

   a. Use a small screwdriver to unwind the spring from the clutch (**Figure 75**).

   b. Press inward on the cam follower (**Figure 76**) to collapse the spring. Use needlenose pliers to pull the cross pin from the clutch. Slowly release the spring tension.

   c. Note the location and orientation of the clutch, cam follower, spring and related components then remove them from the propeller shaft.

1C. On 75-250 hp models (except Model E75), a dual action cam-type shifter (1, **Figure 77**) is used to move the clutch. Detent balls located on the shift slider (3, **Figure 77**) engage slots within the shifter bore to provide smooth shifting and positive engagement.

Perform the disassembly procedure over a box or parts pan as small parts will likely fall from the propeller shaft.

Disassemble the propeller shaft as follows:

   a. Remove the shift actuator (B, **Figure 78**) from the slot in the shifter (A, **Figure 78**).

   b. Use a small screwdriver to unwind the spring (C, **Figure 78**) from the sliding clutch.

   c. With the spring removed, pull or push the cross pin (C, **Figure 79**) from the sliding clutch.

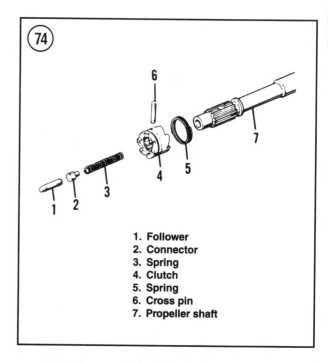

1. Follower
2. Connector
3. Spring
4. Clutch
5. Spring
6. Cross pin
7. Propeller shaft

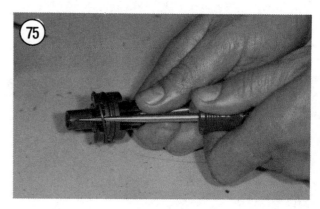

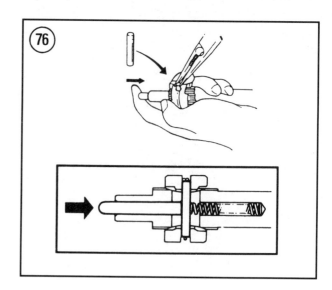

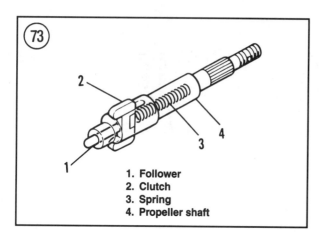

1. Follower
2. Clutch
3. Spring
4. Propeller shaft

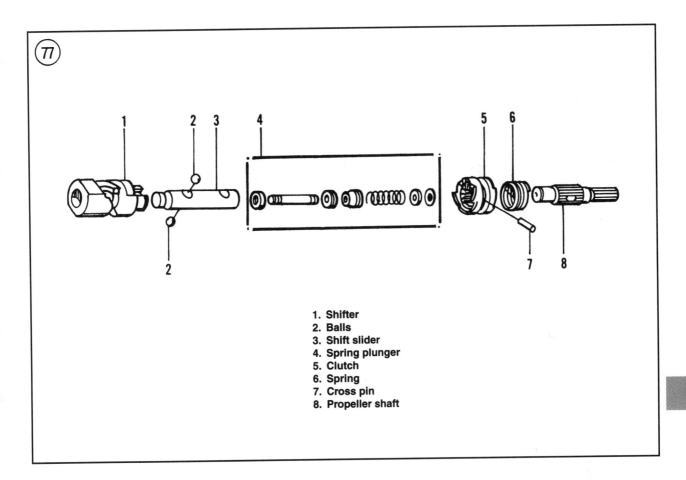

1. Shifter
2. Balls
3. Shift slider
4. Spring plunger
5. Clutch
6. Spring
7. Cross pin
8. Propeller shaft

9

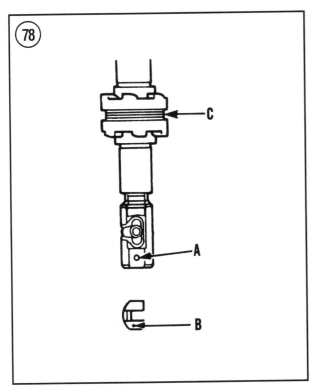

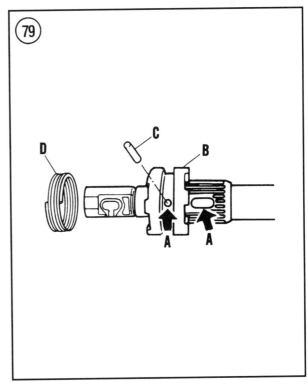

d. Slide the clutch from the propeller shaft. Work slowly and carefully to avoid lost components and use a screwdriver to pry the shifter assembly from the propeller shaft as indicated (**Figure 80**).

e. Remove the balls, springs and followers from the propeller shaft. Separate the shift slider (A, **Figure 81**) from the shifter (B, **Figure 81**).

Drive shaft seal and bearing housing disassembly

On 115-250 hp models, the drive shaft bearings and seals are located within a separate housing attached to the gearcase (**Figure 82**).

Remove the drive shaft bearing *only* if it must be replaced. Refer to *Component Inspection* to determine if replacement is required. Replace the seals any time the bearing housing requires service.

To ensure proper seal location on assembly, use a depth micrometer to measure the seal depth at the location indicated (A, **Figure 83**). Record the measurement.

As with the seals, use a depth micrometer and measure the depth of the bearing within the housing (B, **Figure 83**).

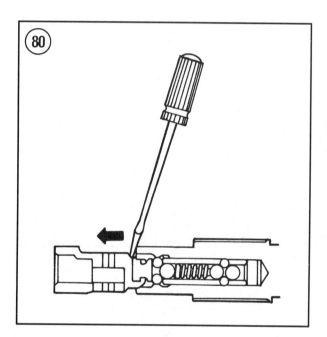

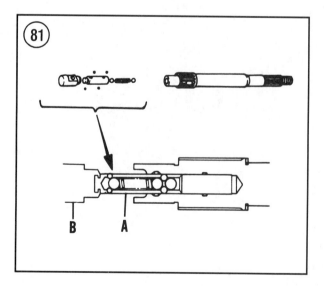

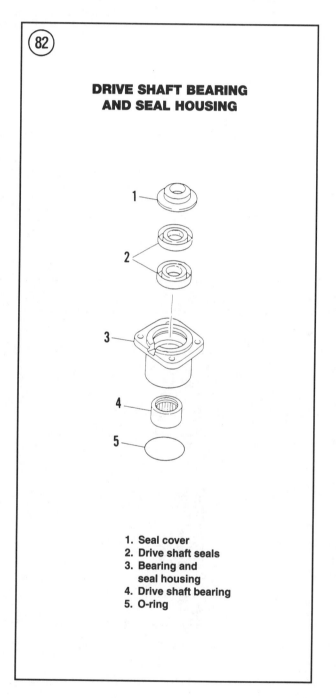

DRIVE SHAFT BEARING AND SEAL HOUSING

1. Seal cover
2. Drive shaft seals
3. Bearing and seal housing
4. Drive shaft bearing
5. O-ring

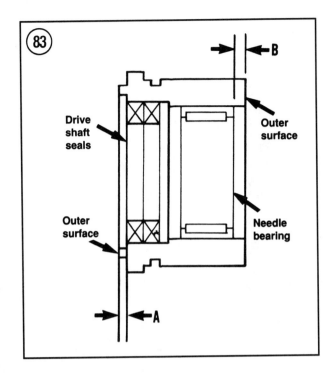

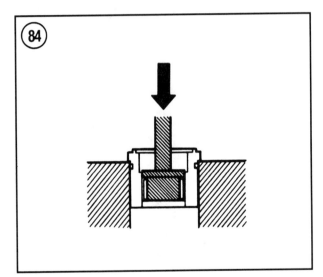

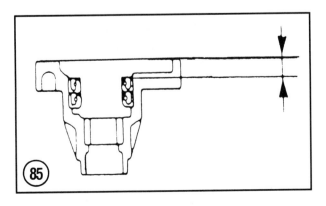

This is required to ensure that the bearing will contact the drive shaft at the proper location when assembled.

Note the orientation of the seals and bearing in the housing prior to removal. Note which direction the numbered side of the bearing is facing. Use the bearing driver and driver rod (part No. YB-6071 and YB-6169) or an appropriately sized socket and extension to remove the bearing. The socket used must be large enough in diameter to contact the bearing case yet not large enough to contact seal and bearing housing. Carefully drive the bearing and seals from the housing (**Figure 84**).

The seals can be replaced without removing the bearing. Note the orientation of the seal lips (2, **Figure 82**) prior to removal. Carefully pry the seals from the housing with a blunt tip screwdriver or suitable pry bar. Do not allow the tool to contact the housing.

On 6-25 hp (two-cylinder) and C30 models, the drive shaft bearing and seals are incorporated into the oil seal/bearing housing at the base of the water pump (**Figure 85**). Remove the bearing or bushing only if replacement is required. Refer to the *Component Inspection* section in this chapter.

Use a depth micrometer and measure the depth of the drive shaft seals at the point indicated (**Figure 85**). Record the measurement and carefully pry the seals from the housing with a blunt tip screwdriver or suitable pry bar. Do not allow the tool to contact the housing.

Use a depth micrometer and measure the depth of the bearing or bushing at the point indicated (**Figure 86**). Record the measurement. Use an appropriately sized socket and extension to remove the bearing or bushing. The socket selected must contact the bearing body and not contact the housing during removal of the bearing or

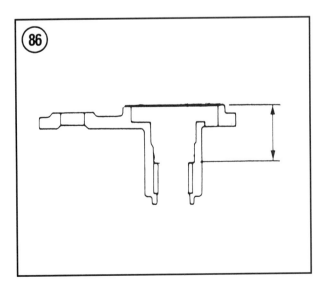

bushing. Work from the end opposite the seals and drive the bearing or bushing from the housing.

Lower drive shaft bearing removal

Do not remove the lower drive shaft bearing unless replacement is required. Refer to *Component inspection* to determine if replacement is required.

Remove the lubrication sleeve (A, **Figure 87**) from the gearcase. Prior to removal of the bearing, measure its depth within the drive shaft bore. This is necessary to ensure that the bearing will contact the drive shaft at the proper location when assembled. Use a suitable depth micrometer and measure the distance from the top or mating surface of the gearcase to the top of the bearing (C, **Figure 87**). Record the measurement.

Note the orientation (facing up or down) of the numbered side of the bearing. Use an appropriately sized socket and extension or a pipe to drive the bearing from the housing. The tool used must be large enough to contact the bearing yet not large enough to contact the gearcase. Apply heat to the outside surfaces of the gearcase near the bearing to aid in removal of the bearing.

On 2-15 hp models, use bushing removal tool part No. YB-6178 and a slide hammer to remove the drive shaft bushing as indicated in **Figure 88**.

Shift shaft seal removal

On 3-5 hp models, a bellows (C, **Figure 89**) is used to seal the shift shaft. Remove the retainer and carefully pull

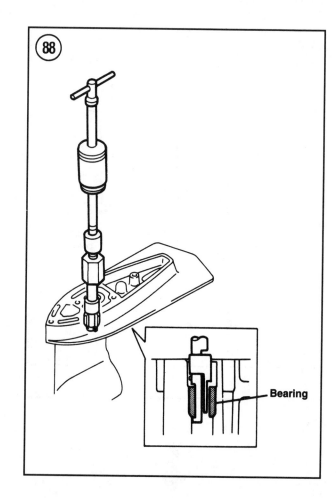

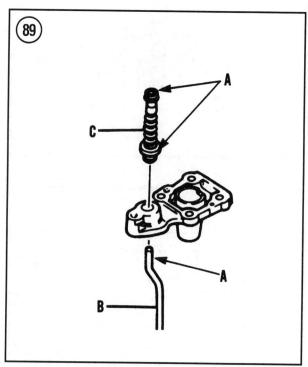

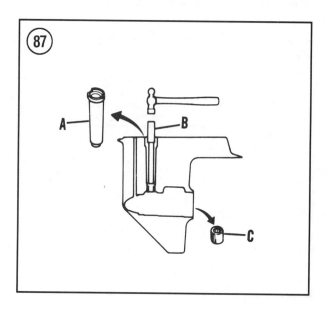

the shift shaft bellows from the water pump base. Slide the bellows over the end of the shift shaft.

A typical oil seal arrangement is used on other models to seal the shift shaft. The oil seal is housed in either the water pump base or a separate housing. Remove the fasteners and shift shaft bushing/seal housing on models so equipped. Slide the housing over the top of the shift shaft.

Note the seal lip orientation. Measure the depth of the seal within the housing at the point indicated (**Figure 90**). Record the measurement. Carefully pry the seal(s) from the housing with a small blunt tip screwdriver. Do not allow the screwdriver to contact the housing.

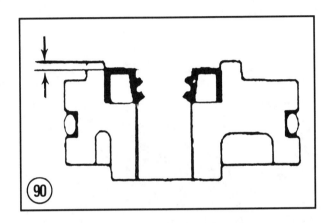

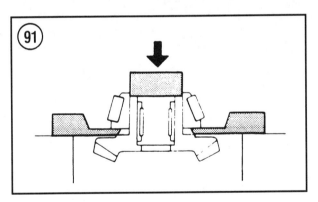

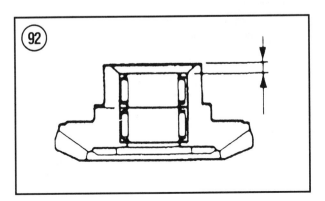

Forward driven gear bearing removal

Remove the tapered roller bearing and propeller shaft needle bearing only if replacement is required. Refer to *Component Inspection* in this chapter to determine if replacement is required.

Select an appropriately sized socket or piece of pipe that will contact the hub of the gear yet not contact the bearing (**Figure 91**). Position the bearing separator (part No. YB-06219) between the bearing and gear as indicated in **Figure 91**. Provide support to prevent the gear from dropping and use a press to push the gear from the bearing.

NOTE
The propeller shaft forward needle bearing arrangement varies by model. Either a single or double needle bearing arrangement is used.

Prior to removal, use a depth micrometer to measure the bearing(s) depth in the gear at the point indicated in **Figure 92**. This is required to ensure that the bearing will contact the propeller shaft at the proper location on assembly. Record the measurement.

Carefully secure the gear in a soft jaw vise. Use slide hammer part No. YB-06096 and bearing puller part No. YB-06523 to remove the needle bearing(s) from the gear (**Figure 93**). Note the orientation (forward or rearward facing) of the numbered side of the bearing.

9

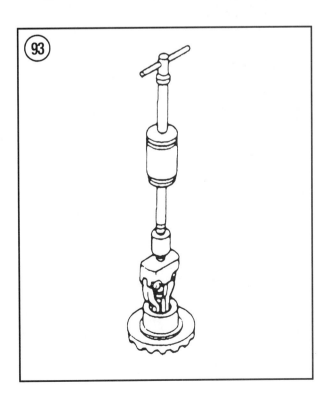

COMPONENT INSPECTION

This section provides instruction on the proper inspection of the gearcase components.

Never compromise a repair by using damaged or questionable components. Component failure may cause damage that costs far more to repair than the component itself.

Prior to inspection thoroughly clean all components using a suitable solvent. Make note of component orientation prior to cleaning when necessary. Use compressed air to dry all components. Never allow bearings to spin while using compressed air to dry them. The bearing will suffer irreparable damage if allowed to spin with compressed air.

> *WARNING*
> *Never allow bearings to spin when using compressed air to dry them. The bearing may spin at high speed and fly apart resulting in serious bodily injury or death.*

Make sure all components are removed and use pressurized water to clean the gearcase. When cleaning is required with components installed, clean the gearcase with a suitable solvent instead of water. Use compressed air to thoroughly dry the gearcase.

Propeller Shaft Inspection

Inspect the propeller shaft for bent, damaged or worn conditions. Replacement of the propeller shaft is required if defects are noted. Repair or straightening is not recommended.

Position the propeller shaft on V-blocks or other stable supports that will allow rotation of the shaft. Rotate the shaft and note if any deflection or wobble is present. Replace the propeller shaft if visible deflection or wobble is noted.

Inspect the propeller shaft surfaces (A, **Figure 94**) for corrosion and damaged or worn areas. Inspect the propel-

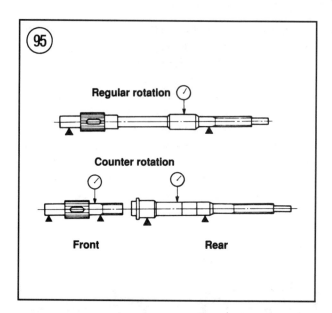

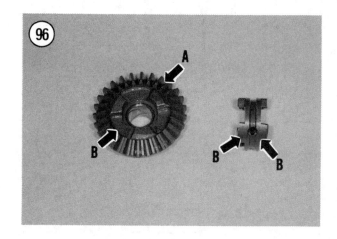

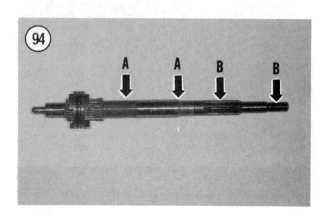

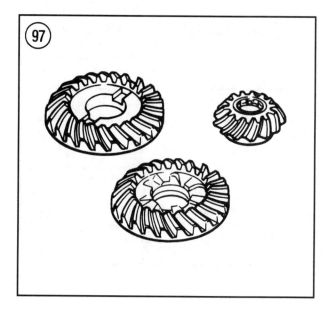

ler shaft splines and threaded area (B, **Figure 94**) for twisted splines or damaged propeller nut threads. Inspect the bearing contact areas at the front and midpoint of the propeller shaft. Replace the propeller if discolored areas, rough surfaces, transferred bearing material or other defects are noted.

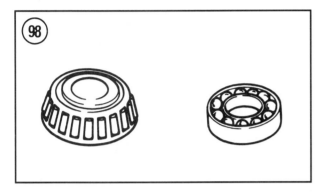

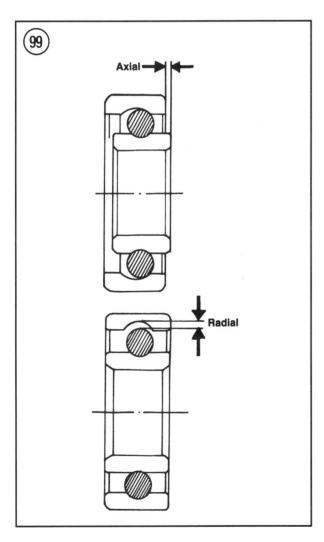

Inspect the propeller shaft at the seal contact areas. Drag a fingernail over the seal contact area. Replace the propeller shaft if deep grooves have worn in the surface or your fingernail will catch in the groove.

Place V-blocks or other suitable supports at the points indicated in **Figure 95**. Use a dial indicator to measure the shaft deflection at the rear bearing support area. Securely mount the dial indicator. Slowly rotate the propeller shaft and observe the dial indicator movement. Replace the propeller shaft if the needle movement exceeds 0.2 mm (0.008 in.).

Gear and Clutch Inspection

The appearance and mounting arrangement of the gears and clutches varies by models. Refer to **Figure 33-44** to locate and identify the components used in your model.

Inspect the clutch and gear surfaces (B, **Figure 96**) for chipped, damaged, worn or rounded over surfaces. Replace the clutch and gears if any of these conditions are found on either component.

Inspect the gear for worn, broken or damaged teeth (A, **Figure 96**). Note the presence of pitted, rough or excessively worn (highly polished) surfaces. Replace the gear if any of these conditions are found.

Although the gears are available individually for some models, they should always be replaced as a set (**Figure 97**). This is especially important for engines with high operating hours. Wear patterns form on the gears in a few hours of use. The wear patterns will be disturbed if a new gear is installed with a used gear. Accelerated wear of the new gear as well as the old gear will result as new wear patterns are formed on the mismatched gears.

Bearing Inspection

Clean all bearings thoroughly in solvent and air dry prior to inspection. Replace bearings if the gear lubricant drained from the gearcase was heavily contaminated with metal particles. The particles tend to collect inside the bearing assemblies and will likely contaminate the gears and other components if the bearings are reused.

Inspect roller bearing and bearing race surfaces (**Figure 98**) for pitting, rusting, discoloration or rough surfaces. Inspect the bearing race for highly polished or unevenly worn surfaces. Replace the bearing assembly if any of these conditions are noted.

Rotate ball bearings in the directions indicated (**Figure 99**). Note the presence of rough operation or *axial* or *radial* looseness. Replace the bearing if rough operation or looseness is noted.

9

Inspect the needle bearing (**Figure 100**) located in the bearing carrier, front driven gear and drive shaft bearing housing. Replace the bearing if flattened rollers, discoloration, rusting, rough surfaces or pitting is noted.

Inspect the propeller shaft and drive shaft at the bearing contact areas. Replace the drive shaft and/or propeller shaft along with the needle bearing if discoloration, transferred bearing material, rough surfaces or pitting is noted.

Shift Cam/Follower and Related Components

Refer to **Figure 33-44** to identify the type of shift components used in your model. Refer to **Figure 101-103** to locate and identify the components described.

    a. For 4-30 hp models, refer to **Figure 101**.

    b. For 40-70 hp and E75 models, refer to **Figure 102**.

    c. For 75-250 hp models, refer to **Figure 103**.

Inspect the bore in the propeller shaft for the presence of debris, damaged or worn areas. Clean debris from the bore. Replace worn or damaged shift components. Inspect the clutch spring for damage, corrosion or weak spring tension and replace if defects are noted.

Inspect the cross pin for damaged, rough or worn surfaces. Inspect the follower/shift slider spring for damage or corrosion. Replace as required.

Inspect the follower/shifter for cracked, broken or worn area. Replace the cam and follower or shifter/slider if defects or worn surfaces are noted.

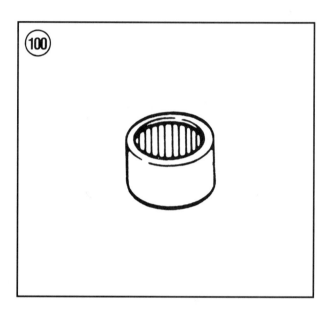

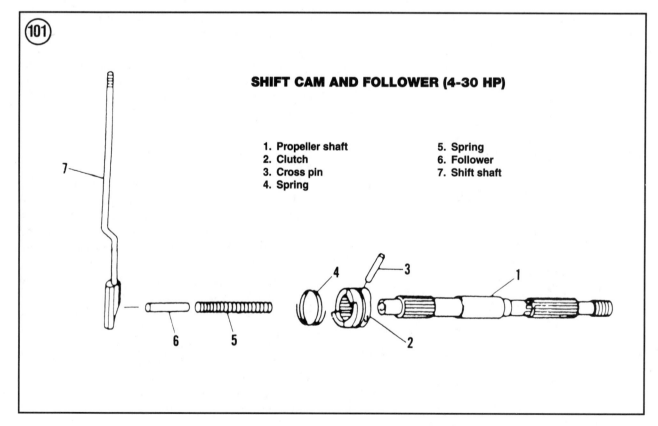

SHIFT CAM AND FOLLOWER (4-30 HP)

1. Propeller shaft
2. Clutch
3. Cross pin
4. Spring
5. Spring
6. Follower
7. Shift shaft

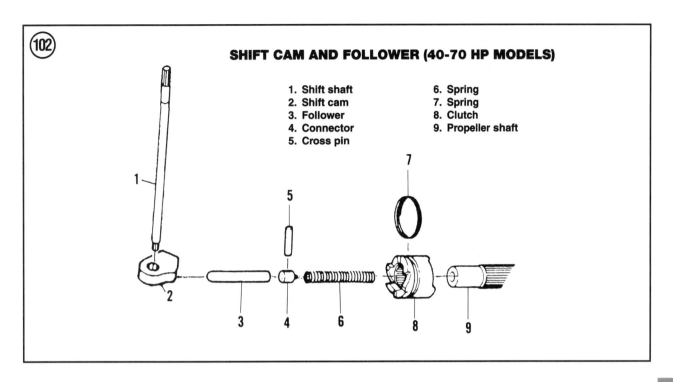

SHIFT CAM AND FOLLOWER (40-70 HP MODELS)

1. Shift shaft
2. Shift cam
3. Follower
4. Connector
5. Cross pin
6. Spring
7. Spring
8. Clutch
9. Propeller shaft

9

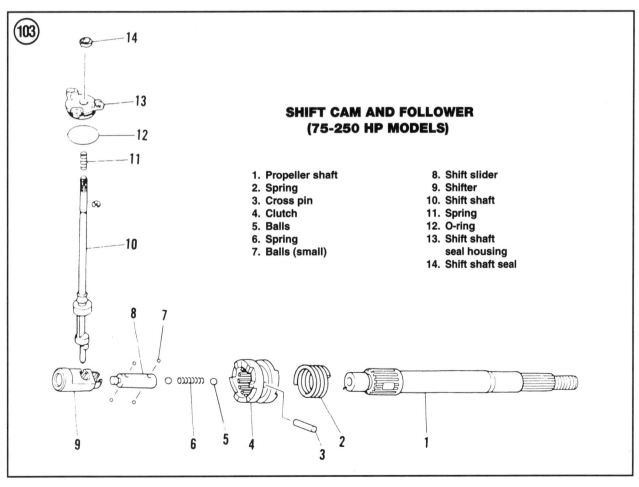

**SHIFT CAM AND FOLLOWER
(75-250 HP MODELS)**

1. Propeller shaft
2. Spring
3. Cross pin
4. Clutch
5. Balls
6. Spring
7. Balls (small)
8. Shift slider
9. Shifter
10. Shift shaft
11. Spring
12. O-ring
13. Shift shaft
    seal housing
14. Shift shaft seal

Check the detent balls for flat spots or pitting and replace as required.

Inspect the shift cam for broken, chipped or worn surfaces. Replace the cam and follower/shifter if defects or worn surfaces are noted.

Inspect the shift shaft for a bent or twisted condition. Inspect the seal/bushing housing for cracks or worn shift shaft bore. Replace the housing and/or shift shaft if defects are noted.

Shims, Spacers, Fasteners and Washers

Inspect all shims for bent, rusted or damaged surfaces. Replace any shim that does not appear to be like new.

Spacers are used in various locations within the gearcase. Replace them if bent, corroded or damaged. Use only the correct part to replace them. In most cases, they are of a certain dimension and made with a specified material.

Replace any locking type nut unless it is in excellent condition. Replace the pinion fastener anytime it is removed from the drive shaft.

Replace any worn or damaged washers located on the pinion gear. These washers are sometimes used as a thrust surface and are subject to wear.

Gearcase Assembly

This section provides procedures to assemble the gearcase. For assistance with component location and identification, refer to **Figure 33-44**.

Perform the shim selection and backlash measurement if gears, bearings, drive shaft or housings are changed from the original components. Shim selection and backlash measurement is provided in this section.

Follow all instructions carefully. Improper assembly can lead to gearcase failure, rapid wear of gears and bearings, sloppy shift operation or noisy operation.

Ensure that all seals are installed with the seals facing the direction noted during removal. Install seals to the proper depth as measured on disassembly. Seal depth specifications are provided in **Table 4**.

Install all bearings with the numbered side facing the direction noted on removal. Generally the numbered side is used when installing the bearing.

Clean the outside surface of all seals and the bore in which the seal is installed with Loctite Primer T. Apply a light coating of Loctite 271 to the outside diameter of all seals. Also, apply a light coat in the bore in which the seal will be installed. Always wipe excess sealant from the surfaces after seal installation.

Apply Yamaha all-purpose grease to the seal lip surfaces. Apply a light amount of Yamaha gearcase lubricant to the surfaces of all needle, roller and ball bearings. Do not apply any lubricant to the gear surfaces as it can interfere with backlash measurement.

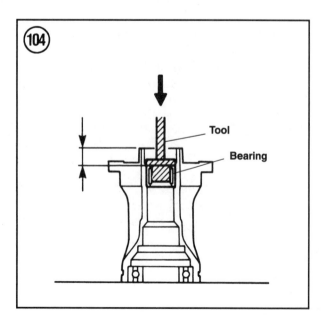

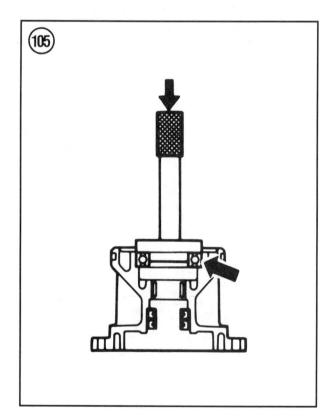

Component Assembly

This section provides assembly procedures for the following components.

1. Gearcase cap/bearing carrier.
2. Propeller shaft and shift components.
3. Drive shaft bearing and drive shaft seals.
4. Lower drive shaft bearing/bushing.
5. Front mounted gear/bearings.
6. Front mounted bearing race and shims.

Gearcase cap/bearing carrier

> *CAUTION*
> *Some gearcase caps and bearing carriers incorporate a step or ledge in the bore for*

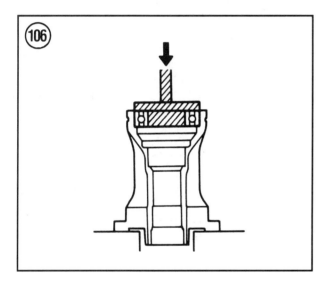

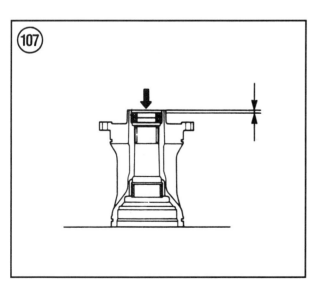

the propeller shaft support bearing. If the bearing is installed from the wrong end of the bore, the step will prevent proper installation of the bearing.

Select an appropriately sized socket or section of pipe, rod or tubing to press the propeller shaft support bearing into the gearcase cap or bearing carrier. The tool used must squarely contact the bearing on the shouldered surface, but not contact the bearing bore. Work carefully and stop often to measure the depth with a depth micrometer. Install the bearing to the depth noted on disassembly (**Figure 104**).

On 4-15 hp models, the reverse gear ball bearing is installed into the gearcase cap or bearing carrier prior to installing the reverse gear. Select a socket or section of pipe, tubing or other appropriate tool to press the ball bearing into the gearcase cap or carrier. The tool selected must contact the outer race or surface of the ball bearing. For 4 and 5 hp models, refer to **Figure 105**. For 6-15 hp models, refer to **Figure 106**.

Position the gearcase cap with the propeller shaft seal side facing down. To ease assembly and prevent damage to the bore, apply a light coating of Yamaha gearcase lubricant or its equivalent to the bearing bore in the cap or carrier. Make sure the tool used is positioned squarely and centered on the bearing and the press. Slowly press the bearing into the cap or carrier until it is firmly seated. Lubricate the bearing and bore with Yamaha gearcase lubricant. Carefully install the reverse gear into the bearing bore and press the gear onto the bearing until seated.

> *WARNING*
> *Always wear safety glasses when you are striking any object with a hammer. When using a hammer, anyone in the area must wear safety glasses.*

> *NOTE*
> *If the seal depth is not known, refer to **Table 4** for required information.*

Apply Loctite 271 to the seal and seal bore surfaces as described at the beginning of this section. Select an appropriately sized socket or short section of pipe or rod that will contact the outer diameter of the seal. The tool selected must be slightly smaller in diameter than the seal diameter yet maintain adequate contact on the seal case. It must not contact the gearcase cap or carrier during installation.

Press the inner seal into the cap or carrier until it is just below the surface (**Figure 107**). For 6 and 8 hp models, refer to **Table 4** for the correct inner seal depth. Press slowly and use a depth micrometer to check the depth several times to avoid pressing the seal in too deep. For all other models, the inner seal depth is set by contact with the outer seal during installation.

Place the outer seal onto the inner seal with the seal lip facing the correct direction. Slowly press the outer seal along with the inner seal (except 6 and 8 hp models) into the carrier. Check the depth frequently with a depth micrometer to avoid pressing the seal in too deep. Press the outer seal to the depth recorded on disassembly.

NOTE
Not all models use the thrust spacer. Refer to **Figure 33-44** *to determine if the spacer is used on your model.*

Place the thrust spacer (**Figure 108**) over the reverse gear with its beveled inner diameter facing the gear. Place the reverse gear on the padded table of the press with the gear tooth side facing down. Select a large socket or plate that will contact the inner race or surface of the ball bearing as indicated in **Figure 108**. Apply Yamaha gearcase lubricant to the inner bore of the ball bearing.

On 200-250 hp (76°) models, install the shims onto the hub of the reverse gear prior to the installation of the ball bearing to the gear. Place the ball bearing with the numbered side facing up (if numbered) and press the ball bearing onto the reverse gear until seated.

Lubricate the inner bearing bore of the bearing carrier with Yamaha gearcase lubricant or its equivalent. Position the gear with the gear tooth side facing down. Position the carrier onto the bearing with the seal side facing up as indicated in **Figure 109**. Use a driver that will squarely contact the rear surface of the carrier.

Slowly press the carrier onto the ball bearing until fully seated within the bearing bore. Lubricate the seal lips with Yamaha all-purpose grease or its equivalent. Install a new O-ring onto the carrier. Lubricate the O-ring and surfaces that contact the gearcase with Yamaha all-purpose grease or its equivalent.

Propeller shaft and shift components

For 3 hp models, refer to **Figure 34** during the assembly procedure. Install the spring into the bore of the propeller shaft. Insert a small screwdriver into the slot of the propeller shaft. Compress the spring by sliding the screwdriver toward the threaded end of the propeller shaft. With the spring compressed, slide the clutch into the slot with the notched side facing forward. Allow the spring to move the screwdriver toward the clutch and carefully remove the screwdriver. Apply Yamaha all-purpose grease to the surfaces of the follower, then insert it into the propeller shaft with the pointed side facing OUT.

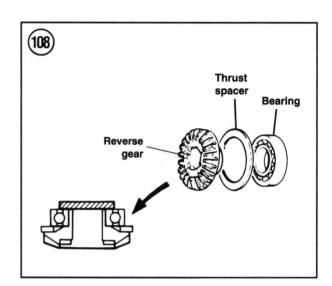

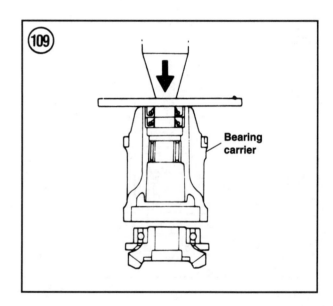

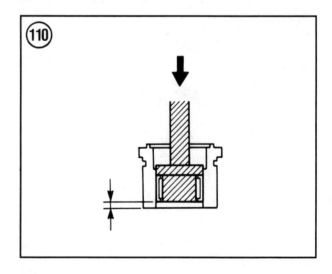

For 4-30 hp models, refer to **Figure 35-39** during the assembly procedure.

Drive shaft bearing

> *NOTE*
> *The drive shaft bearing must be installed to the proper depth within the bearing and seal housing to ensure that the bearing contacts the drive shaft at the proper location. The housing does not provide a step or shoulder for the bearing. Slowly tap the bearing into position. Stop and check the depth frequently during installation.*

1. Select an appropriately sized socket or section of pipe or tubing. The tool used must contact the bearing case, yet not contact the bearing housing during installation.

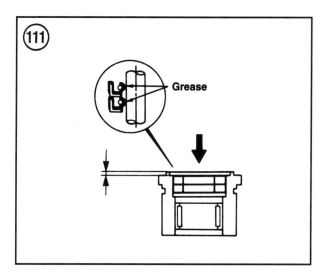

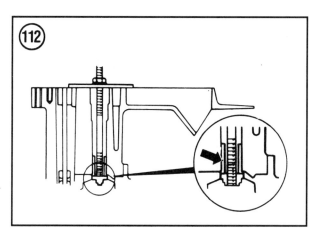

2. Apply Yamaha gearcase lubricant to the bearing bore surfaces of the bearing housing prior to installation. Lubricate all surfaces of the bearing prior to installation.
3. Position the bearing at the opening to the housing with the numbered or lettered side facing UP or toward the oil seal bore.
4. Using the driving tool, slowly tap the bearing into the housing. Stop when the bearing reaches the exact depth (**Figure 110**) recorded prior to removal.

Drive shaft seals

The seals must be installed with the seal lips, positioned as indicated in **Figure 111** to ensure proper contact with the drive shaft.

1. Clean the seal bore in the housing and the outer seal diameter with Loctite Primer T to remove all contaminants.
2. Select an appropriately sized socket, section of tubing or rod for use as an installation tool. The selected tool must contact the outer diameter of the open side of the seal, yet not contact the bore of the housing during installation.
3. Apply a light coat of Loctite 271 sealant to the seal bore and the outer diameter of the seals.
4. Place a seal with the lip (open side) facing up into the seal bore opening.
5. Use the selected tool to carefully drive the first seal in until just below the seal bore opening.
6. Place the second seal into the seal bore with the lip (open side) facing up.
7. Use the tool to carefully drive the seals into the housing to the exact depth recorded prior to removal of the seals (**Figure 111**).
8. Wipe all excess sealant from the housing and apply Yamaha all-purpose grease to the seal lips.

Lower drive shaft bearing/bushing installation

> *NOTE*
> *All bearing and bushings must be installed to the proper depth within the housing. There is **no** step or shoulder in the bearing/bushing bore. The bearing or bushing must be installed to the proper depth to ensure the proper contact location on the drive shaft.*

On 2-8 hp models, use the bushing installation tool (part No. YB-6169, YB-6029 and YB-6028) to install the drive shaft bushings.

1. Install the lower bushing as follows:
   a. Apply Yamaha gearcase lubricant to the bushing surfaces and the bushing bore in the gearcase.
   b. Position the lower bushing and installation tool into the bushing bore as indicated in **Figure 112**.

9

c. Install the threaded rod and nut through the plate and into the drive shaft bore. Thread the rod into the installation tool as indicated in **Figure 112**.

d. Tighten the nut until the bushing installation tool bottoms out on the housing and the nut becomes snug. Remove the installation tools.

2. Install the upper bushing as follows:

a. Apply Yamaha gearcase lubricant to the bushing surfaces and the bushing bore in the gearcase.

b. Use part No. YB-6025, YB-6229 or select an appropriately sized socket or tubing to install the bushing. The tool used must provide adequate contact to the bushing, yet not contact the bushing bore in the housing during installation.

c. Carefully drive the bushing into the housing (**Figure 113**) to the exact depth recorded prior to removal of the bushing.

3. On 9.9-250 hp models, use an appropriately sized socket and extension or section of pipe, rod or tubing to install the lower drive shaft bearing. The tool selected must provide adequate contact for the bearing diameter, yet not contact the bearing bore within the housing. Tap the bearing lightly and slowly into the bore. Stop frequently to measure the depth of the bearing (**Figure 114**).

4. Install the lower drive shaft bearing as follows:

a. Lubricate the bearing surfaces and the bearing bore in the housing with Yamaha gearcase lubricant.

b. Position the bearing into the bore with the numbered or lettered stamping facing up or toward the water pump mounting area. Place a piece of wooden dowel or other suitable rod into the bearing inner bore to ensure the rollers are not dislodged.

c. Stop frequently for measurement and slowly tap the bearing into the bore until it reaches the exact depth (**Figure 114**) that was recorded prior to removal.

Gearcase mounted seals

NOTE
No step or shoulder is provided to position the seal within the gearcase. Install the seals to the depth recorded prior to removal. If the seal depth is not known or you suspect that the seals have moved within the bore, refer to Table 4.

1. On 2-5 hp models, select an appropriately sized socket, tubing or rod to install the drive shaft seals into the gearcase. The tool selected must be of a sufficient diameter to provide adequate contact to the seals (outer diameter of the open side). The tool must *not* contact the seal bore during installation.

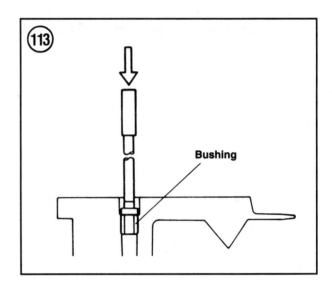

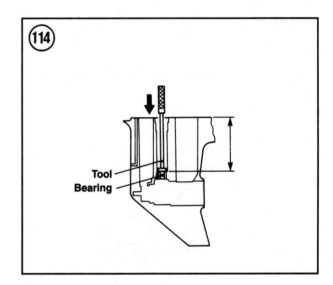

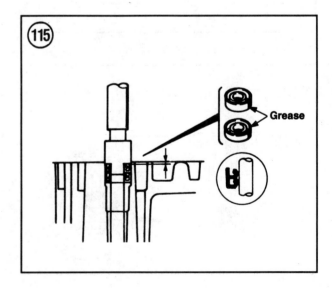

2. Apply Loctite Primer T to the seal bore in the housing and the outer diameter of the seals to remove contaminants. Apply Loctite 271 sealant to the outer diameter of the seal and the seal bore within the housing.

3. Position the first seal into the bore with the seal lip (open side) facing up. Use the selected tool to carefully drive the seal into the bore until just below the gearcase surface.

4. Position the second seal over the first seal (**Figure 115**) with the seal lip (open side) facing up.

5. Use the selected tool to drive both seals into the bore until the second seal just reaches the depth recorded prior to removal (**Figure 115**).

Water pump base mounted seals

The appearance of the water pump base varies by model. Refer to **Figure 33-44** for identification and orientation of

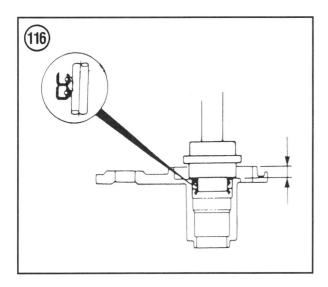

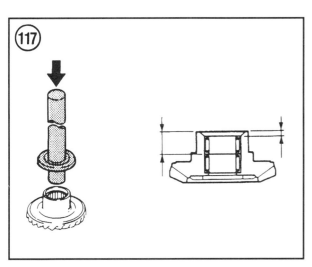

the components. Install the seals to the depth recorded prior to removal. This is necessary to ensure proper contact with the drive shaft.

Refer to **Table 4** if the seal depth is not known or you suspect that the seals have moved within the bore.

1. Select an appropriately sized socket and extension, tubing or rod to install the seals. The tool selected must provide adequate contact to the diameter at the open side of the seals, yet not contact the seal bore within the water pump base during installation.

2. Clean the seal bore and diameter of the seal with Loctite Primer T. Apply a light amount of Loctite 271 sealant to the diameter of the seal and the seal bore within the water pump base.

3. Position the water pump base with the seal bore facing up or toward the water pump impeller when assembled. Provide adequate support for the bottom side. Install the first seal into the bore with the seal lip open side of the seal facing UP.

4. Use the selected tool to slowly drive the first seal into the bore until just below the water pump base surface.

5. Position the second seal over the first seal with the seal lip (open side) facing UP. Stop frequently for measurement and carefully drive the second and first seal into the bore until they just reach the proper installation depth (**Figure 116**).

6. Wipe excess sealant from the water pump base and apply Yamaha all-purpose grease to the seal lips.

Front mounted gear/bearing assembly

The needle bearing within the bore of the front mounted gear will vary in size and quantity within the models. To ensure proper contact of the bearing to the propeller shaft, install the bearing to the depth recorded prior to removal (**Figure 92**).

1. Install the needle bearing into the gear as follows:
   a. Select an appropriately sized socket and extension or section of pipe, tubing or rod to install the bearing. The tool selected must provide adequate contact for the outer diameter of the bearing yet not contact the diameter of the bearing bore in the gear during assembly.
   b. Apply Yamaha gearcase lubricant to the surfaces of the bearing and the bearing bore in the gear.
   c. Carefully press or tap the bearing(s) into the bore. Use a depth micrometer to check the bearing depth. Install the bearing to the exact depth (**Figure 117**) as recorded prior to removal.

2. Install the tapered bearing to the gear as follows:
   a. Select a suitable plate, large socket or section of pipe that will contact the inner bearing race. The tool used

must not contact the bearing cage or the hub of the gear.

b. Position the gear, tooth side facing down, on a suitable press. Apply Yamaha gearcase lubricant to the hub of the gear and the inner bore of the tapered bearing

c. Place the tapered bearing onto the hub of the gear as indicated in **Figure 118**. Place the selected installation tool onto the inner race of the bearing.

d. Press the bearing onto the hub of the gear until fully seated. Inspect the bearing to ensure that no damage occurred during installation.

Front mounted bearing race and shim installation

> *NOTE*
> *When driving a bearing or race into the housing, always use very light taps and listen to the noise when the driver rod is struck. Strike the rod only hard enough to slightly move the bearing or race. Stop driving when the pitch changes or a sharp ring is heard as the rod is struck.*

Refer to *Shim selection* prior to installing any shim when the repair involves the replacement of gears, drive shaft, bearings or gearcase housing. Use the original shims or replacement shims of the same thickness when none of the listed components are replaced. Refer to **Table 3** to determine the available shims. Select a combination of shims that is exactly the same total thickness as the original shims, or the thickness as determined in the *Shim selection* procedure.

Use the specified tool to drive the bearing race into the housing. The use of other tools will likely result in damage to the bearing race.

a. For 6-8 hp models, use part No. YB-6071.

b. For 9.9-30 hp models, use part No. YB-6085.

c. For C40 models, use part No. YB-6109.

d. For 40-50 hp (except E48) models, use part No. YB-06063.

e. For Model E48, use part No. YB-06110.

f. For 60-90 hp models, use part No. YB-6276B.

g. For 115-130 hp models, use part No. TB-06199.

h. For 150-225 hp (90°) models, use part No. YB-06258.

i. For 200-250 hp (76°) models, use part No. YB-06432.

On 6-250 hp models, position the gearcase in a suitable mounting location with the gearcase opening facing UP. Inspect the gearcase for the presence of debris and contaminants and clean if required. Place the shims (A, **Figure 119**) onto the shoulder or step in the gearcase as indicated

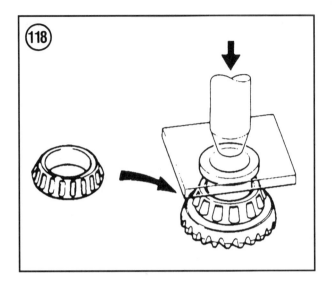

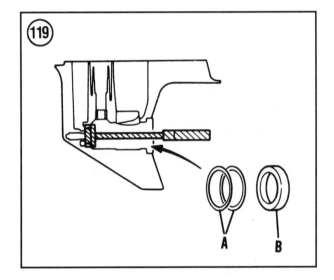

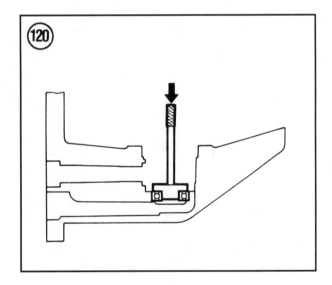

in **Figure 119**. Position the race (B, **Figure 119**) into the housing with the tapered side facing up or out.

Position the bearing race driver tool onto the race with the tapered side down. Use part No. YB-6071 or a suitable rod. Slowly and carefully drive the race into position.

On 2-5 hp models, use part No. YB-6270 and a suitable driver rod or part No. YB-6071 to install the bearing. Inspect the gearcase for debris or contamination and clean if required. Position the gearcase in a sturdy mount with the gearcase opening facing up as indicated in **Figure 120**. Apply Yamaha gearcase lubricant to the bearing and the bearing bore within the gearcase. Install the selected shims into the gearcase. Install the bearing into the gearcase with the numbered side facing out. Place the installation tool

onto the bearing and carefully drive the bearing into the housing until seated.

Gearcase Assembly

This section provides assembly procedures for standard right-hand rotation gearcases. Refer to *Shim selection* when the repair involves the replacement of gears, drive shaft, bearings or gearcase housing

Variations in component appearance and location exist with the models. For assistance with component identification, usage and orientation, refer to **Figure 33-44**.

Shift shaft and shift cam installation

On C40 and 40-70 hp models, position the shift cam (7, **Figure 121**) into the gearcase with the UP mark facing up as indicated in **Figure 121**. Insert the E-clip (5, **Figure 121**) onto the shift shaft groove. Insert the shift shaft into its bore and engage the splines of the shift cam.

Install a new O-ring (4, **Figure 121**) onto the shift shaft seal housing. Lubricate the seal housing, O-ring and seal housing bore in the gearcase with Yamaha gearcase lubricant.

Lubricate the shift shaft seal (2, **Figure 121**) with Yamaha all-purpose grease then install the seal housing over the shift shaft and press into position. Note the shift shaft bore is offset to the forward side of the gearcase. Install a new O-ring over the shift shaft. Install the fasteners (**Figure 122**) and tighten securely.

(121)

1. O-ring
2. Shift shaft seal
3. Shift shaft seal housing
4. O-ring
5. Shift shaft
6. Clip
7. Gearcase housing
8. Shift cam

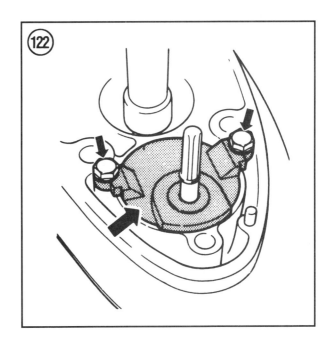

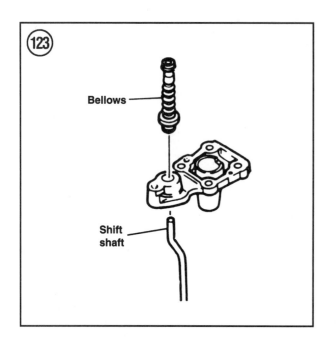

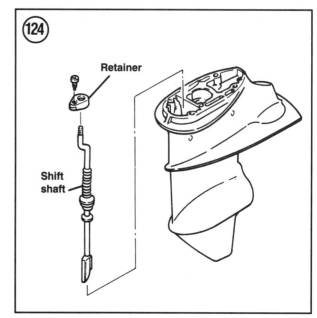

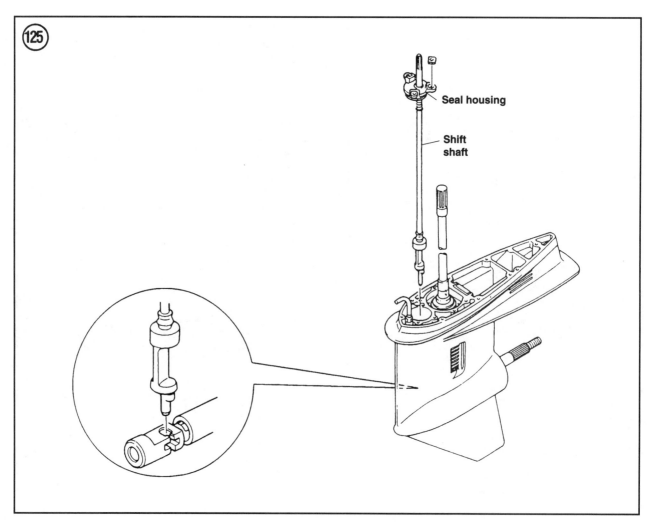

On all other models, the shift shaft and shift cam are installed after the gears and shafts are installed.

On 3-25 hp (two-cylinder) models, the shift shaft bellows (A, **Figure 123**) is held in position with the water pump base.

On 25 hp (three-cylinder) and 30 hp models, the bellows is held down with a separate retainer (**Figure 124**).

Carefully slide the shift shaft into the shift shaft bore. Lubricate the shift shaft with Yamaha gearcase lubricant and slide the shift shaft bushing into position on the gearcase. Apply Yamaha all-purpose grease into the bellow bore to ease assembly. Install the retainer or water pump

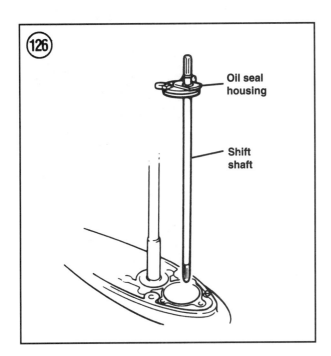

base over the bellow and shift shaft. Tighten the fasteners securely.

On 75-250 hp models, the shift shaft is installed in a similar fashion as the 40-70 hp models. The shaft and seal housing are installed after the gears and shafts.

Apply Yamaha all-purpose grease to the seal lip of the new shift shaft seal. Install a new O-ring over the bottom of the seal housing at the gearcase to seal carrier mating surface. Install a new O-ring onto the shift shaft. Insert the shift shaft into the seal carrier with the grooved side up.

On 115-250 hp models, carefully install the shift shaft into the shift shaft bore with the shift cam oriented as indicated in **Figure 125**. Carefully rotate the shift shaft until the lower end engages the shifter assembly and the shift shaft drops into position. Carefully seat the seal housing. Apply Loctite 572 to the threads and install the fasteners for the seal housing. Tighten the fasteners securely.

On 75-90 hp models, install the shift shaft into the shift shaft bore (**Figure 126**). Carefully rotate the shift shaft until it engages the shift cam and drops into position. Seat the seal housing into the gearcase. Apply Loctite 572 to the fastener threads. Install the fasteners and tighten securely.

Lubrication sleeve installation

On 9.9-225 hp (90°) models, the lubrication sleeve must be installed prior to installation of the tapered bearing race (if so equipped) and the drive shaft. Align the locating boss as indicated in **Figure 127**. Use a large wooden dowel and push the sleeve into the drive shaft bore until fully seated in the gearcase.

Drive shaft bearing race installation

On 40-90 hp models, the drive shaft bearing race and shims must be installed prior to installation of the drive shaft and pinion gear. Refer to *Shim selection* to determine the correct thickness of shims if the repair involves replacement of gears, bearings, drive shaft or gearcase housing.

Use the recommended tools to drive the race into the housing. The use of other tools may result in damage to the bearing race.

    a. For 40-50 hp models, use part No. YB-06110 and driver rod YB-06071.

    b. For 60-90 hp models (excluding Model E60), use part No. YB-6156 and driver rod YB-06071.

    c. For Model E60, use part No. YB-06156 and driver rod YB-06071.

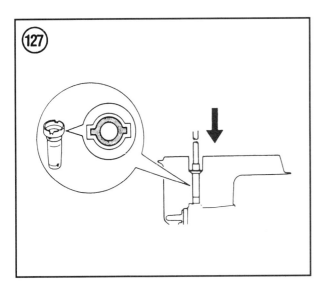

Inspect the step or shoulder in the drive shaft bore for debris and contaminants and clean if required. Apply a light coat of Yamaha gearcase lubricant to the surfaces of the bearing race and the race bore within the gearcase.

Place the selected shims onto the step or shoulder in the drive shaft bore. Place the race into the entrance to the bore with the taper facing UP. Place the driver tool and driver rod onto the race. Carefully tap the driver rod (**Figure 128**) until the race is seated in the housing.

Forward and pinion gear installation

Variation exists in component appearance, usage and orientation. For assistance with component usage, location and orientation, refer to **Figure 33-44**.

Place the forward gear or forward gear and bearing assembly into the housing. On 2 hp models, the driven gear and propeller shaft are installed as a unit. On 2 hp models, install the shim onto the propeller shaft prior to installing the propeller shaft into the gear. Ensure that the gear is fully seated against the bearing. Place any washers, shims or bearings in position above the pinion gear mounting location. Install all parts in the exact orientation as removed.

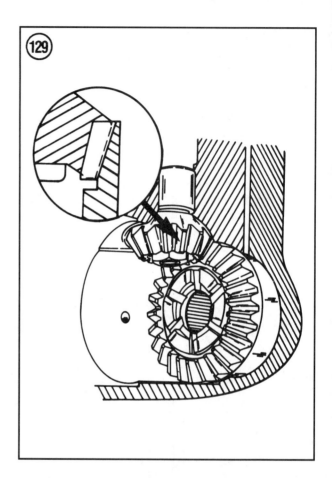

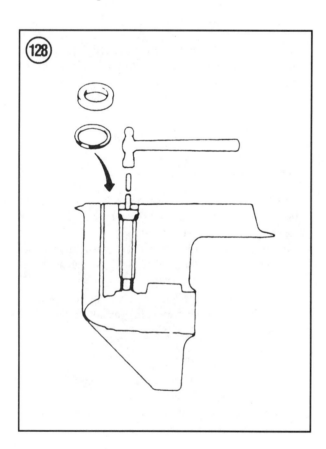

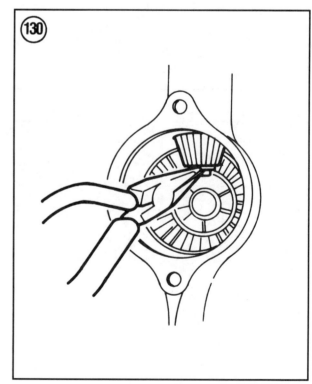

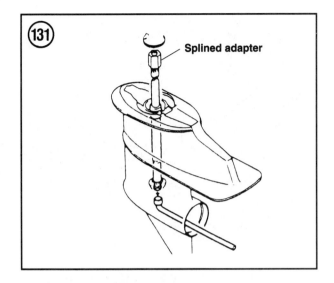

Splined adapter

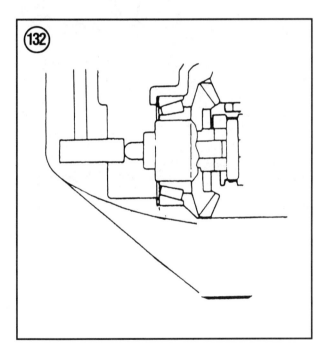

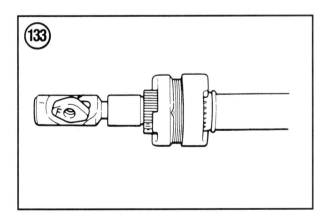

Place the pinion gear into the housing with the teeth engaged to the forward gear (**Figure 129**). Carefully insert the drive shaft into the gearcase. Slowly rotate the drive shaft until it engages the inner splines of the pinion gear. Install the washer (if so equipped) onto the splines. Use needlenose pliers to install a new circlip (**Figure 130**) on the models so equipped. On all other models, apply Loctite Primer T and Loctite 271 to the threads of the drive shaft and the *new* pinion nut. Install the pinion nut and hand tighten for now.

Refer to the disassembly procedures in this chapter for the part number of the splined adapter. Use a socket and breaker bar and a torque wrench (**Figure 131**) to tighten the pinion nut to the specification listed in **Table 1**.

Propeller shaft installation

On 3-70 hp models, install the propeller shaft assembly into the forward gear needle bearing (**Figure 132**). Keep the shaft in a horizontal position to ensure the follower remains within the propeller shaft during installation.

On 75-90 hp models, install the propeller shaft with the shift cam positioned in the shifter as indicated in **Figure 133**. *Do not* rotate the propeller shaft during assembly. The propeller shaft must remain with the cam in a horizontal position until the shift shaft is engaged into the shift cam.

On 115-250 hp models, install the propeller shaft into the needle bearing with the flat surface of the shifter facing UP (**Figure 134**). *Do not* rotate the propeller shaft until the shift shaft engages the shifter and the propeller shaft bearing carrier is installed.

Refer to *Shift shaft installation* in this chapter for further instructions.

9

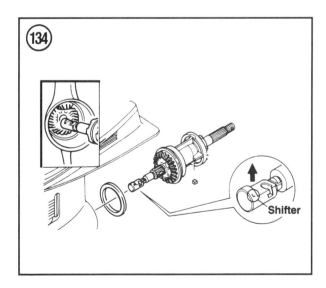

Shifter

Gearcase cap/bearing carrier installation

On 2 hp models, install a new gasket onto the gearcase cap. Apply Yamaha all-purpose grease to the gasket surface, propeller shaft seals and rear bearing surfaces. Slide the gearcase cap over the propeller shaft and into position. Apply Loctite 572 to the fastener threads. Install the fasteners and tighten to the specification listed in **Table 1**.

On 3-5 hp models, install a new O-ring onto the groove in the gearcase cap. Install the thrust washer onto the propeller shaft. Apply Yamaha all-purpose grease to the O-ring, thrust washer, propeller shaft oil seals and gearcase-to-cap mating surface. Slide the gearcase cap over the propeller shaft and press into the gearcase opening. Apply Loctite 572 to the fastener threads. Install the fasteners (**Figure 135**) and tighten to the specification listed in **Table 1**.

On 6-25 hp (two-cylinder) and C30, 40 and 50 hp models, install a new O-ring onto the groove in the bearing carrier. Apply Yamaha all-purpose grease to the O-ring, propeller shaft oil seals and carrier to gearcase mating surfaces. Apply grease to the thrust washer and install it onto the propeller shaft. Carefully slide the carrier over the propeller shaft (**Figure 136**) and press firmly into position. Apply Loctite 572 to the threads of the fasteners. Install the fasteners and tighten to the specification listed in **Table 1**.

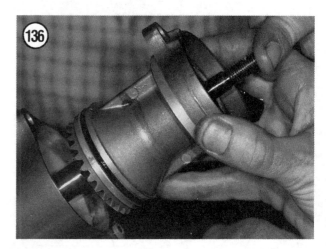

On C40, E48 and 60-225 hp (90°) models, lubricate the thrust washer (if so equipped) with Yamaha all-purpose grease and install it onto the propeller shaft. Install a new O-ring onto the groove formed between the carrier and thrust spacer. Apply Yamaha all-purpose grease to the O-ring, propeller shaft oil seals and carrier-to-gearcase mating surfaces. Slide the carrier over the propeller shaft and carefully press into position. Align the locating key slot in the carrier with the slot in the gearcase (**Figure 137**). Apply Yamaha all-purpose grease to the key and insert it into the slot. Apply Yamaha all-purpose grease to the threads of the cover nut and the threads in the housing. Install a new locking tab washer (A, **Figure 138**) onto the carrier. Ensure that the notch aligns with the boss on the carrier. Install the cover nut (B, **Figure 138**) and thread by hand into the gearcase threads. Refer to the disassembly procedures for the part number of the cover nut tool. Tighten the cover nut to the specification listed in **Table 1**. Bend a locking tab into a gap in the cover nut. Tighten the nut additionally if necessary to allow a tab to enter a gap. Bend the remaining tabs down as indicated in **Figure 138**.

On 200-225 hp (76°) models, apply Yamaha all-purpose grease to the thrust washer and install it onto the propeller shaft. Place new O-rings (1, **Figure 139**) onto grooves of the carrier (2, **Figure 139**). Apply Yamaha all-purpose

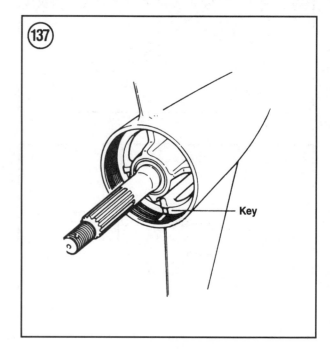

Key

grease to the O-rings, propeller shaft seals and carrier-to-gearcase mating surfaces. Make sure the UP mark on the carrier is facing UP. Slide the carrier over the propeller shaft and carefully press into position in the gearcase. Align the fastener holes in the carrier with the fastener holes in the gearcase. Apply Loctite 572 to the fastener threads. Install the fasteners into the housing and tighten to the specification listed in **Table 1**. Apply Yamaha all-purpose grease to the mating surfaces of the ring (5, **Figure 139**). Install the ring onto the carrier. Align the fastener holes in the carrier with the holes in the ring. Apply Loctite

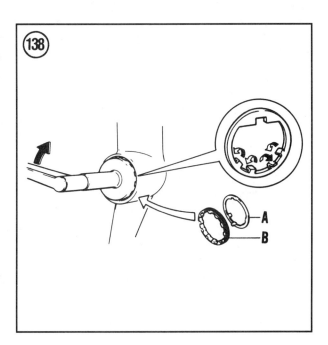

572 to the fastener threads. Install the fasteners and tighten to the specification listed in **Table 1**. Use a grease gun and the grease fitting in the carrier (4, **Figure 139**) to lubricate the mating surface of the carrier to the gearcase. Pump in Yamaha all-purpose grease until it flows from the housings.

On 115-250 hp models, apply grease to the seal lips of the drive shaft bearing/seal housing. Install a new O-ring onto the housing. Lubricate the O-ring with Yamaha gearcase lubricant. Place all shims, washers or bearings onto the drive shaft then slide the bearing/seal housing over the drive shaft. Carefully press the housing into the gearcase. Apply Loctite 572 to the fastener threads. Install the fasteners and tighten to the specifications listed in **Table 1**.

Pressure test the gearcase as instructed in Chapter Three prior to filling with Yamaha gearcase lubricant.

Shim Selection (All Models)

> *CAUTION*
> *The backlash adjustment must be done correctly, or it will result in a noisy gearcase as well as rapid wear of the affected gears. Do not risk damage to a newly installed set of gears with an incorrect adjustment. If you feel unqualified to complete this procedure, have it performed by a Yamaha dealer or qualified machine shop familiar with outboard motors.*

Proper pinion gear engagement and forward and reverse gear backlash are necessary for smooth operation and long gear service life. A shim adjustment is required to achieve

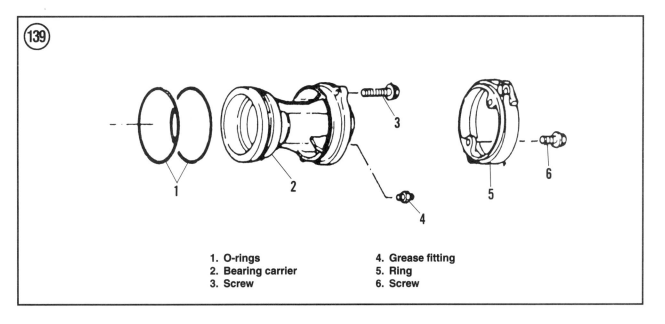

1. O-rings
2. Bearing carrier
3. Screw
4. Grease fitting
5. Ring
6. Screw

the proper tolerances when replacing major internal components such as gears, bearings, drive shaft or the gearcase housing. The marine dealership customarily uses specialized tools and precise measuring equipment to perform the shim selection procedure.

If the use of these tools is not possible, there is a less preferable but usually effective method of shim selection. Use the same shim thickness as removed from all shim locations. Assemble the gearcase, then measure the *gear backlash*. Gear backlash measurements will give a fairly accurate indication of what shim changes are required. Refer to *Measuring Gear Backlash* in this chapter for procedures.

> *NOTE*
> *All water pump components must be removed prior to measuring gear backlash. The drag created by the water pump components will hinder accurate measurements.*

> *CAUTION*
> *Use very light force when moving the drive shaft during backlash measurements. Inaccurate readings are certain if excessive force is used.*

> *NOTE*
> *Make sure that all gearcase lubricant is drained from the gearcase prior to measuring gear backlash. Inaccurate readings will result from the cushion effect of the lubricant on the gear teeth.*

Measuring Gear Backlash (All Models)

Gear backlash measurements and measuring procedures vary by model. Refer to the instructions that apply to your model.

A dial indicator, sturdy mount for the dial indicator, bearing puller assembly and backlash indicator tool are required to accurately measure backlash. For 2-250 hp models, use backlash indicator Yamaha part No. YB-06265/90890-06705. Secure a suitable puller tool or Yamaha part No. YB-06234, YB-06117, YB-90890-6501, YB-90890-6504. A dial indicator and sturdy mount can be purchased through most tool suppliers or use Yamaha part No. YU-03097/90890-01252 and YU-34481/90890-06705.

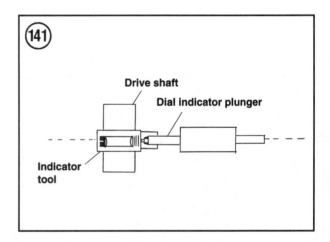

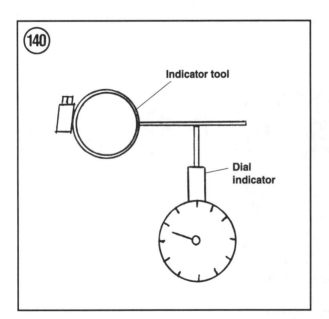

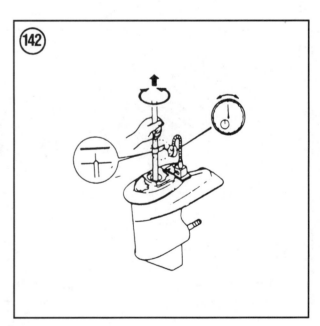

When attaching the dial indicator and indicator tool, always align the dial indicator at a 90° angle to the indicator arm (**Figure 140**) as viewed from the top. The dial indicator must be positioned at the same height and aligned with the backlash indicator on the drive shaft (**Figure 141**) as viewed from the side.

To measure gear backlash, load the propeller shaft in the fore or aft position using hand pressure or a puller to prevent shaft movement. Position the gearcase with the drive shaft facing up or down. Lightly rotate the driveshaft clockwise and counterclockwise while observing the dial indicator. The free movement of the shaft indicates the amount of gear lash or tooth clearance that is present. Read the amount of movement on the dial indicator. Gear backlash specifications are listed in **Table 2**.

1. For 2 hp models, check the gear backlash as follows:

    a. Slide the backlash indicator onto the drive shaft. Position the gearcase with the drive shaft facing UP.

    b. Secure the dial indicator and indicator mount to the gearcase. Align the dial indicator plunger with the mark on the backlash indicator. Secure the indicator to the shaft.

    c. Lightly pull up on the shaft and gently rotate the drive shaft in the clockwise and counterclockwise directions (**Figure 142**). Note the dial indicator reading when the drive shaft reaches its free movement limit in each direction. Record the amount of needle movement as the gear backlash measurement.

2. For 3 hp models, check the gear backlash as follows:

    a. Pull up on the shift shaft to shift the gearcase into forward gear. Slide the backlash indicator onto the drive shaft. Secure the dial indicator and indicator mount to the gearcase.

    b. Align the dial indicator stem with the mark on the backlash indicator. Tighten the indicator to the drive shaft. Position the gearcase with the drive shaft facing down.

    c. Hold the propeller shaft to prevent rotation. Gently rotate the drive shaft in the clockwise and counterclockwise directions (**Figure 143**). Note the dial indicator reading when the drive shaft reaches its free movement limit in each direction. Record the amount of needle movement as the gear backlash measurement.

3. For 4-50 hp and E60 models (except Model E48), check the gear backlash as follows:

    a. Rotate the drive shaft and push down or pull up on the shift shaft (**Figure 144**) until the gearcase is in neutral.

9

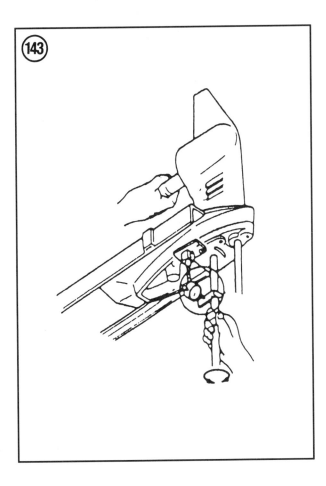

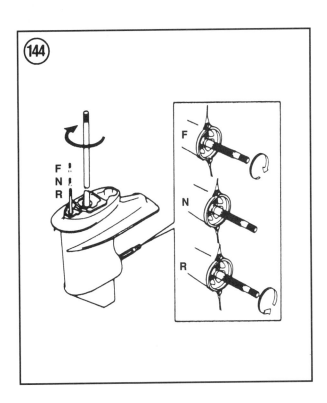

b. Install the puller assembly onto the gearcase as shown in **Figure 145**. Tighten the center bolt to load the propeller shaft forward and prevent free movement of the propeller shaft.

c. Slide the backlash indicator onto the drive shaft. Secure the dial indicator and indicator mount to the gearcase. Align the dial indicator stem with the mark on the backlash indicator. Tighten the backlash indicator to the drive shaft. Position the gearcase with the drive shaft facing down.

d. Lightly pull down on the drive shaft, or away from the gearcase (**Figure 146**), while gently rotating the drive shaft in the clockwise and counterclockwise directions. Note the dial indicator reading when the drive shaft reaches its free movement limit in each direction. Record the amount of needle movement as the *forward* gear backlash measurement.

e. On 4-15 hp models, remove the puller assembly from the propeller shaft (**Figure 147**). Repeat Step d. Record the amount of dial indicator needle movement as reverse gear backlash.

f. On 20-30 hp and 40, 50 and E60 models, install the propeller onto the propeller shaft (**Figure 148**) without the spacer (located forward of the propeller) and with the propeller facing backward. Install the propeller nut and tighten to 5.0 Nm (44.0 in. lb.). This will prevent propeller shaft rotation and pull the propeller shaft in the aft direction. With the drive shaft facing down, repeat Step d. Record the amount of dial indicator movement as *reverse* gear backlash.

4. For E48 and 60-90 hp models (except Model E60), check the gear backlash as follows:

a. Rotate the drive shaft clockwise and move the shift shaft until the gearcase is in neutral.

b. Install the puller assembly onto the gearcase as shown in **Figure 145**. Tighten the puller center bolt to 5.0 Nm (44.0 in. lb.). This will prevent free

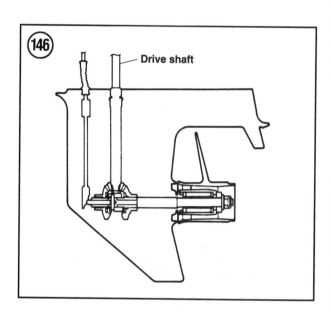

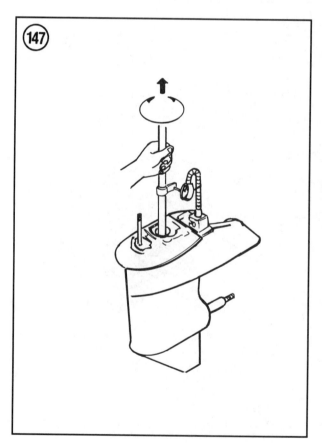

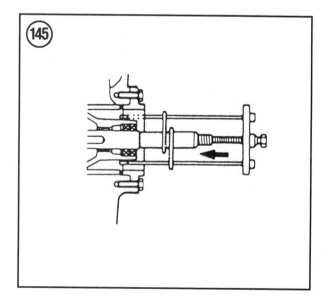

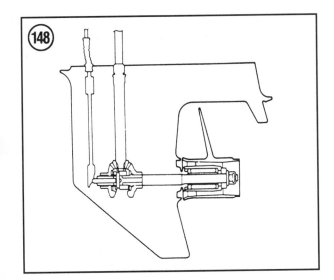

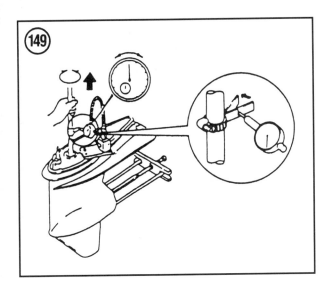

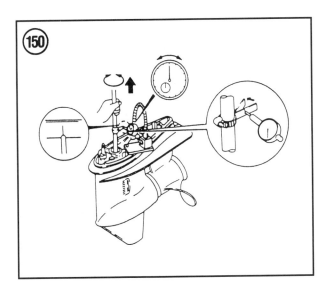

movement of the propeller shaft and load the propeller shaft forward.

c. Slide the backlash indicator onto the drive shaft. Secure the dial indicator and indicator mount with the gearcase. Align the dial indicator stem to the mark on the backlash indicator. Tighten the backlash indicator to the drive shaft. Position the gearcase with the drive shaft facing up.

d. Lightly pull up on the drive shaft then *gently* rotate the drive shaft in the clockwise and counterclockwise directions (**Figure 149**). Note the dial indicator readings when the drive shaft reaches its free movement limit in each direction. Record the amount of needle movement as the *forward* gear backlash.

e. Remove the puller assembly from the gearcase. Install a propeller onto the propeller shaft without the spacer and with the propeller facing backwards (**Figure 148**). Install the spacer and the propeller nut and tighten to 5.0 Nm (44.0 in. lb.). This will prevent free movement of the propeller shaft and load the propeller shaft in the aft direction. Repeat Step d and record the amount of dial indicator movement (**Figure 150**) as the *reverse* gear backlash.

5. For 115-250 hp models, check the gear backlash as follows:

a. Rotate the drive shaft in the clockwise direction, as viewed from the top, and move the shift shaft until the propeller shaft rotates in the clockwise direction (**Figure 151**). Use the shift rod wrench Yamaha part No. YB-06052 to rotate the shift shaft.

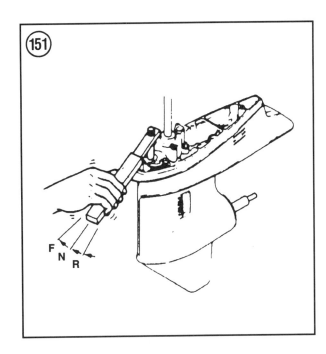

9

b. Install the puller assembly onto the carrier and propeller shaft as indicated in **Figure 152**. Tighten the center bolt (4, **Figure 152**) to 5.0 Nn (44.0 in. lb.). This will prevent free propeller shaft movement and load the propeller shaft forward.

c. Slide the backlash indicator onto the drive shaft. Secure the dial indicator and indicator mount onto the gearcase. Align the dial indicator stem with the mark on the backlash indicator. Tighten the backlash indicator to the drive shaft at the large diameter area. Position the gearcase with the drive shaft facing down.

d. Lightly pull down on the drive shaft, or away from the gearcase, then gently rotate the drive shaft in the clockwise and counterclockwise directions (**Figure 153**). Note the dial indicator readings when the drive shaft reaches its free movement limit in each direction. On standard rotation units, record the amount of dial indicator movement as the *forward* gear backlash. On counter rotation units, record the amount of dial indicator movement as the *reverse* gear backlash.

e. Loosen the backlash indicator from the drive shaft. Remove the puller assembly from the propeller shaft and carrier. Repeat Step a, positioning the shifter until the propeller shaft rotates in the counterclockwise direction. Install the propeller onto the propeller shaft *without* the spacer normally located forward of the propeller. Tighten the propeller nut to 5.0 Nm (44.0 in. lb.).

f. Position the backlash indicator as instructed in Step c. Repeat Step d. On standard rotation units, record the amount of dial indicator movement as *reverse* gear backlash. On counter rotation units (L models), record the amount of dial indicator movement as *forward* gear backlash.

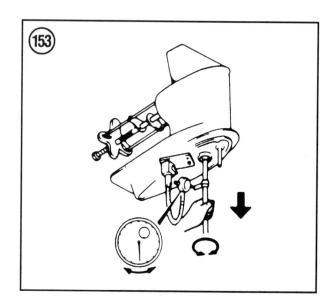

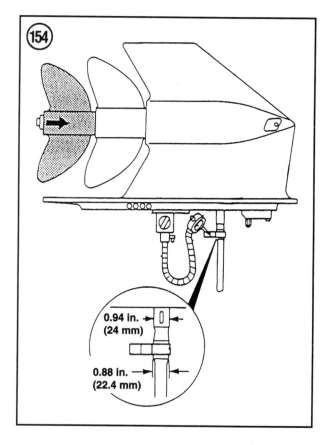

(152)

1. **Housing puller (part No. Yb-06234)**
2. **Universal puller (part No. Yb-06117)**
3. **Stopper plate (part No. Yb-06501)**
4. **Center bolt (part No. Yb-06504)**

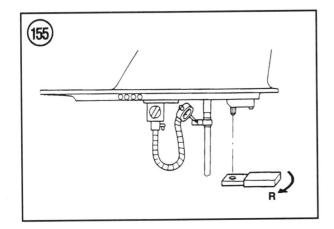

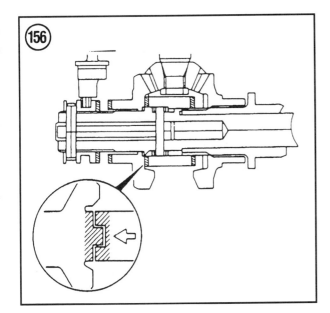

6. For twin propeller units (D150 models), check gear backlash as follows.

   a. Install both propellers onto the gearcase. Position the gearcase with the drive shaft facing down. Install the backlash indicator onto the large diameter portion of the drive shaft (**Figure 154**).

   b. Place the shift rod wrench Yamaha part No. YB-06052 onto the shift shaft. Rotate the shift rod wrench to the reverse gear direction as indicated in **Figure 155**.

   c. Use a block of wood, a suitable scale and an assistant to apply 400 N (90 lb.) of forward pressure to the rear propeller (**Figure 154**). Do not apply any pressure to the front propeller.

   d. With the pressure applied to the rear propeller, slowly turn the drive shaft clockwise until you feel the clutch engage the gear (**Figure 156**).

   e. Shift the gearcase into neutral. Rotate the front propeller approximately 30° in the clockwise direction. Move the shift shaft toward the reverse gear direction (**Figure 157**). The movement toward reverse gear should be difficult. If not, repeat Steps b-e until shift shaft movement is difficult when shifted toward reverse gear.

   f. Rotate the drive shaft approximately 20° in the clockwise direction (**Figure 158**). Install the back-

9

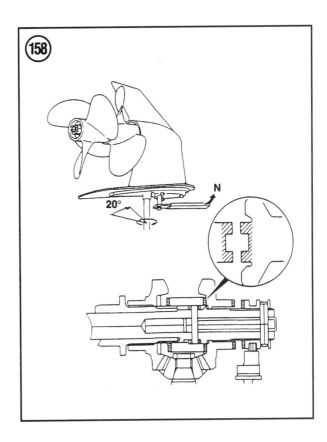

lash indicator onto the drive shaft and align the dial indicator to the mark on the backlash indicator. Move the shift shaft toward the reverse gear.

g. While maintaining the force applied to the rear propeller and the shift shaft held toward reverse gear, carefully rotate the drive shaft in the clockwise and counterclockwise directions. Note the dial indicator readings when the drive shaft reaches its free movement limits in either direction. Record the amount of needle movement on the dial indicator as *front* gear backlash.

h. Remove the backlash indicator from the drive shaft. Remove the force from the rear propeller and apply the same force 400 N (90 lb.) to the front propeller (**Figure 159**).

i. Move the shift shaft toward the forward gear position (**Figure 160**). Watch for propeller movement and rotate the drive shaft clockwise until you feel both clutch dogs engage and both propellers begin to move (**Figure 161**). Ensure that the front propeller rotates in the direction indicated in **Figure 161**.

j. Move the shift shaft to the neutral position (**Figure 162**). Slowly rotate the drive shaft clockwise until the front propeller rotates approximately 20° in the clockwise direction (**Figure 162**).

k. Move the shift shaft toward the forward gear direction and maintain pressure on the shift shaft. Align the dial indicator stem to the mark on the backlash

indicator. Tighten the dial indicator to the large diameter section of the drive shaft. Gently rotate the drive shaft in the clockwise and counterclockwise directions. Note the dial indicator readings when the drive shaft reaches its free movement limits (**Figure 163**) in each direction. Record the amount of needle movement on the dial indicator as *rear* gear backlash.

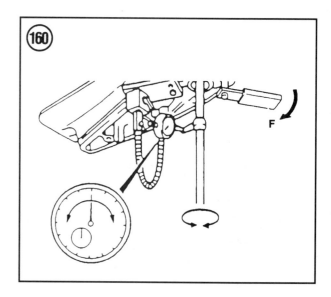

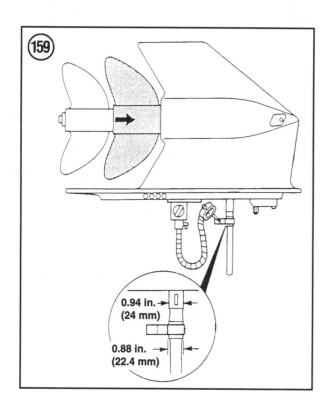

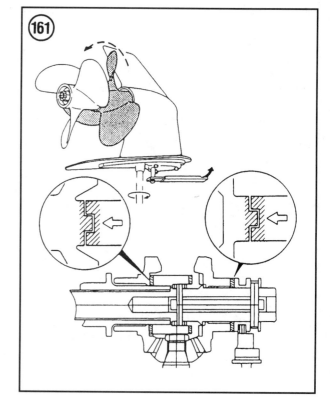

Changes to Shim Thickness

Compare the recorded backlash readings with the specifications listed in **Table 2**. Shim changes are required when one or both backlash readings are beyond the listed specifications. Refer to the description of the backlash readings for recommended shim changes. Available shims are listed in **Table 3**.

NOTE
Shim locations vary within the models. Always note the location of all shims during disassembly and ensure that all shims are installed in the same location.

Make all shim changes in small increments. Aim for the middle of the backlash specification anytime shim changes are required.

In most cases, no change or only a slight change from the original shim thickness is required. Always check for proper assembly prior to making significant changes to shim thickness.

Gearcase disassembly is required to gain access to the shims. Refer to the procedures provided in this chapter.

After any shim change, assemble the gearcase and repeat the backlash measuring procedure. Make required changes until all readings are within the specifications listed in **Table 2**.

Both measurements too high

The pinion gear is probably positioned too high in the gearcase when both readings are above the listed specifications. Shim changes are required to lower the pinion gear closer to both driven gears.

On 2-25 hp models, the shims that set the pinion height (A, **Figure 164**) are located just above the pinion gear. Select a thicker shim or set of shims to position the pinion gear closer to the driven gear(s). This will lower both

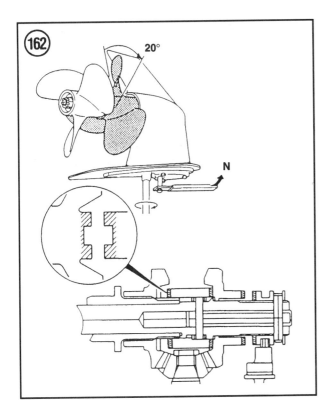

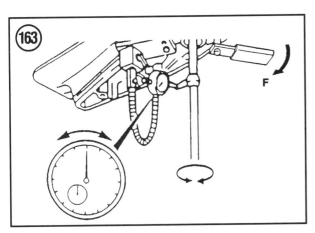

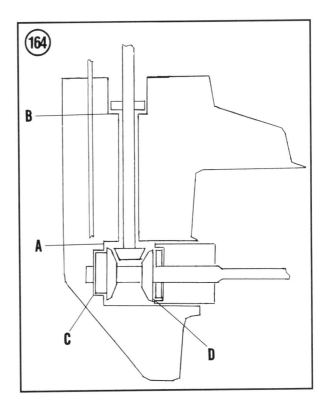

backlash readings. Measure the gear backlash to verify lower readings. Make further changes if necessary until both backlash readings are within the listed specifications.

On 30-250 hp models, the shims that set the pinion height (B, **Figure 164**) are located just below the bearing near the water pump. Select a thinner shim or set of shims to position the pinion gear closer to the driven gear. This will lower both backlash readings. Measure the backlash to verify lower readings. Make further changes if necessary until both readings are within the listed specifications.

Both measurements too low

The pinion gear is probably positioned too low in the gearcase when both readings are below the listed specifications. Shim changes are required to raise the pinion gear away from both driven gears.

On 2-25 hp models, the shims that set the pinion height (A, **Figure 164**) are located just above the pinion gear. Select a thinner shim or set of shims to position the pinion gear further from the driven gear(s). This will increase both backlash readings. Measure the gear backlash to verify higher readings. Make further changes if necessary until both readings are within the listed specifications.

On 30-250 hp models, the shim that set the pinion height (B, **Figure 164**) are located just below the bearing near the water pump. Select a thicker shim or set of shims to position the pinion gear further from the driven gear. This will increase both backlash readings. Measure the backlash to verify higher readings. Make further changes if necessary until both readings are within the listed specifications.

Standard rotation gearcase, forward gear backlash too high

The shims that set the forward gear backlash (C, **Figure 164**) are located just forward of the front gear bearing. Select a thicker shim or set of shims to position the front gear closer to the pinion gear. This will lower the forward gear backlash without affecting the reverse gear backlash. Measure the gear backlash to verify lower readings. Make further shim changes if necessary until backlash is within the listed specification.

Counter rotation gearcase, forward gear backlash too high

The shims that set forward gear backlash (D, **Figure 164**) are located between the *rear* gear and the bearing carrier. Select a thicker shim or set of shims to position the rear gear closer to the pinion gear. This will lower the

forward gear backlash without affecting the reverse gear backlash. Measure the gear backlash to verify lower readings. Make further shim changes if necessary until backlash is within the listed specification.

Standard rotation gearcase, forward gear backlash too low

The shims that set forward gear backlash (C, **Figure 164**) are located just forward of the front gear bearing. Select a thinner shim or set of shims to position the front gear further from the pinion gear. This will increase the forward gear backlash without affecting reverse gear backlash. Measure backlash to verify higher readings. Make further shim changes if necessary until backlash is within the listed specification.

Counter rotation gearcase, forward gear backlash too low

The shims that set forward gear backlash (D, **Figure 164**) are located between the *rear* gear and the bearing carrier. Select a thinner shim or set of shims to position the rear gear further from the pinion gear. This will increase the forward gear backlash without affecting the reverse gear backlash. Measure the gear backlash to verify higher reading. Make further shim changes if necessary until backlash is within the specification.

Standard rotation gearcase, reverse gear backlash too high

On 4-30 hp models, shims are not used to set reverse gear backlash. Check for and correct any condition that prevents the gearcase cap/bearing carrier from seating properly into the gearcase.

On 40-250 hp models, the shims that set reverse gear backlash (D, **Figure 164**) are located between the reverse gear bearing and the bearing carrier. Select a thicker shim or set of shims to position the reverse gear closer to the pinion gear. This will lower the reverse gear backlash without affecting forward gear backlash. Measure the gear backlash to verify lower readings. Make further shim changes if necessary until backlash is within the listed specification.

Counter rotation gearcase, reverse gear backlash too high

The shims that set the reverse gear backlash (C, **Figure 164**) are located between the front gear bearing and the step in the housing. Select a thicker shim or set of shims to position the front gear closer to the pinion gear. This will decrease the reverse gear backlash without affecting the forward gear backlash. Measure the gear backlash to verify lower readings. Make further shim changes if necessary until backlash is within the listed specification.

Standard rotation gearcase, reverse gear backlash too low

On 4-30 hp models, shims are not used to set reverse gear backlash. Check for and correct any condition that prevents the reverse gear from seating properly to the reverse gear bearing. Check for and correct any condition that prevents the bearing from seating properly into the gearcase cap/bearing carrier.

On 40-250 hp models, the shims that set reverse gear backlash (D, **Figure 164**) are located between the reverse gear bearing and the bearing carrier. Select a thinner shim or set of shims to position the reverse gear further from the pinion gear. This will increase the reverse gear backlash without affecting the forward gear backlash. Measure the gear backlash to verify higher readings. Make further shim changes if necessary until backlash is within the listed specification.

Counter rotation gearcase, reverse gear backlash too low

The shims that set reverse gear backlash (C, **Figure 164**) are located between the front gear bearing and the step in the housing. Select a thinner shim or set of shims to position the front gear further from the pinion gear. This will increase the reverse gear backlash without affecting forward gear backlash. Measure the gear backlash to verify higher readings. Make further changes if necessary until backlash is within the listed specification.

Twin propeller gearcase, front gear backlash too high

The shims that set the front gear backlash (C, **Figure 164**) are located between the front gear bearing and the step in the housing. Select a thicker shim or set of shims to position the front gear closer to the pinion gear. This will lower the front gear backlash without affecting the rear gear backlash. Measure the gear backlash to verify lower readings. Make further changes if necessary until backlash is within the specification.

Twin propeller gearcase, front gear backlash too low

The shims that set the front gear backlash (C, **Figure 164**) are located between the front gear bearing and the step in the housing. Select a thinner shim or set of shims to position the front gears further from the pinion gear. This will increase the front gear backlash without affecting the rear gear backlash. Measure the gear backlash to verify higher readings. Make further changes if necessary until backlash is within the specification.

Twin propeller gearcase, rear gear backlash too high

The shims that set rear gear backlash (D, **Figure 164**) are located between the rear gear bearing carrier and the step in the gearcase. Select a thinner shim or set of shims to position the rear gear closer to the pinion gear. This will lower rear gear backlash without affecting front gear backlash. Measure the gear backlash to verify lower readings. Make further changes if necessary until backlash is within the specification.

Twin propeller gearcase, back gear backlash too low

The shims that set rear gear backlash (D, **Figure 164**) are located between the rear gear bearing carrier and the step in the gearcase. Select a thicker shim or set of shims to position the rear gear further from the pinion gear. This will increase the rear gear backlash without affecting front gear backlash. Measure the gear backlash to verify higher readings. Make further changes if necessary until backlash is within the specification.

Special Procedures for L Model Gearcases

Many of the components used on the L (counter rotation) models are identical or similar to the components used on the standard rotation units. When applicable, you will be directed to the information and procedures provided for the standard rotation gearcases. Procedures and information required to repair counter rotation gearcases are provided in this section.

Refer to **Figure 165-167** during disassembly and assembly of the gearcase.

a. For 115 and 130 L models, refer to **Figure 165**.

b. For 150-225 hp (90°) L models, refer to **Figure 166**.

c. For 200-250 hp (90°) L models, refer to **Figure 167**.

9

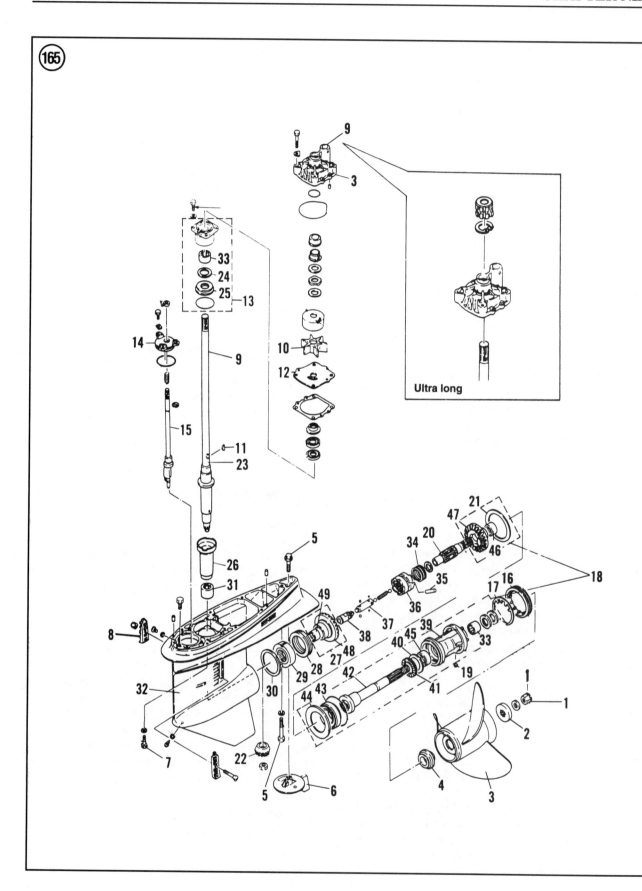

Ultra long

**COUNTER ROTATION GEARCASE
(115 AND 130 HP MODELS)**

1. Propeller nut
2. Spacer
3. Propeller
4. Front spacer
5. Bolt
6. Trim tab
7. Bolt/washer
8. Water inlet
9. Drive shaft
10. Impeller
11. Drive key
12. Wear plate
13. Bearing and seal
    housing assembly
14. Shift shaft
    seal housing
15. Shift shaft
16. Cover nut
17. Locking tab washer
18. Bearing carrier
    and gear assembly
19. Locating key
20. Rear propeller shaft
21. Thrust spacer
22. Pinion gear
23. Drive shaft
24. Shim

25. Bearing
26. Lubrication sleeve
27. Reverse gear
    assembly
28. Bearing carrier
29. Reverse gear bearing
30. Shim
31. Drive shaft
    lower bearing
32. Gearcase housing
33. Drive shaft upper bearing
34. Spring
35. Cross pin
36. Clutch
37. Shift slider
38. Shifter
39. Bearing carrier
40. Shim
41. Bearing
42. Front propeller shaft
43. Forward gear
    bearing carrier
44. Thrust spacer
45. Needle bearing
46. Forward gear assembly
47. Forward gear
48. Reverse gear
49. Needle bearing

9

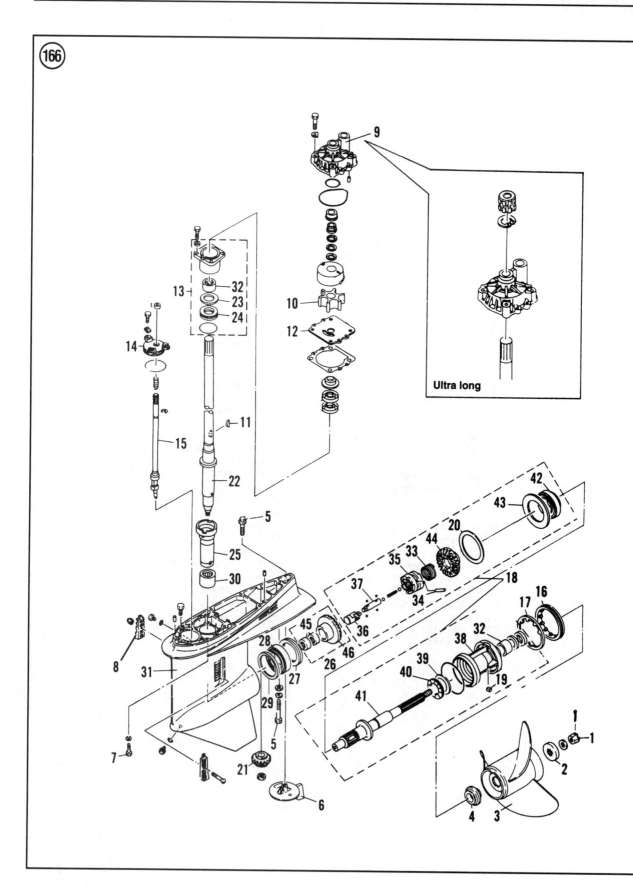

Ultra long

COUNTER ROTATION GEARCASE
(150-225 HP [90°] MODELS)

1. Propeller nut
2. Spacer
3. Propeller
4. Front spacer
5. Bolt
6. Trim tab
7. Bolt
8. Water inlet
9. Pump cover
10. Impeller
11. Drive key
12. Wear plate
13. Bearing and seal housing
14. Shift shaft seal housing
15. Shift shaft
16. Cover nut
17. Locking tab washer
18. Bearing carrier and
    forward gear assembly
19. Locating key
20. Shim
21. Pinion gear
22. Drive shaft
23. Shim
24. Bearing
25. Lubrication sleeve
26. Reverse gear assembly
27. Reverse gear bearing
28. Bearing carrier
29. Shim
30. Drive shaft
    lower bearing
31. Gearcase housing
32. Needle bearing
33. Spring
34. Cross pin
35. Clutch
36. Shifter
37. Shift slider
38. Bearing carrier
39. Shim
40. Bearing
41. Propeller shaft
42. Forward gear bearing
43. Thrust spacer
44. Forward gear
45. Needle bearing
46. Reverse gear

9

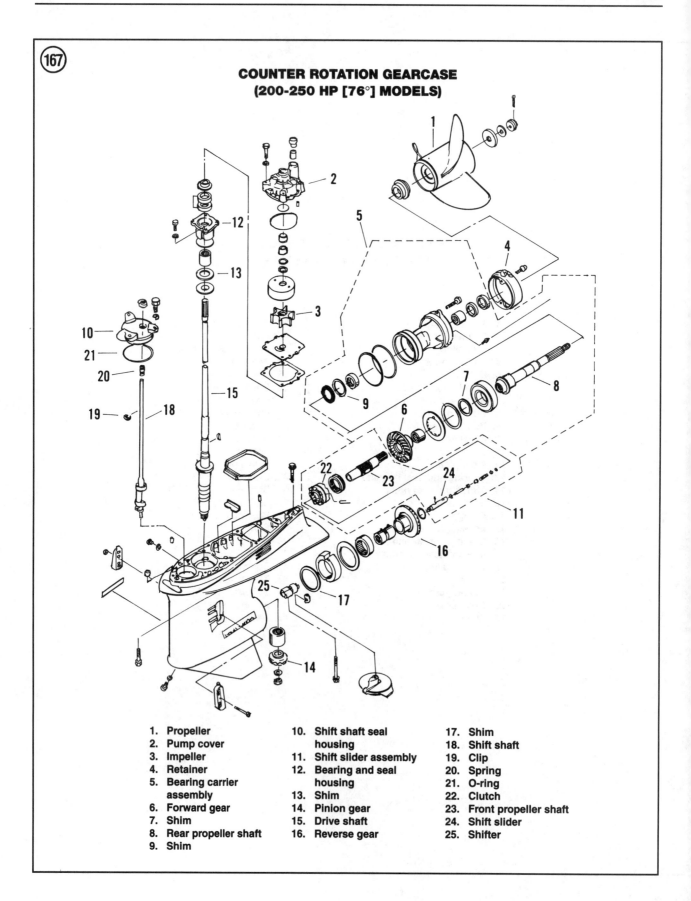

**COUNTER ROTATION GEARCASE
(200-250 HP [76°] MODELS)**

1. Propeller
2. Pump cover
3. Impeller
4. Retainer
5. Bearing carrier assembly
6. Forward gear
7. Shim
8. Rear propeller shaft
9. Shim
10. Shift shaft seal housing
11. Shift slider assembly
12. Bearing and seal housing
13. Shim
14. Pinion gear
15. Drive shaft
16. Reverse gear
17. Shim
18. Shift shaft
19. Clip
20. Spring
21. O-ring
22. Clutch
23. Front propeller shaft
24. Shift slider
25. Shifter

Water pump

Water pump component removal, inspection and assembly procedures are identical to the standard rotation models of the same horsepower. Refer to the *Water Pump* section in this chapter.

Bearing carrier

CAUTION
The shifter and shift shaft components can suffer damage during the propeller shaft re-

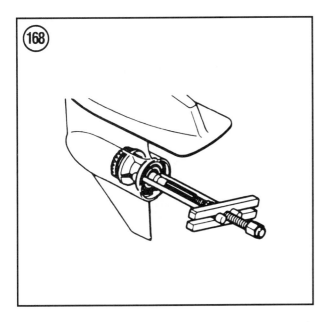

moval process. Always remove the shift shaft from the gearcase prior to pulling the propeller shaft from the housing.

Remove the propeller from the propeller shaft following the procedure listed for the standard rotation model of the same horsepower. Use the cover nut tool, Yamaha part No. YB-34447, to remove the cover nut from the gearcase.

On 115 and 130 models, remove the shift shaft from the gearcase following the procedures listed for the standard rotation models. Use a suitable puller tool or Yamaha part No. YB-06117, YB-06501, YB-06504 to pull the forward gear and carrier assembly from the gearcase as indicated in **Figure 168**. Pull the front propeller shaft from the gearcase.

On 150-250 models, use a slide hammer (Yamaha part No. YB-06096) and puller head (Yamaha part NO. YB-6335) to remove the carrier, propeller shaft and forward gear assembly. Thread the puller head onto the end of the propeller shaft. Thread the slide hammer onto the puller head. Use quick strokes of the slide hammer (**Figure 169**) to remove the assembly from the gearcase. Make certain that you retain the locating key from the bearing carrier upon removal of the carrier. On 200-250 hp (76°) models, pull the front propeller shaft from the gearcase.

On 115-225 hp (90°) models, use a suitable puller or Yamaha part No.YB-06207 to push the propeller shaft and forward gear from the bearing carrier as indicated in **Figure 170**. Note the location and orientation of all bearings, shims, washers and seals prior to removal from the bearing carrier.

9

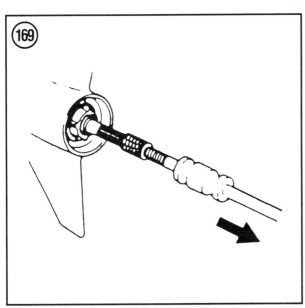

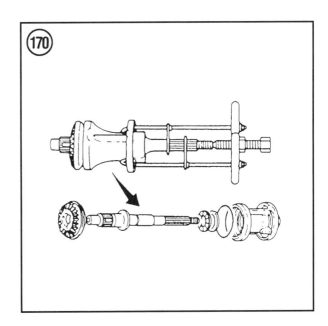

On 200-250 hp (76°) models, secure the bearing carrier into a vise with soft jaws. Use a slide hammer and remove the forward gear from the bearing carrier as indicated in **Figure 171**. Use a screwdriver to bend the locking tab away from the ring nut. With the bearing carrier secured in a vise, use the ring nut removal and installation tool (Yamaha part No. YB-06048/90890-06510) to remove the ring nut and tab washer from the bearing carrier as indicated in **Figure 172**. Use a suitable puller or Yamaha part No. YB-06207 to push the propeller shaft and bearing from the bearing carrier (**Figure 170**). Note the location and orientation of all components prior to removal.

NOTE
DO NOT remove the needle bearings from the bearing carrier unless they must be replaced. They are not suitable for use after removal. As with the standard rotation gearcases, always measure the depth of seals and bearings within the bearing carrier prior to removal. Record the measurements for use when installing the components.

Refer to the procedures listed for the standard rotation units for propeller shaft seal and aft needle bearing removal. Use a depth micrometer to measure the depth of the needle bearing for the forward gear (**Figure 173**). Record the measurements for use when installing the bearing. Secure the carrier into a vise with soft jaws. Use a slide hammer and puller jaws to remove the bearing from the carrier (**Figure 174**).

Propeller shaft

Disassemble the propeller shaft components following the procedures listed for the standard rotation model of the same horsepower.

Gears and bearings

Refer to the standard rotation section for gear and bearing removal and inspection procedures. As with the standard rotation models, measure the installed depth of all needle bearings prior to removal.

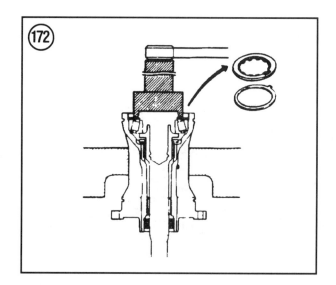

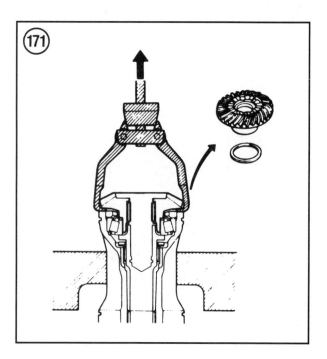

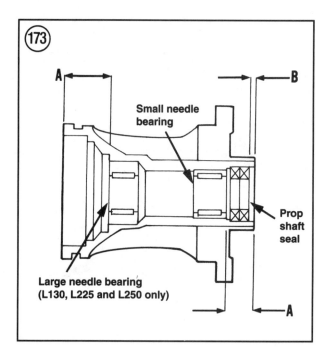

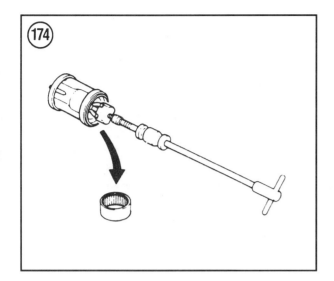

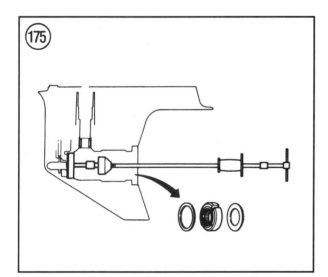

Pull the reverse gear from the gearcase after removal of the propeller shaft and shift shaft. *Do not* remove the roller bearing unless damaged. The roller bearing is not suitable for use after removal. Use a slide hammer (**Figure 175**) and remove the bearing and shims from the gearcase as required.

Shift shaft and shifting components

Removal, inspection and installation of the shift shaft and seal carriers are identical to the standard rotation models. Refer to the procedures for the same horsepower.

Drive shaft and pinion gear

Drive shaft and pinion gear removal, inspection and assembly procedures are identical to the standard rotation models of the same horsepower. Refer to the standard rotation drive shaft, drive shaft bearing and seal removal and installation procedures provided in this chapter.

Assembly

Assembly is the reverse of disassembly. Refer to the procedures for the standard rotation gearcases when the components are identical or similar. Following are special assembly instructions:

On 115-225 hp (90° V) models, use an appropriately sized socket, section of pipe or tubing to drive the roller bearing and shims into the bearing carrier (**Figure 176**). The numbered or lettered side of the roller bearing must face outward. Install the bearing to the depth recorded prior to removal. Install all bearings, washers and shims to

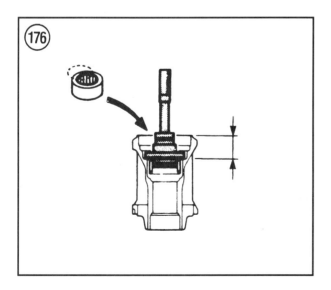

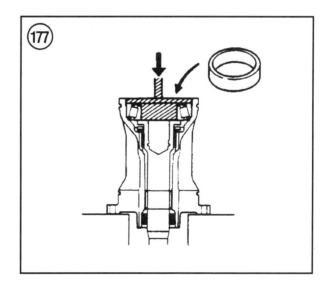

the same location and orientation as removed. Slide or press the propeller shaft and forward gear into the bearing carrier.

On 200-250 hp models, install the forward gear shims, then use Yamaha part No. YB-06071 and YB-06430 to drive the bearing race into position (**Figure 177**). Install all shims washers and bearings into the carrier (**Figure 178**). Press the propeller shaft into the tapered roller bearing. Install the ring nut with the same tools used to remove it (**Figure 179**). Tighten the ring nut to 108 N•m (80 ft.-lb.), then bend the locking tab into a slot on the ring nut. Additional tightening of the ring nut may be required to align the tab with an opening. Install the shim onto the hub of the gear, then press the forward gear into the tapered bearing.

Install the shims into the step at the front of the gearcase. Use a suitable driver to carefully drive the reverse gear roller bearing into the gearcase (**Figure 180**). The tool used must contact the bearing case, yet not contact the gearcase during assembly. Lubricate the thrust bearing with Yamaha all-purpose grease and install onto the reverse gear bearing surface if so equipped.

Complete the assembly using the procedures for the standard rotation models when applicable. Use a dial indicator and mount to measure the amount of propeller shaft end play (**Figure 181**). Move the propeller shaft in the fore and aft direction while observing the dial indicator reading. Check the bearing, shims and washer orientation if the end play is not within 0.25-0.40 mm (0.012-0.016 in.). Increase or decrease shim thickness to correct the end play if necessary.

Refer to the standard rotation model of the same horsepower for procedures and install all water pump components. Refer to Chapter Three for procedures, then pressure test the gearcase prior to filling with gearcase lubricant.

Special Procedures for D Model (Twin Propeller) Gearcases

Many of the components used on D model (twin propeller) gearcases are identical or similar to the components used on standard rotation gearcases. When applicable, you will be directed to the information provided for the stand-

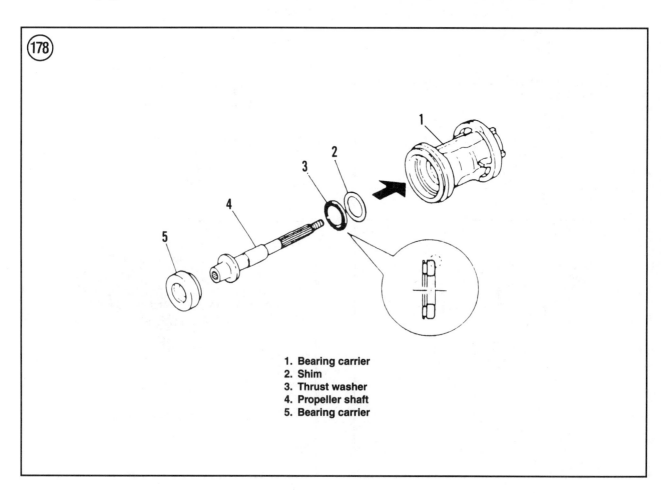

1. Bearing carrier
2. Shim
3. Thrust washer
4. Propeller shaft
5. Bearing carrier

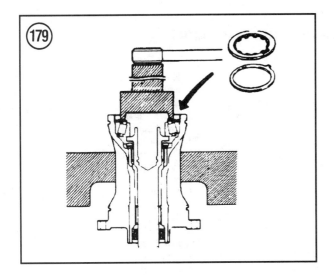

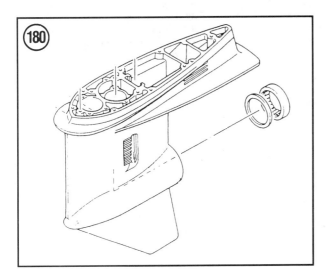

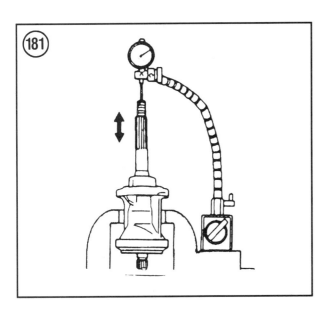

ard rotation gearcases. Information required to repair D model gearcases are provided in this section. For assistance with component identification and orientation, refer to **Figure 182** during the disassembly and assembly procedures.

Use the procedure for the standard rotation 150 hp models for water pump installation.

Refer to Chapter Three and pressure test the gearcase prior to filling with gearcase lubricant.

Water pump

The water pump used on the twin propellers is identical to the water pump used on other 150 hp models. For removal and installation procedures, refer to the *Water pump servicing* section in this chapter.

Propeller removal

> *WARNING*
> *Remove all spark plug leads and disconnect the battery before attempting to remove or install the propeller(s). Never use your hand to hold a propeller during removal or installation of the propeller nut. Place a block of wood between the propeller and the gearcase housing to prevent propeller shaft rotation. Use heavy gloves when handling the propellers.*

1. Disconnect all spark plug leads and both battery cables from the battery before attempting to remove the propellers.

2. Place a block of wood between the rear propeller and the gearcase to prevent propeller rotation.

3. Straighten the cotter pin (1, **Figure 183**) and remove it from the rear propeller shaft. Discard the cotter pin. The threaded end of the shaft is a standard right-hand thread. Turn the nut counterclockwise for removal and clockwise for installation. Use a suitable socket and breaker bar to loosen and remove the rear propeller nut (2, **Figure 183**).

4. Remove the spacer from the shaft. Use heavy gloves to pull the propeller from the shaft. A block of wood can be used as a cushion to carefully drive the propeller (5, **Figure 183**) from the propeller shaft if necessary. Use light blows to avoid damaging the propeller or propeller shaft. Inspect the propeller for damage and replace it or have it repaired as required.

5. Note the orientation of the thrust spacer and remove it from the rear propeller shaft.

9

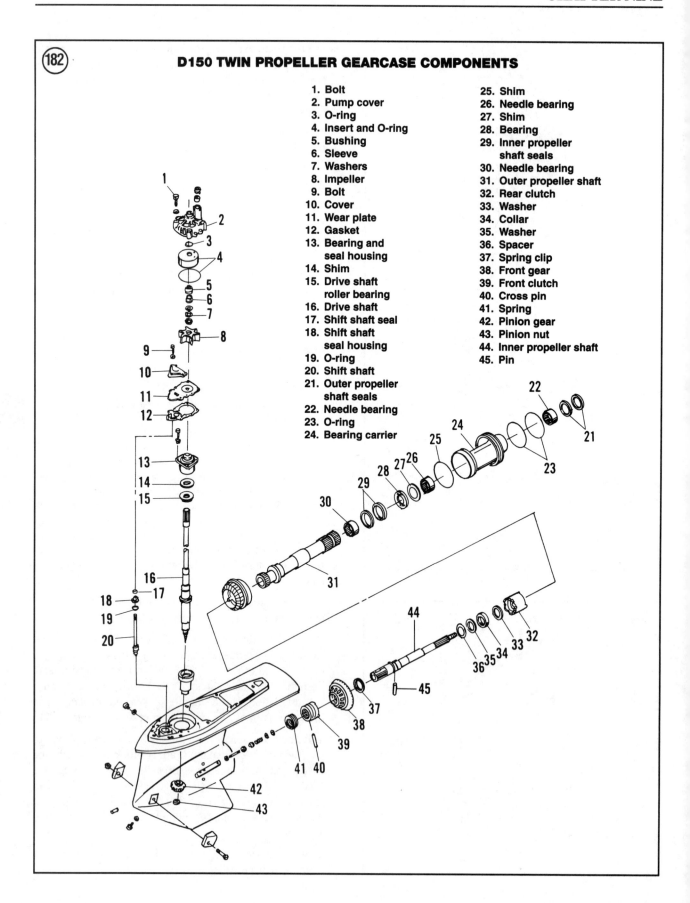

(182)

D150 TWIN PROPELLER GEARCASE COMPONENTS

1. Bolt
2. Pump cover
3. O-ring
4. Insert and O-ring
5. Bushing
6. Sleeve
7. Washers
8. Impeller
9. Bolt
10. Cover
11. Wear plate
12. Gasket
13. Bearing and seal housing
14. Shim
15. Drive shaft roller bearing
16. Drive shaft
17. Shift shaft seal
18. Shift shaft seal housing
19. O-ring
20. Shift shaft
21. Outer propeller shaft seals
22. Needle bearing
23. O-ring
24. Bearing carrier
25. Shim
26. Needle bearing
27. Shim
28. Bearing
29. Inner propeller shaft seals
30. Needle bearing
31. Outer propeller shaft
32. Rear clutch
33. Washer
34. Collar
35. Washer
36. Spacer
37. Spring clip
38. Front gear
39. Front clutch
40. Cross pin
41. Spring
42. Pinion gear
43. Pinion nut
44. Inner propeller shaft
45. Pin

6. Use a screwdriver to bend all tabs on the lockwasher (2, **Figure 184**) away from the front propeller nut. Place a block of wood between the front propeller and the gearcase housing to prevent propeller rotation. The threaded end of the front propeller shaft is a standard right-hand thread. Turn the nut counterclockwise for removal and clockwise for installation. Use a suitable socket and hinge handle,

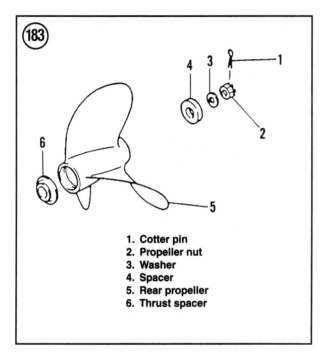

1. Cotter pin
2. Propeller nut
3. Washer
4. Spacer
5. Rear propeller
6. Thrust spacer

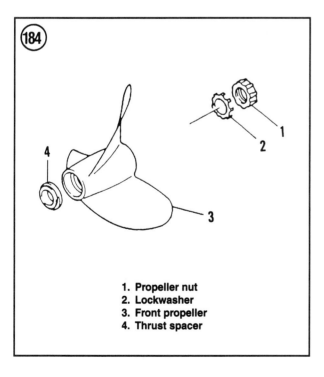

1. Propeller nut
2. Lockwasher
3. Front propeller
4. Thrust spacer

breaker bar, to remove the front propeller nut (1, **Figure 184**).

7. Pull the front propeller nut and lockwasher from the propeller shaft. Replace the lockwasher if corroded or the tabs are cracked or damaged. Use heavy gloves to remove the propeller from the propeller shaft. If necessary, use a block of wood as a cushion, then carefully drive the propeller from the propeller shaft. Use light blows to avoid damaging the propeller or propeller shaft. Inspect the propeller for damage and replace it or have it repaired as required.

8. Note the orientation of the thrust spacer (forward of the propeller) prior to removal. Pull the thrust spacer from the propeller shaft. Lightly tap the spacer if it is seized to the propeller shaft.

Propeller installation

> *WARNING*
> *Always remove all spark plug leads and disconnect both battery cables from the battery prior to installing the propellers. Use heavy gloves when handling the propellers.*

Install the propeller after completion of gearcase repairs. Clean all corrosion and other contaminants from both propellers, propeller shafts, thrust spacers, propeller nuts and the splined bore of the propellers prior to installation. Apply Yamaha all-purpose grease to the tapered and splined section of the propeller shafts prior to installation.

1. Install the front mounted thrust spacer onto the propeller shaft. The tapered bore must mate with the tapered area of the propeller shaft.

2. Slide the propeller (3, **Figure 184**) onto the propeller shaft. Slightly rotate the propeller to align the splines, then push the propeller onto the shaft until firmly seated against the thrust spacer. Place a block of wood between the propeller and the gearcase housing to prevent propeller rotation during installation.

3. Install the lockwasher (2, **Figure 184**) onto the propeller with the bent end of the tabs facing away from the propeller. Install the front propeller shaft nut (1, **Figure 184**) with the flat surface facing the propeller. Use a suitable socket and torque wrench to tighten the nut to the specification listed in **Table 1**. Bend two or more tabs up to engage the propeller nut and two or more tabs down to engage the propeller.

4. Install the thrust spacer for the rear propeller onto the propeller shaft. The tapered bore must mate with the tapered area of the propeller shaft.

5. Slide the propeller onto the propeller shaft. Slightly rotate the propeller to align the splines, then push the propeller onto the shaft until firmly seated against the

9

thrust spacer. Place a block of wood between the propeller and the gearcase housing to prevent propeller rotation during installation.

6. Install the spacer, washer and rear propeller nut onto the propeller shaft. Use a suitable socket and torque wrench to tighten the propeller nut to the specification listed in **Table 1**.

7. Install a new cotter pin through the slot in the propeller nut and the hole in the propeller shaft. Tighten the propeller nut slightly more if necessary to align the hole with the slots. Bend the ends of the cotter pin over.

Bearing carrier and front propeller shaft removal and disassembly

1. Use a screwdriver to bend the tabs of the tab washer away from the cover nut. Standard or right-hand threads are used to retain the cover nut. Use cover nut tool Yamaha part No. YB-42223 to loosen and remove the cover nut (**Figure 185**) from the gearcase.

2. Pull the bearing carrier, front propeller shaft and rear gear from the gearcase. Use the carrier removal procedures listed for standard rotation models if the carrier assembly cannot be easily pulled from the gearcase.

3. Clamp the bearing separator to the rear gear as shown in **Figure 186**. Place the carrier onto a press as indicated in **Figure 187**. Provide support for the propeller shaft to prevent the shaft from dropping. Press the rear gear and propeller shaft from the carrier.

4. Note the orientation of the components prior to removal. Remove the rear gear and bearing (1, **Figure 188**) from the

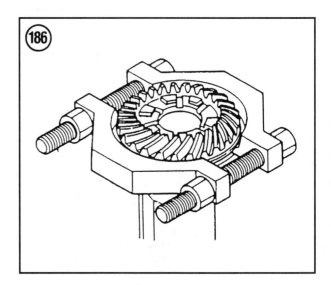

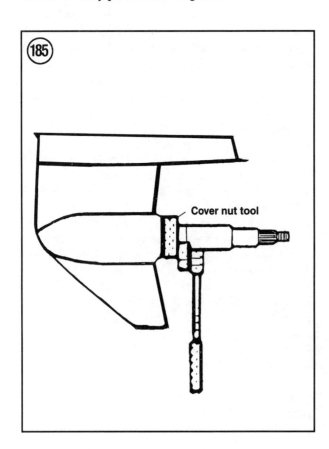

Cover nut tool

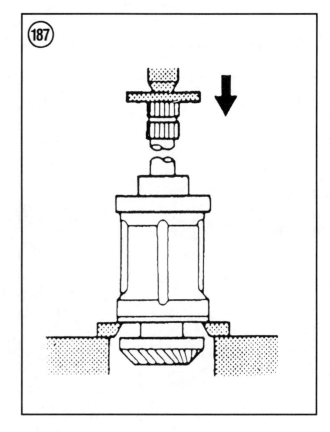

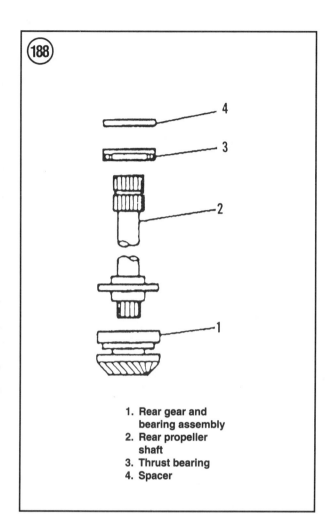

1. Rear gear and bearing assembly
2. Rear propeller shaft
3. Thrust bearing
4. Spacer

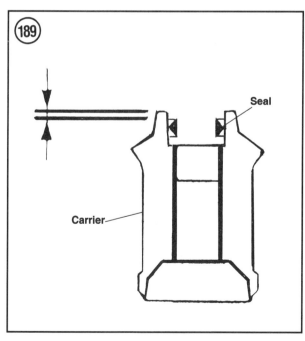

propeller shaft (2, **Figure 188**). Slide the thrust bearing (3, **Figure 188**) and spacer (4, **Figure 188**) off the shaft.

5. Use a depth micrometer to measure the seal depth as indicated in **Figure 189**. Record the measurement. Use a screwdriver to carefully pry the seals from the carrier. Discard the seals.

NOTE
Remove the needle bearing only if it must be replaced. The removal process will probably destroy the needle bearing.

6. Use a depth micrometer to measure the depth of the rear needle bearing at the points indicated in **Figure 190**. Measure the front needle bearing depth at the points indicated in **Figure 191**. Record all measurements.

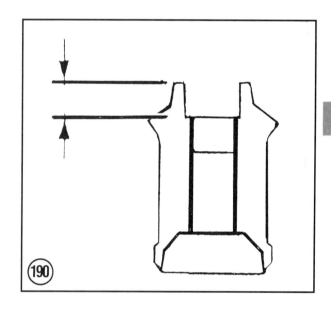

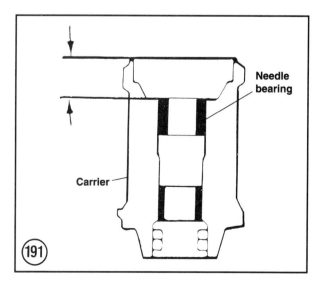

7. Note the orientation of the numbered side of the bearing prior to removal. Use a slide hammer (Yamaha part No. YB-06096) and bearing puller jaws (Yamaha part No. YB-06535) to remove the front and rear needle bearings (**Figure 192**).

Drive shaft and pinion gear removal

Prior to removal of the drive shaft, refer to the procedures for the standard rotation 150 hp gearcase to remove and disassemble the drive shaft seal and bearing housing (**Figure 193**).

Use special pinion nut tool (Yamaha part No. YB-42224) and drive shaft holder (Yamaha part No. YB-06201) to loosen and remove the pinion nut (**Figure 194**). If neces-

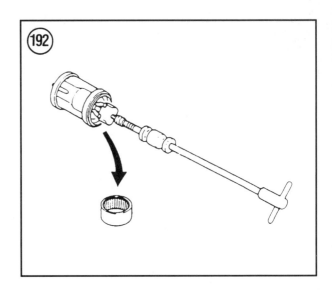

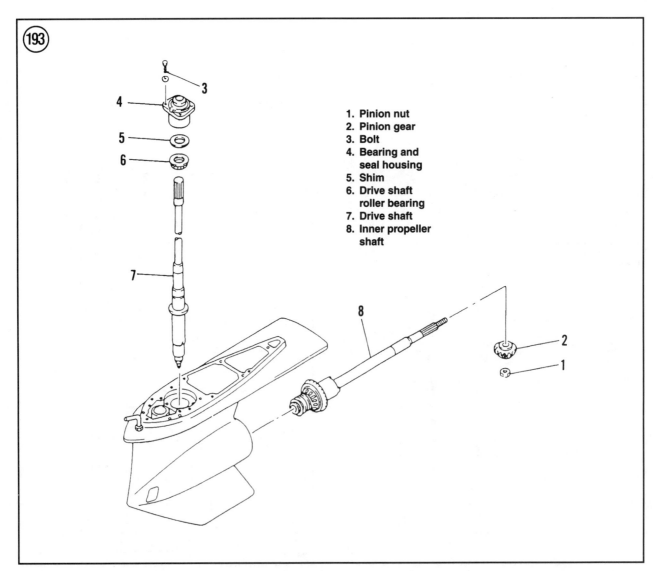

1. Pinion nut
2. Pinion gear
3. Bolt
4. Bearing and
   seal housing
5. Shim
6. Drive shaft
   roller bearing
7. Drive shaft
8. Inner propeller
   shaft

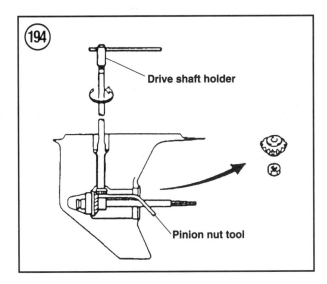

Drive shaft holder

Pinion nut tool

sary, a thin wrench can be used to grip the pinion nut. Pull the drive shaft from the gearcase. Remove the pinion nut and pinion gear from the gearcase.

Rear propeller shaft removal and disassembly

The pinion nut, pinion gear and drive shaft (**Figure 193**) must be removed prior to removal of the propeller shaft. Refer to the standard rotation 150 hp models for instructions, then remove the shift shaft from the gearcase.

Grasp the propeller shaft (8, **Figure 193**) and, without rotating, carefully pull the shaft and front gear assembly from the gearcase.

1. Use a screwdriver to unwind the spring (1, **Figure 195**) from the front clutch (2, **Figure 195**). Push the cross pin

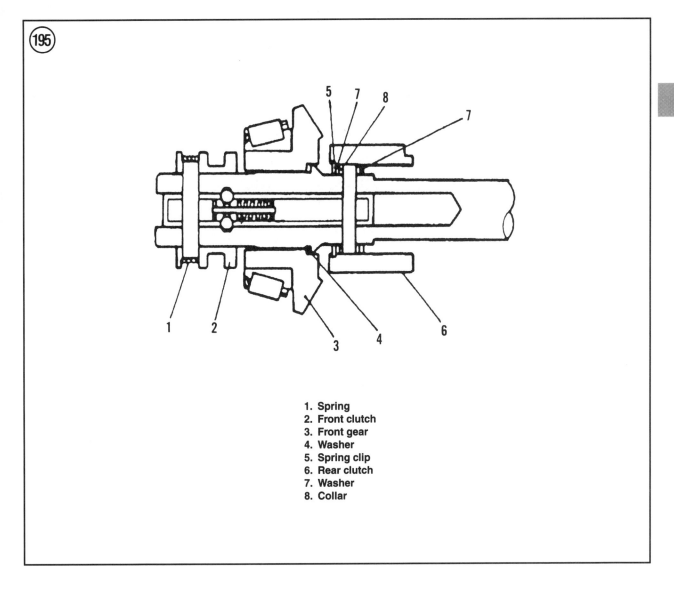

1. Spring
2. Front clutch
3. Front gear
4. Washer
5. Spring clip
6. Rear clutch
7. Washer
8. Collar

9

from the clutch and slide the front clutch from the propeller shaft. Slide the front gear and bearing assembly from the shaft.

2. Use a screwdriver to pry the end of the clip (**Figure 196**) from the groove in the rear clutch (6, **Figure 195**). Use the screwdriver to gradually lift the clip from the groove and work it out of the clutch.

3. Push the cross pin from the clutch, then slide the rear clutch toward the propeller end and off the propeller shaft. Remove the collar (8, **Figure 195**) from the clutch bore.

4. Remove and inspect the washers (7, **Figure 195**). Replace them if they are damaged or worn.

5. Remove the shifter from the propeller shaft bore. Note the orientation of all components, then disassemble the shifter components. Replace any worn or damaged components.

Gears and bearings removal and installation

Refer to the standard rotation 150 hp gearcase for procedures, then remove, inspect and install the front gear, bearing, race, needle bearing and lower drive shaft bearing.

Propeller shaft assembly and installation

Inspect both propeller shafts for a bent condition, worn or damaged areas and replace if defects are noted. Refer to the standard rotation 150 hp models for propeller shaft inspection procedures.

Inspect the cross pin retaining springs for damaged or corroded areas and for lost spring tension. Replace the springs if they are questionable.

1. Slide the spring clip, followed by the washer (5, 6 and 7, **Figure 197**) over the aft end of the propeller shaft.

2. Position the collar (8, **Figure 197**) over the propeller shaft with the cross pin holes aligned with the cross pin slot. Slide the second washer (7, **Figure 197**) over the propeller shaft and position it next to the collar.

3. Lubricate with Yamaha all-purpose grease, then insert the components of the shifter into the bore of the propeller shaft. Make sure the detent balls are positioned into the bore provided in the shift slider. Align the cross pin bore of the shifter shaft with the slot in the propeller shaft and the hole in the collar. Insert the cross pin through the hole

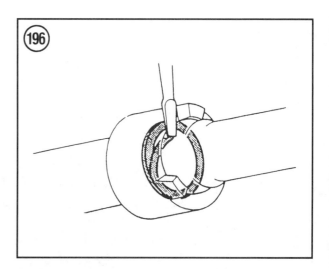

(196)

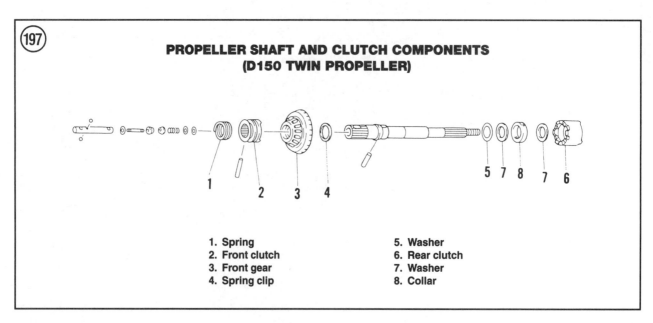

(197)

**PROPELLER SHAFT AND CLUTCH COMPONENTS
(D150 TWIN PROPELLER)**

1 2 3 4   5 7 8 7 6

1. Spring
2. Front clutch
3. Front gear
4. Spring clip

5. Washer
6. Rear clutch
7. Washer
8. Collar

in the collar, the slot in the propeller shaft and the hole in the shifter.

4. Carefully slide the clutch onto the propeller shaft and over the collar and cross pin (**Figure 197**). Use a screwdriver to push the clip into the groove of the rear clutch as shown in **Figure 198**. Make sure the clip is fully seated into the groove.

5. Place the washer (5, **Figure 197**) onto the front end of the propeller shaft. Slide the gear and bearing assembly (3, **Figure 197**) over the propeller shaft and position next to the washer.

6. Align the front clutch (2, **Figure 197**) onto the splined section of the propeller shaft so that the hole for the cross

pin aligns with the slot in the propeller shaft. The dog side of the clutch must face toward the front gear as shown in **Figure 197**.

7. Push the cross pin through the hole in the clutch and the slot in the propeller shaft. Carefully manipulate the shifter shaft until the hole for the cross pin is aligned with the cross pin. Carefully wind the cross pin spring (1, **Figure 197**) over the clutch and into the groove covering the cross pin. Make sure the cross pin spring loops do not cross over one another.

8. Carefully place the propeller shaft and front gear assembly into the gearcase. Refer to the procedures listed for standard rotation 150 hp models and install the shift shaft into position. Rotate the shift shaft until the shaft drops into the position and the shift cam is engaged with the front clutch.

Rear (outer) propeller shaft disassembly and assembly

NOTE
Remove the needle bearing from the propeller shaft only if it must be replaced. The removal process will probably destroy the bearing.

1. Use a depth micrometer to measure the depth of the seals at the points indicated in **Figure 199**. Record the seal depth. Use a blunt tip screwdriver to carefully pry the seals from the seal bore.

2. Use a depth micrometer to measure the depth of the propeller shaft needle bearing at the points indicated in **Figure 200**. Record the bearing depth.

9

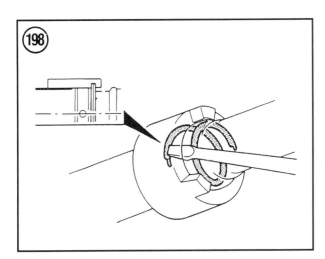

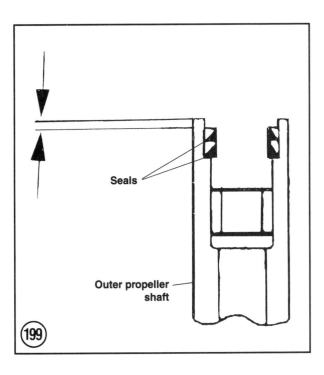

Seals

Outer propeller shaft

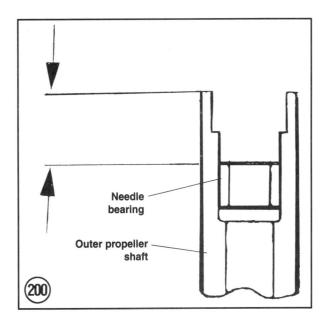

Needle bearing

Outer propeller shaft

3. Use a slide hammer (Yamaha part No. YB-06096) and bearing puller, part No. YB-06535, to engage the needle bearing and remove it from the propeller shaft bore (**Figure 201**). Note the orientation of the numbered side of bearing prior to removal from the bearing puller.

4. Apply Yamaha gearcase lubricant to the needle bearing bore and the outer surface of the needle bearing. Place the needle bearing into the propeller shaft bore with the numbered side facing out or in the position noted prior to removal. The removal tool selected must provide adequate contact with the bearing case yet not contact the propeller shaft bore during assembly. Use an appropriately sized socket and extension (or Yamaha part No. YB-42225 and YB06071) to carefully drive the needle bearing to the depth recorded prior to removal (**Figure 202**). Work slowly and stop frequently to measure the depth. The bearing must be installed to the proper depth to ensure the bearing contacts the propeller shaft at the proper location.

5. Apply Loctite Primer T to the seal bore in the end of the propeller shaft and the outer diameter of both new seals. Apply Loctite 271 to the seal bore and the outer diameter of both seals.

6. Place the first seal into the bore with the open end facing down or away from the propeller. The tool selected to install the seals must provide adequate contact with the seal yet not contact the seal bore during installation. Use an appropriately sized socket and extension (or Yamaha part No. YB-42225) to carefully drive the first seal into the seal bore until just below the seal bore opening.

7. Place the second seal onto the first seal with the open end facing up or away from the propeller shaft. Drive the second and first seal into the seal bore until the second seal just reaches the depth (**Figure 203**) recorded prior to removal of the seals. Wipe excess Loctite from the bore.

8. Lubricate the needle bearing with Yamaha gearcase lubricant. Apply Yamaha all-purpose grease to the seal lips prior to installation.

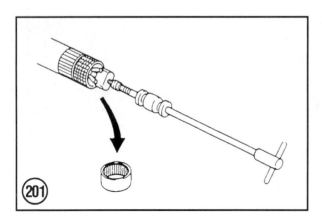

Drive shaft
and pinion gear installation

Install the pinion gear into the gearcase with the pinion gear teeth engaged into the front gear teeth. Clean all contaminants from the drive shaft. Apply Loctite Primer T to the threaded end of the drive shaft. Carefully slide the drive shaft into the drive shaft bore and engage the splines

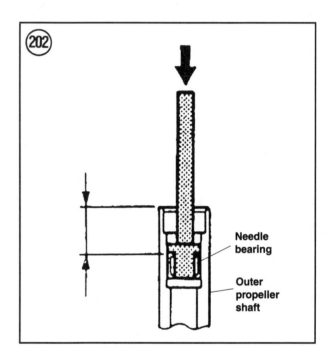

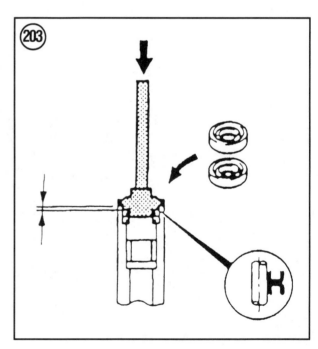

of the pinion gear. Apply Loctite 271 onto the threads of the drive shaft and new pinion nut.

Install the pinion nut onto the drive shaft and use the tools specified during removal to tighten the pinion nut to the specification listed in **Table 1**. Install the upper bearings along with the bearing and seal housing following the procedures for standard rotation 150 hp models.

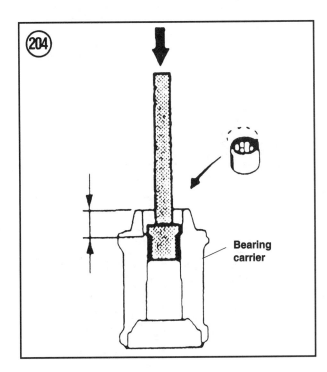

Bearing carrier

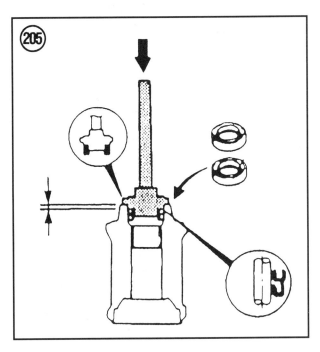

Bearing carrier assembly and installation

1. Apply Yamaha gearcase lubricant to the aft needle bearing housing and the needle bearing bore of the carrier.

2. Position the new needle bearing in the housing bore with the numbers facing up or as noted prior to removal.

3. The tool used to install the new needle bearing must provide adequate contact to the bearing case, yet not contact the bearing bore in the carrier during installation. Select an appropriately sized socket and extension or Yamaha part No. YB-42227 and carefully drive the needle bearing into the bore until it just reaches the depth noted prior to removal (**Figure 204**).

4. Apply Loctite Primer T to the seal bore in the carrier and the outer case of the seals. Apply Loctite 271 to the seal bore diameter and the outer case of the seals.

5. Position the first seal in the seal bore opening with the open end facing up (**Figure 205**). The tool used to install the new seals must provide adequate contact with the seal case, yet not contact the seal bore in the carrier during installation. Use an appropriately sized socket or Yamaha part No. YB-42227 to drive the first seal into the carrier until just below the bore opening.

6. Place the second seal onto the first seal with the open end facing up. Use the same installation tool to drive the second and first seal into the seal bore until the second seal just reaches the depth recorded prior to removal (**Figure 205**). Wipe excess Loctite from the seals.

7. Apply Yamaha gearcase lubricant to the needle bearing. Apply Yamaha all-purpose grease to both seal lips prior to installation.

8. Apply Yamaha gearcase lubricant to the needle bearing case and the housing bearing bore. Place the new needle bearing into the bore opening (**Figure 206**) with the numbered side facing up or the position noted prior to removal.

9. Select an appropriately sized socket and extension or Yamaha part No. YB-42229 and carefully drive the front bearing into the bore until it reaches the depth noted prior to removal (**Figure 206**).

10. Install the spacer (4, **Figure 207**) into the large opening of the bearing carrier. Place the thrust bearing (3, **Figure 207**) onto the shim as shown. Wrap the propeller nut threads and the propeller splines with tape (**Figure 208**) to protect the seals from damage during installation of the propeller shaft into the carrier. Insert the propeller shaft into the bearing carrier until the flange is seated against the thrust bearing. Position the bearing and gear assembly in the carrier and rotate it until the splines in the gear align with those on the propeller shaft.

11. Place the carrier onto a press with the gear side up and the seal side supported as shown in **Figure 209**. Make sure the thrust bearing and propeller shaft are properly seated

then press the gear into the bearing carrier bore until it is seated in the carrier.

12. Place the rear gear (outer shaft) shim (5, **Figure 210**) into the gearcase. Make sure it is positioned on the step or shoulder in the bore. Place the thrust washer (4, **Figure 210**) onto the rear (inner) propeller shaft.

13. Lubricate the bearing carrier (3, **Figure 210**) and carrier contact areas of the gearcase with Yamaha all-purpose grease. Position the *UP* marking on the bearing carrier with the up side facing the antiventilation plate. Carefully slide the bearing carrier, propeller shaft and gear assembly into the gearcase. Rotate the propeller shaft until the pinion and rear gear teeth engage, then press the bearing carrier firmly into the gearcase.

14. Place the locking tab washer onto the bearing carrier with the tab inserted into the opening in the gearcase housing. Lubricate the cover nut (1, **Figure 210**) and the threads in the gearcase with Yamaha all-purpose grease. Thread the cover nut in by hand. Use Yamaha part No. YB-42223 and a torque wrench to tighten the cover nut to the specification listed in **Table 1** (**Figure 211**).

15. Bend one tab into a gap on the cover nut. Bend the other tabs down to prevent restricted exhaust. Tighten the cover nut a little more if necessary to bend the tabs into position.

Perform the gear backlash measurements using the procedures provided in this chapter.

For water pump installation procedures, refer to the procedures for a standard rotation 150 hp gearcase.

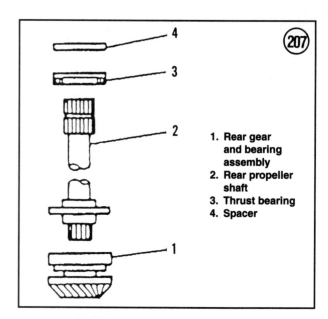

1. Rear gear and bearing assembly
2. Rear propeller shaft
3. Thrust bearing
4. Spacer

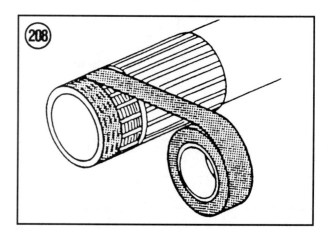

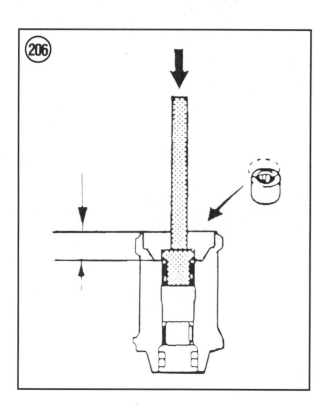

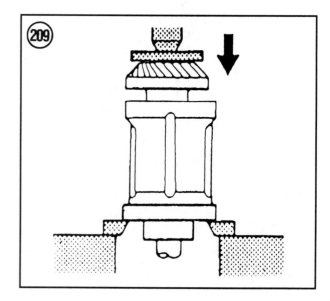

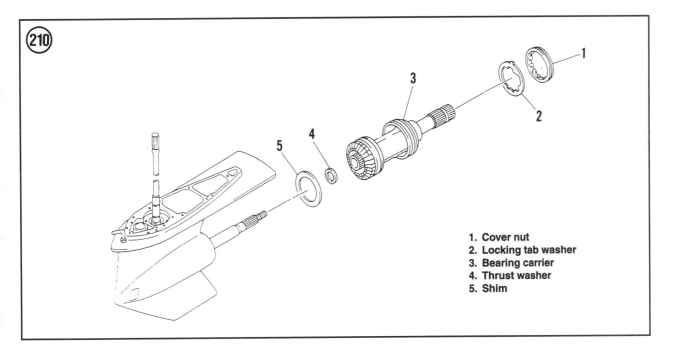

1. Cover nut
2. Locking tab washer
3. Bearing carrier
4. Thrust washer
5. Shim

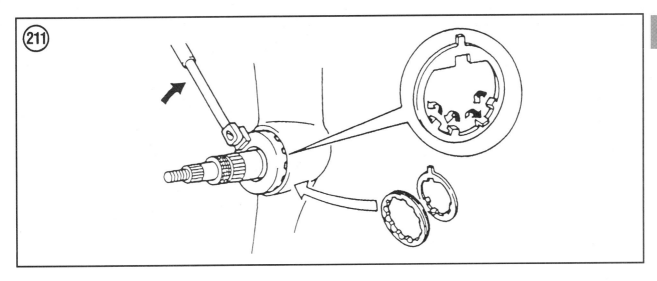

Table 1 TIGHTENING TORQUES

Oil level/ drain plug	
All models	7 N•m (61 in.-lb.)
Pinion gear nut	
9.9 and 15	26 N•m (19 ft.-lb.)
20 and 25 hp (two-cylinder)	51 N•m (37 ft.-lb.)
25 hp (three-cylinder), 30 and C30	50 N•m (36 ft.-lb.)
C40, 40-50 hp	75 N•m (55 ft.-lb.)
60-225 hp (90°)	95 N•m (70 ft.-lb.)
200-250 hp (76°)	142 N•m (104 ft.-lb.)
	(continued)

Table 1 TIGHTENING TORQUES (continued)

Gearcase cap/cover nut	
4 and 5 hp	8 N•m (70 in.-lb.)
C30	11 N•m (97 in.-lb.)
40 and 50 hp	16 N•m (11 ft.-lb.)
E48	130 N•m (95 ft.-lb.)
60-90 hp	145 N•m (106 ft.-lb.)
115 and 130	
150-225 hp (90°) (except D150TR)	190 N•m (140 ft.-lb.)
D150TR (dual props)	145 N•m (106 ft.-lb.)
200-250 hp (76°)	108 N•m (80 ft.-lb.)
Shift rod connector	
4-8 hp	10 N•m (88 in.-lb.)
Gearcase to midsection	
4 and 5 hp	8 N•m (71 in.-lb.)
9.9 and 15	18 N•m (13 ft.-lb.)
20-50 hp (except E48)	40 N•m. (29 ft.-lb.)
E48	
M8 bolts	18 N•m (13 ft.-lb.)
M10 bolts	37 N•m (27 ft.-lb.)
60-225 hp (90°)	40 N•m (29 ft.-lb.)
200-250 hp (76°)	47 N•m (34 ft.-lb.)
Water pump cover	
6 and 8 hp	11 N•m (97 in.-lb.)
Propeller nut	
6-15 hp	17 N•m (12 ft.-lb.)
20 and 25 hp (two-cylinder)	35 N•m (26 ft.-lb.)
25 hp (three-cylinder), 30, C30 and C40	30 N•m (22 ft.-lb.)
40 and 50 hp	30 N•m (22 ft.-lb.)
E48, E60 and E75,	35 N•m (26 ft.-lb.)
60-90 hp	55 N•m (40 ft.-lb.)
115-250 hp (except D150TR)	55 N•m (40 ft.-lb.)
D150TR	
Front prop	65 N•m (47 ft.-lb.)
Rear prop	55 N•m (40 ft.-lb.)
Standard tightening	
Fastener size	
8 mm nut, M5 bolt	5 N•m (44 in.-lb.)
10 mm nut, M6 bolt	8 N•m (70 in.-lb.)
12 mm nut, M8 bolt	18 N•m (13 ft.-lb.)
14 mm nut, M10 bolt	36 N•m (26 ft.-lb.)
17 mm nut, M12 bolt	43 N•m (31 ft.-lb.)

Table 2 GEAR BACKLASH

Model	Forward gear backlash	Reverse gear backlash
2 hp	0.27-0.99 mm (0.010-0.039 in.)	–
3 hp	0.15-1.22 mm (0.006-0.048 in.)	–
4 and 5 hp	0.28-0.71 mm (0.011-0.028 in.)	0.28-0.71 mm (0.011-0.028 in.)
6 and 8 hp	0.25-0.75 mm (0.010-0.030 in.)	0.25-0.75 mm (0.010-0.030 in.)
9.9 and 15 hp	0.19-0.86 mm (0.007-0.034 in.)	0.95-1.65 mm (0.037-0.065 in.)
20 and 25 hp (two-cylinder)	0.32-0.53 mm (0.013-0.021 in.)	0.85-1.17 mm (0.034-0.046 in.)
25 hp (two-cylinder), 30 hp	0.20-0.50 mm (0.008-0.020 in.)	0.70-1.00 mm (0.028-0.040 in.)
C25	0.10-0.25 mm (0.004-0.009 in.)	0.35-0.50 mm (0.014-0.019 in.)
C30	0.31-0.72 mm (0.012-0.028 in.)	0.93-1.65 mm (0.037-0.065 in.)
C40	0.10-0.25 mm (0.004-0.009 in.)	0.40-0.55 mm (0.016-0.022 in.)
40, 50 hp	0.18-0.45 mm (0.007-0.018 in.)	0.71-0.98 mm (0.028-0.039 in.)
E48	0.09-0.27 mm (0.004-0.011 in.)	0.90-1.26 mm (0.035-0.050 in.)
E60, 60 and 70 hp	0.09-0.28 mm (0.004-0.012 in.)	0.75-1.13 mm (0.033-0.044 in.)

(continued)

Table 2 GEAR BACKLASH (continued)

Model	Forward gear backlash	Reverse gear backlash
E75, 75-90 hp	0.08-0.25 mm (0.003-0.009 in.)	0.67-1.00 mm (0.026-0.039 in.)
115, 130 hp RH	0.32-0.50 mm (0.013-0.020 in.)	0.80-1.17 mm (0.032-0.046 in.)
L115 and L130 LH	0.32-0.45 mm (0.013-0.018 in.)	0.80-1.12 mm (0.032-0.043 in.)
150-225 hp (90°)		
(except P150, L150, D150 and L200)	0.25-0.46 mm (0.010-0.018 in.)	0.74-1.29 mm (0.029-0.050 in.)
P150	0.71-1.01 mm (0.028-0.040 in.)	0.79-1.38 mm (0.032-0.054 in.)
L150, L200	0.21-0.43 mm (0.008-0.017 in.)	0.97-1.29 mm (0.038-0.050 in.)
D150 (dual props)	0.19-0.59 mm (0.007-0.023 in.)	0.39-0.70 mm (0.015-0.027 in.)
200-250 hp (76°) RH rotation	0.19-0.40 mm (0.007-0.040 in.)	0.64-0.93 mm (0.026-0.036 in.)
L200, L225 and L250 hp		
(76° V) LH rotation	0.32-0.52 mm (0.013-0.020 in.)	0.64-0.93 mm (0.026-0.036 in.)

Table 3 AVAILABLE SHIM THICKNESS

Model	Pinion shim	Forward shim	Reverse shim
2 hp	*	0.30 mm (0.012 in.)	*
	—	0.40 mm (0.016 in.)	—
	—	0.50 mm (0.020 in.)	—
3 hp	*	2.00 mm (0.079 in.)	*
	—	2.10 mm (0.083 in.)	—
	—	2.20 mm (0.087 in.)	—
	—	2.30 mm (0.091 in.)	—
4 and 5 hp	*	*	*
6 and 8 hp	—	0.10 mm (0.004 in.)	0.10 mm (0.004 in.)
	—	0.12 mm (0.005 in.)	—
	—	0.15 mm (0.006 in.)	—
	—	0.18 mm (0.007 in.)	—
	—	0.30 mm (0.012 in.)	—
	—	0.40 mm (0.016 in.)	—
	—	0.50 mm (0.020 in.)	—
9.9 and 15 hp	1.130 mm (0.045 in.)	0.10 mm (0.004 in.)	0.10 mm (0.004 in.)
	1.200 mm (0.048 in.)	0.12 mm (0.005 in.)	0.20 mm (0.008 in.)
	—	0.15 mm (0.006 in.)	0.30 mm (0.012 in.)
	—	0.18 mm (0.007 in.)	0.40 mm (0.016 in.)
	—	0.30 mm (0.012 in.)	0.50 mm (0.020 in.)
	—	0.40 mm (0.016 in.)	—
	—	0.50 mm (0.020 in.)	—
20 and 25 hp			
(two-cylinder)	1.50 mm (0.060 in.)	1.00 mm (0.040 in.)	1.00 mm (0.040 in.)
	1.60 mm (0.064 in.)	1.10 mm (0.044 in.)	1.10 mm (0.044 in.)
	—	1.20 mm (0.048 in.)	1.20 mm (0.048 in.)
	—	1.30 mm (0.052 in.)	1.30 mm (0.052 in.)
	—	1.40 mm (0.056 in.)	—
40 and 50 hp	0.05 mm (0.002 in.)	0.05 mm (0.002 in.)	0.05 mm (0.002 in.)
E48	0.08 mm (0.003 in.)	0.08 mm (0.003 in.)	0.08 mm (0.003 in.)
	0.12 mm (0.005 in.)	0.12 mm (0.005 in.)	0.12 mm (0.005 in.)
	0.30 mm (0.012 in.)	0.30 mm (0.012 in.)	0.30 mm (0.012 in.)
	0.50 mm (0.020 in.)	0.50 mm (0.020 in.)	0.50 mm (0.020 in.)
E75, 60-90 hp	0.12 mm (0.005 in.)	0.12 mm (0.005 in.)	0.12 mm (0.005 in.)
115 and 130 hp	0.15 mm (0.006 in.)	0.15 mm (0.006 in.)	0.15 mm (0.006 in.)
	0.18 mm (0.007 in.)	0.18 mm (0.007 in.)	0.18 mm (0.007 in.)
	0.30 mm (0.012 in.)	0.30 mm (0.012 in.)	0.30 mm (0.012 in.)
	0.40 mm (0.016 in.)	0.40 mm (0.016 in.)	0.40 mm (0.016 in.)
150-250 hp	0.10 mm (0.004 in.)	0.10 mm (0.004 in.)	0.10 mm (0.004 in.)
	0.15 mm (0.006 in.)	0.15 mm (0.006 in.)	0.15 mm (0.006 in.)
	0.18 mm (0.007 in.)	0.18 mm (0.007 in.)	0.18 mm (0.007 in.)
	0.30 mm (0.012 in.)	0.30 mm (0.012 in.)	0.30 mm (0.012 in.)
	0.40 mm (0.016 in.)	0.40 mm (0.016 in.)	0.40 mm (0.016 in.)
	0.50 mm (0.020 in.)	0.50 mm (0.029 in.)	0.50 mm (0.020 in.)

*Shims are not required in this location.

9

Table 4 DRIVE SHAFT SEALS

Model	Seal depth
2 hp	4.0-4.5 mm (0.12-0.18 in.)
3 hp	1.5-2.0 mm (0.06-0.08 in.)
4 and 5 hp	1.0-1.5 mm (0.04-0.06 in.)
6 and 8 hp	3.0-3.5 mm (0.12-0.14 in.)
9.9 and 15 hp	7.0-8.0 mm (0.28-0.31 in.)
20 and 25 hp (two-cylinder)	8.5-9.0 mm (0.33-0.35 in.)
40 and 50 hp	0.0-0.5 mm (0.00-0.020 in.)
115-225 hp (90°)	0.25-0.75 mm (0.010-0.030 in.)
200-250 hp (76°)	0.3-0.7 mm (0.012-0.027 in.)

Table 5 PROPELLER SHAFT SEALS

Model	Inner seal depth	Outer seal depth
3 hp	*	1.0-1.5 mm (0.04-0.06 in.)
4 and 5 hp	*	Fully seated
6 and 8 hp	10.0-10.5 mm (0.39-0.41in.)	3.0-3.5 mm (0.12-0.14 in.)
9.9 and 15 hp	*	3.0-3.5 mm (0.12-0.14 in.)
20 and 25 hp (two-cylinder)	*	4.5-5.0 mm (0.18-0.20 in.)
40 and 50 hp	*	4.0-4.6 mm (0.16-0.18 in.)
E60 and E75,	60-90 hp*	5.0 mm (0.020 in.)
115-225 hp (90°) (except D150)	*	4.75-5.25 mm (0.187-0.207 in.)
D150 (dual props)		
Inner propeller shaft	*	2.75-3.75 mm (0.108-0.128 in.)
Outer propeller shaft	*	4.75-5.25 mm (0.187-0.207 in.)
200-250 hp (76°)	*	0.3-0.7 mm (0.010-0.020 in.)

*Inner seal is next to and contacting the outer seal when installed.

Table 6 GEAR RATIO AND GEAR TOOTH COUNT

Model	Gear ratio	Driven/drive gear tooth count
2-25 hp (two-cylinder)	2.08 to 1	27/13
25 hp (three-cylinder)-50 hp (except C40)	1.85 to 1	24/13
C40	2.00 to 1	26/13
60 and 70 hp	2.33 to 1	28/12
E75, 75-90 hp	2.00 to 1	26/13
115 and 130 hp	–	–
P150TR (Pro 150)	2.00 to 1	28/14
D150TR (V Max)	2.00 to 1	28/14
150-225 (90°)	1.86 to 1	26/14
L150, L200 (LH Rotation)	1.86 to 1	26/14
200-250 hp (76°)	1.81 to 1	29/16

Table 7 FRONT MOUNTED GEAR NEEDLE BEARING DEPTH

Model	Inner bearing	Outer bearing
115 and 130 hp models	10.25-10.75 mm (0.404-0.423 in.)	
150-225 hp models (90°)	21.0-21.4 mm (0.827-0.843 in.)	4.5-4.9 mm (0.177-0.193 in.)
200-250 hp (76°)	2.3-2.7 mm (0.09-0.10 in.)	–
200-250 hp L models (76°)	11.8-12.2 mm (0.46-0.48 in.)	–

Chapter Ten

Jet Drives

Jet drives (**Figure 1**) offer significant advantages for shallow water operation. The absence of the propeller and gearcase allows the engine to operate in areas much too shallow for a standard propeller drive gearcase. This chapter will provide repair procedures for all Yamaha jet drive units.

JET DRIVE OPERATION

Jet Drive Components

The major components of the jet drive include the impeller (1, **Figure 2**), intake opening (2, **Figure 2**), volute tube (3, **Figure 2**) and discharge nozzle (4, **Figure 2**).

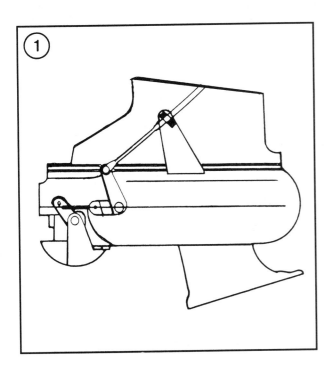

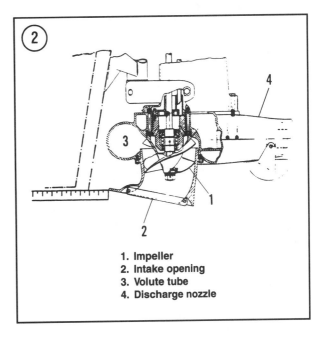

1. Impeller
2. Intake opening
3. Volute tube
4. Discharge nozzle

In normal installation of a jet drive engine, the intake opening will be slightly below the bottom of the boat as indicated in **Figure 2**. Overall performance of a jet drive equipped boat is greatly affected by the engine mounting height.

A higher jet mounting height may enhance top speed. However, the pump may ventilate during acceleration or in turns. Ventilation occurs when the pump is unloaded due to air entering the intake instead of water. The engine speed will increase yet the boat will lose forward thrust.

Mounting the jet pump too low will generally result in excessive water spray and speed loss due to the increased drag.

Contact the boat manufacturer or a boat dealership that is familiar with jet drive equipped boats for mounting height recommendations.

Thrust Control

The impeller is connected to a shaft supported by bearings on one end and connected into the crankshaft at the other end. Anytime the engine is running the impeller is turning.

The rotating impeller pulls water through the intake opening and pushes it through the volute tube (3, **Figure 2**). The volute tube directs the water toward the discharge nozzle. The water flowing from the discharge nozzle provides thrust to move the boat. Thrust is increased as the speed of the impeller increases.

Forward, neutral and reverse operations are provided by raising a scoop into the water stream flowing from the discharge nozzle. The scoop is moved with a cable actuated lever attached to the scoop lever (**Figure 3**). The cable is moved by direct connection of the control box or tiller shift cable.

Maximum forward thrust is provided when the scoop is positioned below the water stream exiting the discharge nozzle (**Figure 3**).

Neutral thrust is provided by raising the scoop to cover about half of the discharge nozzle opening. The scoop directs half of the exiting water in the opposite direction of the water exiting the discharge nozzle (**Figure 4**). The thrust is balanced and very little forward or reverse movement will occur.

Reverse thrust is provided by raising the scoop to virtually cover the entire discharge nozzle opening (**Figure 5**). All exiting water is diverted by the scoop in the opposite direction of the discharge nozzle opening. This will provide reverse thrust for the boat. The reverse thrust is far less efficient than the forward thrust, resulting is far less power in the reverse direction.

Steering the boat is accomplished as the engine is pivoted port or starboard as with the standard propeller drive gearcases.

> *CAUTION*
> *Steering response is limited and unpredictable when reverse thrust is selected. Practice common backing maneuvers in open water until you are comfortable with the jet drive backing characteristics.*

A drawback to having excellent shallow water running ability is a substantial reduction in efficiency. Jet drive model descriptions reflect the reduction in performance associated with the installation of the jet drive unit. The performance is generally equivalent to 70 percent of the

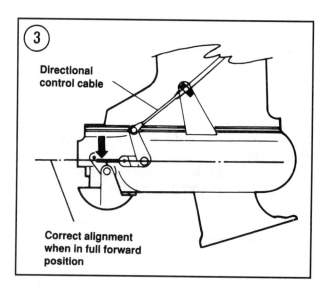

③ Directional control cable

Correct alignment when in full forward position

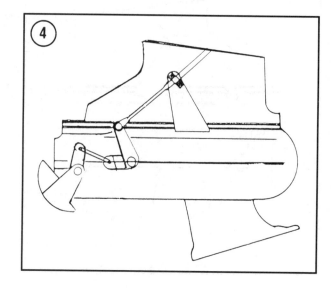

④

same basic engine with a standard propeller drive gearcase. Refer to the following for comparison.

When a jet drive unit is installed:

a. A 40 hp model becomes a 28 jet.

b. A 50 hp model becomes a 35 jet.

c. A 90 hp model becomes a 65 jet.

d. A 115 hp model becomes an 80 jet.

e. A 150 hp model becomes a 105 jet.

Except for the gearcase, a jet drive engine is identical in all respects to the model with a propeller drive gearcase. Refer to the information for the engine horsepower listed when a propeller drive gearcase is installed for repair instructions to components other than the jet drive.

Jet Drive Repair

Since outboards with jet drives may operate in very shallow water, certain components are susceptible to wear. A jet drive unit may ingest a considerable amount of sand, rocks and other debris during normal operation. Compo-

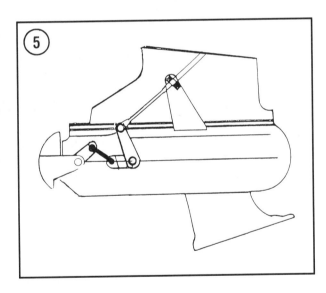

nents that require frequent inspection are the engine water pump, impeller and intake housing. Other components that tend to require frequent inspection include the bearing housing, drive shaft bearings and drive shaft.

Engine water pump

The water pump used to cool the power head is virtually identical to the pumps used on standard propeller drive gearcases. Like the standard propeller drive gearcase, the water pump is connected to and driven by the drive shaft.

Refer to the *Water Pump* section in Chapter Nine for water pump inspection and repair procedures. Use the procedures for the horsepower the engine would be rated at if a propeller drive gearcase were installed.

Flushing the cooling system

> *CAUTION*
> *The water pump impeller is damaged within seconds if the engine is run without a supply of water. Use a test tank or a suitable flush adapter (Yamaha part No. 6EO-28193-00-94) to run the engine out of the water.*

Sand and other debris will quickly wear the impeller and other components of the water pump. Frequently inspect the water pump components if the engine is run in sand or silt laden water. Sand and other debris can collect in the power head cooling passages. These deposits will eventually lead to overheating and increased corrosion. Use the flush adapter to flush debris from the cooling system after running the engine in salt or sand laden water. This important maintenance step can add years to the life of your outboard. For water pump inspection and servicing intervals refer to Chapter Four.

> *CAUTION*
> *Serious engine damage can result from overheating. Constantly monitor the water stream while the engine is running. Stop the engine immediately if the water stream becomes weak or stops.*

1. Disconnect the lubrication hose to gain access to the flush plug (**Figure 6**).

2. Use a large screwdriver to remove the large plug on the port side of the jet drive (**Figure 6**). Discard the gasket located beneath the plug.

3. Thread the flush adapter (Yamaha part No. 6EO-28193-00-94) into the threaded opening for the plug. Attach a

garden hose to the adapter. Turn the water supply to full open.

4. Start the engine and allow it to run for at least 10 minutes at idle speed.

5. Switch the engine off, *then* turn the water supply off.

6. Remove the adapter from the jet drive. Install the plug and new gasket. Tighten the plug securely.

Impeller to housing clearance

Worn or damaged surfaces on the impeller or the intake housing will allow water to slip past the impeller and result in decreased efficiency. Measure the impeller clearance if increased engine rpm is noted along with a loss in top speed or power.

1. Remove all spark plug leads and disconnect both battery cables from the battery.

2. Locate the intake grate on the bottom of the jet drive. Use long feeler gauges to measure the clearance between the impeller edges and the intake housing as indicated in **Figure 7**. Carefully rotate the flywheel and check the clearance in several locations. Determine the *average* clearance measured.

3. Correct average clearance is approximately 0.8 mm (0.030 in.). Small variations are acceptable as long as the impeller is not contacting the intake housing and the engine is not exceeding the maximum rated engine speed. Refer to *Impeller shimming* if excessive clearance is noted or the impeller is contacting the intake housing.

4. Attach all spark plug leads. Connect both battery cables to the correct battery terminals.

Jet drive removal and installation

WARNING
Always disconnect all spark plug leads and both battery cables at the battery terminals before working with the jet drive to prevent accidental starting.

Disconnect the directional control cable from the scoop lever. Remove the intake housing to gain access to the jet drive mounting bolts. Refer to *Intake housing* in this chapter for procedures. Follow the procedures listed in Chapter Nine for the removal and installation of propeller drive gearcase and remove the jet drive unit from the engine. Disregard the references to the shift shaft when removing or installing a jet drive unit.

Install the intake housing, if removed, to gain access to the mounting bolts. Check and correct the directional control cable adjustment after installation. Perform the adjustment procedures to the direction control as described

in Chapter Five. Always check for proper cooling system operation after installation of the jet drive.

Intake housing removal/installation

Remove the intake housing when shimming the impeller or when the impeller and housing require inspection for worn or damaged components. To assist with component identification and orientation, refer to **Figure 8** or **Figure 9** during disassembly and assembly of the jet drive.

1. Disconnect all spark plug leads. Disconnect both battery cables from the battery terminals.

2. Remove the six intake housing mounting bolts (**Figure 8** or **Figure 9**). Pull the intake housing from the jet drive. Carefully tap the housing loose with a rubber mallet if necessary.

3. Clean and inspect the housing mounting bolts. Replace them if found to be corroded or damaged.

4. Clean all debris and contaminants from the intake housing and jet drive mating surfaces.

5. Inspect the inner surfaces of the intake housing liner for deep scratches, eroded or damaged areas. Replace the liner if these conditions are present and excessive impeller clearance was measured. Refer to *Intake housing liner* for procedures.

6. Install the intake housing onto the jet drive housing with the lower end facing the rear. Apply Yamaha all-purpose grease to the threads of the bolts. Tighten them to the specification listed in **Table 1**.

7. Connect all spark plug leads. Connect both battery cables. Run the engine to check for proper operation before putting in back into service.

Intake housing liner replacement

Replacement of the liner is a fairly simple process. Removal of the intake grate may be necessary for proper access to the liner.

1. Refer to *Intake housing* for procedures then remove the intake housing from the jet drive.

2. Locate the bolts on the side of the intake housing that hold the liner to the housing. Note the locations, then remove the bolts.

3. Tap the liner loose with a long punch through the intake grate opening. Place the punch on the edge of the liner and carefully drive it from the housing.

4. Apply a light coat of Yamaha all-purpose grease to the liner bore in the intake housing. Carefully slide the new

liner into position. Align the bolt holes in the liner with the bolt holes in the housing.

5. Apply Yamaha all-purpose grease to the threads of the bolts. Install them and tighten to the specification listed in **Table 1**. Use a file to remove any burrs or bolt material protruding into the intake housing.

6. Refer to *Intake housing* and install the intake housing to the jet drive.

Impeller removal and installation

Removal of the jet drive is required prior to removing the impeller. Access to the drive shaft is necessary when removing the impeller nut.

1. Refer to *Jet drive removal* for procedures, then remove the jet drive from the engine.

2. Refer to *Intake housing*, then remove the intake housing from the jet drive.

3. Select the drive shaft adapter indicated for your model. For 28 and 35 jet, use part No. YB-6079. For 65 jet, use part No. YB-6151. For 80 and 105 jet, use part No. YB-6201.

4. Use the drive shaft adapter to grip the splined end of the drive shaft when removing or installing the impeller.

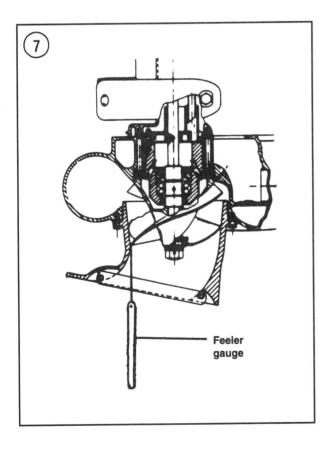

Feeler gauge

5. Use a screwdriver to bend the tabs of the washer (8, **Figure 8** or 8, **Figure 9**) away from the impeller nut (9, **Figure 8** or 9, **Figure 9**). Note the location and orientation of all components prior to removal. Use a suitable socket and adapter to remove the nut, tab washer and lower shims from the drive shaft. Discard the tab washer.

6. Pull the impeller, drive key, sleeve and upper shims from the drive shaft. Use a rubber mallet to carefully tap the impeller loose from the shaft if necessary.

7. Inspect the impeller for worn or damaged areas and replace if defects are noted.

8. Place the sleeve and drive key (4 and 5, **Figure 8** or 4 and 5, **Figure 9**) onto the drive shaft. Apply Yamaha all-purpose grease to the drive key and impeller bore. Slide the upper shims, then the impeller onto the drive shaft.

9. Place the lower shims, new tab washer (8, **Figure 8** or 8, **Figure 9**) and impeller nut onto the drive shaft. Make sure the shims and tab washers are in the proper position. Use the drive shaft adapter and suitable socket to tighten the impeller nut to the specification listed in **Table 1**.

10. Bend the tabs up to secure the impeller nut. Refer to *Intake housing*, then install the intake housing to the jet drive. Refer to *Impeller to intake housing clearance* for procedures, then measure and correct the clearance. Refer to *Jet drive removal and installation* and install the jet drive to the engine.

10

Impeller shimming

Shimming of the impeller is necessary to ensure proper impeller to intake housing clearance. Removal and installation of the intake housing and impeller will be required for each shim change. Refer to the sections in this chapter for removal and installation instructions. For component identification and orientation, refer to **Figure 8** or **Figure 9**.

Refer to *Impeller to intake housing clearance* after each shim change for measurement procedures. Repeat the process until the clearance is correct.

Eight shims are used on 28 jet and 35 jet models to position the impeller. Nine shims are used on 65 jet, 80 jet and 105 jet models. All shims are 0.8 mm (0.030 in.) thick. Normally shims are located both above and below the impeller.

1. Remove the jet drive from the engine. Refer to *Jet drive removal and installation*.

2. Remove the intake housing from the jet drive. Refer to *Intake housing*.

3. Note the location and orientation of all components, then remove the impeller from the drive shaft. Refer to *Impeller removal and installation*.

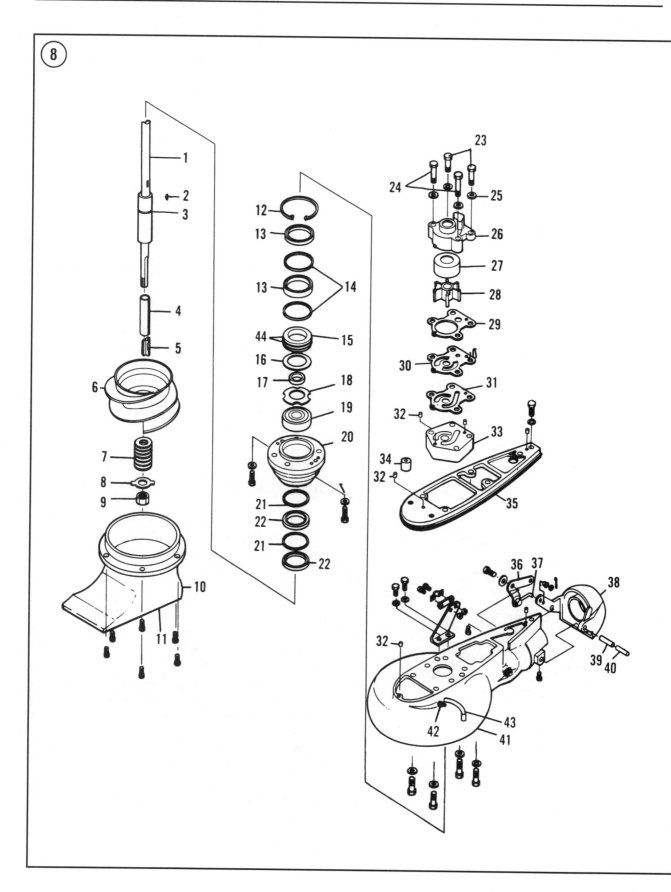

JET DRIVE COMPONENTS
(28 JET AND 35 JET MODELS)

1. Drive shaft
2. Drive key
   (engine water pump)
3. Thrust ring (flange)
4. Sleeve
5. Impeller drive key
6. Impeller
7. Shims
8. Tab washer
9. Impeller nut
10. Intake housing
11. Intake grate opening
12. Snap ring
13. Seal
14. Retaining ring
15. Seal carrier
16. Washer
17. Collar
18. Thrust washer
19. Bearing
20. Bearing housing
21. Seal retainer
22. Seal
23. Bolts (rear)
24. Bolts (front)
25. Washers
26. Water pump cover
27. Insert
28. Impeller
29. Gasket
30. Wear plate
31. Gasket
32. Locating pin
33. Spacer plate
34. Rubber sleeve
35. Adapter plate
36. Scoop lever
37. Linkage
38. Scoop
39. Bushing
40. Pin
41. Jet drive housing
42. Grease fitting
43. Vent hose
44. O-rings

10

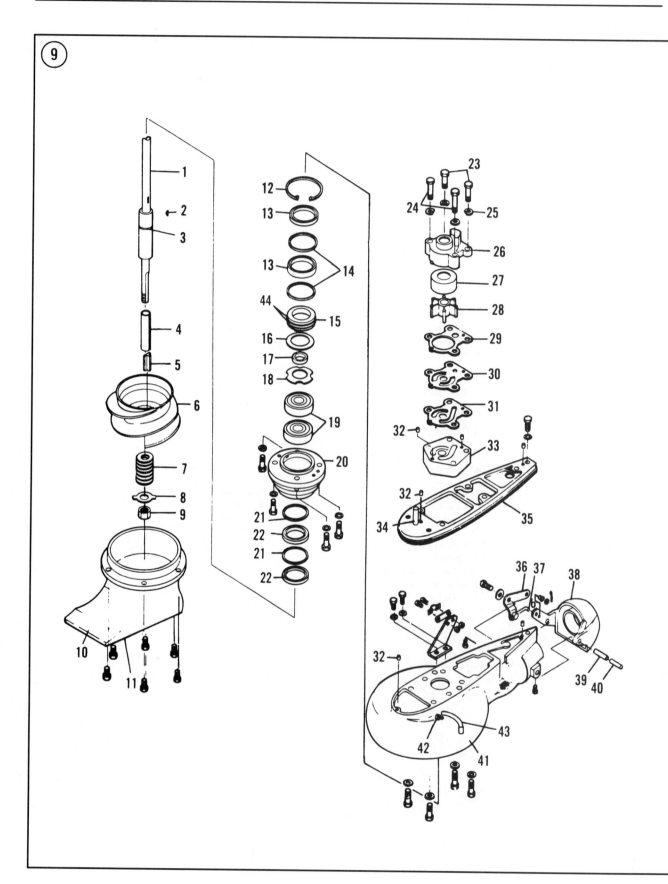

JET DRIVE COMPONENTS
(65 JET, 80 JET AND 105 JET MODELS)

1. Drive shaft
2. Drive key
   (engine water pump)
3. Thrust ring
4. Sleeve
5. Impeller drive key
6. Impeller
7. Shims
8. Tab washer
9. Impeller nut
10. Intake housing
11. Intake grate opening
12. Snap ring
13. Seal
14. Seal retainer
15. Seal carrier
16. Washer
17. Collar
18. Thrust washer
19. Bearings
20. Bearing housing
21. Seal retainer
22. Seal
23. Rear bolts
24. Front bolts
25. Washers
26. Water pump cover
27. Insert
28. Impeller
29. Gasket
30. Wear plate
31. Gasket
32. Locating pin
33. Spacer
34. Locating pin
35. Adapter plate
36. Scoop lever
37. Linkage
38. Scoop
39. Sleeve
40. Pin
41. Jet drive housing
42. Grease fitting
43. Vent hose
44. O-rings

4. If too much impeller clearance is present, remove a shim from below the impeller and place it above the impeller.

5. If too little clearance is present, remove a shim from above the impeller and place it below the impeller.

6. Install the impeller and intake housing onto the jet drive following the instructions listed in this chapter. Refer to *Impeller to intake housing clearance* and measure the clearance. Repeat Steps 1-6 until the clearance is correct.

Bearing housing removal

Drive shaft bearing inspection and/or replacement is required when contaminants or a significant amount of water is found when performing routine maintenance to the jet drive. Replace all seals, gaskets and O-rings anytime they are removed. Removal of the bearing housing is required to gain access to the bearings, shafts, seals and other components.

1. Remove the jet drive from the engine. Refer to *Jet drive removal and installation* for procedures.

2. Remove the intake housing from the jet drive housing. Refer to *Intake housing* for procedures.

3. Remove the impeller from the drive shaft. Refer to *Impeller removal and installation* for procedures.

4. Remove all engine water pump components. Refer to the *Water pump servicing* section in Chapter Nine for procedures. Use the procedures for the horsepower the engine would be rated if a propeller drive gearcase were installed.

5. Remove the spacer plate (33, **Figure 8** or 33, **Figure 9**) from the jet drive housing. Locate and remove the bolts and washers securing the bearing housing (**Figure 10**) to the jet drive housing.

6. Pull the bearing housing from the jet drive housing and place it on a clean work surface.

Drive shaft bearing removal and installation

NOTE
A single bearing is used on the drive shaft for 28 jet and 35 jet models. Two bearings are use for 65 jet, 80 jet and 105 jet models.

WARNING
The components of the bearing housing will become very hot during disassembly and assembly. Take all necessary precautions to protect yourself and others from personal injury.

WARNING
Never use a flame or allow sparks in an area where any combustible material is present. Always have a suitable fire extinguisher

nearby when using a flame or other heat producing device.

CAUTION
Pay strict attention to the direction the bearings are installed onto the drive shaft. The inner race surfaces must be installed correctly to ensure a durable repair. The inner race thrust surfaces are wider on one side versus the other. Refer to the provided illustrations prior to assembly of the drive shaft.

To assist with component identification, refer to **Figure 8** or **Figure 9** during disassembly and assembly procedures. Note the location and orientation of all components prior to removal from the bearing housing. Rotate the drive shaft to check the bearings for rough operation. Replace the bearings if a rough or a loose feel is noted.

Do not remove the bearings from the drive shaft unless replacement is required. Removal of the bearings will require that heat be applied to the housing. The seals will be damaged and require replacement from the heat and/or the removal process.

1. Use a screwdriver to pry the snap ring (1, **Figure 11**) from the housing.

2. Secure the bearing carrier into a soft jaw vise with the impeller end of the drive shaft facing up. Thread the impeller nut onto the shaft to protect the threads. Apply

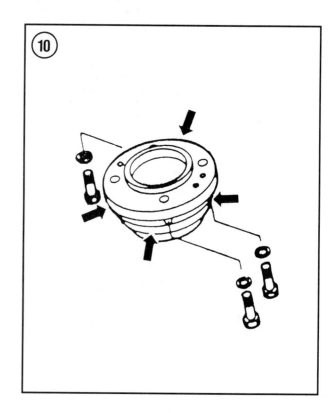

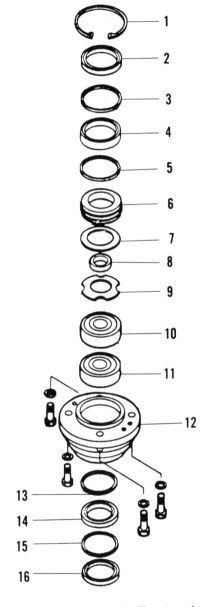

**BEARING HOUSING
COMPONENTS (TYPICAL)**

1. Snap ring
2. Seal
3. Retaining ring
4. Seal
5. Retaining ring
6. Seal carrier
7. Shim
8. Collar
9. Thrust washer
10. Top bearing*
11. Bottom bearing
12. Bearing housing
13. Retaining ring
14. Seal
15. Retaining ring
16. Seal

*A top bearing is not used
on 28 jet and 35 jet models.

moderate heat to the areas noted with arrows (**Figure 10**). Use a block of wood and hammer to tap, on the installed nut end, the shaft and bearing(s) from the housing. Gradually increase the amount of heat until the bearing(s) and drive shaft slide from the housing.

3. Remove the seal carrier (6, **Figure 11**) from the drive shaft. Note the orientation of the seal lips, then use a screwdriver to remove the grease seals (2 and 4, **Figure 11**) and both retaining rings (3 and 5, **Figure 11**) from the seal carrier. Discard the seals. Remove the O-rings from the seal carrier and discard them.

4. Note the location and orientation of the shim, collar and thrust washer (7-9, **Figure 11**), then remove them from the bearing housing.

5. Note the seal lip direction prior to removal. Use a screwdriver to remove the retaining rings (13 and 15, **Figure 11**) and seals (14 and 16, **Figure 11**) from the bearing housing. Discard the seals. Press the bearing(s) from the drive shaft.

6. Inspect the drive shaft for damaged surfaces or excessive wear in the seal contact areas. Replace the drive shaft if any defects are noted.

7. To assist with component location and orientation, refer to **Figures 12-14** during the assembly process. Place the thrust washer, if so equipped, onto the drive shaft. Note the orientation of the bearing thrust surfaces (wide side of the inner race), and slide the bearing(s) onto the shaft. Use a

10

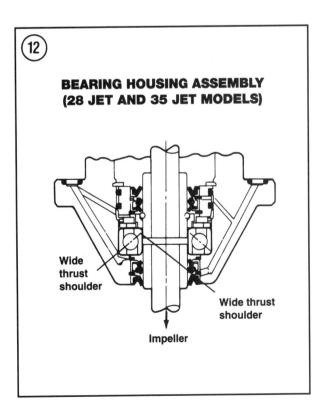

**BEARING HOUSING ASSEMBLY
(28 JET AND 35 JET MODELS)**

Wide
thrust
shoulder

Wide thrust
shoulder

Impeller

section of tubing or pipe to press the new bearing(s) onto the drive shaft. The tool used must contact only the inner race of the bearings.

8. Use Loctite Primer T to clean all contaminants from the seal bore in the bearing housing. Select a large socket or section of pipe to install the seals into the bearing housing. The tool selected must provide adequate contact for the seal, yet not contact the bearing housing during installation.

9. Apply Loctite Primer T to the outer surface of the seal. When dry, apply Loctite 271 to the seal bore in the housing and the seal outer surfaces. Place the seal into the housing with the seal lip (open side) facing in the direction noted prior to removal. Use the selected tool to press the seal into the bearing housing until seated against the retainer. Wipe the excess Loctite from the seals.

10. Install the retaining ring into the housing groove. Apply Loctite 271 to the outer surface of the second seal. Place the seal onto the housing with the seal lip (open side) facing the direction noted during removal. Use the selected tool to press the second seal into the housing until seated against the retaining ring. Place the second retaining ring into the housing groove with the notched area aligned with the small hole in the retaining ring groove. Wipe the excess Loctite from the seal area.

11. Apply Yamaha all-purpose grease to the seal lips and retaining ring prior to installation of the drive shaft and bearings.

CAUTION
Apply only enough heat to allow the bearing housing to expand and slide over the bearing(s). Excessive heat will damage the seals and retainers in the bearing housing. Use a section of appropriately sized pipe and a press, if necessary, to fully seat the bearing(s) into the housing. Press only on the outer bearing race. Use light pressure only. Never drive the bearings into position.

12. Place the drive shaft into a soft jaw or padded vise with the impeller side up. Set the bearing housing onto the drive shaft. Use a heat lamp or torch to apply heat to the bearing housing in the areas indicated (**Figure 10**). Remove the heat and use heavy gloves to push the bearing housing down over the drive shaft bearings. Apply heat gradually until the bearing housing slides fully onto the bearing(s) and the bearing(s) seat in the housing.

13. Install the thrust washer (9, **Figure 11**) onto the shaft with the gray side facing the impeller. Place the collar (8, **Figure 11**) onto the drive shaft. Place the shim (7, **Figure 11**) in the housing in the direction noted prior to removal.

14. Apply Loctite Primer T to the seal bore surfaces in the seal carrier (6, **Figure 11**) and the outer surfaces of the

seals (2 and 4, **Figure 11**). Install the first retaining ring into the seal carrier. Apply Loctite 271 to the seal bore and the outer seal surfaces.

15. Place the seal into the seal bore opening with the seal lip (open side) facing in the direction noted prior to removal or as indicated in **Figure 12-14**. Use an appropriately sized socket or section of tubing to push the first seal into the seal carrier until seated against the retainer. The

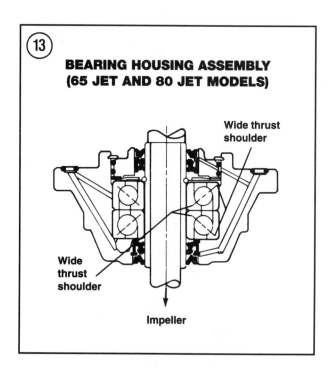

(13)

BEARING HOUSING ASSEMBLY (65 JET AND 80 JET MODELS)

Wide thrust shoulder

Wide thrust shoulder

Impeller

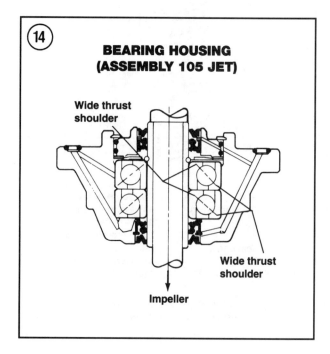

(14)

BEARING HOUSING (ASSEMBLY 105 JET)

Wide thrust shoulder

Wide thrust shoulder

Impeller

tool must provide adequate contact to the seal, yet not contact the seal carrier during installation.

16. Place the second retainer in the seal carrier groove. Push the second seal into the seal carrier as described in Step 15. Place new O-rings onto the seal carrier. Lubricate the seal lips and all seal carrier surfaces with Yamaha all-purpose grease. Carefully press the seal carrier into the bearing housing until fully seated.

17. Use snap ring pliers to install the snap ring into the groove in the bearing housing.

Bearing housing installation

1. Ensure that the mating surface of the bearing housing and jet drive housing are free of debris and contaminants.

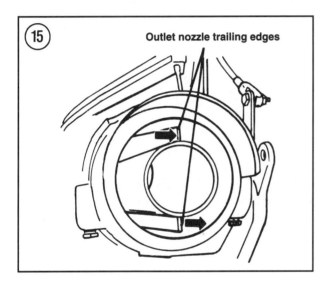

2. Install the housing and drive shaft into the jet drive housing. Apply Yamaha all-purpose grease to the threads of the bolts that retain the bearing housing, then install them. Tighten the bolts to specification listed in **Table 1**.

3. Install the aluminum spacer (33, **Figure 8** or 33, **Figure 9**) onto the jet drive housing. Refer to Chapter Nine for procedures, then install the water pump onto the jet drive housing. Use the procedures listed for the horsepower the engine would be rated if a propeller drive gearcase were installed.

4. Install the impeller and related components. Refer to *Impeller removal and installation*.

5. Install the intake housing. Refer to *Intake housing*.

6. Refer to *Impeller to housing clearance* and measure the clearance as described. Correct the clearance as required.

7. Install the jet drive onto the engine. Refer to *Jet drive removal and installation*. Removal of the intake housing may be required to access the fasteners on some models.

8. Perform the lubrication procedures as described in Chapter Four. Perform the direction control adjustments as described in Chapter Five.

Correcting Steering Torque

Steering torque will cause the boat to steer to the starboard or port side with the engine pointed straight ahead. The tabs (**Figure 15**) in the water discharge opening can be used to correct the steering torque.

Use pliers to bend the trailing end of *both* tabs approximately 1.6 mm (1/16 in.) toward the starboard side of the outlet if the boat steers to the starboard direction (**Figure 15**).

Bend both tabs toward the port side of the outlet if the boat steers toward the port direction.

10

Table 1 TIGHTENING TORQUE

Component	Torque specification
Jet drive mounting bolts	31.2 N•m (23 ft.-lb.)
Intake housing mounting bolts	10.9 N•m (96 in.-lb.)
Intake housing liner retaining bolts	11.3 N•m (100 in.-lb.)
Bearing housing mounting bolts	7.9 N•m (70 in.-lb.)

Table 2 STANDARD TIGHTENING TORQUE

Fastener size	Torque specification
8 mm bolt, M5 nut	5 N•m (44 in.-lb.)
10 mm bolt, M6 nut	8 N•m (70 in.-lb.)
12 mm bolt, M8 nut	18 N•m (13 ft.-lb.)
14 mm bolt, M10 nut	36 N•m (26 ft.-lb.)
17 mm bolt, M12 nut	43 N•m (31 ft.-lb.)

Chapter Eleven

Rewind Starter

This chapter provides repair procedure for all rewind starter assemblies. **Tables 1-3**, located at the end of this chapter, provide rewind starter tightening torque specifications and rewind rope length.

All manual start models and some electric start models are equipped with a rewind type starter (**Figure 1**). On 2-5 hp models, the rewind starter is the only means for cranking the engine for starting. An electric starter, rewind starter or both types are present on 6-50 hp models and models E48, E60 and E75. The rewind starter on the electric start models functions as the backup starter should the electric starting system fail.

The major components of the rewind starter include:

1. Starter rope.
2. Sheave.
3. Drive pawl.
4. Rewind spring.
5. Housing.
6. Rope guide.

Except for the rope guide and lockout assembly, all of the above are encased within the housing.

As the rope (1, **Figure 2**) is pulled, the sheave (2, **Figure 2**) assembly will rotate in the clockwise direction as viewed from the top. The rotation of the sheave will cause the drive pawl (3, **Figure 2**) to pivot from its normal position and engage the starter pulley which is mounted to

the flywheel. The starter spring will wind up within the housing as the rope is pulled.

As the rope is released, the starter spring will unwind causing the sheave to rotate in the counterclockwise direction as viewed from the top. As the sheave rotates in the counterclockwise direction, the drive pawl spring (10, **Figure 2**) will pivot the drive pawl to the normal position, releasing the starter from the pulley. The rope will wind around the sheave when released.

The rope guide (7, **Figure 2**) is supported by a bracket on most models and protrudes into an opening on the top motor cover.

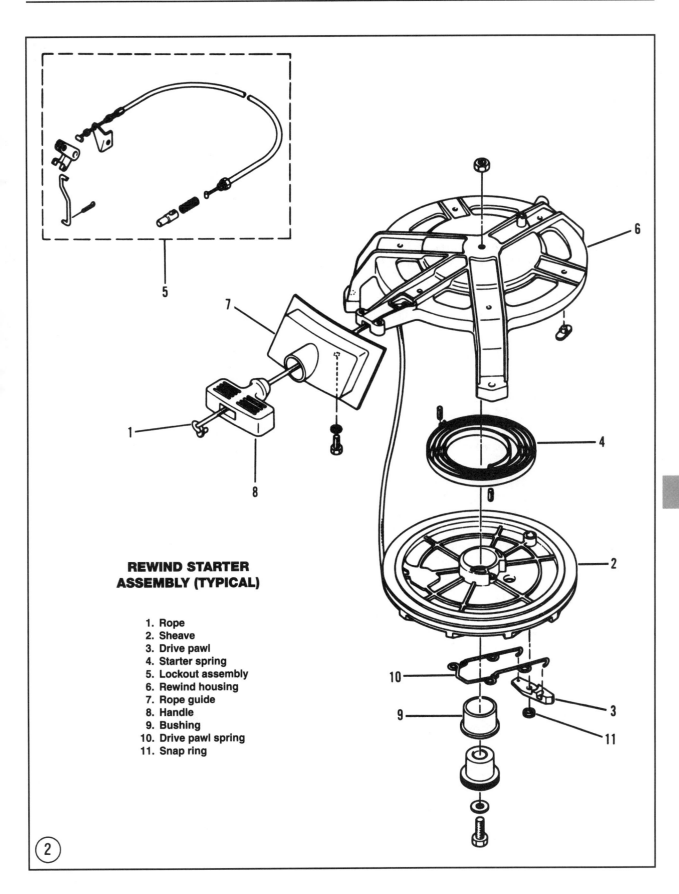

**REWIND STARTER
ASSEMBLY (TYPICAL)**

1. Rope
2. Sheave
3. Drive pawl
4. Starter spring
5. Lockout assembly
6. Rewind housing
7. Rope guide
8. Handle
9. Bushing
10. Drive pawl spring
11. Snap ring

11

To prevent the engine from starting when in gear, all 4-75 hp manual start models are equipped with a lockout assembly (**Figure 3**). The lockout is cable actuated and will prevent the starter sheave from rotating when the shift is engaging forward or reverse gear. The gear shift linkages on the engine operate the lockout assembly. Adjustment is required when any components of the lockout assembly are changed or the assembly is removed from the linkage or rewind housing. Refer to Chapter Five for adjustment procedures.

> *CAUTION*
> *When servicing the rewind starter, wear suitable eye protection, gloves and adequate covering over all exposed portions of the body. The starter spring may release from the housing with considerable force and result in serious bodily injury. Follow all instructions carefully and wear suitable protection to minimize the risk.*

Cleaning and lubrication of the internal components are required when the drive pawl is not engaging properly or the starter is binding when activated.

Use only the correct starter rope. Other types of rope will not withstand the rigorous use and will fail quickly. Contact a Yamaha dealership to purchase the correct starter rope.

Apply Yamaha all-purpose grease or its equivalent to all bushing, drive pawl, springs and pivot surfaces. Also apply grease to the starter spring and housing. Use Loctite type 572 or 271 on the starter shaft retaining bolt and other fasteners that mount the starter to the engine.

Refer to **Table 1** for tightening torque specifications. Use the standard torque specifications listed in **Table 2** when a specific torque is not indicated for a fastener.

Refer to **Figure 4-10** for component identification and orientation. The appearance of the components may differ slightly from the illustration. Note of all component loca-

tions and orientations prior to disassembly to ensure proper assembly.

   a. For 2 and 3 hp models, refer to **Figure 4**.
   b. For 4 and 5 hp models, refer to **Figure 5**.

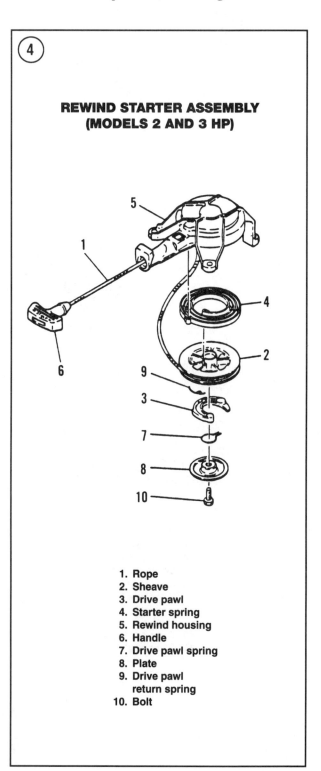

④

**REWIND STARTER ASSEMBLY
(MODELS 2 AND 3 HP)**

1. Rope
2. Sheave
3. Drive pawl
4. Starter spring
5. Rewind housing
6. Handle
7. Drive pawl spring
8. Plate
9. Drive pawl
   return spring
10. Bolt

③

⑤

REWIND STARTER ASSEMBLY (MODELS 4 AND 5 HP)

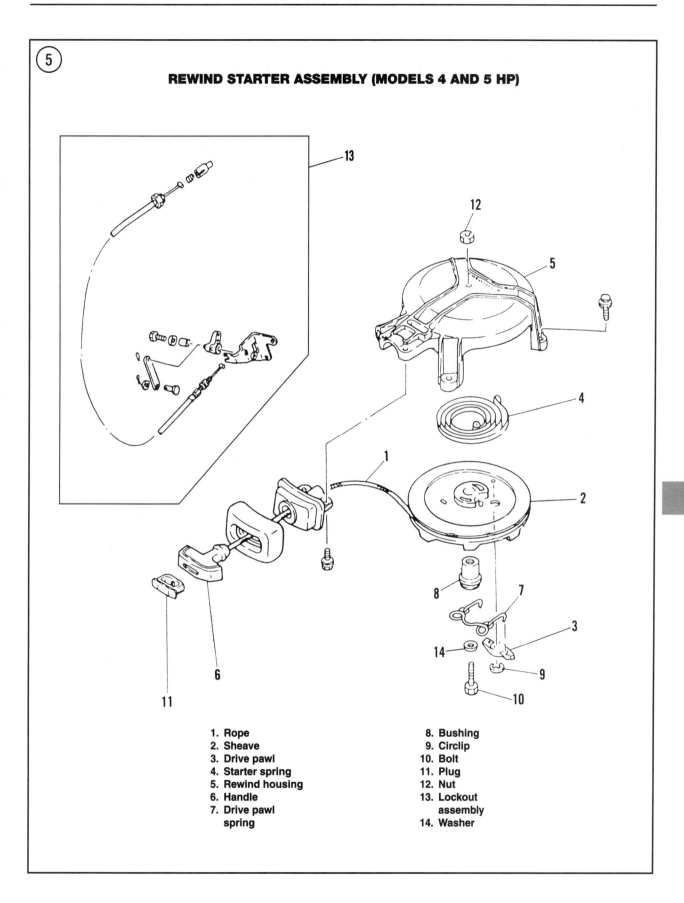

1. Rope
2. Sheave
3. Drive pawl
4. Starter spring
5. Rewind housing
6. Handle
7. Drive pawl
   spring
8. Bushing
9. Circlip
10. Bolt
11. Plug
12. Nut
13. Lockout
    assembly
14. Washer

11

c. For 6 and 8 hp models, refer to **Figure 6**.

d. For 9.9 and 15 hp models, refer to **Figure 7**.

e. For 20 and 25 hp models, refer to **Figure 8**.

f. For 28 jet and 30-50 hp models, refer to **Figure 9**.

g. For models E48, E60 and E75, refer to **Figure 10**.

The repair procedures for the 2 and 3 hp models will vary from the 4-75 hp models. Refer to the procedures for the required model.

**Rewind Starter Removal and Disassembly
(2 and 3 hp Models)**

1. Remove the three bolts that retain the rewind starter to the power head. Remove the rewind starter from the power head (**Figure 11**). Inspect the pulley mounted on the flywheel for wear or damage and replace if required. Position the rewind starter on a clean work surface with the top of the rewind housing facing down.

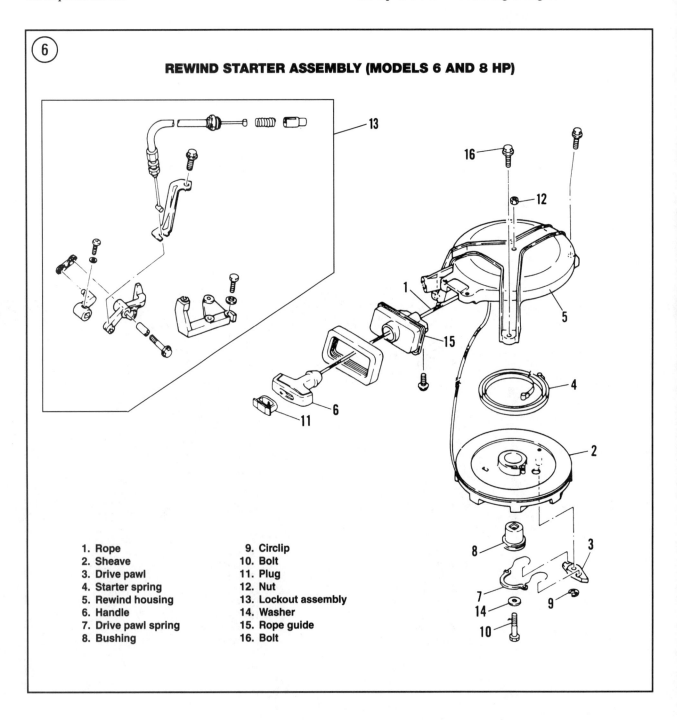

(6)

REWIND STARTER ASSEMBLY (MODELS 6 AND 8 HP)

1. Rope	9. Circlip
2. Sheave	10. Bolt
3. Drive pawl	11. Plug
4. Starter spring	12. Nut
5. Rewind housing	13. Lockout assembly
6. Handle	14. Washer
7. Drive pawl spring	15. Rope guide
8. Bushing	16. Bolt

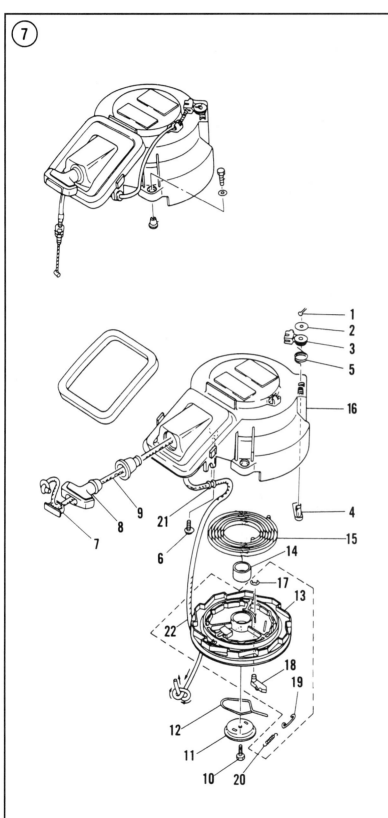

**REWIND STARTER ASSEMBLY
(MODELS 9.9 AND 15 HP)**

1. Pin
2. Washer
3. Bushing mount
4. Lockout lever
5. Spring
6. Bolt
7. Plug
8. Handle
9. Rope
10. Bolt
11. Plate
12. Drive pawl spring
13. Sheave
14. Bushing
15. Starter spring
16. Rewind housing
17. Circlip
18. Drive pawl
19. Link
20. Return spring
21. Guide bushing
22. Rope groove

11

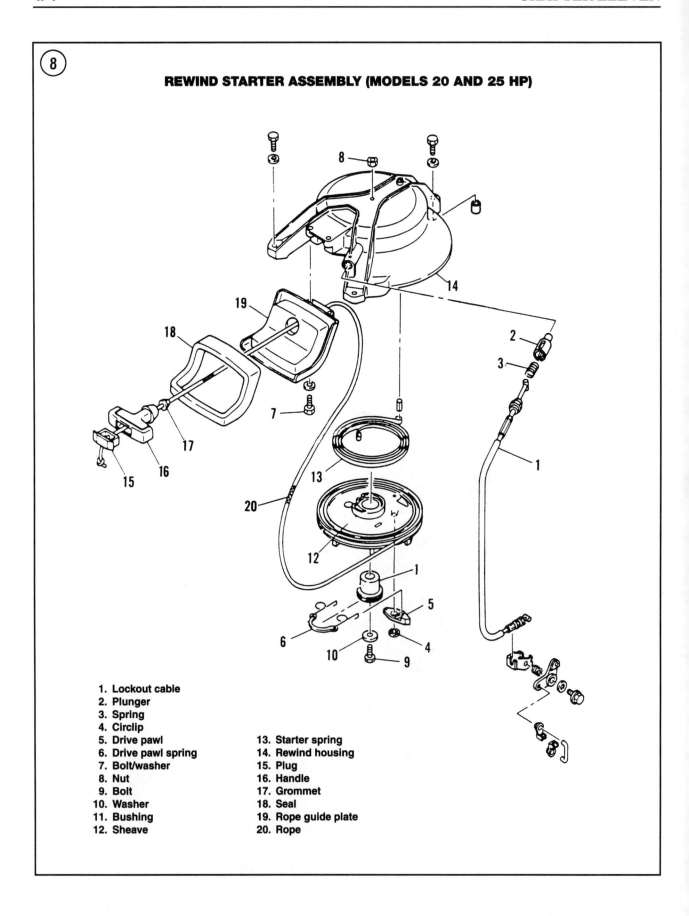

REWIND STARTER ASSEMBLY (MODELS 20 AND 25 HP)

1. Lockout cable
2. Plunger
3. Spring
4. Circlip
5. Drive pawl
6. Drive pawl spring
7. Bolt/washer
8. Nut
9. Bolt
10. Washer
11. Bushing
12. Sheave
13. Starter spring
14. Rewind housing
15. Plug
16. Handle
17. Grommet
18. Seal
19. Rope guide plate
20. Rope

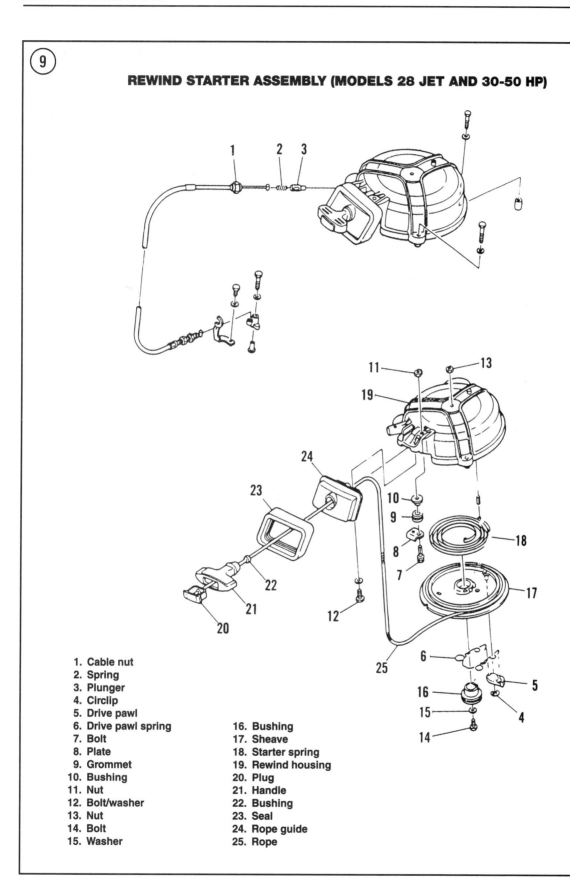

REWIND STARTER ASSEMBLY (MODELS 28 JET AND 30-50 HP)

1. Cable nut
2. Spring
3. Plunger
4. Circlip
5. Drive pawl
6. Drive pawl spring
7. Bolt
8. Plate
9. Grommet
10. Bushing
11. Nut
12. Bolt/washer
13. Nut
14. Bolt
15. Washer
16. Bushing
17. Sheave
18. Starter spring
19. Rewind housing
20. Plug
21. Handle
22. Bushing
23. Seal
24. Rope guide
25. Rope

11

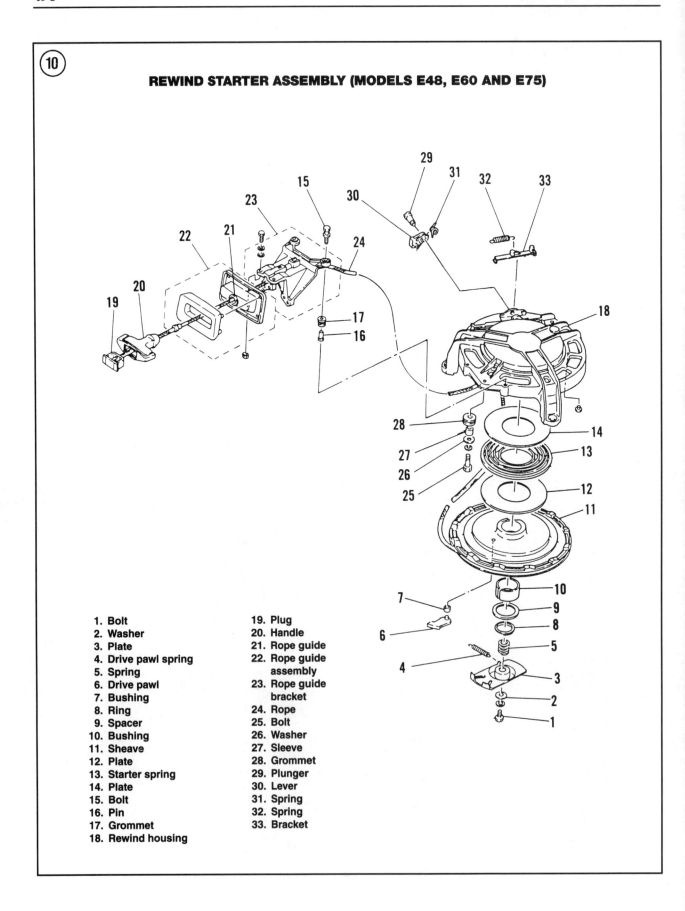

REWIND STARTER ASSEMBLY (MODELS E48, E60 AND E75)

1. Bolt
2. Washer
3. Plate
4. Drive pawl spring
5. Spring
6. Drive pawl
7. Bushing
8. Ring
9. Spacer
10. Bushing
11. Sheave
12. Plate
13. Starter spring
14. Plate
15. Bolt
16. Pin
17. Grommet
18. Rewind housing
19. Plug
20. Handle
21. Rope guide
22. Rope guide assembly
23. Rope guide bracket
24. Rope
25. Bolt
26. Washer
27. Sleeve
28. Grommet
29. Plunger
30. Lever
31. Spring
32. Spring
33. Bracket

2. If the rope is not broken, pull it out approximately 6 inches and clamp it at the rope guide with vise grips or pliers. This will prevent the rope from winding into the housing when the handle is removed.

3. Use a screwdriver to pry the plug and rope from the handle. Untie the knot and pull the handle from the rope.

4. Grip the rope and rewind housing and remove the vise grips or pliers. Allow the rope to slowly wind onto the sheave until the rope is relaxed.

5. Remove the starter shaft bolt and plate (8 and 10, **Figure 4**). Lift the drive pawl (3, **Figure 4**) and drive pawl springs (7 and 9, **Figure 4**) from the rewind starter assembly.

6. Insert a small tip screwdriver into the hole in the starter sheave (**Figure 12**) and press down to hold the starter spring into the housing (5, **Figure 4**). Maintain downward pressure on the spring and lift the sheave (2, **Figure 4**) and rope from the rewind housing. Remove the screwdriver when the sheave has cleared the housing.

7. Place the housing on the floor with the spring side facing down. Hold the housing down and lightly tap the top of the housing with a mallet until the starter spring (4, **Figure 4**)

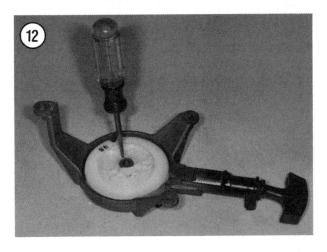

drops from the housing and is completely unwound or relaxed.

Inspection (2 and 3 hp Models)

Clean all components except the rope in a solvent suitable for composite or plastic components. Use hot soapy water if a suitable solvent is not available. Dry all components with compressed air.

1. Inspect the plate (8, **Figure 4**) for damaged or worn areas and replace if required.

2. Inspect the drive pawl (3, **Figure 4**) for cracks or worn areas. Replace the pawl if damage or wear is noted.

3. Inspect the drive pawl springs (7 and 9, **Figure 4**) for broken or bent springs and worn surfaces. Replace if any defects are noted.

4. Inspect the entire length of the starter spring for cracked, broken or damaged areas. Pay particular attention to the hook or bent end at the end of the spring.

5. Inspect the sheave (2, **Figure 4**) for warped, damaged or worn surfaces and replace if required.

6. Inspect the entire length of the rope (1, **Figure 4**) for cuts and worn or frayed areas. Pay particular attention to the length nearest the handle. Replace with the proper type of rope if not in excellent condition.

7. Inspect the rope guide for damaged or worn areas. To prevent rapid wear on the replacement rope, replace the housing if sharp areas are present or a groove has worn in the rope guide.

Starter Assembly and Installation (2 and 3 hp Models)

Measure the length of the starter rope and compare the length to the specifications listed in **Table 3**. Trim the rope to the *exact* length as specified. To prevent the end of the rope from unraveling, carefully melt the cut end of the rope with a small flame. While still molten use thick gloves and shape the end of the rope into a compact nub. Trim loose pieces from the end when cooled.

1. Wipe the surfaces in the rewind housing where the spring is installed with Yamaha all-purpose grease or its equivalent.

2. Position one end of the rope through the hole in the sheave and tie a knot as indicated (**Figure 13**). Position the knot into the recess in the sheave. Install the plug into the handle.

> *CAUTION*
> *DO NOT remove the retainer from the replacement starter spring until the spring is properly installed in the rewind housing.*

11

3. Position the hooked or bent end of the starter spring over the tab in the rewind housing as indicated (**Figure 14**). Carefully wind the spring into the housing in the direction indicated until all loops are installed and the spring is positioned fully into the housing.

4. Position the sheave with the flywheel end (rope knot is visible) facing up. Wrap the rope 3 1/2 turns *counterclockwise* around the sheave. Route the remaining length of rope into the notch in the sheave as indicated in **Figure 15**.

5. Apply a light coat of Yamaha all-purpose grease or its equivalent to the flat surfaces of the sheave. Install the sheave into the rewind housing. Make sure the hook or bent end of the rewind spring engages the tab on the sheave. Insert a screwdriver through the hole in the sheave to align the hook with the tab if necessary.

6. Apply a light coat of Yamaha all-purpose grease or its equivalent to the drive pawl. Install the pawl return spring (9, **Figure 4**), drive pawl (3, **Figure 4**) and drive pawl spring (7, **Figure 4**).

7. Install the plate (8, **Figure 4**) into the sheave. Make sure the open end of the pawl spring engages the tab on the drive pawl.

8. Apply Loctite 572 or 271 to the threads of the bolt (10, **Figure 4**). Install the bolt and torque to the specification listed in **Table 1** or **Table 2**.

9. Position the rewind housing on a work surface with the flywheel end up. Hold down on the sheave and rotate it three complete turns *counterclockwise*. While maintaining light downward pressure, route the rope through the rope guide and handle. Tie a knot in the rope as indicated (**Figure 16**). Insert the knot into the opening in the handle. Install the plug into the handle.

10. Release the sheave while allowing the rope to slowly feed into the rewind starter. Operate the rewind starter several times to check for proper operation. Disassemble and inspect if binding or rough operation is noted. Install the starter onto the engine and tighten the fasteners to the specification listed in **Table 1** or **Table 2**. Check for proper operation.

Rewind Starter Removal and Disassembly (4-75 hp Models)

To assist with the location and identification of components, refer to **Figure 5-10** and locate the illustration that applies to your model. Refer to this illustration during the removal, assembly and installation procedures.

1. Locate and disconnect the starter lockout cable from the rewind housing. Remove the plunger and spring from the end of the cable.

2. Remove all bolts, nuts and washers that attach the rewind starter to the engine. Remove the rewind starter and position it on clean work surface with the flywheel side up.

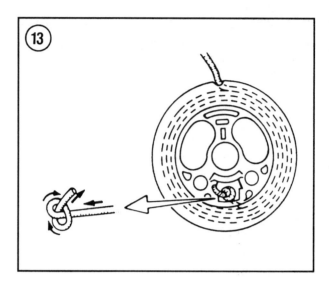

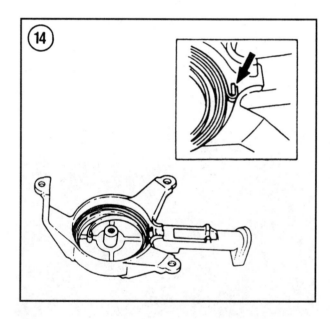

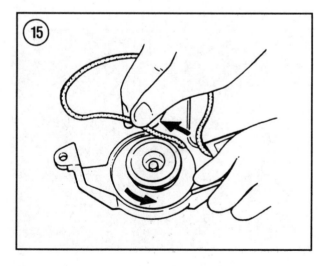

3. Remove the circlip that retains the drive pawl (excluding Models E48, E60 and E75). Remove the drive pawl and spring (**Figure 17**).

4. If the rope is not broken, pull the rope handle out approximately 6 inches and clamp the rope at the guide with vise grips or pliers. Pry the plug and rope from the handle and untie the knot in the rope. Grasp the rope end and rewind housing. Maintain downward pressure on the sheave. Release the vise grip or pliers and allow the rope

to slowly wind into the groove on the starter sheave until the spring tension is relieved.

5. Remove the bolt, nut, washers and bushings from the rewind housing (**Figure 18**). On Models E48, E60 and E75, remove the plate, drive pawl and springs.

6. Rotate the sheave clockwise (**Figure 19**) until the starter spring releases from the sheave and the slot in the sheave aligns with the rope guide.

7. Locate the access hole in the sheave and insert a screwdriver into the hole (**Figure 20**). Push the starter spring down while carefully removing the sheave from the rewind housing.

8. Maintain constant downward pressure on the starter spring and carefully remove the starter spring from the rewind housing by gently lifting and pulling one loop at a time.

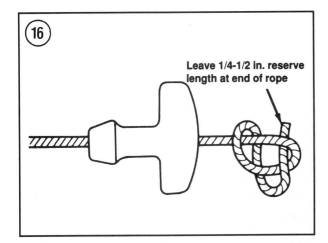

Leave 1/4-1/2 in. reserve length at end of rope

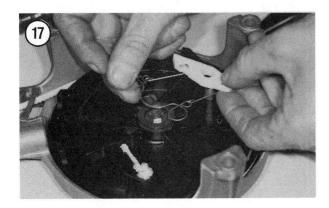

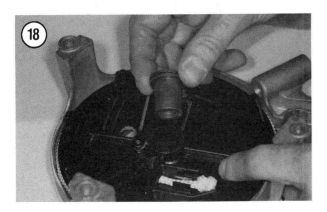

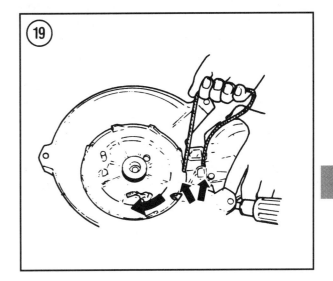

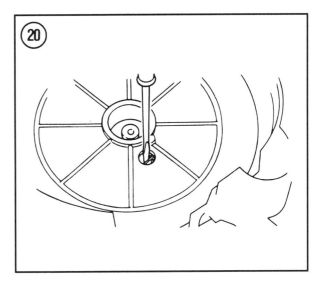

11

9. On the 9.9, 15, E48, E60 and E75 models, remove the lockout lever, pins, bushing, spring and fasteners from the rewind housing.

Inspection (4-75 hp Models)

Clean all components except the rope in a light solvent that is suitable for plastic or composite material. Use hot soapy water if a suitable solvent is not available. Dry all components with compressed air.

1. Inspect the drive pawl for cracks or worn areas and replace if not in excellent condition.

2. Inspect the drive pawl springs for broken or bent loops. Replace the springs if defects are noted or worn areas are found on the spring.

3. Inspect the entire length of the starter spring for cracked, bent, corroded or broken areas. Pay particular attention to the hook or bent end at the end of the spring.

4. Inspect the sheave for warped, damaged or worn areas. Check the fit of the bushing or bolt to the hole in the sheave. Worn components will result in a loose fit and improper starter operation. Replace worn components as required.

5. Inspect the entire length of the rope for cuts and worn or frayed areas. Pay particular attention to the length nearest the handle. Replace with the proper type rope if not in excellent condition.

6. Inspect the rope guide for worn or damaged areas. Replace the rope guide if sharp edges are noted or a groove has worn in the surfaces.

7. Inspect the starter shaft bolt and bushings for damaged or worn areas and replace as required. On E48, E60 and E75 models, inspect the plate near the bolt for worn or damaged areas and replace if any defect is noted.

8. Inspect the lockout plunger and spring and other components of the assembly. Replace the plunger and spring if cracked, broken or worn areas are noted. Check for proper operation of the cable and levers. Replace the components if binding of the cable or worn linkages are noted.

Rewind Starter Assembly and Installation (4-75 hp Models)

Measure the length of the replacement rope and compare the measurement to the specification listed in **Table 3**. Cut the rope to the *exact* length as specified. To prevent the rope from unraveling, melt the cut end with a small flame. While still molten use thick gloves to shape the end into a compact nub. Trim loose pieces from the end when cool.

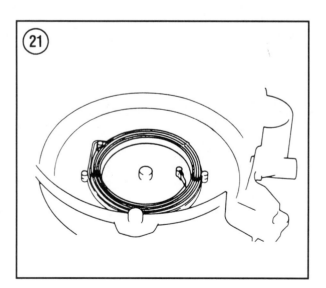

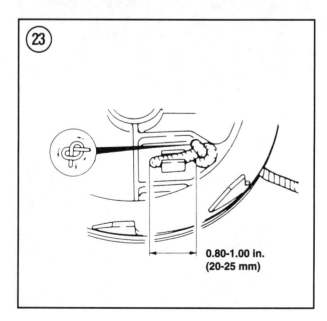

0.80-1.00 in.
(20-25 mm)

1. Wipe a light coating of Yamaha all-purpose grease or its equivalent into starter spring cavity of the rewind housing.

CAUTION
DO NOT remove the retainer from a replacement starter spring until the spring is properly installed into the rewind housing.

2A. Position the rewind housing on a stable work surface and clamp the unit down to hold the unit securely. Install the end of the starter spring over the tab in the rewind housing and carefully wind the spring counterclockwise into the housing (**Figure 21**).

2B. When installing a replacement spring, install the spring fully into the rewind housing (**Figure 22**). Hold the spring into position with a glove protected hand and carefully remove the retainers.

3. Pass the end of the rope through the hole in the sheave and tie a knot as indicated (**Figure 23**). Make sure that the proper length of rope remains as indicated in **Figure 23**.

4. With the flywheel end of the sheave facing up, wind the rope *counterclockwise* 2 1/2 turns around the sheave.

5. Place the end of the rope into the notch in the sheave groove. Apply a light coating of Yamaha all-purpose grease to the upper and lower surfaces of the sheave. Install the sheave into the rewind housing. Ensure that the hooked end of the rewind spring engages the tab on inner portion of the sheave. Use the access hole in the sheave to verify spring engagement.

6. On Models E48, E60 and E75, install the drive pawl, springs and plate. Apply Loctite 572 or 271 to the threads and install the bolt, nut, washers and bushings into the sheave. Refer to **Table 1** for tightening torque specification.

7. Hold the sheave down into the rewind housing and rotate the sheave five turns *counterclockwise*. While maintaining the downward pressure, route the end of the rope through the rope guide and handle. Tie a knot in the end of the rope as indicated in **Figure 16**. Install the plug into the handle.

8. Slowly release the rope as the spring winds the rope onto the sheave groove. Operate the rewind several times to check for proper operation. Disassemble and inspect the components if binding or rough operation is noted.

9. For all models (except E48, E60 and E75), install the drive pawl, springs and retaining clip. Lubricate the drive pawl and springs with Yamaha all-purpose grease or its equivalent.

10. On the 9.9, 15, E48, E60 and E75 models, lubricate the lockout lever, pin and bushing with Yamaha all-purpose grease or its equivalent. Install the components onto the rewind housing. Tighten all fasteners securely.

11. Install the rewind assembly onto the power head. Refer to **Table 1** or **Table 2** for fastener tightening torque. Lubricate the lockout plunger with Yamaha all-purpose grease or its equivalent and install the lockout cable. Tighten the retainer securely. Refer to Chapter Five for lockout cable adjusting procedures.

11

Table 1 TIGHTENING TORQUE

	Torque specification
Rope guide/bracket bolts	
4, 5 hp	6 N•m (53 in.-lb.)
6, 8 hp	5 N•m (44 in.-lb.)
Starter shaft bolt	
4, 5 hp	3 N•m (26 in.-lb.)
6, 8 hp	4 N•m (35 in.-lb.)
E48, E60, E75	8 N•m (70 in.-lb.)

Table 2 STANDARD TIGHTENING TORQUE

Fastener size	Tightening torque
8 mm nut, M5 bolt	5 N•m (44 in.-lb.)
10 mm nut, M6 bolt	8 N•m (70 in.-lb.)
12 mm nut, M8 bolt	18 N•m (13 ft.-lb.)
14 mm nut, M10 bolt	36 N•m (26 ft.-lb.)
17 mm nut, M12 bolt	43 N•m (31 ft.-lb.)

Table 3 STARTER ROPE LENGTH

Model	Rope length
2 hp	1300 mm (51.2 in.)
3 hp	1650 mm (65.0 in.)
6 and 8 hp	1850 mm (72.8 in.)
9.9 and 15 hp	1800 mm (70.9 in.)
20 and 25 hp	1950 mm (76.8 in.)
30-50 hp	2095 mm (82.5 in.)
E48, E60 and E75	2300 mm (90.6 in.)

Chapter Twelve

Power Trim/Tilt and Mid-Section

This chapter will provide removal, installation and minor repair to the hydraulic trim and tilt systems. Procedures for removal, inspection and assembly of the mid-section components are provided in this chapter as well.

POWER TRIM

Table 1 and **Table 2** provide tightening torque specifications for trim/tilt and mid-section components. **Table 3** provides electric trim motor specifications. **Tables 1-3** are located at the end of the chapter.

> ### WARNING
> *Never work under any part of the engine without providing suitable support. The engine mounted tilt lock or hydraulic system may collapse and allow the engine to drop. Support the engine with suitable blocks or an overhead cable **before** working under the engine.*

Manual Tilt System Removal and Installation

Fastener location and component appearance vary by model. Mark or make note of component location and orientation prior to removal to ensure a proper assembly.

Apply Yamaha all-purpose grease or its equivalent to all bushings (5, **Figure 1**) and pivot points on assembly. Apply Loctite 572 to the threads of the tilt lever bolt (2, **Figure 1**) and the clamp bracket fastener threads (6, **Figure 1**).

1. Remove both battery cables from the battery terminals. Disconnect *all* spark plug leads. Refer to **Figure 1** during the removal and installation procedures.

2. Activate the tilt lever and pivot the engine in the full *up* position. Use an overhead hoist or other secure means to support the engine as indicated in **Figure 2**.

3. Remove the clamp bracket bolts (6, **Figure 1**).

4. Pivot the bracket spacer (3, **Figure 1**) out of the clamp brackets and carefully drive the lower pin (4, **Figure 1**) from the assembly. Take care to avoid damaging the pivot surfaces or bushings (5, **Figure 1**).

5. Remove the circlip and upper pivot pin from the swivel bracket. Carefully drive the upper pivot pin from the tilt unit cylinder. Remove the tilt system from the engine.

6. Inspect the circlip for corrosion or weak spring tension and replace if its condition is questionable. Inspect all bushings and pins for damaged or worn surfaces and replace as required.

7. Installation is the reverse of removal. Tighten all fasteners to the specifications provided in **Table 1** or **Table 2**. Check for proper operation on completion.

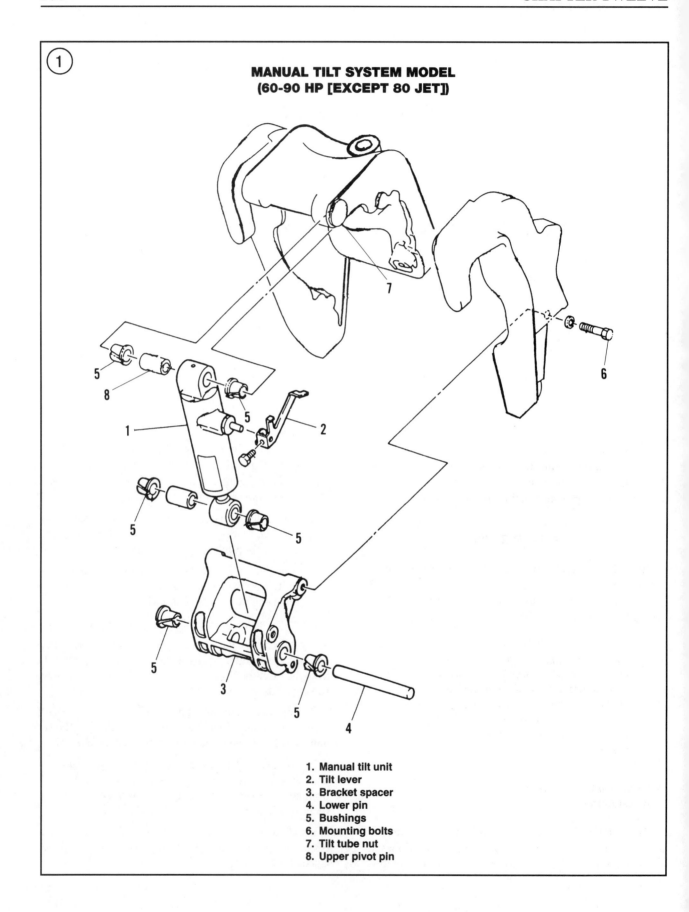

**MANUAL TILT SYSTEM MODEL
(60-90 HP [EXCEPT 80 JET])**

1. Manual tilt unit
2. Tilt lever
3. Bracket spacer
4. Lower pin
5. Bushings
6. Mounting bolts
7. Tilt tube nut
8. Upper pivot pin

Hydraulic Tilt and Trim System Removal and Installation (Single Trim Cylinder)

Fastener location and component appearance vary by model. Mark the location and orientation of all components prior to removal to ensure a proper assembly. Make a sketch of the trim wire routing before removal. Apply Yamaha all-purpose grease to all bushing and pivot points on assembly. Apply Loctite 242 to the threads of the tilt/trim system fasteners.

1. Disconnect both battery cables from the battery terminals. Disconnect *all* spark plug leads. Refer to **Figure 3** during the removal and installation procedures.

2. Locate the manual relief valve and access opening on the starboard side clamp bracket. Rotate the valve 3-4 turns counterclockwise. Tilt the unit to the full up position and securely tighten the manual relief valve.

3. Use an overhead hoist or other secure means to support the engine as indicated in **Figure 2**.

4. Trace the wires from the trim system to the power head and disconnect the wires. Route the wires out the cover openings to allow for removal of the tilt/trim system.

5. Remove the screws (3 and 5, **Figure 3**) and ground wires (4 and 6, **Figure 3**) from the clamp brackets.

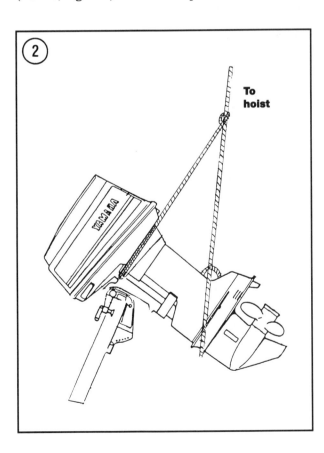

(2)

To hoist

6. Remove the nuts (8 and 13 **Figure 3**) and the washers and mounting stud (9 and 10, **Figure 3**). Pivot the bracket spacer out of the clamp brackets.

7. Pull the bracket spacer from the tilt/trim system and remove the bushings (12, **Figure 3**).

8. Remove the circlip (14, **Figure 3**). Support the trim/tilt system and carefully drive the pivot pin (15, **Figure 3**) from the swivel housing.

9. Inspect the circlip for corrosion and weak spring tension. Replace if its condition is questionable. Inspect all bushings and pins for damaged or worn surfaces. Replace if required.

10. Lower the tilt/trim system and remove the bushings and bushing sleeve from the cylinder.

11. Installation is the reverse of removal. Tighten all fasteners to the specification listed in **Table 1** or **Table 2**. Route all trim wires carefully to avoid interference with other components. Check for proper operation on completion.

Three Cylinder Power Trim System Removal and Installation

Fastener location and component appearance vary by model. Note the component location and orientation prior to removal to ensure a proper assembly. Make a sketch of the trim wire routing before removal. Apply Yamaha all-purpose grease to all bushings and pivot points on assembly.

1. Remove both battery cables from the battery terminals. Disconnect all spark plug leads. Refer to **Figure 4** during the removal and installation procedures.

2. Trace the wires leading from the trim system to the connections on the power head. Disconnect the wires from the power head and route them out of the engine cover. Remove all clamps along the wires.

3. Locate the manual relief valve access hole on the port clamp bracket. Rotate the valve counterclockwise 2-3 turns (**Figure 5**). Carefully tilt the engine to the full up position. Support the engine with a hoist or other suitable means as indicated in **Figure 2**. Securely tighten the manual relief valve.

4. Disconnect all ground wires (2, **Figure 4**). Clean and inspect the ground wire mounting location.

5. Remove the pivot pin circlips. Carefully drive the lower pin from the clamp bracket.

6. Support the trim system and remove the upper pin from the swivel bracket. Remove the trim system.

7. Inspect all bushings and pins for damaged or worn surfaces and replace as required.

8. Installation is the reverse of removal. Route the trim system wires carefully to avoid interference with other components.

12

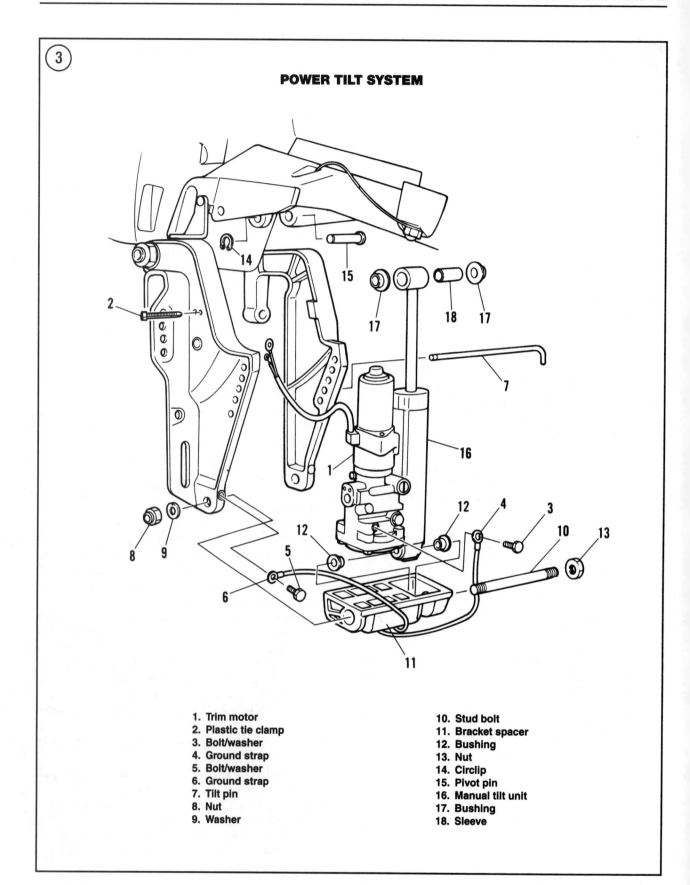

POWER TILT SYSTEM

1. Trim motor
2. Plastic tie clamp
3. Bolt/washer
4. Ground strap
5. Bolt/washer
6. Ground strap
7. Tilt pin
8. Nut
9. Washer
10. Stud bolt
11. Bracket spacer
12. Bushing
13. Nut
14. Circlip
15. Pivot pin
16. Manual tilt unit
17. Bushing
18. Sleeve

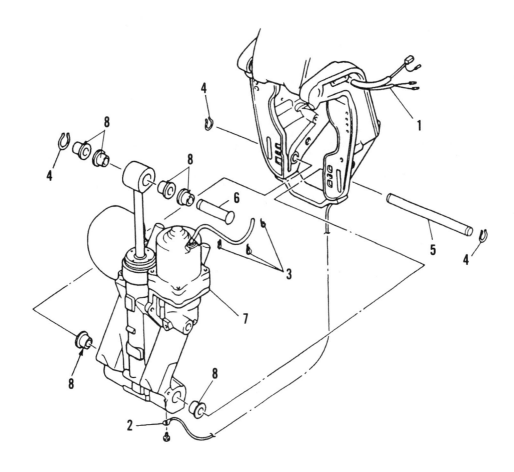

**THREE CYLINDER
POWER TRIM/TILT SYSTEM**

1. Trim system wires
2. Ground wire
3. Plastic tie clamp
4. Circlip
5. Lower pin
6. Upper pin
7. Trim system
8. Bushings

12

9. Check and correct the fluid level before operating the system. Refer to *Hydraulic System Filling and Bleeding* located in this chapter. Check for proper operation on completion.

Trim/Tilt Relay(s) and Relay Unit Replacement

The engine may be equipped with a relay unit or individual relays (**Figure 6**). The mounting location for the relays will vary by model. Refer to the wire charts located near the back of the manual and identify the wire colors for the relays. Trace the wires to the component on the engine. The relay unit must be replaced if either the up or down circuit has failed. With individual relays, only the faulty relay must be replaced. Removal and installation procedures for both types are similar.

1. Disconnect both battery cables at the battery terminals.
2. Trace the wires to the component on the engine. Mark each wire connection location and orientation before removal.
3. Remove the fasteners for the trim relay after making note of their locations. Clean the mounting location and

the threaded holes for the mounting fasteners. Clean and inspect all terminal connections.

4. Installation is the reverse of removal. Tighten all fasteners securely. Clean battery cable connection prior to installation. Check for proper operation upon completion.

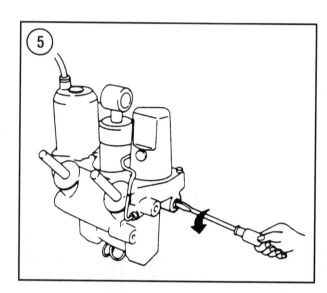

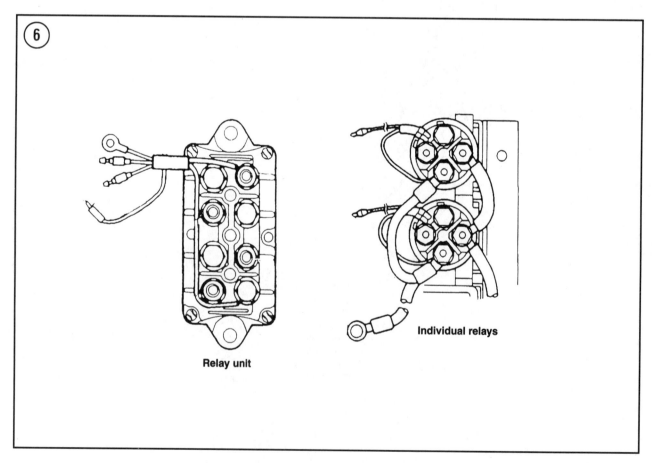

Relay unit   Individual relays

Trim Sender Replacement

The trim sender is located on the inside of the port clamp bracket (**Figure 7**). The sender appearance and wire connections vary by model. The sender used on the 60-90 and 200-250 (76°) models differ from other models. The removal and installation procedure is similar. Make a sketch of the sender wire routing and connections prior to removal to ensure a proper installation.

NOTE
Always adjust the trim sender after replacement. An improperly adjusted trim sender can result in the trim system not reaching its required trim ranges and also inaccurate gauge readings.

Perform trim sender adjustments after installation. Refer to Chapter Five for adjustment.

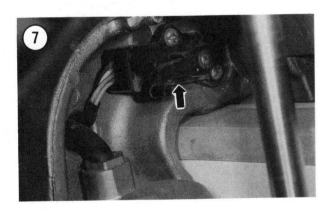

1. Position the engine to full tilt and engage the tilt lock lever. Support the engine with blocks or a suitable overhead cable (**Figure 2**).
2. Trace the sender wires (**Figure 8**) to the harness connection inside the motor cover and disconnect them. Route the wires out of the motor cover to allow removal of the wire and sender. Remove all clamps prior to removal. Inspect the clamps for corrosion or damage and replace if required.
3. Use a felt tip marker to trace the sender outline on the mounting location. This will allow for quicker adjustments and proper orientation on installation. Remove both fasteners and the sender (**Figure 9**). Route the wires through the opening in the port clamp bracket and remove the assembly.
4. Clean corrosion and contaminants from the mounting location and threaded holes.
5. Installation is the reverse of removal. Align the sender with the markings and securely tighten the attaching screws.
6. Refer to Chapter Five for the procedures and adjust the trim sender. Check for proper operation.

Trim/Tilt System Electric Motor Removal/Installation

WARNING
The trim system may contain fluid under high pressure. Always use protective eyewear and gloves when working with the trim system. Never remove components or plugs without first bleeding the pressure from the system. Follow the instructions carefully.

The electric trim motor appearance and mounting arrangement vary by model. Refer to the illustration for your

12

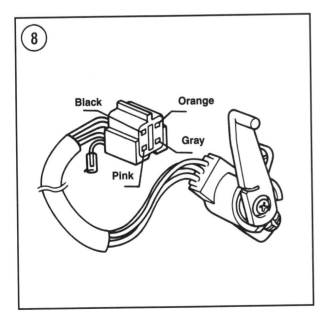

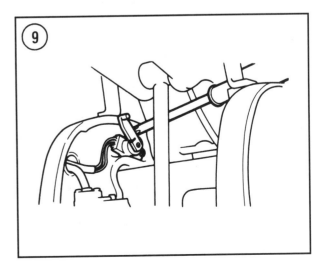

model during the removal and installation procedures. The appearance of the components may vary slightly from the illustration.

    a. For 28 jet and 30-90 hp (except 80 jet), refer to **Figure 10**.

    b. For 80 jet and 115-250 hp models, refer to **Figure 11**.

Removal of the port clamp bracket is usually required when removing the electric trim motor on triple hydraulic cylinder system. Refer to *Mid-section* in this chapter for clamp bracket removal and installation procedures.

> *CAUTION*
> *Never direct pressurized water (pressure washer) at the seal surfaces when cleaning debris or contaminants from the trim system. The water may pass by the seal surface and contaminate the fluid.*

The trim system must operate with clean fluid. A small amount of contaminants can wreak havoc with the trim system operation. Thoroughly clean the trim system external surfaces with soapy water to remove all debris and contaminants. Use compressed air to dry the trim system.

Work in a clean area and use lint free towels to wipe fluids and debris from components upon removal. Cover any openings immediately after removing the trim motor to prevent accidental contamination of the fluid.

> *CAUTION*
> *To avoid unnecessary disassembly and potential wire interference, always note the orientation of the electric trim motor and wire harness. Use a paint dot or piece of tape to mark the location. Never scratch the housing as it will promote corrosion.*

Follow Steps 1-11 to replace the trim/tilt system electric motor.

1. Disconnect both battery cables from the battery terminals. Locate the manual relief valve access opening on the starboard side clamp bracket for models with a single hydraulic cylinder or port side for models with triple hydraulic cylinders.

2. Locate the manual relief valve. Refer to 1, **Figure 10** for single trim cylinder system and 1, **Figure 11** for triple trim cylinder systems. Slowly rotate the manual relief valve 2-3 turns counterclockwise. Manually tilt the engine to the full up position and tighten the manual relief valve to the specification listed in **Table 1** or **Table 2**.

3. Engage the tilt lock mechanism and block or support the engine with an overhead support. Trace the electric trim motor wires to the terminal locations on the power head.

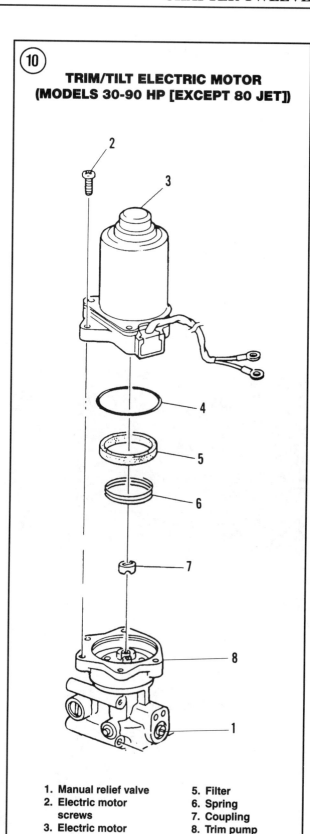

(10)

TRIM/TILT ELECTRIC MOTOR (MODELS 30-90 HP [EXCEPT 80 JET])

1. Manual relief valve	5. Filter
2. Electric motor screws	6. Spring
3. Electric motor	7. Coupling
4. O-ring	8. Trim pump

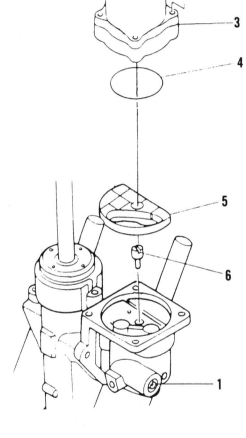

TRIM/TILT ELECTRIC MOTOR (80 JET AND 115-250 HP MODELS)

1. Manual relief valve
2. Electric motor screws
3. Electric motor
4. O-ring
5. Filter
6. Coupling

Note the wire locations to ensure proper connections on assembly. Disconnect the electric trim motor wires.

4. Route the wires out of the motor cover area. Remove all clamps along the wires. Make a note or sketch of the wire harness routing and trim motor wire orientation prior to removal. Remove the screw or fasteners (2, **Figure 10** or 2, **Figure 11**) for the electric trim motor. Carefully lift the electric motor from the trim system.

5. Making sure all fasteners are removed, carefully use a flat scraper or dull putty knife to pry the motor from the housing. Be careful to avoid damaging the electric motor mounting surface. A fluid or water leak can occur if the surfaces are damaged.

6. Remove and discard the O-ring (4, **Figure 10** or 4, **Figure 11**). Remove the filter (5, **Figure 10** or 5, **Figure 11**). Clean the filter in solvent and air dry. Replace the filter if damaged or if debris remains on the filter after cleaning. Complete trim system disassembly and inspection is required if a considerable amount of debris is present in the filter. Remove and clean the spring (6, **Figure 10**) on 30-90 hp models (except 80 jet).

7. Note the top and bottom orientation of the coupling (7, **Figure 10** or 6, **Figure 11**). Compare the coupling surfaces with the electric motor shaft. Determine correct orientation if the coupling was disturbed during removal of the electric trim motor.

8. Clean and inspect the trim motor mounting surface for corrosion, pitting or scratches. Replace any components that have scratches that can be felt with a fingernail.

9. Installation is the reverse of removal. Lubricate with Yamaha all-purpose grease and install a new O-ring onto the electric trim motor to pump sealing surface. Apply Yamaha all-purpose grease to the coupling mating surfaces during installation. Position the electric motor on the pump (8, **Figure 10**) and rotate the electric trim motor until the coupling aligns and the electric trim motor drops into position.

10. Slowly rotate the electric trim motor to obtain correct orientation of the wires and install the fasteners. Tighten the fasteners in a crossing pattern to the specification listed in **Table 1**.

11. Perform the *Hydraulic System Filling and Bleeding* as described in this chapter.

Trim/Tilt System Electric Motor Repair

This section covers the disassembly, inspection and assembly of trim/tilt system electric motors. The procedures vary slightly from one model to the next. Instruction is provided for the individual motor variations.

Work in a clean environment to avoid contaminants. Use electrical contact cleaner to remove contaminants and debris from the electric motor components. Electrical con-

12

⑫

TRIM MOTOR COMPONENTS (28 JET AND 30-50 HP MODELS)

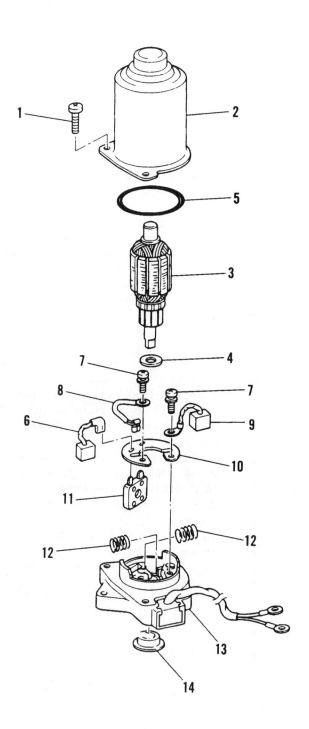

1. Screws
2. Frame assembly
3. Armature
4. Washer
5. O-ring
6. Brush
7. Brush retainer screw
8. Wire
9. Brush
10. Brush plate
11. Bi-metal switch
12. Brush springs
13. Lower cover
14. Coupling

tact cleaner is available at most electrical supply sources. It evaporates rapidly and leaves no residue to contaminate the components. Avoid touching the brushes and commutator after cleaning. Naturally occurring oils on your fingers will contaminate these components.

NOTE
Mark the top cover, frame and bottom cover of the electric motor prior to disassembly. Use paint dots or removable tape. Never

scratch the components as it will promote corrosion of metal components.

The arrangement of the components in the tilt/trim electric motor varies by model. Refer to the illustration that applies to your model during the disassembly and assembly procedures.

a. For 28 jet and 30-50 hp models, refer to **Figure 12**.
b. For 60-90 hp models (except 80 jet), refer to **Figure 13**.

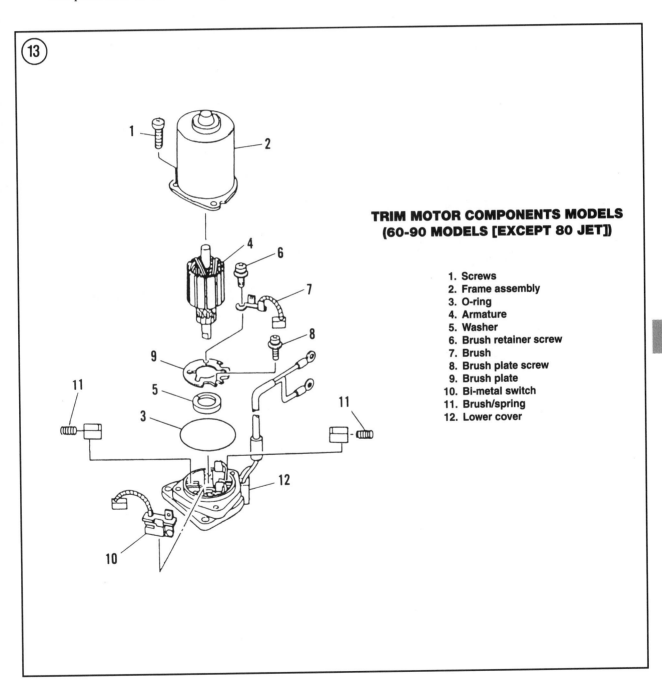

(13)

TRIM MOTOR COMPONENTS MODELS (60-90 MODELS [EXCEPT 80 JET])

1. Screws
2. Frame assembly
3. O-ring
4. Armature
5. Washer
6. Brush retainer screw
7. Brush
8. Brush plate screw
9. Brush plate
10. Bi-metal switch
11. Brush/spring
12. Lower cover

12

c. For 80 jet and 115-225 hp (90°) models, refer to **Figure 14**.

d. For 200-150 hp (76°) models, refer to **Figure 15**.

Tilt/trim system electric motor disassembly

CAUTION
Use caution when working around the permanent magnets in the frame assembly. These magnets are quite powerful. Fingers are easily pinched between the components. Never drop or strike the frame assembly. The magnets might break and damage other components during operation.

1. Remove the electric motor from the trim system. Refer to *Trim/Tilt System Electric Motor Removal/Installation.* Mark all components (**Figure 16**) prior to disassembly to ensure proper orientation on assembly.

2A. On 28 jet and 30-225 (90°) models, remove the screws that retain the frame assembly to the bottom cover. Remove the cover and discard the O-ring.

2B. On 200-250 (76°) models, remove the throughbolts that retain the top cover to the frame and bottom cover.

NOTE
The magnets in the frame assembly are quite strong. Considerable effort may be required to remove the frame assembly from the armature. Make sure all fasteners are removed

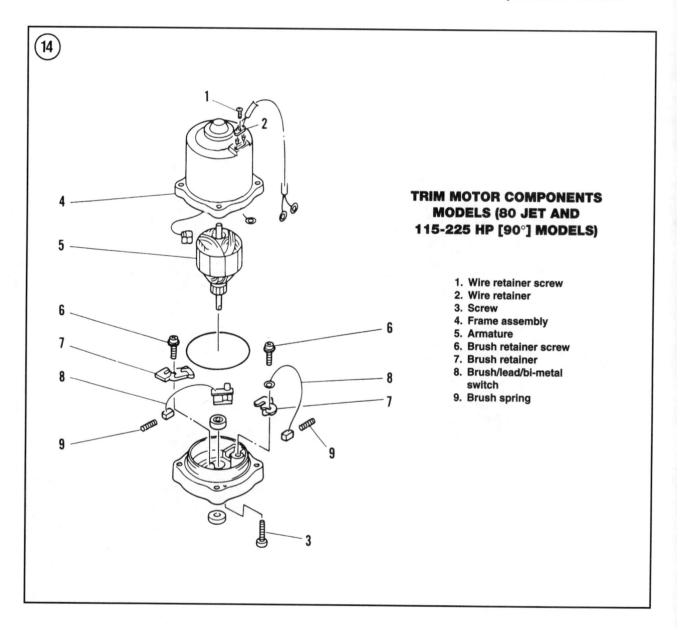

TRIM MOTOR COMPONENTS MODELS (80 JET AND 115-225 HP [90°] MODELS)

1. Wire retainer screw
2. Wire retainer
3. Screw
4. Frame assembly
5. Armature
6. Brush retainer screw
7. Brush retainer
8. Brush/lead/bi-metal switch
9. Brush spring

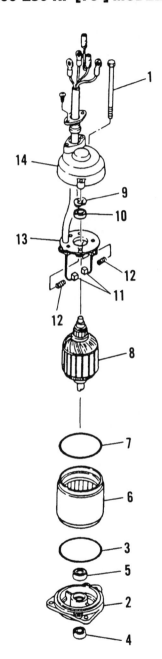

**TRIM MOTOR COMPONENTS
(200-250 HP [76°] MODELS)**

1. Throughbolts
2. Lower cover
3. O-ring
4. Seal
5. Bearing
6. Frame assembly
7. O-ring
8. Armature
9. Wave washer
10. Bushing
11. Brushes
12. Brush springs
13. Brush plate
14. Upper cover

and carefully pull the frame and armature apart.

3A. On 28 jet and 30-225 (90°) models only, grasp the armature shaft with pliers and a shop towel as indicated (**Figure 17**). Pull the armature and bottom cover from the frame assembly.

3B. On 200-250 hp (76°) models, pull the bottom cover from the frame assembly and top cover. Remove and discard the O-ring. While holding the armature firmly into the top cover, remove the frame assembly from the armature. Remove and discard the armature.

4. Use two small screwdrivers to carefully collapse the brush spring and move the brush away from the commu-

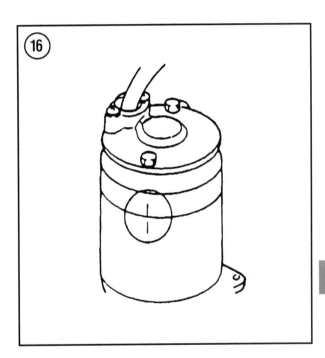

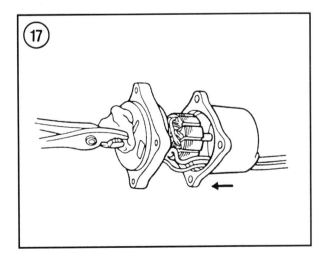

12

tator. Be careful to avoid damaging the brush or commutator. Carefully pull the armature from the cover while the brushes are pulled away from the comutator.

5. Remove the washer on the armature. Refer to the proper illustration and remove the screws, brushes and retainers from the cover.

6. Disconnect and remove the bi-metal switch from the cover.

7. Use compressed air to blow debris from the components. Clean contaminants from all components with electrical contact cleaner.

Trim/tilt motor component inspection and testing

Prior to performing any test or measurement, clean debris and contaminants from all components. Inspect the magnets in the frame assembly for broken or loose magnets and replace the frame assembly if defects are noted.

1. Select the ohms or resistance function of a volt/ohm meter. Select the 1 ohm scale. Connect the positive test lead to the green wire connection on the cover assembly. Connect the negative lead to the respective brush lead for that wire (**Figure 18**). Note the meter reading. Repeat this test with the blue wire and its respective brush lead. Continuity should be indicated for each lead. Replace the harness or cover assembly if an open circuit or very high resistance is indicated.

2. Connect the meter leads to the brush retainers (**Figure 19**). Make certain that the harness connectors are separated from the other leads. Note the meter reading. An open circuit should be indicated. Replace the brushes and leads if an incorrect reading is noted.

3. Connect the meter positive test lead to one of the terminals or brush lead connection at the bimetal switch (**Figure 20**). Connect the negative test lead to the other terminal of the bimetal switch. Note the meter reading. Continuity should be indicated. Replace the bimetal switch if no continuity is noted.

4. Carefully grip the armature in a soft-jawed vise (**Figure 21**). Use only enough clamping force to retain the component. Polish the commutator surfaces with 600 grit wet or dry abrasive paper or carburundum. Periodically rotate the

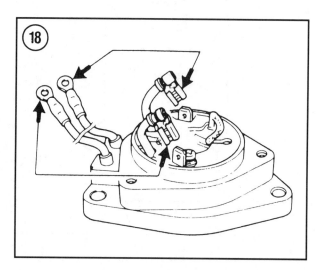

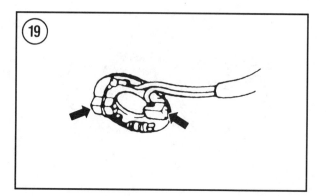

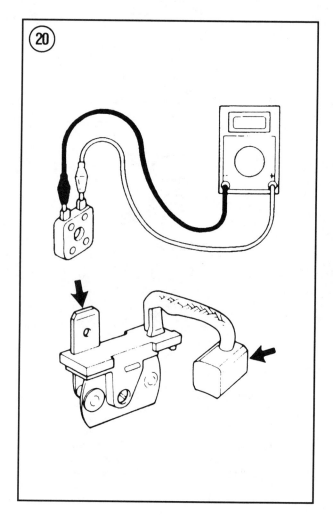

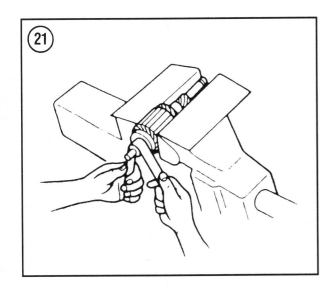

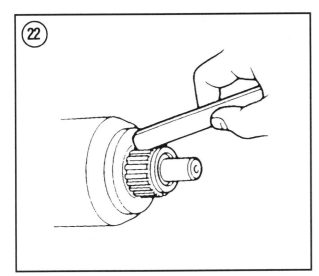

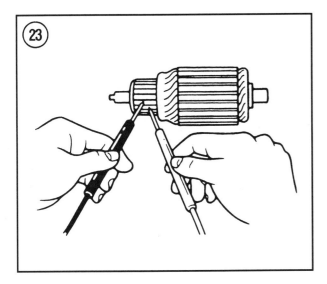

armature to polish evenly. Avoid removing too much material.

5. Use a disposable fingernail file to remove the mica and brush material from the undercut surfaces (**Figure 22**).

6. Select the ohms or resistance function of a volt/ohm meter. Select the 1 ohm scale. Connect the positive test lead to one of the segments on the commutator. Connect the meter negative test lead to another segment on the commutator (**Figure 23**). Note the meter reading. Repeat the test until all segments are tested. Continuity should be present between any pair of segments. Replace the armature if any incorrect readings are noted.

7. Connect the meter positive test lead to one of the segments on the comutator. Connect the negative test lead to one of the laminated areas of the armature (**Figure 24**). Note the meter reading. Connect the negative test lead to the armature shaft and note the meter reading (**Figure 24**). No continuity should be indicated on each test. Replace the armature if an incorrect reading is noted.

8. Using a micrometer or vernier caliper, measure the commutator diameter (**Figure 25**). Compare the measurement with the specification in **Table 3**. Replace the armature if not within the listed specification. Inspect the bearing surfaces on the armature for wear or damaged surfaces and replace as required. Inspect the bushings in

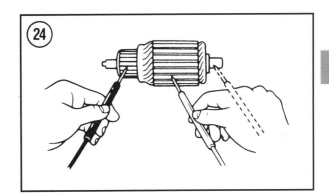

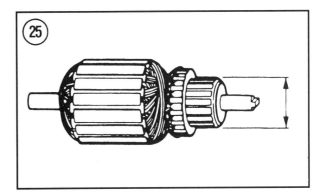

12

the covers or frame assembly and replace if worn or damaged.

9. Using a depth micrometer, measure the depth of the undercut to the mica material (**Figure 26**). Compare the measurement with the specification listed in **Table 3**. Replace the armature if not within the specification. Some models do not require this measurement. Disregard this measurement if the specification is not listed in **Table 3**.

10. Inspect the brush springs for damage or corrosion. Replace the brush springs if any doubts exist about their condition. Measure the brush length (**Figure 27**). Replace both brushes if either brush is at or below the wear limit listed in **Table 3**.

Trim/tilt system electric motor assembly

1. Clean and dry all components. Apply a light coating of Yamaha all-purpose grease to the bushing and armature shaft at the bushing contact surface. Do not allow any grease to contact the brushes or commutator surfaces.

2. Install the brush springs, brush retainers, bimetal switch and brushes into the cover. Tighten the screws securely.

3. Use two small screwdrivers to position the brushes fully into the brush holders (the springs are collapsed). Carefully install the commutator end of the armature into the cover and release the brushes. Never force the armature into the cover as the brushes may be damaged.

4A. On 28 jet and 30-225 (90°) models, use pliers and a shop towel to maintain the position of the armature and cover (**Figure 17**). Install a new O-ring and place the armature into the frame. Make sure the armature shaft end enters the bushing inside the frame.

4B. On 200-250 (76°) models, install a new O-ring onto the top cover. Install the frame assembly over the armature assembly. Position the armature assembly onto the top cover. Make sure that the O-ring is properly positioned onto the frame.

5. Install the washer, if so equipped, onto the armature shaft. Install a new O-ring onto the bottom cover and carefully guide the bottom cover onto the armature shaft and frame.

6. Align the marks made prior to disassembly and install the throughbolts or attaching screws. Do not tighten the screws at this time

7. Make sure the O-ring is properly positioned to prevent water leakage. Tighten the throughbolts or screws to the specification listed in **Table 3**.

8. Install the motor onto the trim system. Refer to *Tilt/trim Electric Motor Removal/Installation*.

Manual Relief Valve Removal/Installation

Replacement of the manual relief valve is simple if the screwdriver slot in the end of the valve is intact. If this is not the case, the valve can usually be removed by other means. Heat the tip of a screwdriver and then hold it against the remnants of the valve. The valve material will melt into the shape of the screwdriver tip. Allow the material to cool and use the same screwdriver to remove the valve. Never drill the valve out or the seating surfaces for the O-ring will suffer irreparable damage.

Inspect the O-rings on the valve even though they will be discarded. Problems may surface if large portions are missing or torn away from the O-rings. They will usually migrate to a valve or other component within the trim system and cause the system to malfunction.

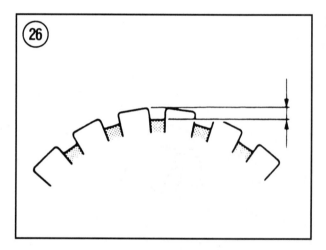

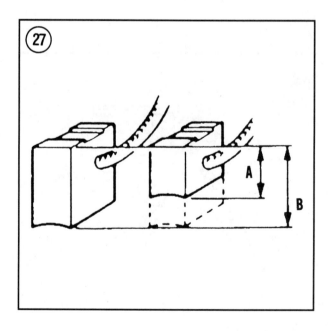

1. Position the engine in the full up tilt position. Engage the tilt lock lever *and* support the engine with an overhead cable or suitable blocks.

2. Locate the manual relief access hole in the clamp bracket. Slowly loosen the valve by rotating it 2-3 turns in the counterclockwise direction (**Figure 28**). Remove the locking ring from the valve (**Figure 29**) and unthread the valve from the trim system. Remove the valve from the opening.

3. Use a suitable light and small pick or screwdriver to remove any remnants of the valve or O-ring from the opening. Avoid damaging any of the machined surfaces in the opening.

4. Lubricate the new manual relief valve with Dextron II automatic transmission fluid and install *new* O-rings onto the valve. Lubricate the O-rings with Dextron II automatic transmission fluid and install the valve into the opening. DO NOT tighten the valve at this time.

5. Rotate the valve clockwise until slight resistance can be felt. Rotate the valve 1/4 turn clockwise and 1/8 turn counterclockwise. Repeat this process until the valve is seated. Tighten to the specification listed in **Table 1**. Refer

to *Hydraulic System Filling and Bleeding* in this chapter to correct the fluid level and purge air from the system.

WARNING
The trim/tilt system creates very high pressures. Always wear protection for the eyes and gloves for the hands. Never disconnect any hydraulic lines or remove any fittings without relieving the pressure in the system. Tilt the engine to the full up position and provide adequate support against falling. Open the manual relief valve 2-3 complete turns to relieve the pressure.

Hydraulic System Filling and Bleeding

Refer to *Filling procedures* if the unit has lost a large amount of fluid or after a major component has been removed.

Refer to *Bleeding procedures* if the trim system exhibits symptoms of air in the fluid.

Filling procedure

This process starts during the assembly process. The pump housing and cylinder(s) are filled with fluid during the repair procedure. This procedure is performed to correct the level after assembly is completed or a component such as the manual relief valve or pump motor is replaced. Use Dextron II automatic transmission fluid in both the single hydraulic cylinder and triple hydraulic cylinder systems.

12

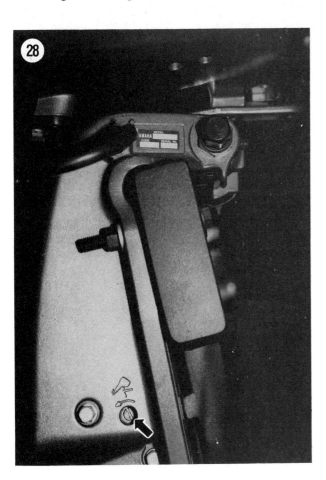

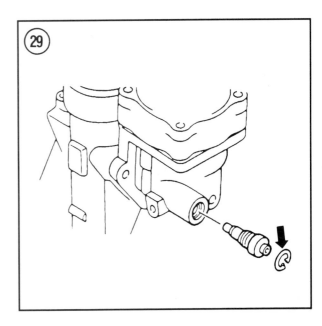

1. Use the power trim/tilt system or open the manual relief valve (A, **Figure 30**) to position the engine in the full UP position. Engage the tilt lock lever and support the engine with suitable blocks or overhead cable. Close the manual relief valve.

2. Locate and clean the area around the reservoir fill plug. Slowly loosen and remove the reservoir fill plug. Refer to **Figure 31** for single trim hydraulic cylinder systems and B, **Figure 30** for triple hydraulic cylinder systems.

3. Fill the unit to the bottom of the opening (**Figure 32**) with the engine in the full up position. Install the fill plug. Remove the supports and disengage the tilt lock lever.

4. Cycle the trim to the full up then down position several times. Check and correct the fluid level as necessary. Tighten the plug to the specification listed in **Table 1**.

Bleeding procedure

A spongy feel or inability to hold trim under load is a common symptom when air is present in the passages. The engine will usually tuck under when power is applied and tilt out when power is reduced. Minor amounts of air in the system will purge into the reservoir during normal operation. When major components have been removed, a significant amount of air can enter the system. Bleeding of the air is then required.

1. Operate the trim system or open the manual relief valve to position the engine fully up. Correct the fluid level as indicated in Step 3 of *Filling procedure*. Install the plug and tighten the manual relief valve.

2. Operate the trim system until the engine is positioned in the full down position. Operate the trim in the up position. Stop the trim immediately if the electric pump motor begins to run faster or sounds different (pump is ventilating). Open the manual relief valve and position the engine in the full up position and support the engine with blocks or an overhead hoist. Check and correct the fluid level. Close the manual relief valve and install the reservoir plug.

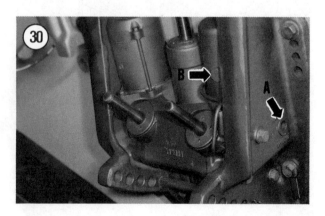

3. Continue to repeat Step 2 until the motor will reach full tilt without ventilating the pump. If a large amount of foam is noted in the reservoir, allow the engine to set for 1 hour and repeat the process.

4. Cycle the trim full up and down several times to purge the remaining air from the system.

MID-SECTION

Clamp Bracket and Swivel Bracket

Repairs to the mid-section usually involve the replacement of worn motor mounts or bushings. Broken mid-section components usually result from impact with underwater objects.

Component appearance and mounting arrangement vary by model. Refer to **Figure 33-40** and locate the illustration that applies to your model. Refer to the illustration for fastener location and component orientation. Component appearance may vary slightly from the illustration. Note

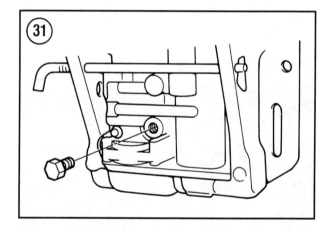

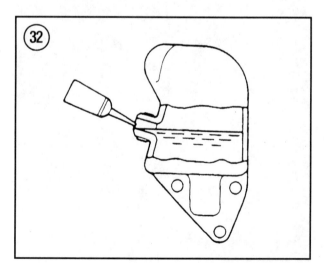

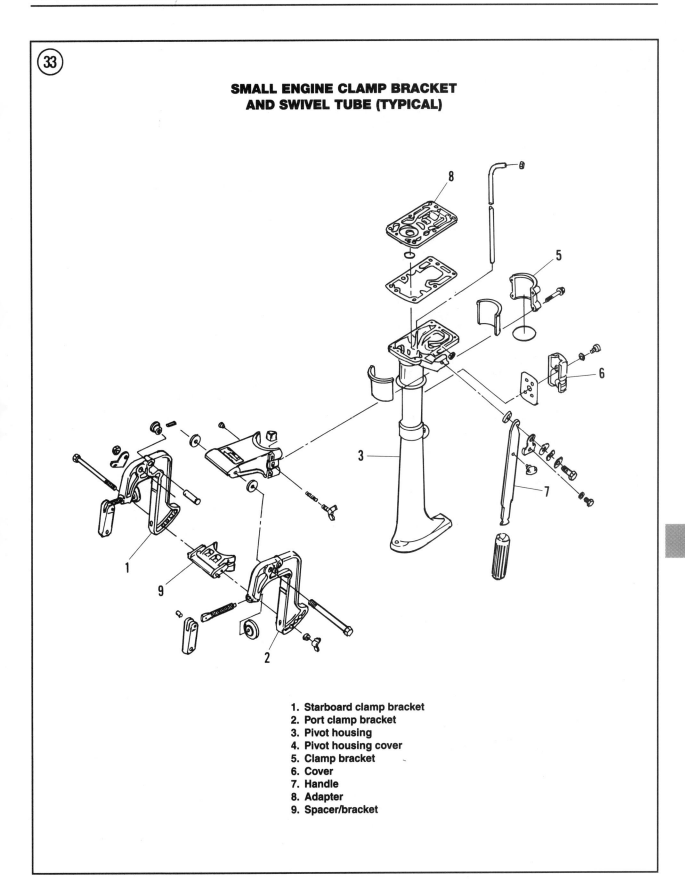

**SMALL ENGINE CLAMP BRACKET
AND SWIVEL TUBE (TYPICAL)**

1. Starboard clamp bracket
2. Port clamp bracket
3. Pivot housing
4. Pivot housing cover
5. Clamp bracket
6. Cover
7. Handle
8. Adapter
9. Spacer/bracket

12

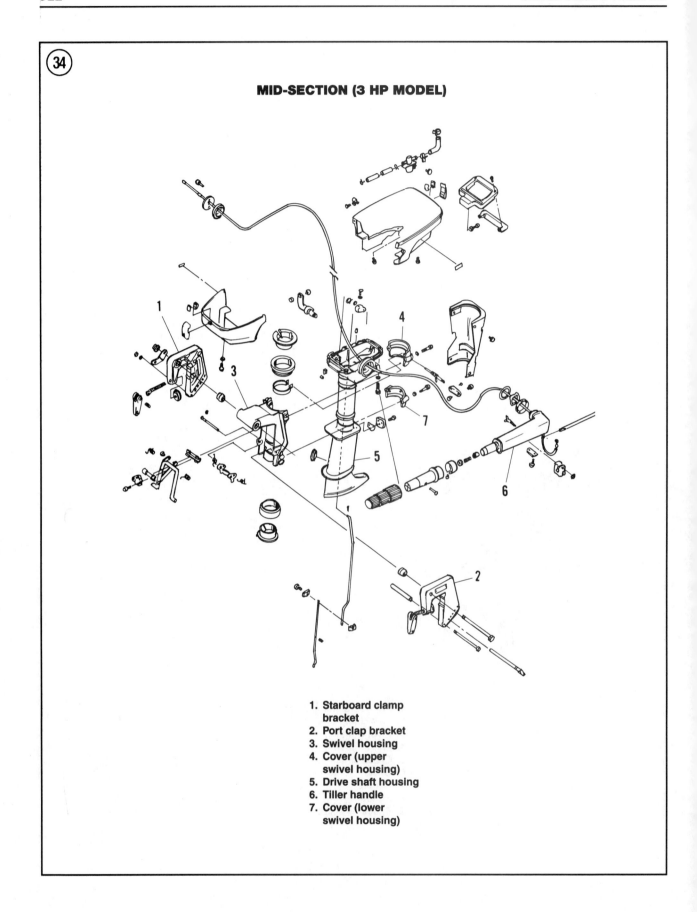

MID-SECTION (3 HP MODEL)

1. Starboard clamp
   bracket
2. Port clap bracket
3. Swivel housing
4. Cover (upper
   swivel housing)
5. Drive shaft housing
6. Tiller handle
7. Cover (lower
   swivel housing)

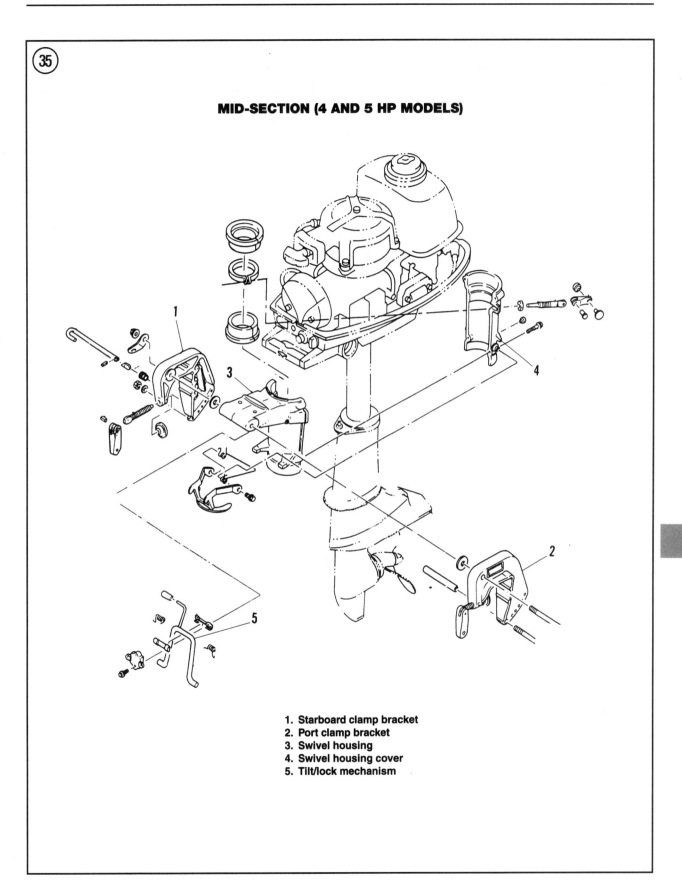

MID-SECTION (4 AND 5 HP MODELS)

1. Starboard clamp bracket
2. Port clamp bracket
3. Swivel housing
4. Swivel housing cover
5. Tilt/lock mechanism

12

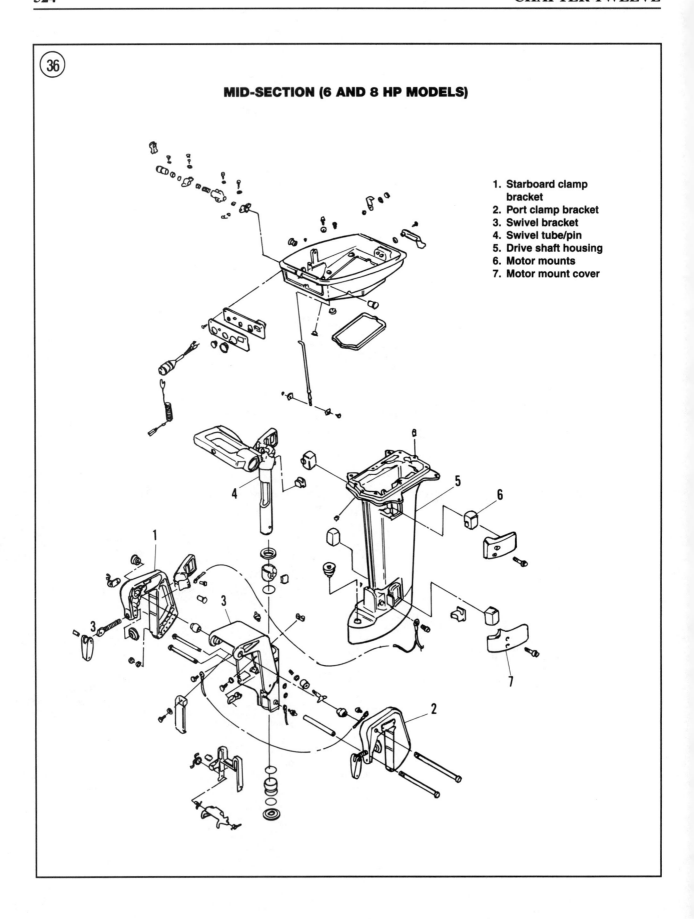

36

MID-SECTION (6 AND 8 HP MODELS)

1. Starboard clamp bracket
2. Port clamp bracket
3. Swivel bracket
4. Swivel tube/pin
5. Drive shaft housing
6. Motor mounts
7. Motor mount cover

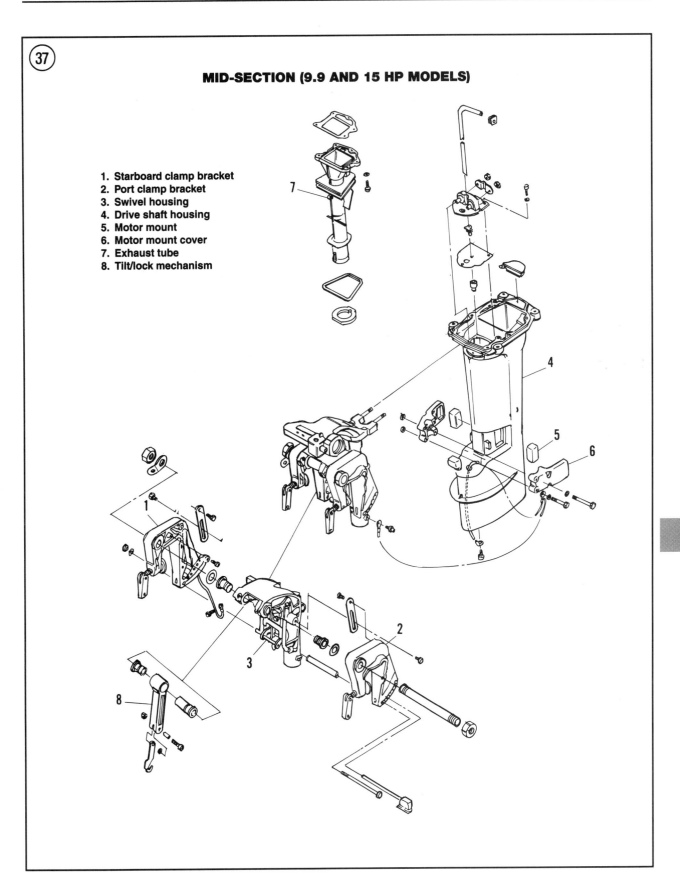

MID-SECTION (9.9 AND 15 HP MODELS)

1. Starboard clamp bracket
2. Port clamp bracket
3. Swivel housing
4. Drive shaft housing
5. Motor mount
6. Motor mount cover
7. Exhaust tube
8. Tilt/lock mechanism

12

MID-SECTION (20 AND 25 HP [TWO-CYLINDER] MODELS)

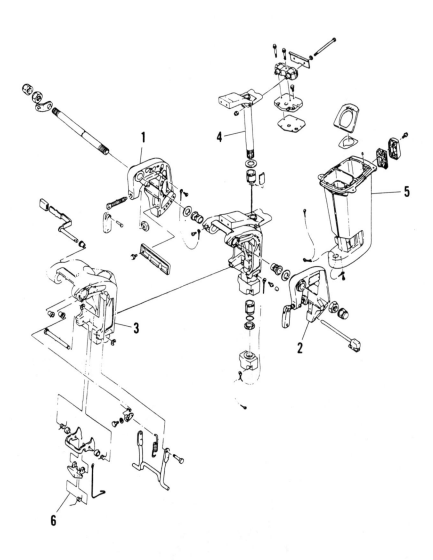

1. Starboard clamp bracket
2. Port clamp bracket
3. Swivel housing
4. Swivel tube
5. Drive shaft housing
6. Tilt lock mechanism

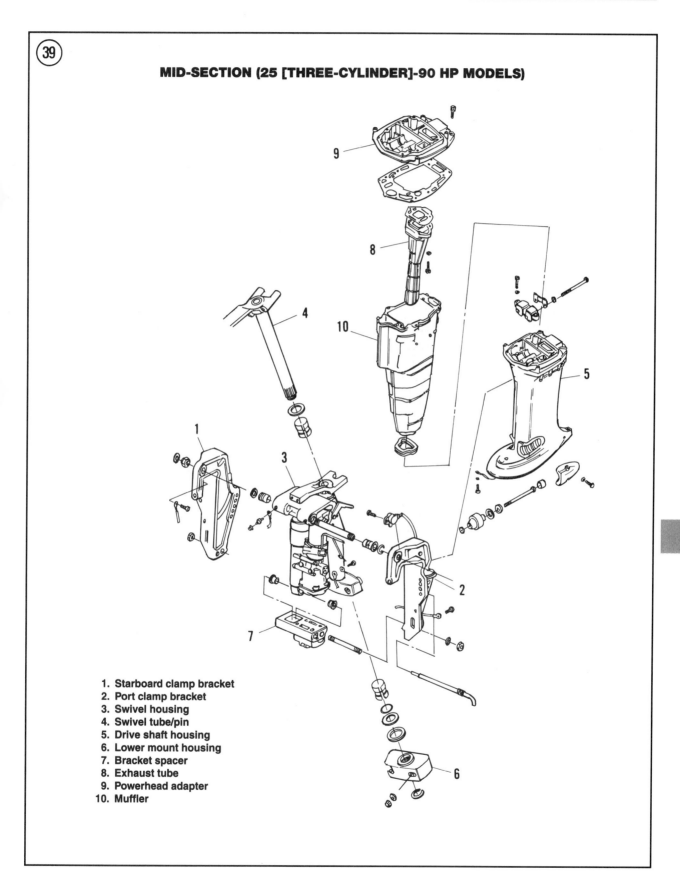

39

MID-SECTION (25 [THREE-CYLINDER]-90 HP MODELS)

1. Starboard clamp bracket
2. Port clamp bracket
3. Swivel housing
4. Swivel tube/pin
5. Drive shaft housing
6. Lower mount housing
7. Bracket spacer
8. Exhaust tube
9. Powerhead adapter
10. Muffler

12

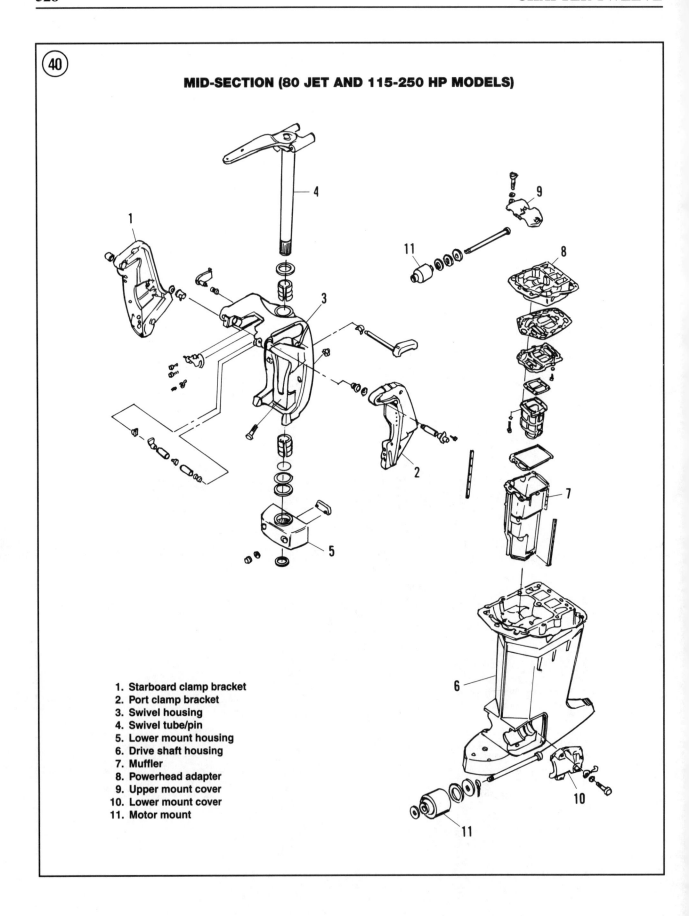

MID-SECTION (80 JET AND 115-250 HP MODELS)

1. Starboard clamp bracket
2. Port clamp bracket
3. Swivel housing
4. Swivel tube/pin
5. Lower mount housing
6. Drive shaft housing
7. Muffler
8. Powerhead adapter
9. Upper mount cover
10. Lower mount cover
11. Motor mount

the location and orientation of all components prior to removal.

    a. For 2 hp models, refer to **Figure 33**.

    b. For 3 hp models, refer to **Figure 34**.

    c. For 4 and 5 hp models, refer to **Figure 35**.

    d. For 6 and 8 hp models, refer to **Figure 36**.

    e. For 9.9 and 15 hp models, refer to **Figure 37**.

    f. For 20 and 25 hp models (3-cylinder), refer to **Figure 38**.

    g. For 25 hp (3-cylinder)-90 hp models (except 80 jet), refer to **Figure 39**.

    h. For 80 jet and 115-250 hp models, refer to **Figure 40**.

Removal of mid-section components will usually require that the gearcase and power head be removed. A commonly replaced component is the motor mount. The lower motor mounts on 6-250 hp models can be replaced without major disassembly. Power head removal is required when replacing the upper motor mounts.

On the larger engines, the power head and the clamp brackets must be removed from the vessel to replace major components of the mid-section. The major components can be replaced on the smaller engines without removing the power head provided the power head is supported adequately. Procedures will vary by model and the components involved. Always provide adequate engine support before removing any component. Use Loctite 572 on the threads of all fasteners. Use Yamaha all-purpose grease on all bushings and pivoting surfaces. Use a *marine* sealant in the drilled holes for the fasteners that attach the clamp brackets to the vessel. Refer to **Table 1** for tightening torque specifications on all fasteners.

Inspect all components and fasteners for wear or damage. Never use a questionable component. Replace all gaskets and seals in the exhaust portion of the driveshaft housing on assembly.

Tiller Handle Components

Refer to the provided illustrations for location and orientation of tiller handle components.

    a. For 2 hp models, refer to **Figure 33**.

    b. For 3 hp models, refer to **Figure 34**.

    c. For 4 and 5 hp models, refer to **Figure 41**.

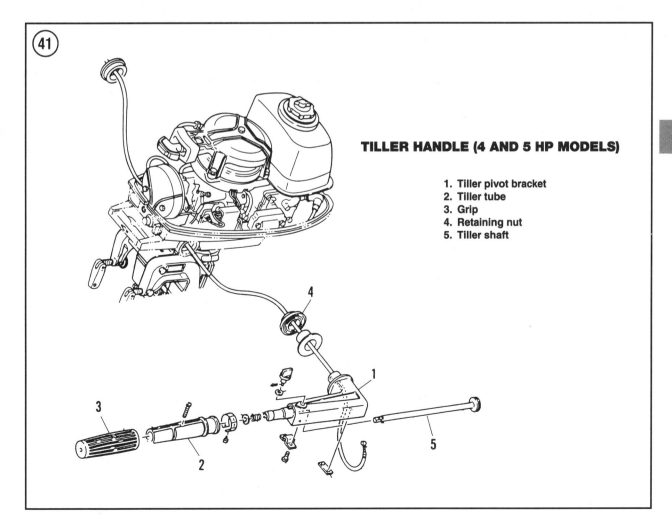

TILLER HANDLE (4 AND 5 HP MODELS)

1. Tiller pivot bracket
2. Tiller tube
3. Grip
4. Retaining nut
5. Tiller shaft

12

④

TILLER HANDLE (6-25 HP [TWO-CYLINDER] MODELS)

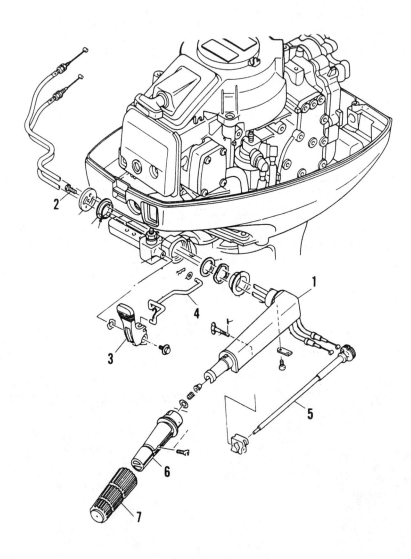

1. Tiller pivot bracket
2. Tiller retaining screw
3. Shift handle
4. Shift linkage
5. Tiller shaft

d. For 6-25 hp (2-cylinder) models, refer to **Figure 42**.

e. For 25 hp (3-cylinder)-75 hp models, refer to **Figure 43**.

Shift/throttle cables

On 4-75 hp tiller models, the throttle and/or shift cables are routed through the tiller handle. Replace any cables that have damaged or worn outer jacket surfaces. Push and pull the core wire in the outer jacket. Replace the cable if it does not move smoothly. Refer to Chapter Five for cable adjustment procedures. Adjust the shift and throttle linkages anytime shift or throttle components are removed.

Pivot points and bushings

Inspect all bushings and pivot bolts or tubes. Replace these and other components if corrosion is present or worn or damaged areas are noted.

Refer to **Table 1** for tightening torque specifications. Use Loctite 572 on all fasteners upon assembly. Apply Yamaha all-purpose grease or its equivalent to all bushings, pivot bolts and sliding surfaces. Check for proper steering and tilting when assembly is complete. Disassemble and check for worn, damaged or improperly installed components if binding or stiff operation is noted.

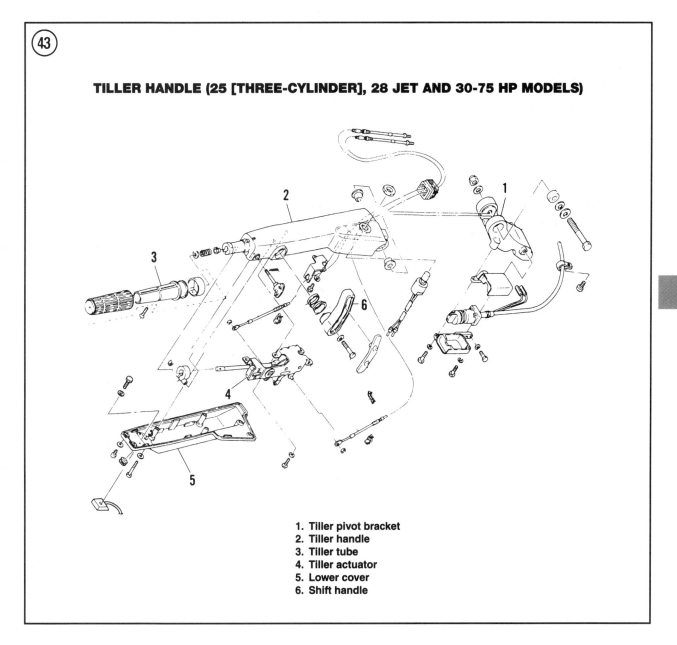

43

TILLER HANDLE (25 [THREE-CYLINDER], 28 JET AND 30-75 HP MODELS)

1. Tiller pivot bracket
2. Tiller handle
3. Tiller tube
4. Tiller actuator
5. Lower cover
6. Shift handle

12

Table 1 TIGHTENING TORQUE

Fastener location	Torque specification
Tilt/trim motor retaining bolt	
40-90 hp models (excludes 80 jet)	4 N•m (35 in.-lb.)
80 jet and 115-250 hp models	5 N•m (44 in.-lb.)
Fluid reservoir retaining bolt	6 N•m (53 in.-lb.)
Fluid reservoir plug	1 N•m (9 in.-lb.)
Manual relief valve	
28 jet and 30-50 hp models	3 N•m (26 in.-lb.)
60-250 hp models	4 N•m (35 in.-lb.)
Pump to housing bolts	9 N•m (79 in.-lb.)
External trim lines	15 N•m (11 ft.-lb.)
Swivel housing cover bolts	
3 hp	8 N•m (70 in.-lb.)
Tilt tube/pin retaining nut	
3, 6 and 8 hp	7 N•m (61 in.-lb.)
4 and 5 hp	13 N•m (115 in.-lb.)
20-25 (two-cylinder)	45 N•m (33 ft.-lb.)
25 (three-cylinder), and 30 hp model	15 N•m (11 ft.-lb.)
40-50 hp models (except E48)	24 N•m (17 ft.-lb.)
60-225 hp (90°)	15 N•m (11 ft.-lb.)
200-250 hp (76°)	15 N•m (11 ft.-lb.)
Upper and lower motor mount nut	
60-90 hp (except 80 jet)	24 N•m (17 ft.-lb.)
115-225 hp (90°)	53 N•m (39 ft.-lb.)
200-250 (76°)	72 N•m (53 ft.-lb.)
Motor mount cover	
9.9 and 15 hp	13 N•m (115 in.-lb.)
20 and 25 hp (two-cylinder)	24 N•m (17 ft.-lb.)
Grounding lead bolt	18 N•m (13 ft.-lb.)
Exhaust tube to adapter bolts	21 N•m (15 ft.-lb.)
Striker plate bolt (3 trim cylinder)	37 N•m (27 ft.-lb.)
Clamp bracket to vessel (upper nut)	53 N•m (39 ft.-lb.)
Clamp bracket to vessel (lower nut)	73 N•m (53 ft.-lb.)

Table 2 STANDARD TORQUE

Fastener size	Torque specification
8 mm nut, M5 bolt	5 N•m (44 in.-lb.)
10 mm nut, M6 bolt	8 N•m (70 in.-lb.)
12 mm nut, M8 bolt	18 N•m (13 ft.-lb.)
14 mm nut, M10 bolt	36 N•m (26 ft.-lb.)
17 mm nut, M12 bolt	43 N•m (31 ft.-lb.)

Table 3 TILT/TRIM ELECTRIC MOTOR SPECIFICATIONS

Minimum brush length	
28 jet and 30-50 hp	3.5 mm (0.14 in.)
60-225 hp (90°)	4.8 mm (0.19 in.)
200-250 hp (76°)	4 mm (0.16 in.)
Minimum commutator diameter	
28 jet and 30-50 hp	21 mm (0.83 in.)
60-225 hp (90°)	21 mm (0.83 in.)
200-250 hp (76°)	24 mm (0.95 in.)
Mica undercut	
Wear limit	
80 jet and 115-250 hp	0.85 mm (0.03 in.)
Standard size (new)	
80 jet and 115-250 hp	1.35 mm (0.05 in.)

Chapter Thirteen

Oil Injection System

This chapter provides removal, inspection and installation procedures for all oil injection components. Pump adjustment and air bleeding procedures are provided as well. In addition, the warning system modes of operation and related instructions are included. **Tables 1-4**, located at the end of this chapter, provide oil injection system information and tightening torque specifications.

All Yamaha outboards from 20-250 horsepower may be factory equipped with oil injection. Models with a *C* in the model name and Models E48, E60 and E75 *do not have oil injection*. Premixing of the fuel and oil is required on all models without oil injection. Premixing of the fuel and oil is required with oil injected models during the break-in period or after a major power head repair.

Refer to Chapter Three for testing and troubleshooting for oil injection and warning system components.

SYSTEM OPERATION

Oil from the engine mounted oil supply tank (1, **Figure 1**) is gravity fed to a crankshaft/gear driven oil injection pump (2, **Figure 1**). The oil pump is a variable ratio unit that provides the precise amount of oil required at a given engine speed. A linkage attached to the oil injection pump and throttle shaft allows changes to the oil/fuel ratio to occur with throttle changes. Fuel to oil ratio at idle is approximately 200 to 1 for 20-50 hp models and approximately 100 to 1 for 60-250 hp models. Fuel to oil ratio at wide-open throttle is approximately 100 to 1 for 20-50 hp models and approximately 50 to 1 for 60-250 hp models.

Changes in fuel/oil ratio occur when the pump lever and shaft are rotated (1, **Figure 2**). This changes the pump stroke. Changing the pump stroke increases or decreases the volume of oil supplied to the engine.

The oil is injected directly into the air and fuel mixture supplied to the engine at the carburetor. The oil is injected directly into the vapor separator tank on EFI models.

The engine mounted oil supply tank (1, **Figure 1**) is the only oil reservoir on 20-90 hp models (except 80 jet).

A remote mounted oil supply tank (**Figure 3**) is used with 80 jet and 115-250 hp models. Oil is pumped by an electric oil pump (A, **Figure 3**) to the engine mounted tank

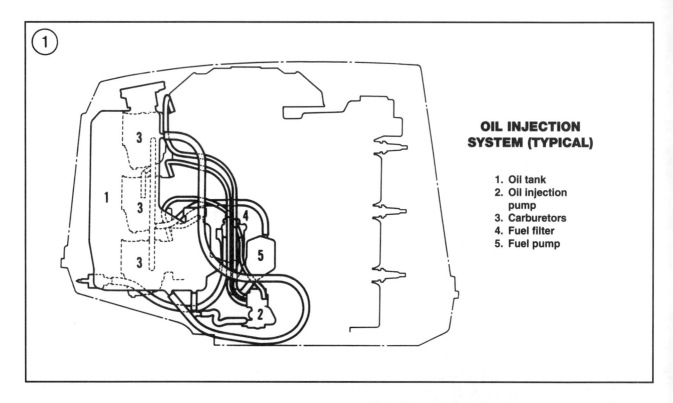

**OIL INJECTION
SYSTEM (TYPICAL)**

1. Oil tank
2. Oil injection
   pump
3. Carburetors
4. Fuel filter
5. Fuel pump

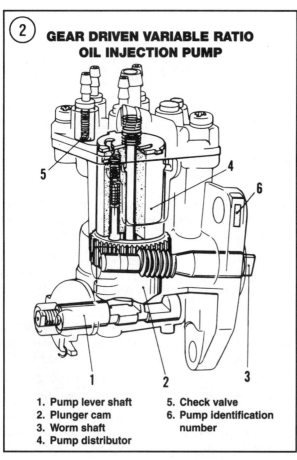

**GEAR DRIVEN VARIABLE RATIO
OIL INJECTION PUMP**

1. Pump lever shaft
2. Plunger cam
3. Worm shaft
4. Pump distributor
5. Check valve
6. Pump identification
   number

when the level in the engine mounted oil supply tank drops to a specified point. The oil pump is controlled by the YMIS microcomputer on V-6 models and a separate oil control module on some V-4 models (**Figure 4**). The remote pump will operate each time the key switch is cycled ON to purge air from the oil lines.

An optional dash mounted oil level gauge allows the operator to monitor the oil level in the remote mounted tank. Oil injection warning lamps are incorporated into the gauge to warn the operator of a problem with the level in the oil supply tank. The sending unit (B, **Figure 3**) is mounted directly to the remote mounted tank. It provides an indication of the oil level in the remote tank.

Oil Filling Procedure

Check the oil level before operating the engine and after running for two or more hours at high speed. Refer to Chapter Four for oil requirements. Never overfill the tank. Fill the tank to the full level mark located on the side of the oil supply tank. The oil may expand from heat and spill over into the engine compartment if overfilled. The full level mark will allow air space at the top of the tank for heat expansion.

Access locations for the oil fill opening vary by model. On two- and three-cylinder models, use the opening on the top engine cover (**Figure 5**) to add oil directly to the engine

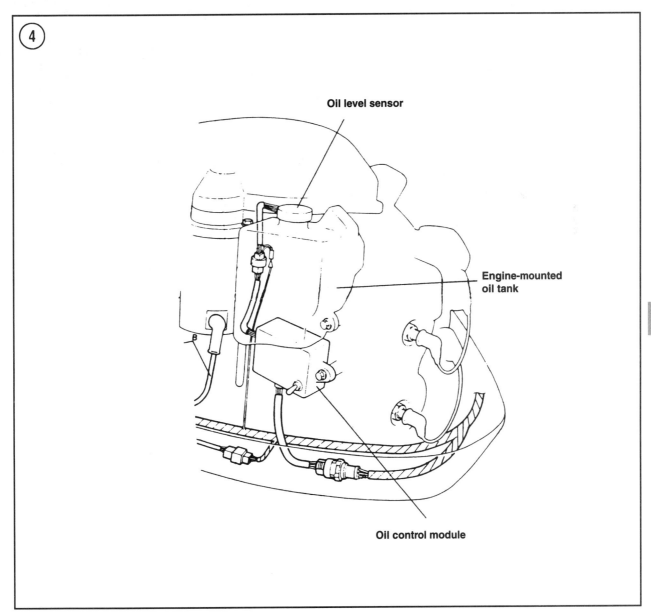

(4)

Oil level sensor

Engine-mounted oil tank

13

Oil control module

mounted oil supply tank. On some models, it is necessary to remove the top motor cover to access the fill opening.

With remote mounted oil tanks, the oil is added directly to the tank through a special boat mounted fill adapter. A large diameter hose connects the adapter to a large fitting on the remote mounted oil tank (**Figure 6**). The venting of the tank is provided by the vent opening near the fill adapter mounting location. Make sure that the fill hose does not cover the tank vent during installation. The boat mounted oil fill adapter resembles the fuel fill adapter. Be careful to avoid selecting the wrong fill adapter when adding oil or fuel to the vessel.

Warning System Operation
20-25 hp Models

The warning system components consist of the CDI unit, tank mounted oil level sensor and LED warning lamps. Electric start remote control models will also use a warning buzzer mounted in the control box or control station.

If the oil level in the engine mounted oil supply tank drops to approximately 10% of capacity, the red LED lamp on the lower motor cover will illuminate. The engine will be limited to approximately 2000 rpm. Also, the warning horn will sound on electric start remote control models. Shut the engine off. Fill the oil tank to turn the horn and lamp off. Normal operation can resume after the tank is filled.

The CDI unit provides the power for the warning lamp. The power for the warning horn on electric start remote control models is supplied by the cranking battery.

> *NOTE*
> *The lamp will also illuminate, engine speed will be limited and a warning horn will sound (on electric start remote control models) if an overheat condition occurs. Check for a cooling system problem when the warning system is activated. The engine must be turned* **off** *to reset the warning horn, warning lamp and stop the power reduction. Failure to do so will result in limited engine speed when no faults are present.*

> *CAUTION*
> *Never operate the engine with the warning system activated. Serious engine damage can occur if the engine is operated without sufficient water for cooling or without sufficient lubrication to the power head.*

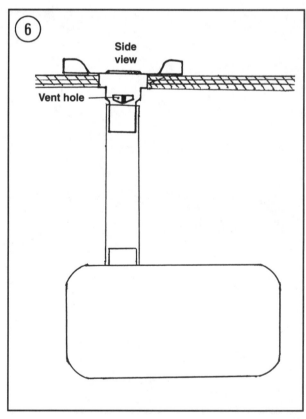

25-90 hp (Three-Cylinder) Models

The warning system components consist of the CDI unit and tank mounted oil level sensor. A lower engine cover mounted warning lamp is used on tiller controlled models. A warning horn and optional dash mounted warning lamp assembly is used on electric start remote control models.

The green LED lamp will illuminate when the oil level is at a satisfactory level in the oil supply tank. Shut the engine off and check the oil level immediately if the green lamp does not illuminate when the engine is started.

When the level in the oil supply tank drops to approximately 0.471 liter (1 qt.) the oil level sensor will switch the yellow lamp on. The engine mounted oil supply tank should be filled as soon as possible.

If the oil level continues to drop, the oil level sensor will switch the red LED lamp on. The warning horn will sound on electric start remote control models and the engine speed will be limited to approximately 2000 rpm. Shut the engine off immediately. Check the cooling system for a water stream and correct the oil level in the oil supply tank. Normal operation can resume begin after the low oil level or overheating condition is corrected.

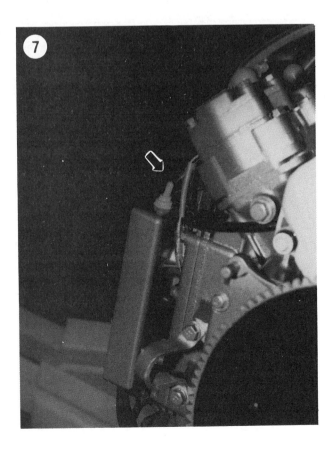

80 Jet and 115-250 hp Models

The warning system components consist of the YMIS microcomputer, oil level sensor, combination oil level gauge/oil warning lamp and warning horn.

The green lamp (if so equipped) will illuminate when the oil level is satisfactory. When the oil level drops to a specified level, the microcomputer will activate the remove tank mounted oil pump. When the remote tank mounted oil pump has pumped sufficient oil to raise the level, it is switched off.

Oil will not be transferred from the remote tank to the oil supply tank if a faulty condition occurs in the remote tank mounted oil pump, filters, hoses or control system. When the supply tank oil level drops to a specified point, the warning horn will sound and the dash mounted warning lamp will illuminate. The engine speed will be limited to approximately 2000 rpm.

The fault could be with the oil level sensor or remote tank mounted oil pump. The microcomputer, oil control module, hoses, filters or wiring could be faulty as well.

An emergency switch is located beneath the upper engine cover (**Figure 7**). Toggle the switch to the on position to activate the remote tank mounted pump manually. The pump should transfer oil from the remote tank to the oil supply tank when activated. Hold the switch *on* until the oil level is at the full level mark on the side of the oil supply tank. Fill the engine mounted tank with oil through the oil level sensor opening if the emergency switch will not activate the remote mounted oil pump. Refer to *Oil Level Sensor* in this chapter for sensor removal and installation.

Test the emergency switch, microcomputer, remote tank mounted oil pump, filters and hoses when the emergency switch will not initiate the oil fill mode. Test the oil level sensor, microcomputer wiring and connections when the only means to operate the remote mounted oil pump is the emergency switch. Refer to Chapter Three for testing and troubleshooting procedures.

> *CAUTION*
> *Operating the engine with insufficient oil or without sufficient cooling water can result in serious power head damage or seizure. Stop the engine immediately when the warning lamp or warning horn sounds. Correct the oil level and/or overheat condition.*

Oil Level Sensor Removal/Installation

Refer to Chapter Three for troubleshooting and testing.

Work in a clean environment. A small amount of debris can wreak havoc with the oil injection system operation.

13

1. Locate the oil level sensor at the top of the oil supply tank. Disconnect the sensor leads at the harness connector.

2. Grasp the oil level sensor between the forefinger and thumb. Squeeze and carefully pull the assembly from the tank (**Figure 8**). Inspect the O-ring at the cap location and replace if damaged.

3. Note the alignment of the oil strainer to the oil level sensor. Alignment marks are provided in most cases. If necessary, mark the sensor and strainer to ensure proper alignment on assembly. Carefully pull the strainer (2, **Figure 9**) from the oil level sensor (1, **Figure 9**). Clean with a suitable solvent. Dry completely and inspect the strainer for torn or damaged surfaces. Replace it if damaged.

4. Remove and inspect the gasket (3, **Figure 9**) from the strainer. Replace if damaged. Drain and remove the oil supply tank and retain the gasket if it was not positioned on the strainer on removal.

5. Align and install the clean strainer onto the oil level sensor. Install the washer onto the bottom of the strainer.

6. Note the alignment marks on the cap and oil supply tank (**Figure 10**). Lubricate the O-ring on the sensor with Yamalube or its equivalent. Avoid pinching the O-ring. Align and install the oil level sensor into the oil supply tank. Make sure the projection on the bottom of the strainer is positioned into the recess for the hose on the bottom of the tank. Carefully press into position.

7. Connect the oil level sensor wires to the harness. Fill with oil and bleed air from the system following the procedures listed in this chapter.

Engine-Mounted Oil Supply Tank

Removal of the engine mounted oil supply tank is a fairly simple process. Refer to the illustrations in this chapter to identify the tank and hose connections. Remove the oil hose leading to the oil pump or the water drain hose and drain the oil into a suitable container placed below the hose fitting. Refer to *Oil Level Sensor* for sensor removal instructions. Remove and inspect the fill cap and sealing gasket for damage or wear (two- and three-cylinder only). Replace the cap and sealing gasket if damaged. Mark all hose connections to the tank and remove all hoses. Remove the fasteners that secure the tank. Note the location and the position of the grommets at the attaching points. Install the replacement tank, grommets and fasteners. Tighten the fasteners securely. Fill the unit with Yamalube 2-cycle outboard oil or its equivalent. Refer to *Bleeding Air from the System* and follow the steps as indicated.

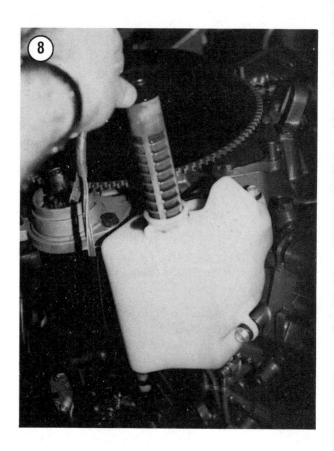

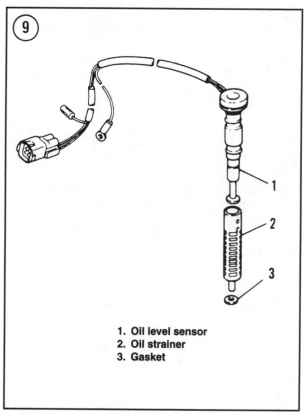

1. Oil level sensor
2. Oil strainer
3. Gasket

Remote Mounted Oil Tank

Service to the remote mounted oil tank includes replacing the oil level sensor, replacing the oil supply pump or cleaning and inspecting the filter on the oil pickup. Clean and inspect the tank for leaks or physical damage. Work in a clean environment. Clean all components thoroughly. A small amount of debris in the system can disable the oil injection system operation. Note the size and location of plastic locking tie clamps and replace them when removal is necessary.

Oil level sensor
removal/installation

1. Locate the oil level sensor on the remote mounted oil tank (**Figure 11**). Disconnect the sensor wires from the harness at the harness connector (1, **Figure 12**). Clean debris and contaminants from the remote mounted oil tank before removing the sensor.

2. Grasp the sensor and carefully pull it from the tank. Inspect the O-ring on the sensor cap and replace if damaged.

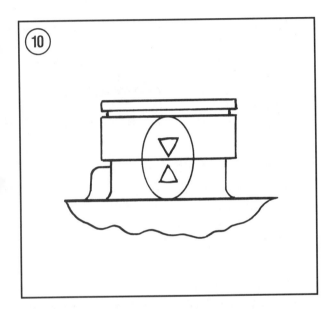

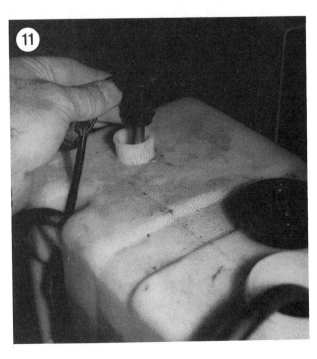

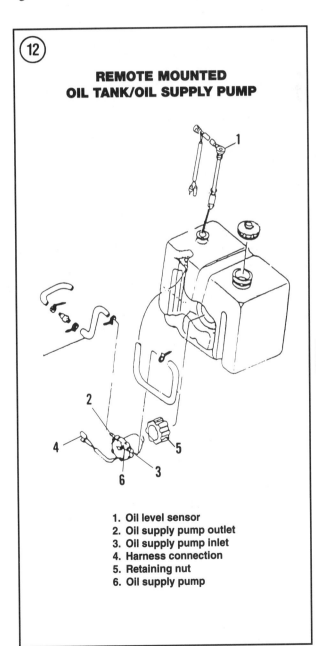

REMOTE MOUNTED OIL TANK/OIL SUPPLY PUMP

1. Oil level sensor
2. Oil supply pump outlet
3. Oil supply pump inlet
4. Harness connection
5. Retaining nut
6. Oil supply pump

13

3. Lubricate the O-ring with Yamalube or its equivalent and carefully install the sensor into the remote mounted tank. Connect the sensor wire connector to the harness connection. Check for proper gauge operation.

Remote tank mounted oil supply pump

The hose routing and the appearance of the components may vary from the illustration shown. Some models use an in-line style filter in the oil line. Work in a clean environment as a small amount of debris in the system can wreak havoc with the oil injection system operation. Clean all components thoroughly. Note the size and location of plastic tie clamps and replace them when removed.

1. Clean debris and contaminants from external surfaces of the remote mounted oil tank. Remove the tank from its mount and drain the oil into a suitable container for storage.

2. Disconnect the oil hoses (2 and 3, **Figure 12**) and electrical connections (4, **Figure 12**) from the oil supply pump (6, **Figure 12**).

3. Twist the retaining nut (5, **Figure 12**) counterclockwise to remove the oil supply pump from its mount. Check the oil line filter (if so equipped). Replace it if contaminants are present.

4. Install the replacement oil supply pump and tighten the retaining nut securely. Refer to **Figure 12** while attaching the oil lines to the oil supply pump. Tighten the hose clamps securely. Connect the oil supply pump wire connector to the harness.

5. Install the remote mounted oil tank to its mounting location. Strap the unit down securely. Connect the hose for the vessel mounted fill adapter (if so equipped). Tighten all clamps securely. Fill the tank with Yamalube or its equivalent through the fill cap or vessel mounted fill adapter.

6. With the key switch in the ON position, the oil warning lights should illuminate and the warning horn should sound. The remote pump will operate for approximately 3 minutes to supply oil to the engine mounted tank. This will purge any air from the line. If the tank is not filled within the 3 minute interval, switch the key switch OFF and repeat the procedure until the engine mounted tank is full. Check all hoses and connections for oil leaks and repair as required.

Oil Hoses and Check Valves

This section provides instructions for removal, inspection and installation of oil hoses and oil line check valves. Oil hose routing and check valve location and orientation will vary by model. Refer to **Figure 13-22** for the routing, location and orientation for your model.

 a. For 20 and 25 hp (two-cylinder) models, refer to **Figure 13**.
 b. For 25 (three-cylinder) and 30 hp models, refer to **Figure 14**.
 c. For 28 jet, 35 jet and 30-50 hp models, refer to **Figure 15**.
 d. For 60 and 70 hp models, refer to **Figure 16**.
 e. For 65 jet and 75-90 hp models (except 80 jet), refer to **Figure 17**.
 f. For 80 jet and 115-130 hp models, refer to **Figure 18**.
 g. For 105 jet and 150-200 hp (90°) models (except models P200, S200 and 225), refer to **Figure 19**.
 h. For P200, S200 and 225 (90°) models, refer to **Figure 20**.
 i. For 1996 225 and 250 (76°) carbureted models, refer to **Figure 21**.
 j. For 200-250 (76°) EFI models, refer to **Figure 22**.

Hose removal and inspection

Work in a clean environment. A small amount of debris can wreak havoc with the operation of the oil injection system. Mark or make note of hose routing and connections prior to removal to ensure correct routing on assembly.

Carefully cut, remove and replace all plastic locking tie clamps when it is necessary to remove them. Inspect spring type hose clamps and replace any that are corroded or have lost spring tension.

Remove multiple hose connections in a cluster with their oil injection system components whenever possible. This will reduce the chance of incorrect connections and the time needed to bleed air from the system.

Inspect all hoses for cuts or abrasions and replace them if defects are noted. Replace any hose that feels hard or brittle. Hoses that feel too soft or spongy should be replaced as well. Clear hoses are used at the crankshaft/gear driven oil pump. Inspect these hoses and replace any that are cloudy in appearance.

Oil line check valves

The oil line check valves prevent oil from flowing out of the oil lines when the engine is not running. Before removing them from the oil lines, note the direction of the arrow on the check valve. The arrow indicates the direction the check valve will allow oil flow. The arrow must always lead to the oil discharge fitting on the intake manifold. Refer to **Figure 13-22** for check valve orientation and

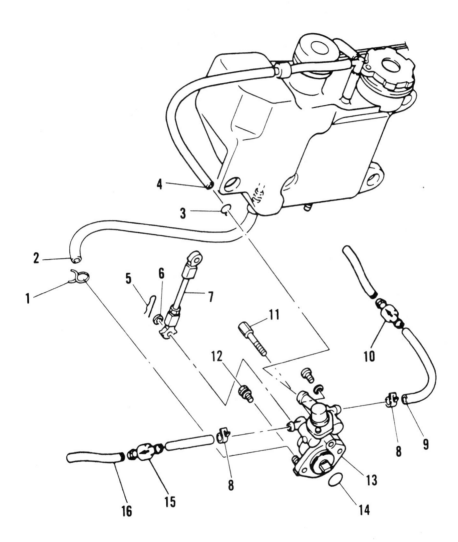

**OIL HOSE ROUTING
(20 AND 25 HP [TWO-CYLINDER] MODELS)**

13

1. Clamp
2. Inlet hose connection
3. Clamp
4. Water drain hose
5. Clip
6. Washer
7. Oil pump linkage
8. Plastic locking tie clamp

9. Hose to No. 1 cylinder
10. Oil line check valve
11. Oil pump retaining bolt
12. Retaining screw
13. Oil pump
14. O-ring
15. Oil line check valve
16. Hose to No. 2 cylinder

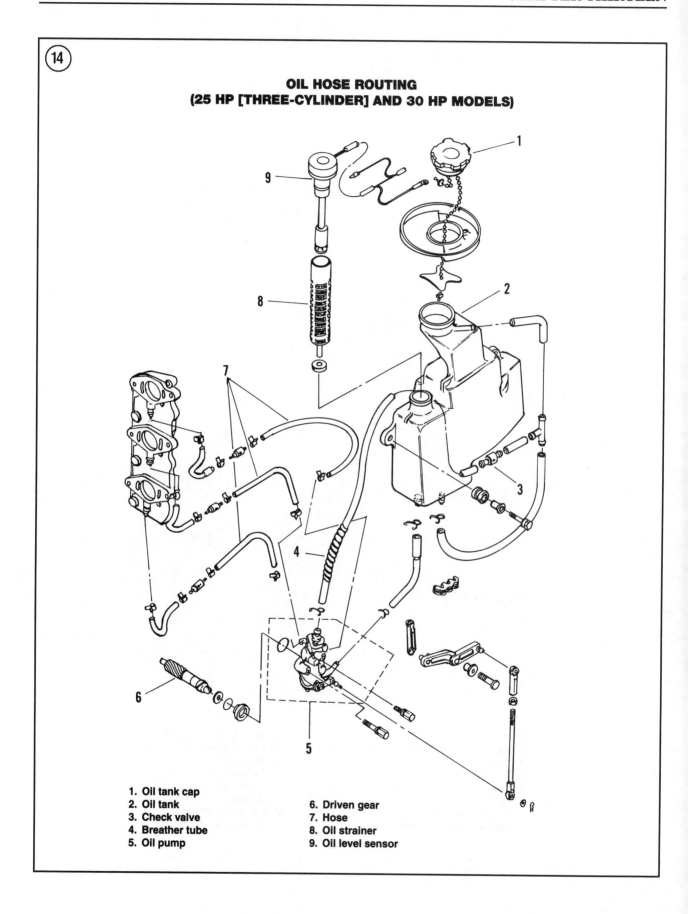

⑭

**OIL HOSE ROUTING
(25 HP [THREE-CYLINDER] AND 30 HP MODELS)**

1. Oil tank cap
2. Oil tank
3. Check valve
4. Breather tube
5. Oil pump
6. Driven gear
7. Hose
8. Oil strainer
9. Oil level sensor

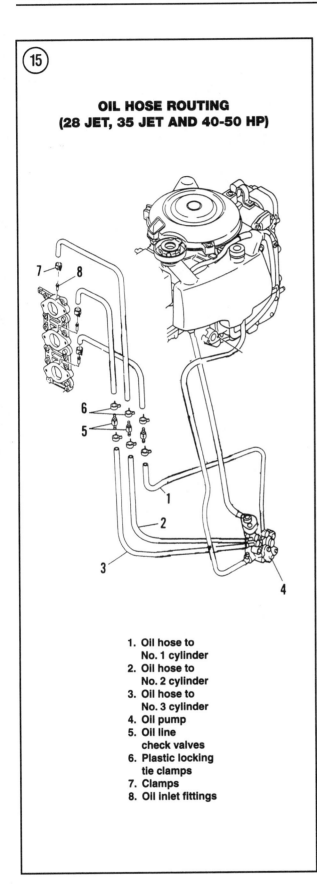

(15)

OIL HOSE ROUTING
(28 JET, 35 JET AND 40-50 HP)

1. Oil hose to
   No. 1 cylinder
2. Oil hose to
   No. 2 cylinder
3. Oil hose to
   No. 3 cylinder
4. Oil pump
5. Oil line
   check valves
6. Plastic locking
   tie clamps
7. Clamps
8. Oil inlet fittings

location. Inspect all spring type clamps and replace any that are corroded or have lost spring tension. Refer to Chapter Three *Oil Line Check Valve Testing* to test the check valve.

CAUTION
Use caution when installing oil line check valves. The engine will suffer serious power head damage if a check valve is installed in the wrong direction. The arrow on the check valve indicates the direction of oil flow. It must point towards the oil discharge fitting on the intake manifold or vapor separator tank.

Oil Pump Removal/Installation

The oil pump is precisely matched to deliver the proper amount of oil to the engine. The oil requirements and oil pumps vary by model. Never use a pump that is not designated for use on the engine. Insufficient or excessive lubrication may occur. Most pumps have an identification number stamped on them. The typical location is near the pump lever. Compare the stamped identification number with the information provided in **Table 1**.

Parts or repair instructions are not provided for the oil pump. Replace the complete unit if it is faulty. Oil pump appearance and mounting location varies by model. Refer to **Figure 13-22** to locate the oil pump or oil hose connections for your model. Mark all hoses prior to removal to ensure correct connections on assembly. Note the size and location of plastic locking tie clamps and replace them when removed. To assist with component identification and orientation, refer to the correct model listed in **Figure 13-22** during the removal and installation of the oil pump.

1. Carefully pry the linkage connector (4, **Figure 23**) from the pump lever. Do not disturb the link rod adjustment.

2. Remove the clamp and hose from the inlet side of the oil pump and quickly plug the hose with a suitable object such as a dowel rod or golf tee.

3. Mark all hose locations at the outlet fittings and remove them from the oil pump connection. Plug the hoses as described in Step 2.

4. Remove the two retaining bolts (3, **Figure 23**) and pull the oil pump (2, **Figure 23**) from the cylinder block. Remove and discard the O-ring (1, **Figure 23**).

5. Install a new O-ring (2, **Figure 24**) onto the oil pump (1, **Figure 24**). Lubricate the O-ring with Yamalube 2 cycle outboard oil or its equivalent.

6. Position the oil pump at the mounting location and carefully insert the oil pump drive shaft into the drive gear

13

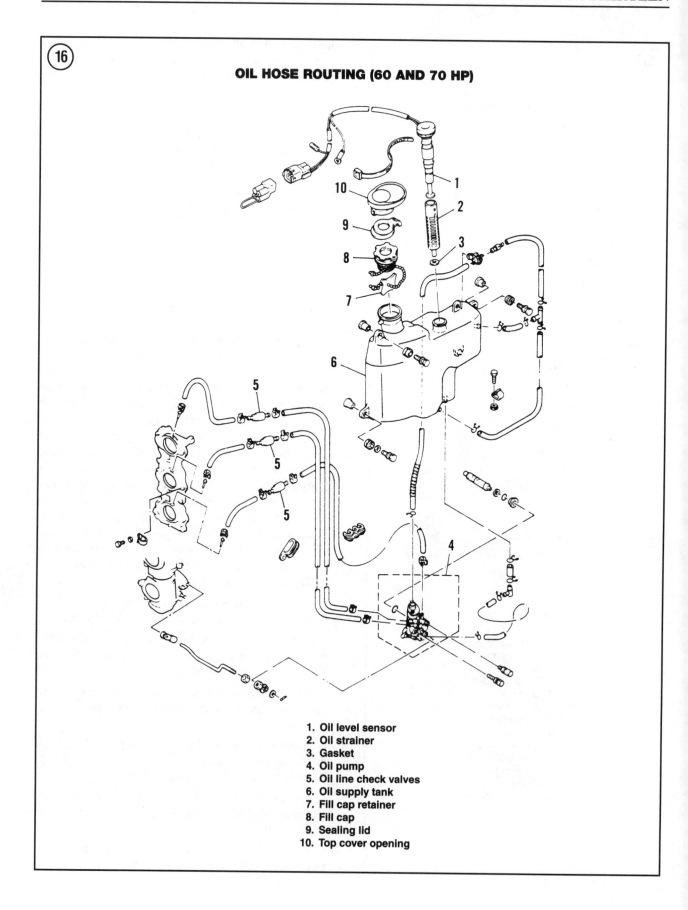

16

OIL HOSE ROUTING (60 AND 70 HP)

1. Oil level sensor
2. Oil strainer
3. Gasket
4. Oil pump
5. Oil line check valves
6. Oil supply tank
7. Fill cap retainer
8. Fill cap
9. Sealing lid
10. Top cover opening

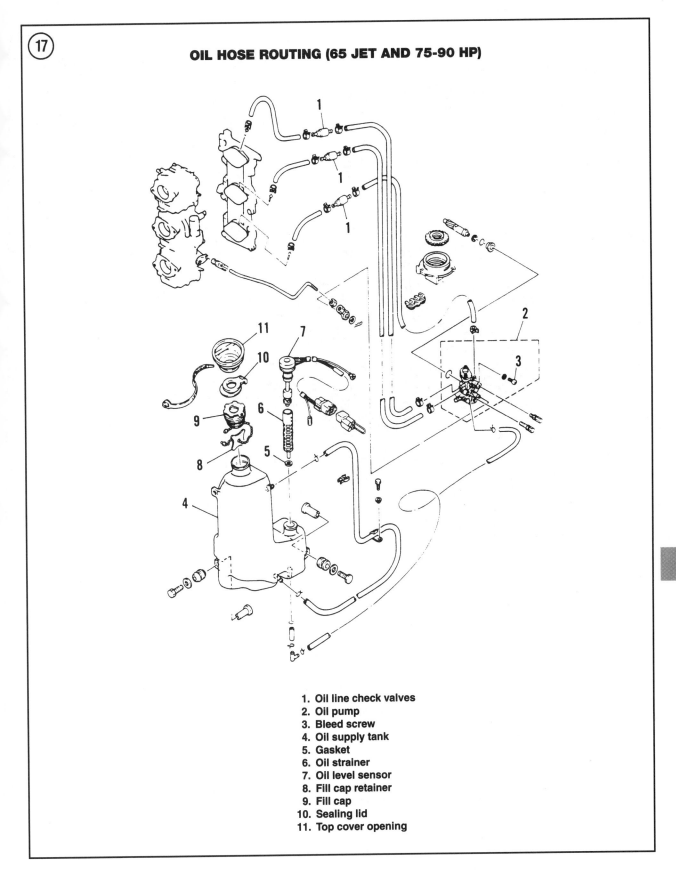

OIL HOSE ROUTING (65 JET AND 75-90 HP)

1. Oil line check valves
2. Oil pump
3. Bleed screw
4. Oil supply tank
5. Gasket
6. Oil strainer
7. Oil level sensor
8. Fill cap retainer
9. Fill cap
10. Sealing lid
11. Top cover opening

13

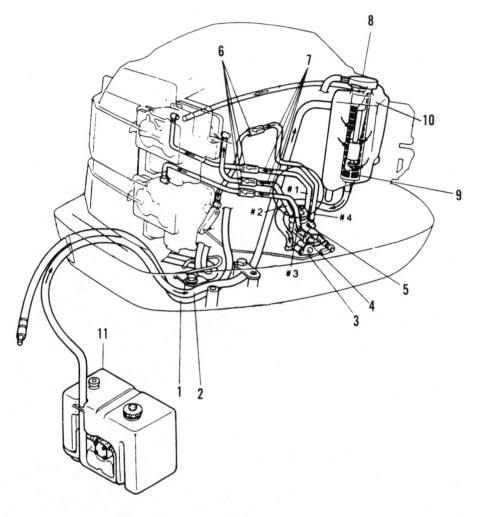

(18)

OIL HOSE ROUTING (80 JET AND 115-130 HP)

1. Fuel hose
2. Oil hose
3. Pump control lever
4. Oil pump
5. Oil outlet fitting
6. Oil line check valve
7. Oil outlet hose
8. Oil level sensor
9. Oil strainer
10. Oil supply tank
11. Remote mounted tank

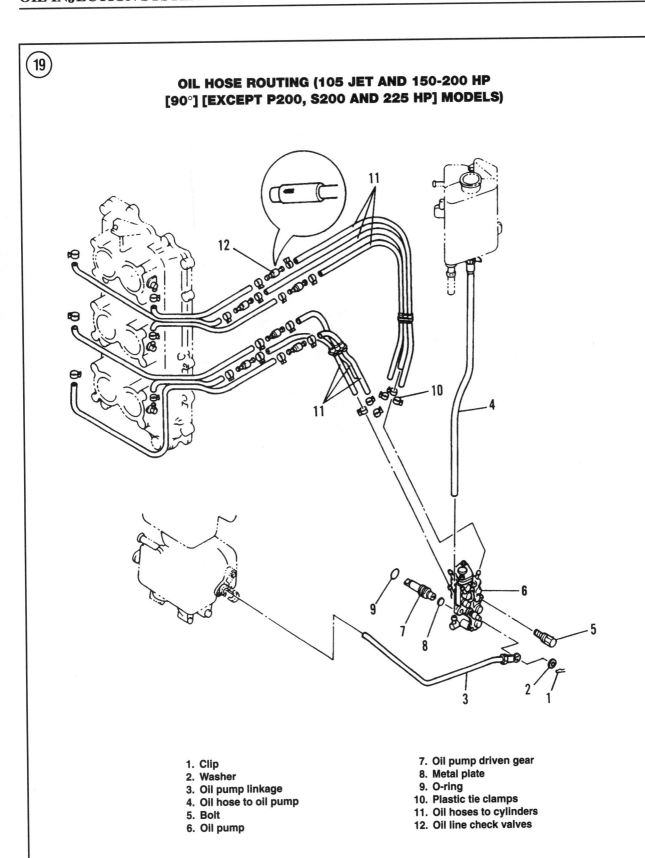

OIL HOSE ROUTING (105 JET AND 150-200 HP
[90°] [EXCEPT P200, S200 AND 225 HP] MODELS)

1. Clip
2. Washer
3. Oil pump linkage
4. Oil hose to oil pump
5. Bolt
6. Oil pump
7. Oil pump driven gear
8. Metal plate
9. O-ring
10. Plastic tie clamps
11. Oil hoses to cylinders
12. Oil line check valves

13

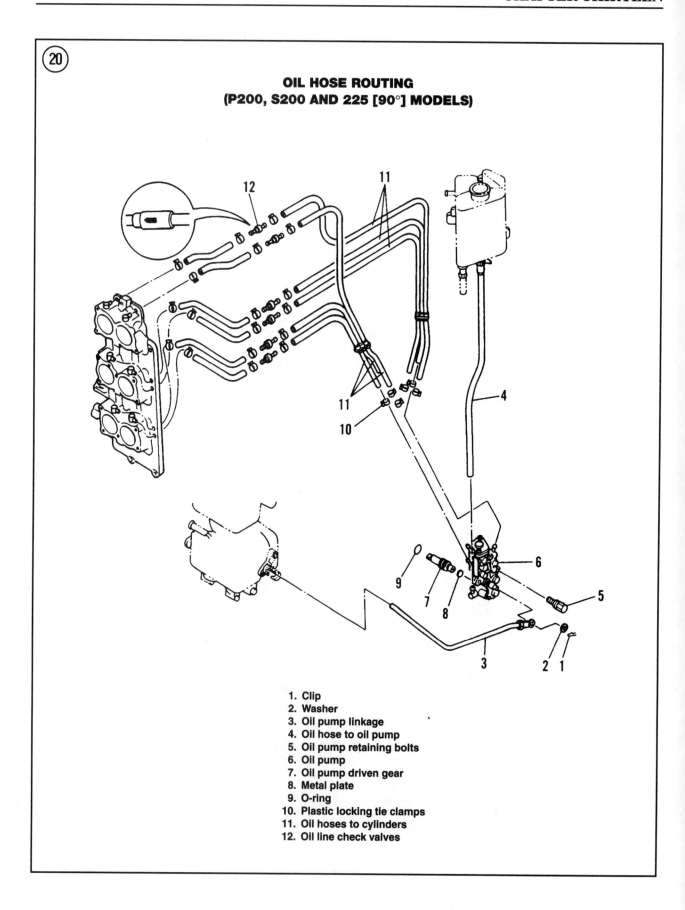

20

**OIL HOSE ROUTING
(P200, S200 AND 225 [90°] MODELS)**

1. Clip
2. Washer
3. Oil pump linkage
4. Oil hose to oil pump
5. Oil pump retaining bolts
6. Oil pump
7. Oil pump driven gear
8. Metal plate
9. O-ring
10. Plastic locking tie clamps
11. Oil hoses to cylinders
12. Oil line check valves

collar and seals (3-6, **Figure 24**). Rotate the oil pump until the oil pump drive shaft (7, **Figure 24**) is aligned with the slot in the drive gear. The drive shaft will fall in when aligned. Never force the pump into position. Rotate the pump until the retaining bolts (3, **Figure 23**) align with the threaded holes, then install the bolts. Torque the bolts to the specification listed in **Table 1**.

7. Fill with Yamalube or its equivalent and connect all hoses to the correct location. Clamp all hoses securely. Operate the throttle and shift linkages to ensure that the

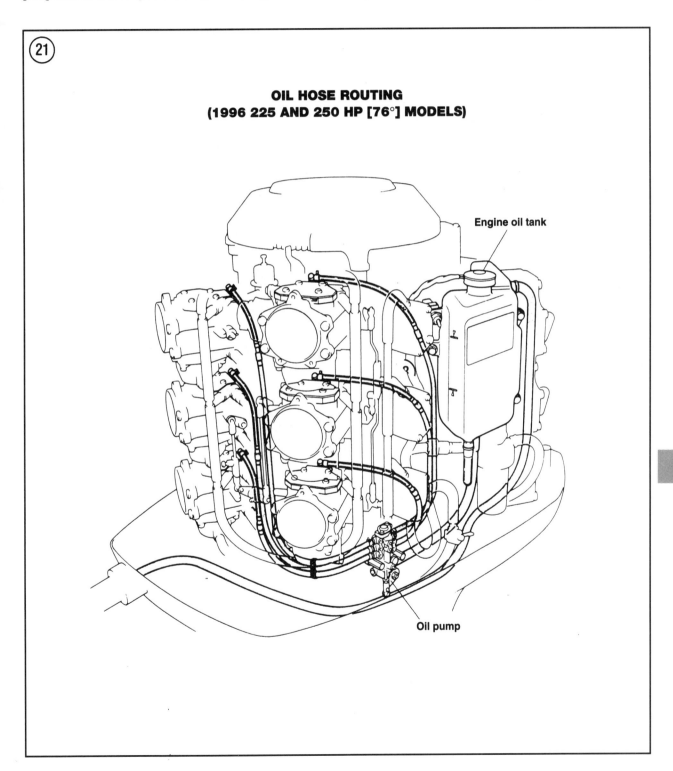

㉑

**OIL HOSE ROUTING
(1996 225 AND 250 HP [76°] MODELS)**

Engine oil tank

Oil pump

13

hoses do not contact any moving parts. Correct hose routing as required. Refer to *Oil Pump Linkage Adjustment* to adjust the pump lever position.

8. Refer to *Bleeding Air from the System* and follow the instructions.

Driven Gear Removal/Installation

Refer to **Figure 25-27** to determine the correct orientation of components for your model. Inspect the driven gear for damaged or worn gear teeth and replace if required. On V4 and V6 models only, inspect the bearing end (opposite the oil pump) for wear or damage and replace if required. The *drive* gear should be inspected when substantial wear is noted or damage is found on the driven gear or shaft. Refer to Chapter Eight for *drive* gear replacement procedures.

a. For 20-90 hp models (except 80 jet), refer to **Figure 25**.

b. For 80 jet and 115-225 hp (90°) models, refer to **Figure 26**.

c. For 200-250 hp models (76°) models, refer to **Figure 27**.

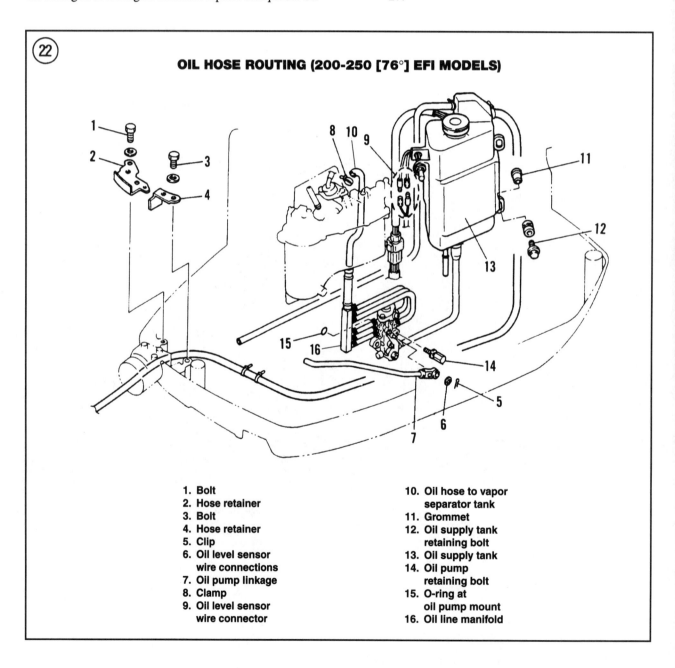

(22)

OIL HOSE ROUTING (200-250 [76°] EFI MODELS)

1. Bolt
2. Hose retainer
3. Bolt
4. Hose retainer
5. Clip
6. Oil level sensor wire connections
7. Oil pump linkage
8. Clamp
9. Oil level sensor wire connector
10. Oil hose to vapor separator tank
11. Grommet
12. Oil supply tank retaining bolt
13. Oil supply tank
14. Oil pump retaining bolt
15. O-ring at oil pump mount
16. Oil line manifold

23

OIL PUMP MOUNTING

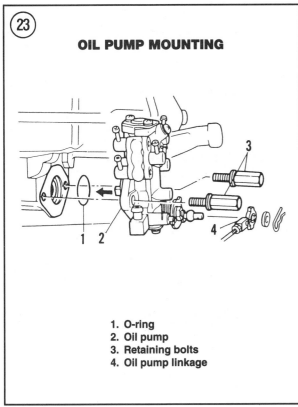

1. O-ring
2. Oil pump
3. Retaining bolts
4. Oil pump linkage

24

PUMP DRIVE COMPONENTS

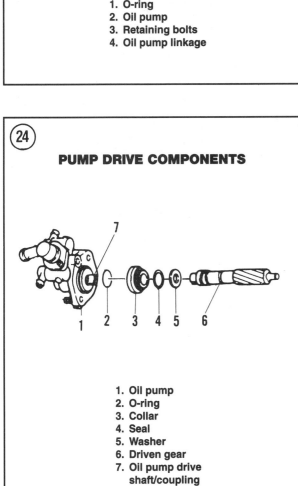

1. Oil pump
2. O-ring
3. Collar
4. Seal
5. Washer
6. Driven gear
7. Oil pump drive
   shaft/coupling

25

DRIVEN GEAR (20-90 HP [EXCEPT 80 JET] MODELS)

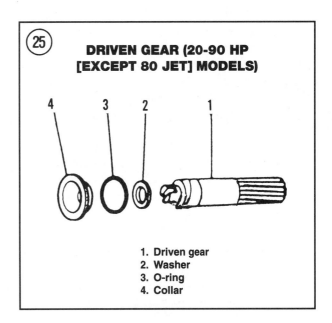

1. Driven gear
2. Washer
3. O-ring
4. Collar

26

DRIVEN GEAR (80 JET AND 115-225 HP [90°] MODELS)

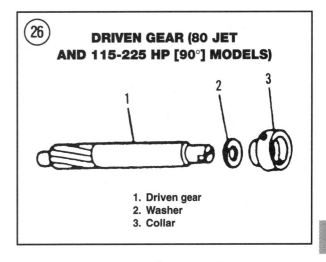

1. Driven gear
2. Washer
3. Collar

13

27

DRIVEN GEAR (200-250 HP [76°] MODELS)

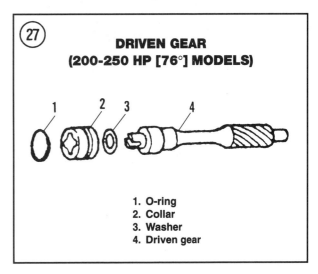

1. O-ring
2. Collar
3. Washer
4. Driven gear

1. Remove the oil pump. Refer to *Oil Pump Removal/Installation* in this chapter.

2. Refer to **Figure 25-27** and determine the correct illustration for your model. Refer to the illustration during the removal and installation procedures.

3. Note the location and orientation of the components. Remove the collars, washers and O-rings from the mounting location. Discard the O-rings. Inspect the collars and washers for wear or damage and replace if required.

4. Use a pair of needle nose pliers to pull the driven gear from the cylinder block. Pull the gear from the protruded coupling end.

5. Lubricate the gear, O-rings and collars with Yamalube or its equivalent. Use needle nose pliers and carefully insert the gear into the opening. Slowly rotate the gear during installation to mesh the driven gear teeth with the drive gear teeth. Ensure that the bearing end of the gear enters the bushing in the cylinder block (V4 and V6 only).

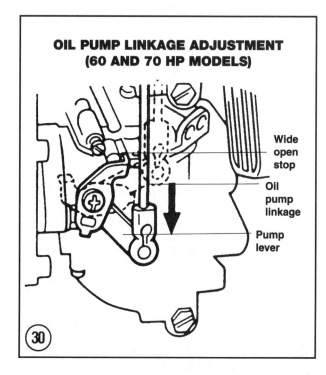

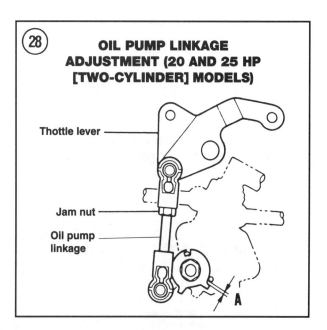

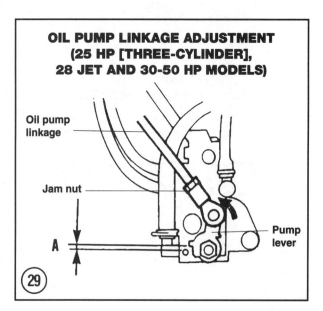

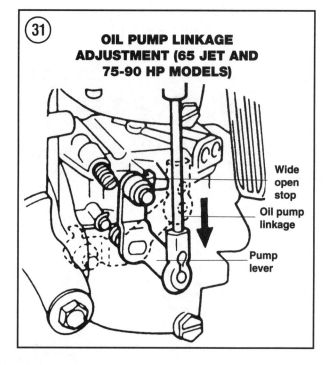

6. Install the collars, washers and *new* O-rings. Refer to the illustrations during installation.

7. Refer to *Oil Pump Removal/Installation* located in this chapter and install the oil pump.

Oil Pump Linkage Adjustment

Oil pump linkages vary by model. Refer to **Figure 28-32** to determine the correct orientation for your model.

   a. For 20-25 hp (two-cylinder) models, refer to **Figure 28**.

   b. For 25 hp (three-cylinder), 28 jet and 30-50 hp models, refer to **Figure 29**.

   c. For 60-70 hp models (except 65 jet), refer to **Figure 30**.

   d. For 65 jet and 75-90 hp models (except 80 jet), refer to **Figure 31**.

   e. For 80 jet and 115-250 hp models, refer to **Figure 32**.

1. Carefully pry the oil pump linkage connector from the pump lever.

2. Position the carburetor throttle valve in the full throttle position.

3A. For 20-90 hp models (excluding 80 jet), rotate the pump lever in the direction indicated until the lever contacts the wide open stop.

3B. For 80 jet and 115-250 hp models, rotate the pump lever until it contacts the stop pin on the oil pump.

4. Refer to **Table 4** for linkage adjustment stop clearance specification. Back the lever away from the stop until the linkage adjustment clearance between the lever and the stop matches the listed specification.

5. Loosen the jam nut if so equipped. Set the carburetor throttle valve in the full throttle position. Set the pump lever to the specified clearance. Adjust the oil pump linkage to the length required. Install the oil pump linkage onto the connection without changing the stop clearance. Check to ensure that adequate thread engagement is present in the linkage connector (**Figure 33**). Adjust the linkage at the throttle valve end if necessary.

6. Tighten the jam nut, if so equipped, and install the linkage onto the pump lever.

7. Operate the throttle from idle to wide open position several times and check the stop clearance. Perform the adjustment again if the clearance is not correct. Perform the adjustment again if binding of the linkage occurs when the throttle is moved or if the carburetor/throttle valve will not achieve wide open throttle.

Bleeding air from the system

1. Refer to *Oil filling procedure* in this chapter. Fill all tanks as indicated. Manually fill any oil supply hoses with Yamalube 2-cycle outboard oil.

2. Mix a 50:1 fuel/oil mixture in a portable tank following the procedures listed in Chapter Four. Connect the portable tank fuel hose to the fuel inlet hose on the engine.

OIL PUMP LINKAGE ADJUSTMENT MODELS 80 JET AND 115-250 HP

Wide open stop

Pump lever

Oil pump linkage

Jam nut

(32)

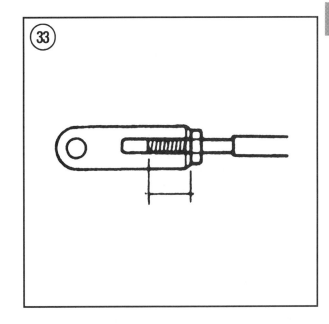

(33)

13

3. Use a test tank or flush/test adapter and run the engine on the fuel/oil mix while performing Steps 4 and 5.

4. Locate the air bleed screw on the oil pump (**Figure 34**). The air bleed screw will have a sealing gasket under the screw head.

5. Position a shop towel under the screw. With the engine running at idle speed, loosen the air bleed screw 3 to 4 turns counterclockwise. Tighten the screw fully clockwise when oil begins to flow out of the air bleed screw opening.

6. Check the hoses leading into and out of the oil pump. Repeat Steps 4 and 5 if air is noted in the hoses.

7. Run the engine for an additional 5-10 minutes on the premix and check for the presence of air in the oil hoses.

Oil Injection Control Module

The oil injection module (**Figure 35**) is mounted to the port side of the power head on some 115-130 hp models. Replacement of the module is usually required when the oil injection warning system is malfunctioning and all other components test correctly. Check all connections for faulty or dirty connectors before replacing the module. To remove the module, unplug the wire connectors and remove the module retaining screws. Clean the mounting area of debris and contaminants. Install the module and tighten the fasteners securely. Connect the wires at the connectors and check for proper operation.

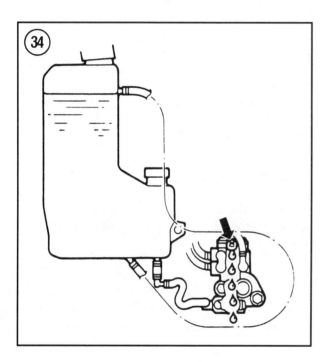

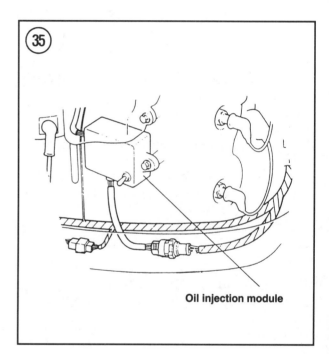

Oil injection module

Table 1 TIGHTENING TORQUE

	Torque specification
Oil pump mounting bolt	
20-50 hp	6.5 N•m (57 in.-lb.)
60-90 hp models (except 80 jet)	7.0 N•m (61 in.-lb.)
80 jet, 105 jet and 150-250 hp	6.5 N•m (57 in.-lb.)
Standard fastener torque	
Fastener size	
8 mm nut, M5 bolt	5 N•m (44 in.-lb.)
10 mm nut, M6 bolt	8 N•m (70 in.-lb.)
12 mm nut, M8 bolt	18 N•m (13 ft.-lb.)
14 mm nut, M10 bolt	36 N•m (26 ft.-lb.)
17 mm nut, M12 bolt	43 N•m (31 ft.-lb.)

Table 2 OIL PUMP IDENTIFICATION

Model	Identification mark
40 and 50 hp	63D00
60 and 70 hp	6H302
65 jet and 75-90 hp (excludes 80 jet)	6H102
80 jet and 115 hp	6N600
130 hp	6N700
105 jet, 150-175 hp	6R400
200-225 (90° V)	6R510
200-250 (76° V)	65L00

Table 3 OIL INJECTION SYSTEM SPECIFICATIONS

	Capacity
Engine mounted oil reservoir	
20 and 25 hp (two-cylinder)	0.7 L (0.74 qt.)
40 and 50 hp	1.5 L (1.6 qt.)
60 and 70 hp	2.8 L (2.96 qt.)
65 jet and 75-90 hp (except 80 jet)	3.3 L (3.49 qt.)
80 jet and 115-130 hp	0.9 L (0.95 qt.)
105 jet and 150-225 hp (90°)	0.9 L (0.95 qt.)
200-250 hp (76°)	1.2 L (1.27 qt.)
Remote mounted oil tank	10.5 L (11.1 qt.)

Table 4 STOP CLEARANCE SPECIFICATIONS

Model	Stop clearance
20-25 hp (two-cylinder)	0.5 mm (0.02 in.)
25 hp (three-cylinder) and 28 jet	1.0 mm (0.039 in.)
30-90 hp (except 80 jet)	1.0 mm (0.039 in.)
80 jet and 115-250 hp	Light contact against stop

13

Chapter Fourteen

Remote Control

The remote control provides a means to control throttle, shifting and other engine operations from a location well beyond reach of the engine (**Figure 1**). It is the boat operator's link to the engine. This chapter will provide neutral throttle operating instructions, shift cable removal/installation procedures and remote control disassembly and assembly procedures.

CAUTION
Always refer to your owner's manual for specific operating instructions for the re-

mote control. Become familiar with all control functions before operating the engine.

Neutral Throttle Operation

Two common types of controls are used on your Yamaha outboard. The most commonly used type is the 703 control or *pull for neutral throttle control* (**Figure 2**). To activate the neutral throttle function, position the handle in neutral. Pull the handle straight out or away from the control

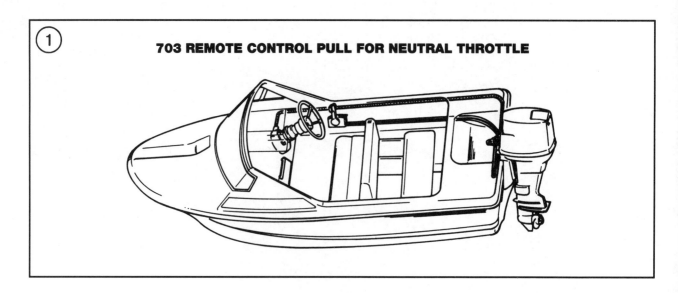

① 703 REMOTE CONTROL PULL FOR NEUTRAL THROTTLE

(Figure 3). The throttle can then be advanced without shifting the engine into gear. This feature will assist with starting and warming up the engine. To return to normal operation, position the handle to neutral and push the handle toward the control.

The other type of control used is the 705 control or push for neutral throttle control (**Figure 4**). To activate the neutral throttle function, position the handle in neutral. Push in and hold the throttle-only button. The button can

be released after the throttle is advanced. The throttle can be advanced without shifting the engine into gear as long as the handle does not reach the neutral position. To return to normal operation, position the handle to the neutral position. The throttle-only button will return to the normal position. Normal operation with shifting can resume.

WARNING
A malfunction in the remote control can lead
to lack of shift and throttle control. Never

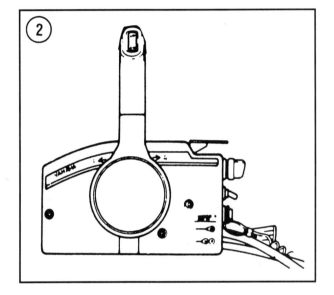

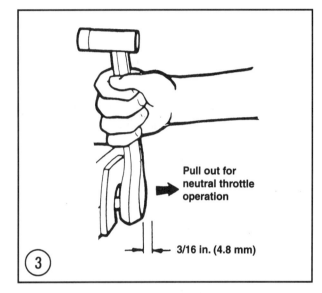

Pull out for neutral throttle operation

3/16 in. (4.8 mm)

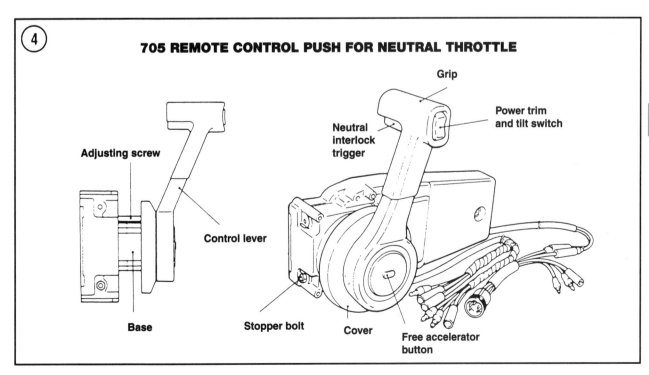

705 REMOTE CONTROL PUSH FOR NEUTRAL THROTTLE

Grip

Power trim and tilt switch

Neutral interlock trigger

Adjusting screw

Control lever

Base

Stopper bolt

Cover

Free accelerator button

14

operate an outboard when any malfunction is noted with the remote control. Damage to property, serious bodily injury or death can result if the engine is operated without proper control. Check the control for proper remote control operation before operating the engine or after performing any service or repair.

Throttle/Shift Cable Removal/Installation

Throttle/shift cable replacement is required when the cable becomes hard to move or excessive play occurs due to cable wear. Replace both the throttle and shift cable at the same time. The conditions that caused one cable to require replacement are likely to be present in the other cable. Mark the cables prior to removal to ensure that the throttle and shift cables are installed to the proper attaching points. Remove and attach one cable at a time to avoid confusion.

Procedures are provided for both the 703 and 705 remote controls. For assistance with control box identification, refer to neutral throttle operation.

703 Remote Control

1. Disconnect both battery cables from the battery.

2. Remove the screws or bolts attaching the remote control to the boat structure.

3. Remove the cover from the lower side of the control (**Figure 5**).

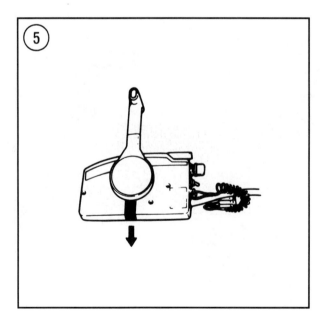

4. Remove the two screws and the lower back cover from the control (**Figure 6**).

5. Identify the cable that requires replacement. Move the control handle to provide access to the circlip on the cable end (**Figure 7**).

6. Note and/or mark the location of the cable and cable grommet to the clamp groove (**Figure 8**). Remove the

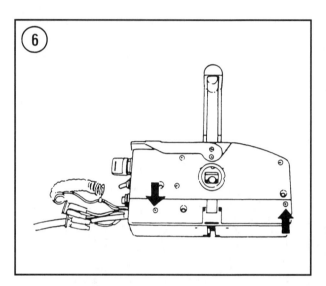

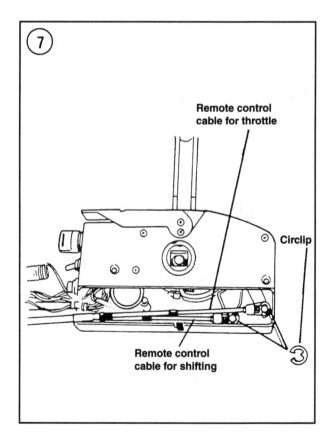

Remote control cable for throttle

Circlip

Remote control cable for shifting

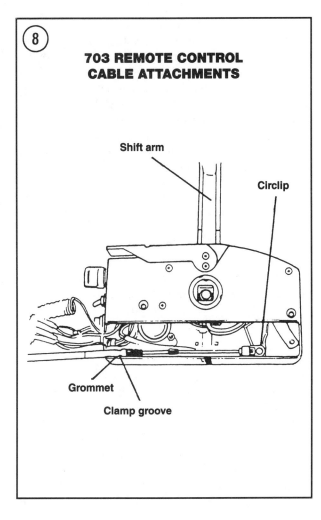

**703 REMOTE CONTROL
CABLE ATTACHMENTS**

Shift arm

Circlip

Grommet

Clamp groove

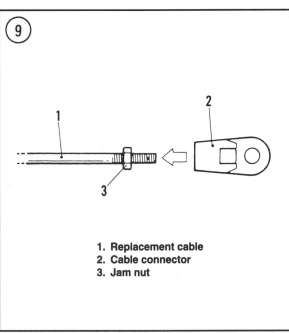

1. Replacement cable
2. Cable connector
3. Jam nut

circlip (**Figure 7**), then lift the cable from the clamp groove and pin on the lever. Inspect the circlip for corrosion, damage or lost spring tension. Replace if any defects are noted.

7. Apply Yamaha marine grease or its equivalent to the threaded end of the replacement cable (1, **Figure 9**). Thread the cable connector (2, **Figure 9**) onto the threaded end until 11.0 mm (0.4 in.) of the threaded end is in the cable connector. Tighten the jam nut (**Figure 9**) securely against the cable connector.

8. Place the cable and grommet into the clamp groove in the control box as indicated in **Figure 8**. Apply Yamaha marine grease to the attaching points of the cables. Position the cable connector over the pin on the lever then install the circlip. Make sure the circlip is properly installed into the groove in the pin.

9. Repeat Steps 5-8 for the other cable.

10. Install the lower back cover and screws (**Figure 6**). Install the cover (**Figure 5**). Install the control and attaching screws to the boat. Tighten all fasteners to the specifications listed in **Table 1**. Adjust the throttle and shift cables at the engine as instructed in Chapter Five. Connect both battery cables to the battery.

705 Remote Control

1. Disconnect both battery cables at the battery.

2. Remove the screws or bolts attaching the control to the boat structure.

3. Remove the five screws (1, **Figure 10**) from the back cover. Support the cables, then carefully pry the back cover (2, **Figure 10**) from the control.

14

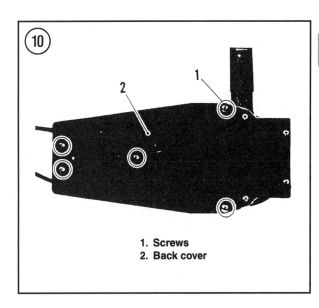

1. Screws
2. Back cover

4. Refer to **Figure 11** to identify the shift cable. Mark it accordingly.

5. Make note of the position of the shift cable and grommet (**Figure 11**) in the clamp groove.

6. Move the shift handle to provide access to the circlip on the cable connector. Use needle nose pliers to remove the circlip from the shift arm attaching pin. Carefully lift the throttle cable from the shift arm and clamp groove.

7. Thread the cable connector onto the threaded end is the shift cable until 11.0 mm (0.4 in.) of the threaded end in the connector (Figure 9).

8. Apply Yamaha marine grease to the attaching points for the cable. Place the cable and grommet into the clamp groove of the control. Place the cable connector over the pin on the lever or arm. Install the circlip onto the pin. Make sure the circlip is properly installed into the groove in the pin.

9. Repeat Steps 5-8 for the throttle cable. Inspect the cables to ensure that both are properly aligned into the clamp groove (**Figure 11**). Place the back cover onto the control. Hold the back cover firmly in position while you install the five screws (**Figure 10**). Tighten all fasteners to the specifications listed in **Table 1**.

10. Install the control to the boat structure. Tighten the attaching screws securely. Adjust the shift and throttle cables at the engine as instructed in Chapter Five. Connect both battery cables. Check for proper shift and throttle operation.

Remote Control Disassembly and Assembly

This section provides procedures for disassembly and assembly of the remote control. Separate procedures are provided for the 703 and 705 controls.

The major components or systems of the control include the:

1. Throttle control mechanism.
2. Shift control mechanism.
3. Neutral throttle mechanism.
4. Tilt/trim switch.
5. Ignition/start switch.
6. Fuel enrichment switch.
7. Warning buzzer.

When complete disassembly is not required to access the faulty component(s), perform the disassembly steps until the desired component is accessible. Reverse the disassembly steps to assemble the remote control.

To save a great deal of time on assembly and to ensure proper assembly, make notes, markings or drawings prior to removing any component from the remote control. Improper assembly can cause internal binding or reversed cable movement.

Clean all components, except electric switches and the warning buzzer, in a suitable solvent. Use compressed air to blow debris from the components. Inspect all components for damaged or worn surfaces. Replace any defective or suspect component. Apply Yamaha all-purpose grease or its equivalent to all pivot points or sliding surfaces on assembly. Test all electrical components when they are removed to ensure proper operation upon assembly. Refer to Chapter Three for testing procedures for all electrical switches and the warning buzzer.

703 Control, disassembly and assembly

1. Disconnect both battery cables from the battery.

2. Remove the screws or bolts that attach the control to the boat structure. Mark all wires leading to the control to ensure proper connections on installation. Disconnect all leads. Place the control handle in the neutral position.

3. Mark the cable location for reference, and then remove the throttle and shift cables from the remote control as instructed in *Throttle/shift cable removal/installation* in this chapter. Place the control on a clean work surface.

4. Remove the back cover plate (1, **Figure 12**) from the control. Remove the throttle-only lever and shaft (13 and 4, **Figure 12**). Remove the retaining bolt, then lift the throttle arm and shift arm from the control. Remove any accessible bushings, grommets and retainers at this point.

5. Remove the retainer (5, **Figure 12**), then lift the leaf spring and neutral switch from the control.

6. Note the position of the gear (7, **Figure 12**) and carefully lift it from the control. Remove any accessible bushings, grommets and retainers. Note the trim wire routing and remove the control handle from the control.

7. Remove the neutral position lever from the handle. Note the wire routing, then pull the trim switch and wires from the handle.

8. Make note of all wire connections and routing prior to removal. Disconnect the wires, then remove the start switch, lanyard switch and fuel enrichment switch from the control. Note the location and orientation of any remaining components, then remove them from the control.

9. Assembly is the reverse of disassembly. Apply Yamaha all-purpose grease to all bushing, pivot points and sliding surfaces. Apply Loctite 271 to the threads of all bolts and screws on assembly.

10. Install the throttle and shift cables as instructed in *Throttle/shift cable removal/installation* in this chapter. Install both back covers (**Figure 13**). Tighten all fasteners to the specifications listed in **Table 1**. Reattach all disconnected leads to the control. Install both battery cables to the battery. Adjust the cables at the engine as instructed in

Chapter Five. Check for proper operation before putting the engine into service.

705 Control, disassembly and assembly

To assist with component identification and orientation, refer to **Figure 14**. Mark the location and orientation of *ALL* components prior to removal.

1. Disconnect both battery cables from the battery.

2. Remove the screws that retain the control to the boat structure. Mark or make note of the throttle and shift cable locations. Remove both cables from the remote control as instructed in *Throttle/shift cable removal/installation*.

3. Mark or make note of all wires and connections leading into the control, then disconnect them.

4. Mark or make notes or drawings to indicate the location and orientation of each component prior to removal.

5. Place the control handle in neutral position. Remove the circlip (1, **Figure 15**) from the throttle lever pivot. Lift the cam plate and dwell plate from the control (2 and 3, **Figure 15**).

6. Slide the throttle lever toward the back of the control to access the two screws (1, **Figure 16**) that retain the drive plate (2, **Figure 16**). Remove the screws. Note the orientation of the drive plate and the drive limiter (26, **Figure 14**), then lift them from the control.

7. Count the number of turns as you tighten the throttle friction until fully seated. Record the number of turns. Loosen the screw back to the original position. Remove the circlip (1, **Figure 17**). Note the orientation of the components, then lift the washer, throttle arm, throttle friction and bushings (2, 3 and 5, **Figure 17**) from the control. Remove the friction screw (6, **Figure 17**) from the remote control housing.

8. Remove the two hex bolts, then lift the throttle shaft (**Figure 18**) from the remote control housing. Note the position of the shift lever (3, **Figure 19**). It must be installed in the same position as removed. Remove the bolt (1, **Figure 19**) and washer (2, **Figure 19**), then lift the throttle lever from the control.

9. Remove the screws (22, **Figure 14**), then carefully lift the gear cover from the remote control housing. Loosen the locking nut (11, **Figure 14**) without turning the stopper

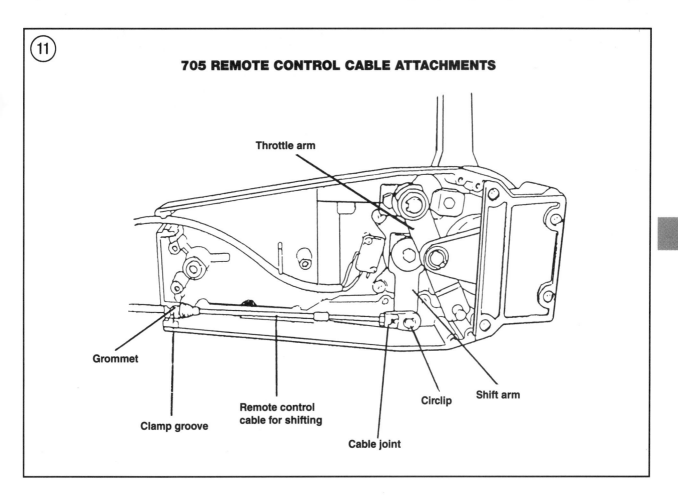

11

705 REMOTE CONTROL CABLE ATTACHMENTS

Throttle arm

Grommet

Clamp groove

Remote control
cable for shifting

Cable joint

Circlip

Shift arm

14

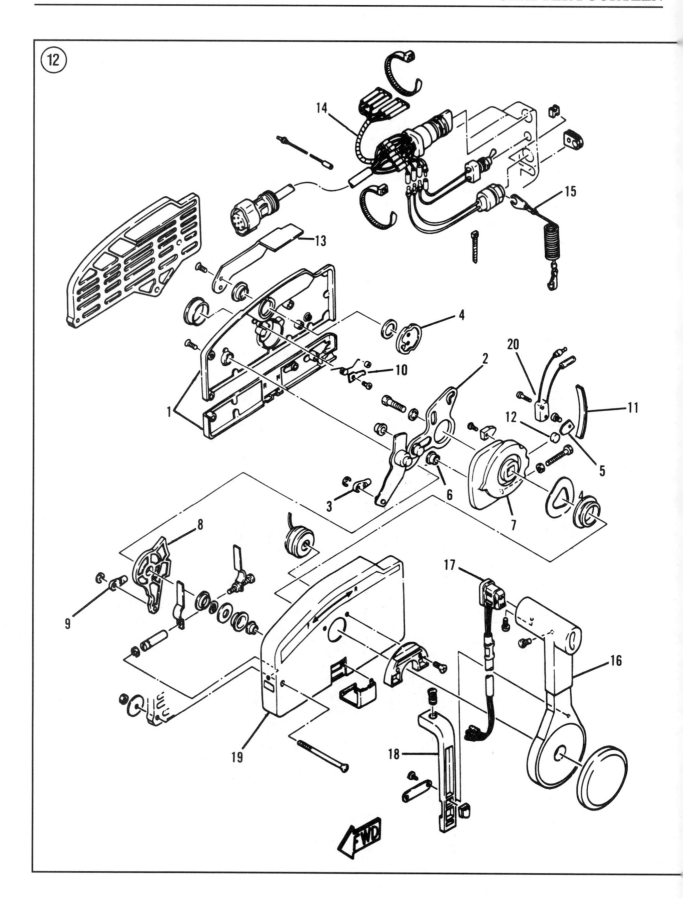

703 REMOTE CONTROL INTERNAL COMPONENTS

1. Back covers
2. Throttle arm/lever
3. Cable connector
4. Throttle only shaft/cam
5. Retainer
6. Bushing
7. Gear
8. Shift arm
9. Cable connector
10. Detent roller
11. Leaf spring
12. Throttle only roller
13. Throttle only lever
14. Start switch
    lead connectors
15. Lanyard
16. Control handle
17. Trim switch*
18. Neutral position lever
19. Control housing
20. Neutral switch

*Used only on tilt/trim models

screw (15, **Figure 14**). Count the turns while turning the stopper screw clockwise (15, **Figure 14**) until fully seated. Record the number of turns then remove the screw and locking nut.

10. Carefully pry the throttle-only cover (56, **Figure 14**) from the throttle-only shaft (57, **Figure 14**). Use pliers to pull the throttle only shaft from the control. The shaft may break during the removal procedure. Remove the two screws (59, **Figure 14**) from the washer. Note the routing of the trim wires, then pull the control handle and trim wires from the remote control. Disconnect the trim wires from the instrument harness. Remove the decal cover (66, **Figure 14**) and neutral lock assembly (55, **Figure 14**) from the control.

11. Mark all components prior to removal. Remove the screws (61, **Figure 14**) along with the cover/mount from the control. Remove the circlip (39, **Figure 14**) from the drive shaft (37, **Figure 14**). Note the orientation of the lock plate, shift plate and gear (31, 32 and 35, **Figure 14**) then slide them from the drive shaft. Note the location and orientation of all remaining components, then remove them.

12. Remove the neutral switch (13, **Figure 14**), trim switch and leads (50 and 67, **Figure 14**) along with the key switch, enrichment switch and warning buzzer (if so equipped). Refer to Chapter Three for test procedures for these components.

13. Assembly is the reverse of disassembly. Apply Yamaha all-purpose grease to all pivot points and sliding surfaces. Install the throttle friction screw and stopper screw until seated, then back out the recorded number of turns. Tighten the jam nut securely. Apply Loctite 271 to the

14

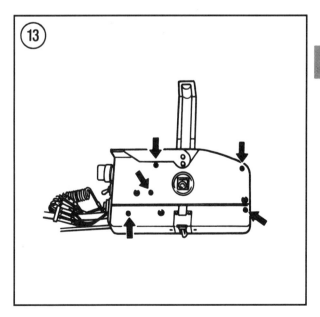

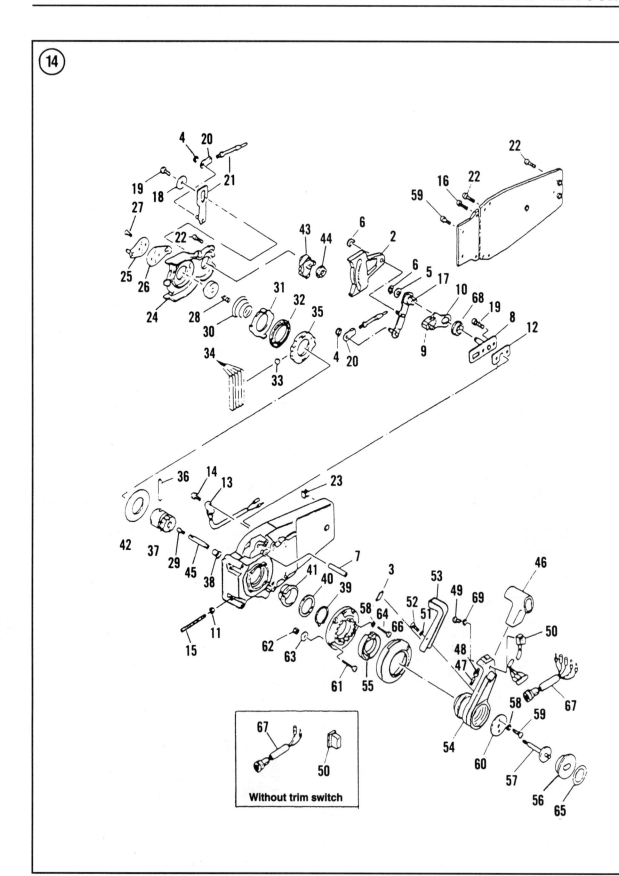

Without trim switch

705 REMOTE CONTROL INTERNAL COMPONENTS

1. Back cover
2. Cam plate
3. Cap
4. Circlip
5. Washer
6. Circlip
7. Friction shaft
8. Throttle shaft
9. Throttle friction
10. Adjusting plate
11. Nut
12. Spacer
13. Neutral switch
14. Screw
15. Screw
16. Screw
17. Throttle lever
18. Washer
19. Bolt
20. Cable connector
21. Shift cable
22. Screw
23. Cable grommet
24. Gear cover
25. Drive arm
26. Drive arm limiter
27. Screw
28. Spring
29. Screw
30. Spring
31. Locking plate
32. Shifting plate
33. Throttle only roller
34. Spring
35. Gear

36. Pin
37. Shaft
38. Bushing
39. Circlip
40. Washer
41. Bushing
42. Washer
43. Gear
44. Bushing
45. Shaft
46. Handle grip
47. Spring
48. Screw
49. Screw
50. Trim switch
51. Washer
52. Screw
53. Neutral lock lever
54. Control handle
55. Neutral lock plate
56. Cover
57. Throttle only shaft
58. Washer
59. Screw
60. Washer
61. Screw
62. Nut
63. Washer
64. Screw
65. Decal
66. Decal
67. Wire
68. Bushing
69. Washer

14

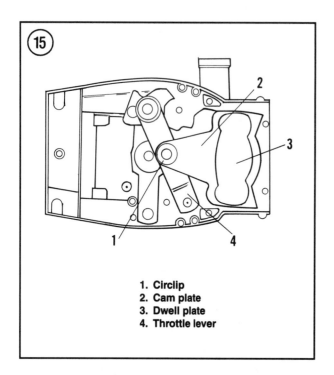

15

1. Circlip
2. Cam plate
3. Dwell plate
4. Throttle lever

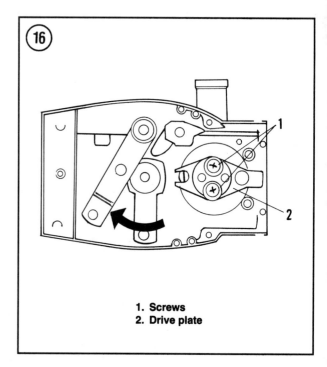

16

1. Screws
2. Drive plate

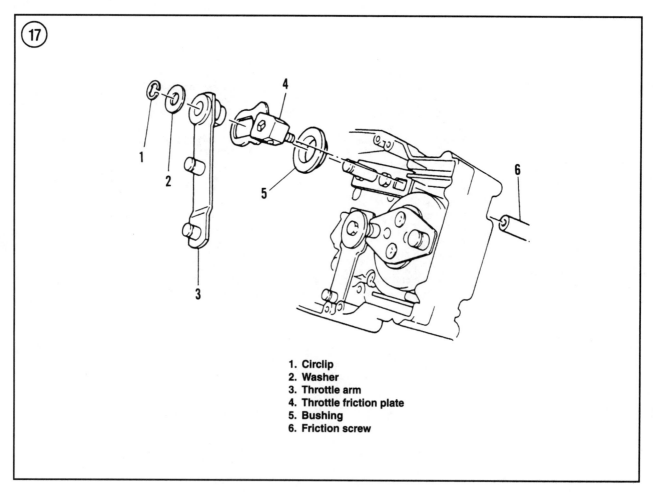

17

1. Circlip
2. Washer
3. Throttle arm
4. Throttle friction plate
5. Bushing
6. Friction screw

threads of all fasteners (excluding the throttle friction screw and stopper screw). Tighten all fasteners to the specifications listed in **Table 1**.

14. Install the throttle and shift cables into the remote control as instructed in *Throttle/shift cable removal/instal-*

lation. Install the control to the boat and tighten the screws or bolts securely. Adjust the cables at the engine as instructed in Chapter Five.

15. Check the throttle and shift for proper operation and correct as required.

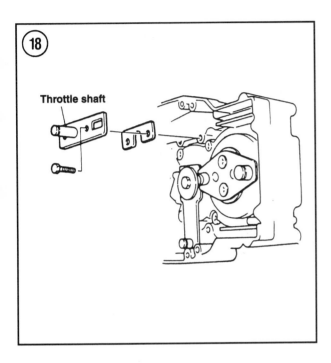

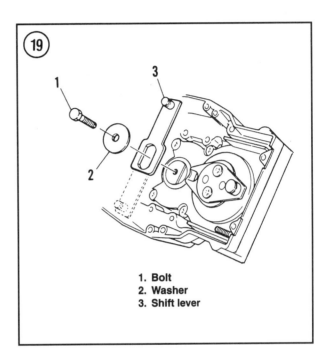

1. Bolt
2. Washer
3. Shift lever

Table 1 TIGHTENING TORQUE

Component fastener	Torque specification
Neutral lock holder (703 Control)	1.2-1.5 N•m (11-13 in.-lb.)
Neutral throttle lever screws (703 Control)	1.5-1.8 N•m (13-16 in.-lb.)
Throttle stopper locknut (705 Control)	5.0-8.0 N•m (44-70 in.-lb.)
Throttle lever (705 Control)	5.0-8.0 N•m (44-70 in.-lb.)
Control handle screw (703 Control)	6.0-6.5 N•m (52-56 in.-lb.)
Control handle mounting screws (705 Control)	3.0-4.5 N•m (26-39 in.-lb.)
Cover/mount (705 Control)	5.0-8.0 N•m (44-70 in.-lb.)
Drive plate screws (705 Control)	5.0-8.0 N•m (44-70 in.-lb.)
Standard tightening torque	
Fastener size	
8 mm nut, M5 bolt	5.0 N•m (44 in.-lb.)
10 mm nut, M6 bolt	8.0 N•m (70 in.-lb.)
12 mm nut, M8 bolt	18.0 N•m (13 ft.-lb.)
14 mm nut, M10 bolt	36.0 N•m (25 ft.-lb.)
17 mm nut, M12 bolt	43.0 N•m (31 ft.-lb.)

14

Index

15

2 HP MODELS (1996-ON)

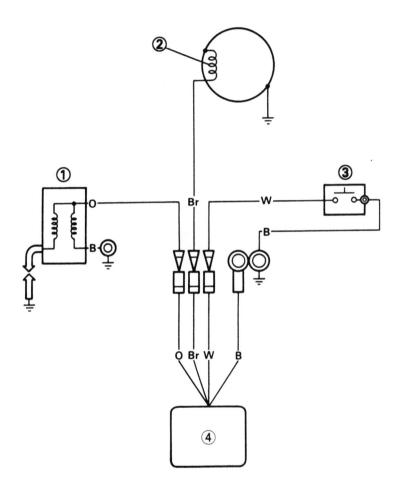

1. Ignition coil
2. Charge coil
3. Stop switch
4. CDI unit

B : Black
Br : Brown
O : Orange
W : White

16

3 HP MODELS (1996-ON)

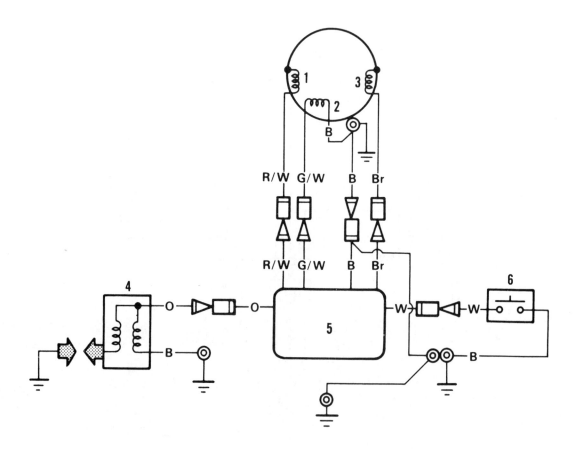

1. Pulser coil No. 1   B : Black
2. Pulser coil No. 2   Br : Brown
3. Charge coil   G : Green
4. Ignition coil   O : Orange
5. CDI unit   R : Red
6. Stop switch   W : White

4 AND 5 HP MODELS

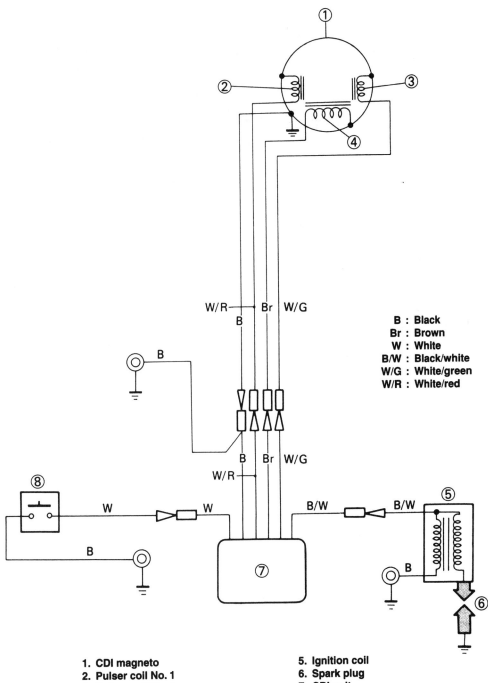

B : Black
Br : Brown
W : White
B/W : Black/white
W/G : White/green
W/R : White/red

1. CDI magneto
2. Pulser coil No. 1
3. Pulser coil No. 2
4. Charge coil
5. Ignition coil
6. Spark plug
7. CDI unit
8. Stop switch

16

6 AND 8 HP MODELS (MANUAL START)

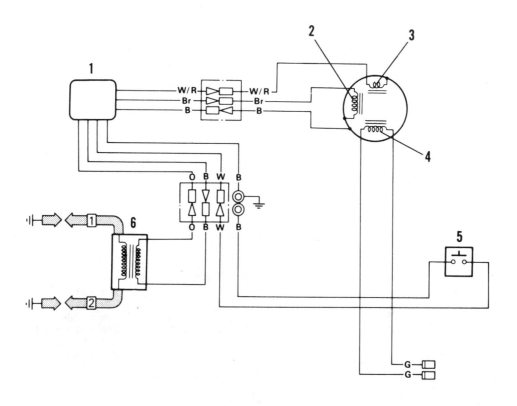

1. CDI unit
2. Charge coil
3. Pulser coil
4. Lighting coil
5. Engine stop switch
6. Ignition coil

B : Black
Br : Brown
G : Green
G/W : Green/white
O : Orange
R : Red
W : White
W/R : White/red

6 AND 8 HP MODELS (ELECTRIC START)

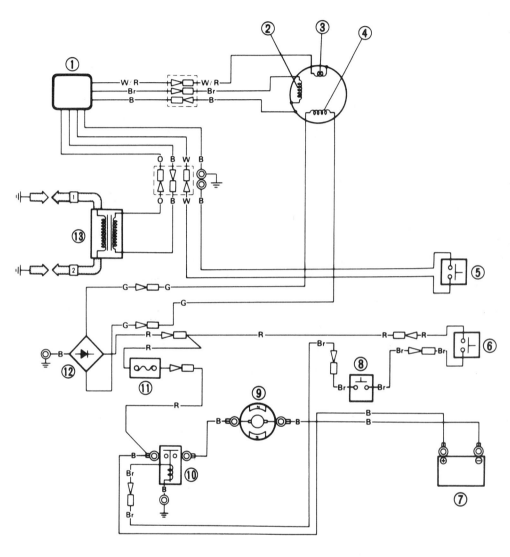

1. CDI unit
2. Charge coil
3. Pulser coil
4. Lighting coil
5. Engine stop switch
6. Starter switch
7. Battery
8. Neutral switch
9. Starter motor
10. Starter relay
11. Fuse
12. Rectifier
13. Ignition coil

B : Black
Br : Brown
G : Green
G/W : Green/white
O : Orange
R : Red
W : White
W/R : White/red

16

9.9 AND 15 HP MODELS (MANUAL START, TILLER)

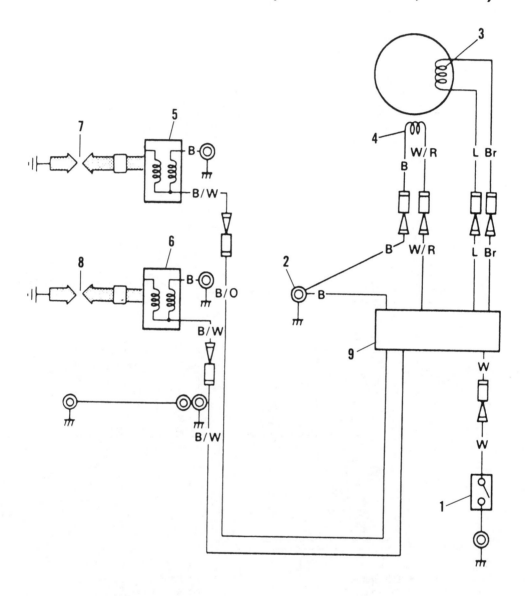

1. Engine stop switch
2. Engine ground terminal
3. Pulser coil
4. Ignition charge coil
5. Ignition coil No. 1
6. Ignition coil No. 2
7. Spark plug No. 1
8. Spark plug No. 2
9. CDI unit

B : Black
Br : Brown
L : Blue
W/R : White/red
B/W : Black/white
B/O : Black/orange

9.9 AND 15 HP MODELS (ELECTRIC START, TILLER)

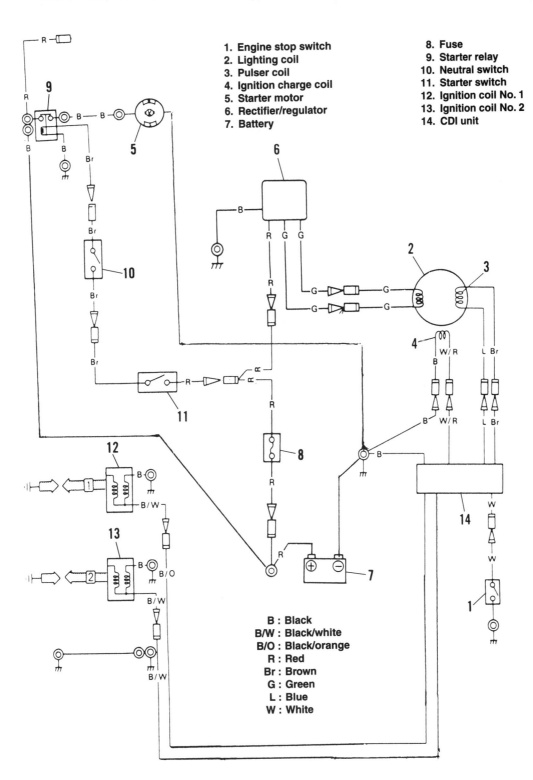

1. Engine stop switch
2. Lighting coil
3. Pulser coil
4. Ignition charge coil
5. Starter motor
6. Rectifier/regulator
7. Battery
8. Fuse
9. Starter relay
10. Neutral switch
11. Starter switch
12. Ignition coil No. 1
13. Ignition coil No. 2
14. CDI unit

B : Black
B/W : Black/white
B/O : Black/orange
R : Red
Br : Brown
G : Green
L : Blue
W : White

16

9.9 AND 15 HP MODELS (ELECTRIC START, REMOTE CONTROL)

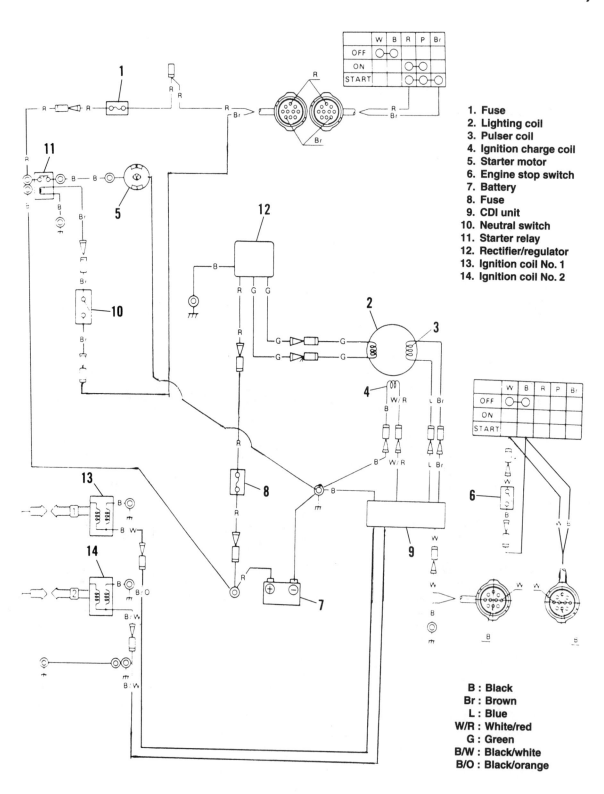

1. Fuse
2. Lighting coil
3. Pulser coil
4. Ignition charge coil
5. Starter motor
6. Engine stop switch
7. Battery
8. Fuse
9. CDI unit
10. Neutral switch
11. Starter relay
12. Rectifier/regulator
13. Ignition coil No. 1
14. Ignition coil No. 2

B : Black
Br : Brown
L : Blue
W/R : White/red
G : Green
B/W : Black/white
B/O : Black/orange

20 AND 25 HP TWO-CYLINDER MODELS
(MANUAL START, TILLER)

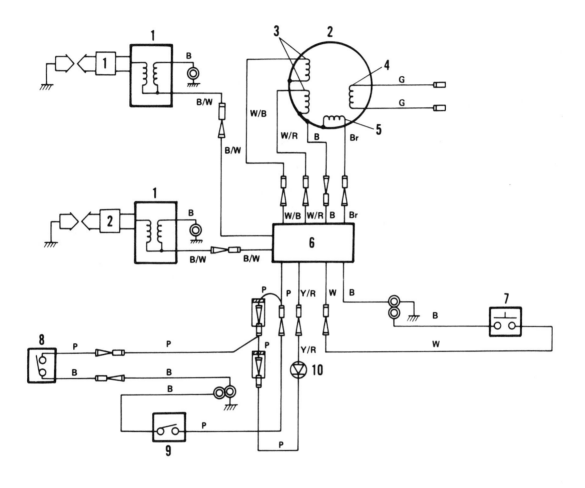

1. Ignition coil
2. CDI magneto
3. Pulser coil
4. Lighting coil
5. Charge coil
6. CDI unit
7. Emergency stop switch
8. Thermoswitch
9. Oil level sensor
10. Warning lamp

B : Black
Br : Brown
G : Green
P : Pink
W : White
B/W : Black/white
W/B : White/black
Y/R : Yellow/red
W/R : White/red

16

20 AND 25 HP TWO-CYLINDER MODELS (ELECTRIC START, TILLER)

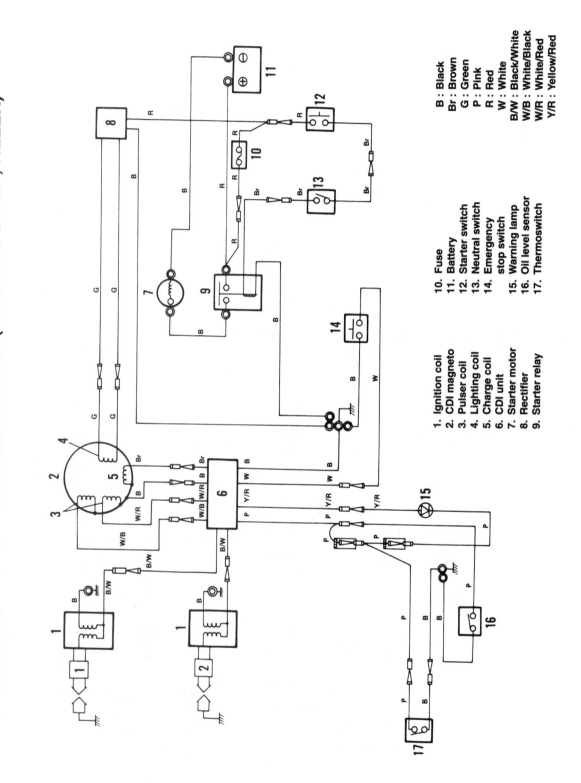

1. Ignition coil
2. CDI magneto
3. Pulser coil
4. Lighting coil
5. Charge coil
6. CDI unit
7. Starter motor
8. Rectifier
9. Starter relay
10. Fuse
11. Battery
12. Starter switch
13. Neutral switch
14. Emergency
    stop switch
15. Warning lamp
16. Oil level sensor
17. Thermoswitch

B : Black
Br : Brown
G : Green
P : Pink
R : Red
W : White
B/W : Black/White
W/B : White/Black
W/R : White/Red
Y/R : Yellow/Red

20 AND 25 HP TWO-CYLINDER MODELS (ELECTRIC START, REMOTE CONTROL)

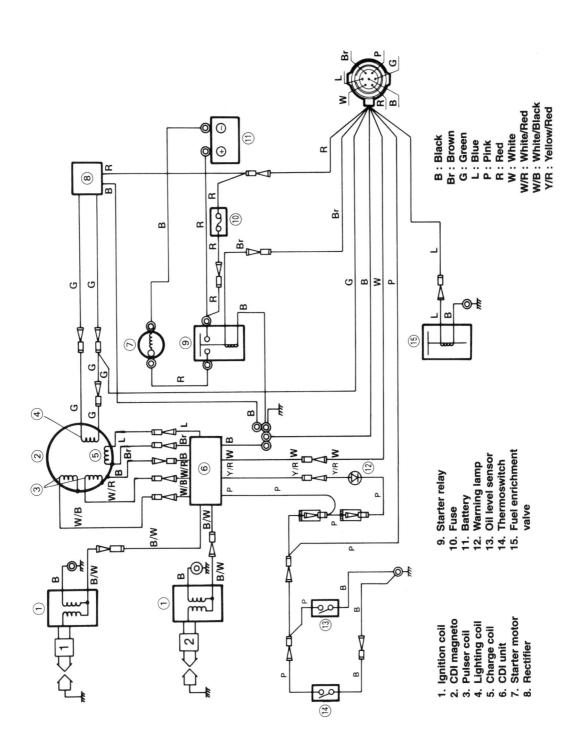

B : Black
Br : Brown
G : Green
L : Blue
P : Pink
R : Red
W : White
W/R : White/Red
W/B : White/Black
Y/R : Yellow/Red

1. Ignition coil
2. CDI magneto
3. Pulser coil
4. Lighting coil
5. Charge coil
6. CDI unit
7. Starter motor
8. Rectifier

9. Starter relay
10. Fuse
11. Battery
12. Warning lamp
13. Oil level sensor
14. Thermoswitch
15. Fuel enrichment
    valve

16

25 HP THREE-CYLINDER MODELS
(MANUAL START, TILLER)

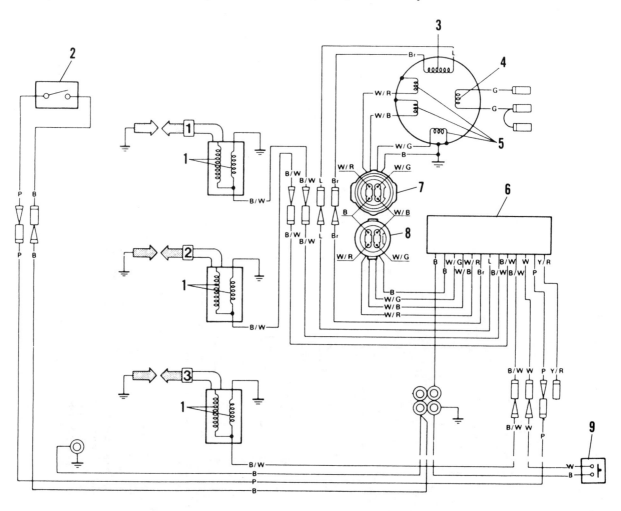

1. Ignition coil
2. Thermoswitch
3. Charge coil
4. Lighting coil
5. Pulser coil
6. CDI unit
7. Magneto coil connector
8. CDI connector
9. Emergency stop switch

B : Black
Br : Brown
G : Green
L : Blue
P : Pink
R : Red
W : White
B/O : Black/orange
B/W : Black/white
W/B : White/black
W/R : White/red
W/G : White/green
Y/R : Yellow/red

C25 MODELS (ELECTRIC START, TILLER)

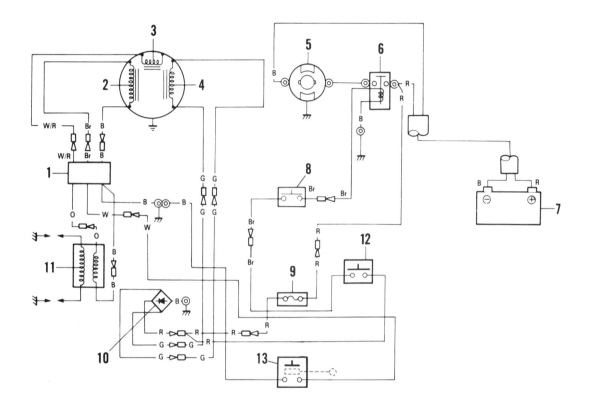

1. CDI unit
2. Charge coil
3. Pulser coil
4. Lighting coil
5. Starter motor
6. Starter relay
7. Battery
8. Neutral switch
9. Fuse
10. Rectifier
11. Ignition coil
12. Starter switch
13. Stop switch

B : Black
Br : Brown
G : Green
L : Blue
O : Orange
R : Red
W : White
W/R : White/red

16

C25 MODELS (ELECTRIC START, REMOTE CONTROL)

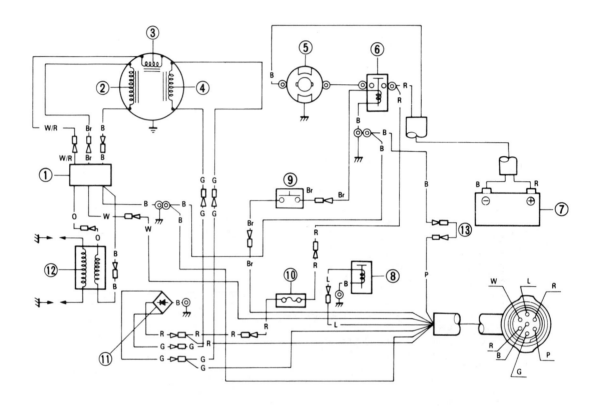

1. CDI unit
2. Charge coil
3. Pulser coil
4. Lighting coil
5. Starter motor
6. Starter relay
7. Battery
8. Choke solenoid
9. Neutral switch
10. Fuse (20A)
11. Rectifier
12. Ignition coil
13. Cover lead wire

B : Black
Br : Brown
G : Green
L : Blue
O : Orange
R : Red
W : White
W/R : White/red

C25 MODELS (MANUAL START, TILLER)

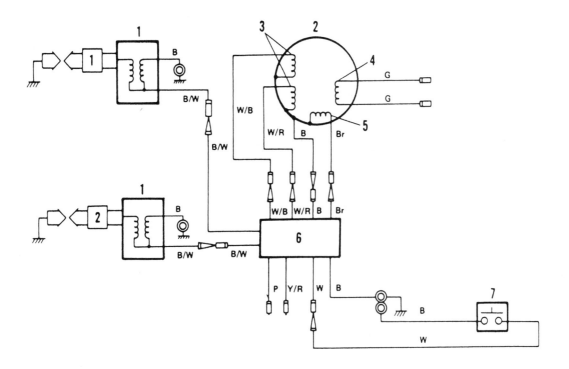

1. Ignition coil
2. CDI magneto
3. Pulser coil
4. Lighting coil
5. Charge coil
6. CDI unit
7. Emergency
   stop switch

B : Black
Br : Brown
G : Green
W : White
P : Pink
Y/R : Yellow/red
B/W : Black/white
W/B : White/black
W/R : White/red

16

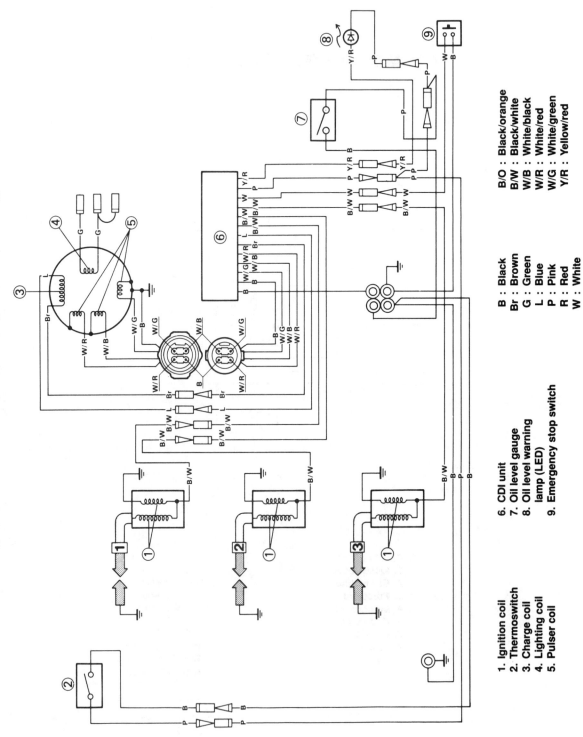

30 HP THREE-CYLINDER MODELS
(MANUAL START, TILLER [EXCEPT C30])

1. Ignition coil
2. Thermoswitch
3. Charge coil
4. Lighting coil
5. Pulser coil

6. CDI unit
7. Oil level gauge
8. Oil level warning lamp (LED)
9. Emergency stop switch

B : Black
Br : Brown
G : Green
L : Blue
P : Pink
R : Red
W : White

B/O : Black/orange
B/W : Black/white
W/B : White/black
W/R : White/red
W/G : White/green
Y/R : Yellow/red

30 HP THREE-CYLINDER MODELS
(ELECTRIC START, TILLER [EXCEPT C30])

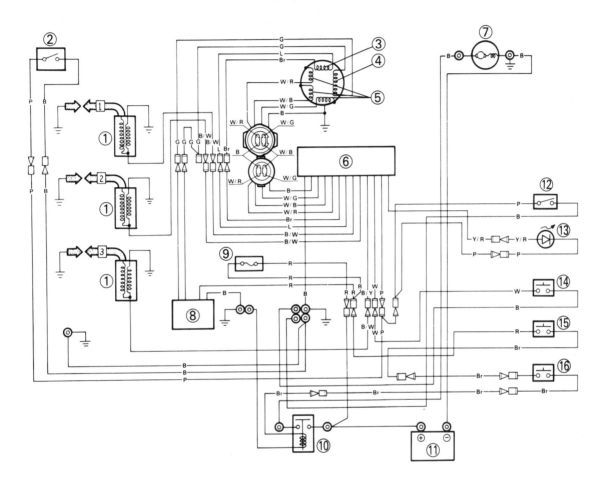

1. Ignition coil	B : Black
2. Thermoswitch	Br : Brown
3. Charge coil	G : Green
4. Lighting coil	L : Blue
5. Pulser coil	P : Pink
6. CDI unit	R : Red
7. Starter motor	W : White
8. Rectifier	Y : Yellow
9. Fuse (10A)	B/O : Black/orange
10. Starter relay	B/W : Black/white
11. Battery	W/B : White/black
12. Oil level sensor	W/R : White/red
13. Oil level warning	W/G : White/green
lamp (LED)	Y/R : Yellow/red
14. Engine stop switch	
15. Starter switch	
16. Neutral switch	

16

30 HP THREE-CYLINDER MODELS
(ELECTRIC START, REMOTE CONTROL [EXCEPT C30])

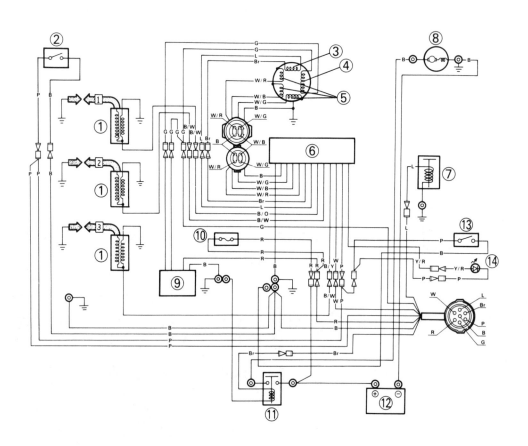

1. Ignition coil
2. Thermoswitch
3. Charge coil
4. Lighting coil
5. Pulser coil
6. CDI unit
7. Fuel enrichment valve
8. Starter motor
9. Rectifier
10. Fuse (10A)
11. Starter relay
12. Battery
13. Oil level sensor
14. Oil level warning lamp (LED)

B : Black
Br : Brown
G : Green
L : Blue
O : Orange
P : Pink
R : Red
W : White
Y : Yellow
B/O : Black/orange
B/W : Black/white
W/B : White/black
W/R : White/red
W/G : White/green
Y/R : Yellow/red

C30 TWO-CYLINDER MODELS
(MANUAL START, TILLER)

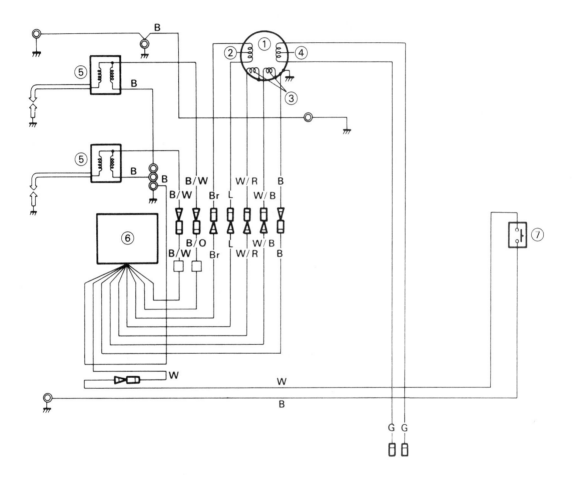

1. CDI magneto
2. Charge coil
3. Pulser coil
4. Lighting coil
5. Ignition coil
6. CDI unit
7. Engine stop switch

B : Black
Br : Brown
G : Green
L : Blue
W : White
B/O : Black/orange
B/W : Black/white
W/B : White/black
W/R : White/red

16

C30 TWO-CYLINDER MODELS
(ELECTRIC START, REMOTE CONTROL)

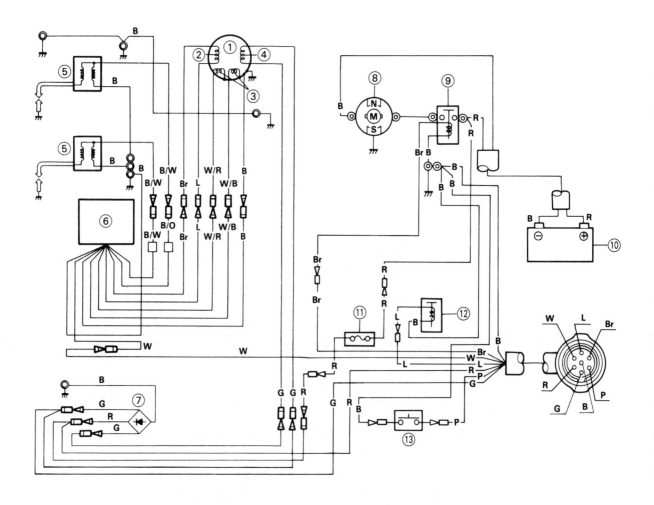

1. CDI magneto
2. Charge coil
3. Pulser coil
4. Lighting coil
5. Ignition coil
6. CDI unit
7. Rectifier
8. Starter motor
9. Starter relay
10. Battery
11. Fuse
12. Fuel enrichment solenoid
13. Thermoswitch

B : Black
Br : Brown
G : Green
L : Blue
P : Pink
R : Red
W : White
B/O : Black/orange
B/W : Black/white
W/B : White/black
W/R : White/red

C40 TWO-CYLINDER MODELS
(ELECTRIC START, REMOTE CONTROL)

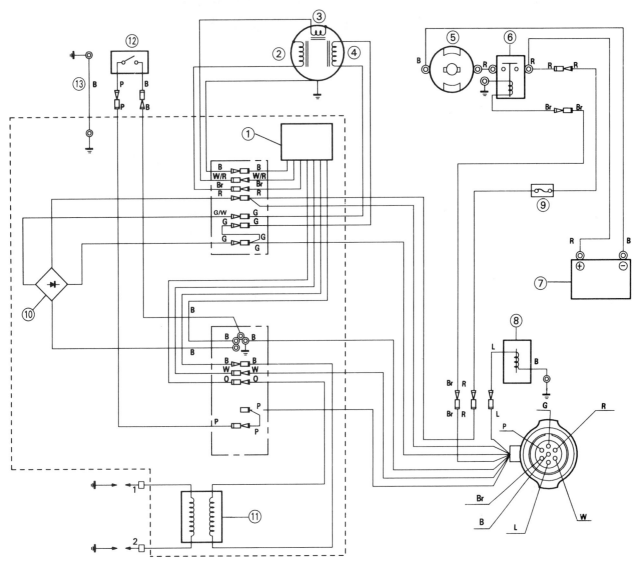

1. CDI unit
2. Charge coil
3. Pulser coil
4. Lighting coil
5. Starter motor
6. Starter relay
7. Battery
8. Choke solenoid
9. Fuse (10A)
10. Fuse (10A)
11. Ignition coil
12. Thermoswitch
13. Ground wire

B : Black
Br : Brown
G : Green
L : Blue
O : Orange
P : Pink
R : Red
W : White
G/W : Green/white
W/R : White/red

16

28 JET, 35 JET, 40 AND 50 HP THREE-CYLINDER MODELS (POWER TRIM AND TILT SYSTEMS)

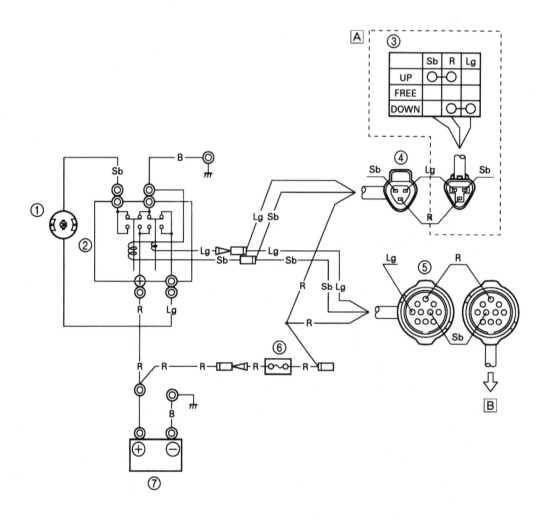

1. **Power trim/tilt motor**
2. **Power trim/tilt relay**
3. **Power trim/tilt switch**
4. **Three-pin electrical connector (black)**
5. **Ten-pin electrical connector**
6. **Fuse**
7. **Battery**

A : **Bottom cowl PTT switch model**
B : **To remote control**

R : **Red**
LG : **Light green**
Sb : **Sky blue**
B : **Black**

28 JET, 35 JET, 40 AND 50 HP THREE-CYLINDER MODELS (CHARGING SYSTEM)

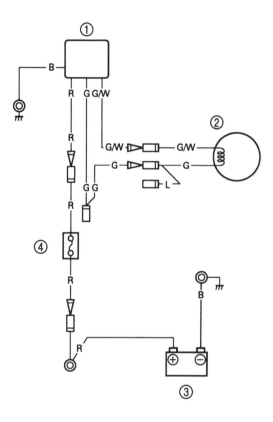

1. Rectifier/regulator
2. Lighting coil
3. Battery
4. Fuse

G : Green
G/W : Green/white
R : Red
B : Black

16

28 JET, 35 JET, 40 AND 50 HP THREE-CYLINDER MODELS (IGNITION SYSTEM)

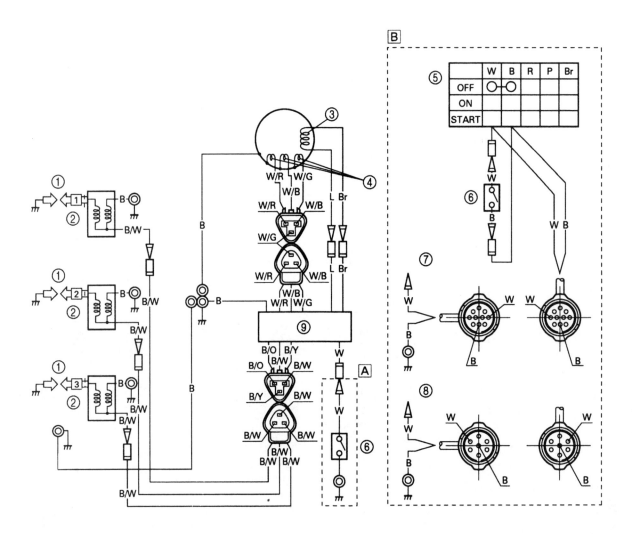

1. Spark plug
2. Ignition coil
3. Charge coil
4. Pulser coil
5. Main switch
6. Engine stop switch
7. Ten-pin connector
8. Seven-pin connector
9. CDI unit

A : Tiller models
B : Remote control models

B : Black
Br : Brown
L : Blue
W : White
B/O : Black/orange
B/W : Black/white
B/Y : Black/yellow
W/B : White/black
W/R : White/red
W/G : White/green

28 JET, 35 JET, 40 AND 50 HP THREE-CYLINDER MODELS (WARNING SYSTEM, CONTROL SYSTEM)

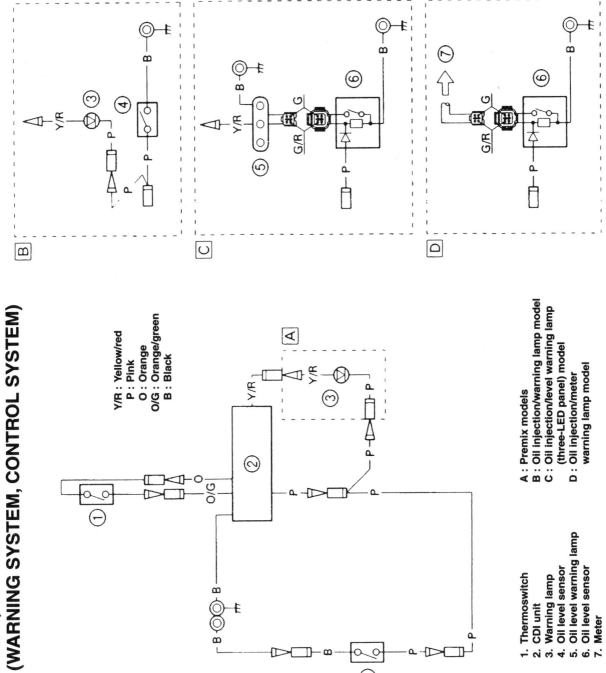

Y/R : Yellow/red
P : Pink
O : Orange
O/G : Orange/green
B : Black

A : Premix models
B : Oil injection/warning lamp model
C : Oil injection/level warning lamp (three-LED panel) model
D : Oil injection/meter warning lamp model

1. Thermoswitch
2. CDI unit
3. Warning lamp
4. Oil level sensor
5. Oil level warning lamp
6. Oil level sensor
7. Meter

16

28 JET, 35 JET, 40 AND 50 HP THREE-CYLINDER MODELS (STARTING SYSTEM)

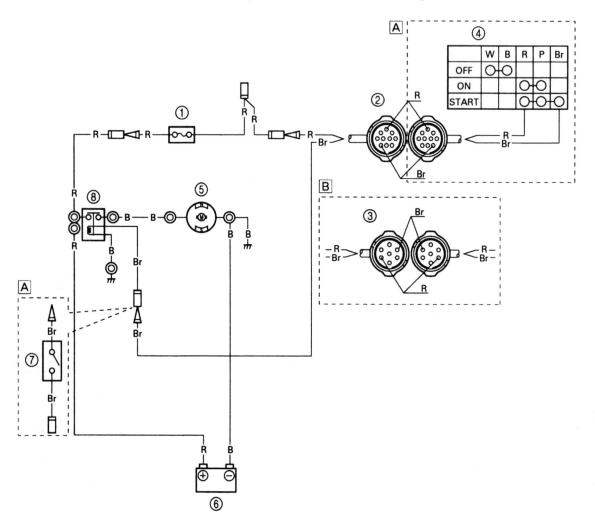

1. Fuse
2. Ten-pin electrical connector
3. Seven-pin electrical connector
4. Main switch
5. Starter motor
6. Battery
7. Neutral switch
8. Starter relay

B : Black
Br : Brown
R : Red

A : Except remote control models
B : Remote control models

MODEL E48

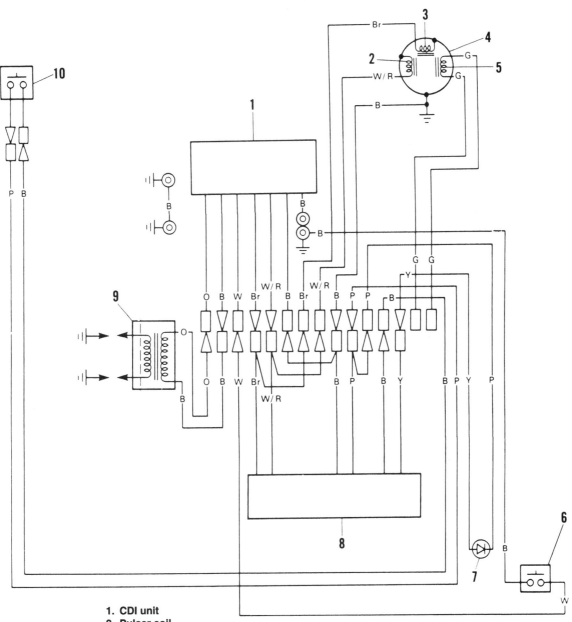

1. CDI unit
2. Pulser coil
3. Charge coil
4. CDI magneto
5. Lighting coil
6. Engine stop switch
7. Warning lamp (LED)
8. Power reduction control unit
9. Ignition coil
10. Thermoswitch

B : Black
Br : Brown
G : Green
O : Orange
P : Pink
W : White

16

MODEL E60

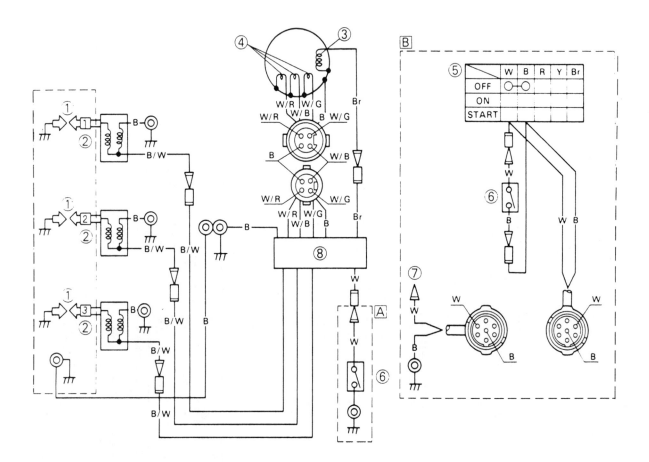

1. Spark plugs
2. Ignition coil
3. Charge coil
4. Pulser coil
5. Main switch
6. Engine stop switch
7. Seven-pin connector
8. CDI unit

A : Tiller models
B : Remote control models

B : Black
Br : Brown
W : White
W/B : White/black
W/G : White/breen
W/R : White/red
B/W : Black/white

MODEL E75

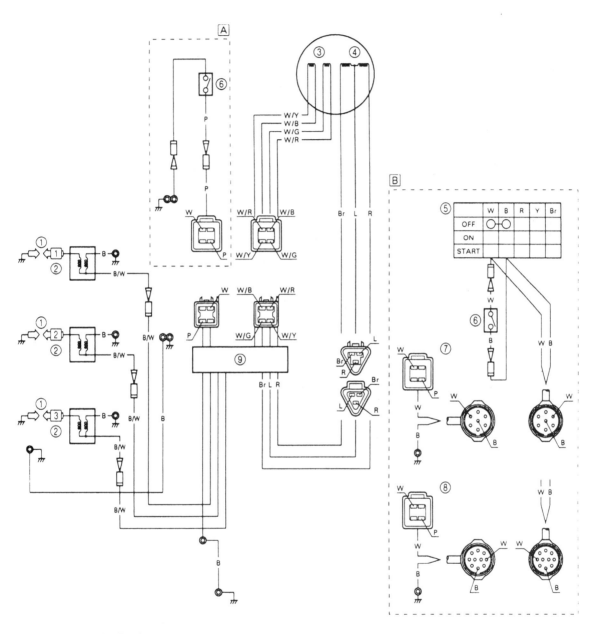

B : Black	**1.**	**Spark plugs**
Br : Brown	**2.**	**Ignition coil**
L : Blue	**3.**	**Pulser coil**
R : Red	**4.**	**Charge coil**
P : Pink	**5.**	**Main switch**
W : White	**6.**	**Engine stop switch**
Y : Yellow	**7.**	**Seven-pin connector**
B/W : Black/white	**8.**	**Ten-pin connector**
W/B : White/black	**9.**	**CDI unit**
W/G : White/green		
W/R : White/red	**A :**	**Tiller models**
W/Y : White/yellow	**B :**	**Remote control models**

16

C60, 60 AND 70 HP MODELS

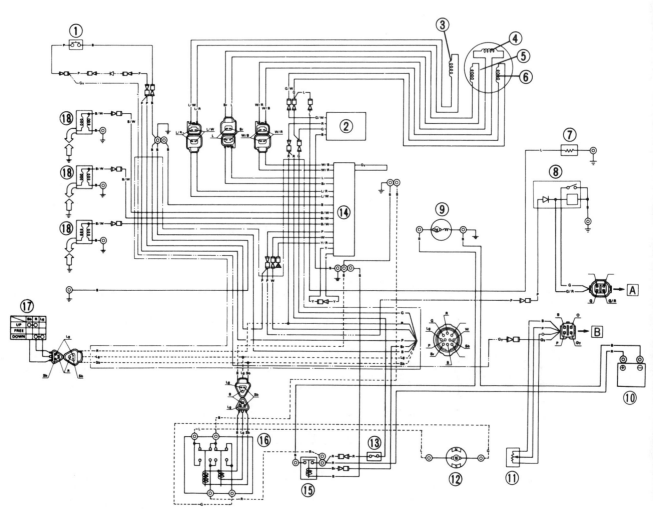

A : To oil level gauge
B : To trim gauge

— — — —	PTT models
— — — —	Digital meter models
— — — —	Oil injection models

1. Thermoswitch
2. Rectifier/regulator
3. Crank position sensor
4. Pulser coil
5. Charge coil
6. Lighting coil
7. Electrothermal valve
8. Oil level sensor (oil injection models)
9. Starter motor
10. Battery
11. Trim sensor (power trim/tilt models)

12. Power trim and tilt motor (power trim/tilt models)
13. Fuse (20A)
14. CDI unit
15. Starter relay
16. Power trim and tilt relay (power trim/tilt models)
17. Power trim and tilt switch (power trim/tilt models)
18. Ignition coil
19. Oil warning lamp

B : Black	Y : Yellow
Br : Brown	Lg : Light green
G : Green	W/R : White/red
Gy : Gray	W/B : White/black
L : Blue	B/W : Black/white
O : Orange	L/R : Blue/red
P : Pink	L/W : Blue/white
R : Red	G/W : Green/white
Sb : Sky blue	G/R : Green/red
W : White	

C75 AND C85, 1996 MODELS (PRIOR TO SERIAL NO. 351385)

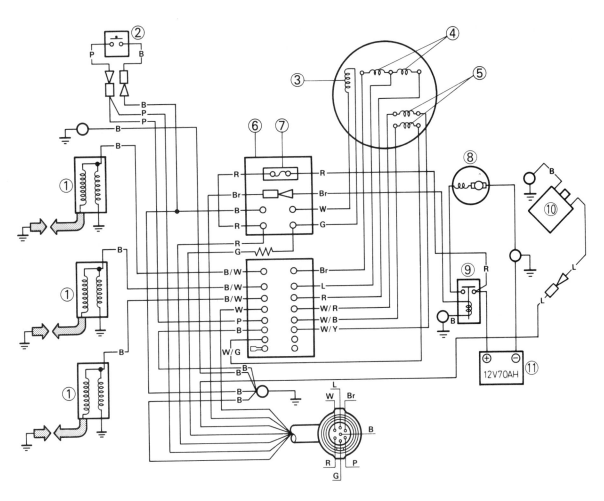

1. Ignition coil
2. Thermoswitch
3. Lighting coil
4. Charge coil
5. Pulser coil
6. Rectifier/regulator
7. Fuse
8. Starter motor
9. Starter relay
10. Choke solenoid
11. Battery

B : Black
Br : Brown
G : Green
Gy : Gray
L : Blue
O : Orange
P : Pink
R : Red
Sb : Sky blue
W : White
Y : Yellow
Lg : Light green
B/W : Black/white
W/G : White/green

16

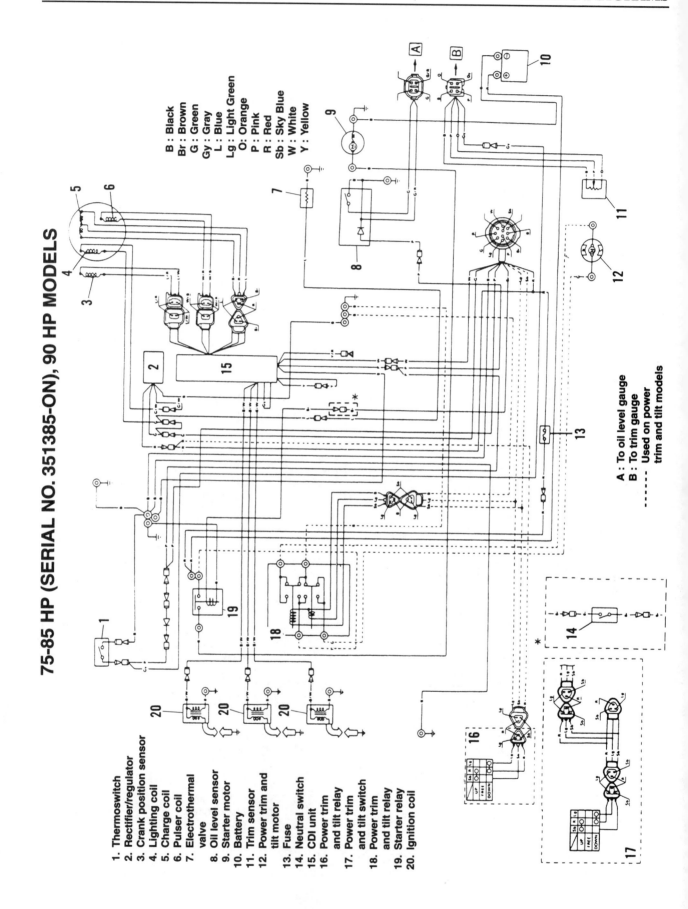

75-85 HP (SERIAL NO. 351385-ON), 90 HP MODELS

B : Black
Br : Brown
G : Green
Gy : Gray
L : Blue
Lg : Light Green
O : Orange
P : Pink
R : Red
Sb : Sky Blue
W : White
Y : Yellow

A : To oil level gauge
B : To trim gauge
------ : Used on power
trim and tilt models

1. Thermoswitch
2. Rectifier/regulator
3. Crank position sensor
4. Lighting coil
5. Charge coil
6. Pulser coil
7. Electrothermal
valve
8. Oil level sensor
9. Starter motor
10. Battery
11. Trim sensor
12. Power trim and
tilt motor
13. Fuse
14. Neutral switch
15. CDI unit
16. Power trim
and tilt relay
17. Power trim
and tilt switch
18. Power trim
and tilt relay
19. Starter relay
20. Ignition coil

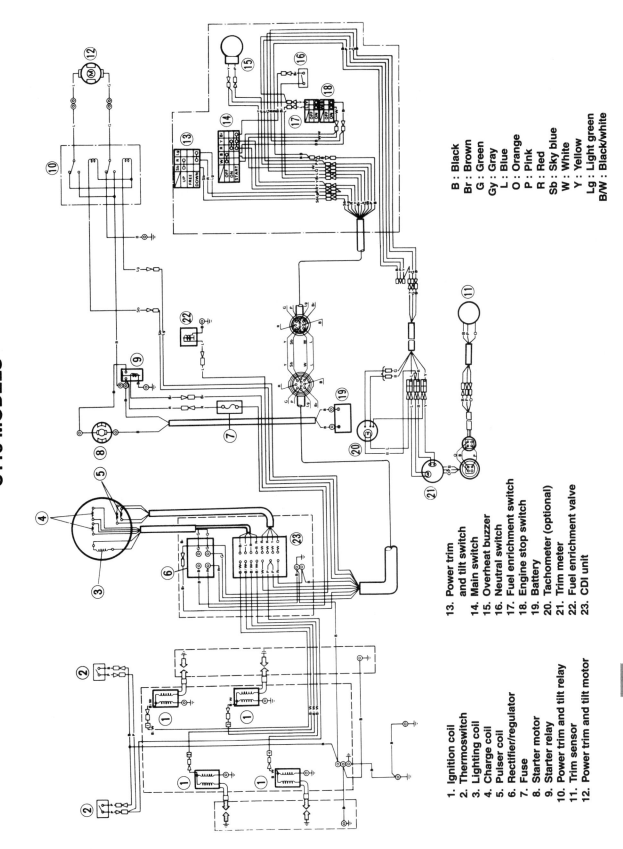

C115 MODELS

B : Black
Br : Brown
G : Green
Gy : Gray
L : Blue
O : Orange
P : Pink
R : Red
Sb : Sky blue
W : White
Y : Yellow
Lg : Light green
B/W : Black/white

1. Ignition coil
2. Thermoswitch
3. Lighting coil
4. Charge coil
5. Pulser coil
6. Rectifier/regulator
7. Fuse
8. Starter motor
9. Starter relay
10. Power trim and tilt relay
11. Trim sensor
12. Power trim and tilt motor
13. Power trim and tilt switch
14. Main switch
15. Overheat buzzer
16. Neutral switch
17. Fuel enrichment switch
18. Engine stop switch
19. Battery
20. Tachometer (optional)
21. Trim meter
22. Fuel enrichment valve
23. CDI unit

115 AND 130 HP OIL-INJECTED MODELS

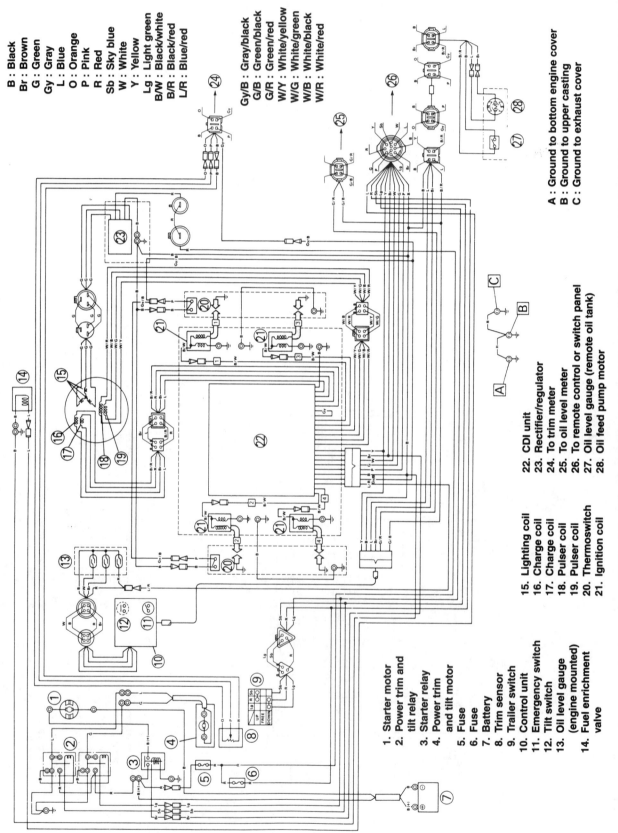

B : Black
Br : Brown
G : Green
Gy : Gray
L : Blue
O : Orange
P : Pink
R : Red
Sb : Sky blue
W : White
Y : Yellow
Lg : Light green
B/W : Black/white
B/R : Black/red
L/R : Blue/red

Gy/B : Gray/black
G/B : Green/black
G/R : Green/red
W/Y : White/yellow
W/G : White/green
W/B : White/black
W/R : White/red

A : Ground to bottom engine cover
B : Ground to upper casting
C : Ground to exhaust cover

1. Starter motor
2. Power trim and tilt relay
3. Starter relay
4. Power trim and tilt motor
5. Fuse
6. Fuse
7. Battery
8. Trim sensor
9. Trailer switch
10. Control unit
11. Emergency switch
12. Tilt switch
13. Oil level gauge (engine mounted)
14. Fuel enrichment valve
15. Lighting coil
16. Charge coil
17. Charge coil
18. Pulser coil
19. Pulser coil
20. Thermoswitch
21. Ignition coil
22. CDI unit
23. Rectifier/regulator
24. To trim meter
25. To oil level meter
26. To remote control or switch panel
27. Oil level gauge (remote oil tank)
28. Oil feed pump motor

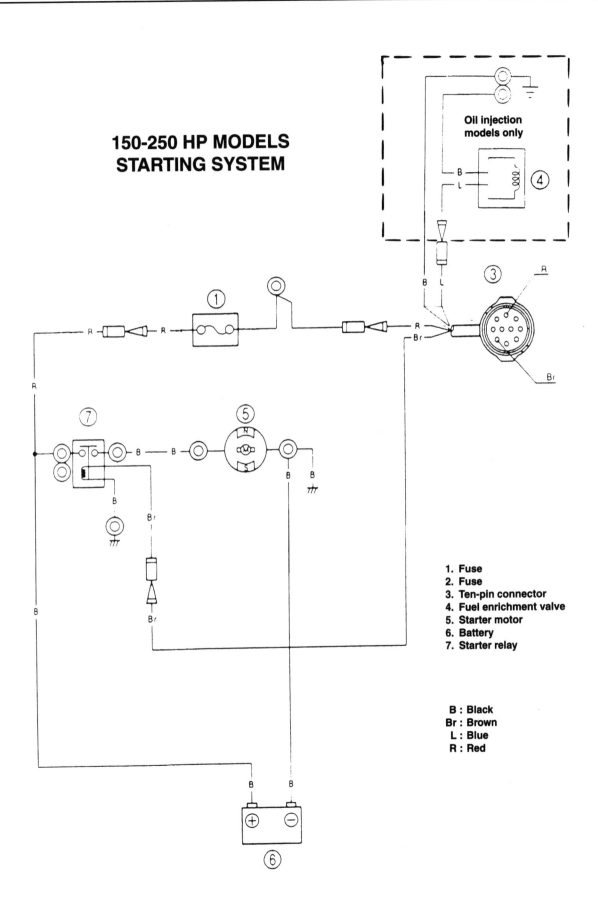

150-250 HP MODELS
STARTING SYSTEM

Oil injection models only

1. Fuse
2. Fuse
3. Ten-pin connector
4. Fuel enrichment valve
5. Starter motor
6. Battery
7. Starter relay

B : Black
Br : Brown
L : Blue
R : Red

16

CHARGING SYSTEM
150-225 HP (90°) MODELS

OIL INJECTED MODELS

PREMIX MODELS

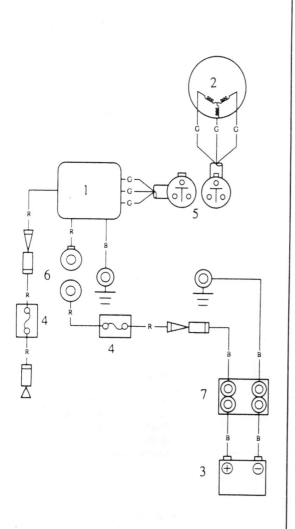

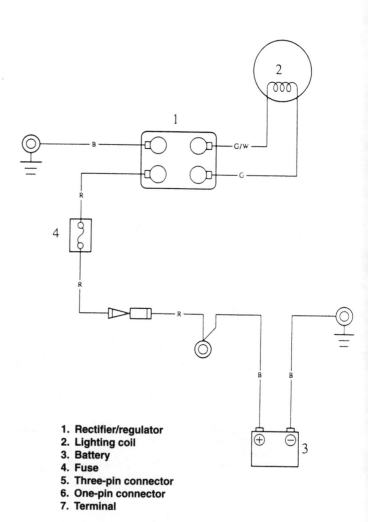

1. Rectifier/regulator
2. Lighting coil
3. Battery
4. Fuse
5. Three-pin connector
6. One-pin connector
7. Terminal

G : Green
G/W : Green/white
R : Red
B : Black

CHARGING SYSTEM
200-250 HP (76°) MODELS

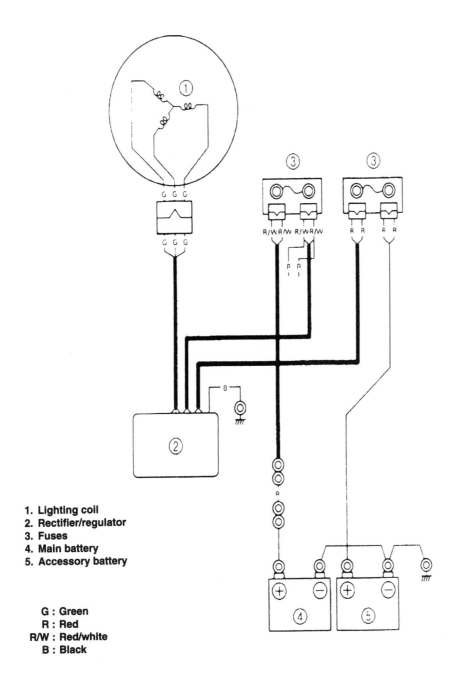

1. **Lighting coil**
2. **Rectifier/regulator**
3. **Fuses**
4. **Main battery**
5. **Accessory battery**

    G : Green
    R : Red
R/W : Red/white
    B : Black

16

TRIM SYSTEM
150-225 HP (90°) MODELS

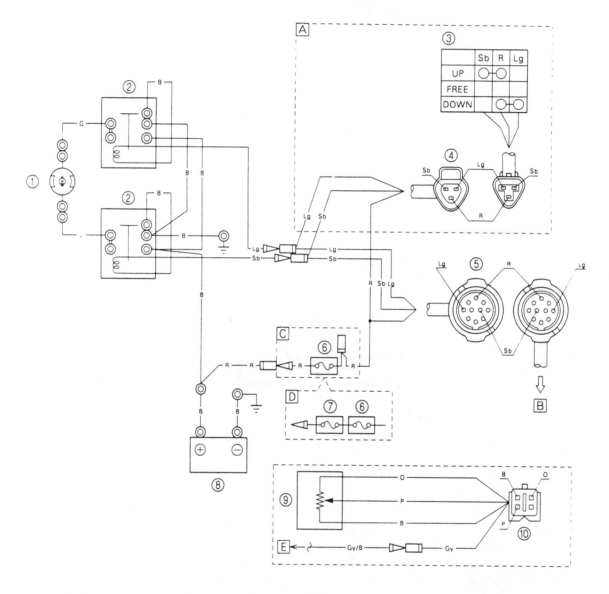

1. Power trim and tilt motor
2. Power trim and tilt relay
3. Trailer switch
4. Three-pin connector
5. Ten-pin connector
6. Fuse
7. Fuse
8. Battery
9. Trim sensor
10. Four-pin connector

A : Bottom engine cover trim switch
B : To remote control
C : Premix models
D : Oil injection models
E : Power supply lead

B : Black
G : Green
Gy : Gray
L : Blue
Gy/B : Gray/black
Lg : Light green
O : Orange
P : Pink
R : Red
Sb : Sky blue

TRIM SYSTEM
200-250 HP (76°) MODELS

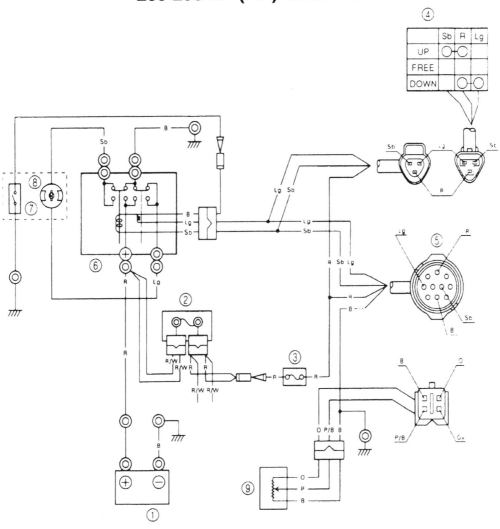

B : Black
R : Red
Lg : Light green
Sb : Sky blue
O : Orange
Gy : Gray
P/B : Pink/black
P : Pink
R/W : Red/white

1. Main battery
2. Fuse
3. Fuse
4. Trailer switch
5. Ten-pin connector
6. Power trim and tilt relay
7. Thermoswitch
8. Trim sensor

16

IGNITION SYSTEM
150-225 HP (90°) OIL-INJECTED MODELS

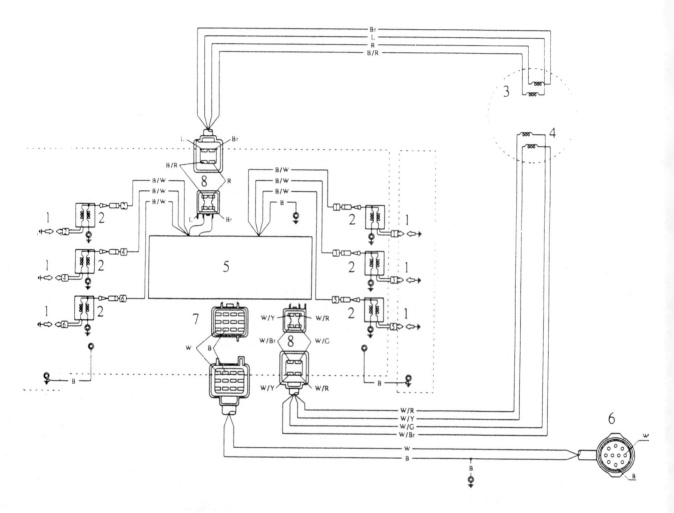

B : Black
Br : Brown
B/R : Black/red
B/W : Black/white
L : Blue
R : Red
W : White
W/Br : White/brown
W/G : White/green
W/R : White/red
W/Y : White/yellow

1. Spark plugs
2. Ignition coils
3. Charge coil
4. Pulser coil
5. CDI unit
6. Ten-pin connector
7. 12-pin connector
8. Four-pin connector

IGNITION SYSTEM
150-225 HP (90°) PREMIX MODELS

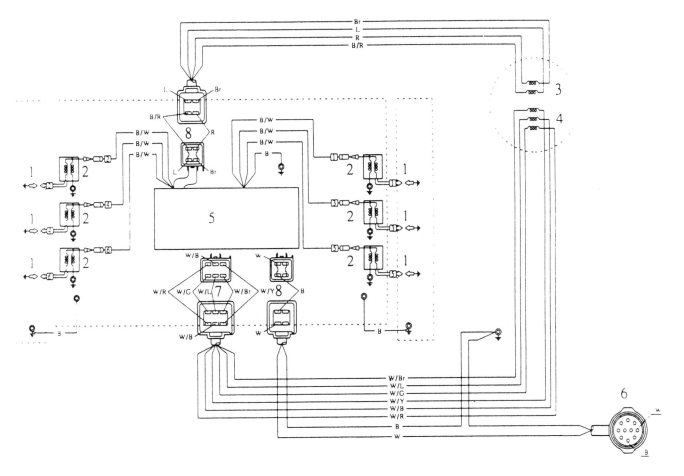

B : Black
Br : Brown
B/R : Black/red
B/W : Black/white
L : Blue
R : Red
W : White
W/B : White/black
W/Br : White/brown
W/G : White/green
W/L : White/blue
W/R : White/red
W/Y : White/yellow

1. Spark plugs
2. Ignition coil
3. Charge coil
4. Pulser coil
5. CDI unit
6. Ten-pin connector
7. Six-pin connector
8. Four-pin connector

16

IGNITION SYSTEM
200-250 HP (76°) EFI MODELS

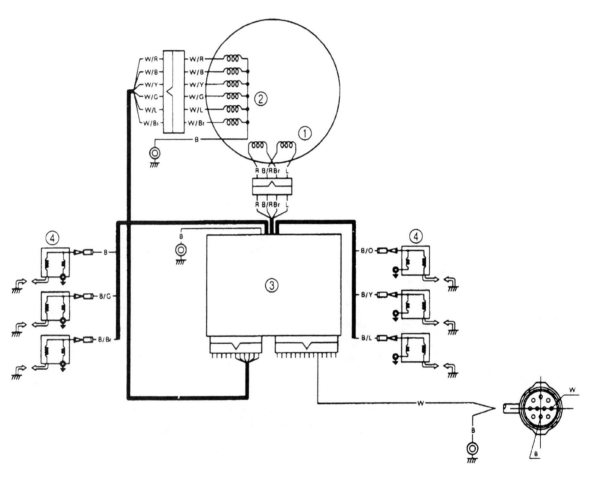

1. Charge coil
2. Pulser coil
3. CDI unit
4. Ignition coil

B : Black
W : White
B/L : Black/blue
B/Y : Black/yellow
B/O : Black/orange
B/G : Black/green
B/Br : Black/brown
R : Red
Br : Brown
B/R : Black/red
W/R : White/red
W/B : White/black
W/Y : White/yellow
W/G : White/green
W/L : White/blue
W/Br : White/brown
G/W : Green/white
G/L : Green/blue

IGNITION CONTROL/WARNING SYSTEM
150-225 HP (90°) PREMIX MODELS

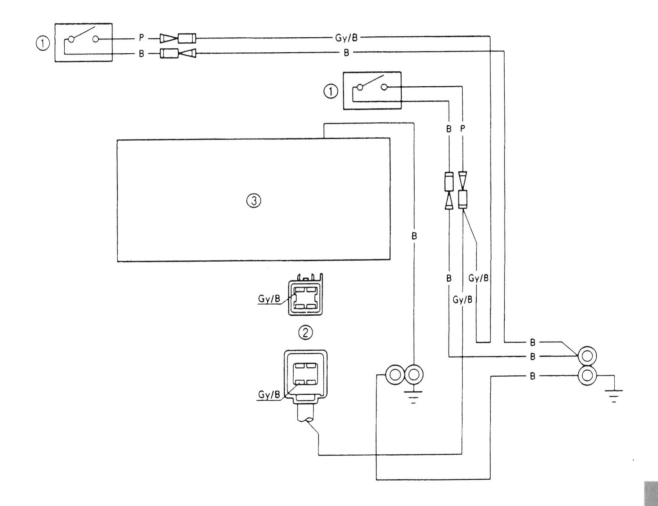

1. Thermoswitch
2. Four-pin connector
3. CDI unit

B : Black
Gy/B : Gray/black
P : Pink

16

IGNITION CONTROL/WARNING SYSTEM
150-225 HP (90°) OIL-INJECTED MODELS

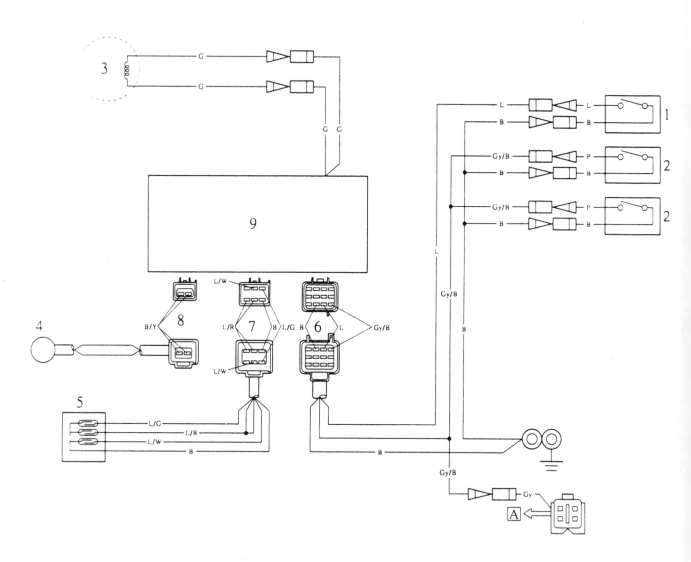

1. Emergency switch
2. Thermoswitch
3. Crank position sensor
4. Thermosensor
5. Oil level sensor
6. 12-pin connector
7. Six-pin connector
8. Two-pin connector
9. CDI unit

B : Black
B/Y : Black/yellow
Gy/B : Gray/black
L : Blue
L/G : Blue/green
L/R : Blue/red
L/W : Blue/white
P : Pink

IGNITION CONTROL/WARNING SYSTEM
200-250 HP (76°) MODELS

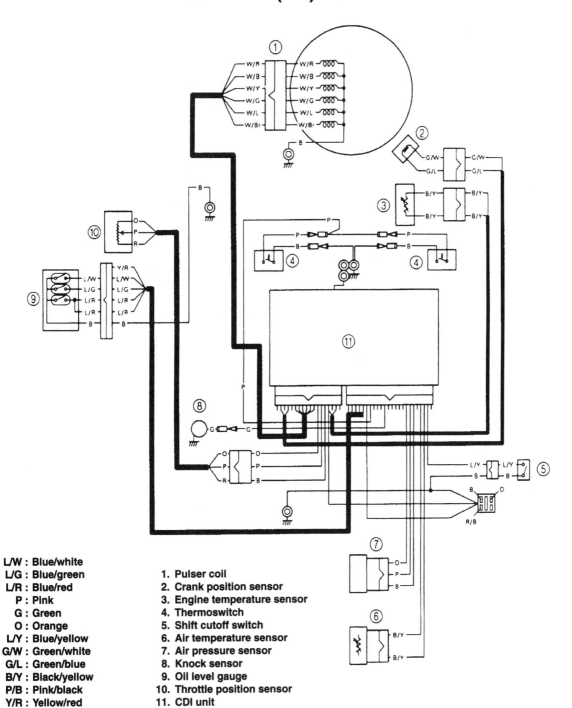

L/W : Blue/white
L/G : Blue/green
L/R : Blue/red
P : Pink
G : Green
O : Orange
L/Y : Blue/yellow
G/W : Green/white
G/L : Green/blue
B/Y : Black/yellow
P/B : Pink/black
Y/R : Yellow/red

1. Pulser coil
2. Crank position sensor
3. Engine temperature sensor
4. Thermoswitch
5. Shift cutoff switch
6. Air temperature sensor
7. Air pressure sensor
8. Knock sensor
9. Oil level gauge
10. Throttle position sensor
11. CDI unit

16

225-250 HP (76°) 1996 MODELS

1. Throttle position sensor
2. Fuel enrichment valve
3. Power trim and tilt switch
4. Oil level gauge (engine tank)
5. Emergency switch
6. Electromagnetic fuel feed pump
7. Emergency connector
8. Diagnosis connector
9. Pulser coil
10. Thermoswitch
11. Ignition coil
12. Spark plug
13. Knock sensor
14. Overspeed stop lead
15. Lighting coil
16. Charge coil
17. CDI unit
18. Crank position sensor
19. Thermosensor
20. Fuse
21. Fuse
22. Starter motor
23. Power trim and tilt relay
24. Starter motor relay

25. Rectifier/regulator
26. Shift cutoff switch
27. Battery
28. Auxiliary battery
29. Oil level gauge (remote tank)
30. Oil feed pump
31. Trim sensor
32. Power trim and tilt motor thermoswitch
33. Power trim and tilt motor
34. Primer pump lead
35. To remote control
36. To digital meter
37. Negative lead

B : Black
Br : Brown
G : Green
Gy : Gray
L : Blue
O : Orange
P : Pink
R : Red

Sb : Sky blue
W : White
Y : Yellow
Lg : Light green
B/W : Black/white
B/R : Black/red
L/R : Blue/red
Gy/B : Gray/black

G/B : Green/black
G/R : Green/red
W/Y : White/yellow
W/G : White/green
W/B : White/black
W/R : White/red

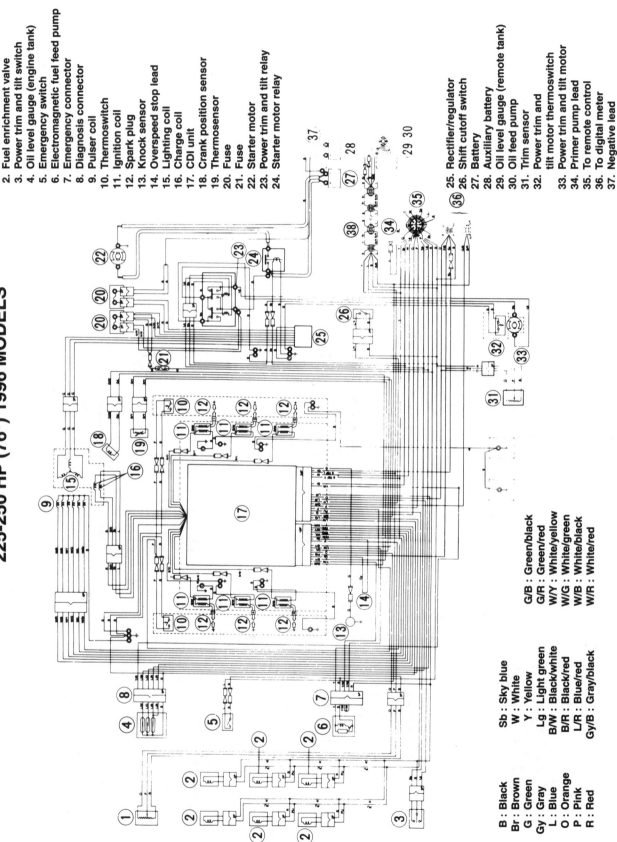

FUEL INJECTION SYSTEM 200-250 (76°) MODELS

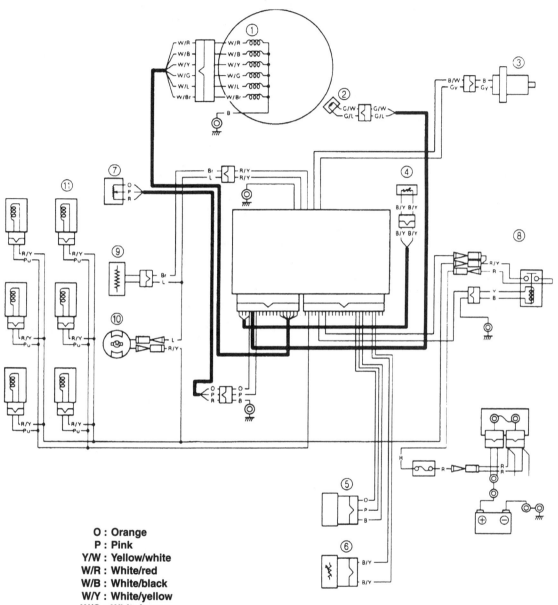

O : Orange
P : Pink
Y/W : Yellow/white
W/R : White/red
W/B : White/black
W/Y : White/yellow
W/G : White/green
W/L : White/blue
W/Br : White/brown
B/Y : Black/yellow
G/W : Green/white
G/L : Green/blue
Pu : Purple
G : Green
R : Red
B : Black
Y : Yellow
Gy : Gray

1. Pulser coil
2. Crank position sensor
3. Oxygen density sensor
4. Engine temperature sensor
5. Air pressure sensor
6. Air temperature sensor
7. Throttle position sensor
8. Injection system relay
9. Resistor
10. High pressure fuel pump
11. Fuel injectors

16

OIL FEED PUMP CONTROL 200-225 (76°) MODELS

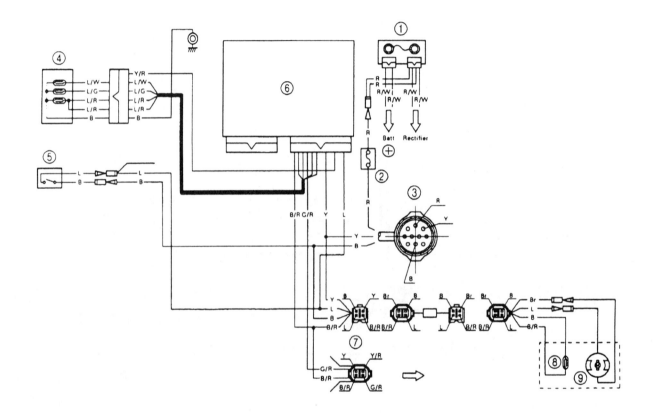

Y/R : Yellow/red
L/W : Blue/white
L/G : Blue/green
L/R : Blue/red
B : Black
L : Blue
R : Red
R/W : Red/white
Y : Yellow
Br : Brown
B/R : Black/red
G/R : Green/red
B/R : Black/red

1. Fuse
2. Fuse
3. Ten-pin connector
4. Oil level gauge
   (engine tank)
5. Emergency switch
6. CDI unit
7. Four-pin connector
8. Oil level gauge
   (remote tank)
9. Oil feed pump

DIGITAL METER WIRING DIAGRAM

1. Digital tachometer
2. Digital speedometer
3. Fuel management meter
4. Lamp switch
5. Fuse
6. Fuel sensor

B : Black
Br : Brown
G : Green
Gy : Gray
L : Blue
Lg : Light green
O : Orange
P : Pink
R : Red
Sb : Sky blue
W : White
Y : Yellow

A : To remote control box
B : To trim sensor
C : To oil level gauge

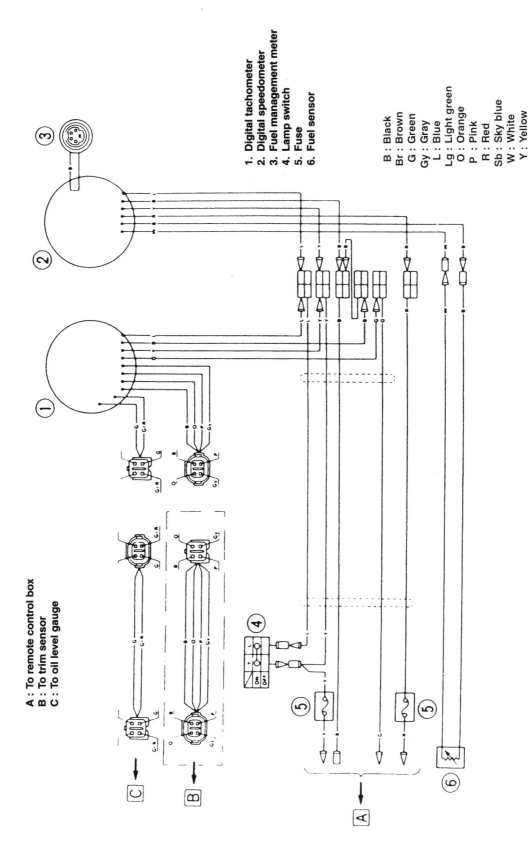

16

REMOTE CONTROL WIRING DIAGRAM

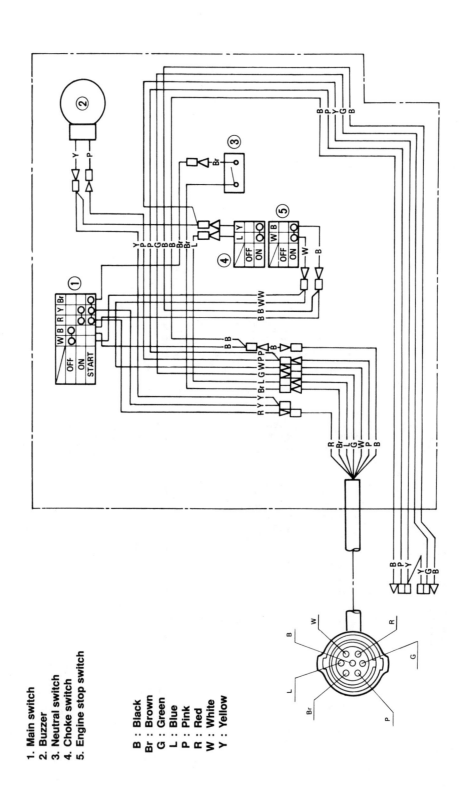

1. Main switch
2. Buzzer
3. Neutral switch
4. Choke switch
5. Engine stop switch

B : Black
Br : Brown
G : Green
L : Blue
P : Pink
R : Red
W : White
Y : Yellow

NOTES

NOTES

NOTES

MAINTENANCE LOG

Date	Maintenance Performed	Engine Hours